MW00582050

A Reader in Sociophonetics

edited by
Dennis R. Preston
Nancy Niedzielski

De Gruyter Mouton

The hardcover edition was published in 2010 as volume 219
of the series *Trends in Linguistics. Studies and Monographs.*

ISBN 978-1-934078-05-1
e-ISBN 978-1-934078-06-8

The Library of Congress has cataloged the hardcover edition as follows:

A reader in sociophonetics / edited by Dennis R. Preston, Nancy Niedzielski.
p. cm. – (Trends in linguistics. Studies and monographs ; 219)
Includes index.
ISBN 978-1-934078-04-4 (hardcover : alk. paper)
ISBN 978-1-934078-06-8 (ebook)
1. Grammar, Comparative and general – Phonology. 2. Dialectology – Research. 3. Sociolinguistics I. Preston, Dennis Richard. II. Niedzielski, Nancy A., 1964–
P217.3.R43 2010
414'.8–dc22

2010013190

Bibliographic information published by the Deutsche Nationalbibliothek

The Deutsche Nationalbibliothek lists this publication in the Deutsche Nationalbibliografie; detailed bibliographic data are available in the Internet at http://dnb.d-nb.de.

Cover image: Hemera/Thinkstock
Typesetting: IBT Global, Troy, NY
Printing: Hubert & Co. GmbH & Co. KG, Göttingen
∞ Printed on acid-free paper

Printed in Germany.

www.degruyter.com

Contents

Introduction: Sociophonetics Studies of Language Variety Production and Perception

Dennis R. Preston, Oklahoma State University and
Nancy Niedzielski, Rice University

Introduction

In 2002 Erik Thomas suggested that the "[m]elding of sociolinguistics and phonetics is sometimes referred to as *sociophonetics* . . ." (189), and it is not at all odd that phonetics would qualify for this singling out, for the variables treated in the history of the sociolinguistic enterprise have very often been phonetic. In the journal *Language Variation and Change*, 133 articles appeared in the ten-year period 1999–2008 (vols. 11–20); of these, 61, just under 46%, dealt with phonetic topics exclusively, and many more included phonetic variables among others or used them as a major consideration in determining the distribution of other variables, most notably morphological ones.

There is little doubt, then, that phonetics is particularly important to current work in sociolinguistics, nor that it was important to the sociolinguistic side of traditional dialectology, the most direct forerunner of the modern enterprise, as evidenced, for example, in the age- and sex-related variable features uncovered by Gauchat in Charmey, Switzerland (1905), some of which were later confirmed as participants in real-time change by Hermann (1929), or in the work of McDavid (1948) on post-vocalic /r/ in South Carolina, subtitled "A social analysis." Even the allied social sciences have attended to phonetic variation (e.g., Fischer 1958, who found that good boys said "walking" and not-so-good-boys said "walkin'").

One might argue, then, that sociophonetics is has always been simply one branch of the linguistic part of sociolinguistics, rather than the more current melding Thomas mentions. In other words, if sociolinguistics designates the social as well as linguistic factors that must be taken into consideration to account for the distribution of linguistic variables, whether stable or in flux, then the phonetic level is just one of those that must be included and has no theoretical privilege over phonology, morphology, syntax, semantics, or pragmatics, nor would its concerns be excluded from historical linguistics, psycholinguistics, neurolinguistics, applied linguistics, etc. . . . There are, however, several reasons that phonetics has the special status Thomas suggests and, perhaps most tellingly, even a name, as the other levels do not. ("Sociopragmatics," however, seems to have some currency; the 2009 issue of the *Journal of Historical Pragmatics* was entitled "Historical Sociopragmatics.")

First, phonetic variation is not just long-standing in formal study, as shown previously, but also in the public mind. From the Gileadites inability to realize palatal sibilants (Old Testament, Judges 12: 5–6) to Johnnie L. Cochran's criticism during the O. J. Simpson trial of the idea that a Black person could be identified on the basis of voice as "racist," public attention to so-called accents has been notable.

Second, the mechanics of instrumental or acoustic phonetics, although important contributors to the earliest modern work on variation (e.g., Labov 1962; Labov, Yaeger, and Steiner 1972), are now freely available to any investigator who has a computer, a considerable reduction from the thousands of dollars one would have had to invest to carry out such work only a few decades ago. The sound analysis program Praat (Boersma and Weenink 1992–2009) and its add-on Akustyk (Plichta 2009) are the most widely used, along with PLOTNIK, a vowel plotting and normalization software package developed by William Labov (2009). Most recently, NORM (2009), a web-based vowel normalization program, provides even further tools for analysis cost-free.

Third, there has been a reawakening of the importance of phonetics to phonology, and, to the extent that sociolinguistics must keep up with general theoretical advances in the field, attention to such integration and dependency is necessary. Variationist implications in both optimality theory (e.g., Boersma and Hayes 1991) and exemplar theory (Pierrehumbert 1994) have been particularly influential in sociophonetics. For some time the contributions of William Labov in particular have contributed to this interface in the areas of vowel shifts and mergers by proposing phonetics-based generalizations that appear to be influential in the development of a systematic phonology (e.g., Labov 1994).

Fourth, the area of speech science, although long associated with sophisticated phonetics research, is now better attuned to the goals and findings of general linguistics and, even more recently, to the interests of sociolinguistics in particular. There is a review of a great deal of this work in the introductory sections of Chapter 8.

Finally, the phonetic level is convenient, not only because even a short interview with a respondent is likely to contain a considerable portion of both the sounds and environments one would like to study, but also because, except for some phonetic caricatures or stereotypes, it is also the level where both variation and change may go undetected in the speech communities where phonetic variation, nevertheless, plays an important role. This often subconscious awareness of variation also lends itself well to experimental work, both in production and perception.

In summary, we suggest that sociophonetics is the sub-branch of the discipline that has attracted the greatest attention over the last few decades, although the interest in phonetic factors in language variation studies is long-standing. Recent advances in speech science and inexpensive computer implementations of them allow increasingly sophisticated studies of the progress of language variation, contact, and change, and on-going studies of many dramatic changes show that language variety is not only robust in the modern age, a fact often denied by popular media pundits, but also socially embedded in interesting ways. Even more recently, instrumental studies of language variety, contact, and change have focused on the role of social categories and attitudes in perception as well as production.

The studies presented here look at the role of social factors—age, sex, status, ethnicity, network, and ideology—in the formation, progress, and deterrence of intra- and interlingual contact and change at the phonetic level; they also look at the ways in which social identities and beliefs shape and influence a listener's ability to identify and even comprehend as well as socially evaluate varieties.

The book is organized into three parts; the first deals with the correlation of variable phonetic facts and aspects of social identity and relationships, the second with the perception of phonetic variables (including social facts about speakers as well as perceivers), and the last with studies that combine elements of both production and perception.

Part I: Production

The first part, on production, begins with a chapter on historical sociolinguistics that explores one of the Labovian contributions mentioned previously—the puzzle of near-mergers (e.g., Labov 1994). Faber, Di Paolo and Best explore *ɛ̄ (Middle English long ɛ), contending from internal evidence (following the uniformitarian principle) and traditional dialect accounts that a path in which it nearly merged with *ē (Middle English long e), merged with *ɛ̂ (Middle English lengthened short ɛ), nearly merged with *ǣ (Middle English long a, e.g., "name") and/or *æj (the Middle English diphthong, e.g., "day"), and finally merged with *ē is the only reasonable story that can account for the resulting modern standard (where "feed"—Middle English long e, "heap"—Middle English long ɛ, and "speak"—Middle English lengthened short ɛ) as well as the variety of attested dialect forms. As they put it, "Only in a theory of language which distinguishes between near and true mergers can this sequence of developments have occurred in the history of a single language variety" (34).

In Chapter 2, Hay and Maclagan investigate the social and linguistic conditioning of the intrusive /r/ ("clawring" for "clawing" or "ma'r and pa" for "ma and pa") in New Zealand English. They look at social factors as well as those of the linguistic environment, particularly the emergence of intrusive /r/ after /aʊ/ and alternative realizations of that diphthong locally as well as the degree of "r-ness" of the variable. They find intrusive /r/ to be sensitive to lexical items, affix identity, class, and gender and that the "r-ness" of intrusive /r/ is sensitive to the same factors. In this chapter use is made of the logistic regression option of the open-source statistical program R; since logistic regression is the backbone of the VARBRUL/GOLDVARB programs popular among sociolinguists for decades (most recently available for Macintosh, PC, and Linux frameworks at http://individual.utoronto.ca/tagliamonte/Goldvarb/GV_index.htm), it is interesting to see this established treatment in new clothing. An R add-on making use of the full power of logistic regression, specifically written for variationists (Rbrul), is available at www.ling.upenn.edu/~johnson4/Rbrul.R.

In Chapter 3 Roeder assesses the influence of one aspect of the Northern Cities Chain Shift (NCCS)—the raising and fronting of /æ/—on a Mexican-American community in Lansing, Michigan, USA. Such work as this brings second language acquisition (and its reflexes in subsequent generations) into the concerns of sociophonetics. Roeder's major finding is that the NCCS is indeed having an influence on the emerging vowel system of the community, although details of that influence do not necessarily match up with the surrounding community, a finding that supports Labov's distinction between those members of a speech community to whom a change is incrementally *transmitted* over generations as opposed to those to whom it is *diffused* more rapidly and usually with a loss of subtle environmental factors (e.g., Labov 2007). This chapter also distinguishes between those predictable or natural phonetic processes that might have an influence on a system being acquired from those that are idiosyncratic to the target system itself. Social factors (sex, education) are also strongly correlated with the influence of the new target norm (i.e., the NCCS).

Chapter 4 is a further examination of heritage language communities, in this case a study of the degree to which North African (Arabic, Berber) language backgrounds may account for rhythmic differences in the speech of *banlieue* (multi-ethnic, immigrant, working-class suburbs) residents in Paris. Fagyal begins with a careful analysis of methods used to compute cross-linguistic rhythmic differences, an important contribution to the area in general since nonsegmental studies have been rare. Her conclusions are that that the stress-timed background languages of the immigrants have had a small but noticeable influence on their French, not removing it from the group of generally syllable-timed European Romance languages but providing it with vowel reduction and consonant clustering characteristics related to rate of articulation.

Chapter 5 is another contribution to nonsegmental characteristics and is an interesting example of cross-linguistic research in the sociophonetic field. Yaeger-Dror, Takano, Granadillo, and Hall-Lew seek to uncover the prosodic contours associated with NEG in English, Japanese, and Spanish, using pitch, duration, and amplitude in all three languages to determine lexical (syllable) prominence. The authors employ a considerable array of social and linguistic factors to study (treated in a VARBRUL analysis) the choice of prominence for NEG. They conclude that news announcing rather than casual interactions, positions other than end-or-sentence for NEG, full rather than clitic morphology of NEG itself, supportive (rather than informative or remedial) footing, and women are factors that promote prominence in NEG, along with interesting detail about region and other factors.

Chapter 6 is the first of two studies included in this book on Japanese vowel devoicing, a feature long thought to have only regional and/or standard language significance on the social side and relatively categorical environmental conditioning on the linguistic. Imai shows, however, interesting social variation within Tokyo Japanese, particularly in the interaction between age and sex, in which young men (but not middle-aged and older ones) are considerably more frequent devoicers. This study, like many of the others in this book, also makes a straightforward contribution to a much more detailed understanding of linguistic environmental influences on phonetic variables, here ones that promote and demote devoicing in a considerably more fine-tuned way than was previously thought, although Hibiya (1999: 119) hints at greater variability and change for this feature in Tokyo.

Part II: Perception

The first chapter in the section on perception continues to look at the variable of Japanese vowel devoicing. Popular belief suggests that native speakers think devoicing of /i/ and /u/ between voiceless consonants and at the ends of words is standard Kanto area (Tokyo) Japanese and that speakers from other regions, particularly the Kansai area (Osaka) do not devoice or do not devoice as frequently, although, as documented in Chapter 7, research evidence for greater Kanto devoicing is slim. In this study, Yonezawa Morris asks respondents from Tokyo and Osaka to listen to voiced and devoiced tokens of lexical items and phrases as well as items that have distinctive and shared pitch accent patterns and identify the city of the speaker. She shows that respondents from both areas are not only able to identify devoicing but also attribute voiced and devoiced tokens to the areas indicated by the stereotypical beliefs outlined above. This chapter also hints at the intriguing possibility that many tokens of voiced vowels were identified as devoiced (and attributed to Tokyo) on the basis of their occurring between voiceless consonants that have a particularly high promoting effect on devoicing. If this is so, it is an interesting linguistic parallel to the social redirection of acoustic facts outlined in Chapter 11.

In Chapter 8, Clopper investigates how well (or how poorly) nonlinguists identify the regional provenience of US dialect samples. She provides speech samples of group classification (with no labels or regions suggested by the experimenter) and a second test in which paired samples were used, again with no suggested identification, and the respondents rated how much one sample was like the other. Although gross differences were fairly well recognized (Northern and Southern US varieties were distinguished, for example), more subtle aspects of dialect differences were not detected, although both an enhanced ability to recognize one's own variety and an experience factor (based on geographical mobility) of familiarity with other varieties were significant. Clopper concludes by suggesting that an exemplar model of phonology is best equipped to account for her findings.

Chapter 9 explicitly tests the ability of participants in a vowel shift (the Northern Cities Chain Shift—NCCS) and nonparticipants to identify an intended vowel along a continuum of signals from an unshifted to shifted position. Plichta and Rakerd recruited listeners from urban southeastern Michigan (shifted) and the Upper Peninsula of Michigan (nonshifted) and presented them with the second step of the NCCS—the fronting of /ɑ/. The seven-step continuum tested the location of F2 that caused a respondent to switch his or her identification of the vowel from that of "sock" or "hot" to that of "sack" or "hat." One would expect the shifted NCCS speakers to tolerate a much higher (fronter) F2 and still report "sock," and the nonshifted respondents to identify a much lower (backer) F2 boundary for the switchover to a "sack" interpretation. The results were somewhat more complicated; when the test words were presented in isolation, the two sets of respondents exhibited a crossover point at the same step (mean scores of 4.7 and 4.8). When the same seven-step items were embedded in carrier phrases which contained other examples of NCCS-shifted or nonshifted vowels, the nonshifted listeners were not influenced by the embedding, but the shifted respondents relocated their crossover points in line with the expectations, moving the crossover from 4.5 to 5.4, a strong suggestion that, at least in part, the normalization routine involved in by speakers is dependent on both speaker system and other contextual clues (e.g., Ladefoged and Broadbent 1957).

In Chapter 10 Preston continues the search begun in Chapter 9 by asking not only if locals understand locally changing systems better but also if demographic subdivisions of speakers within those areas have advantages and if the linguistic units of the shift itself play a role. By presenting shifted NCCS single-item tokens, he is able to show that groups more centrally associated with the shift are indeed better comprehenders of these tokens, although the best are far below the comprehension scores for such studies as Peterson and Barney (1952) and Hillenbrand et al. (1995). This study also shows that misunderstood vowels are overwhelmingly understood in the "pre-shift" or conservative position, not in the shifted position actually used by the most advanced of these respondents. For example, when a word like "bat" is misunderstood, it is taken to be "bet," even though, in the NCCS, "bet" will have moved to "bat" or "but," and the closest vowel to the shifted "bat" would be that of stable /e/ ("bait") or shifted /ɪ/ ("bit"). Finally, this chapter suggests that a number of characteristics of individual vowels (recency in the shift, historical complexity) also contribute to degree of misunderstanding.

Chapter 11 is the most exploitative of the speech science influence on sociophonetics and reports on a number of studies that clearly show the importance of implicit knowledge, explicit knowledge, and social identity in speech perception. Niedzielski illustrates this by reporting on studies such as Koops, Gentry, and Pantos 2009, which discusses the undoing of the previously merged /ɪ/-/ɛ/ before nasals in Houston, Texas, USA. Production studies show that, along with shifting most other vowels away from Southern variants, many younger speakers now make the "pin-pen" distinction. To test awareness of this change, they asked hearers to indicate what word a speaker produced, from a set of words such as "rinse" or "rents," while their eye movements were tracked. The decision was influenced by a picture presented in the middle of the screen, along with the "rinse" and "rents" choices and two unrelated words. In some cases, the picture was that of a younger speaker, and, indicating awareness of the distinction being made by that group, respondents showed little or no eye movement back and forth between the two reasonable choices when "rinse" was spoken; they focused on "rinse." When the accompanying picture was that of an older person and the pronunciation was "rinse," however, the respondents indicated an awareness of age as a factor in the merger by eye movements that went back and forth between the two choices. Such experiments as these and others reported by Niedzielski in this chapter reveal a sophisticated merger of speech science and sociophonetic investigation in studying implicit and explicit knowledge of language variation.

Chapter 12 is the first of two that focus on group or ethic identification from speech alone by nonspecialist listeners. Here Thomas, Lass, and Carpenter ask if African American English can be identified, and, if so, if there are demographic differences among those who make such identifications with different degrees of reliability and if there are specific phonetic details that permit the identification. They focus on two regional groups and European American and African American listeners' perceptions of the fronting of /o/ (as in "hope"), a feature associated with European American but not African American speakers in the US South, and on the raising of /æ/ (the vowel of "bag"), a feature associated with southern African Americans but not European Americans. Sample sentences were presented unmodified, monotonized, and with all vowels converted to schwa. The local groups were superior, regardless of ethnicity, but considerably hampered in correct identification when the vowel qualities were changed to schwa, and female voices were identified less correctly than male. In a second experiment, the same two vowels were presented along with sentences that contained no samples of vowels known to be distinctive in the varieties under investigation in an attempt to directly contrast prosodic clues with those of vowel quality. The results show that both cues are important, making ethnic voice identification dependent on complexes of features rather than single elements.

Part III: Production and Perception

Chapter 13 continues the question of untrained listeners' ability to identify groups and includes new work on the characteristics of such groups. Purnell first characterizes potentially salient linguistic features of German heritage speakers of English in Wisconsin and African American English. His general goal is to determine what relationship there is between the strength of distinctiveness in these various aspects of the speech signal and the relative salience of those features to identification. In the first experiment, a study is made of the acoustic correlates to final consonant devoicing, first showing that younger speakers in the German heritage area are more aligned with the oldest speakers in this community, a relationship often uncovered in such second language background speech communities. The results show the effectiveness of a trading model for devoicing, in which glottal pulse is inversely correlated to consonant duration, in both perception and production rather than an enhancement model, in which an increase in one factor is accompanied by an increase in the other. This sophisticated multivariate treatment of what are often taken to be single variables (e.g., voicing) leads to the conclusion that hearers are attuned to very low-level features of the signal. Purnell goes on to show that the different groups of hearers use these elements differently. In recalculation of previous work, Purnell also shows that identification of African American, Chicano, and European American voices in a matched-guise experiment is dependent on low-level aspects of the features presented in the signal (the word "hello"). In this case filter (e.g., formant values), source (e.g., pitch) and source-filter (e.g., intensity) characteristics of the signal were considered. He concludes that the relative position of /ɛ/ and /o/ in the vowel space, particularly vowel height, is the major contributing phonetic factor in ethnic identification.

Chapter 14 introduces an interesting twist on the problem of gender identification. Although fundamental frequency (f0) is usually the best clue, it can be unreliable in cases of overlap and idiosyncratic voices and is, therefore, particularly unreliable in the case of young children. Foulkes, Docherty, Khattab, and Yaeger-Dror investigate the possibility that gender related phonetic details other than F0 in a speech community are salient to listeners as gender identity clues. They conducted an experiment in Tyneside, the large conurbation in the northeast of England, with the city of Newcastle upon Tyne as its hub, to investigate this possibility. They first report on production studies that establish gender related voiceless stop variation. In Tyneside, laryngealized (i.e., partially voiced) versions of voiceless stops in medial position are much more common among men, and in word-final (pre-pause) position, preaspirated voiceless stops are preferred by women. Tyneside, non-local UK respondents, and speakers of American English judged lexical items spoken by young children (three to four years of age) as "boy" or "girl" on the basis of samples that incorporated both these variables and were also coded for F0, amplitude, rate of articulation, and vocal quality. F0 returned an interesting result—higher F0 was associated with the "boy" rather than the "girl" response, but amplitude was clearly associated with boys (and these two factors may have interacted). Nevertheless, the features themselves (laryngealization and preaspiration) were significant for locals; Tynesiders more frequently identified laryngealized medial tokens as "boy" and did not reverse the pattern of identification for preaspirated final tokens (where the nonlocal UK and American respondents identified them as "boy"). As in many of the other studies reported here, untrained listeners, particularly local ones, seem remarkably sensitive to low level phonetic variation.

Chapter 15 studies the distribution of and reactions to the lowering of the onset of the /ɛi/ diphthong in an emerging variety here called "Avant-garde Dutch," one associated with younger, well-educated women. Van Bezooijen and van Heuven first establish, from talk-show data, that that social distribution is correct and go on to detail the acoustics of the shift. In this stage, they employ, in addition to a Herz-to-Bark normalization procedure, an "end-point" normalization routine, in which the extremes of /i/ and /a/ are measured to determine the relative height of the lowering of the onset of the diphthong under question for individual respondents. This procedure shows as well a female preference for lowering, although there is a great deal of intra-personal variation in both sexes and glide-weakening appeared to accompany some onset lowering, perhaps an influence on the first stage of the study. Respondents from a variety of regional backgrounds listened to speakers of Standard Dutch, Amsterdam Dutch, "Randstad" Dutch (the Amsterdam conurbation), and Avant-garde Dutch in a typical Likert-scale experiment. Young women showed not only a consistent ability to distinguish Avant-garde Dutch in their rankings, regardless of regional background, but also had more positive attitudes towards it.

In Chapter 16 Evans explores the idea that untrained respondents cannot effectively imitate the linguistic details of another variety. Her respondent, "Noah," is an Inland Northern speaker who spent some time in the North Midlands-South Midlands area of Morgantown, West Virginia, USA. Although most of his associates were also Northern during his time there, he acquired an ability to imitate the local variety, but one that he characterized as no more efficient than that of many of his friends. An acoustic investigation of his imitation speech (from a set passage and word list), however, reveals his relative mastery of important details of the Southern Vowel Shift when he was asked to "read like a West Virginian": reversal of the tense-lax and peripheral character of the pairs /ɪ/-/i/ and /ɛ/-/e/, fronting of back vowels, and monophthongization of diphthongs. This sample was then played for local, West Virginia respondents along with three authentic West Virginia voices and typical Northern and South Midlands speakers from Michigan and southern Indiana, respectively; the respondents were asked to rate how likely it was that each speaker was West Virginian. The imitation variety tied one authentic West Virginia speaker and bested the two others; only very few respondents felt that there was "something wrong" with the imitation; one said it was "over the top," but most had no inkling that one of the voices was an imitation. Perhaps most importantly, as the Atlas of North American English clearly shows, the southern features Noah used in his imitation are, in fact, not all that common in West Virginia, perhaps another victory for stereotype over acoustic fact.

Chapter 17 reports on ongoing work on the vowel system of Memphis, Tennessee in the United States and reactions to it. More than any other chapter here, it suggests that attitudes and perceptions are not just the byproducts of variation but also contributors. Fridland first reports on production studies that seek to determine the degree to which European American and African American Memphians participate in the Southern Vowel Shift. For example, all respondents show the reversal of tense-laxness and peripherality in the /ɛ/-/e/ pair, but not for /ɪ/-/i/; there was considerable back-vowel fronting, no confusion in the low-back area, and extensive /ay/-monophthongization. Fridland then resynthesized tokens of these vowels and others on both the F1 and F2 dimensions and asked local respondents to rate the degree to which each token was "Southern." Her results showed a sensitivity that matched relatively closely the degree of southernness with the active participation of the vowels in the local shift. Respondents also rated these tokens for their "pleasantness" and "education," and degree of southernness was correlated with both unpleasantness and lack of education, although the front vowel reversals had a much stronger influence than back vowel fronting. In an overt ranking task for correctness and pleasantness with no voice samples, however, local respondents found local speech to be uneducated but pleasant, suggesting that there is often a disconnect between overt and covert responses to attitude surveys. In a final perception study, these same Southern vowels were found to be more "rural," another possible explanation for their downgrading.

References

Boersma, Paul and Bruce Hayes. 2001. Empirical tests of the gradual learning algorithm. *Linguistic Inquiry* 32 (1): 45–86.

Boersma, Paul and David Weenink. 1992–2009. Praat: Doing phonetics by computer. http://www.praat.org (accessed February 2, 2010).

Fischer, John L. 1958 Social influences on the choice of a linguistic variant. *Word* 14: 47–56.

Gauchat, Louis. 1905. L'unité phonétique dans le patois d'une commune. In *Aus Romanischen Sprachen und Literaturen; Festschrift Heinrich Morf*, 175–232.

Hermann, Edward. 1929. Lautveränderungen in der Individualsprache einer Mundart. *Nachrichtigen der Gesellsch. Der Wissenschaften zu Göttingen*. Phil.-his Kll., 11, 195–214.

Hibiya, Junko. 1999. Variationist sociolinguistics. In Natsuko Tsujimura (ed.), *The handbook of Japanese linguistics*. Malden, MA and Oxford, UK: Blackwell, 101–120.

Hillenbrand, James, Laura A. Getty, Michael J. Clark, and Kimberlee Wheeler. 1995. Acoustic characteristics of American English vowels. *Journal of the Acoustical Society of America* 97 (5): 3099–3111.

Koops, Christian, Elizabeth Gentry, and Andrew Pantos. 2008. The effect of perceived speaker age on the perception of PIN and PEN vowels in Houston, Texas. *University of Pennsylvania Working Papers in Linguistics* 14: 2 (Selected papers from NWAV 36). http://repository.upenn.edu/pwpl/vol14/iss2/.

Labov, William. 1962. The social motivation of a sound change. *Word* 19: 273–309.

Labov, William. 1994. *Principles of linguistic change: Internal factors*. Oxford, UK: Blackwell.

Labov, William. 2007. Transmission and diffusion. *Language* 83 (2): 344–387

Labov, William. 2009. PLOTNIK. http://www.ling.upenn.edu/~wlabov/Plotnik.html (accessed February 2, 2010).

Labov, William, Malcah Yaeger, and Richard Steiner. 1972. *A quantitative study of sound change in progress*. Philadelphia: US Regional Survey.

Ladefoged, Peter and D. E. Broadbent. 1957. Information conveyed by vowels. *Journal of the Acoustical Society of America* 1 (29): 99–104.

McDavid, Raven I., Jr. 1948 Postvocalic /-r/ in South Carolina: A social analysis. *American Speech* 23: 194–204.

NORM. 2009. NORM: The vowel normalization and plotting suite. http://ncslaap.lib.ncsu.edu/tools/norm/ (accessed February 10, 2010).

Peterson, Gordon E. and Harold L. Barney. 1950. Control methods used in a study of the vowels. *The Journal of the Acoustical Society of America* 24 (2): 175–184.

Pierrehumbert, Janet. 1994. Knowledge of variation. In Katharine Beals, J. Denton, R. Knippen, L. Melnar, H. Suzuki and E. Zeinfeld (eds), *CLS 30*, Volume 2, Papers from the parasession on variation in linguistic theory. Chicago: Chicago Linguistic Society, 232–256.

Plichta, Bartłomiej. 2009. Akustyk: A free Praat plug-in for sociolinguists. http://bartus.org/akustyk/ (accessed February 10, 2010).

Thomas, Erik 2002 Instrumental phonetics. In J. K. Chambers, Peter Trudgill, and Natalie Schilling-Estes (eds), *The handbook of language variation and change*. Malden MA/Oxford: Blackwell, 168–200.

Part I
Studies of Production

Chapter 1

The Peripatetic History of Middle English *ε̄†

Alice Faber, Haskins Laboratories; Marianna Di Paolo, University of Utah; Catherine T. Best, University of Western Sydney & Haskins Laboratories

1. Introduction

In Modern English, descendants of Middle English *ē, *ε̄, and *ε (when lengthened in open syllables) are merged in /i/. Examination of the historical sources and of modern dialects suggests that things were a bit more complicated, however. In particular, while *ε̄ (whether merged with *ε, as in Standard English, or not, as in some scattered dialects) approached *ē in the 14th century, it did not merge with *ē until the 17th century. In the interim, *ε̄ (but not *ē) approached *ǣ (or *æj), an approximation that is reflected both in contemporary prescriptive records and in scattered modern dialects. These historical developments are best understood in terms of a view of language change that is not restricted to investigating historical antecedents of prestige and standard dialects and that takes as a given that languages of the past were typologically and structurally comparable to languages of the present. Thus, for example, if near mergers are observed in present languages, the possibility of near merger cannot be excluded in discussions of past languages. A further consequent of our reexamination of *ε̄ is that additional doubt is cast on the chronological and conceptual unity of the Great English Vowel Shift.

1.1 Background

Modern sociolinguistic research in the Labovian paradigm has documented instances of near mergers. In a near merger, two sounds in a particular language or dialect are measurably and reliably different even though speakers generally behave as if the sounds do not contrast phonologically. In the near merger that we have studied the most, that of tense and lax vowels before /l/ in Utah, speakers produce the contrasting words POOL[1] and PULL with statistically reliable acoustic differences (Di Paolo and Faber 1990; Faber and Di Paolo 1995), yet they often have substantial difficulty in correctly labeling randomly presented words as either POOL or PULL (Di Paolo and Faber 1990; Faber, Best, and Di Paolo 1993a, 1993b). That is, in circumstances that require meta-linguistic reflection, such as a perceptual identification experiment, speakers with a near merger cannot easily access the phonetic distinction that they make in their own speech (Labov, Karen, and Miller 1991; Labov 1994: 357–370, 377–418; Faber, Di Paolo, and Best, ms). Similarly, near merged CHILL and DEAL are perceived to rhyme, as attested in a Salt Lake Valley advertising sign observed in the Spring of 1993: "TAKE OFF THE CHILL WITH/ A D I SWEATER DEAL."[2] For the near merger of /ɑ/ and /ɔ/ in the Intermountain West, listeners in a matched guise experiment rated speakers more favorably on factors associated with Standard English in guises that manifested the typical near merger than in guises with a complete merger or with no examples of /ɔ/ (Di Paolo 1992a). This result suggests that speakers with a near merger are sensitive to the near merged contrast under some circumstances, even though they cannot access it explicitly for linguistic purposes.

As pointed out by Harris (1985), the existence of near mergers follows from the theory of merger propounded by Trudgill and Foxcroft (1978). Trudgill and Foxcroft distinguish between merger-by-transfer and merger-by-approximation (See Figure 1.1). In merger-by-transfer (1a), lexical items move from the class defined by one phoneme to the class defined by another without a phonetically intermediate stage. In merger-by-approximation, in contrast, two phonemes gradually approach, or approximate, each other, until the regions in phonetic space occupied by the two coincide (1b). Such mergers are characterized by phonetically intermediate values. In cases of merger-by-approximation, there may well be a stage in which two phonemes are very close in phonetic space, but have not yet coalesced.

Since the concept of near merger entered sociolinguists' theoretical repertoire (Labov, Yaeger, and Steiner 1972), a substantial number of near mergers have been isolated and studied. These include FOOL/FULL in Albuquerque, NM (Labov et al. 1972) and the Salt Lake Valley (Di Paolo 1988; Di Paolo and Faber 1990; Faber and Di Paolo 1995); SAUCE/SOURCE in New York City (Labov et al. 1972); HERE/HAIR in Norwich, England (Trudgill 1974: 120–125) and possibly in Wellington, NZ (Holmes and Bell 1992); COD/CARD in eastern New England (Costa and Mattingly 1981); HOCK/HAWK in Western Pennsylvania (Labov et al. 1972) and the Intermountain West (Di Paolo 1992a, 1992b); MERRY/MURRAY in Philadelphia (Labov, Karen, and Miller 1991); $C^{j}jV$[3]-$C^{j}ijV$ in Russian (Diehm and

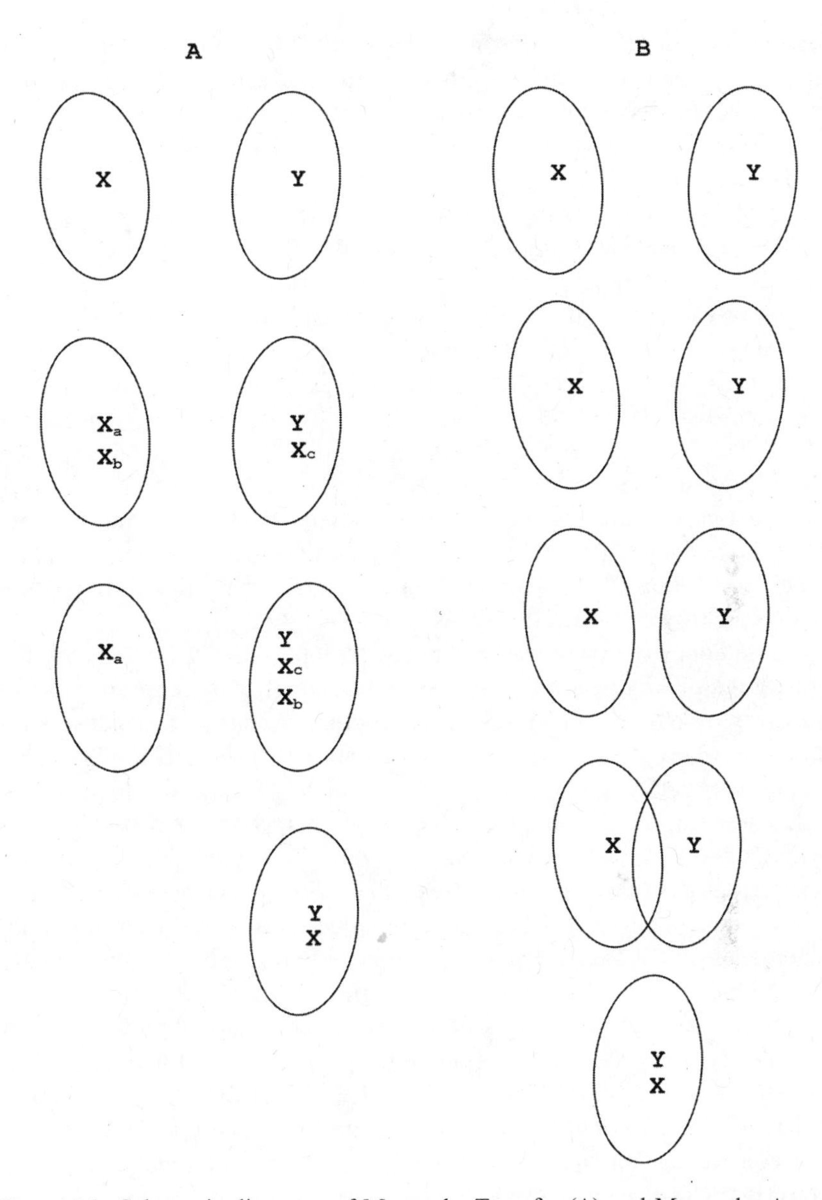

Figure 1.1 Schematic diagrams of Merger-by-Transfer (A) and Merger-by-Approximation (B) of two phonemes /X/ and /Y/. In merger-by-transfer, lexical items containing /X/ gradually come to contain /Y/ instead. In merger-by-approximation, the realizations of /X/ and /Y/ gradually approach each other in phonetic space, until they cannot be differentiated.

Johnson 1997); and, /ɛ/-/æ/ in some varieties of Swedish (Janson and Schulman 1983). And, some situations that have in the past been treated as complete merger have been reanalyzed as near mergers (Miller 1976; Nunberg 1980). Given the general uniformitarian assumption (Labov 1994: 21–45) that past stages of languages, stages that are not directly observable today, were qualitatively the same as modern, directly observable languages, it should be the case that near mergers occurred in the past as well. Clearly the methods used to diagnose near mergers—acoustic analysis and direct interrogation of speakers—are not available for past language stages. However, in languages with a written history and a metalinguistic tradition, it might be possible to discern traces of past near mergers. In fact, Labov (1975), in a paper entitled "Using the present to explain the past," suggested that the early Modern English reflexes of Middle English *ɛ̄ as in MEAT and *ā as in MATE were in fact nearly rather than fully merged. In the precursors of Standard English, the two vowels subsequently diverged, so that *ɛ̄ ultimately merged with *ē as in MEET in Modern English /i/. However, the near merger is still observed in contemporary Belfast vernacular (Harris 1985: 241–248; Milroy and Harris 1980; Milroy 1992: 160).

While Labov (1975) is heavily cited by sociolinguists, this work has been virtually ignored by historical linguists, and especially by those focusing on the history of English. The more general notion of near merger is explicitly dismissed, where it is noted at all. Thus, Lass (1980: 94, n17) refers to the "uncertain empirical and theoretical status" of near mergers in his rejection of the possibility that *ɛ̄ and *æj were nearly merged in the speech of John Hart.[4] Likewise, Stockwell and Minkova (1988: 415) express skepticism about the spectrograms presented in Labov et al. (1972) as evidence of near mergers; it is unclear, however, whether they are questioning the generality of the phenomenon or Labov's interpretation of the spectrographic evidence. In any case, the work cited in the previous paragraph suggests that near mergers are more widespread than might have been supposed based only on a close reading of Labov et al. (1972), providing the phenomenon with a more secure empirical status. In other work (Faber, Di Paolo, and Best Ms.), we address the theoretical status of near mergers, arguing that the existence of near mergers is consistent with current models of speech perception and of language acquisition. Consequently, when it comes to diachronic developments, the only appropriate basis for questioning reconstructions involving near merger is the extent to which they account for known facts. In the remainder of this paper, we will argue that, in the case of MEAT/MATE, no competing explanations have comparable coverage, and that, therefore, the near merger explanation is the most powerful one available.

2. MEAT/MATE revisited

2.1 The problem and the evidence

Because Labov's treatment of the MEAT/MATE facts has not been widely accepted, we felt that a complete re-examination of all the evidence was in order. We soon realized that it would be inappropriate to focus specifically on the MEAT/MATE developments. Instead, we found it necessary to focus more broadly on the changing place of the reflexes of Middle English *ɛ̄ among the English front vowels. Rather than attempt to prove that any one development in the history of the English front vowels exemplifies near merger, we will construct a diachronic scenario in which near mergers play a role. To the extent that this scenario proves illuminating we will have provided support for near merger as a diachronic construct, supplementing the varied synchronic evidence in the literature.

Our scenario will be constructed, as much as possible, on the idealization that changes observed in Standard British English and its ancestors reflect internal developments alone. It is clearly the case that the language of invaders and migrants had an indelible influence on the face of the language; nonetheless, in many instances explicit evidence correlating a specific immigrant group with a specific feature or set of features is at best highly speculative. Milroy (1992) describes the common but inappropriate imposition of modern socially-based notions of standard, prestige, and vulgarism on speech communities of the past. To this we would add that current models relating the structured heterogeneity evident in any speech community to the socioeconomic structure of that speech community are based on the class structure of modern industrialized society. The value of models of language change that find Lower Middle-Class women to be in the vanguard is clearly questionable for societies in which the social role of women is different than in modern societies, societies in which the educational opportunities available to all members, especially to women, were much more limited than today, and societies without a clearly identifiable Middle Class.[5] When outside influences are appealed to in efforts to account for developments in Standard English, these appeals generally hide assumptions about the geographic origin of migrants to London in particular centuries, and how well integrated these migrants were in London speech communities. They also hide assumptions about what sorts of in-migrants would have been in a position to influence the speech of native Londoners. Milroy and others have shown that the responsiveness of vernacular speakers in modern societies to the linguistic norms of standard varieties of their language is much more limited than conservative politicians and educators would like to be the case (Milroy and Milroy 1992: 109–115, with references). Adherence to non-standard, sometimes covert, community norms is a way of showing solidarity with one's community (Labov 1963; Trudgill 1983). It seems unlikely that vernacular speakers in the past would have been more responsive to external normative pressures than those of the present. In any case, appeal to outside influences to explain particular linguistic developments reflects, in large measure, biases that linguistic change must have external causes (see Faber 1992 for further discussion). Instead, our goal here is to construct, insofar as possible, a scenario in which evolution of the Modern English vowel system can be explained on the basis of internal factors alone. Such a scenario seems to us to be a necessary precursor to empirical determination of the actual role of cross-dialect influences and other external factors in shaping the modern English system. While we are not uninterested in either the causes of particular sound changes or in the causes of sound change in general, we prefer to start with a description of what happened. In the case of MEAT/MATE and the allied Great English Vowel Shift, even a cursory review of the literature suggests that adequate description poses a sufficient challenge.

Sources of evidence for the vowel system of English in various times and places are varied. In addition to changing spelling conventions and poetic rhymes, we have orthoepical evidence from various periods, to the extent that this is interpretable. There is also considerable evidence for modern variants in the *Survey of English Dialects* (SED). As with the other sources of evidence, this evidence must be interpreted with caution. Particular variants observed by SED fieldworkers in the middle of the twentieth century cannot be assumed to have had highly comparable distributions 300–400 years ago (similarly, Stockwell and Minkova 1988). Aside from the spread of standard and standard-like forms at the expense of regional variation, the existence at other times of competing regional standards emanating from other centers of influence, especially in the north and in the north Midlands cannot be excluded. Nonetheless, the SED records provide presumptive evidence for the validity of particular systems that might be posited for earlier stages of the language.

One sort of evidence we will not be using is literary puns. Although extensive studies are available of puns in Shakespeare's works (e.g., Kökeritz 1953), in an era that is surely relevant to our topic, we are not convinced that all (or even any) of these puns are necessarily based on complete or perceived homonymy. As Kökeritz (1953: 53*ff*) notes, phonological reconstruction is necessary to distinguish true homonymic puns from those that are not truly homonymic. If phonological reconstruction is necessary to determine which puns are homonymic, then the existence of a particular class of putatively homonymic puns cannot be used to argue for a particular reconstruction without risking circularity. As a result, we will not be using puns as evidence in the present investigation.

2.2 The 'top half' shifts and their chronology

Table 1.1. Late Middle English Front Vowels

Long Vowels	Keywords	Short Vowels	Keywords	Diphthongs	Keywords
ī	BITE	ɪ	BIT	ɪj	NIGHT
ē	FEED				
ɛ̄, ɛ̂	HEAP, SPEAK	ɛ	BET		
(ɔ̄), æ̂	(STONE), NAME	æ	CAT	æj	DAY

The Middle English front vowel space, in Table 1.1, was quite crowded. In addition to the short vowels /ɪ ɛ æ/, there were long vowels /ī ē ɛ̄ ǣ/ and diphthongs /ɪj/ (< *ɪg) and /æj/ (< *ɛg, *æg). We follow Dobson (1968), Stockwell (1985), and Stockwell and Minkova (1988; 1990; 2002) in interpreting the short vowels as qualitatively as well as quantitatively distinct from their long counterparts. This interpretation is based on the fact that there were different numbers of long and short vowels. If both the short vowels and the long vowels were evenly distributed in the front vowel space, there would necessarily have been qualitative differences between the short vowels and their long counterparts. These differences would have been most striking for *ɛ, which would, in the ideal case, have been equidistant from *ē and *ɛ̄, while *ɪ and *æ would have been relatively close to *ī and *ǣ, respectively. Further, when *ɛ lengthened in open syllables the resulting vowel was not identical with *ɛ̄ or with *ē (see section 2.3.1), supporting the suggestion that *ɛ was qualitatively distinct from both *ɛ̄ and *ē. In what follows, we will use the symbol ɛ̂ to refer to this lengthened *ɛ; we will likewise use æ̂, when it is necessary to distinguish original long from lengthened æ. Lass (1980, 1989, 1992b) bases his opposing interpretation that short vowels differed from their long counterparts only in quantity primarily on the fact that 16th-century orthoepists, especially John Hart, do not describe any qualitative differences. However, it is worth noting that John Hart is describing a vowel system several hundred years more advanced than that of Middle English. In particular, the upper half vowel shifts had already taken place. Thus, the fact that post-shift /ī/

in FEED might have been qualitatively identical to *ɪ, or nearly so, in no way means that the pre-shift *ī in BITE was. And if BET and HEAP had vowels of the same quality for Hart, this qualitative identity may reflect raising of *ɛ̄ incidental to the Vowel Shift. In any case, the system in Table 1.1, more or less, provided the input to the Vowel Shift, which we agree should be separated into two; as regards the front vowels, the diphthongization of *ī BITE and raising of *ē FEED must be separated, both chronologically and areally, from the raising of *ɛ̄ HEAP and of *ǣ/*æj DAY/NAME (Johnston 1992; Stockwell and Minkova 1988; Lass 1989).

Stockwell and Minkova suggest that the impetus for the top-half shifts involving *ī BITE and *ē FEED was the early creation of a diphthong in *ɪj NIGHT following the full lenition of velar and palatal fricatives *ɣ/ʑ (and epenthesis of /w/ or /j/ before their voiceless counterparts). Words in the BITE *ī class gradually transferred to the *ɪj NIGHT class, an example of merger-by-transfer. Then, according to Stockwell and Minkova, the onset in *ɪj NIGHT lowered, as *ē FEED, already fairly high, raised further, to fill the gap vacated by the lowering of *ɪj NIGHT (similarly, Jespersen 1909: 233*ff*). We agree with Stockwell and Minkova that *ī BITE diphthongized before *ē FEED rose. However we disagree that merger of *ī BITE and *ɪj NIGHT necessarily played a crucial role in the development of [aj]-like diphthongs for either class. Our disagreement is based on the existence of SED (Orton and Barry 1969) sites in the far north of England in which the *ī BITE and *ɪj NIGHT classes are still distinct. In these locales, the reflex of *ī in BITE is /aj, /æj/, or /ɛj/. At most of these sites, *ɪj NIGHT merged with *ē FEED rather than with *ī BITE. However, at five sites,[6] *ī BITE, *ɪj NIGHT, and *ē FEED are all distinct. At these sites, *ē FEED emerges as a mid central diphthong, /əj/ or /ɛ̈j/,[7] and *ɪj NIGHT is /ī/. Thus diphthongization of *ī BITE, as far as /æj/, is dependent neither on raising of *ē FEED nor on merger with *ɪj NIGHT.

The dialectological evidence regarding the relation between the diphthongization of *ī BITE and the raising of *ē FEED is consistent with the historical attestations of these changes in Southern and Eastern sources, as summarized by Dobson (1968). The merger of *ī BITE and *ɪj NIGHT was complete by 1400, although it is primarily observed in Eastern (e.g., Norfolk) sources in the 15th century (§140), and the diphthongization of the merged phoneme had begun by 1400 as well (§137). The raising of *ē FEED to /i/ was complete by 1450 (Stockwell and Minkova 1988) or 1500 (Dobson, 1968: §132). These chronologies suggest that, at least for the front vowels, diphthongization of the high vowel preceded raising of the mid-high vowel.

Lass (1989; 1992a), following Luick (1964: §482), Wolfe (1972) and others, suggests instead that the raising of *ē FEED (and *ō) pushed *ī/ɪj BITE/NIGHT (and *ū/ʊw) out of the way; as Luick observed, *ū did not diphthongize in dialects in which *ō had previously fronted. Lass' chronological argument (most recently, 1992a) is based primarily on an overt parallelism with the back vowels. That is, if *ō raised before *ū diphthongized, it must also be the case that *ē raised before *ī diphthongized. It seems to us that, rather than being a premise in an argument for a particular chronology, this parallelism is one possible consequent of a demonstration that the chronologies for diphthongization and raising are the same for the front and back vowels. In particular, while, as described before, the dialectological evidence suggests that *ī diphthongized before *ē raised, there is dialectological evidence suggesting that *ō raised before *ū diphthongized. According to the SED (Orton and Barry 1969), in a small region of west central Gloucestershire,[8] *ō has raised to [ū], while *ū is only marginally a diphthong [ᵁū] (similarly, Stockwell and Minkova 1988).[9] This evidence, combined with that adduced earlier, clearly supports an ordering of *ō raising followed by *ū diphthongization. However, the chronological and dialectological evidence suggests that *ī BITE diphthongized before *ē FEED rose.

Further evidence for this chronology comes, paradoxically, from a handful of forms in which *ē raising is attested quite early, especially in eastern and south-eastern sources, as collated by Wełna (2004). In a group of French borrowings (e.g., *friar, inquire, entire, choir, contrive, dice*), many ending in /r/, /ē/ raised to [ī] early enough to merge with *ī, and subsequently diphthongize. Thus, even if the chronologies described previously allowed for ordering *ē raising before *ī diphthongization, they would not support positing a causal link. Rather, they suggest that the two changes spread independently. In some areas, *ē raising began early enough to feed *ī diphthongization, but in the vast majority of the area in which both changes occurred, *ī diphthongization occurred first, so that the subsequent raising did not lead to merger.

2.3 The 'bottom half' shifts

Stockwell and Minkova (1988) treat the changes involving *ǣ NAME as resulting from merger with *æj DAY < *æj, ɛj. The dialectological evidence in SED summarized by Anderson (1987) suggests that this change originated in the north Midlands and eventually spread to virtually all of England, except for a corner in the northwest Midlands. Based on late medieval spellings (c. 1350–1450), especially of *lady*, Johnston (1992) likewise suggests that the bottom-half shifts originated in the Yorkshire Dales (similarly, Luick 1964: §515) by the late 14th century. These shifts may have begun even earlier. Johnston (1992) presents evidence that [ǣ] had raised in some Yorkshire dialects prior to the top half shifts described in section 2.2, and, indeed, prior to open syllable lengthening (OSL). In these dialects (and in other northern dialects), Old English *ā STONE had not backed to /ɔ̄/. In most of these dialects, NAME and STONE ultimately merged; that is, *æ, when it lengthened to [æ̂], merged with *ā. However, in a few parts of the West Riding of Yorkshire, STONE merged with HEAP/SPEAK, as /ɪə/, while NAME varies between /ɪə/ and /eə/. Assuming that OSL affected all short vowel qualities at the same time, Johnston's reconstruction involves an early merger of reflexes of OE *ā STONE and *ɛ̄ HEAP; following OSL, *ɛ̂ SPEAK merged with STONE/HEAP while *æ̂ NAME remained distinct.

Minkova (1982) demonstrates that OSL was a concomitant of the loss of final *-e*. According to the authorities cited by Minkova, both OSL and loss of *-e* were underway in the north early in the 13th century. It follows then that the bottom half shifts began, at least in some areas, by the start of the 13th century. The merger of *æ̂ NAME and *æj DAY did not reach southern Standard English until the early 17th century. The raising of *ɛ̂/ɛ̄ SPEAK/HEAP to /i/ (and the consequent merger with *ē FEED) did not take place until the 16th century in non-standard (especially northern) speech and late in the 17th century in the standard (Dobson §106, §107); thus, Stockwell and Minkova (1988) exclude this final raising to merger from the vowel shift proper. However, in our view, the ultimate merger of *ɛ̂/*ɛ̄ HEAP/SPEAK with *ē FEED in /i/ is the last step in a sequence of events set in motion by the late Middle English lengthening of *ɛ SPEAK in stressed open syllables.

*2.3.1 Step 1: The lengthening of *ɛ*

Despite the crowded Middle English front vowel space, the lengthening of *ɛ SPEAK did not immediately lead to merger. This claim is supported by two pieces of evidence. First of all, *ɛ̂ SPEAK remained distinct from *ɛ̄ HEAP at least until the middle of the last century in a wide area of northwestern England, according to the SED, and more scattered areas elsewhere.[10] This area (indicated in Figure 1.2) includes Lancashire and the West Riding of Yorkshire, as well as Cheshire, Derbyshire, and parts of Staffordshire, Shropshire, Suffolk, Cornwall, Devon, Hampshire, Gloucestershire, Wiltshire, Oxfordshire, and Buckinghamshire. The typical contrast is something like /ɪə/ in HEAP vs. /ɛj/ in SPEAK (Orton and Barry 1969). In much of the area in which *ɛ̄ HEAP and *ɛ̂ SPEAK are distinct, they are distinct from *ē FEED as well. As in Standard English, the reflex of *ē FEED tends to be /i/. Given the retention of a distinction between *ɛ̄ and *ɛ̂ in some areas, with both patterning as long vowels, ordinary comparative methodology requires reconstructing a two-stage process in the ancestors of Southern Standard English (cf. Lass 1988):

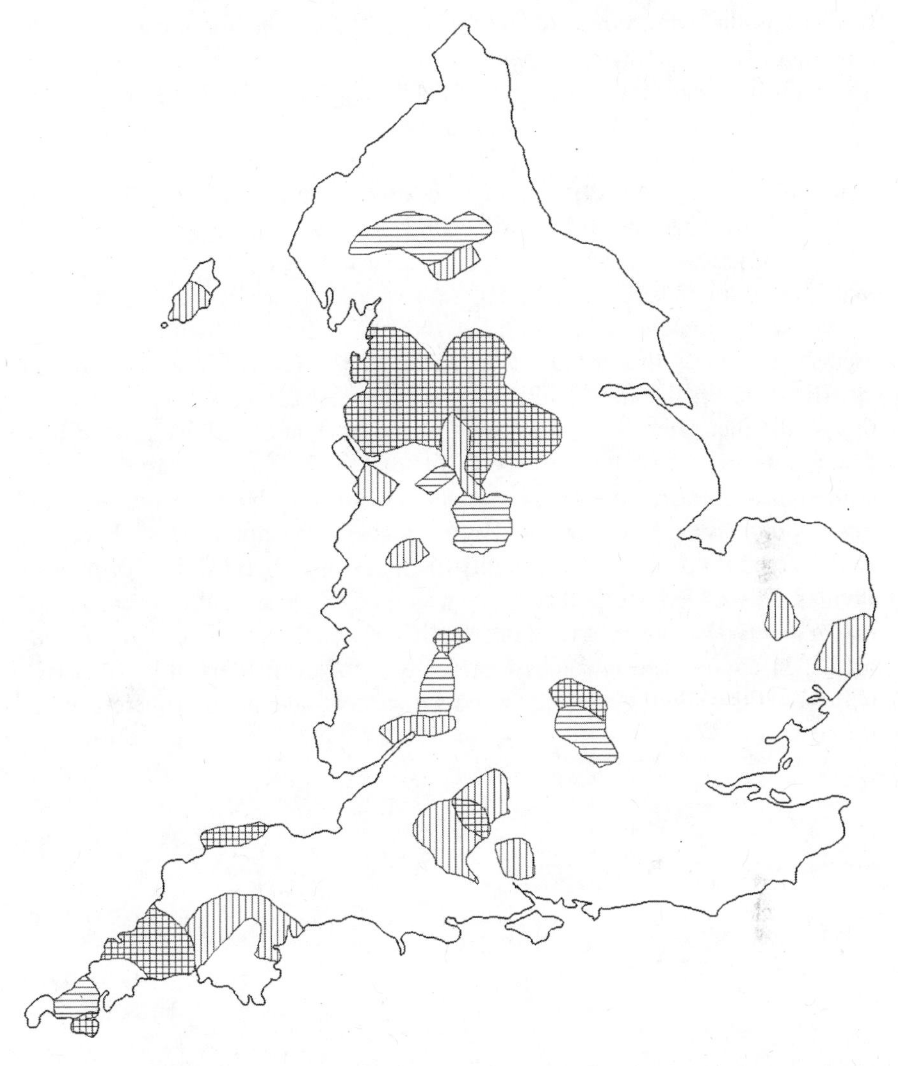

Figure 1.2 Regions of England in which the SPEAK and HEAP classes remain distinct, according to the Survey of English Dialects. Key: cross-hatching indicates that the SPEAK class is distinct from both the HEAP class and the FEED class; vertical stripes, that HEAP and FEED have merged, and are distinct from SPEAK; and horizontal stripes, that SPEAK has merged with FEED, and both are distinct from HEAP. (In all maps, Scotland and Wales are not shown, because they were not surveyed for SED.)

first *ɛ̂ lengthened in virtually all of England; later, in a more restricted area, reflexes of *ɛ̂ merged with those of *ɛ̄.

In any case, this three-way contrast of *ē FEED, *ɛ HEAP, and *ɛ̂ SPEAK was earlier more widespread than indicated in SED. In a study of rhyming patterns used by Chaucer and contemporary poets, Ogura (1980; 1987, ch. 2) found that in the late 14th century, *ɛ̂ SPEAK rhymed with *ɛ̄ HEAP and with *ē FEED, but *ɛ̄ HEAP and *ē FEED did not rhyme with each other. Ogura interprets these facts as reflecting lexical diffusion leading to the ultimate merger of *ē FEED and *ɛ̄ HEAP. However, if, as Ogura suggests, this merger was complete by the middle of the 15th century, subsequent developments are difficult to interpret. Consequently, we would like to suggest that *ɛ̄ HEAP, *ē FEED, and *ɛ̂ SPEAK were phonetically very close, but nonetheless distinct. That is, as illustrated in Figure 1.3a, *ɛ̂ SPEAK stood in a near merger relationship to both *ē FEED and to *ɛ̄ HEAP. Recall that in the modern near mergers that we have studied, words may be perceived as rhyming without having phonetically identical nuclei. We want to stress that these near merged rhymes are conceptually distinct from so-called false or inexact rhymes. The difference is that in near merged rhymes, neither rhymers nor readers are conscious of any phonetic differences between the rhyming elements. In contrast, in inexact rhymes, rhymers and readers alike treat two words as if they rhyme, despite their awareness of phonological differences.

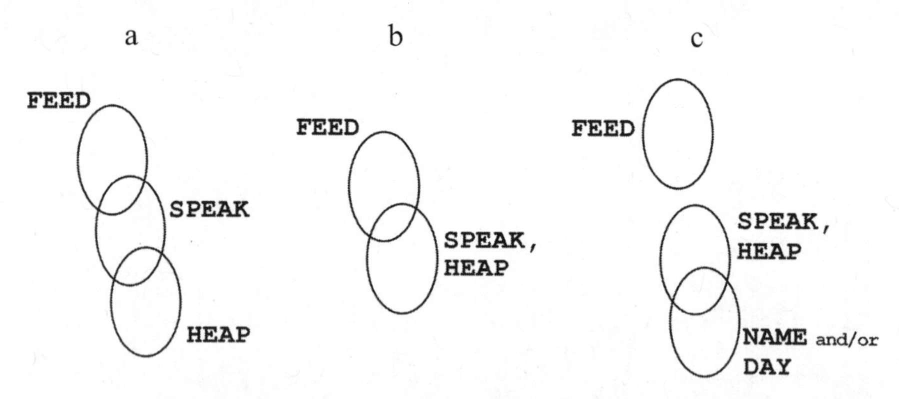

Figure 1.3 Schematic diagrams representing hypothetical overlap of reflexes of Middle English front long vowels and diphthongs. In A, the SPEAK class overlaps with both the FEED class and the HEAP class. In B, the SPEAK and HEAP classes have fallen together, with the result that both overlap with the FEED class. In C, the FEED class has diverged from the SPEAK/HEAP class, which has now come to overlap with the NAME class or the DAY class, neither of which is represented in A or B.

*2.3.2 Step 2: Merger of *ɛ̂ with *ɛ̄ and convergence with *ē*

Ogura also found that by the first part of the 15th century, *ē FEED, *ɛ̄ HEAP, and *ɛ̂ SPEAK all rhymed with each other. She interprets this to mean that all three sounds had merged. We agree with Ogura that the change in rhyming patterns between the late 14th and early 15th centuries is evidence for phonological change. However, we disagree with her as to what that change was. We suspect that two things had happened. First of all, in Chaucer's language, *ɛ̂ SPEAK totally merged with *ɛ̄ HEAP. Secondly, *ɛ̄ HEAP (now including *ɛ̂ SPEAK) moved into a near merger relationship with *ē FEED. If the merger of *ɛ̂ SPEAK and *ɛ̄ HEAP proceeded by *ɛ̄ HEAP moving into the phonetic space occupied by *ɛ̂ SPEAK, as indicated in Figure 1.3b, then the near merger of *ē FEED and *ɛ̄ HEAP would have been a consequence of the earlier near merger of *ē FEED and *ɛ̂ SPEAK, and the two changes are reduced to one. We distinguish between the true merger of *ɛ̄ HEAP and *ɛ̂ SPEAK and the near merger of *ē FEED and *ɛ̄ HEAP based on subsequent developments: *ɛ̄ HEAP and *ɛ̂ SPEAK shared subsequent developments, while *ē FEED and *ɛ̄ HEAP diverged in descendants of Chaucer's language.

*2.3.3 Step 3: Divergence of *ɛ̂/ɛ̄ from *ē and convergence with *ǣ and/or *æj*

Several pieces of evidence suggest that *ɛ̄ HEAP and *ē FEED diverged. First of all, around the turn of the 16th century, the spelling <ea> was reintroduced for *ɛ̄ HEAP, on old Saxon models (Scragg 1974), and this spelling was the norm by the early 17th century. Secondly, according to Dobson (1968) and others, /i/ in FEED was the norm by the turn of the 16th century. Third, also starting in the 16th century, *ɛ̄ HEAP, but not *ē FEED, approximated *ǣ NAME and/or *æj DAY, as illustrated in Figure 1.3c. This near merger continued into the early 18th century in some speech varieties, and, as we will show (in section 2.3.4) into at least the mid-20th century in some parts of England. Contemporary evidence for the approximation of HEAP to NAME and/or DAY, cited by Dobson (1968), Labov (1975, 1994: 298–303), Harris (1985), and others, indicates that HEAP had the same vowel as NAME and/or DAY for some speakers in some areas. Most of this evidence is from non-orthoepical sources. Labov (1994: 302) suggests a socio-economic factor. The few orthoepists who report a system in which HEAP and NAME have the same value were the sons of tradesmen, while their contemporaries who did not report such a system were from landed gentry or noble families. Further, as noted by Milroy (1992), rejection of evidence in support of system (1.3c) (e.g., by Luick 1964: §489, Wolfe 1972, and Cercignani 1981) has been based in large measure on the presumption that sounds once merged cannot unmerge. This presumption is only valid for true mergers, not for near mergers.

Here we have the crux of the matter. It is relatively straightforward to derive the modern English system in which reflexes of *ǣ NAME and *æj DAY contrast with reflexes of *ē FEED, *ɛ̄ HEAP, and *ɛ̂ SPEAK without the intermediate stage in which *ɛ̄ HEAP and *ɛ̂ SPEAK had apparently merged with *ǣ NAME or *æj DAY, as in (1.3c). However, if the speech form in which NAME and DAY contrast with FEED, HEAP, and SPEAK is a direct descendant of one in which HEAP, SPEAK, and NAME and/or DAY were truly merged, there are severe difficulties. There are several 'solutions' in the literature.

The first 'solution' is to deny the validity of the sources suggesting system (1.3c) in the precursor of Standard English. This is the 'solution' adopted by Luick (1964), Wolfe (1972), and Cercignani (1981), among others. One problem with this 'solution' is that, while much of the evidence suggesting system (1.3c) comes from sources that are relatively easy to explain away, John Hart, generally considered the 'best' orthoepist, clearly reports the same vowel in HEAP and DAY, one that differed from his vowel in NAME (see Wolfe 1972: 35*ff* for discussion).

The second 'solution' is to assert that the contemporary standard pronunciation of HEAP/SPEAK with /i/ rather than /e/ was borrowed from another dialect in which system (1.3c) had not occurred because (1.3b) had led to true merger of *ɛ̄/ɛ̂ HEAP/SPEAK with *ē FEED; in such dialects, HEAP/SPEAK would have raised to /i/ when FEED did, in the 15th century. Dobson (§108) notes that the dialects most likely to have influenced the standard, those of Essex, Suffolk, and Norfolk, also apparently had (1.3c). If the raised variant of HEAP/SPEAK was borrowed from any of these dialects to the standard, it is still necessary to explain how HEAP and NAME diverged in them. Further, it seems to us unlikely that any source dialect would have had exactly the same words in the HEAP/SPEAK class as the standard. Whether the dialect borrowing hypothesis is to be interpreted as borrowing lexical items or as changing the pronunciation of lexical items under the influence of the source dialect, changes in the lexical inventories of the dialects would have led to a residue of words in the HEAP/SPEAK class with /e/ rather than /i/. Such a residue clearly exists, in the well known set of 'exceptions' *great, break, steak.*[11] However, the dialect borrowing hypothesis provides no such handy account of words from the NAME and DAY classes which surface in the standard with /i/ rather than /e/. Chief among these are *measles*, from ME *maseles*, with *ā, and *pleat*, a doublet from *plait.* (Other anomalous outcomes, like 19th-century *raisin* with /i/, have been leveled out.)

As a result of difficulties with the dialect borrowing hypothesis, Dobson (§108) suggests that *all* words in the HEAP/SPEAK class had variants with

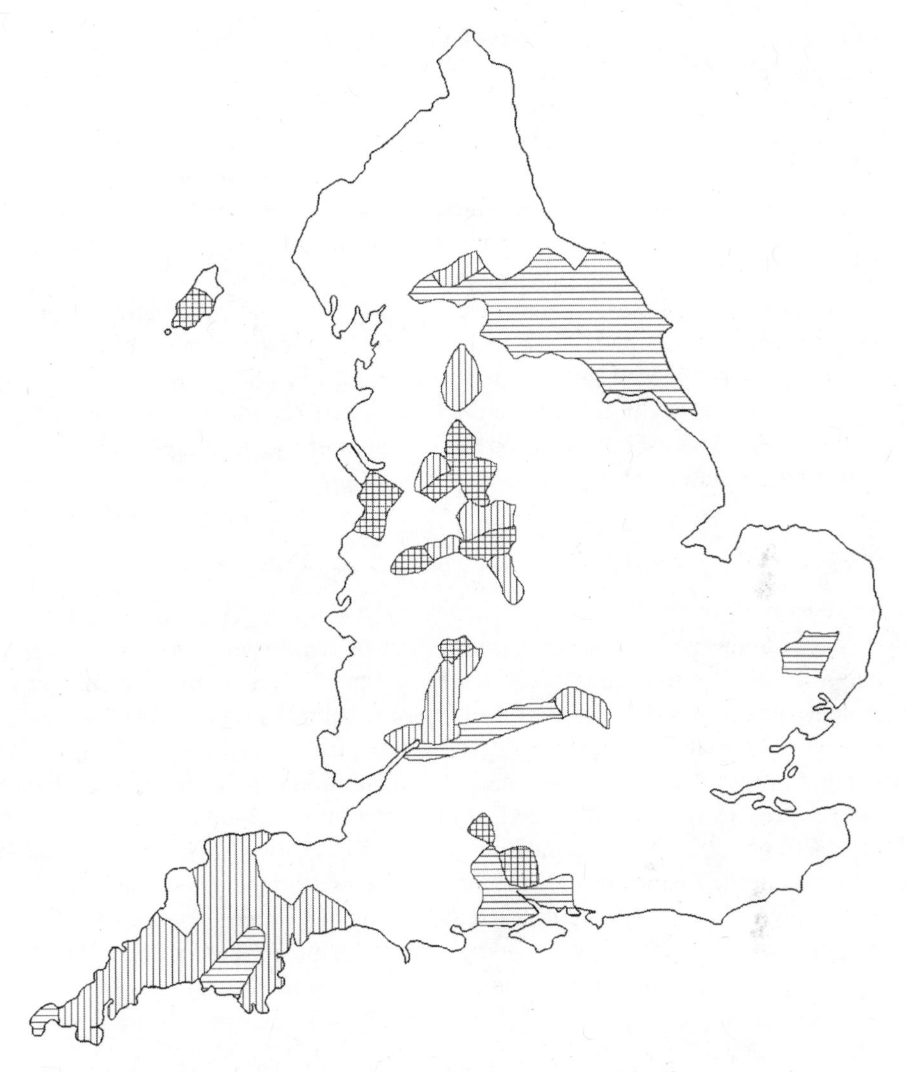

Figure 1.4. Regions of England in which the SED found relics of a merger of SPEAK/HEAP with NAME and/or DAY. Key: horizontal stripes, indicate that SPEAK and/or HEAP is merged with NAME; vertical stripes, that SPEAK and/or HEAP is merged with DAY; and cross-hatching, that SPEAK and/or HEAP is merged with both NAME and DAY.

/ɛ̄/ *and* variants with /ē/, starting as early as the 14th century. Thus, in effect, systems (1.3b) and (1.3c) existed simultaneously in the precursor to Standard English. As *ǣ NAME raised to /ɛ̄/, the lower variant in the HEAP class merged with NAME, and, at the same time, the higher variant merged with

FEED, and, with FEED, raised to /i/ in the 15th century. In Dobson's view, the HEAP/SPEAK variants with /ɛ̄/ dominated through the 17th century, but the higher variants in /i/ (< *ē) ultimately won out.

As Labov (1975) pointed out, the diachronic problem disappears if we assume that the 16th and 17th century *ɛ̄/ɛ̂ HEAP/SPEAK and *ǣ NAME and/or *æj DAY merger was a near merger and not a true merger. It is important to note that Labov's analysis is not a special instance of the first 'solution' described before, that there never was a merger of HEAP/SPEAK with NAME and/or DAY. That solution requires explaining away the observations from the 16th century. In contrast, Labov's near merger account does not require discarding this evidence, since 16th-century speakers who treated HEAP and NAME words as rhyming were behaving exactly like modern speakers with near mergers. That is, Labov's account incorporates a psycholinguistic explanation rather than carelessness for the observations of these speakers.

*2.3.4 Step 4: Merger of *ɛ̂/ɛ̄ with *ē and of *ǣ with *æj*

The near merger of HEAP/SPEAK with NAME and/or DAY did not necessarily occur in the same wide geographical area as the earlier merger of HEAP and SPEAK. However the widely dispersed reports of a comparable merger in contemporary dialects (Figure 1.4) suggest that it too was relatively widespread. (The transcriptional identity of reflexes of *ɛ̄ and *ǣ in SED reports for these areas may, of course, mask a contemporary near merger like that observed by Harris (1985) in Belfast.) In addition to the approximation and repulsion of HEAP/SPEAK and NAME and/or DAY, two additional changes occurred in the history of the standard. These are the merger of *ǣ NAME and *æj DAY already mentioned and the raising of *ɛ̂/ɛ̄ HEAP/SPEAK to /i/, merging with *ē FEED. These changes are in principle independent. Thus, there are eight possible descendants of the system in (2c). These outcomes are listed in Table 1.2. Seven of these possible outcomes are attested in the SED records.

The first possible outcome is no change. That is, *ɛ̄ HEAP, *ɛ̂ SPEAK, and *ǣ NAME would continue to be distinct from *ē FEED and from *æj DAY. This pattern is attested in the North Riding of Yorkshire, in Hampshire, and in parts of Gloucestershire, Devon, Cornwall, and Suffolk.[12] The second outcome is reversal of the near merger, with no additional change. This pattern is attested in parts of Cumberland, Lancashire, and NW Yorkshire, as well as in scattered locations in Staffordshire, Dorset, Cornwall, and Essex.[13] (This pattern may, of course, be a direct continuation of (1.3b) rather than an outcome of (1.3c) with re-splitting of *ɛ̄ HEAP and/or *ɛ̂ SPEAK from *ǣ NAME.) As

Table 1.2 Possible Descendants of Vowel System (1.3c)

Outcome	*# of Different Vowels*	*Changes from 1.3c*	*Contrasting Word Classes*	*Where Attested*
1.	3	no change	HEAP/SPEAK/ NAME vs. DAY vs. FEED	Yorks, Hamps, parts of Gloucestershire, Cornwall, Devon, Suffolk
2.	4	Resplit	HEAP/SPEAK vs. NAME vs. DAY vs. FEED	parts of Cumberland, Lancs, parts of NW Yorks, Dorset, Essex
3.	2	Merger 1	HEAP/SPEAK/ NAME/DAY vs. FEED	SED site Ch 6 (Hanmer, Flintshire)
4.	3	Resplit + Merger 1	HEAP/SPEAK vs. NAME/DAY vs. FEED	Central Yorks and Lincolnshire, Westmorland
5.	2	Merger 2	HEAP/SPEAK/ NAME/FEED vs. DAY	Scattered locations in N Yorks, Hamps, Staffordshire
6.	3	Resplit + Merger 2	HEAP/SPEAK/ FEED vs. NAME vs. DAY	East Anglia, Kent, Wilts, Somerset, Oxfordshire, Herefordshire; earlier and independently in far North
7.	2	Resplit + Merger 1 + Merger 2	HEAP/SPEAK/ FEED vs. NAME/ DAY	SE England, S Midlands (Standard English)
8.	1	Merger 1 + Merger 2	HEAP/SPEAK/ FEED/NAME/ DAY	Not attested

already indicated, the merger of *ǣ NAME and *æj DAY probably began in the West Riding of Yorkshire. In the West Riding of Yorkshire and in Lancashire, this was the only merger to occur in the front vowel system, although the pronunciation of the vowels has changed. The third possible outcome then is superposition of this merger on the preceding *ɛ̄/*ɛ̂/*ǣ HEAP/SPEAK/ NAME merger or near merger, giving rise to a system in which *ɛ̄/*ɛ̂/*ǣ/*æj

HEAP/SPEAK/NAME/DAY contrast with *ē FEED. This system is attested only in Cheshire (C6 Hanmer [Flintshire]). Anderson (1987) suggests, however, that it was formerly more widespread in the South Midlands. The fourth outcome is reversal of the near merger, coupled with merger of *ǣ NAME and *æj DAY, giving rise to a system with a three-way contrast of *ɛ̄/*ɛ̂ HEAP/SPEAK, *ǣ/*æj NAME/DAY, and *ē FEED. This system is attested in central Yorkshire, in Lincolnshire, and in southern Westmorland.

The fifth possible outcome is merger of *ɛ̄/*ɛ̂/*ǣ HEAP/SPEAK/NAME with *ē FEED. This system is attested only in a few isolated locations in Hampshire, Yorkshire, and Staffordshire.[14] There are, in addition, dialects in which *ɛ̄/*ɛ̂ HEAP/SPEAK diverged from *ǣ NAME, merging instead with *ē FEED. This is the sixth possible outcome, and it is attested in East Anglia and Kent, as well as in Somerset, Herefordshire, Wiltshire, and Oxfordshire, and in Derbyshire (and parts of adjacent counties). In the seventh possible outcome, everything happened. That is, *ɛ̄/*ɛ̂ HEAP/SPEAK diverged from *ǣ NAME; *ǣ NAME then merged with *æj DAY, and *ɛ̄/*ɛ̂ HEAP/SPEAK with *ē FEED. This is the Standard English system, indicated with small cross-hatches in Figure 1.5. Aside from the coastal areas where it is probably a late intrusion (Bristol, Isle of Man, coastal Northumberland and Durham), this system is attested in two large areas, the Southeast of England (including London), and the South Midlands. (The eighth possible outcome of system (1.3c), collapse of all five vowel classes into a single category, is not attested anywhere.)

Because the *ǣ/*æj NAME/DAY and *ɛ̄/*ɛ̂/*ē HEAP/SPEAK/FEED mergers are logically independent, they could have occurred in different orders in different areas. As already noted, the *ǣ/*æj NAME/DAY merger originated in the West Riding of Yorkshire. Most of the area in which this merger took place but not the merger of *ɛ̄/*ɛ̂/*ē HEAP/SPEAK/FEED is in the north. This area is marked with horizontal stripes in Figure 1.5. In contrast, most of the area in which *ɛ̄/*ɛ̂/*ē HEAP/SPEAK/FEED merged but not *ǣ/*æj NAME/DAY is in the east and south. This area is marked with vertical stripes in Figure 1.5. This geographical location is consistent with Dobson's observation that the earliest indications of the *ɛ̄/*ɛ̂/*ē HEAP/SPEAK/FEED merger are in eastern sources.

To our puzzlement, Anderson (1987) describes the *ǣ/*æj NAME/DAY merger as atypical for the south. He attributes its spread to a South Midlands koine in which HEAP/SPEAK/NAME/DAY were merged (outcome 3 on Table 1.2). Although SED records such a system only in Flintshire (Cheshire 6), it was attested in various locations in the South Midlands in the 19th century. However, it is difficult to see how such a system could have provided the basis for a merger of *æj DAY with *ǣ NAME rather than with *ɛ̄/*ɛ̂ HEAP/SPEAK,

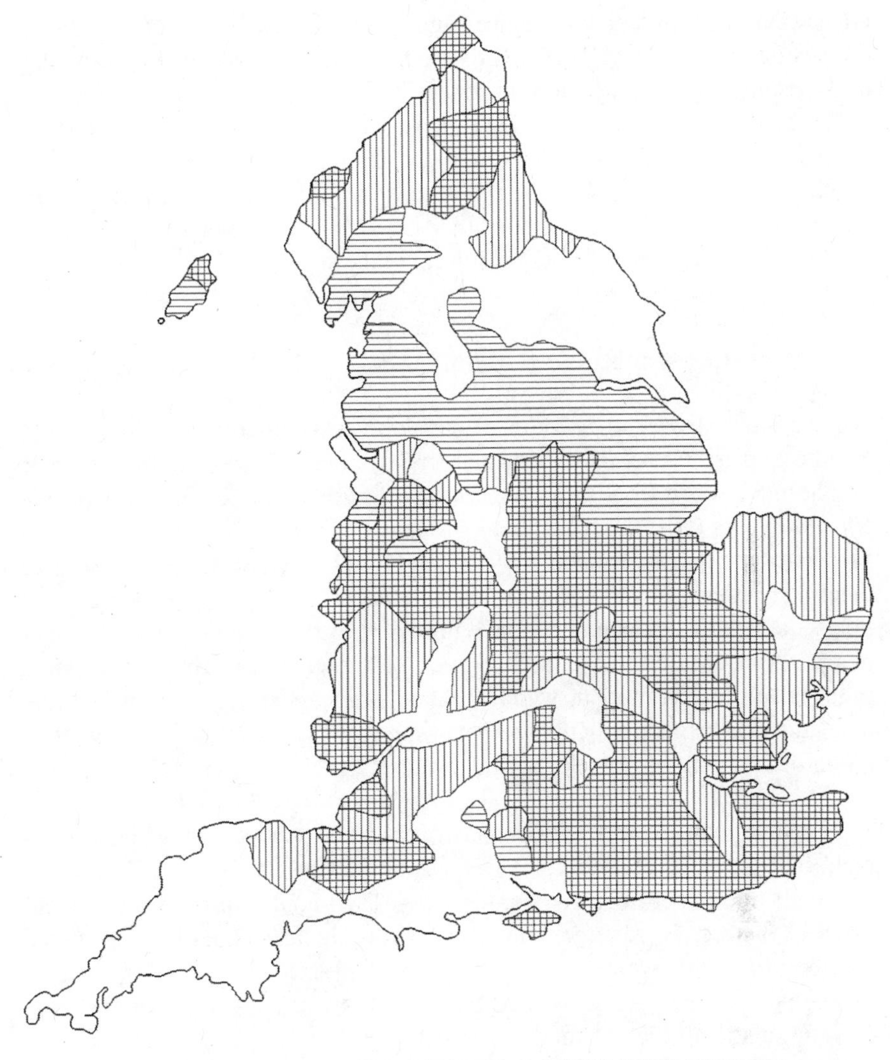

Figure 1.5 Geographic extent of NAME/DAY and SPEAK/HEAP/FEED mergers, in SED. Key: horizontal stripes indicate that NAME is merged with DAY; vertical stripes, that SPEAK/HEAP is merged with FEED; and cross-hatching, that both mergers occurred.

unless this system in fact reflected a near merger of *ɛ̄/*ɛ̂ HEAP/SPEAK with *ǣ/*æj NAME/DAY. In any case, we prefer to interpret the apparent atypicality of the *ǣ/*æj NAME/DAY merger in the Southeast as reflecting the late spread of this change from the West Riding of Yorkshire to the Southeast.

Given that the geographic evidence suggests a southern or eastern origin for the raising of *ɛ̄/*ɛ̂ HEAP/SPEAK to /i/, and the diachronic evidence provided by Dobson suggests an eastern origin, it is likely that the two large areas in which both the *ǣ/*æj NAME/DAY merger and the raising of *ɛ̄/*ɛ̂ HEAP/SPEAK to /i/ are attested underwent these changes in different orders. In the Southeast, *ɛ̄/*ɛ̂ HEAP/SPEAK raised to /i/ before the *ǣ/*æj NAME/DAY merger, while in the Midlands, *ǣ NAME and *æj DAY merged before *ɛ̄/*ɛ̂ HEAP/SPEAK raised to /i/, both resulting in the same system.

3. Summary and Conclusion

We can summarize our account of developments undergone by reflexes of Middle English *ɛ̄ as a series of mergers and near mergers, culminating in Southern Standard English, in a merger with reflexes of *ē. Over a period of 500-600 years (20–24 generations), *ɛ̄ nearly merged with *ē, merged with *ɛ̂, nearly merged with *ǣ and/or *æj, and finally merged with *ē. Only in a theory of language which distinguishes between near and true mergers can this sequence of developments have occurred in the history of a single language variety. While we certainly do not wish to claim that there are isolated villages in the Pennines in which Elizabethan English has been preserved, unchanged, our reconstruction derives support from the contemporary attestation of comparable vowel systems to those that we have posited for earlier stages of the language.

Further, our reconstruction constitutes an extended plausibility argument that the modern English vowel system can be attributed to a series of internally motivated, natural sound changes, without requiring recourse to external factors. To reiterate some of our introductory remarks, we are not claiming that there were no such externally-motivated changes in the history of English. Rather, just as our reconstruction is true to what is known from sociolinguistic studies of modern speech communities, so too any account relying on attested pre-modern population movements must be true to what is known from modern studies of language change in contact situations. While our account relies on modern descriptions of near mergers in a variety of speech communities, to the extent that it is plausible, it also provides presumptive evidence for the validity of the concept of near merger.

In our account we distinguish between the radiation of a linguistic innovation outward from its area of origin and the borrowing of innovated forms. The Standard English contrast of HEAP/SPEAK/FEED with NAME/DAY can be explained as the result of a series of ordinary linguistic innovations originating in different parts of England, without recourse to dialects in which different innovations occurred, and without recourse to otherwise unattested diglossic situations. Rather, we hope to have demonstrated that the concept of near merger, imported from modern sociolinguistic studies, can indeed, as Labov suggested 35 years ago, shed light on the development of the Modern English vowel system.

Notes

† The research reported in this paper was supported by NIH grants HD-01994 and DC-00403. A preliminary version was presented at the January 1994 meeting of the Linguistic Society of America. We would like to take this opportunity to thank those who commented on that presentation, as well as Bill Labov for his thoughtful comments on the written text.

1 Here and throughout, words in capital letters represent classes of words with the same vowel nucleus. Thus, we use "FOOL/FULL" to refer to those words containing /ul/ and those words containing /ʊl/, respectively.

2 We are grateful to Tom D. Pratt for bringing this sign to our attention.

3 C^j refers to any palatalized consonant. The functional load of the contrast between C^jjV and C^jijV is, according to Diehm and Johnson, quite low. Nonetheless, the sequences are acoustically distinct, but not perceived as categorically different by Russian speakers.

4 See section 2.3.3 for further discussion of the *ɛ̄/æj problem. In later work, Lass (1992b: 10) seems more open to the possibility of a "marginal (but cooptable) difference" between sounds in his discussion of possible quality differences between *ī and *ɪ. See section 2.2 for further discussion.

5 For similar caveats, see Guy (1990). On changes in British society and class structure in the early Modern period, see Coward (1988) and Earle (1989).

6 Du 4 Witton-le-Wear, Du 5 Bishop Middleham, We 4 Stavely-in-Kendall, Y 3 Skelton, and Y 13 Horton-in-Ribblesdale.

7 With the exception of Y 3 Skelton, where *ē FEED is /ɪə/, and is merged with reflexes of *ɛ̄ HEAP, *ɛ̂ SPEAK, *æ̂ NAME, and *ā STONE.

8 Gl 6 Slimbridge and 7 Latteridge.

9 Stockwell and Minkova (1988) phonemicize these Gloucestershire reflexes of *ō and *ū as /ū/ and /ʊu/, while Orton, Sanderson, and Widdowson (1978) phonemicize both as /ū/. In light of the consistency of the fieldworker's transcriptions (of 20 items containing *ū in the first two parts of Orton and Barry (1969), 18 have [^{ʊ}ū] at Gl 6 and 19 at Gl 7; of 13 items containing *ō, 9 have [ū] at Gl 6 as do all 13 at Gl 7; the remaining 4 items with *ō are missing at Gl 6 or have a vowel other than [ū] or [^{ʊ}ū], including one token of *broody* with [aʊ]), it seems likely that the

contrast is real. However, given the phonetic similarity between [ū] and [^{ʊ}ū], the possibility of a near merger cannot be excluded.

10 Our claims about the distribution of dialect forms in England are based on Kolb (1966), Anderson (1987), Orton et al. (1978), Kolb, Glauser, Elmer, and Stamm 1979, and our own independent collation of the SED Basic Materials (Orton and Barry 1969; Orton and Halliday 1962; Orton and Tilling 1969; Orton and Wakelin 1967), guided by the phonemicizations implicit in Orton et al. (1978). Our interpretations of the SED material differ from Anderson's in several respects. Aside from trivial differences in the exact placement of boundaries and differences resulting from the fact that we collated a different subset of the lexical material than did Anderson, there are two fundamental differences. First, we recorded forms that were identified in the Basic Materials as "older" at the expense of those reflecting Standard English, even if the latter were more typical of a site, while Anderson gave equal weight to each form recorded. Secondly, Anderson's treatment of *ɛ̄ and *ɛ̂ is somewhat confused. In his introduction (p. 11) and in the key to maps 59A and B (p. 90), *ɛ̄ is designated E_1, and *ɛ̂ E_2; however, in the discussion of long front vowels (p. 85), *ɛ̂ is designated E_1. While the reference on p. 85 may be a simple typographical error, it is precisely with regard to those areas in which *ɛ̄ and *ɛ̂ are still distinct that our maps are most different from Anderson's.

Because of the importance to our argument of the non-standard systems in the West Midlands, the first and second authors independently collated materials from twenty-six sites in this region and seven Gloucestershire sites, using distinct but overlapping sets of items from the Basic Materials. For twenty out of these thirty-three sites, our initial classifications agreed. Differences in interpretation for nine additional sites were resolved through negotiation. In four remaining cases, Ch 1 Kingsley, Db 3 Burbage, Db 4 Youlgreave, and St 1 Warslow, no agreement was reached. For these sites, we used the classifications of the first author.

With regard to the systems mapped, a further caveat is in order. The areas in which *ɛ̄, *ɛ̂, and *ē, for example, are still distinct may differ with regard to both the phonetic realizations of these categories and with regard to other mergers. Thus, in some parts of the cross-hatched area in Figure 1.2, *ɛ̂ has merged with *æj, while in others it is distinct from *ɛ̄, *ē, *ǣ, and *æj, although not, perhaps, from reflexes of OE *ā STONE.

11 More plausibly, Luick (1964: §500) treats *great* and *break* as borrowings, while forms like *heap* represent the normal development. Throughout the 17th century, the orthoepists treat *great* and *break* as regular. Anomalous pronunciations with [e] first appear in the early 18th century. Until late in that century pronunciations of *great* with [i] still occurred, but were considered affected. SED also records scattered instances of *break* with [i], e.g., Sa 2 Prees, Db 4 Youlgreave, St 1 Warslow, St 2 Mow Cop. The anomalous vowel in *yea* is generally explained as parallelism with that in *nay*. The only thing exceptional about *steak* is its spelling. The source for its nucleus is Old Norse /ei/, which has [e] as its normal reflex (Jesperson 1909: 76; Luick 1964: §389; Bloomfield 1984: 360–361). Other forms with ON /ei/

are *raise*, *swain*, *nay*, *they*, *bait*, *hale* and *wail*; *weak* is anomalous in that it fell in with ME *ɛ̄ rather than *æj.

12 Dv 10 Cornwood, Dv 9 Widecombe-in-the-Moor, Cornwall 6 St. Buryan, Sf 5 Kersey, Gl 5 Sherborne, Gl 6 Slimbridge.

13 Cu 6 Gosforth, La 1 Coniston, St 1 Warslow, Wa 2 Hockley Heath, Ess 11 Netteswell.

14 Y 3 Skelton, St 3 Alton, Ha 1 Hatherden.

References

Anderson, Peter M. 1987. *A structural atlas of the English Dialects*. London: Croom Helm.

Bloomfield, Leonard. [1933] 1984. *Language*. Chicago: University of Chicago Press.

Cercignani, Fausto.. 1981. *Shakespeare's works and Elizabethan pronunciation.* Oxford: Clarendon Press.

Costa, Paul and Ignatius G. Mattingly. 1981. Production and perception of phonetic contrasts during phonetic change. *Haskins Laboratories Status Report on Speech Research* SR 67/68: 191–196.

Coward, Barry. 1988. *Social change and continuity in early modern England 1550–1750.* (Seminar Studies in History). London: Longman.

Diehm, Erin and Johnson, Keith. 1997. Near-merger in Russian palatalization. *OSU Working Papers in Linguistics* 50: 11–18.

Di Paolo, Marianna. 1988. Pronunciation and categorization in sound change. In Kathy Ferrara, Becky Brown, Keith Walters, and John Baugh (eds), *Linguistic change and contact: Proceedings of the Sixteenth Annual Conference on New Ways of Analyzing Variation in Language*. Austin: Texas Linguistic Forum 30, 84–92.

Di Paolo, Marianna. 1992a. Hypercorrection in response to the apparent merger of (ɑ) and (ɔ) in Utah English. *Language and Communication* 12: 267–292.

Di Paolo, Marianna. 1992b. Evidence for the instability of a low back vowel 'merger.' Paper presented at the 21st Annual Conference on New Ways of Analyzing Variation in Language. Ann Arbor, Michigan.

Di Paolo, Marianna and Alice Faber. 1990. Phonation differences and the phonetic content of the tense-lax contrast in Utah English. *Language Variation and Change* 2: 155–204.

Dobson, Eric J. 1968. *English pronunciation, 1500–1700*. Vol. II. *Phonology*. Oxford: Clarendon.

Earle, Peter. 1989. *The making of the English middle class: Business, society and family life in London, 1660–1730*. Berkeley: University of California Press.

Faber, Alice. 1992. Articulatory variability, categorical perception, and the inevitability of sound change. In Garry Davis and Greg Iverson (eds), *Explanation in historical linguistics*. Amsterdam: John Benjamins, 58–75.

Faber, Alice, Catherine T. Best, and Marianna Di Paolo. 1993a. Cross-dialect perception of nearly merged forms. Paper presented at the Annual Meeting of the LSA. Los Angeles, California.

Faber, Alice, Catherine T. Best, and Marianna Di Paolo. 1993b. Dialect differences in vowel perception. Paper Presented at the Fall Meeting of the Acoustical Society of America. Denver, Colorado.

Faber, Alice and Marianna Di Paolo. 1995. The discriminability of nearly merged forms. *Language Variation and Change* 7: 35–78.

Faber, Alice, Marianna Di Paolo, and Catherine T. Best. Ms. Perceiving the unperceivable: The acquisition of near merged forms.

Guy, Gregory R. 1990. The sociolinguistic types of language change. *Diachronica* 7: 47–67.

Harris, John. 1985. *Phonological variation and change: Studies in Hiberno English.* Cambridge: Cambridge University Press.

Holmes, Janet and Allan Bell. 1992. On shear markets and sharing sheep: The merger of EAR and AIR diphthongs in New Zealand speech. *Language Variation and Change* 4: 251–273.

Janson, Tore and Richard Schulman. 1983. Non-distinctive features and their uses. *Journal of Linguistics* 19: 321–336.

Jespersen, Otto. 1909. *A modern English grammar on historical principles.* Part 1: *Sounds and spelling.* Heidelberg: Carl Winters.

Johnston, Paul A. 1992. English vowel shifting: One great vowel shift or two small vowel shifts? *Diachronica* 9: 189–226.

Kastovsky, Dieter and Gero Bauer (eds). 1988. *Luick revisited.* Tübingen: Gunter Narr Verlag.

Kökeritz, Helge. 1953. *Shakespeare's pronunciation.* New Haven: Yale University Press.

Kolb, Eduard. 1966. *Phonological atlas of the northern region: The six northern counties, North Lincolnshire and the Isle of Man.* Bern: Francke Verlag.

Kolb, Eduard, Beat Glauser, Willy Elmer, and Renate Stamm. 1979. *Atlas of English sounds.* Bern: Francke Verlag.

Labov, William. 1963. The social motivation of a sound change. *Word* 19: 273–309.

Labov, William. 1975. On the use of the present to explain the past. *Proceedings of the Eleventh International Congress of Linguists.* Vol. 2. Bologna: Società Editrice Il Mulino, 825–851.

Labov, William. 1994. *Principles of linguistic change: Internal factors.* Oxford: Blackwell.

Labov, William, Mark Karen, and Corey Miller. 1991. Near mergers and the suspension of phonemic contrast. *Language Variation and Change* 3: 33–74.

Labov, William, Malcah Yaeger, and Richard C. Steiner. 1972. *A quantitative study of sound change in progress.* Philadelphia: US Regional Survey.

Lass, Roger. 1980. John Hart *Vindicatus*? A study in the interpretation of early phoneticians. *Folia Linguistica* 1: 75–96.

Lass, Roger. 1988. Vowel shifts, great and otherwise: Remarks on Stockwell and Minkova. In Kastovsky and Bauer (eds), 395–410.

Lass, Roger. 1989. How early does English get modern? Or, what happens if you listen to orthoepists and not to historians. *Diachronica* 6: 75–110.

Lass, Roger. 1992a. What, if anything, was the Great Vowel Shift? In Matti Rissanen, Ossi Ihalainen, Terttu Nevalainen, and Irma Vitsainen (eds), *History of Englishes: New methods and interpretations in historical linguistics*. Berlin: Mouton, 144–155.

Lass, Roger. 1992b. The Early Modern English short vowels *noch Einmal*, again: A reply to Minkova and Stockwell. *Diachronica* 9: 1–13.

Luick, Karl. [1914–1929] 1964. *Historische Grammatik der englischen Sprache*. Oxford: Blackwell.

Miller, D. Gary. 1976. Glide deletion, contraction, Attic reversion, and related problems of Ancient Greek phonology. *Die Sprache* 22: 137–156.

Milroy, James. 1992. *Linguistic variation and change*. Oxford: Blackwell.

Milroy, James and John Harris. 1980. When is a merger not a merger? The MEAT/MATE problem in a present-day English vernacular. *English World Wide* 1: 199–210.

Milroy, James and Lesley Milroy. 1992. *Authority in language: Investigating language prescription and standardization*, 2nd. ed. London: Routledge.

Minkova, Donka. 1982. The environment for open syllable lengthening in Middle English. *Folia Linguistica Historica* 3: 29–58.

Nunberg, Geoffrey. 1980. A falsely reported merger in eighteenth-century English: A study in diachronic variation. In William Labov (ed.), *Locating language in time and space*. New York: Academic Press, 221–250.

Ogura, Mieko. 1980. The development of ME *ε̄: A case of lexical diffusion. *Studies in English Literature*, 39–57.

Ogura, Mieko. 1987. *Historical English phonology: A lexical perspective*. Tokyo: Kenkyusha.

Orton, Harold and Michael V. Barry. 1969. *Survey of English dialects*, B: Vol. 2: *The West Midland Counties*. Leeds: E. J. Arnold.

Orton, Harold and Wilfred J. Halliday. 1962. *Survey of English dialects*, B: Vol. 1: *The Northern counties and the Isle of Man*. Leeds: E. J. Arnold.

Orton, Harold, Stewart Sanderson, and John Widdowson. 1978. *The linguistic atlas of England*. London: Croom Helm.

Orton, Harold and Philip M. Tilling. 1969. *Survey of English dialects*, B: Vol. 3: *The East Midland counties and East Anglia*. Leeds: E. J. Arnold.

Orton, Harold and Martyn F. Wakelin. 1967. *Survey of English dialects*, B: Vol. 4: *The Southern counties*. Leeds: E. J. Arnold.

Scragg, D. G. 1974. *A history of English spelling*. New York: Barnes & Noble.

SED (Survey of English Dialects) = Orton and Barry 1969; Orton and Halliday 1962; Orton and Tilling 1969; Orton and Wakelin 1967.

Stockwell, Robert P. 1985. Assessment of alternative explanations of the Middle English phenomenon of high vowel lowering when lengthened in the open syllable. In

Roger Eaton, Olga Fischer, Willem Koopman, and Frederike van der Leek (eds), *Papers from the 4th ICEHL*. Amsterdam: John Benjamins, 303–318.

Stockwell, Robert P. and Donka Minkova. 1988. The English Vowel Shift: Problems of coherence and explanation. In Kastovsky and Bauer (eds), 355–394.

Stockwell, Robert P. and Donka Minkova. 1990. The Early Modern English vowels, more o'Lass. *Diachronica* 7: 199–214.

Stockwell, Robert P. and Donka Minkova. 2002. Interpreting the Old and Middle English close vowels. *Language Sciences* 24: 447–457.

Trudgill, Peter. 1974. *The social differentiation of English in Norwich*. Cambridge: Cambridge University Press.

Trudgill, Peter. 1983. Sex and covert prestige: Linguistic change in the urban English of Norwich. *On Dialect*. Oxford: Blackwell, 169–195.

Trudgill, Peter and Tina Foxcroft. 1978. On the sociolinguistics of vocalic merger: Transfer and approximation in East Anglia. In Peter Trudgill (ed.), *Sociolinguistic patterns in British English*. London: Edward Arnold, 69–79.

Wells, John. 1982. *Accents of English*. 3 Volumes. Cambridge: Cambridge University Press.

Wełna, Jerzy. 2004. Middle English ē raising: A prelude to the Great Vowel Shift. *Studia Anglica Posnaniensia* 40: 75–85.

Wolfe, Patricia M. 1972. *Linguistic change and the Great Vowel Shift in English*. Berkeley: University of California Press.

Chapter 2

Social and Phonetic Conditioners on the Frequency and Degree of "intrusive /r/" in New Zealand English[1]

Jen Hay and Margaret Maclagan, University of Canterbury

1. Background

This paper investigates the use of intrusive /r/ in New Zealand English (NZE). Intrusive /r/, together with linking /r/, is often referred to as /r/-sandhi. Most non-rhotic dialects of English exhibit /r/-sandhi (see e.g., Docherty and Foulkes 1999; Foulkes 1997a, b, Tollfree 1999, Bauer 1984, Trudgill 1974, Wells 1982, Williams and Kerswill 1999). Linking /r/ refers to cases in which the /r/ is orthographically present, and is produced across a morpheme or word boundary when followed by a vowel (e.g., *fea**r**ing, ca**r** alarm*). Intrusive /r/ occurs in the same environments, but when there is no orthographic /r/ present (e.g., *cla_wing, ma_and pa*). Most theories analyze linking /r/ and intrusive /r/ as synchronically identical—differing only in historical status (intrusive /r/ arose later than linking /r/) and orthographic form.

The use of intrusive /r/ is phonologically conditioned—in most dialects it occurs only after non-high monophthongs or after diphthongs with non-high offglides. However many young New Zealanders are also beginning to use intrusive /r/ after a new vowel: /au/, in uses such as *now-/r/-and then*, or *plough/r/ing.*

Phonological accounts of /r/-sandhi vary in terms of whether they analyze the /r/ as underlyingly present, inserted, or some combination of the two (see, e.g., McCarthy 1993, Harris 1994, Vennemann 1972, Johansson 1973, McMahon, Foulkes and Tollfree 1994, McMahon 2000). However virtually all of this literature models /r/-sandhi as a categorical phenomenon, assuming implicitly that word external /r/-sandhi processes are obligatory in the dialects that contain them.

Despite the phonological predictions, production of /r/ across word boundaries is reported to be variable (Jones 1964, Gimson 1980, Wells 1982). Linking /r/ appears to occur at higher rates than intrusive /r/, perhaps because the latter may be associated with a certain amount of stigmatisation (see, e.g., Lewis 1975; 1977, Pring 1976, Fox 1978; Brown 1988). Linking /r/ and intrusive /r/ also behave differently with respect to the nature of the following boundary. Word-internally, linking /r/ "almost invariably occurs," while there are "occasional" instances of word-internal intrusive /r/ (Wells 1982: 224). Gimson and Cruttenden (1994: §12.4.7) claim that in RP "the insertion of /r/ is obligatory before a suffix beginning with a vowel, where the /r/ is historically justified," whereas "the insertion of intrusive /r/ before a suffix is strongly resisted."

Hay and Sudbury (2005) investigate how /r/-sandhi emerged in New Zealand English in the late 19th century, concurrent with the decline of rhoticity. There was never a period of complete /r/-lessness in New Zealand English—linking and intrusive /r/ arose before rhoticity was gone. Linking /r/ across morpheme boundaries remained categorically present. Across word-boundaries, it declined with the loss of rhoticity, but at a much slower rate than non-prevocalic /r/. Intrusive /r/ across word boundaries arose gradually. Intrusive /r/ across morpheme boundaries was a later innovation, which seems to have largely postdated the disappearance of rhoticity in New Zealand. This historical trajectory makes sense of the observations that intrusive /r/ is less frequent than linking /r/ (it's more recent), and that across morpheme boundaries linking /r/ is categorically present (it always has been), and that intrusive /r/ is resisted.

The identity of the preceding vowel has also been reported to play some role in conditioning the likelihood that /r/ will arise. Jones (1964) and Gimson (1980) claim that intrusive /r/ is more likely following schwa than other vowels. It is also claimed to be less stigmatized in this context (Crystal 1984: 43; Brown 1988: 149). Wells claims intrusive /r/ after /ɔ/ is more stigmatized than after other vowels because it was a later innovation (1982: 225). Hay and Sudbury's (2005) study of 19th-century New Zealand English shows the lowest rates of intrusive /r/ after /ɔ/, supporting Wells' claim.

In addition to linguistic conditioners, there may also be social conditioners in some dialects. The most comprehensive contemporary corpus-oriented study was conducted by Foulkes (1997a, b), who studied /r/-sandhi in a stratified sample of speakers from both Newcastle upon Tyne and Derby. While social categories appeared to play no role in Derby, there were clear class and age differences in Newcastle, suggesting that /r/-sandhi may be socially conditioned in some dialects.

No large-scale systematic study has investigated rates of /r/-intrusion following different vowels. And while it has been claimed that /r/-sandhi is more common across word boundaries than morpheme boundaries, no one has investigated whether different types of suffixes may give rise to different rates of /r/-intrusion. Empirical data on the possible conditioners of intrusive

/r/ are virtually non-existent, and all work on this topic has analyzed intrusive /r/ as a discrete variable.

The lack of empirical data on intrusive /r/ likely relates to the scarcity of appropriate environments for its occurrence. In the studies reported here, then, we decided to sacrifice the advantages of natural speech in favor of reading and production studies, which ensured collection of sufficient data, enabled us to systematically manipulate potentially relevant linguistic factors, and facilitated recording of comparable environments across different speakers. Some preliminary analysis of the data-set used here was reported in Hay and Warren (2002). That paper presented a simple binary analysis of rates of /r/ production and concentrated on the role that different affixes played in facilitating /r/-production.

This paper analyzes these recordings with four research questions in mind. First, does the use of intrusive /r/ act as a sociolinguistic variable in New Zealand English? Second, can the variability be predicted by any linguistic conditioners? Third, can the likelihood of /r/ insertion after /au/ be predicted by the phonetic quality of a speaker's /au/ vowel, i.e., is the documented change in production of /au/ in NZE (Gordon et al. 2004, Maclagan, Gordon and Lewis 1999, Woods 2000) affecting the rate of /r/ insertion? And finally, is there any evidence for socially or linguistically conditioned variation in the degree of constriction of the /r/? That is, we hypothesized that there may be interesting variation not only in the likelihood of /r/ being produced, but also in how /r/-like the /r/ is when it is produced.

Introductory sociolinguistics textbooks drive home the important difference between "discrete" (or categorical) sociolinguistic variables and continuous ones (see e.g., Milroy and Gordon 2003: 138–139), acknowledging that perhaps continuous ones are sometimes analyzed as categorical for statistical convenience. However our analysis reveals that NZE intrusive /r/ acts both as a categorical and as a continuous sociolinguistic variable. A straightforward analysis of the presence vs absence of /r/ reveals socially conditioned variation in the likelihood /r/ will be produced. However when an /r/ is produced, the degree of the constriction is also socially conditioned. This difference in degree echoes the more straightforward difference in frequency.

2. Methodology

Because relevant environments for /r/-intrusion are relatively rare in spontaneous speech, we set out to answer these questions through a series of sentences containing relevant environments, which participants were asked to read aloud. This allowed for direct comparability of environments across participants. Sixteen University of Canterbury students received chocolate fish for their participation in the task. All students were non-rhotic, and native speakers of New Zealand English.

Because our participants were students, social class was assessed by recording the Elley-Irving scores of the participants' parents. The Elley-Irving scale is a New Zealand-specific index of social stratification which assigns scores from one (highest) to six to New Zealand occupations (Elley and Irving 1985). We added the scores for the parents together to give a rough social class index. This index ranged from 3 to 11 (mean: 6.7; median: 6.5). The participants were aged between 19 and 44 (mean: 26; median 23). There were 4 males and 12 females.

The participants were recorded reading 48 sentences targeting intrusive /r/. The 48 sentences were randomized together with 86 filler sentences which were designed to test hypotheses unrelated to /r/-sandhi. A total of 768 target sentences (16 * 48) were analyzed. All sentences were read from index cards, and recorded on Digital Audio Tape. Recordings were made using Sony DAT walkman recorders (TCD-D8) and Sony tie clip microphones, (ECM-T145).

Table 2.1 Experiment 1 Base Words and Environments

Base word	***Following environment***
Sofa	-ing
Oprah	-y
Ma	-ism
Bra	-ify
Claw	-ish
Plough	-ese
	-ize
	in

The 48 sentences consisted of one of 6 base words, combined with one of 8 following environments. 7 of these environments were affixes and one was a word boundary. Table 2.1 shows the base words and environments tested. The base words were chosen to represent a range of different vocalic environments. All base words were combined with all affixes listed. The base *plough* was included to assess the degree to which intrusive /r/ is used after /au/, which appears to be an emerging feature of New Zealand English, occurring concurrently with a change in the phonetics of /au/.

The sentences are listed in the appendix, and a quick glance over them will reveal that we sacrificed a great deal of "naturalness" in order to record the full paradigms. Participants were warned that some of the sentences they would be asked to read would be a bit weird, and they were asked just to humor us! Note that the filler sentences, with which the test sentences were randomized, were relatively normal.

Each utterance was given a binary analysis, indicating whether an /r/ was produced at the boundary or not. Six examples were excluded from the overall analysis due to misreading by the participant. Of the 48 environments in which each speaker could potentially produce an intrusive /r/, the range of /r/s actually produced was between 0 and 36, with the mean being 13 and the median 10.5. Overall 206 tokens were analyzed as containing an intrusive /r/.

For those tokens which were analyzed as containing an intrusive /r/, we also took an F3 measurement at the lowest point of F3 during the /r/, the most salient acoustic correlate of /r/. Acoustic analysis was carried out using Praat (http://www.fon.hum.uva.nl/praat/) using the standard settings (25 ms analysis frame, Gaussian window, 10 pole LPC filter) with formants manually corrected when it was clear that Praat's reading was incorrect. Correction was most often needed when the female speakers' fundamental frequency was so high that accurate reading of the first formant was difficult. Figures 2.1 and 2.2 give examples of where the measurement was taken. Both are male speakers producing the word *clawify*, and in both cases an /r/ was produced. Note, however, that the F3 descends relatively lower for the first speaker (Speaker 14) than for the second speaker during this word. We will return to the potential relevance of this difference.

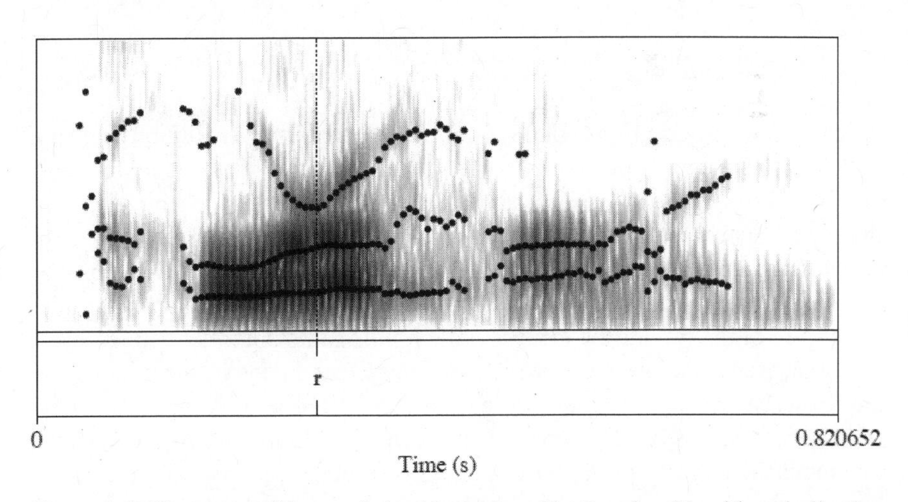

Figure 2.1 Utterance of the word clawify produced by Speaker 14, with an indication of where the F3 reading was taken.

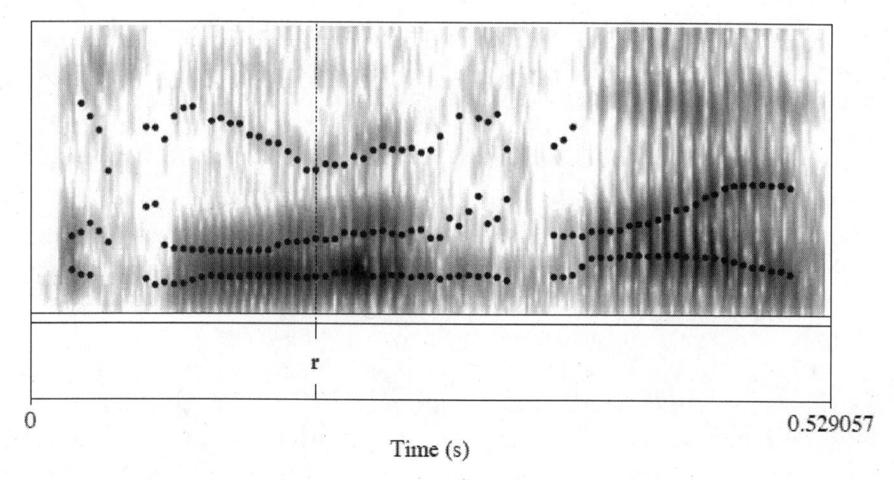

Figure 2.2 Utterance of the word clawify produced by Speaker 2, with an indication of where the F3 reading was taken.

We first investigated the factors affecting the likelihood that an /r/ would be produced at all. We then turned our attention to the cases where /r/ was produced, in order to assess whether there was any meaningful variation in the F3 values.

3. Results

3.1 Likelihood of Intrusive /r/

First, we fit a logistic regression model investigating the likelihood of use of intrusive /r/. Independent factors considered were the speaker gender, age, and social class, as well as the base word, and the identity of the affix. All factors but age and gender proved significant predictors of /r/-insertion. Gender was significant to .06, and so we have left it in the model. This allows us both to consider the direction of this near-significant effect and to consider the nature of the remaining effects while holding this potential gender effect constant. Recall, however, that there are only four males in the data set, so any observed effect of gender is tentative at best. In addition to the effect of the affix, the model also includes a significant interaction between social class and the identity of the base. The model details are given in Tables 2.2 and 2.3. For factors involved in interactions, the significance level in Table 2.2 incorporates both the main effects and the relevant interactions (i.e., Factor + Higher Order Factors).

Table 2.2 Wald Statistics for Model Predicting Likelihood of /r/-insertion

Factor	Chi-Square	d.f.	P
Gender	3.76	1	0.0525
Social class	70.64	6	<.0001
Base	79.93	10	<.0001
Affix	28.09	7	0.0002
Social class x base	18.3	5	0.0026
TOTAL	131.33	19	<.0001

Table 2.3 Coefficients for Model Predicting Likelihood of /r/-insertion

Intercept	-4.834077
Gender=Male	0.408924
Class	0.542852
base=claw	2.206757
base=ma	-0.830365
base=oprah	0.667502
base=plough	-0.887871
base=sofa	3.421577
affix=ify	0.27231
affix=ism	0.028013
affix=ing	1.000898
affix=ish	0.607396
affix=word	-1.055286
affix=y	0.570314
affix=ize	0.633545
Social class x base=claw	-0.264542
Social class x base=ma	-0.002005
Social class x base=oprah	-0.424215
Social class x base=plough	-0.067133
Social class x base=sofa	-0.446194

The model effects are plotted in Figures 2.3–2.5 where the y-axes show the predicted likelihood that an intrusive /r/ will be present. The predicted probability of insertion is calculated by deriving the log odds of insertion from the coefficients in Table 2.3, and then converting the log odds to a probability using the inverse logit function (exp(x)/(1+exp(x)). Figure 2.3 shows the (near-significant) effect of gender. Male participants are more likely to use intrusive /r/.

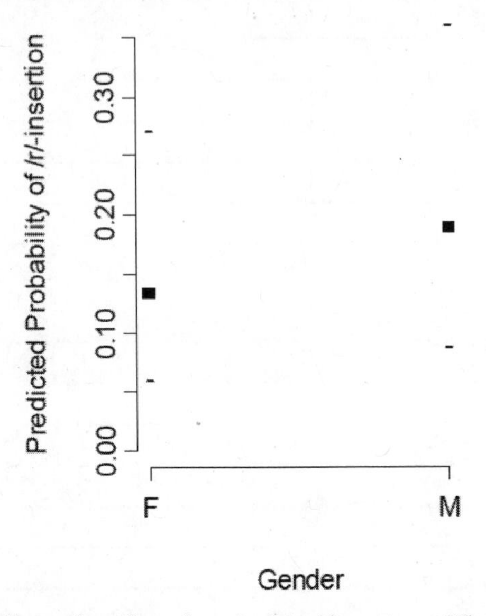

Figure 2.3 Model prediction for effect of gender (significant to p<.06). Here, and in other figures, 95% confidence limits are added.

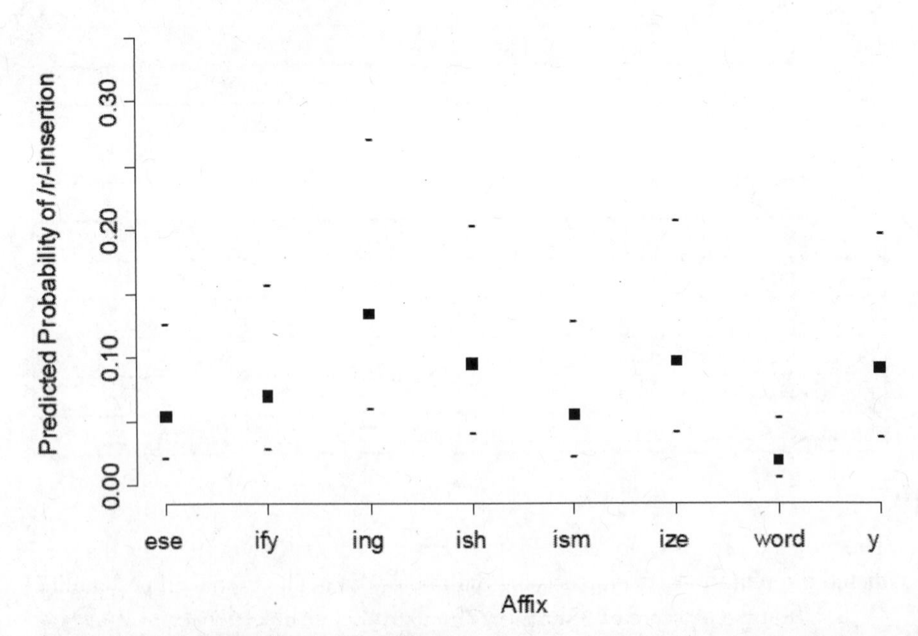

Figure 2.4 Model predictions for affix-type.

The effect of the identity of the affix is shown in Figure 2.4. As reported in Hay and Warren (2002), the rate of /r/ insertion differs across affixes, with affixes marking more word-like boundaries more likely to attract an /r/. Hay and Warren explain: "*-ing* is the affix with the strongest (most word-like) boundary and attracts the highest rate of intrusive /r/. *-ish* is also a relatively productive, relatively separable affix. This contrasts with affixes like *-ese* and *-ify*, which are less frequent, less separable, and more likely to occur with bound roots (see, e.g., Hay and Baayen 2002)." They demonstrate that the rate of /r/ use with these affixes correlates with various measures of their parsability. The more word-like the affix boundary is, the more likely intrusive /r/ is to occur.

Finally, Figure 2.5 shows the predicted effect of social class, which interacts with the identity of the base. Confidence intervals have been left off the graph to reduce the visual clutter. Note that the y-axis spans a much greater range than the previous figures—reflecting the fact that the effects of base and social class are of a greater magnitude than the effects of gender and affix.

A number of things are apparent from the graph. First, intrusive /r/ is relatively rare after *Oprah* and much more common after *sofa* and *claw*. The relatively low rate of intrusive /r/ after *Oprah* reflects the fact that many participants

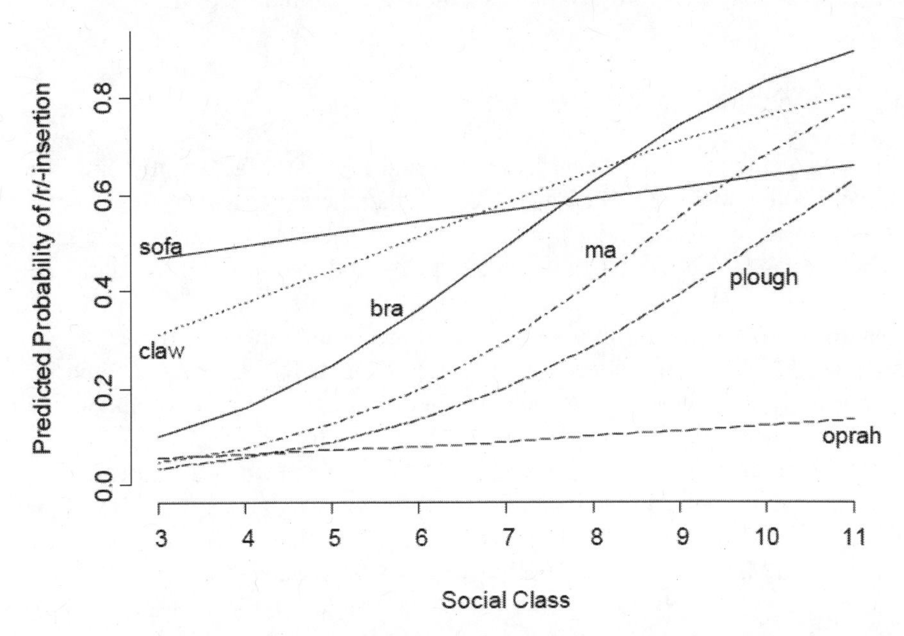

Figure 2.5 Model predictions showing interaction between Social Class and base type. A score of 3 represents a relatively higher social classes and 11 a relatively lower social class.

omitted the second syllable of the base, leading to productions such as *Oprese* and *Oprish.* Because of its low overall rate of intrusive /r/, *Oprah* does not show strong effects of social class. Interestingly, *sofa* also does not show strong effects of social class. This would seem to reinforce the observations from other dialects that intrusive /r/ may be somewhat less stigmatized following schwa than following stressed vowels (Crystal 1984: 43; Brown 1988: 149). *Claw*, and especially *bra*, *ma* and *plough*, show a stronger effect of social class, with higher social classes using dramatically less intrusive /r/. This is not surprising for *plough*—as this is a relatively new, incoming variant and is also (as we will argue) associated with innovativeness in the phonetics of the /au/ vowel. It is perhaps also not so surprising for *claw*, given that intrusive /r/ with /ɔ/ is rare in some dialects, and seems to have evolved later in New Zealand English than with some other vowels. It is interesting to note, however, that the overall rate of /r/ after /ɔ/ is actually relatively high in this data-set—which is an interesting difference from work on early speakers of New Zealand English, where rate of /r/ after /ɔ/ (Varbrul weight .290) was considerably lower than the rate of /r/ after either /a/ (Varbrul weight .840) or /ə/ (Varbrul weight .502) (Hay and Sudbury 2005: 813). It is difficult to know, however, whether the relative influence of the vowels has changed, or whether there is something about this particular base word that makes it unusually facilitative of /r/.

3.2 Degree of /r/-ness of intrusive /r/s

Having established that there are social and linguistic factors affecting the likelihood of intrusive /r/, we hypothesized that there may also be more subtle differences in the articulation of the /r/ when it is produced. Namely, the same factors that lead an /r/ to be more likely to be produced, may also lead it to be more /r/-like when it is produced. Comparing Figures 2.1 and 2.2 reveals that there is some variation in how low F3 is. In the utterance in Figure 2.1, F1, F2 and F3 look approximately equidistant, whereas in Figure 2.2, F1 and F2 appear closer together. We wondered whether such variation was random, or whether there might be some structured variation to uncover here.

There are a variety of differences in articulation which could lead to a decreased F3—including increased retroflexion, increased "bunching" or constriction in the palatal region, and increased liprounding (Fant 1968, Ladefoged and Maddieson 1996, Guenther et al. 1999). We do not want to speculate about the most likely articulatory correlates of a lower F3 in a NZE context, but will simply refer to /r/s with lower F3s as having an increased constriction (relative to /r/s with higher F3s, all else being equal), without being specific about where that constriction may be. Regardless of the articulatory means, it seems fair to say that, if a speaker increases the magnitude of the articulatory gestures associated with /r/ (whatever they may be for that speaker) so that the realization becomes more strongly /r/ like, the result will be a lowered F3. Our general hypothesis was that there may be structured variation in how /r/-like our recorded /r/s were.

In this analysis, we considered only tokens which had been analyzed as containing an /r/. We excluded 14 examples of *sofa* words which contained an intrusive /r/, but were produced without the base-final vowel (as in, e.g., "sof/r/ish" rather than "sofa/r/ish"). These were excluded from the analysis, in order to maintain comparability—i.e., all of the analyzed /r/s are clearly intervocalic. We also excluded the *Oprah* bases from this analysis. As seen in Figure 2.3, tokens of *Oprah* were highly unlikely to be produced with intrusive /r/—this is because they were most often produced without the second syllable of *Oprah* as in, e.g., *Oprese.* Only 7 *Oprah* tokens were actually produced with an intrusive /r/. Because we expected the identity of the base to be a contributer to the F3 of /r/, we excluded these *Oprah* tokens from this analysis. All other bases were produced with reasonable frequency (between 20 tokens (for *plough*) and 54 (for *claw*)). The total data set analysed in this section contains 192 observations.

Obviously, comparing the raw, non-normalized F3 measurement is problematic, because of the inherent differences in this value due to vocal tract length. Rather than measure the entire vowel space in order to normalize the formant values, we chose to measure, for each speaker, their F3 during "regular" non-intrusive /r/s. The read materials contained four instances of the name *Sarah* (see Appendix 2.1). For each speaker we used Praat to measure the lowest point of F3 during the /r/ for all *Sarah* instances where the spectrogram was clear enough for us to be confident of the analysis. The main analysis problems occurred, as indicated previously, when the female speakers used particularly high fundamental frequencies, so that it was difficult to distinguish F1 clearly.

We then included this mean value as a predictor in an ordinary least squares linear regression analysis. If the degree of constriction of intrusive /r/ is not sociolinguistically variable, then the value of F3 during *Sarah* should theoretically account for all of the variation in F3 in intrusive /r/. This measurement, then, effectively acts as a vocal tract length normalizer. We might also expect some differences across speakers depending on which bases they produced intrusive /r/ with, since the identity of the preceding vowel could affect the value of F3. However by including the identity of the base in the model, this variation should be accounted for.

Indeed, both the identity of the base and the F3 of the "real" /r/ were significant predictors of F3 of intrusive /r/. Strikingly, on top of these effects, there is a significant effect of social class. Holding real F3 and base identity constant, people from higher social classes produce higher F3 (i.e., produce the /r/ with less constriction).

The model statistics are shown in Tables 2.4 and 2.5. The effect of the average F3 during *Sarah* is shown in Figure 2.6. As one would predict, the greater the F3 is during *Sarah*, the greater it is during intrusive /r/. Including this effect in the model, then, has a normalizing effect. The effect of the identity of the base is shown in Figure 2.7. Some of the variation seen here may relate to the effect of the preceding vowel, although we don't expect radical differences in F3 amongst these vowels. The lower value for *bra* than *ma* probably reflects the fact that it also has an /r/ earlier in the word.

Figure 2.8 shows the effect of social class. When the base word and the "real" /r/ F3 are held constant, individuals from lower social classes (and so higher Elley-Irving scores), produce a lower F3 during the intrusive /r/. We interpret this as reflecting the fact that their intrusive /r/ is more /r/-like.

Table 2.4 Anova Table for Ordinary Least Squares Model Predicting F3 of /r/

Factor	d.f.	Partial SS	MS	F	P
"real" /r/ F3	1	1483982	1483982	36.29	<.0001
Social class	1	167535.2	167535.3	4.1	0.0445
Base	4	1398549	349637.2	8.55	<.0001
REGRESSION	6	2594777	432462.8	10.58	<.0001
ERROR	178	7278811	40892.2		

Table 2.5 Coefficients for Ordinary Least Squares Model Predicting F3 of /r/

	Value
Intercept	1008.15
"real" /r/ F3	0.4454
Social class	-15.2102
base=claw	111.3187
base=ma	204.0661
base=plough	83.1766
base=sofa	-57.3682

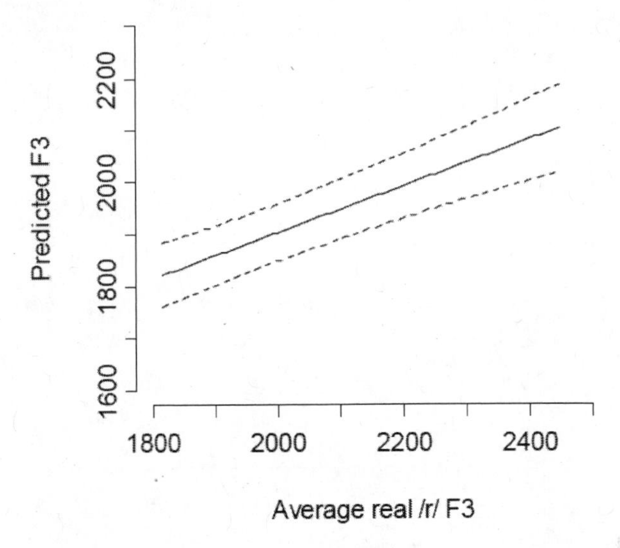

Figure 2.6 Effect of the average "real" /r/ F3 (from utterances of the word *Sarah*) in predicting the F3 of the intrusive /r/.

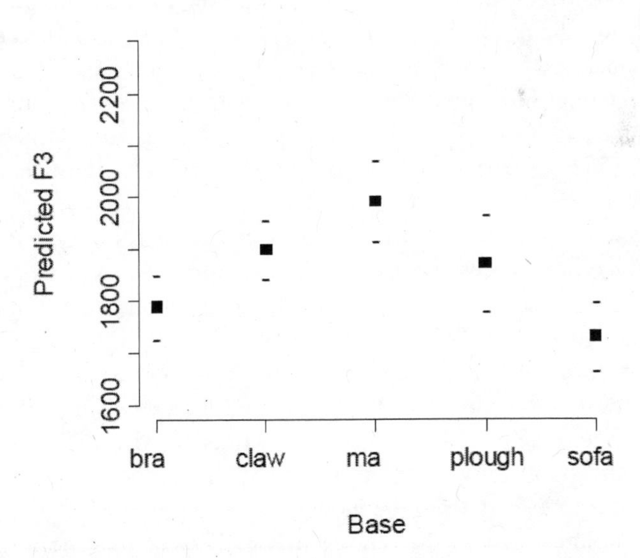

Figure 2.7 Effect of the base-type in predicting the F3 of intrusive /r/.

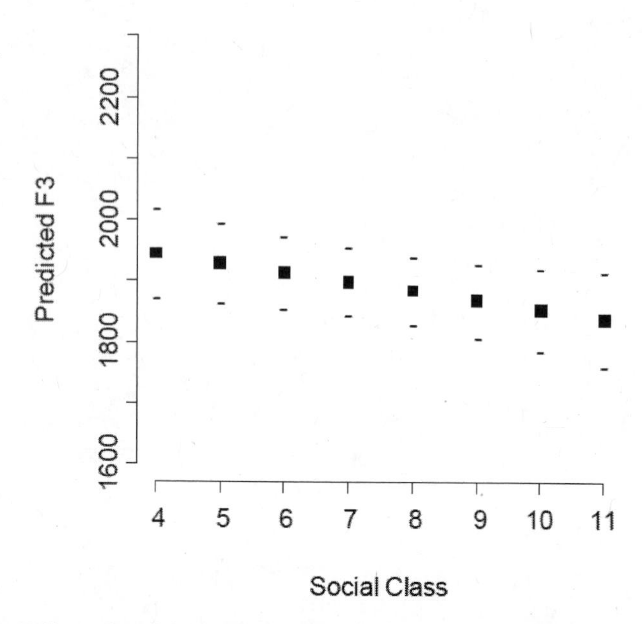

Figure 2.8 Effect of social class in predicting the F3 of intrusive /r/. Lower index scores are associated with higher social classes.

We wondered whether this effect resulted from speakers of different classes producing slightly different sets of preceding vowels. To double-check this, we tried fitting the model with just a single base word, *sofa* (the base which has a reasonable frequency of intrusive /r/ production regardless of social class). In a model fit on just the *sofa* data, both the F3 of /r/ during *Sarah* ($p<.001$), and social class ($p<.005$) are significant predictors of the F3 during intrusive /r/. This confirms that social class still remains significant when all variation attributable to the different base words is removed.

In order to double-check that our strategy for pseudo-normalizing the values was having the desired effect, we also attempted to fit a model which excluded the normalizing value. In the resulting model the most significant predictor is gender ($p<.0001$). The base type is still significant ($p<.0001$). Social class does not quite reach significance ($p<.07$). Gender is not significant in the model which includes the speaker F3 for a "real" /r/, but it is highly significant in a model which excludes it. We interpret this difference as indicating that the "real" /r/ F3 measurement is doing a decent job of removing vocal tract length effects from the model.

We were interested in the degree to which there may be a direct link between the rate of /r/ insertion and the degree to which the /r/ is constricted.

That is—is social class playing a significantly separate role for each, or is there a more direct relationship between frequency and degree? We refit the model predicting the F3 of the intrusive /r/, this time including the rate of /r/ insertion for that speaker as a predictor. The effects of the "real" /r/ F3 and the base word remained significant. Social class was no longer significant; instead the rate of /r/ insertion proved a significant factor ($p<.01$). This effect is shown in Figure 2.9.

The more frequently an individual produced an intrusive /r/, the lower their F3 was when they did so. Both high rates of intrusive /r/ and low F3s are associated with speakers from lower classes. This may be because social class independently affects both of these factors. Or it may be because there is some more direct link between them (e.g., high rates of intrusive /r/ somehow more directly *lead* to lower F3s). That the rate of /r/-insertion is a better predictor of

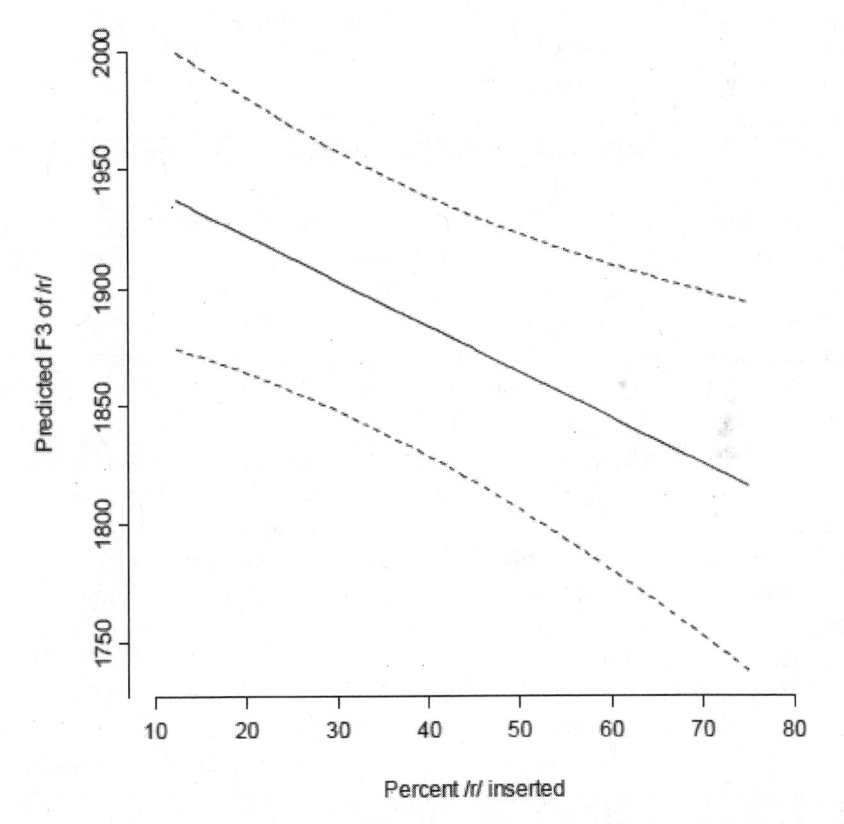

Figure 2.9 Model predictions for the F3 of /r/, on the basis of the percent /r/ produced by that speaker. Dashed lines represent 95% confidence intervals.

the F3 than social class suggests the latter may be more likely. We will return to speculation about how such a link might arise in the discussion.

3.3 Is the variation in F3 perceivable?

Given the results outlined before, we were interested in whether it was possible to "hear" degrees of intrusive /r/. For variation to be socially meaningful, it presumably has to be accessible to the listener. Yet it is not clear whether individuals are really able to hear subtle differences in the degree of constriction of an /r/.

We asked a trained linguist to listen to each /r/ in the data-set and distinguish between whether it was a "strong" /r/ which could plausibly form a syllable onset, or whether it was a weaker form of /r/ which seemed to contain a reduced degree of constriction. She coded 165 of the 192 intrusive /r/s analyzed in section 3.2 as strong /r/s, and 27 as lesser /r/s. Obviously what we were asking the analyst to do here was to impose an artificial boundary on what is likely to be a continuum. Nonetheless, we were interested in whether degrees of "/r/-ness" (even if just two) could be perceived by a listener.

A logistic regression of this analysis reveals that the single best predictor is the F3 of the consonant—the lower the F3 was, the more likely the listener was to rate the /r/ as a "strong" /r/ ($p<.01$). The variation in F3, then, seems to have been at least one criterion that this listener used, suggesting that the variability in F3 was to some degree audible. Interestingly the rate of /r/-insertion of the speaker also reaches significance ($p<.05$). That is, speakers are more likely to produce an audibly more /r/-like /r/ if they are also speakers who have high levels of /r/-insertion overall. The model is shown in Tables 2.6 and 2.7, and the predicted analysis based on the percent /r/ produced by the speaker and the F3 of the token is shown in Figure 2.10. This binary analysis echoes the result shown before, which demonstrated that the F3 of a consonant was well predicted by the degree to which the speaker producing the consonant tended to produce intrusive /r/, over all.

This suggests that it is at least plausible that this F3 variance is behaving as a sociolinguistic variable which carries social meaning. It is possible for a trained linguist, who is permitted to listen to the signal as many times as she wants to, to distinguish between degrees of /r/-ness. Of course, whether this is also true of the general listener, on a single fleeting occasion, is not so clear. This suggests interesting lines of enquiry for future perceptual work.

Table 2.6 Wald Statistics for Logistic Regression Model Predicting Likelihood of Analysis as "strong" /r.

Factor	Chi-Square	d.f.	P
Speaker rate of intrusive /r/	4.47	1	0.0346
F3 of /r/	7.01	1	0.0081
TOTAL	12.41	2	0.002

Table 2.7 Coefficients for Logistic Regression Model Predicting Likelihood of Analysis as "strong" /r/

	Coef
Intercept	5.110738
Speaker rate of intrusive /r/	0.021752
F3 of /r/	-0.0022

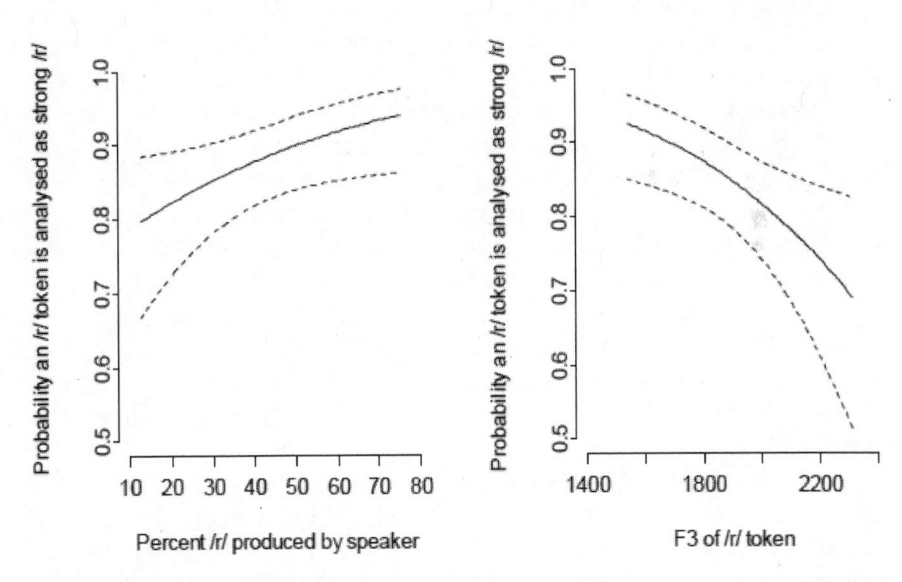

Figure 2.10 Model effect showing the likelihood that /r/ is analyzed as a "strong" consonant, as a function of the frequency with which the speaker produces intrusive /r/ (left panel), and the F3 of the /r/ itself (right panel).

3.4 Likelihood of /r/-insertion after /au/

Finally, having established that both the frequency and the degree of intrusive /r/ act as sociolinguistic variables, we then turned to a closer investigation of the *plough* paradigm. This vowel is a relatively recent addition to potential environments for intrusive /r/, and it is not a vowel that facilitates intrusive /r/ in other dialects. Theoretically, the high /u/ offglide of the vowel should prevent intrusive /r/ from appearing. The vowel /au/, however, has undergone relatively extreme phonetic change in New Zealand English. Where many New Zealand speakers born in the late 19th century still produced /au/ as a closing diphthong with the second element approximating their /ɔ/ vowel (Gordon et al. 2004), modern NZE speakers usually have a very central second element, approximating schwa (Maclagan 1982). In addition, the first element has raised from [a] or [æ] to closer to [ɛ], so that for many speakers /au/ is now realized as [ɛə]. One effect of this change is to lessen the difference between the two targets so that the vowel is relatively less diphthongal and relatively more monophthongal in production.

We therefore speculated that the likelihood of intrusive /r/ appearing may be partially predicted by the phonetic quality of the /au/ vowel produced by that speaker. This would be intriguing—providing an interesting insight into the interface between phonetics and phonology.

Assessing this link is not straightforward, as the presence of /r/ will itself affect the formants of the preceding vowels, so directly comparing the target words of /r/-inserters and non-/r/-inserters is not practical. Any difference found during the preceding vowel could be due to the presence of the /r/ rather than to any inherent difference in the quality of the vowel.

Fortuitously, the test sentences included four instances of the word *plough* in non-intrusive environments (see Appendix 2.1). Using Praat, we took measurements of F1 and F2 at two target points during the diphthong. The first measurement was taken at the first steady state portion of the vowel or where the F2 was highest, and the second at the second steady state or where F2 was lowest. The second target was measured before F2 started to lower for the following consonant, which was /m/ in all cases. For two tokens, the vowel was in fact, a triphthong, /æʊə/, and we took measurements at the first and the last target of the vowel.

In attempting to relate these raw values to the quality of the vowel, the normalization problem rears its ugly head again. Raw formant values will, of course, be affected by the length of the vocal tract. Rather than compare raw values, then, we calculated the Euclidean distance, in F1/F2 space, between the two targets of each vowel. This value would be zero for an entirely monophthongal vowel, and it would be high for a vowel which contained a high degree of internal movement. Figures 2.11 and 2.12 give examples of tokens with

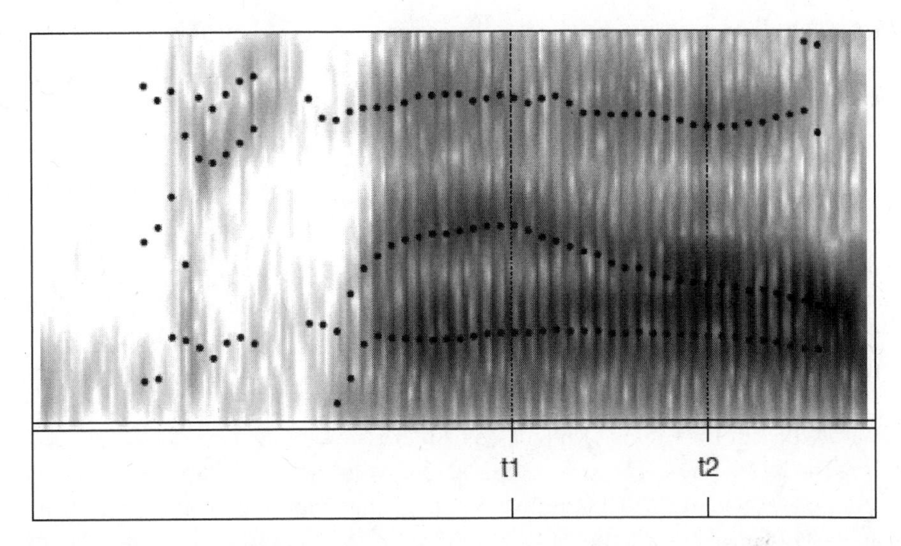

Figure 2.11 Spectrogram of the word plough produced by speaker number 4. This shows the location of measurements for the first (t1) and second (t2) targets. The Euclidean distance between the two targets in this token is 525 Hz.

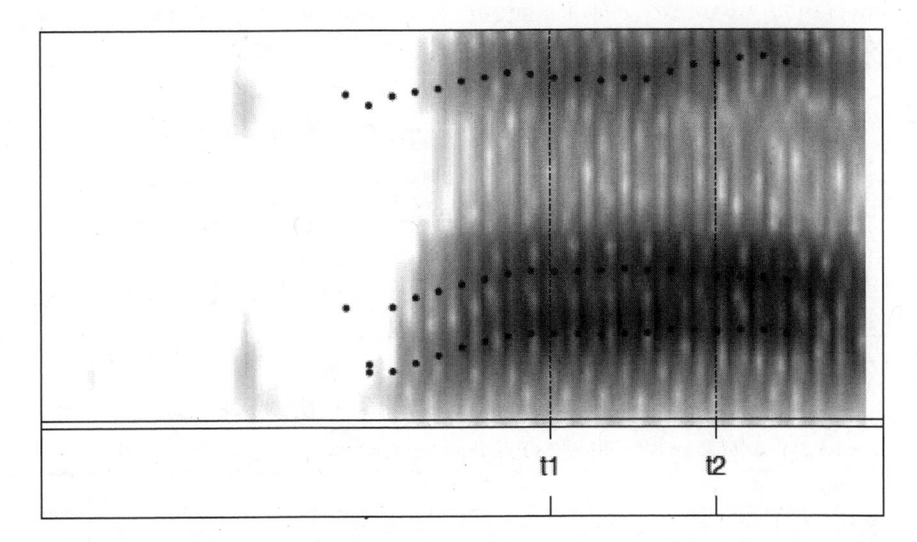

Figure 2.12 Spectrogram of the word plough produced by speaker number 14. This shows the location of measurements for the first (t1) and second (t2) targets. The Euclidean distance between the two targets in this token is 54 Hz.

relatively high and low Euclidean distances, respectively, to give a sense of the variation here. The places where the targets were taken are marked. For each speaker, we then calculated their average Euclidean distances, to get an overall index of the degree to which their /au/ tends to be monophthongal.

We then fit a logistic regression model, over just the *plough* paradigm, attempting to predict the likelihood that /r/ would be produced. We found significant effects of gender and social class, as well as a significant effect of the degree of monophthongization of the /au/ vowel.

The model statistics are given in Tables 2.8 and 2.9. Figures 2.13–2.15 plot the effects from the model. Males were significantly more likely to use intrusive /r/ after /au/ (Figure 2.13), and there is a significant effect of social class, such that individuals from higher social classes do not use /r/ after /au/ at all, but then rates of intrusive /r/ increase with decreasing social class (Figure 2.14). These two effects are as one would expect from the previous analysis—they work the same way as those described in section 3.1, in the analysis of the entire data-set. Figure 2.15 shows the effect of monophthongization of /au/. Speakers with highly diphthongal /au/ are very unlikely to produce /r/ after /au/. Speakers with an /au/ which contains less movement are much more likely to produce intrusive /r/ after /au/.

Note that there are no speakers for whom /au/ is entirely monophthongal. That is, it is not merging with a second vowel (such as /a:/), and thus becoming eligible for intrusive /r/. Rather this phonetic change in the quality of the vowel is making it eligible for participation in a phonological rule.

Table 2.8 Wald Statistics for Model Predicting the Likelihood of /r/-insertion After /au/

Factor	Chi-Square	d.f.	P
Gender	5.08	1	0.0242
Social class	14.45	1	0.0001
Monophthongization of /au/	10.2	1	0.0014
TOTAL	15.72	3	0.0013

Table 2.9 Coefficients for Model Predicting the Likelihood of /r/-insertion After /au/

	Coef
Intercept	-6.83224
gender=Male	1.89032
Social class	1.01736
Monophthongization of /au/	-0.01296

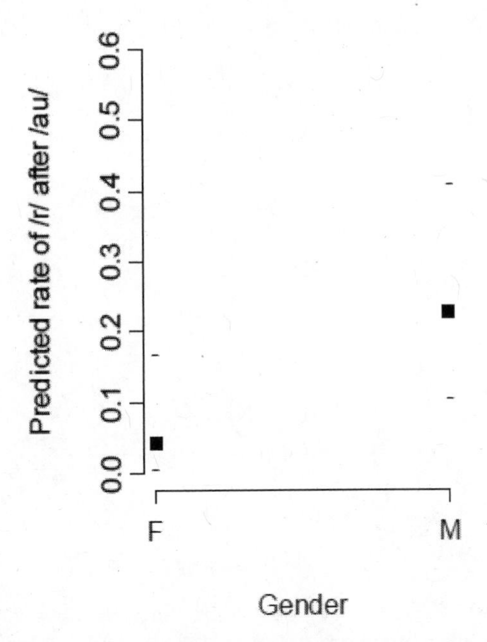

Figure 2.13 Model predictions for the effect of gender on /r/ insertion after /au/.

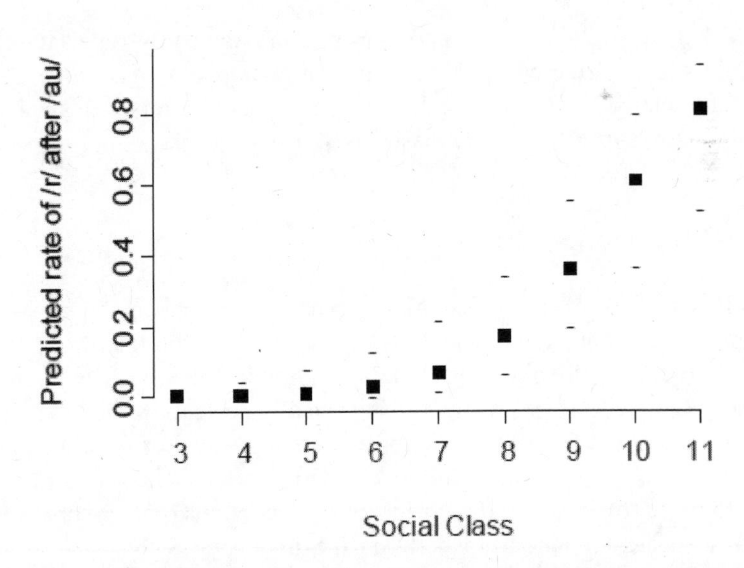

Figure 2.14 Model effects for the effect of social class on rate of /r/-insertion after /au/. Lower index scores are associated with higher social classes.

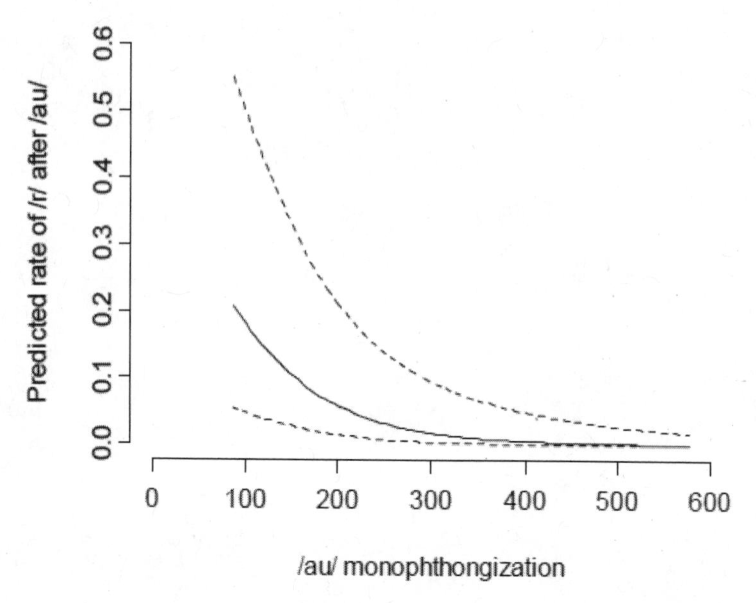

Figure 2.15 Model effects for the effect of /au/ monophthongization on the rate of /r/-insertion after /au/. The x-axis shows the Euclidean distance between the two targets of /au/, the lower the Euclidean distance, the more monophthongal the /au/.

As there are only 20 tokens across 6 speakers, this sadly makes it impractical for us to examine whether the degree of monophothongization of /au/ is gradiently related to F3. This will be an interesting question to consider as the rate of intrusive /r/ after /au/ increases in NZE.

4. Discussion

Phonological theories tend to model /r/ as a categorical phenomenon. We have shown that it is non-categorical in two senses. First, the likelihood that /r/ will be produced is highly variable, and conditioned by a range of social and linguistic factors. It is by no means categorically present. Second, when /r/ is present, the degree of the constriction varies in a way that is both linguistically and socially constrained. Individuals from lower social classes are more likely to use intrusive /r/, and their intrusive /r/ contains greater constriction.

This apparent relationship between the frequency with which a consonant is produced and the quality of that consonant is intriguing, and raises the question of whether this link between frequency and degree may be echoed in other variables. That such a link could exist follows well from exemplar models of speech production and perception, in which lexical representations consist of distributions of remembered exemplars (see, e.g., Johnson 1997; Pierrehumbert 2001, 2002). In such models, speech perception proceeds by matching the acoustic signal to the distribution which it most resembles. Speech production proceeds by activating a subpart of the stored distribution. Pierrehumbert (2002) describes the process associated with producing a particular vowel: "to produce an /i/, for example, we activate the exemplars in some area of the /i/ region in the vowel space. This group of /i/s serves as a goal for the current production, much as a perceived object can serve as a goal for a reaching motion."

Hay and Sudbury (2005) have argued that the historical evolution of intrusive /r/ in NZE is best modeled by an exemplar theoretic approach in which words and frequent phrases are stored, and in which "the alternation exists as a set of correspondences between /r/-ful and /r/-less exemplars in the lexicon" (819). Hay and Gibson (2005) have also argued for an exemplar account of intrusive /r/. They conducted an /r/ phoneme-monitoring experiment involving linking, intrusive and "real" /r/s. New Zealanders "heard" the intrusive /r/ much less than other /r/s, and were more accurate across word-internal morpheme boundaries than across word boundaries. Hay and Gibson argue that their results can be well accounted for if one assumes that the more the /r/ is present in the representation of a word, the more participants "hear" it in this task.

If the production target constitutes an averaging over a subpart of the exemplar space, it follows that the production target could potentially gradiently vary depending on the nature of that exemplar space. Certainly if all previously encountered exemplars of the appropriate type were produced with /r/, this should lead to an /r/-ful production. It should also lead to a robustly /r/-ful production, given the overwhelming force of evidence in favour of the /r/. However if the exemplar space is variable, it is possible that averaging over /r/-ful and /r/-less exemplars could lead to an /r/-ful target with a relatively weak constriction. That is, variability in the probability of /r/-production, may lead to variability in the /r/-fulness of /r/s that are produced.

In this way, speakers of lower social classes will have encountered more /r/s, and so will be both more likely to produce an /r/, and the /r/ that they produce will be relatively /r/-ful. For speakers of higher social classes, a smaller proportion of their stored exemplars will be /r/-ful.

This account may also help explain some reports in the literature that intrusive /r/ may involve a lesser constriction than linking /r/, or than "real" onset /r/ (Mullooly 2004; McCarthy 1993). An onset /r/ is lexically present, and will be produced for all exemplars of a particular word. Linking /r/ is also categorically present across a word-internal morpheme boundary, and so should resemble onset /r/s. Indeed Hay and Gibson (2005) show that these behave alike in perception. Linking /r/ across word boundaries is variable, but occurs at higher rates than intrusive /r/. This exemplar account would therefore predict that intrusive /r/ should contain a weaker constriction than the other /r/s.

Further work will be needed to reveal whether an exemplar account of speech production is responsible for the relationship between frequency of /r/ use and degree of constriction. Certainly, such an account would predict that there should be other variables where there is a link between the frequency of occurrence of the variable and its phonetic quality. For example /hw/ may involve reduced aspiration in environments facilitating merger with /w/ in dialects which contain this as a variable. Consonants in environments facilitating consonant cluster reduction may be reduced. In the early loss of rhoticity in NZE, /r/ may have undergone a gradual weakening. As Thomas (2002) points out, acoustic work on consonants has been sadly lacking in the history of sociophonetics. We are being highly speculative here, but it is certainly within the bounds of possibility that the sociophonetics of consonants may be much more gradient and intriguing than has hitherto been thought.

The relationship between the phonetic realization of /au/ and the likelihood of /r/-insertion is also intriguing. Under a traditional phonological account of the alternation, one would have to argue that the phonetics of /au/ has now changed so much that it is being reclassified, for some speakers, as [-high] and so eligible for the /r/-insertion rule (or not eligible for the deletion rule, depending on one's analysis). We think it is more likely that a more gradual analogical process is taking place. As the phonetics of /au/ changes, it gradually starts to resemble phonetically other vowels which are associated with intrusive /r/—in particular, the offglide begins to resemble schwa, which does participate in the alternation. It may be particularly relevant that there is a related triphthong (as in *flour, sour*), which always has an associated orthographic r and so attracts linking /r/. As the second target of /au/ begins to more closely resemble schwa, the distinction between the second two targets of the triphthong will be considerably lessened, increasing the overall resemblence between, e.g., *flour* and *plough*. Indeed, some of our students have even reported informally to us that they think these words rhyme. Thus just as intrusive /r/ arose after /a/ in the late 19th century (e.g., *ma/r/-and* by analogy to *ca/r/-and*), the same type of analogical process may be leading intrusive /r/ to arise after /au/ in contemporary NZE (e.g., *plough/r/-and* by analogy to *flou/r/-and*). In order to more directly test this interpretation, we will need to record productions of the relevant "triphthongs" from speakers. It may also be useful to elicit rhyming judgements.

5. Conclusion

In our logistic regression analysis of the likelihood of /r/-insertion, we found a strong social class effect, with speakers from higher social classes significantly less likely to use intrusive /r/. We also found linguistic factors—the identity of the preceding vowel and the identity of a following affix considerably affect the likelihood of /r/-insertion.

We also conducted a linear regression analysis in an attempt to predict the F3 of the /r/s that were produced (where F3 is a measure of the degree of consonantal constriction). We included in the model a "baseline" measurement for each speaker of average F3 measurements for "real" /r/s (from utterances of the word *Sarah*). Any further factors retained in the model, then, index the degree to which an individual's intrusive /r/ differs from their "real" /r/. We found that social class is retained in the model, such that speakers from higher social classes have higher F3s (and so less constriction relative to their "real" /r/) than lower social classes do. Thus, intrusive /r/ is a gradient sociolinguistic variable, which differs not only in frequency of occurrence, but also in degree of realization.

In terms of /r/ after /au/, we demonstrated that the likelihood that an individual will insert /r/ in this environment is significantly correlated with the degree to which their /au/ vowel is monophthongal (as measured by the average Euclidean distance (in F1/F2 space) between two target points during /au/ vowels produced in a non /r/-inserting environment). This is significant as it demonstrates that a phonetic change can make an environment eligible for an ostensibly phonological rule.

These results cast considerable doubt on current phonological analyses which regard intrusive /r/ as a straightforward, categorical, non-variable phonological process. Both the frequency and degree of the /r/ are considerably influenced by both linguistic and social factors. These results also raise the more general question of how often "frequency" may also equate with "degree" in other phonological sound changes that have historically been analyzed as categorical.

Appendix 2.1

When Sarah got her first bra, she couldn't talk about anything else. She could only talk bra-ese.

Bendon plans to completely bra-ify New Zealand

When Sarah got her first bra, she couldn't talk about anything else. Her speech was just full of bra-isms.

Bendon is bra-ing up the country.
Sarah decided not to buy the bikini, because it looked a little bra-ish.
Susan put her bra in the wash.
Sarah decided not to buy the bikini, because it looked a little too bra-y.
Bendon plans to completely bra-ize New Zealand

My flatmate belongs to a weird club called "the claws," and their speech is unintelligible to me—they just speak claw-ese all the time.
My flatmate stuffs animals, and his job is to claw-ify the leopards.
My flatmate belongs to a weird club called "the claws," and their speech is just full of weird claw-isms.
The cat walked up to the cushion and started clawing it.
Be careful of the cat, because she can be fairly claw-ish.
The cat caught a claw in the cushion.
Be careful of the cat, because she can be fairly claw-y.
My flatmate stuffs animals, and his job is to claw-ize the leopards.

Sue is always saying "do this" and "do that"—her speech is just full of Ma-ese.
Sue has always been just like Ma, and now she's trying to Ma-ify our house.
Sue is always saying "do this" and "do that"—her speech is just full of Ma-isms.
Sue is decorating the house just like Ma would, she's really Ma-ing the place up.
I thought about wearing fur, but that would be such a Ma-ish thing to do.
Sue went inside to get the bags, and left her Ma in the van.
I thought about wearing fur, but that would be such a Ma-y thing to do.
Sue has always been just like Ma, and now she's trying to Ma-ize our house.

All teenagers these days are speaking Oprah-ese.
The broadcasters are trying to Oprah-ify television in New Zealand
My cousin always comes out with weird Oprah-isms
The bookstores are Oprah-ing up all their displays
The show was pretty Oprah-ish.
My cousin went to see Oprah in Chicago
The show was pretty Oprah-y.
The broadcasters are trying to Oprah-ize television in New Zealand

The plough marketing person is really boring, she just talks plough-ese all of the time.
The plough manufacturing company plans to completely plough-ify farms in New Zealand.
The plough marketing person is really boring, she is just full of plough-isms, and can't talk about anything else.
The farmer is out ploughing in the field.
The machine is kind of a lawnmower, but is also kind of plough-ish.

The farmer left the plough in the field.
The machine is kind of a lawnmower, but is also kind of plough-y.
The plough manufacturing company plans to completely plough-ize farms in New Zealand

There's an obsession with sofas sweeping the town, and everyone seems to be speaking sofa-ese.
I personally like to sit on the floor, but my flatmate plans to sofa-ify the flat.
The furniture salesperson is really annoying, his speech is just full of bed terminology, table jargon and sofa-isms.
We're considering sofa-ing up our lounge.
The chair looks pretty sofa-ish.
The movers put the sofa in the garage.
The chair looked pretty sofa-y.
I personally like to sit on the floor, but my flatmate plans to sofa-ize the flat.

Notes

1 Preliminary analysis of some of this data has appeared in Hay and Warren (2002). We thank Malcah Yaeger-Dror for helpful comments on an earlier version of this paper. We are grateful to Andrea Sudbury for recording some of the participants, and to Alice Murphy for her contribution to the phonetic analysis.

References

Bauer, Laurie 1984. Linking /r/ in RP: Some facts. *Journal of the International Phonetic Association* 14: 74–79.

Brown, Adam. 1988. Linking, intrusive, and rhotic /r/ in pronunciation models. *Journal of the International Phonetic Association* 18 (2): 144–151.

Crystal, David. 1984. Should intruders keep out? In David Crystal (ed.), *Who cares about English usage?* London: Penguin, 36–44.

Docherty, Gerard and Paul Foulkes. 1999. Derby and Newcastle: Instrumental phonetics and variationist studies. In Foulkes and Docherty (eds), 47–71.

Elley W.B and J.C Irving. 1985. The Elley-Irving socio-economic index: 1981 census revision. *New Zealand Journal of Educational Studies* 20: 115–128.

Fant, Gunnar. 1968. Analysis and synthesis of speech processes. In Bertil Malmberg (ed.), *Manual of phonetics*. North-Holland: Amsterdam, 171–272.

Foulkes, Paul. 1997a. Rule inversion in a British English dialect: A sociolinguistic investigation of [r]-sandhi in Newcastle upon Tyne. *University of Pennsylvania Working Papers in Linguistics*, 4 (1): 259–270.

Foulkes, Paul. 1997b. English [r]-sandhi: A sociolinguistic perspective. *Histoire Epistemologie Langage* 19: 73–96.

Foulkes, Paul and Gerard Docherty (eds). 1999. *Urban voices: Accent studies in the British Isles.* London: Arnold

Fox, Anthony. 1978. To "r" is human? Intrusive remarks on a recent controversy. *Journal of the International Phonetic Association* 8: 72–74.

Gimson, A.C. 1980. *An introduction to the pronunciation of English* (3rd ed), London: Arnold.

Gimson, A.C. and Alan Cruttenden. 1994. *An introduction to the pronunciation of English* (5th ed), London: Arnold.

Gordon, Elizabeth, Lyle Campbell, Jennifer Hay, Margaret Maclagan, Andrea Sudbury, and Peter Trudgill. 2004. *New Zealand English: Its origins and evolution.* Cambridge: Cambridge University Press.

Guenther, Frank, Carol Y. Espy-Wilson, Suzanne E. Boyce, Melanie L. Matthies, Majid Zandipour, and Joseph S. Perkell. 1999. Articulatory tradeoffs reduce acoustic variability during American English /r/ production. *Journal of the Acoustical Society of America* 105: 2854–2865.

Harris, John. 1994. *English sound structure.* Oxford: Blackwell.

Hay, Jennifer and Harald Baayen. 2002. Parsing and productivity. In Geert Booij and Jaap van Marle (eds), *Yearbook of morphology 2001.* Dordrecht: Kluwer, 203–235.

Hay, Jennifer and Andrew Gibson. 2005. Hearing /r/-sandhi. Paper presented at the New Zealand Linguistic Society Conference, Auckland, November.

Hay, Jennifer and Andrea Sudbury. 2005. How rhoticity became /r/-sandhi. *Language* 81 (4): 799–823.

Hay, Jennifer and Paul Warren. 2002. Experiments on /r/-intrusion. *Wellington Working Papers in Linguistics* 14: 47–58.

Johansson, Stig. 1973. Linking and intrusive /r/ in English: A case for a more concrete phonology. *Studia Linguistica* 27: 53–68.

Johnson, Keith. 1997. Speech perception without speaker normalization. In Keith A. Johnson and J. W. Mullennix (eds.), *Talker variability in speech processing.* San Diego: Academic Press, 145–66.

Jones, Daniel. 1964. *An outline of English phonetics* (9th edition). Cambridge: Heffer and Sons.

Ladefoged, Peter and Ian Maddieson. 1996. *Sounds of the world's languages.* Oxford: Blackwell.

Lewis , J. Windsor. 1975. Linking /r/ in the General British pronunciation of English. *Journal of the International Phonetic Association.* 5: 37–42.

Lewis, J. Windsor. 1977. The r-link business—a reply. *Journal of the International Phonetic Association* 7: 28–31.

Maclagan, Margaret. 1982. An acoustic study of New Zealand English vowels. *The New Zealand Speech Therapists Journal* 37: 20–26.

Maclagan, Margaret A., Elizabeth Gordon, and Gillian Lewis. 1999. Women and sound change: Conservative and innovative behavior by the same speakers. *Language Variation and Change.* 11 (1): 19–41.

McCarthy, John. 1993. A case of surface constraint violation. *Canadian Journal of Linguistics* 38: 169–195.

McMahon, April, Paul Foulkes, and Laura Tollfree. 1994. Gestural representation and lexical phonology. *Phonology* 11: 227–316.

McMahon, April. 2000. *Lexical phonology and the history of English.* Cambridge: Cambridge University Press.

Milroy, Lesley and Matthew Gordon. 2003. *Sociolinguistics:Method and interpretation.* Oxford: Blackwell.

Mullooly, Richard. 2004. An electromagnetic articulograph study of alternating [ɹ] and the effects of stress on rhotic consonants. PhD Thesis, Queen Margaret University College.

Pierrehumbert, Janet. 2001. Exemplar dynamics: Word frequency, lenition, and contrast. In Joan Bybee and Paul Hopper (eds), *Frequency effects and the emergence of linguistic structure.* Amsterdam: John Benjamins, 137–157.

Pierrehumbert, Janet. 2002. Word-specific phonetics. In C. Gussenhoven and N. Warner (eds), *Laboratory Phonology VII.* Berlin: Mouton de Gruyter, 101–140.

Pring, Julian. 1976. More thoughts on the /r/-link business. *Journal of the International Phonetic Association* 6: 92–95.

Thomas, Erik. 2002. Instrumental phonetics. In J.K. Chambers, Peter Trudgill, and Natalie Schilling-Estes (eds), *The handbook of language variation and change.* Cambridge: Blackwell, 168–200.

Tollfree, Laura. 1999. South-east London English: discrete versus continuous modelling of consonantal reduction. In Foulkes and Docherty (eds), 163–184.

Trudgill, Peter. 1974. *The social differentiation of English in Norwich.* Cambridge: Cambridge University Press.

Vennemann, Theo. 1972. Rule inversion. *Lingua* 29: 209–242.

Wells, John C. 1982. *Accents of English* (3 Volumes). Cambridge: Cambridge University Press.

Williams, Ann and Paul Kerswill. 1999. Dialect leveling: Change and continuity in Milton Keynes, Reading and Hull. In Foulkes and Docherty (eds), 141–162.

Woods, Nicola J. 2000. New Zealand English across the generations: an analysis of selected vowel and consonant variables. In Allan Bell and Konrad Kuiper (eds), *New Zealand English.* Wellington: Victoria University Press and Amsterdam/Philadelphia: John Benjamins, 84–110.

Chapter 3

Effects of Consonantal Context on the Pronunciation of /æ/ in the English of Speakers of Mexican Heritage from South Central Michigan

Rebecca Roeder, University of North Carolina Charlotte

1. Introduction

This study investigates whether coarticulatory effects on the pronunciation of /æ/ display previously unattested patterns in the English of Mexican Americans from Lansing, Michigan. The analysis is based on wordlist data from sixteen lifelong residents of Michigan who are also native speakers of English. Findings show extreme raising of /æ/ pre-nasally—a feature that is prevalent in local Anglo speech—in female respondents under 25 years of age. T-tests reveal no statistically significant raising of /æ/ before nasals in the other ten speakers, however, providing a counterexample to Labov's hypothesis that some raising of /æ/ in a pre-nasal environment occurs in almost every dialect of American English (Labov 1994: 197). These results concur with Thomas (2001), who found a lack of /æ/-raising in a pre-nasal environment in Mexican American speakers of English in Texas. Results for other phonetic environments agree with previous sociophonetic and laboratory phonology findings.

1.1 Background

Laboratory studies on the conditioning effects of phonetic environment on vowel formant frequencies in English have generally paid little attention to dialect variation. Throughout his work, Kenneth Stevens has provided evidence that the majority of coarticulatory effects found in language are not speaker-controlled but are instead due to "inherent dynamic properties of the articulatory structures and of the neuromuscular system that controls them" (Stevens and House 1963: 122). Stevens and House do state that speakers can manipulate phonetic cues for the functional purpose of increasing perceptual contrast, and they give the categorical example of vowel lengthening in English before voiced consonants (122)—an adjacency effect that is not purely the result of physical limitations in the human voice mechanism. Stevens (1998: 288) also briefly discusses the variation in overall vowel patterns that occurs across regional dialects, but the degree to which edge effects vary based on dialect has not been fully investigated.

The current study addresses the question of whether adjacent phonetic environment—specifically consonantal context—displays the same patterns in Mexican American speakers from a Northern Cities Shifted (NCS) area as were found in earlier studies—namely Hillenbrand, Clark and Nearey (2001) and Stevens and House (1963). Although the participants in the Hillenbrand et al. study were also NCS speakers, the results did not conflict significantly with the results of the Stevens and House study. Therefore, any variation found in the Mexican American speakers may indicate either 1) unique characteristics attributable to the influence of Spanish or 2) distinctive characteristics of NCS English which emerged because the elicited speech was more natural.

Stevens and House (1963) measured formant frequency values for three men pronouncing the eight vowels /i, ɪ, ɛ, æ, ɑ, ʌ, ʊ, u/ in the following three environments: 1) in isolation, 2) in /hVd/ syllables, and 3) in stressed, symmetrical CVC syllables, preceded by unstressed /hə/ (e.g., /həbVb/, /hədVd/, etc.) with the 14 consonants /p, t, k, b, d, g, f, v, s, z, θ, ð, ʧ, ʤ/. Surprisingly, no significant F1 or F2 differences were found between the first two environments—vowels in isolation and in /hVd/ syllables; therefore, these two sets of tokens were combined into a category that was somewhat confusingly labeled the *null* context (Stevens and House 1963: 116) for purposes of comparison to other environments. Reflecting the contemporary perspective of the field, no additional demographic information was offered on the three informants.

The over-arching result of the Stevens and House study was that consonantal environment (excluding the /hVd/ environment) causes vowel centralization, or undershoot. A number of more specific systematic effects, some of which are discussed further below, were also found to correlate with manner, voicing, and place of articulation features of the adjacent consonants.

Hillenbrand et al. (2001) expanded on Stevens and House (1963) in several ways. They interviewed six men and six women, all but one of whom were from the same general Northern Cities Shifted dialect area. In order to maintain comparability with the earlier study, they chose the same eight vowels, and used a subset of the consonants (initial /h, b, d, g, p, t, k/ and final /b, d, g, p, t, k/). The vowels were recorded in isolation, and in CVC syllables read from a wordlist. The main difference in procedure from Stevens and House was that every combination of initial and final consonantal context was tested for each vowel instead of being limited to symmetrical syllables. Therefore, although this study eliminated the variable of manner by using only stop consonants, the researchers were able to comment on differences in effect between initial and final consonants. Overall, conditioning environment had minimal effect on vowel pronunciation in the Hillenbrand et al. study, but this may be because natural speech was not elicited due to the extremely controlled nature of the experiment. The effects they did see largely agreed with Stevens and House, with the additional finding that preceding consonants showed larger effects, in general, than following consonants, especially for F2.[1] With regard to social factors, Hillenbrand et al. found the same effects in both men's and women's speech.

Although the vowel patterns found in these two studies suggest different dialects, the similarity of results suggests universal tendencies in the coarticulation of specific consonants and adjacent vowels. The issue of whether coarticulatory effects may, in fact, differ across dialects is not directly addressed in either article. As mentioned previously, this analysis is concerned with the same general Northern Cities Shifted dialect area investigated by Hillenbrand et al. (2001), but it takes a more sociolinguistic approach. For example, in the Hillenbrand et al. study, speakers who were familiar with linguistics were asked to read phonetic transcriptions that were blocked by vowel (not scattered) from a word list.[2] In the current study, however, naïve speakers were asked to read actual words, written in regular orthography, and presented one at a time on a computer screen to avoid the intonational effects that often accompany reading a list.

Several other sociolinguistic studies on the effects of phonetic environment on vowel production have been done in this dialect region. Ito (1999) analyzed Anglo speakers in rural Lower Michigan; Evans (2001) analyzed speakers in Ypsilanti, near Detroit, who were originally from Appalachia; and Jones (2003) analyzed African Americans in Lansing. The methodology of the current study is very similar to that used in these three earlier Michigan studies, enabling a comparison of results. Labov (1994: 100) discusses the fronting and raising of /æ/ together as "advancement" of the NCS. He provides ordered lists of environments that promote this advancement, based on the results of a few major studies, including his own, in several Northern Cities Shifted regions, including Detroit. The two environments on which he comments are following manner of articulation[3] and point of articulation (not specified as preceding or following).[4] The combined results of these studies are discussed in the following section.

2. Methods and Setting

2.1 Physical and Linguistic Setting

Data collection was conducted in Lansing, the capitol of Michigan, located in the south central part of the state—about 90 miles from the larger cities of Grand Rapids and Detroit, and only several hours from Chicago. Michigan falls in the center of the dialect area defined by the *Atlas of North American English* (Labov et al. 2006) as the Inland North. The most distinctive regional speech feature that has been discovered in this area is the sound change in progress known as the Northern Cities Shift (NCS). This shift, illustrated schematically in Figure 3.1, is a vowel change that affects six vowels and has been under way among Anglos in urban areas across the northern-central United States for 35 years or more.

The status of the NCS as a chain shift is under some debate, and the diachronic order of change and direction of movement of several of the vowels involved are also disputed. However, a number of researchers, including Labov (1994: 195), accept the hypothesis that /æ/ was the first vowel to shift—the catalyst that began the chain reaction. In any case, shifted /æ/ is now perhaps the most distinctive feature of the NCS. In advanced NCS

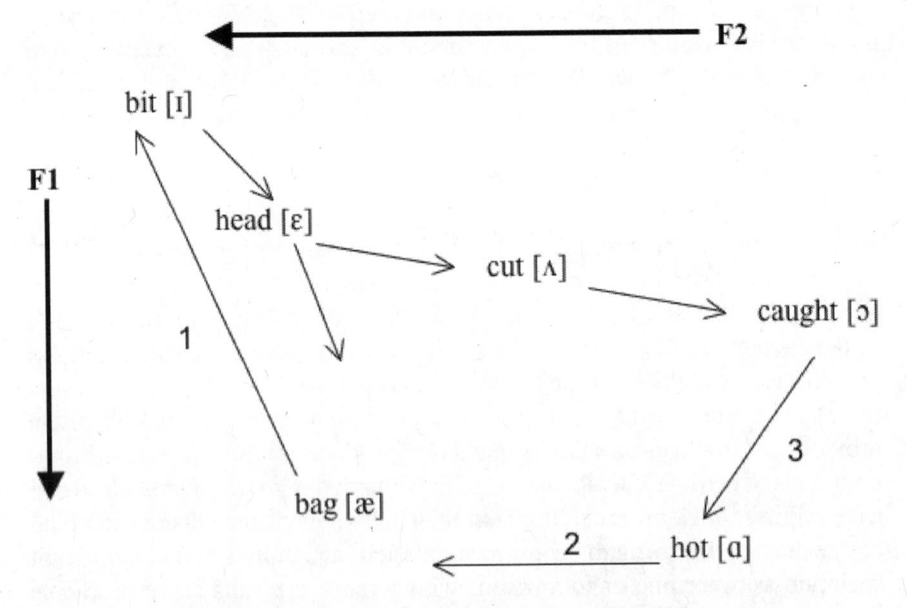

Figure 3.1 The Northern Cities Shift (based on Labov 1994: 191).

speakers, /æ/ is realized in a high front position in all phonetic environments, nearing [ɪ] in its most extreme form—a position referred to as *fronted and raised* in the vowel space because F2 is higher than older attested positions for this vowels and F1 is lower. In the second step, /ɑ/ moves forward towards [æ]. In the third step, /ɔ/ centralizes and fronts in the vowel space, and is ultimately produced as [ɑ]. The other movements seen in Figure 3.1 appear to follow these first three in speakers native to shifted areas. Evans, Ito, Jones and Preston (2000) found the NCS to be well advanced among younger Anglos in Lansing, as would be expected from a sociolinguistic perspective, given its status as a capitol city and its proximity to several large urban centers.

In the year 2000, according to US Census data, Latinos made up 10% of Lansing's total population of 120,000, with people of Mexican heritage comprising the majority of this group at nearly 7%. Migrants of Mexican heritage began settling in the Lansing area in substantial numbers during World War II, when workers were needed in the factories, and the population has been growing steadily since then—unlike the Anglo population which, incidentally, is decreasing in number. Firm ties to Texas are still maintained by many, and a strong sense of solidarity is apparent in this close-knit community; but Mexican Americans are now well integrated throughout the Lansing area, and many families have been in Michigan for one, two or even three generations. Several thousand undocumented migrants continue to come to Lansing each summer, and the group mobility and the constant influx of people help to keep both Texas English and Spanish alive here—although many second and third generation residents are monolingual.

2.2 Participants

This study focuses on 16 people chosen from a total group of 32 Mexican American residents of Lansing who were participants in a larger study. The initial stage of the larger project was to compare average F1 and F2 of the vowels /æ, ɛ, ɑ, ɔ/ from wordlist data across the social factors of sex, age, socioeconomic status and generation of residence in Michigan. Results of the larger study revealed that the dialect spoken by Mexican Americans in Lansing is clearly influenced by the NCS, but it is not as advanced in this group as in Anglos in the area, and shows a different order of accommodation than has been observed through geographic spread of the shift. There is significant variation between men and women, with women showing more NCS-like characteristics than men for every variable, but there is very little significant variation across apparent time within gender. These findings are consistent with other studies that show sustained resistance to accommodation to local norms by members of ethnic minority groups.

The one exception is that Mexican American women under the age of 25 who were born and raised in Lansing show the same F1/F2 values for /æ/ as the young Detroit women who were used as a control group. These speakers also show accommodation to the off-glide that is characteristic of NCS /æ/, whereas first generation speakers do not. It is, therefore, likely that any effects on vowel pronunciation from adjacent consonantal context that are found in the speech of these young women in particular represent features of the NCS—not features from Spanish.

Of the 32 speakers analyzed in the larger study, half are both native speakers of English and lifetime residents of Lower Michigan. This half was chosen for further analysis of the influence of conditioning phonetic environment on the pronunciation of /æ/. Respondents for this part of the study consisted of ten men, ages 14 to 71, and six women, ages 14 to 23. All but two are second or third generation residents of Lansing. Of the remaining two, one is a 35-year-old man who has only lived in Lansing for 10 years, but has lived in south central Michigan his entire life. The other is a 71-year-old man who came to Lansing at the age of 3.

2.3 Methodology

All interviews were conducted entirely in English. Analog recordings were made using a Marantz PMD201 portable cassette recorder for some speakers, a Marantz PMD222 for the rest, and an AT831b Audio-technica uni-directional clip-on microphone. The recordings were then digitized to 16-bit, 10,000 Hz digital format using the acoustic software Praat. First and second formant measurements were taken through Praat, using the sociophonetic software program Akustyk. When possible, the vowel was measured during the steady state. For diphthongs, a single measurement was taken just after the perceptual end of the transition from the preceding consonant. The larger study used a Nearey normalization procedure (without F3) to produce regularized data, whereas the phonetic conditioning results discussed in the following section are based on raw data. Analysis was performed on 31 words containing /æ/ as the stressed vowel, which were taken from recordings of each speaker reading a longer wordlist as part of a session that included the reading of a short passage, a dialect perception test, and a conversational question-based sociolinguistic interview.

3. Results

3.1 Relative positions of /æ/ and /ɛ/

As illustrated in Figure 3.1, /æ/ is acoustically further front and higher than /ɛ/ in the most advanced NCS speakers, with /æ/ ultimately approaching high front vowel territory in some speakers. This pattern is much different from what has been found in south Texas. As documented by Thomas (2001), /ɛ/ is close to [e] with respect to F1 and F2 values in the English of Mexican Americans in south Texas. Also, the vowel /æ/ is usually well below and behind /ɛ/ in these Texas speakers, although /æ/ in this speech community does tend to be somewhat higher in relation to the total vowel space than /æ/ in the speech of Texas Anglos. As one indicator of the degree to which a speaker had accommodated to the NCS, therefore, the relative positions of the mean unnormalized F1 and F2 values for tokens of /æ/ and /ɛ/ were calculated for each individual separately and are shown in Table 3.1.

Table 3.1 Relative Positions of /æ/ and /ɛ/ in Native Speakers of Michigan English

Pseudonym	*F1(norm) of /æ/ (in Hertz)*	*/æ/ relative to /ɛ/ (based on F1/F2 means)*	*Sex*	*Age*	*College Degree*	*SES*
Judith	765	fronted and raised /æ/	F	21	No	W
Jose	696	fronted and raised /æ/	M	35	Yes	M
Lucy	729	fronted /æ/	F	14	N/A*	M
Estela	703	fronted /æ/	F	17	N/A*	W
Emelia	694	fronted /æ/	F	20	No	W
Solana	731	fronted /æ/	F	22	Yes	M
Ralph	662	fronted /æ/	M	41	No	M
Edmund	680	fronted /æ/	M	45	Yes	M
Andy	722	/æ/ = /ɛ/	M	14	N/A*	W
Rodolfo	702	/æ/ = /ɛ/	M	27	No	W
Melito	677	/æ/ = /ɛ/	M	29	No	W
Martin	684	/æ/ = /ɛ/	M	48	No	M
Walter	743	backed /æ/	M	71	No	W
Melinda	798	/æ/ below /ɛ/	F	16	N/A*	M
RonaldB	657	/æ/ below /ɛ/	M	16	N/A*	M
Jesse	668	/æ/ below /ɛ/	M	28	No	W

Note: * indicates that the speaker was too young to be in college at the time of the interview.

The second column of Table 3.1 lists normalized F1 means for /æ/ and shows that only two speakers have a normalized F1 above 750 Hz. 700 Hz or lower (normalized) is considered Northern Cities Shifted by Labov, Ash and Boberg (2006), indicating that most of these speakers are shifted or close to shifted in their pronunciations of /æ/. Comparison of the F1/F2 means for /æ/ to the F1/F2 means for /ɛ/ in the speech of each individual further distinguishes the respondents.

The third column in Table 3.1 gives the position of the average for tokens of /æ/ relative to the position of the average for tokens of /ɛ/ in the vowel space, based on t-tests done in Plotnik. For example, Lucy has a mean F2 for /æ/ that is different from her mean F2 for /ɛ/ at a probability level of $\leq .05$, such that /æ/ is significantly further front in the vowel space than /ɛ/. But her F1 means for the two vowels are not significantly different. The difference in means for /æ/ and /ɛ/ is significant in both F1 and F2 for only two speakers, Judith and Jose, who are at the top of the list. In these speakers, /æ/ is fronted and raised in relation to /ɛ/, which is typical of an advanced NCS system and suggests that Judith and Jose are more advanced into the NCS than any of the other speakers.

The next six speakers have an /æ/ that is fronted in relation to /ɛ/ but is not raised above /ɛ/. This is not surprising given that many Anglo NCS speakers, including the young Detroit women used as a control group in the larger study, do not raise /æ/ above /ɛ/ either. The F1/F2 means for /æ/ and /ɛ/ in the next four speakers on the list are not significantly different between vowels. Overlapping means are common in the speech of people who exhibit only incipient or conservative accommodation to the NCS, as may be the case with these speakers. Finally, the last four respondents listed in Table 3.1 have conservative non-NCS vowel configurations, in which /æ/ is backer or lower than /ɛ/.

In the following analysis of environment, the top eight speakers in Table 3.1, who appear to be more affected by local Michigan norms than the others, are grouped together and referred to as Group A. Both gender and level of education have been strongly correlated with accommodation to local standards in previous studies, and it is notable that, out of these sixteen participants, the three who have college degrees (Jose, Solana, Edmund) and all but one of the women under the age of 25 are included in Group A. Ralph, the only Group A respondent who is neither a woman nor a college graduate, is a monolingual speaker of English who works in sales at an upscale department store and presumably must conform to accepted norms to fulfill the requirements of his occupation.

To summarize, Table 3.1 illustrates that—with regard to the vowels /æ/ and /ɛ/—these second and third generation speakers fall along a continuum from fairly typical Northern Cities shifters (Group A) to unshifted (Walter,

Melinda, Ronald and Jesse). The next section presents an analysis of the degree to which Group A correlates with how /æ/ patterns allophonically. If some environments promote the shift more than others, this should be observable in terms of relative variation among tokens across individuals. If phonological environment has no relationship to the shift, then there should be no difference in environmental effects in people who are strongly influenced by the shift, as compared to people whose speech is not strongly influenced.

3.2 Phonetic conditioning of [ae]

Table 3.2 presents an ordered list that ranks the effectiveness of conditioning environment on the pronunciation of /æ/, based on a comparison of Labov's (1994) results to those of the three Lower Michigan studies mentioned before.

Table 3.2 Ranked List of the Influence of Consonantal Environment on the Production of /æ/, Based on the Combined Findings of Labov (1994), Ito (1999), Evans (2001) and Jones (2003)

<table>
<tr><td>Preceding Consonant</td><td rowspan="5">/æ/</td><td>Following Consonant</td></tr>
<tr><td>VELAR</td><td>NASAL</td></tr>
<tr><td>APICAL</td><td>VOICED STOP
VOICED FRICATIVE
VOICELESS FRICATIVE</td></tr>
<tr><td>LABIAL</td><td rowspan="2">VOICELESS STOP</td></tr>
<tr><td>LIQUID</td></tr>
</table>

Although the four studies did not find identical rankings, they are in agreement with respect to the first and last feature in each environment. The leftmost column in Table 3.2 provides an ordered list of preceding consonant features, beginning at the top with the factor that most promotes the fronting and raising of /æ/ (velar consonants), and ending at the bottom with the least promoting factor (liquids). Following the methodology used in Plotnik, these studies did not test every preceding manner and place environment separately, but rather tested for only those environments that had been shown previously to have the strongest conditioning influence.

The rightmost column gives a similarly ordered list of following consonant manner features. Although Labov (1994) does include a ranked ordering for following place of articulation, this factor had little effect on /æ/ in any of the Michigan studies.

Table 3.2 indicates, for example, that /æ/ in a word such as *gamble*—where it is preceded by a velar consonant and followed by a nasal consonant—should be more raised and fronted than /æ/ in any other environment.

Eight ANOVA's were run for each individual. The dependent variables were F1 and F2, analyzed for the following environmental factors: preceding manner and voice, preceding place of articulation, following manner and voice, and following place of articulation. Unlike previous studies, manner and voice were separated from place of articulation for preceding environment, so that every possible combination of features could be tested. In accordance with the findings of previous studies, the influence of following place of articulation was minimal. No significant difference between the effects of any two following place of articulation features was found in more than two speakers, so those results are not presented here. In addition, only results for other environments that are significant in at least four speakers will be discussed. As mentioned before, the discussion notes, in particular, the number of Group A speakers for whom these categories are significant, since that may shed light on the relevance of each feature to the NCS.

3.3 Following Manner and Voice

Five following manner and voice environments were tested: voiced and voiceless stops, voiced and voiceless fricatives, and nasals. Table 3.3 lists words used by environment.[5]

Table 3.3 Following Manner and Voice Features and Words

Manner/Voice	**Words**
Voiced Stop	tab, cabin, dad, Saginaw, brag, rag
Voiceless Stop	apple, nap, zap, pat, mattress, rack, black
Voiced Fricative	have, has, jazz
Voiceless Fricative	Bath, laugh, ask, past, cash, mash
Nasal	Sam, Lansing, plant

Excluded (singleton): pal (liquid); badge (affricate); gamble, gang, thank, banker (velar)

The only feature that is significant in at least two speakers is following nasal, and the effects on F1 in this environment are dramatic. Table 3.4 indicates the effects of following nasal environment on the production of /æ/ for each individual.

Table 3.4 Results for Position of /æ/ Before Nasal Consonants (X = Statistical Significance ≤ .05 Level of Probability between Mean for Pre-nasal /æ/ and Mean for /æ/ in all other Environments)

Name	*Age*	*Overall F1/F2 means (/æ/ relative to /ɛ/)*	*Pre-nasal /æ/, raised (F1)*	*Pre-nasal /æ/, fronted (F2)*
Judith	21	fronted and raised /æ/	X	
Jose	35	fronted and raised /æ/		
Lucy B	14	fronted /æ/	X	
Estela	17	fronted /æ/	X	X
Emelia	20	fronted /æ/	X	
Solana	22	fronted /æ/	X	X
Ralph	41	fronted /æ/		X
Edmund	45	fronted /æ/		
Andy	14	/æ/ = /ɛ/		X
Rodolfo	27	/æ/ = /ɛ/		
Melito	29	/æ/ = /ɛ/		
Martin	48	/æ/ = /ɛ/		
Walter	71	backed /æ/		
Melinda	16	/æ/ below /ɛ/	X	
Ronald B	16	/æ/ below /ɛ/		
Jesse	28	/æ/ below /ɛ/		

T-test results show that all six young women, but none of the men, raise /æ/ in front of nasals to a degree that is statistically significant at or below the .05 level of probability. In addition, the only two speakers whose pre-nasal /æ/ is both fronted and raised are young women who also have an overall mean for /æ/ that is fronted, indicating NCS accommodation. There are two other people (out of the 32 participants) who show statistically significant fronting and raising of /æ/ before nasals. Both are women under the age of 40 who, although they are speakers of English as a second language, learned English in Lansing and have lived in Lansing for most or all of their lives. The fact that statistical significance is achieved for these speakers based on only three words per speaker in which /æ/ appears before a nasal—*Sam, Lansing, plant*—underscores how dramatically different pre-nasal /æ/ is from /æ/ in other environments.

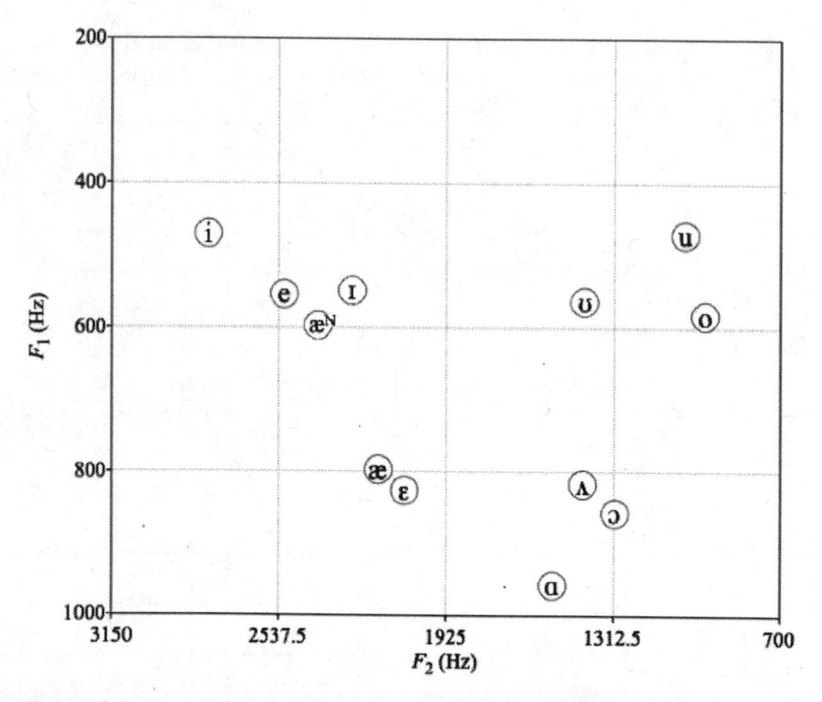

Figure 3.2 Vowel chart for Solana, age 22, third generation. Pre-nasal /æ/ = $æ^N$.

Figure 3.2 is the vowel chart of Solana, one of the two young women whose pre-nasal /æ/ is both fronted and raised above non-pre-nasal /æ/. Solana's mean for /æ/ before nasals is very high in her vowel space, near both [e] and [ɪ]. Figure 3.3 shows individual tokens of /æ/ in Solana's speech, as graphed in the software Plotnik.

Except for the word *dad*, which contains /æ/ between voiced alveolar stops—an environment that may cause fronting and raising because the constriction involved in the articulation of /d/ causes a lowered F1 and a raised F2—Solana's pre-nasal tokens of /æ/ are the highest /æ/ tokens in her vowel system.

A dramatically raised position for tautosyllabic pre-nasal /æ/ is common in NCS speech (Labov 1994: 266). To explain this, Labov and others have posited that raising of /æ/ before nasals is a default feature in American English that is simply exploited to a more extreme degree in the Northern Cities Shift. However, Thomas (2001) found that some of the Mexican American speakers of English he interviewed in Texas did not have an /æ/ that was raised at all before nasals,[6] suggesting that there are dialects of American English in

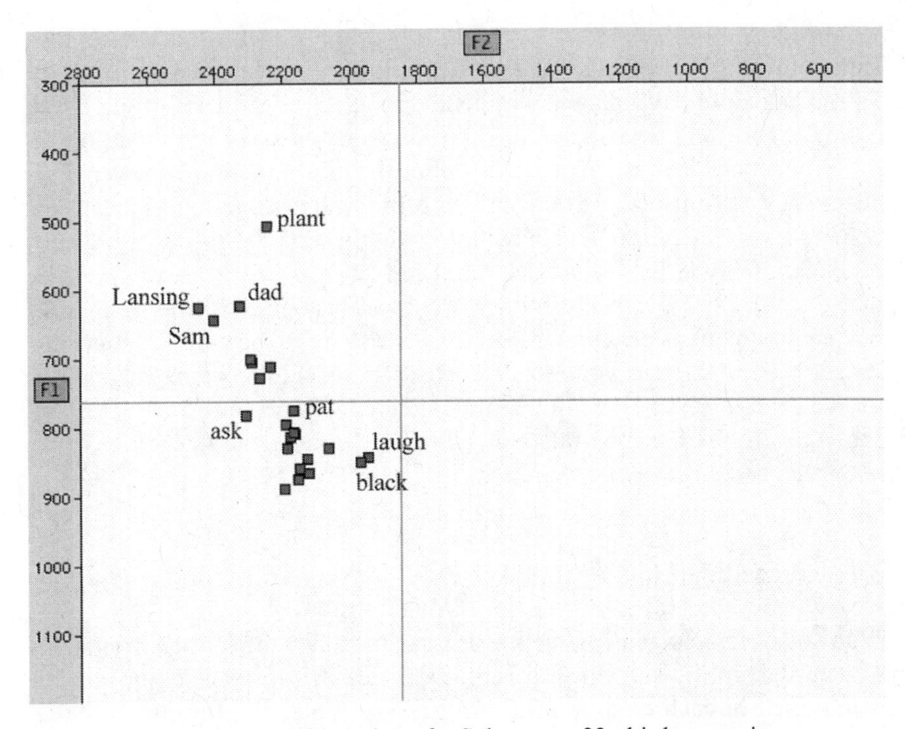

Figure 3.3 Plotnik chart of /æ/ tokens for Solana, age 22, third generation.

which pre-nasal raising of /æ/ is not a diagnostic feature. More importantly for the present study, none of the Texas Mexican American speakers whose vowels charts are shown in his 2001 book have a dramatically raised pre-nasal /æ/. Therefore, the presence of a high position for pre-nasal /æ/ in all six women under the age of 25 in the present study indicates strong NCS influence. In the Mexican American speech community in Lansing, raising of /æ/ before nasals may be as indicative of NCS influence as any overall change in vowel means. Furthermore, if young women are the leaders of change in this speech community as in many others, this finding also indicates that the Mexican American speech community in Lansing is headed towards fuller accommodation to NCS patterns in the production of /æ/.

Neither Stevens and House (1963) nor Hillenbrand et al. (2001) examined vowels in the nasal environment. Stevens and House state "nasal consonants were not included because of the difficulties of measuring formant frequencies for nasalized vowels" (112). Hillenbrand et al. focus on stop consonants and make no comment about nasal environments.

Technology has advanced considerably since Stevens and House published their article in 1963. For the current study, measurement of vowel tokens in a nasal environment was done through careful identification of the nasal formant, followed by individual readings for F1 and F2 in Praat.

Production does not match perception in this situation, however. Evidence shows that listeners average the first oral and nasal formants when perceiving a vowel (Beddor and Hawkins 1990, Stevens 1998). As pointed out by Plichta (2004), this means that nasalized /æ/ will be perceived as higher than oral /æ/. Plichta (2004) discovered that nasalization of vowels, even in an oral environment, is a common feature of NCS speech, but perhaps it is most salient perceptually in a pre-nasal context. If so, this provides an impetus for the genesis of the NCS, in that pre-nasal /æ/ was perceived as raised and subsequently produced as raised by children learning the dialect as a first language, creating the first step in the chain shift.

3.4 Preceding Manner and Voice

With regard to preceding manner and voice, the following four environments were tested: voiced and voiceless stops, voiceless fricatives, and liquids. The words used in each environment are listed in Table 3.5. Results show that preceding voiced stops are correlated with a significantly lower F1 for /ae/ in four of the sixteen speakers. Only one of these four is in Group A, supporting previous hypotheses that raising after voiced stops is a universal tendency.

Table 3.5 Preceding Manner and Voice Features and Words—Excluded (singletons): zap (voiced fricative), jazz (affricate)

Manner/Voice	Words
Voiced Stop	banker, bath, dad, gamble, gang, badge
Voiceless Stop	cabin, cash, pal, past, pat, tab
Voiceless Fricative	Saginaw, Sam, thank
Liquid	black, brag, Lansing, laugh, plant, rack, rag
Nasal	mash, mattress, nap
/h/ *or* Vowel Initial	apple, ask, has, have

Although preceding manner and voice were not tested separately in the previous sociolinguistic studies mentioned, these findings coincide with Stevens and House (1963) and Hillenbrand et al. (2001). Since Stevens and House tested vowels in symmetrical CVC environments only, they make no claims about the influence of preceding versus following environment. They do, however, consider /hVd/ as a *null* environment, which may imply that preceding /d/ has more influence than following /d/. Hillenbrand, Clark and Nearey provide inconclusive evidence on the effects of initial versus final voiced consonants, although, as mentioned previously, they found that preceding consonants have more influence overall.

Hillenbrand et al. (2001: 755) suggest that one physical characteristic of voiced consonants that may contribute to the raising effect they have on adjacent vowels is that the larynx is slightly lower in the production of voiced consonants than it is in the production of voiceless consonants. Although this in itself may not cause a lowering of F1, Stevens (1998: 474) discusses changes in F1 that occur in conjunction with the changes in airflow, transglottal pressure, vocal tract volume, and vocal tract stiffness that are all associated with the production of voiced stops.

3.5 Preceding Place of Articulation

The environments tested for the effects of preceding place of articulation were labial, apical, liquid apical, velar, /h/ and vowel initial. The words used are listed by environment in Table 3.6. Results show that preceding apicals and velars were correlated with significantly raised [æ] in four speakers. All four of the speakers for whom this result is significant were men. Also, only two of the Group A speakers showed any significance for this feature, indicating again that this effect is not correlated specifically with the Northern Cities Shift.

Table 3.6 Preceding Place of Articulation Features and Words—Excluded (singleton): jazz (palato-alveolar)

Place of Articulation	**Words**
Labial	badge, banker, bath, pal, past, pat, mash, mattress
Apical	thank, dad, tab, zap, Saginaw, Sam, nap
Liquid	brag, rack, rag, black, Lansing, laugh, plant
Velar	gamble, gang, cabin, cash
/h/ *or* Vowel Initial	has, have, apple, ask

Independent factors indicate that raising in the context of velars is a universal feature. The tongue body is high during the articulation of the velar consonants [k, g, ŋ], and these are the only consonants of English that are classified with the feature [+high] by Stevens (1998: 254). In addition, the CV and VC transitions are slower for velars than for labials or alveolars (365). It follows, therefore, that the velar environment may lead to undershoot in the articulation of a vowel, resulting in a lower F1, especially for non-high vowels.

Although apicals are not classified as [+high] by Stevens, the tongue tip is in a high position for the articulation of the consonant, and this is correlated with a raising and fronting effect on the transition into following front vowels. However, the transition out of this constricted position should occur more quickly than it does with velars (Stevens 1998: 354). Despite the rapid transition time, depending on the duration of the vowel and the place of articulation of the following consonant, the vowel trajectory may never reach the target position. Especially with a non-high vowel such as /æ/ is in these speakers, undershoot may cause lower F1.

The only preceding environment that had a conditioning effect on F2 in the present study was preceding liquids. When tested against other preceding manners, it was significantly correlated with backing in five speakers, particularly in comparison to preceding voiced stops, which have already been shown to promote raising. Three of the five speakers who showed this effect are from Group A.

When liquids were separated from other apicals and tested against place features for following consonant, they were found to correlate with a backed /æ/ in ten speakers, six of whom are in Group A. This was the most widespread finding in this study, but is probably due to the fact that four of the seven words used end with a velar consonant, which further promotes backing and therefore exaggerated the results for liquids. Since this result appears in both Group A and other speakers and has articulatory motivation, it again suggests a universal, default tendency.

4. Conclusion

In summary, results for the conditioning effects of following consonant manner and voice are the most striking and suggest that dramatic raising of /æ/ in front of nasals is a marker of accommodation to the NCS among Mexican American speakers of English in Lansing. The results for preceding environment provide clear evidence in support of previous conclusions about the conditioning effects on /æ/ of several specific consonantal environments.[7] Overall findings show that preceding voiced stops, velars, and apicals promote raising of /æ/. Preceding liquids are significantly correlated with a low F2, or backed /æ/. All of these findings except the pre-nasal raising of /æ/ agree with results found in studies on laboratory phonology and therefore suggest universal rather than area-specific effects. Findings on pre-nasal /æ/ raising were not possible in the Hillenbrand et al. (2001) study, since the nasal environment was not tested.

In general, therefore, no previously unattested coarticulatory effects on the production of /æ/ are apparent in the speech of Mexican Americans in Lansing who are native speakers of English. However, there is evidence of complex social stratification in one local feature. Very low F1 in tautosyllabic pre-nasal /æ/—ubiquitous in the local Anglo population—is present among those interviewed for the present study only in women under 25 who were born in Lansing and speak English as a native language. This supports the hypothesis that young women are the leaders of change, but it also raises the question of whether raising in the production of /æ/ before nasals is a distinctly female marker in this group. Given the accommodation to NCS /æ/ found in these young women—as evidenced by their pronunciation of both raised pre-nasal /æ/ and the centralizing off-glide that is distinct in the pronunciation of NCS /æ/, it is apparent that lack of assimilation to the pronunciation of vowels other than /æ/ in these speakers cannot be attributed to lack of contact with the Anglo community or lack of perceptual acuity. Subtle and accurate assimilation to local mainstream norms appears to be occurring in only some aspects of the phonetics and phonology for other reasons. Communicative competence in Lansing's Mexican American community clearly involves more than just the ability to assimilate to Anglo speech characteristics.

Notes

1 This study also included a perceptual experiment, which found unexpected results when production and perception were compared. The tokens that were most often confused in the perceptual experiment were not those that were most acoustically displaced due to phonetic conditioning. The authors offer an explanation based on relative distance of the token from a prototype.

2 Stevens and House (1963) does not indicate whether or not the three male speakers recorded were linguistically trained or not. The speakers were asked to read words in the form of "bisyllabic nonsense utterances in iambic form" (112), but it is not clear if they were presented as phonetic transcription or using regular orthography.

3 "The relative degree of advancement is influenced by the manner of articulation of the following segment, in the order nasals > voiceless fricatives > voiced stops > voiced fricatives > voiceless stops" (Labov 1994: 100).

4 "[The relative degree of advancement caused by] point of articulation follows the ordering palatal > apical > labial, velar" (Labov 1994: 100).
5 Although the words *gamble, gang, thank* and *banker* contain /æ/ in a pre-nasal environment, they were removed from this part of the analysis in order to separate nasal effects from velar effects, because the raising effects of velar consonants are so strong.
6 Personal communication.
7 The number of words used was fairly small in this study, and all possible environments were not tested. Therefore, a lack of statistical significance with regard to the coarticulatory effects of any given environment does not necessarily constitute conclusive evidence about that environment.

References

Beddor, Pamela and Sarah Hawkins. 1990. The influence of spectral prominence on perceived vowel quality. *Journal of the Acoustical Society of America* 87 (6): 2684–2704.

Evans, Betsy. 2001. *Dialect contact and the Northern Cities Shift in Ypsilanti, Michigan.* PhD Dissertation. Lansing, MI: Michigan State University.

Evans, Betsy, Rika Ito, Jamila Jones, and Dennis R. Preston. 2000. Change on top of change: Social and regional accommodation to the Northern Cities Chain Shift. In Hans Bennis, Hugo Ryckeboer, and Jan Stroop (eds), *De Toekomst van de Variatielinguïstiek* (a special issue of Taal en Tongval to honor Dr. Jo Daan on her ninetieth birthday), 61–86.

Hillenbrand, James, Michael Clark, and Terrance Nearey. 2001. Effects of consonant environment on vowel formant patterns. *Journal of the Acoustical Society of America* 109 (2): 748–763.

Ito, Rika. 1999. *Diffusion of urban sound change in rural Michigan: A case of the Northern Cities Shift.* PhD Dissertation. Lansing, MI: Michigan State University.

Jones, Jamila. 2003. *African Americans in Lansing and the Northern Cities Vowel Shift: Language contact and accommodation.* PhD Dissertation. Lansing, MI: Michigan State University.

Labov, William. 1994. *Principles of linguistic change: Internal factors.* Oxford: Blackwell.

Labov, William, Sharon Ash, and Charles Boberg. 2006. *The atlas of North American English.* Berlin: Mouton de Gruyter.

Plichta, Bartłomiej. 2004. *Interdisciplinary perspectives on the Northern Cities Chain Shift.* PhD Dissertation. Lansing, MI: Michigan State University.

Stevens, Kenneth and House, A. 1963. Perturbation of vowel articulations by consonantal context: An acoustical study. *Journal of Speech and Hearing Research* 6: 111–128.

Stevens, Kenneth. 1998. *Acoustic phonetics*. Cambridge, MA: MIT Press.

Thomas, Erik. 2001. *An acoustic analysis of vowel variation in New World English*. Publication of the American Dialect Society 85. Durham, NC: Duke University Press.

Chapter 4

Rhythm Types and the Speech of Working-Class Youth in a Banlieue of Paris: The Role of Vowel Elision and Devoicing

Zsuzsanna Fagyal, University of Illinois at Urbana–Champaign

1. Introduction

1.1 From teenage talk to "French of the suburbs"

Adolescents in multi-ethnic working-class suburbs (henceforth, *banlieues)* of Paris have been repeatedly portrayed as the "movers and shakers" of language change in French. The recurrent theme of "French being in the process of giving birth to a new language" (Gadet 2003: 85), however, raises many issues that are seldom examined. One such issue is the notion of novelty.

Verlan,[1] the most salient example of adolescent language use in France and, reportedly, a hallmark of innovation by the multi-ethnic working-class youth, goes back several centuries in the history of French as a type of word-formation process based on the inversion of syllables and segments within the word (Antoine 1998). Voltaire (1694–1778), the famous 18th-century French writer and philosopher, resorted to this process to form his pseudonym from the place name *Airvault*, the closest city to the village of Saint-Loup-sur-le-Thouet in the Poitou region where his grandfather was born (Merle 2000). Hiding the writer's humble origins[2], the "verlanized" pseudonym seems to have defined the symbolic boundaries of an individual social self within the larger community in much the same way as *verlan* is used today by the multi-ethnic urban youth, reportedly "twisting French in every direction, modifying, splitting, and inverting its words"[3] (Goudailler 1997: 9). Thus, rather than a symbol identifying one social group at one point in time, *verlan* is probably better understood as a way of indexing in the lexicon one's adherence to, or denial of, certain group values at a given time in the history of the language.

The "recycling" of old linguistic material in teenage talk is not unique to French. Stenström et al. (2002: 158–159) analyze the use of *well* as an adjective modifier (e.g., *well bored*, *well hard)* in the speech of London teenagers as a feature that goes "all the way back to *Beowulf* and the eighth century [but] in dormant existence until the late 20th century when it was taken up again and revived in the London teenage talk." Known as *exaptation* in historical linguistics, the recombination of former linguistic processes was attested in tense marking in Old-High German (Lass 1990) and in rhythm in English poetry (Haverkort and De Roder 2003). Thus, when measured on an extended time-scale, new is not always as novel as it might appear. Why is it, then, that despite the age-old processes it employs, adolescent language use in the French *banlieues* is consistently perceived as innovative?

One answer could be age. Newly (re)discovered structural features of the language in teenage talk have been argued to serve the purpose of stylistic distinctions in social interactions within and between adolescent peer groups. Of all periods of life, the adolescent years[4] in Western cultures are a time of self-invention, during which "young people continue a process, begun in late childhood, of equipping themselves to be full members of society" (Brown and Larson 2002: 6). Children begin to experiment with variable speech patterns for their own needs of self-expression long before puberty. Through gradual adjustments in their ways of conveying social-indexical meaning through language in the broader community, children begin to probe the limits of their participation in local social categories during the adolescent years. Adolescence is a coming of age of full sociolinguistic competence (Eckert and Rickford 2001), characterized by an intense quest for self-expression through the discovery of new, and the rediscovery of old, styles in language, dress (Eckert 2000), adornment (Mendoza-Denton 1999), and music (Epstein 1995). Invented and reinvented by each generation, these means of self-expression can signal distinctive social practices within the broader community, referred to as youth culture.[5] Thus, rather than novelty, distinctiveness in interactions is what seems to underlie perceptions of innovative language use in adolescence; it seems that something new is only as novel as it can be distinctive in everyday local practice.[6] And yet, the distinctiveness of age-related linguistic behavior does not explain why teenagers in the French *banlieues* are perceived as altering the structure of French as we know it today.[7]

Patterns of variation foreshadowing future change (in apparent time), rather than variation related to a specific period in life (age-grading), have been concurrent interpretations in many longitudinal studies of variable speech phenomena, with age-grading almost invariably turning out to be the best interpretation. "Teenagers use slang items that they will not use when they become adults," Preston (2004: 152) argues, and youth language "is not necessarily the way in which "the youth" will speak when they will reach their forties,"[8] according to Carton (2000: 25–26). While panel studies of generational change indicate that the speech of older speakers, often times individuals with unique personal histories, can show important changes over time as these speakers become late adopters of the innovative variant in the community (Sankoff and Blondeau 2007), such lifespan changes seem to be "the exception rather than the rule" (Sankoff 2004: 136).

How is it, then, that locally distinctive linguistic patterns of teenage talk in the Parisian *banlieues* are unanimously considered as signs of on-going language change in the broader speech community?

Reasons could be related to contact. Sankoff's (2004) review of well-known longitudinal studies reveals that virtually all observations of long-term stability of phonemic patterns over the life course of individuals had been made in some of the wealthiest Western societies. Social-demographic conditions in these nation-states can be rightly considered "remarkably stable", as Sankoff (2004: 136) observes with respect to Brink and Lund's studies of phonetic variation in Copenhagen. Often conducted over a relatively short time period, speech communities in countries such as Denmark, Switzerland, the UK,[9] and even the United States in the nineteen sixties and seventies,[10] were not subject to "catastrophic" societal changes such as massive population movements or conquests and subsequent long-term colonization. Language varieties spoken by "speakers who are fairly well-settled" or by speakers living in more or less "insular societies" (Chambers 2003: 108) not exposed to intense contact with other populations are considered "stationary" dialects by historical linguists (Hock 1991). In such communities, characterized by relatively little mobility and primary reliance on natural birth rate for population growth, age-grading could appear more salient than slow incremental changes observed over a relatively short time period. But what happens in communities known to have been affected by large-scale social-demographic changes? How are we to build into models of language variation and change the effect of sudden massive alterations of local dynamics of language use and related patterns of first language acquisition?

Working-class suburbs of Paris have been targeted by several large waves of immigration throughout the 20th century. The relatively late and rapid industrialization of France, combined with massive immigration of low-skilled foreign labor, altered social structures and modes of production in a country that was still predominantly rural after World War II. During the three prosperous decades (*les Trente Glorieuses*) following the war, for the first time in the history of the country, large populations from outside Europe settled in the peripheral urban working-class neighborhoods, traditionally home to newcomers integrating into French society at the bottom of the social hierarchy. These immigrants came predominantly from rural areas of Portugal and North Africa. As opposed to the Portuguese who were the most numerous but who spoke a Romance language, North Africans, the second most numerous group, had the disadvantage of what Chambers (2003: 97) calls "the language gap": although they came from former French colonies, being mostly illiterate, they did not speak French. Their native Semitic languages, typically dialects of spoken Arabic and Berber, were typologically different from Indo-European languages with which Metropolitan varieties of French had been previously in contact[11] (see Lodge 2004). A final factor singling out North Africans as "focal points [with] disparate bonds to the social mainstream" is "the integration gap" (Chambers 2003: 102–103), i.e., "the immigrants' attitudes toward the national language" and various cultural attributes that define membership in the host society. This factor could be of particular importance in a country like France where full-fledged membership in society is tied to the endorsement of specific cultural values in the public sphere. As Posner (1997: 48) reminds us, "Frenchness is not a question of genetics but of cultural allegiance." France is known to have rejected throughout its history regional and ethnic communities and local languages (*patois*) that could have represented viable alternatives to its political and linguistic unity. Despite the successful assimilation of immigrant groups in the past (see Noiriel 1988), the "anxiety of national fragmentation" (Mathy 2000: 142) in the face of multiculturalism is real, going back at least to the French Revolution. Thus, demonstrating one's allegiance to the rules of "appropriate cultural behavior" in public, among them standard language use or the lack of display of religious symbols,[12] is expected of all newcomers wishing to integrate into French society.[13]

At the local level, the newcomers have the burden of embedding themselves into tightly knit networks "based on sentiment, trust, and sharing of lifestyles" (Lin 2001: 66), and favoring the maintenance and reinforcement of existing resources, among them local vernaculars (Milroy 1980). The populations at the receiving end have to expect to loosen up some of these strong ties, and learn to communicate, live, and compete for resources with the newly arrived. The influx of a large number of immigrants showing significant linguistic homogeneity and receiving institutional help to integrate into French society could, in principle, favor the borrowing and blending of indigenous and incoming linguistic features in neighborhoods where these populations settled down. If, on the other hand, the newcomers were kept in relative isolation from mainstream society with other immigrants and/or locals because of numerous "gaps" hindering their immediate integration, then Chambers' (2003: 105–107) "inverse assimilation" hypothesis would apply: "certain variants in the native speech of (otherwise) assimilated second-generation speakers" diffused beyond the incoming ethnic group and became a marker of region or neighborhood. Confirming this interpretation is the fact that the variety of French spoken by descendents of North African immigrants is commonly referred to by the type of neighborhood in which these populations reside: *le français des banlieues* (*banlieue* French).

1.2 The talk of the suburbs

Cités 'housing projects' and *banlieues* 'suburbs' are some of the bywords that proverbially represent "socially disadvantaged peripheral areas of French cities containing relatively dense concentrations of minority ethnic groups" (Hargreaves and McKinney 1997: 12). Three decades after the end of the last waves of immigration from outside Europe, these areas of the French capital found themselves at the bottom of the social spectrum. According to the 1990 census data, residents of the department of Seine Saint-Denis, northeast of Paris, had the lowest annual income of all departments (Soulignac 1993). The global impoverishment of the population further deteriorated a decade later, with residents earning six to fifteen times less than those in the wealthiest areas southwest of the capital (ORGECO 2001). Social separatism, a term that French sociologists have long preferred over ghettoization,[14] has become apparent in urban areas where "disadvantaged neighborhoods [. . .] are considered, and rightly so, enclaves of foreign populations of recent immigrant origin,"[15] according to Maurin (2004). These signs point to a highly polarized outcome of contact between the locals and the newly settled immigrants. Polarized settlement patterns, with "the rich and the educated on the one side, and the poor immigrant on the other forming the two extreme poles of territorial segregation"[16] (Maurin 2004: 17) are known to have had lasting consequences on language use and the formation of new dialect varieties in many other contexts around the world (see e.g., Mufwene 2001).

But does the speech of second generation speakers from North Africa carry traces of heritage language[17] use strong enough to spread beyond working-class neighborhoods, as folk reports of on-going language change seem to predict?

1.3 Linguistic features

The emergence of specific lexical and phonetic features in the Parisian *banlieues* is frequently evoked. Christian Bachmann, the first ethnographer to conduct participant observation in some of the poorest housing projects of the town of *La Courneuve*, perceived a whole-scale restructuring of spoken French of the "youth of the *cités*": "the whole linguistic system is affected: intonation, lexicon, and even syntax, which is the most difficult to imitate,"[18] he insisted already in the 1980s. Evoking social isolation of peer groups, Bachmann suggested that male speakers using *verlan* (*keum* inverted from *mecs* 'guys') could be the loci of innovation and transmission of this massive change. Linguists upheld some of these claims but rejected others. Gadet (1998: 22), for instance, considers lexical and prosodic features the most innovative in the "new version of working-class French", but rejects hypotheses of a whole-scale restructuring of the vernacular. Duez and Casanova (2000: 69) note rhythmic irregularities, and a "specific use of the rhythmic properties of French", but they insist that these represent a recognizable part of the "French substrate" and therefore cannot be considered innovations. Recently, Cerquiglini (2001: 62) proposed that the perception of an uneven speech rhythm and the predominantly consonantal character of what he called the *talk of the cités* could come from the nativization of certain phonological features borrowed from French spoken by descendants of immigrants from North Africa, called *Beurs*:[19]

> "Certain vowels tend to fall. Consonants, on the other hand, particularly among Arabs in the *banlieues*, become more explosive. This is a type of pronunciation that rap musicians [. . .] have picked up. For instance, instead of *partir*, one says *p'r't'r*: the vowels disappear almost completely. And the consonants explode, like in *Rrrspect*! (*Respect*). This is the *Beur* way of speaking. French is perfectly well integrating this new influence, just as it had integrated Italian, English, and came out with even more vitality as a result."[20]

While rap musicians' use of certain pronunciation features might point to salient stereotypes (Fagyal 2007), the idea that local features of working-class Parisian French show traces of contact with immigrant languages from North Africa is noteworthy. The description of phonetic phenomena is especially revealing: "instead of *partir* one would say *p'rt'r*: vowels disappear almost entirely" seems to point to extreme vowel reduction, perhaps even elision of full (non-schwa) vowels, not yet reported in European varieties of French. One would, consequently, expect consonants to play a more predominant role, which is confirmed in the next phrase: "and consonants explode, such as in *Rrrspect!*" Knowing that the lack of vowel reduction and the tendency to equalize the duration of unaccented syllables (*l'égalité syllabique* 'isosyllabicity') has been reported for all varieties of French spoken in Europe (see e.g., Valdman 1993), one could hypothesize that contact with Semitic languages of north-west Africa, languages with a strong tendency towards vowel reduction, could alter some of these well-known characteristics of French. The goal of this paper is to measure these effects empirically.

1.4 Empirical measurements of speech rhythm

Empirical studies of speech rhythm have a tumultuous history marked by attempts at finding the best acoustic phonetic measures, allowing the classification of languages in distinct rhythm types. The most recent approaches to rhythmic typology have focused on perception. Psycholinguists observed that young infants could discriminate between their mother tongue and another language before even developing the ability to segment speech. Infants' discrimination patterns closely matched dichotomous distinctions proposed earlier between so-called syllable-timed and stressed-timed languages. The former were characterized by syllables that "tend to come at more-or-less evenly recurring intervals so that, as a result, phrases with extra-syllables take proportionately more time" (Pike 1945: 35), while the latter were thought to display uniform spacing of metrically strong, accented syllables. Mora-timing, with Japanese as the most well-known representative of this third rhythm class, was later added to this dichotomy.

Approaching the issue from its perceptual underpinnings, recent psycholinguistic experiments have shown that infants can successfully discriminate between a stress-timed and a mora-timed language, e.g., English and Japanese, but are less able to discriminate between two stressed-timed languages, such as English and Dutch (Mehler et al. 1996, Nazzi, Bertoncini, and Mehler 1998). Taking these studies as their input, Ramus, Nespor, and Mehler (1999) (henceforth, RNM) hypothesized that infants' perception of rhythm types is centered on the alternation of vocalic intervals of variable length with "noisy" portions of the speech signal. However, rather than computing a raw measure of sonority derived from spectral information, RNM resorted to identifying and then collapsing into longer stretches of vocalic and consonantal intervals discrete phonological units, i.e., vowels and consonants.[21] They claimed that "a simple segmentation of speech into consonants and vowels" is all that is needed to arrive at language-specific auditory patterns reminiscent of the syllable- vs. stress-timed distinction that forms the basis of infants' successful discrimination between various languages. Rhythm types were conceived as a continuum. It was hypothesized that languages with predominantly simple CV-type syllable structure, absence of vowel reduction, and relatively little variation in vowel durations produce a speech signal that contains more vocalic than consonantal material. This would translate in an overall higher ratio of vocalic intervals per utterance. Such languages were expected to pattern separately from languages with complex syllable structure and a strong tendency towards vowel reduction.

The measure capturing the ratio of vocalic portions in the signal was %V, the sum of vocalic interval durations divided by the total duration of utterances. ΔC, the standard deviation of consonantal intervals, indicated a greater variety of syllable types in a language (i.e., light and heavy onsets and codas), resulting in greater variation of consonantal interval durations. These measures allowed RNM to distinguish between the clearest cases of rhythm type. English and Dutch patterned together with Polish, all three having complex codas and onsets, which resulted in the expected high ΔC but low %V values. Italian, Spanish, Catalan, and French, although showing variable tendencies within the group, exhibited the opposite tendency. Japanese patterned separately from both types, showing low ΔC and high %V values, pointing to simple onset and coda structures, as well as the absence of diphthongization.

The third dispersion measure, the standard deviation of vocalic interval durations, or ΔV, was expected to be low in European varieties of French with no diphthongization and/or vowel reduction. ΔV was expected to be high, on the other hand, in languages like Dutch or English that showed a wide dispersion of vocalic interval durations, indicating the presence of short, reduced vowels as well as long diphthong-like segments. This measure, however, proved to be less successful than %V and ΔC in differentiating between rhythm types, which led RNM to conclude that "the ΔV scale seems less related to rhythm classes," although it "still reflects phonological properties of the language" (RNM 1999: 275). Based on utterances elicited in tightly controlled conditions, RNM's findings empirically confirmed the existence of rhythm types and clusters of languages patterning along a continuum of main phonotactic characteristics.

There seemed to be only one caveat: %V, ΔC, and ΔV are continuous measures of phonotactic differences between languages. In less tightly controlled corpora, standard deviation was argued to be sensitive to "spurious variability introduced by changes in speaking rate" (Grabe and Low 2002: 521). A formula by Grabe et al. (1999), used in many subsequent studies, proposed to normalize vocalic and intervocalic interval durations in order to minimize the impact of speech rate.[22] As we shall see, however, neutralizing rate-induced variation could result in the loss of socially meaningful variation.

2. Method

2.1 Questions and hypotheses

Recordings from five French speakers of European origin (henceforth, EF speakers) and five French speakers of North-African origin (henceforth, AF speakers), born in the same community, were examined. It was hypothesized that the speech of AF speakers would show influence from their heritage languages, and thus characteristics of stress-timed languages. EF speakers were expected to pattern with syllable-timed languages, thus separately from both AF speakers and stress-timed languages. If rhythmic patterns of heritage languages from North Africa were the main factor influencing AF speakers' rhythm type in French, then the patterning of the ten speakers in two distinct groups should not be obscured by individual speaker differences.

Vernacular Arabic spoken in Western parts of North Africa, the dialect area of origin of AF speakers in the corpus, has been classified as stress-timed. These dialects exhibit "short vowel deletion in open syllables, resulting in various consonant clusters and types of syllables with complex onsets and codas" (Ghazali et al. 2002: 332, Miller 1984). Stress is lexically distinctive, heavy syllables tend to attract it (weight-sensitivity), and syllables are parsed into trochaic feet with the metrically strong syllable on the left. Dialects of Berber, in contact with Arabic in North Africa, could also be a factor in comparisons of rhythm type, because of their well-known characteristics of licensing long voiceless obstruents in both onset and coda positions. In some dialects, entire words can be composed of voiceless segments (Dell and Elmedlaoui 1985, Ridouane 2003). Northern varieties of French, on the other hand, show widely different characteristics. They are considered syllable-timed, marking accentual prominence at the phrase level, and showing no weight-sensitivity with a tendency to parse predominantly light (CV) syllables into iambic feet, i.e., with the metrically strong syllable on the right.

Thus, if AF speakers' speech shows heritage language influence, it can also be expected to show signs of vowel deletion and/or reduction, which might lead to a preference for heavy and closed, rather than light and open, syllables. Substantial vowel reduction, if present, should be manifest in low %V values, indicating that AF speakers' readings are more "consonantal." The alternation of full and reduced vocalic intervals is expected to be manifest in high ΔV values, and similar degrees of alternation between the duration of consonantal intervals should also yield higher ΔC values. AF speakers' speech samples might also show evidence of transfer of other phonological constraints from Arabic. Specifically, they can show the presence of vowel epenthesis breaking up consonant clusters, as well as the insertion of glottal stops. Vowel epenthesis could parallel findings from second-language acquisition, such as Youssef and Mazurkewich's 1998 study of Cairene Arabic L2 learners of English, whose readings showed traces of epenthetic vowels, analyzed as "phonological transfer" from Arabic. Shortening and/or deletion of vowels in stressed or unstressed positions in the word would confirm previous reports of "high frequency of consonants" and "staccato rhythm" in the speech of multi-ethnic working-class youth by Duez and Casanova (2000) and Cerquiglini (2001) (see previous discussion).

2.2 Speakers and community

Recordings were made during fieldwork, which was carried out in educational settings (tutoring) in a *collège* 'middle/junior high school' in *La Courneuve*, a working-class suburb near Paris, between 2000 and 2002. Speakers are represented in Table 4.1 by their pseudonyms chosen randomly by the researcher from the fifty most frequent Arabic and European French first names. These ethnically easily identifiable names bear no resemblance to speakers' real names, places of residence, or exact geographic origins. They merely provide shortcuts to speakers' reported language use: 'AF' for Arabic/Berber[23] and French, 'EF' for French only.

Speakers were between eleven and fifteen years of age. The youngest speakers were sixth graders, the oldest third graders.[24] On average, AF speakers were a year older (4th grade) than EF speakers (5th grade). Students' standing in school was based on their *moyenne générale*, obtained from school officials at the end of the semester when the recordings took place. Sixth graders' *moyenne générale* was based on their first semester-final grades.

AF speakers were heritage speakers of a Semitic language from North Africa, to which they unanimously referred as Arabic. Four speakers' parents came from Algeria, and one speaker did not wish to communicate information about his parents' country of origin. The speakers were at least passive bilinguals,[25] i.e., they understood their heritage language but did not necessarily speak it natively. EF speakers reported that their family members have been monolingual speakers of French for more than three generations. All speakers were born in the immediate vicinity of *La Courneuve*, a town of about thirty-five thousand people and one of the poorest peripheral areas of the French capital. About 23% of the town's population is younger than 14-years-old, and almost as many are children of recent immigrants.[26] Between 30 to 38% of the

Table 4.1 Demography of Speakers of North African (AF) and European (EF) Descent

Speaker (code name)	Grade in school	Age	*Moyenne générale**	Parents' birth country
AF				
Khatib	4	13	8.30	Algeria
Laith	5	12	9.20	
Mousa	5	13	9.93	
Yasin	3	14	15.90	
Ramey	4	13	8.90	*NA*
mean	*4.2*	*13.0*	*10.45*	
EF				
Alain	6	11	13.73^{+}	France
Chris	6	11	10.77^{+}	
Jacob	6	11	10.86^{+}	
Octave	4	13	12.96	
Karl	4	13	8.66	
mean	*5.2*	*11.8*	*11.4*	

*(*Moyenne générale* is based on average grade in school from the preceding year or, for the 6th graders ($^{+}$), on the first semester in middle school $^{+}$).

active population are regularly out of work, 59% of them for a year or longer. The town is known for its housing projects, among them *La Cité des Quatre-Mille,* infamous for riots that shook France for the first time in the 1980s. Its residents are routinely depicted in the French and foreign media as involved in drug dealings, clashes with the police, collective rape, and even Islamic Jihad.[27] Several speakers from both ethnic groups in the corpus live in one of the many housing projects in town.

2.3 Task, corpus, and measurements

The short paragraph in Appendix A was submitted to each of the speakers at the end of a picture-naming task. The speakers were recorded individually and instructed to read the text in a natural fashion. They could study the text prior to reading it in order to minimize hesitations and false starts that would have made it impossible to obtain continuous speech data.

Since speakers in this study were recorded reading the same text in the same language and in the same dialect area, RNM's central and dispersion measures were used to examine individual and group rhythm type characteristics. These measures were used to relate acoustic properties of the speech signal to phonotactic constraints observed in the speakers' speech.

Although RNM implicitly resorted to a joint phonemic and acoustic segmentation of the speech signal into "vocalic" and "consonantal" portions, they qualified the segmentation process "straightforward with the exception of glides" (p. 271). But many phonetic phenomena, among them vowel devoicing, challenge this assumption. Should a devoiced high vowel uttered with a friction-like noise be considered vocalic based on phonemic analysis or consonantal because of its acoustic characteristics? Furthermore, segmentation issues related to allophones of /r/ that surface as approximants in various languages are also omitted. The most frequent approximants, /j/ and /w/, are singled out, but the steps taken to segment these continuous articulations into discrete units are not explained. RNM specify, for instance, that prevocalic glides are segmented as consonants and post-vocalic glides are treated as vowels, but they provide no indications as to how the acoustic boundaries of these segments were determined. Delimiting approximants in intervocalic positions can be a dubious process, as formant movements and voicing are continuous, and therefore often leave no discontinuities that can be taken as boundary cues on the spectrogram.

In the present study, devoiced vowels were considered consonantal when voicing was undetectable through most of the duration of the vowel. Boundaries of glides were determined by joint acoustic and auditory evaluation. The palatal front glide /j/ was considered consonantal whenever its presence was indicated by a clear formant and/or amplitude change in the speech signal. The front and back glides /ɥ/ and /w/ were considered vocalic, and included with the following vowel. Pauses and marks of hesitation were excluded.

Although the %V, ΔC, and ΔV indices were intended by RNM to be relative measures, values calculated for each individual utterance or phrase were averaged out to yield one measure per speaker in most earlier studies.[28] Since average values are highly sensitive to major deviations from central tendencies in a distribution, phrase length could become an issue when calculating these indices. This is especially problematic when length is not measured in number of syllables, but in absolute duration of a phrase or an utterance. RNM controlled for the average duration (about three seconds) of the isolated utterances in their corpus by selecting utterances of roughly comparable length. However, such a control is impossible in fieldwork data with speakers freely selecting their articulatory rates. The present study follows Grabe and Low's (2002: 525) in taking as few "subjective and intuitive decisions as possible when taking measurements." However, since %V, ΔC, and ΔV indices were calculated on utterances or prosodic phrases in previous studies, the present study aimed at replicating calculations of these indices on prosodic domains of similar length. Individual intonation phrases delimited by silent pauses and major pitch movements in the text systematically overlapped with syntactic clauses and short utterances, representing the closest possible approximation to units over which rhythm type indices were calculated in RNM's (1999) and Ghazali et al.'s (2002: 332) studies. Whenever disfluencies occurred, phrases shorter than five syllables were collapsed with the shortest surrounding phrase. The length of phrases obtained in this way ranged from 13 to 17 segments.

3. Results

3.1. %V, ΔV, ΔC indices

Table 4.2 shows the total durations, the total number of intonation phrases, vocalic and consonantal intervals, the mean articulatory rates and lengths of phrases with standard deviations for each speaker. The total number of measurements varied across speakers.[29] The difference between the highest and lowest numbers of vocalic intervals was comparable to inter-speaker differences in RNM's 1999 study. Inter-speaker differences in the number of consonantal interval measurements, however, were more than three times higher than in their study. Possible reasons for this will be discussed later in the study.

Articulatory rates varied between 10 and 13 segments per second for most speakers. Since previous studies, including RNM's, gave no information about individual speakers' articulatory rates, it is difficult to compare the extent of these differences to previous observations. On average, speakers in the AF group were one year older, articulated two segments per second faster, and completed the reading task in average four seconds faster than speakers in the EF group.[30] Laith, an AF speaker, had the longest intonation phrases and Jacob, an EF speaker, had the shortest intonation phrases in the sample.

Average %V and ΔC values for AF and EF speakers together with average values of various languages representing main rhythm types in RNM's study are represented in Figure 4.1. Since standard error values were not published by these authors, they could not be represented on the figure.[31] AF and EF speakers patterned closer to syllable-timed languages, such as Italian, Spanish, French,

Table 4.2 Total Durations, Total Number of Intonation Phrases, Vocalic Intervals, Consonantal Intervals, Mean Articulatory Rates, Length of Phrases, and Their Standard Deviations for Speakers of North African (AF) and European Descent (EF)

	Total duration (sec)	N of intonation phrases*	N of vocalic intervals	N of consonantal intervals	Articulatory rate (interval/sec)		Average length of intonation phrases (N intervals/phrase)	
					Mean	Std	Mean	Std
AF								
Khatib	27.66	20	136	183	11.53	2.05	16	6
Laith	24.30	17	139	159	12.91	1.86	18	7
Mousa	26.69	23	136	134	10.45	1.35	12	5
Yasin	17.87	15	144	109	14.25	2.33	17	8
Ramey	23.98	17	133	139	11.08	1.77	16	7
mean	*24.10*	*18.40*	*137.60*	*144.80*	*12.04*	*1.87*	*15.80*	*6.60*
EF								
Alain	29.44	18	133	137	9.71	2.00	18	8
Chris	27.92	22	140	140	10.17	1.44	13	5
Jacob	30.64	31	149	151	10.02	1.88	10	5
Octave	25.81	20	144	144	11.24	1.36	14	5
Karl	26.71	24	137	134	10.24	1.39	12	6
mean	*28.45*	*22.75*	*141.50*	*143.00*	*10.29*	*1.67*	*13.75*	*5.75*

*Phrases with less than five segments were collapsed with the preceding phrase.

and Catalan than to stress-timed languages, exemplified by English, Dutch, and Polish, with the latter representing a different rhythm type.

The speakers' readings appeared to be more vocalic (higher %V values) but roughly as consonantal (similar ΔC values) as some of the Romance languages are in RNM's study. Having uttered more vocalic sequences, and uttered them more slowly then AF speakers, the EF group had higher average %V than the EF group. There were no differences in terms of ΔC values.

As for average ΔC and ΔV values, Figure 4.2 reveals that AF and EF speakers patterned closer to each other and the Romance language group than to any of the stress-timed languages or Japanese. EF speakers exhibited slightly more vocalic duration variations (ΔV). As in RNM's study, within-group variations for languages and speakers in this corpus seemed more prevalent when plotted as functions of %V and ΔV. Rather than isolated subgroups, however, the main rhythm types appeared as a continuum. Figure 4.3

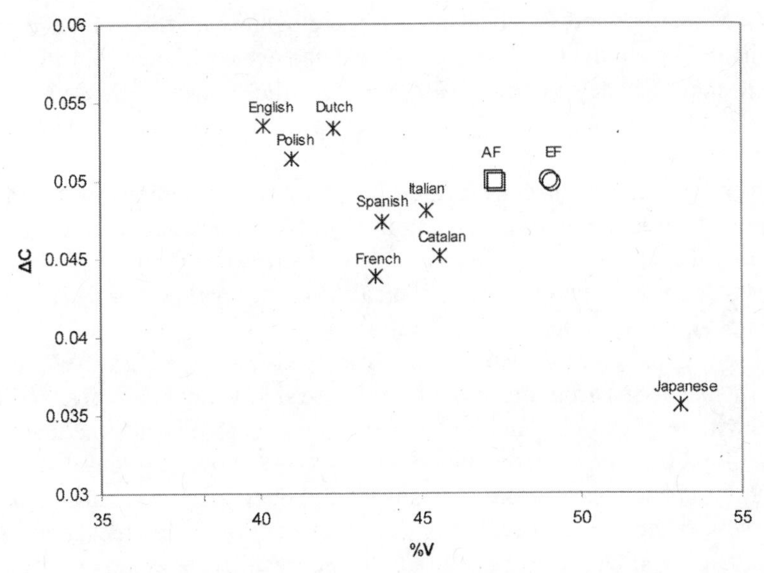

Figure 4.1 Average %V and ΔC values for French speakers of North African (AF) and European descent (EF) and languages representing main rhythm types (Ramus et al. 1999: 273).

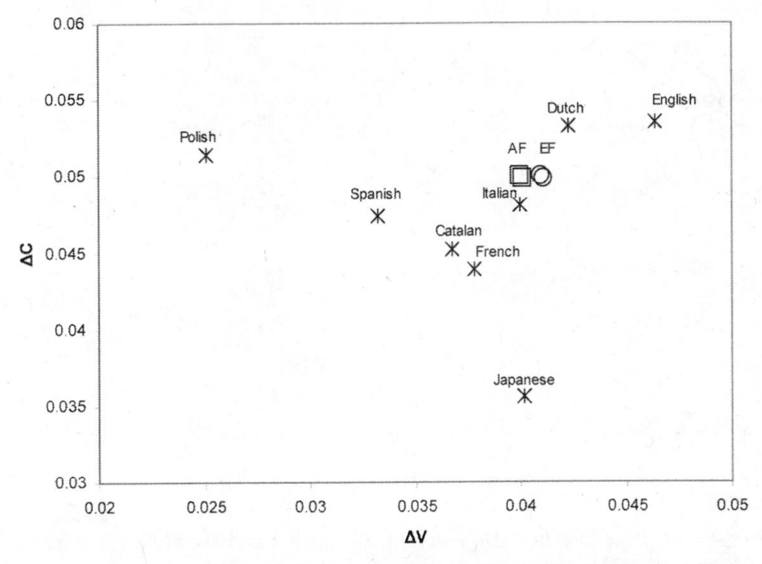

Figure 4.2 Average ΔV and ΔC values for French speakers of North African (AF) and European descent (EF) and languages representing main rhythm types (Ramus et al. 1999: 274).

indicates that AF and EF speakers patterned again with the Romance group and differed from the Germanic group that had overall higher ΔV values. The ten speakers' speech samples were more vocalic, however, than previously measured for French. The EF group again appeared more vocalic, but vocalic interval durations (ΔV) varied to the same extent in both groups.

Neither vocalic nor consonantal durations varied homogenously in this sample.[32] While a log transformation of measurements rendered the variance of consonantal duration measurements more homogenous, and therefore allowed the use of parametric statistical tests, no mathematical trick could accomplish the same for vocalic durations.[33]

The non-parametric version of one-way ANOVA, the Kruskal-Wallis test, with speaker as the grouping variable indicated significant inter-speaker differences with respect to the length of vocalic intervals ($H=191.635$, $median=8.85$, $df=9$, $p<0.001$) and consonantal intervals ($H=27.299$, $median=9.41$, $df=9$, $p<0.001$). The longest vocalic and consonantal intervals were measured in the slowest speaker, Alain's reading, followed by four other EF speakers: Chris, Jacob, Karl, and Octave. They were followed by all AF speakers who tended to have short vocalic and consonantal intervals. Yasin's reading showed the shortest vocalic and consonantal interval durations, and he was also the fastest speaker in the corpus. Notice, however, that this ranking only partially overlapped with speakers' articulatory rate: Octave from the EF group for

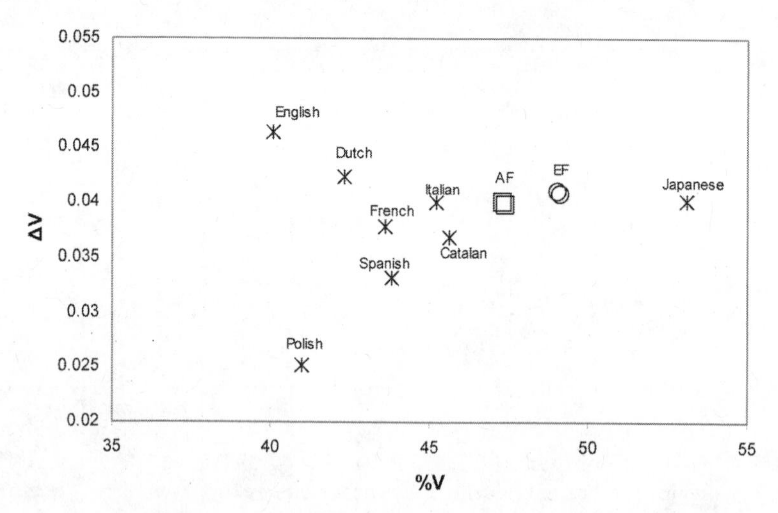

Figure 4.3 Average %V and ΔV values for French speakers of North African (AF) and European descent (EF) and languages representing main rhythm types (Ramus et al. 1999: 273).

instance read overall faster that Ramey and Mousa from the AF group (Table 4.2). The U Mann-Whitney non-parametric t-test for vocalic intervals as dependent variable and ethnicity as grouping variable also showed significant differences (U=165432.00, z = 4.249, p<0.001, two-tailed). The EF group's mean duration (778 ms) was significantly higher than the AF group's (582 ms). As for consonantal interval length, there were also significant differences between the two groups (U=210862.00, z = -3.175, p<0.001, two-tailed), with the EF group's mean consonantal durations (718 ms) significantly higher than the AF group's (650 ms).

3.2 Rhythm type and inter-speaker variation

Regression analyses were carried out to explore what information about the speakers and their speech led to their grouping in two distinct categories. In the first stepwise analysis, the dichotomous outcome variable, ethnicity, was tested against five rhythmic predictor variables: the three rhythm type indices %V, ΔV, and ΔC, speakers' articulatory rate, and the total number of segments per phrase. In a second series of analyses, two external predictor variables, age (as grade in school) and performance in school (*moyenne générale*), were added (see Table 4.1). These variables have been introduced, since speakers' degree of proficiency and/or choice of a more or less careful reading style could be expected to have an effect on the hyper- vs. hypo-articulation of vowels and consonants. Grade in school (approximate age) was expected to inversely correlate with reading proficiency and the ability to reproduce a careful reading style learned in school. Overall performance in school, based on the official score *moyenne générale* put out by the school each year, could also show positive correlation with reading style, as better students could be expected to read more carefully and thus have a lesser tendency to reduce or elide vowels. In the third stepwise regression analysis, the speaker as an additional source of variations was added to the model.

Three backward stepwise regression analyses were performed. The first was carried out with five rhythmic predictor variables, the second and third were performed with grade in school (approximate age) and *moyenne générale*, respectively, added to the model. The fourth analysis combined rhythmic predictors with grade in school and *moyenne générale*, while the fifth analysis added speaker to all the other predictor variables. The initial step in each analysis consisted in building a model with all available predictor variables included. After this initial step, several runs were carried out to test whether any of the predictors could be removed from the model without having a substantial effect on its fit of the observed data. The predictor variable removed first was the one that had the least impact on the model, while the predictor removed next was, each time, the one without substantial contribution. The elimination criterion at each step was statistical significance, with a cut-off point of $p<0.05$. The analyses ran until the best possible fit (no more improvement) was obtained.

Among all predictors, five were significant at the initial step. These were: number of segments in the phrase, articulatory rate, grade-level in school, *moyenne générale*, and speaker. The initial fit of the observed data, however, was barely above chance: 54.3%. After three consecutive runs with several iterations each, this picture improved. Analyses performed with five rhythm type predictor variables resulted in an overall fit of 68.6% of the model, with only articulatory rate contributing significantly (cut-off $p<0.05$) to the overall improvement ($r^2 = 0.521$). The addition of grade in school as the first and only external variable produced a 67.1 % overall prediction accuracy, while the addition of *moyenne générale* alone produced a ratio of 73.1 %. The combination of the last two variables resulted in 75.9 % accuracy. The addition of speaker as an independent variable alone led to 80.1 % accuracy in predicting what speaker belonged to the EF or the AF group.

Table 4.3 shows correlation coefficients for all predictor variables.[34] Out of five rhythmic predictors, only articulatory rate and the number of segments in the phrase correlated significantly and positively with the outcome variable ethnicity.[35] These two variables also showed co-linearity: their positive relationship means that the higher was the articulatory rate, the more intervals (vocalic and consonantal) speakers tended to include in a phrase.[36] Thus, AF speakers tended to speak faster and inserted overall more segments in their phrases than EF speakers.

Although none of the rhythm type indices (%V, ΔC or ΔV) predicted significantly which speakers can be grouped in which of the two categories of ethnic origin, the inverse correlations of %V and ΔC values with ethnicity indicate that as the outcome variable increases speakers' %V and ΔC values would decrease. AF speakers, although slightly, tended to have less vocalic intervals (low %V) and less variation in the duration of consonantal intervals (low ΔC values) in their readings. They also showed slightly greater ΔV values, which is indicative of greater vocalic interval duration variations.

Speakers' grades in school (approximate ages) and *moyennes générales* were statistically significant and showed inverse correlation with ethnicity. Thus EF speakers who were slightly younger, that is enrolled in at a younger grade level, also tended to be better students than AF speakers. The individual speaker as a predictor variable brought the single most important

Table 4.3 Linear Regression Coefficients with Eight Predictor Variables and "ethnicity" (AF or EF) as Outcome Variable[37]

Pearson correlation coefficients (*p<.05, **p<.001)	ethnicity	N of segments in phrase	articulatory rate	%V	ΔV	ΔC	grade	GPA	*individual speaker*
ethnicity EF (1) AF (2)	1.000	.184*	.323**	-.053	.080	-.004	-.459**	-.234**	*.580***
N segments in phrase	.184**	1.000	.280**	-.245**	-.107	.045	-.158*	.064	*.106*
articulatory rate	.323**	.280	1.000	-.219**	-.321**	-.256**	-.278**	.164**	*.205***
%V	-.053	-.245**	-.219*	1.000	.297**	-.125*	.136*	-.284**	*-.070*
ΔV	.080	-.107	-.321**	.297**	1.000	.109	-.096	.068	*.058*
ΔC	-.004	.045	-.256**	-.125*	.109	1.000	.050	.052	*-.092*
age (as grade in school)	-.459**	-.158*	-.278**	.136**	-.096	.050	1.000	.114	*-.841***
GPA (*moyenne générale*)	-.234**	.064	.164**	-.284*	.068	.052	.114	1.000	*-.357***
individual speaker	*.580***	*.106*	*.205***	*-.070*	*.058*	*-.092*	*-.841***	*-.357***	1.000

contribution to the model (r^2=0.58). It was positively correlated with ethnicity, which means that, individually, AF speakers contributed more to the observed variations than EF speakers. The main question, however, still remained: did the three rhythm type indices account for any variation in any way at all in the sample?

Residual variations of %V, ΔV, and ΔC not accounted for by the regression model showed a normal but bimodal distribution, split in two parts respectively at +1 and -1 standard deviation from the sample mean. Since %V, ΔV, and ΔC were inversely correlated with articulatory rate (see Table 4.3), this split could be due to some extent to fast speech processes, known to induce the compression of segmental durations, and thus making AF speakers pattern differently from the more "slowly articulating" EF speakers.

The general conclusion is that ethnic origin and related heritage language use in this sample is tied to a large extent to differences in articulatory rate, splitting speakers in two well-defined groups: the group of the younger, more slowly articulating EF speakers who also tended to be better students, and the group of the somewhat (one grade) older, fast articulating AF speakers who also had overall lower average grades in school. As it turns out, these parameters proved to be meaningful within the adolescent male peer-group social order (see Discussion).

What remains of heritage language influence? One can hypothesize that AF speakers' readings were slightly more consonantal (see negative correlation with %V), because these speakers tended to elide more vowels, and therefore had more complex onsets and codas than EF speakers. Since devoiced vowels were considered consonantal, the slight amount of devoicing could have reduced the number of syllables in the AF group, and contributed to a decrease in %V and an increase in ΔV values. This hypothesis was examined next.

3.3 Beyond global measures: Syllable structure

Figure 4.4 shows the number of different types of syllables in EF and AF speakers' speech. The magnitude of differences between the categories was reduced on a logarithmic scale for easier reading. As one would expect it in French, CV syllables were the most numerous (61%) in both groups' readings. They were four times more frequent than the next most frequent type of syllable: CVC (14%). With the exception of complex codas (CVCC), found only in the syllable /jabl/ of the word *incroyable* 'incredible' in two EF speakers' readings, all other types of syllables showed virtually identical percentages:

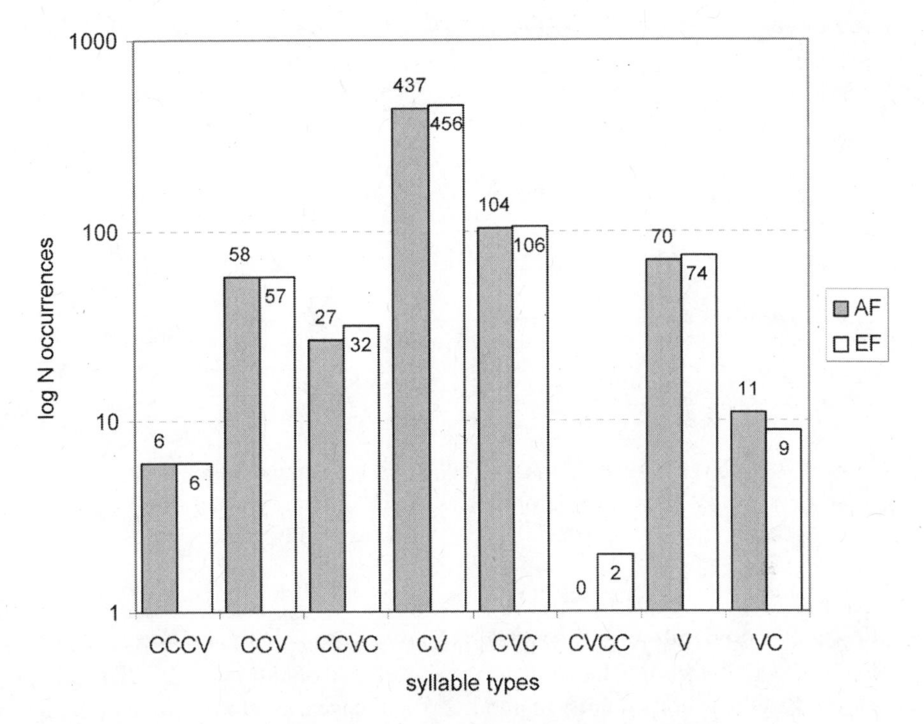

Figure 4.4 Types of syllables in the readings of French speakers of North African (AF) (N=713) and European (EF) (N=742) descent.

V (10%), CCV (8%), and CCVC (4%). This suggests that speakers in the two groups did not differ with respect to the type and complexity of the syllables that they used. If vowel elision, insertion, or reduction occurred in AF speakers' speech, it did not lead to substantial inter-group differences. Numerical differences between the two groups were, in fact, so small that inferential statistics were not computed.

And yet, near-dichotomous differences exist between the two groups at a lower level of phonetic contrast. This level of allophonic differences usually remains unexplored in studies of rhythm type distinctions, because contrasting patterns are often too scarce to be modeled statistically. But, as we shall see, even a few percent of variability at perceptually salient points in the acoustic signal can carry important information.

Figure 4.5 shows that four out of seven acoustic variables, although numerically not substantial to account for statistically significant effects,

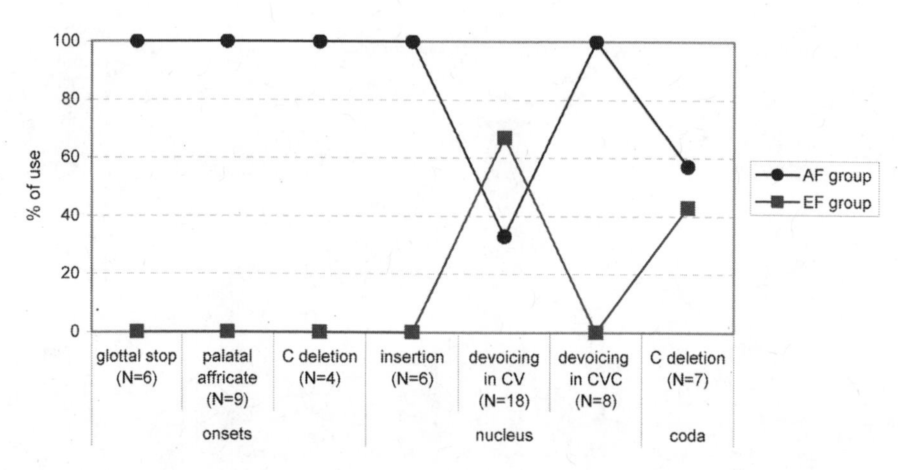

Figure 4.5 Types of onset, nucleus, and coda in the readings of French speakers of North African and European descent (N of total syllables =1455).

allow a clear separation of the speakers in two groups. About 89% (N=1293) of syllables in the sample had at least one onset consonant, but only AF speakers realized these consonants, in about 2.6% of cases, as glottal stops or palatalized affricates. Deletion of onset consonants occurred only in AF speakers' speech (0.15%). Similarly, schwa insertion and vowel devoicing in CVC syllables only characterized AF speakers, while there were nearly identical proportions of coda deletion in the two groups. Devoicing of syllable nuclei in CV syllables, on the other hand, was twice as frequent in the EF group (67%) than in the AF group (33%).

While deletion and, perhaps to some extent devoicing, could be considered fast speech processes, i.e., resulting from the fact that AF speakers, overall, articulated somewhat faster than EF speakers, it is unlikely that schwa insertion, glottalization, and the affrication of palatalized stop consonants could be attributed to rate differences. Clearly, something else other than articulatory rate must lie behind AF speakers' tendency to dissolve consonant clusters with epenthetic vowels, and to prevent vowel coalescence (*enchaînement vocalic*) through the insertion of glottal stops.

Figure 4.6 shows intra-speaker variations in the frequency of onset, nucleus, and coda types. Ample variations within the AF group (the first five speakers from the top), contrasting sharply with a greater uniformity of allophonic realizations in the EF group (the last five speakers), can be observed. Speakers in both groups resorted to coda consonant deletion (1) and devoicing of syllable nuclei in CV syllables (2):

(1) *c'est une histoire incroyab**(le)*** (Karl, EF)
'this is an incredible story'

(2) *ce qu'il est deve**nu*** (Khatib, AF)
'what happened to him'

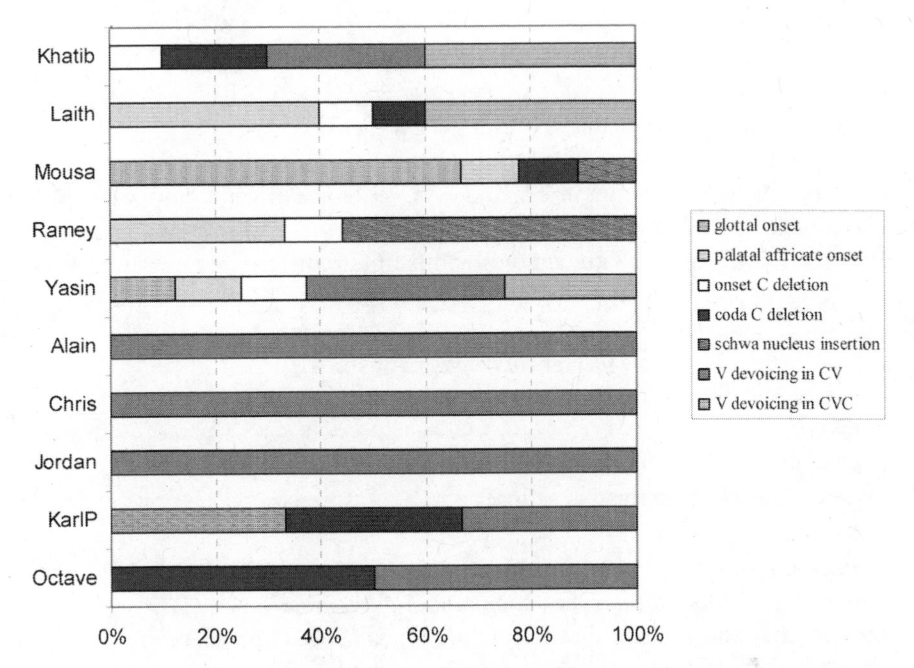

Figure 4.6 Intra-speaker variations in the frequencies of onset, nucleus, and coda types for French speakers of North African (top five) and European (bottom five) descent.

Yasin, the fastest speaker in the sample, combined as many different allophonic realizations as Mousa, Laith, Karl, and Khatib who articulated more slowly. Schwa insertion (examples (3) and (4)) have also occurred, which goes against the logic of fast speech processes that tend to reduce and compress rather than increase vocalic segment durations:

(3) *c'est sû**r*** [schwa] *qu'on ne l'a plus jamais revu* (Ramey, AF)
'it is certain that he has not been seen ever since'

(4) *not**re** prof d'anglais a disparu* (Octave, EF)
'our English teacher has disappeared'

The affrication of stop consonants, as in example (5), arising from the lengthening of the friction phase following the closing gesture of stops (see Corneau 2000), represents a well-known characteristic of Canadian French, and was reported in the vernacular of working-class youth of North African descent and their peers (see Jamin 2005, Jamin, Trimaille, and Gasquet-Cyrus 2006). Thus their occurrence cannot be attributed to fast speech processes or individual speaker characteristics:

(5) *alors qu'un élève l'a vu descendre* ***du*** *RER* (Laith, AF)
'even though a student saw him get off the RER'

Similarly, vowel devoicing in CV and CVC syllables, illustrated in examples (2), (6) and (7), has been shown to occur in informal and formal contexts in Parisian French, with no known or obvious link to differences in articulatory rate (Fagyal and Moisset 1999, Smith 2003):

(6) *il est* ***dis****paru sans laisser de traces* (Yousfi, AF)
'he has disappeared without a trace'

(7) *il (n')est jamais arrivé à l'é****cole*** (Khatib, AF)
'he has never arrived at school'

And finally, glottal onsets similar to example (8) in Mousa's speech, also appeared in Karl's reading who articulated slightly more slowly (1.39 segments/second) than the average speaker in the corpus (1.67 segments/second):

(8) *il n'est jamais ʔarrivé ʔà l'école* (Mousa, AF)
'he has never arrived at school'

Not only there was a greater variety of acoustic means used by AF speakers in producing syllable onsets and nuclei (Figure 4.6), there was also a greater variety of prosodic positions affected by this wider inventory of phonetic realizations. Even though vowel devoicing in CV syllables was common in both groups (see Figure 4.5), it was applied variably by AF and EF speakers. While devoicing occurred only in word-final high vowels in EF speakers' readings, it affected both high vowels (*dis* of *disparu* 'disappeared') and low vowels (*cole* of *école* 'school') word-initially (7) and word-finally (3) in AF speakers' speech. One such contrasting context is shown by the spectrograms in Figure 4.7 (see also Fagyal 2007).

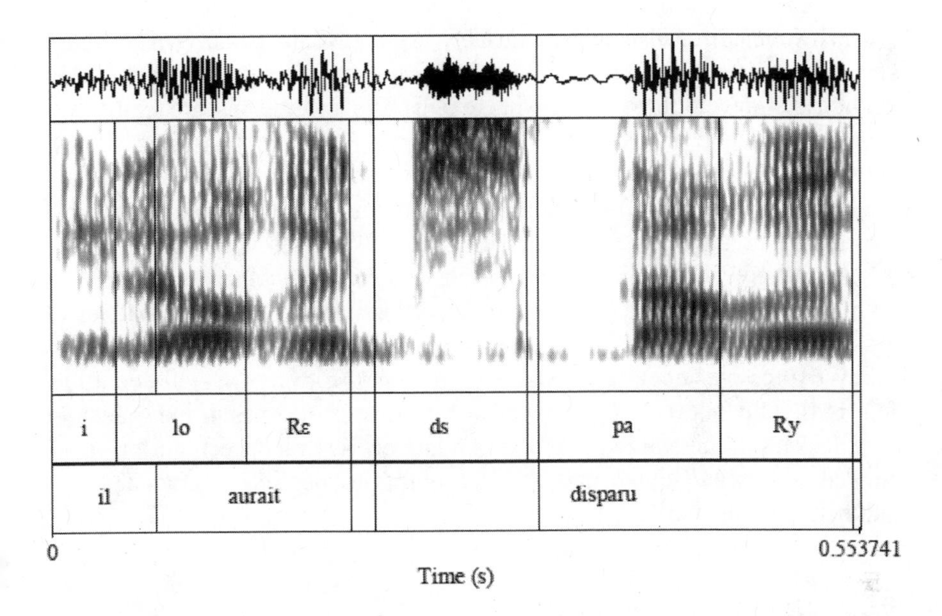

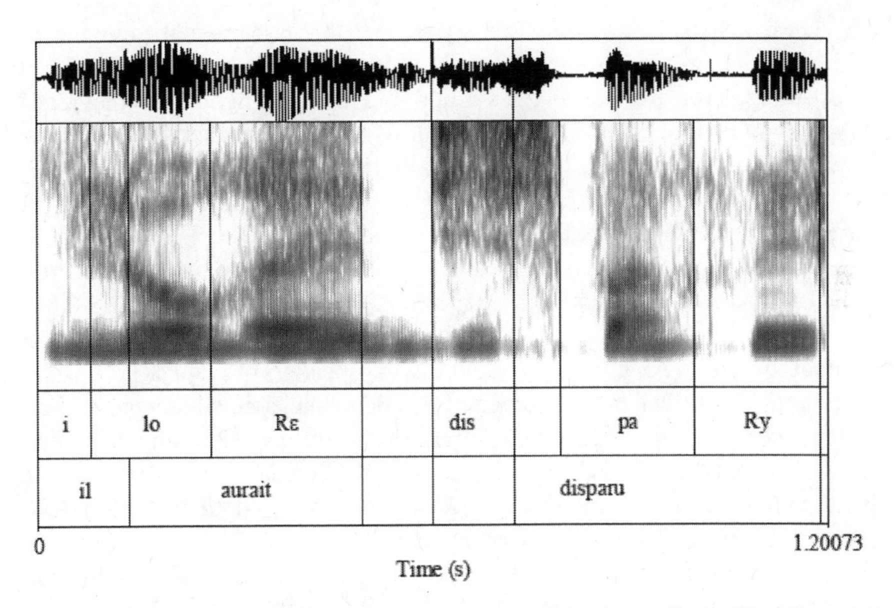

Figure 4.7 Devoicing of *dis* in *disparu* 'disappeared' in the reading of Yousfi, an AF speaker (top spectrogram), and the same unaccented closed syllable in an all-voiced rendition by Alain, an EF speaker (bottom spectrogram).

Schwa insertion also applied variably. As one would expect it in Northern varieties of French in France, AF and EF speakers inserted schwas phrase-medially to prevent three consonants to cluster in a single onset, e.g., in *notre prof* 'our teacher' in example (4), but only AF speakers inserted schwas between two single consonants, such as between the words *sur* 'certain' and *que* 'that' in example (3). Not altogether foreign to French, such patterns of schwa insertion are typical in Southern French varieties. Finally, glottalized onsets that prevent the linking of adjacent vowels (*enchaînement vocalique*) within the same accentual phrase are also possible in Northern varieties of French, but reserved exclusively to emphatic contexts, referred to as 'emphasis by expressive juncture' (*emphase par joncture expressive*) (Léon 1993: 143–144). The fact that glottal stops occurred several times in the speech of AF speakers in the reading of a text, a relatively neutral speech performance elicited in a relatively formal context, points to possible contact features retained from the heritage language.

4. Summary of findings

This study revealed uniformity and differences in the segmental components of rhythm type distinctions in the readings of two groups of male adolescents recorded in a French working-class suburb of Paris. The hypothesis that readings of native French heritage speakers of Arabic (AF speakers) would show influence from the heritage language was confirmed, but contrary to expectations it was not borne out by statistically significant central and dispersion measures of variation. It was detectable only in greater allophonic variation, fine-grained acoustic characteristics of segments that constitute the essential building blocks of syllables in these speakers' speech.

Central and dispersion measures revealed uniformity between bilingual heritage speakers (AF group) and monolingual speakers of French (EF group): both groups patterned closer to each other and syllable-timed languages than to any of the stress-timed languages on the rhythm type continuum established in previous studies. Thus, the hypothesis that AF speakers' readings would pattern closer to stress-timed languages had to be rejected: their rhythm were just as characteristically syllable-timed as EF speakers'.

Significant differences were found in the distribution of vocalic and consonantal interval durations, and regression analyses revealed that the contribution of fine-grained rhythm type predictors was outweighed by social-demographic and performance-related factors. One year of average grade (approximate age) difference and a one point average difference in students' average grade (*moyenne générale*) in school were better predictors of their patterning in two groups than either %V, ΔV, or ΔC. Articulatory rate and the number of segments in a phrase, with the two factors tied together, were the only individually significant predictors.

AF speakers' readings appeared slightly less vocalic (low %V values) than non-heritage speakers', while both groups showed similar amounts of consonantal duration variations (ΔC). AF speakers showed somewhat more variability in the length of vocalic intervals (higher ΔV values). Thus, the hypothesis that AF speakers' speech would be more consonantal was confirmed, but greater ΔV or ΔC variations, as one would have expected it in stress-timed languages with more complex syllable structure, were not found. All these effects were not statistically significant.

Traces of heritage language use were found in vowel epenthesis, unusual in Northern varieties of French, glottal onset consonants that appeared in three AF and one EF speakers' readings. Contrary to predictions, all speakers showed strong tendencies towards open syllabicity, and heritage language influence did not extend beyond the acoustic realizations of individual sounds. Closed syllables with non-branching onsets, nuclei, and codas were the second most frequent syllable type in both groups. These patterns of uniformity were statistically more important than differences in vowel epenthesis and types of onset realizations. Thus, the hypothesis that AF speakers would prefer heavy and closed rather than light and open syllables was not confirmed.

The most unexpected finding was the tendency of AF speakers to devoice vowels in closed syllables in word-initial positions where EF speakers did not show such tendency. This might be part of the factors that lead to the slightly more consonantal character of AF speakers' speech. Since devoicing can drastically reduce the amplitude of vowels, from a perceptual point of view it represents a type of vowel reduction. Thus some degree of vowel reduction was present in AF speakers' readings. But to what extent should such fine details of acoustic realization be worthy of our attention?

5. Discussion

Fine-grained acoustic characteristics of speech segments are rarely examined in studies of rhythm type distinctions, because such distinctions are often not salient enough to be detected by averages and dispersion measures. On the basis of non-normalized vocalic and consonantal duration distributions, Ghazali et al. (2002) showed evidence of rhythm type distinctions between Western and Eastern dialects of Arabic. Based on normalized and non-normalized measures, Low, Grabe, and Nolan (2000) and Deterding (2001) concluded that Singapore English is more syllable-timed than British English, as the latter shows greater amount of vowel reduction. Other studies, however, found only slight differences or concluded on negative results. With respect to rhythm type differences in Spanish, English, and Hispanic Spanish spoken in North Carolina, Carter (2005: 72), for instance, noted that "no clear pattern [was] easily discernible, but some trends [could] be noted." Thomas and Carter (2006) also found that present-day African Americans' and European Americans' spontaneous speech samples did not differ significantly in their degrees of stress- or syllable-timing.[38]

Compared to previous studies, speakers in this study were maximally similar: they shared the same socio-demographic background, grew up in the same neighborhood, and spoke the same dialect of the same language natively. Heritage language influence, if any, was expected to be subtle, and it was indeed found to be subtle. Neither patterns of schwa insertion, nor glottalized onsets or high vowel devoicing in closed syllables were prevalent enough to be statistically significant. Therefore, one might ask: was a digging down to such "atomic" levels of phonetic contrast useful at all?

Fine-grained phonetic details of rhythm type distinctions are more important than they might appear at a first glance. Phonetic realizations, i.e., the precise acoustic make-up of the segmental components of speech rhythm, have been claimed to play an important role in sound change, and perhaps in linguistic change in general. With respect to various patterns of cliticization that could be induced by shifts in syllabicity "along with [the] a vast body of segmental changes." Labov (2001: 12) states: "[. . .] it can be argued that change in the surface phonetics remains the driving force behind a very large number of linguistic changes, perhaps the majority." Alone or in competition with indigenous features, phonetic features borrowed in contact with other varieties and recycled at the lowest segmental level of speech rhythm could act, if not as triggers, then as catalysts in on-going change: "*adstratum* effects that appear to motivate or accelerate language change in progress" Labov (2001: 246). Minute acoustic differences have also been shown to trigger correct identification of a speaker's dialect, as convincingly demonstrated, for instance, by Graff, Labov and Harris (1986) in their classic study of /aw/ fronting in Philadelphia speech. Purnell, Salmons and Tepelli's (2005) work on word-final obstruent devoicing in a German-speaking community in Wisconsin brought evidence for a similar role played by fine-grained, allophonic realizations of consonants: in their study gradient cues to laryngeal constriction did allow the identification of the German-English bilingual speakers' heritage language.

Let us consider the case of allophonic variations in French. Glottal stops as onset consonants, presumably left over from contact with heritage languages from North Africa in this corpus, are not altogether foreign to French: vowel-initial words with emphatic phrase-initial accent (*accent initial*) can have glottalized onsets, as in the often-quoted example of the single-word utterance *ʔIncroyable!* 'Incredible' or another example from Léon's (1993: 144) radio corpora: *des documents ʔimportés* 'imported documents.' "More or less perceptually salient depending on the degree of emphasis", Léon (ibid.) notes, glottal stops are part of an arsenal of means (together with silent pauses and *accent initial*) conveying emphasis by breaking the "expected linking of [consecutive] vowels at the word boundary" (p. 144). If novelty is defined as suggested in the Introduction, i.e., something new and not "recycled," than the novelty in the phonetic system of AF speakers in this corpus is not the mere occurrence of glottal stops, but their contextual polymorphism: in these speakers' speech, glottal stops appeared in non-emphatic readings of a text elicited in a school-like setting. In all but one case, EF speakers' readings showed seamless linking of two adjacent vowels (*enchaînement vocalique*). Unless one considers the unlikely case of speakers' greater emotional involvement in discourse triggering the realization of some onsets as glottal stops, such segments are not bound to appear in middle-class varieties of Parisian French, and they remain unattested in working-class varieties (*français populaire*).

Vowel devoicing shows a different type of remotivation, and could have even more important implications, as it could be a contributing factor in prosodic change, whose phonetic underpinnings in languages have so far been "only dimly perceived" (Labov 2001: 12). Devoicing has been shown to occur in open and closed syllables in Northern Metropolitan varieties of French, but only in word-final positions (Fagyal and Moisset 1999, Smith 2003). As Smith (2003: 177) points out, this is a relatively atypical phenomenon: "From a cross-linguistic perspective, the distribution of devoicing in French is unusual. Final position is prosodically prominent in French, whereas in many languages devoicing is a form of vowel reduction associated with lack of prominence." As a relative novelty, bilingual heritage speakers in this corpus applied devoicing word-initially and word-finally, regardless of the type of syllable. Thus, contrary to the laxing and devoicing of high vowels that occurs word-medially in unaccented positions in Canadian French (see Martin 2004), vowel reduction occurred in metrically strong prosodic positions in AF speakers' speech.[39] One can speculate that such joint patterns of devoicing, if spread beyond the speakers' inter-language, can have important implications for the future development of the accentual system.

If devoicing amounts to vowel reduction, as argued before, then devoicing in these prosodic positions could interact, and to some extent even compete, with each other. Their on-going competition within the system could mean that not only unaccented word-medial syllables but also metrically strong word-final syllables could occasionally be heard as reduced, leaving the penultimate syllable the perceptually most salient full syllable in the accentual phrase. Accentual shift onto the penultimate has, indeed, been one of the most widely discussed features of working-class Parisian French (Straka 1952) and French spoken in the *banlieues* (Conein and Gadet 1998, Fagyal 2003, 2005). Louder and longer syllables in prosodic positions where one would not expect them in middle-class varieties of Parisian French, reinforced by the reduction of prominent (final) syllables, could therefore lend support to previous observations of stress-timed characteristics of French spoken in the Parisian *banlieues.*

Thus, North African heritage language influence in the form of widespread vowel devoicing brought into working-class neighborhoods by recent waves of immigration could act, just as Labov had speculated, as catalysts. In this case, through allophonic enrichment, they would reinforce patterns of accentual shift onto the penultimate, already attested in the local vernacular.

Schwa insertion and the affrication of palatalized onset consonants also show a two-way split between speakers in this study and also have a long history of variation and change in many French varieties. Following their subsequent evolution in working-class Parisian French could provide an opportunity for the observation of the recombination of these features. "Speakers exhibit variations in their pronunciation which they and the listeners do not recognize as variations," Ohala (1989: 175) argues, but these variations represent the pool of synchronic variations from which future changes might draw. The affrication of palatalized stops in present-day working-class Parisian French, also a known feature of French spoken in North Africa (Lanly 1962), seems to be already engaged on the path of incipient change, indexing class and ethnic origin, but also widening in scope and spreading beyond working-class neighborhoods (Jamin et al. 2006).

To return to one of the burning questions raised in the Introduction: could the widening separation between the 'rich districts' (*les beaux quartiers*) of the White upper- and middle-classes and the 'suburbs' (*les banlieues*) of the multi-ethnic working-classes put Parisian French on two separate paths of evolution? Findings in this study point to slight differences in acoustic realizations. Still very much "under the radar," these features seem to have been reanalyzed at the lowest, allophonic level of speech rhythm. Glottalization seemed to have spread to non-emphatic contexts, while devoicing seems to have affected high and non-high vowels in a variety of prosodic positions. These findings, however, remain indicative.

In certain circumstances, that are likely to be the exception rather than the rule, to reiterate Sankoff's (2004) conclusion, these features could spread "as the combined results of numerous individual acts of 'misapprehended pronunciation' by listeners" (Ohala 1989: 177–178). Folk linguistic reports (see Introduction) already provide useful indications that devoicing, the acoustic aspects of syncopation, is recognized as a marker of heritage speakers in the community, but also as an index of the neighborhood itself. Thus, Chamber's (2003) scenario of "inverse assimilation" seems to apply: certain linguistic features "in the native speech of (otherwise) assimilated second-generation speakers, in later generations, leads to the establishment of these features as markers of region (community) rather than ethnicity." Do these features characterize only the speech of non-heritage speakers of Arabic or they appear as aerial features because of the numerical dominance of North Africans and their descendents in the community? This question remains to be investigated. If the first scenario is true, then the next question to ask would be: who holds the key to the spreading of such potential innovations?

In this study, Karl deserves particular attention, as he is the only EF speaker whose reading shows several instances of glottal onsets. He, on the other hand, shows no traces of devoicing in closed syllables in unaccented accentual phrase-medial position. The fast-speaking Yasin, on the other hand, does combine several novel accent features. Ethnographic evidence established independently from this investigation shows that motor skills such as faster articulatory rate is a highly prized verbal skill in adolescent peer-groups in this community. Lepoutre (1997: 132), in his extensive ethnography of pre-adolescents in *La Courneuve*, notes the following:

> To make oneself be heard in the peer group, one must not only speak loud but also speak fast. The speaking rate of certain adolescents in this respect is quite astonishing. This fast pace is apparent not only in articulation, but also the linking of words, phrases, and even turn taking [. . .]. On the other hand, a speaker who is much too slow and lets his syllables drag out too long [. . .] exposes himself to systematic sarcasm and laugher. . . . [40]

Interestingly, or perhaps quite predictably, leaders tend to belong to the first, while the followers in the second category. In Yasin's case, there is all the more reason to retain articulatory rate as a meaningful sociophonetic variable, as this AF speaker was one of the uncontested leaders recorded during fieldwork. A third grader (last grade in middle school), whose strong and tall body and low voice already showed signs of full maturity, was also one of the best students in school, with an average grade (*moyenne générale*) so high that most students can only dream about receiving such a grade for a single assignment in a single subject matter (15.9 out of 20). Respected by all, Yasin was in the same time one of the most brilliant public speakers, readily engaging adults (among them the fieldworker) in political debates and, if necessary, putting down youngsters who dared to tease him (see the practice of *vannes*, a type of crude joking, in Lepoutre 1997). Yasin was well aware of his charisma and age, the oldest possible in middle school, and a pivotal age between intense focusing on peer group membership as opposed to a future professional life. Doran (2002), who studied the use of *verlan* in working-class middle schools and high schools, concludes:

> [. . .] whereas in *collège*, youths are mainly focused on the immediate peer universe and their place in it, as they enter high school years, they begin to think more about how their educational choices will impact on their future social and economical lives in the larger society. (247)

It is through "stylistic icons" like Yasin, who fulfill rather than challenge institutional requirements of brilliant school performance and peer-group practices, that new and novel patterns of phonetic variation could become "noticed" and imitated by peers. In the EF group only Karl comes close to the uncontested status of Yasin as a leader. All other EF speakers, younger than Karl and Yasin, could at this specific age in their pre-adolescent years, pretend to nothing more than the role of followers. It comes as no surprise that they do not even try (yet) to embody the *personae* of fast speaking popular leaders like Yasin and Laith in the EF group. If complex rhythmic phenomena, such as articulatory rate, indeed carry information about the leadership status of a speaker in the local community of practice, as they seem to in adolescent peer groups in *La Courneuve*, then there are good reasons not to discard them early in the analysis as "spurious" variations of speech rhythm (see e.g., Grabe and Low 2002). Thus, the normalization of interval durations is only desirable once one made sure that no potential source of meaningful social variations would be eliminated.

But what kind of social meaning should be attributed to fast-articulatory rate and many other phonetic features displayed by Yasin and other leaders? "By virtue of their location in time and social and cultural space, immigrant adolescents have special knowledge, and in working with this knowledge—in making new meanings—they construct authenticity of a new kind," Eckert (2003: 115) reminds us. When thinking about Yasin, it would be tempting to think of a bridge between two cultural spheres, i.e., the monolingual mainstream society and the multilingual peer group. It could be that novel phonetic features, such as the ones shown in this study, are imitated and spread through the daily actions and interactions of leaders like Yasin, negotiating fast and with brilliant efficiency their positions of intermediaries between two cultures, while embodying an authentic social *persona* of a new kind.

Appendix 4.1

Text read by the speakers in French

C'est une histoire incroyable. Notre prof d'anglais a disparu. Il n'est jamais arrivé à l'école, alors qu'un élève l'a vu descendre du RER le matin. Il aurait disparu sans laisser de traces. Il n'est plus jamais revenu. Sur le chemin de la gare, plusieurs l'avaient reconnu, mais personne ne sait ce qu'il est devenu. En tous cas, c'est sûr qu'on ne l'a plus jamais revu. Et toi, qu'est-ce que tu en penses ? Qu'est-ce qui lui est arrivé ? Invente la suite de l'histoire, imagine que tu es le principal ou l'inspecteur de police. Qu'est-ce que tu ferais ?

Translation of the text to English

This is an incredible story. Our English teacher has disappeared. He has never arrived at school, even though a student saw him get off the RER in the morning. He has disappeared without a trace. He's never come back. On the way from the station [to school], many recognized him, but nobody knows what happened to him. In any case, it is certain that he has not been seen ever since. And you? What do you think? What might have happened to him? Invent the end of the story. Imagine that you are the principal or a detective from the police. What would you do?

Notes

1 *Verlan* (from *envers* 'backwards'): *bizarre* → *zarbi* 'strange' (Méla 1991, 1997; Azra and Cheneau 1994).
2 Contrary to many royal courtiers, Voltaire was of non-noble, provincial origin (Gay 1965: 117).
3 "*faire usage d'une langue française qu'ils tordent dans tous les sens et dont ils modifient les mots en les coupant.*"
4 Adolescence is defined as the period "extending from the first notable changes of puberty to the attainment of adult status [. . .] i.e., from age 10 to the end of secondary school at 18 or 19" (Arnett 2002: 309–310).

5 The central role of peer groups and the notion of youth culture seem to be a Western specificity. Peers still contribute little to adolescent development, for instance, among girls in the Arab world (Booth 2002).
6 Lexical "innovations," ephemeral in nature, are frequent in peer group interactions. They can take as input foreign-sounding words or existing words fallen out of use, but "recycled" in playful interactions, teasing, and verbal sparring matches between peers (Fagyal 2004).
7 Certain aspects of adolescent language use were perceived as age-related behavior several decades ago, but the focus had shifted to social and ethnic factors (Boyer 1994).
8 *Ce n'est pas forcément ainsi que les "jeunes" parleront quand ils seront quadragénaires.*
9 Besides studies in Montreal and Brink and Lund's study of phonetic variation in Copenhagen (cited in Sankoff 2004), the following projects are singled out: Gauchat's (1905) research in Charmey, Switzerland and its restudy by Hermann (1929), Labov's department store study in New York City (Labov 1972) and its restudy by Fowler (1986), and Trudgill's (1974, 1988) study in Norwich. Cedergren's (1973, 1988) Panama City location is the only fieldwork site outside Europe and the United States.
10 Compared to mass immigrations during "The Great Deluge" (1879–1920), the period after 1920 is characterized by a low influx of immigrants, and is thus a period of relative stability, according to the social geographer W. Zelinsky (2001: 23).
11 Languages that are thought to have massively affected working-class Parisian French prior to the latest waves of immigration from outside Europe are Picard, an *oïl* dialect, and Breton, a Celtic language.
12 See the full-fledged national debate known as "the battle of the veils", when "three female Muslim students were expelled from a middle school north of Paris for having gone to class wearing a *hidjab* or *khiemar*, a religious veil/scarf/headdress" (Mathy 2000: 109).
13 Immigration with assimilation into mainstream French society is institutionally supported by the Department of Immigration, Integration, National Identity, and Codevelopment since June 1, 2007.
14 Sociologists first doubted the reality of social-territorial segregation (Wacquant 1989), then came to see it as an "undeniable dimension" (Lepoutre 1997), to finally call it "ghettoization" (Maurin 2004).
15 *Les quartiers défavorisés sont considérés à juste titre comme des enclaves où se massent les populations étrangères ou issues de l'immigration.*
16 *Riches et diplômés, d'un côté, et pauvres et immigrés, de l'autre forment donc les pôles extrêmes de la ségrétation territoriales.*
17 Heritage speakers are people raised in a home where one language is spoken who subsequently switch to another dominant language" (Polinsky and Kagan 2007: 368)
18 *Tout le système linguistique est affecté: intonation, lexique, et même la syntaxe qui reste la moins imitable.*

19 *Beur, -ette* (n.m./f.) descendent of immigrants from North Africa, born in France,

20 *Certaines voyelles ont tendance à tomber. Mais les consonnes—c'est manifeste dans les milieux arabes des banlieues—deviennent beaucoup plus explosives. Un type de prononciation que les rappeurs [. . .] ont reprise. Par exemple, au lieu de "partir", on dira " p'rt'r": les voyelles disparaissent presque totalement. Et les consonnes explosent, comme dans "Rrrspect!" (respect). C'est l'accent beur. Le français intègre parfaitement cette influence nouvelle, comme il a intégré celles de l'italien, de l'anglais, pour sa plus grande vitalité!*

21 The idea of raw spectral measures of sonority was explored recently by Galves and his colleagues (2002) who found that such measures lead to the same clustering of rhythmic classes conjectured by Pike, first shown by Ramus and his colleagues' 1999 study.

22 White and Mattys (2007) have proposed the VarcoV and VarcoC indexes, accomplishing essentially the same task as Grabe et al.'s various PVI indexes. These two measures were tested on an extended corpus of speech samples recorded in *La Courneuve* in Fagyal (in press).

23 AF speakers in this corpus referred to their heritage language as "Arabic," and reported to have at least passive knowledge of the language. Although none of them reported speaking Berber, some speakers might have used "Arabic" as a unifying label for a language from North Africa (see Fagyal in press).

24 Some of the students might have repeated classes, and did not communicate this information during or after the interview. Therefore, their exact age might not always correlate with their grade.

25 The terms active or productive vs. passive or receptive bilingual refer to an active vs. passive knowledge of languages, following established terminology in studies of bilingualism (see Romaine 1989).

26 These numbers are based on the 1999 census data, analyzed and publicly available in the *Centre de Documentation* of La Courneuve (ORGECO 2001).

27 Headline in *The New York Times* published on October 16, 2001.

28 Ramus et al. (1999) and Ghazali et al. (2002) measured vocalic and consonantal intervals in utterances, while Low et al. (2000) did so in intonation phrases. Grabe and Low (2002) later broke this tradition, and computed rhythm type measurements on the entire paragraph, regardless of the length of prosodic units.

29 Despite the instructions, some of the speakers omitted the title and the last sentence in the text. Tiredness and informality with the fieldworker (speakers were volunteers and knew the fieldworker well) might be among the reasons why not all speakers stayed on task until the end of the recording session.

30 The two speakers who omitted the reading of the title and/or the last sentence came from the AF group.

31 The graphical representation of means and standard errors in the Ramus et al. (1999: 273) article, however, suggests relatively normal distributions, without substantial skewing to higher or lower %V and ΔC values, close to the distribution of measurement points for AF and EF speakers.

32 Thus, contrary to RNM who were able to compute single-factor ANOVAs with rhythm type as their main factor, such a comparison could not be carried out here. Levene's test of equality of error variances was non significant ($F(9,1359) = 1.632$, $p< 0.101$).

33 Levene's test of equality of error variances was non significant ($F(9,1359) = 1.632$, $p< 0.101$).

34 Stepwise regression analyses in SPSS do not return correlation coefficients allowing to check for cross-linearity effects. For this reasons, Pearson linear regression analyses were conducted (see Field 2005).

35 EF speakers were coded with value 1, AF speakers with value 2 for the dichotomous variable "ethnicity."

36 The possible impact of this co-linearity effect on the model can be evaluated by other statistical means.

37 Model summaries:

—5 predictors (rhythmic variables only): adjusted $r^2 = 0.156$, standard error of estimate = 0.464, F change (5,210) = 7.783, $p<0.01$.

—6 predictors (rhythmic variables and grade): adjusted $r^2 = 0.256$, standard error of estimate = 0.430, F change (6,209) = 13.329, $p<0.01$.

—6 predictors (rhythmic variables and GPA): adjusted $r^2 = 0.253$, standard error of estimate = 0.431, F change (6,209) = 13.130, $p<0.01$.

—6 predictors (rhythmic variables and speaker): adjusted $r^2 = 0.393$, standard error of estimate = 0.410, F change (6,209) = 24.194, $p<0.01$.

—7 predictors (rhythmic variables, grade, and GPA): adjusted $r^2 = 0.324$, standard error of estimate = 0.410, F change (7,208) = 15.731, $p<0.01$.

—8 predictors (all predictors in): adjusted $r^2 = 0.413$, standard error of estimate = 0.435, F change (8,207) = 19.890, $p<0.01$

38 However, such differences existed in archival recordings of speakers born in the 19th century.

39 In Northern varieties of European French, both syllables can be accented (*accent initial* and *accent final*).

40 "*Pour se faire entendre dans les groupes des pairs, il faut non seulement parler fort, il faut aussi parler vite. La rapidité d'élocution de certains adolescents est en ce sens tout à fait étonnante. Cette vitesse s'applique aussi bien à l'articulation qu'à l'enchaînement des mots et des phrases, et au rythme des échanges. [. .] A l'inverse, un locuteur trop lent, qui s'exprime en faisant traîner ses syllabes [. . .] s'expose de façon quasi systématique aux sarcasmes appuyés, aux éclats de rire . . .*"

References

Antoine, Fabrice. 1998. Des mots et des oms: verlan, troncation et recyclage formel dans l'argot contemporain. *Cahiers de Lexicologie* 72 (1): 41–70.

Arnett, Jeffrey Jensen. 2002. Adolescents in western countries in the 21st Century. In B. Bradford Brown et al. (eds), 307–343.

Azra, Jean-Luc and V. Cheneau. 1994. Language games and phonological theory: Verlan and the syllabic structure of French. *Journal of French Language Studies* 4 (2): 147–170.

Booth, Marylin. 2002. Arab adolescents facing the future. In Brown et al. (eds), 207–242.

Boyer, Henri. 1994. Le *jeune* tel qu'on en parle. *Langage et Société,* 70: 85–92.

Brown, B. Bradford and Reed W. Larson. 2002. The kaleidoscope of adolescence. In Brown et al. (eds), 1–20.

Brown, B. Bradford, Reed W. Larson, and T. S. Saraswathi (eds). 2002. *The world's youth: Adolescence in eight regions of the globe.* Cambridge: Cambridge University Press.

Carter, Phillip M. 2005. Quantifying rhythmic differences between Spanish, English, and Hispanic English. In Randall Scott Gess and Edward J. Rubin (eds), *Theoretical and experimental approaches to Romance Linguistics: Selected papers from the 34th Linguistic Symposium on Romance Languages (LSRL),* Salt Lake City, Utah/ Amsterdam, Philadelphia: Benjamins, 63–75.

Carton, Fernand. 2000. La prononciation. In Gérald Antoine and Bernard Cerliquini (eds), *Histoire de la langue française (1945–2000).* Paris: Editions du CNRS, 25–60.

Cedergren, Henrietta. 1973. *The interplay of social and linguistic factors in Panama.* PhD dissertation, Ithaca, NY: Cornell University.

Cedergren, Henrietta. 1988. The spread of language change: Verifying inferences of linguistic diffusion. In Peter H. Lowenberg (ed.), *Language spread and language policy: Issues, implications, and case studies* (Georgetown University Round Table on Languages and Linguistics 1987), Washington DC: Georgetown University Press, 45–60.

Cerquiglini, Bernard. 2001. Le français aujourd'hui, ça bouge. *Construire* (7), le 13 février, 61–63. http://www.migrosmagazine.ch/pdfdata/pdfarchiv/co/Co-2001/07/CO07p61.pdf.

Chambers, J. K. 2003. Sociolinguistics of immigration. In David Britain and Jenny Cheshire (eds), *Social dialectology: In honor of Peter Trudgill.* Amsterdam/Philadelphia: John Benjamins, 97–113.

Conein, Bernard and François Gadet. 1998. Le "français populaire" des jeunes de la banlieue parisienne entre permanence et innovation. In Jannis K. Androutsopoulos and Arno Scholz (eds), *Jugendsprache / Langue des jeunes / Youth language.* Frankfurt: Peter Lang, 105–123.

Corneau, Caroline. 2000. An EPG study of palatalization in French: Cross-dialect and inter-subject variation. *Language Variation and Change* 12 (1): 25–49.

Dell, François and Mohamed Elmedlaoui. 1985. Syllabic consonants and syllabification in Imdlawn Tashlhiyt Berber. *Journal of African Languages and Linguistics* 7: 105–130.

Deterding, David. 2001. The measurement of rhythm: A comparison of Singapore and British English. *Journal of Phonetics* 29 (2): 217–230.

Doran, Meredith Christine. 2002. *A sociolinguistic study of youth language in the Parisian suburbs: Verlan and minority identity in contemporary France*. PhD Dissertation, French Department. Ithaca, NY: Cornell University.

Duez, Daniéle and Marie-Hélène Casanova. 2000. Quelques aspects de l'organisation temporelle du parler des banlieues parisiennes. *Revue Parole* 1: 59–73.

Eckert, Penelope. 2000. *Linguistic variation as social practice*. Malden, MA: Blackwell.

Eckert, Penelope. 2003. Language and adolescent peer groups. *Journal of Language and Social Psychology* 22 (1): 112–118.

Eckert, Penelope and John R. Rickford. 2001. *Style and sociolinguistic variation*. Cambridge: Cambridge University Press.

Epstein, Jonathon S. 1995. *Adolescents and their music*. New York: Garland.

Fagyal, Zsuzsanna. 2003. The matter with the penultimate: Prosodic change in the vernacular of lower-class immigrant youth in Paris, *Proceedings of the 14th International Congress of Phonetic Sciences*, Vol. 1, Barcelona, 671–674.

Fagyal, Zsuzsanna. 2004. Action des médias et interactions entre jeunes dans une banlieue ouvrière de Paris: Remarques sur l'innovation lexicale [Notes on lexical innovation: action of the media and interactions between adolescents in a working-class suburb of Paris]. *Cahier de Sociolinguistique* 9: 41–60.

Fagyal, Zsuzsanna. 2005. Prosodic consequences of being a Beur: French in contact with immigrant languages in Paris. Selected papers from NWAV 32, Vol. 10 (2). Working Papers in Linguistics, Philadelphia, Department of Linguistics, University of Pennsylvania, 91–104.

Fagyal, Zsuzsanna. 2007. Syncope : de l'irrégularité rythmique dans la musique rap au dévoisement des voyelles dans la parole des adolescents dits « des banlieues ». *Nottingham French Studies* 46 (2): 119–134.

Fagyal, Zsuzsanna. In press. *L'Accent des banlieues: Aspects prosodiques du français populaire en contact avec les langues de l'immigration*. Paris: L'Harmattan.

Fagyal, Zsuzsanna and Christine Moisset. 1999. Sound change and articulatory release: Where and why are high vowels devoiced in Parisian French? *Proceedings of the 14th International Congress of Phonetics Science, Vol. 1*. San Francisco, 309–312.

Field, Andy. 2005. *Discovering statistics using SPSS for Windows*. London/Thousand Oaks/New Delhi: SAGE Publications.

Fought, Carmen (ed.). 2004. *Sociolinguistic variation: Critical reflections,* Oxford: Oxford University Press.

Fowler, Joy. 1986. The social stratification of (r) in New York City department stores, 24 years after Labov. New York University, manuscript.

Gadet, Françoise. 1998. Des fortifs aux técis: persistance et discontinuités dans la langue populaire. In Dawn Marley, Marie-Anne Hintze, and Gabrielle Parker (eds), *Linguistic identities and policies in France and the French-speaking world*, London: Centre for Information and Language Teaching Research, 11–26.

Gadet, François. 2003. Youth language in France: Forms and practices. In Eva Neuland (ed.), *Jugendsprachen—Spiegel der Zeit*, Frankfurt a.M: Peter Lang, 77–89.

Galves, Antonio, Jesus Garcia, Denis Duarte, and Charlotte Galves. 2002. Sonority as a basis for rhythmic class discrimination. Paper presented at Aix-en-Provence, France, April 11–13. http://www.isca-speech.org/archive/sp2002 (accessed February 5, 2010).

Gauchat, Louis. 1905. L'unité phonétique dans le patois d'une commune. *Aus Romanischen Sprachen und Literaturen: Festschrift Heinrich Morf*, Halle: Niemeyer, 175–232.

Gay, Peter. 1965. *Voltaire's politics: The poet as realist.* New York: Vintage Books.

Ghazali, Salem, Rym Hamdi, and Melissa Barkat. 2002. Speech rhythm variation in Arabic dialects. Paper presented at Speech Prosody 2002 conference: Aix-en-Provence, France, April 11–13. http://www.isca-speech.org/archive/sp2002 (accessed February 5, 2010).

Goudailler, Jean-Pierre. 1997. *Comment tu tchatches! Dictionnaire du français contemporain des cités* (Première ed.). Paris: Maisonneuve-Larose.

Grabe, Esther, and Ee Ling Low. 2002. Durational variability in speech and the rhythm class hypothesis. In Carlos Gussenhoven and Natasha Warner (eds), *Laboratory Phonology* 7. Berlin: Mouton de Gruyter, 515–546.

Grabe, Esther, Brechtje Post, and Ian Watson. 1999. The acquisition of rhythmic patterns in English and French. *Proceedings of the 14th International Congress of Phonetic Science*: San Francisco, August.

Graff, David, William Labov, and Wendell A. Harris. 1986. Testing listeners' reactions to phonological markers. In. David Sankoff (ed.) *Diversity and diachrony.* Amsterdam/Philadelphia: John Benjamins, 45–58.

Hargreaves, Alec Gordon and Mark McKinney. 1997. *Post-colonial cultures in France.* London/New York: Routledge.

Haverkort, Marco and Jan H. de Roder. 2003. Poetry, language, and ritual performance. *Journal of Historical Pragmatics* 4 (2): 269–286.

Hermann, Edward. 1929. Lautveränderungen in der Individualsprache einer Mundart. *Nachrichten der Gesellschaft des Wissenschaften zu Göttingen, Phl.-his.* Kll 11: 195–214.

Hock, Hans Henrich. 1991. *Principles of historical linguistics* (2nd revised and updated ed.). Berlin: Mouton de Gruyter.

Jamin, Mikaël. 2005. Sociolinguistic variation in the Paris suburbs. PhD dissertation, Department of French Studies, University of Kent at Canterbury.

Jamin, Mikaël, Cyril Trimaille, and Médéric Gasquet-Cyrus. 2006. De la convergence dans la divergence: le cas des quartiers pluri-ethniques en France. *Journal of French Linguistic Studies* 16 (3): 335–356.

Labov, William. 1972. *Sociolinguistic Patterns.* Philadelphia: University of Pennsylvania Press.

Labov, William. 2001. *Principles of linguistic change: Social factors.* Oxford: Blackwell.

Lanly, André. 1962. *Le Français d'Afrique du Nord: étude linguistique.* Paris: Press Universitaire de France.
Lass, Roger. 1990. How to do things with junk: Exaptation in language evolution. *Journal of Linguistics* 26 (1): 79–102.
Léon, Pierre. 1993. *Précis de phonostylistique: Parole et expressivité.* Paris: Nathan Université.
Lepoutre, David. 1997. *Coeur de banlieue.* Paris: Odile Jacob.
Lin, Nan. 2001. *Social capital: A theory of social structure and action.* Cambridge: Cambridge University Press.
Lodge, Anthony R. 2004. *A sociolinguistic history of Parisian French.* Cambridge: Cambridge University Press.
Low, Ee Lin, Esther Grabe, and Francis Nolan. 2000. Quantitative characterizations of speech rhythm: Syllable-timing in Singapore English. *Language and Speech* 43 (4): 377–401.
Martin, Pierre. 2004. Le dévoisement vocalique en français. *La Linguistique* 40 (2): 3–21.
Mathy, Jean-Philippe. 2000. *French resistance: The French-American culture wars.* Minneapolis: University of Minnesota Press.
Maurin, Éric. 2004. *Le ghetto français.* Paris: Seuil.
Mehler, Jacques, Emmanuel Dupoux, Thierry Nazzi, and Ghislaine Dehaene-Lambertz. 1996. Coping with linguistic diversity: The infant's viewpoint. In James L. Morgan and Katherine Demuth (eds), *Signal to syntax: Bootstrapping from speech to grammar in early acquisition.* Mahwah, NJ: Lawrence Erlbaum Associates, 101–116.
Méla, Vivienne. 1991. Le verlan ou le langage du miroir. *Langages* 101: 73–94.
Méla, Vivienne. 1997. Verlan: 2000. *Langue Française* 114: 16–34.
Mendoza-Denton, Norma. 1999. Fighting words: Latina girls, gangs, and language attitudes. In D. Letticia Galindo and María Dolores Gonzales (eds), *Speaking Chicana: Voice, power, and identity.* Tucson: University of Arizona Press, 39–56.
Merle, Pierre. 2000. *Argot, verlan, tchatches.* Paris: Editions de Milan.
Miller, D. M. 1984. On the perception of rhythm. *Journal of Phonetics* 12 (1): 75–83.
Milroy, Lesley. 1980. *Language and social networks* (2nd ed.). Oxford: Blackwell.
Mufwene, Salikoko. 2001. *The ecology of language evolution.* Cambridge: Cambridge University Press.
Nazzi, Thierry, Josianne Bertoncini, and Jacques Mehler. 1998. Language discrimination by newborns: Towards an understanding of the role of rhythm. *Journal of Experimental Psychology: Human Perception and Performance* 24 (3): 756–766.
Noiriel, Gérard. 1988. *Le Creuset Francais.* Paris: Seuil.
Ohala, John J. 1989. Sound change is drawn from a pool of synchronic variation. In Leiv E. Breivik and Ernst Håkon Jahr (eds), *Language change: Contributions to the study of its causes.* Berlin/New York: Mouton de Gruyter, 173–198.

ORGECO. 2001. Analyse des Résultats exhaustifs du recensement INSEE pour la Ville de La Courneuve (93): Centre de Documentation, Mairie de La Courneuve.

Pike, Kenneth L. 1945. *The intonation of American English*. Ann Arbor: University of Michigan Press.

Polinsky, Maria and Olga Kagan. 2007. Heritage languages: In the "wild" and in the classroom. *Language and Linguistics Compass* 1 (5): 368–395.

Posner, Rebecca. 1997. *Linguistic change in French*. Oxford: Clarendon Press.

Preston, Dennis R. 2004. Three kinds of sociolinguistics: A psycholinguistic perspective. In Fought (ed.), 140–158.

Purnell, Thomas, Joseph Salmons, and Dilara Tepeli. 2005. German substrate effects in Wisconsin English: Evidence for final fortition. *American Speech* 80, 2: 135–164.

Ramus, Franck, Marina Nespor, and Jacques Mehler. 1999. Correlates of linguistic rhythm in the speech signal. *Cognition* 73 (3): 265–292.

Ridouane, Rachid. 2003. Suite de consonnes en berbère chleuh: phonétique et phonologie. Institut de Phonétique. Paris, Paris III. Doctoral dissertation. http://www.afcp-parole.org/article.php3?id_article=604 (accessed February 5, 2010).

Romaine, Suzanne. 1989. *Bilingualism*. Oxford: Blackwell.

Sankoff, Gillian. 2004. Adolescents, young adults, and the critical period: Two case studies from "Seven Up." In Fought (ed.), 121–139.

Sankoff, Gillian and Hélène Blondeau. 2007. Language change across the lifespan: /r/ in Montreal French, *Language* 83 (3): 560–588.

Smith, Caroline L. 2003. Vowel devoicing in Contemporary French. *Journal of French Language Studies* 13 (2): 177–194.

Soulignac, Françoise. 1993. *La banlieue parisienne: Cent cinquante ans de transformations*. Paris: La Documentation Française.

Stenström, Anna-Brita, Gisle Andersen, and Ingrid Kristine Hasund. 2002. *Trends in teenage talk: Corpus compilation, analysis and findings*. Amsterdam/Philadelphia: John Benjamins.

Straka, Georges. 1952. La prononciation parisienne, ses divers aspects et ses traits généraux. *Bulletin de la faculté des lettres de Strasbourg* 30 (5)-6: 212–253.

Thomas, Erik R. and Philip M. Carter. 2006. Prosodic rhythm and African American English. *English World-Wide* 27: 331–355.

Valdman, Albert. 1993. *Bien entendu! Introduction à la prononciation française*. Englewood Cliffs, NJ: Prentice Hall.

Wacquant, Loïc. 1989. Banlieues françaises et ghetto noir américain: de l'amalgame à la comparaison. *Comparative Studies* 10 (4): 81–103.

White, Laurence and Sven L. Mattys. 2007. Calibrating rhythm: First language and second language studies. *Journal of Phonetics* 35 (4): 501–522.

Youssef, Amani and Irene Mazurkewich. 1998. The acquisition of English metrical parameters and syllable structure by adult native speakers of Egyptian Arabic (Cairene Dialect). In Suzanne Flynn, Gita Martohardjono, and Wayne O'Neil (eds),

The generative study of second language acquisition, Mahwah, NJ: Lawrence Erlbaum Associates, 303–332.
Zelinsky, Wilbur. 2001. *The cultural geography of the United States* (revised ed.). Englewood Cliffs, NJ: Prentice Hall.

Chapter 5

The Sociophonetics of Prosodic Contours on *NEG* in Three Language Communities: Teasing apart Sociolinguistic and Phonetic Influences on Speech

Malcah Yaeger-Dror, University of Arizona; Tania Granadillo, University of Western Ontario; Shoji Takano, Hokusei Gakuen University; Lauren Hall-Lew, Oxford University[1]

1. Introduction

Negatives provide cognitively critical information and are also interactively significant. The present study compares the prosodic realization of negatives in three languages, and in two social settings for each language. The study will provide evidence for three loci of prosodic variation in negatives as they are used in amicable social interactions and in informative newscasts in American English, Latin American Spanish,[2] and Japanese. Comparative evidence from adversarial interactions will be cited where relevant.

1.1 Language

Each of these three languages shows unique patterns for how prominence is acoustically accomplished (Pierrehumbert and Beckman 1988; Hirst and Di Cristo 1998; Grabe et al. 2003; Jun 2005). Each has its own default negative morphology with a given default syntactic position, and it is that most common form of negation that will be studied here. Rather than refer to each specific lexical item in this discussion, each language's 'default' lexical negative will be referred to as *NEG.*

1.2 Social situation

Within a given linguistic community, prosody varies radically with the social situation. This chapter will discuss parallel results for the three languages in only two situations: friendly phone calls will be compared with recordings of newscasts. Analyses of other situations can be found elsewhere (e.g., Yaeger-Dror 2002a, b; Yaeger-Dror, Hall-Lew, and Deckert 2002, 2003; Takano 2002, 2008; Kato 2004).

1.3 Culture

In different societies, prosodic prominence is manipulated in various ways, even in apparently similar social situations. Some of these dissimilarieties are purely linguistic (e.g., Grabe et al. 2003; Mennen 2006; Ladd et al. 2009), while others appear to be culturally variable and may be dependent on societal norms of power and solidarity (Brown and Gilman 1960; McLemore 1991; Watts 2003; Locher 2004). The present study argues that neither source of variation should be ignored.

This study will permit cross-cultural and cross-linguistic comparisons, showing that there are nontrivial language-specific and culture-specific components. Cognitive, linguistic, situational, and cultural factors must all be incorporated as variables for any analysis of the prosody of negation strategies.

2. Review of the relevant literature

2.1 Parameters of prosodic variation

There are three primary phonetic parameters of prosodic variation which can be mined for sociophonetic detail: loudness, measured acoustically as amplitude (in decibals: dB), pitch variation, measured acoustically from a speaker's fundamental frequency, or F0 (in HZ), and duration (where the duration of the word or its linguistic subcomponents can be compared with the duration of nearby equivalent tokens and is measurable in milliseconds—or msec). Figure 5.1 shows that all three are measurable using commonly available software:[3] F0 is found on the lowest vertical axis"Pitchtrack" and "Amplitude" has its own vertical axis immediately above it; "Duration" is measured along the horizontal axis. Each of these parameters is manipulated to varying degrees in different languages. Fortunately, in all three languages investigated here, the primary perceptual and productive parameter for prominence is fundamental frequency (F0) and is measurable from the pitchtrack itself (Yaeger-Dror and Fagyal, forthcoming).

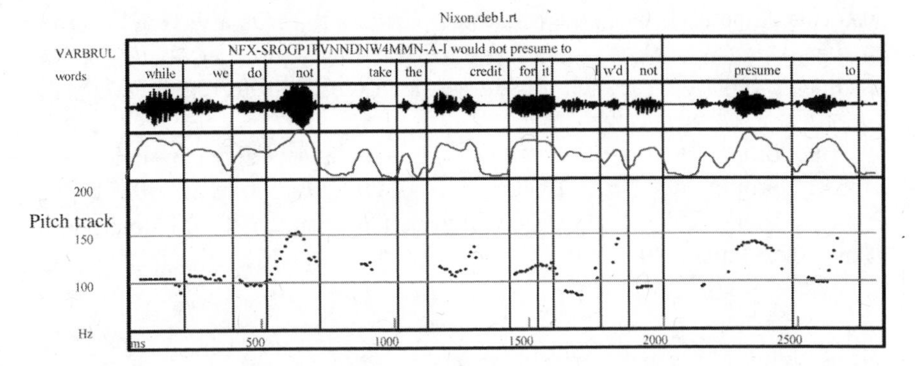

Figure 5.1 Examples of Pitch (F0), amplitude, and duration measures.

Experimental studies have shown that for speakers of Standard American English, amplitude generally appears to co-vary with fundamental frequency; duration appears to be correlated with both sentential position and focal prominence. While amplitude increments can be 'perceived' as 'accenting' a word even in the absence of a fundamental frequency change, this is not common even in a carefully read corpus (Cutler, Dahan, van Donselaar 1997).

In Japanese (as in English), experimental studies demonstrate that fundamental frequency plays the primary role in both production and perception of focal prominence (Pierrehumbert and Beckman 1988; Venditti 2005), whereas amplitude and duration also participate as subsidiary parameters (Sugitou 1982; Koori 1989a, b; Azuma 1992).

In Spanish (Navarro-Tomás 1944; Sosa 1999; Face 2001, 2002; Estebas-Vilaplana 2007) and other Romance languages as well (Di Cristo 1998; Dahan and Bernard 1997), focal prominence is produced primarily by varying fundamental frequency, while amplitude and durational prominence are used primarily for other purposes.

In short, each of the three languages investigated here permits us to measure and code this primary parameter for prominence (F0) directly from the pitchtrack, as shown on the example in Figure 5.1, taken from the first Kennedy/Nixon debate.

2.2 Cognition and prosodic salience

Bolinger (1978) proposed that prosodically emphasizing critical semantic information is a cross-linguistic universal. Prosodic focal prominence maximizes the ability of conversational partners to focus attention on information which is critical to mutual understanding (Cutler et al. 1997). The assumed motivation for such prosodic salience will be referred to here as the *Cognitive Prominence Principle.*

In addition, even within a single language dialects differ in their use of prosodic prominence (e.g., Beckman et al. 2002; Grabe et al 2002; Fagyal 2004; O'Rourke 2005; Thomas and Carter 2006; Mennen 2007; Estebas-Vilaplana 2007; Ladd et al 2009).

2.3 Sentential position and prosody

Syntactic position within a sentence influences prosodic options (Ladd 2008), and it is possible to manipulate focus by altering such positions (e.g., Ochs, Schegloff, Thompson 1996; Danieli et al. 2004; Coussé et al. 2004; Swerts and Wijk 2005, inter alia). The unmarked sentence contour in most languages permits an early prosodic peak with downstep narrowing the permissible F0 range later in the sentence. Many studies have documented that critical information is more likely to be placed early in the sentence, and that material presented early in the sentence is most likely to be prosodically prominent (e.g., Cutler et al. 1997; Horne 2000; Jun 2005; Ladd 2008).

In theory, the closer the ***NEG*** is to the beginning of the sentence, the greater the range and manipulability of prosodic prominence, so a speaker's option to exploit the position of ***NEG*** to emphasize or neutralize its cognitive salience is relevant to the discussion. Discussion of variation of placement to manipulate prosodic prominence can be found in Horne (2000), Jun (2005) and Takano (2008).

In declarative sentences, the unmarked placement for negatives analyzed here—***NEG***—includes 'verbal- *no*' for Spanish, *not* for English, *nai* for Japanese: Spanish verbal-*no* occurs before the verb, near the beginning of the sentence; English *not* immediately follows the English 'AUX' verb, and precedes the main verb, while *nai* generally occurs near the end of the sentence (Takano 2008; Jun 2005).

Even given that there is a strong preference for the unmarked position, it is reasonable to assume that the likelihood of prominence in any given case is mediated by the ***NEG***'s unmarked position in the sentence.

Considering both production and perception studies, Cutler et al. (1997) conclude that "speakers seldom de-accent (critical) information, and if they do, this hinders listeners." They show that while a prominent syntactic position can be neutralized by the overriding significance of other words in the environment, focally informative words are unlikely to be reduced because of their syntactic position. That is, words that carry critical information will be prosodically prominent even if their syntactic position would minimize prominence. Cutler et al.'s conclusion will be referred to as *Cutler's Corollary.* Note that studies which support the corollary claim have been carried out on both English (cf., op cit. and references therein) and French corpora (Benguerel 1970; Dahan and Bernard 1997).

A large segment of this chapter is devoted to the analysis of ways in which negatives are either prosodically prominent (supporting that claim) or not (possibly refuting the claim). Consequently, the relative importance of the *Cognitive Prominence Principle* and *Cutler's Corollary* with regard to actual *NEG* positions and prosody in each of these languages will be discussed further in Section 3.4.

2.4 *NEG* and prosody

The point of departure for studies of negation and prosody was developed in the work of Bolinger (1978), who claimed that cross-linguistically *NEG* will receive "negative prominence." We have taken that to mean prominence that would be represented in ToBI[4] transcription with L*, and which would have F0 no higher than nearby prosodically neutral words; analyses to date do not support this claim.

O'Shaughnessy and Allen (1983) looked specifically at negatives as carriers of critical information. They elicited isolated sentences with negatives that carried information which 'focal prominence' is intended to highlight: they found that *NEG* were almost categorically prominent which they attributed to their conveying cognitively critical information. While O'Shaughnessy did not characterize this "prominence," the pitchtracks of the elicited sentences revealed that overwhelmingly the *NEG* were either rising, rise-fall or high level—all variations on the ToBI theme of H*, rather than the L* proposed by Bolinger (1978).

Subsequently, Hirschberg (1990, 1993) analyzed news reports read by WBUR radio announcers (http://www.ldc.upenn.edu/Catalog/CatalogEntry.jsp?catalogId=LDC96S3; henceforth "BUR"); the newscasters were re-reading National Public Radio stylized newscasts. Like O'Shaughnessy, she found that the vast majority of prominences on *NEG* were H*. More recent studies (Syrdal et al. 2001; Hirschberg 2000) present similar results; in fact, both English *not* tokens (Hirschberg 1990, 1993) and French *pas* tokens (Morel 1995; Jun 2005) are reported as consistently pitch-raised in read speech, as would be projected from the *Cognitive Prominence Principle*, although (contrary to *Cutler's Corollary*) French negatives inside relative clauses are not necessarily prominent in isolated read sentences (Jun 2005).

2.5 Social situation and prosodic salience

Sociolinguists have shown that vowel positions, consonant realizations, and even intonational contours vary with social situation (Labov 1972; Yaeger 1974; Yaeger-Dror 2001; Eckert and Rickford 2001; Tucker 2007). Social situation had initially been shown to influence intonation contours for quite stylized genres of English such as story-telling, sports reporting, and political or religious speeches, or direction-giving in a narrowly defined "game" setting. (See, for example, Levin, Schaeffer, and Snow 1982; Grosz and Sidner 1986; Liberman 1992; Nevalainen 1992; Blaauw 1995; Hirschberg and Nakatani 1996; Hirschberg 2000.) More recent studies have begun to look at less stylized interactive situations (e.g., Bunnel and Idsardi 1996; IEEE 1997ff; Sagisaka et al. 1997; Chu-Carroll and Green 1998; COLING-ACL 1998ff), but the vast majority of prosodic studies are still carried out on de-contextualized, read sentences, or, at best, on newscasts, such as those in the "BUR" corpus discussed earlier. This study will contrast the results of analysis of news-broadcast data with results of a study using conversational speech.

2.6 Social situation, prosody and *NEG*: *The Social Agreement Principle*

Both the *Cogntive Prominence Principle* and *Cutler's Corollary* claim that prominence is directly correlated with the importance of the information being conveyed; all the read negatives which have been analyzed acoustically support that claim. However, negatives must also be considered from another point of view. One situational variable quite important to their analysis is the distinction between informative and socially interactive situations (Yaeger-Dror 1985, 1996, 2002a; Yaeger-Dror et al. 2002). That distinction will be implicated in the study reported here.

We have already seen that both in isolated read sentences (O'Shaughnessy and Allen 1983) and in informative readings (Hirschberg 1990) *NEG* carry important information, and (therefore) are pitch prominent; however, conversation analysts have shown that "preference for agreement" characterizes the conversations they have analyzed (Schegloff, Jefferson, and Sacks 1977; Sacks 1992). We will refer to that claim here as the *Social Agreement Principle*; *NEG* should be prosodically reduced or deleted if they carry new information which might be inferred as disagreeing with—or nonsupportive of—an earlier speaker.

"Preference for agreement" is obviously irrelevant for newscasts, or even for read materials in general, but it is instructive to consider read dialogue: when one reads from books, the F0 on *NEG* tokens is generally prominent in descriptive passages but is significantly less likely to be prominent in dialogue (Yaeger Dror, Hall-Lew and Deckert 2002, 2003; Yaeger-Dror 1996, 2002a).

NEG are more likely to be prominent in adversarial situations, whether or not the information conveyed by the *NEG* is critical to the hearer's understanding of what is said: *NEG*-prominence is also preferred in talk shows with an adversarial stance (Hutchby 1996; Scott 2002; Kiesling and Paulston 2005; Englebretson 2007; Hedberg and Yaeger-Dror 2008), certain types of political interviews (Heritage 2002a, b), US courtroom interaction (but see Kurzon 2001), or televised political debates (Yaeger Dror 2002a; Yaeger-Dror et al. 2002, 2003; Takano 2008).[5] The *Social Agreement Principle* may also be abrogated (in some cultures at least) in highly informative situations like classroom interactions (e.g., Kakavá 2002) or in children's game playing (e.g., Goodwin, Goodwin, and Yaeger-Dror 2002; Goodwin 2006a, b, and citations therein).

On the other hand, percentages are low in actual conversations between friends, with the lowest prominence percentages in face-to-face friendly conversations (Yaeger-Dror 1985; Yaeger-Dror, Hall-Lew, and Deckert 2002). Similar results were found for French friendly conversations (Yaeger-Dror 2002a). In fact, while read news or descriptive passages have a high percentage of prominent negatives, only a very low percentage of "remedial"[6] negatives were prominent in either French or English face to face friendly conversations studied (Yaeger-Dror 1985, 2002a). Thus, there appears to be a direct correlation between H* prominence and an informative social situation and an inverse correlation between prominence and socially supportive situations, or even read dialogue that is intended to sound friendly.

Since negatives not only provide crucial cognitive information but also provide the key to the expression of social agreement (i.e., supportive turns) and disagreement (i.e., remedial turns), analysis of the prosodic realization of negatives provides interesting data for the comparison of the relative importance of the *Cognitive Prominence* and *Social Agreement Principles.*

2.7 Negatives and cultures of power and solidarity

Just as the *Cognitive Prominence Principle* is assumed to be a cognitive universal, conversation theorists initially assumed that rules such as the "preference for agreement" (Sacks 1992; Schegloff et al. 1977), referred to here as the *Social Agreement Principle*, are cultural quasi-universals. However, all cultures don't have the same expectations.

Brown and Gilman (1960) showed that even *Tu/Vous* (T/V) choice varies with both relative solidarity and the relative power of speakers and recipients, that the dominance of power or solidarity vector is societal rather than linguistic, and that the vector preferred in a given culture may change over time. Just as they found that T/V usage can be correlated primarily with either a solidarity vector or a power vector, depending on whether choice of T or V is reciprocal or not, it is reasonable to hypothesize that prominent face-threatening negatives could possibly be used reciprocally in a solidarity-oriented society and nonreciprocally in a power-oriented society (Watts 2003; Mills 2003, 2004; Locher 2004). While this may be a critical factor in prosodic variation on *NEG*, the conversations in the present corpus were chosen to permit the analysis of solidary intimate *NEG* usage and to minimize the importance of possible power differences between the speakers. In fact, the phone calls chosen for analysis exclude probable sources of asymmetry between the coparticipants. (That is, primarily conversations in which interlocutors were the same age, and sex were included.)

Brown and Levinson (1978) chose to emphasize the importance of face concerns, whether the cultural motivation for variation was solidarity or power-based. Like Brown and Gillman, they also presented strong evidence that there is a wide variation in face concerns in different cultures. Not only does the importance of power and solidarity vary, but the situations considered face-threatening vary radically as well, as found in the studies of Blum-Kulka, House, and Kasper (1989). Evidence has shown that interlocutors from different cultures don't request or apologize in the same way (or for the same "infringement" of a coparticipant's "face"), and we hope to show that they definitely don't disagree in the same way.

Wierzbicka (1994) describes Japanese culture as far more sensitive to the *Social Agreement Principle* and Polish culture as far less sensitive to it. On the other hand, even within Japanese culture, well-known for its norms of interpersonal harmony and collective unity, management of interpersonal conflict is more flexible than the cultural stereotype would suggest and therefore is also situation-dependent (Befu 1980; Ishida 1984; Krauss, Rohlen, and Steinhoff 1984; Yamada 1992). Moreover, since power assymmetries are more important in Japanese culture than in Western Cultures (Wierzbicka 1994; Yamada 2002), the "powerful" member of a dyad appears to have the right to express disagreement more directly than speakers from more symmetrical cultures, while in relatively symmetrical interactions neither speaker has the same latitude for expressing disagreement directly (Yamada 1992, 2002).

Even within more similar cultures, different expectations for appropriateness can obtain. While the broadcast debate requires an adversarial stance in English, French political adversaries for the Prime Ministerial position (at least in the 1990s) were more likely to use a superficially less adversarial stance, which native speakers considered critical to a demeanor appropriate to an aspirant for such a political position (Yaeger-Dror 2002a, b). On the other hand, situations which were initially limited to a single society appear to have become cross-cultural genres: e.g, the universality of television "culture" has led to the creation of a cross-cultural hyper-adversarial political "discussion" television genre (Yaeger-Dror 2002a, b).

2.8 Subcultures of power and solidarity

Tannen (1981, 2005), Schiffrin (1984), Maynard (1989), Goodwin and Goodwin (1995), Goodwin et al. (2002), and Jefferson (2002) have all shown the degree to which **sub**culture is also a relevant variable for remedial disagreement strategies or use of negatives even within the English-speaking world, as Gumperz (1982), Licari and Stame (1990), Couper-Kuhlen (1992), Okamoto (1994), Song (1994), Ting-Toomey et al. (1991), Ambady, Koo, Lee, and Rosenthal (1996), Pike and McKinney (1996), Holtgraves (1997), and Yaeger-Dror (2002b) all demonstrate that variation in disagreement strategies is even greater in cross-language, or cross-cultural comparisons.

For example, Tannen (1981, 1984/2005) and Schiffrin (1984) proposed that New Yorkers and Ashkenazi Philadelphians (respectively) are relatively less sensitive to the *Social Agreement Principle* than other Americans. Kakavá (2002) suggested that Greek Americans are also less sensitive to the *Social Agreement Principle.* Similarly, Applefield (1997), Carroll (1988) and Platt (1998) claim that Francophones from the Old World are less sensitive to the *Social Agreement Principle* than Americans (including New Yorkers).

However, while these studies present evidence for a sliding scale of face concerns, they all assume a cross-cultural consensus on a continuum from supportive to remedial turn stance.

One question which arises is to what extent can Spanish, Japanese and English negative prosody be regarded as a cultural, rather than purely linguistic, variable? To what extent can variation within a given language, but in different locales, be traced to subcultural variation which corresponds with the purported face concerns which can be independently verified, such as those which correspond with T/V usage patterns?

2.9 Negatives and stance within a situation

Labov and Fanshel (1977), Goffman (1981), Jacobs (2002) and Clayman (2002) have shown that within a given social setting turn stance may vary—with one participant required to be guardedly neutral (the interviewer, the therapist, the mediator, or the moderator), while other participants are less constrained (the interviewee, the patient, the panel participant). To take a dramatic example, a debate participant may use adversarial stance (as debater), a neutral to supportive stance (as moderator), or even a pseudo-informative position (the rôle affected, for example, by Perot in the 1992 debates). Other interactional factors that influence turn stance have also been isolated (Goffman 1981; Schilling-Estes 1998; Suleiman, O'Connell and Kowal 2002.)

Clayman and Heritage (2002) ascertained that what is considered an appropriate turn stance may vary over a number of years even within a single society. They found that in the 1950s reportorial stance was deferential and supportive of US presidents during a news conference, but register expectations altered so radically during the Nixon years that the appropriate turn stance for a US reporter is now adversarial. They found that this change has not occurred in England, or at least not to the same degree.

Speaker stance should always be considered as a possible factor in any study of any interpersonal pragmatic and prosodic variation; however, since the phone calls chosen were supportive stance, while the news broadcasts analyzed were limited to purely informative monologues, stance was conflated with corpus, and need not be coded separately, so in the present study there are only two stances: supportive (since all conversations were friendly) and informative (in the newscasts). However, speaker stance should always be considered as a possible factor in any study of any interpersonal pragmatic and prosodic variation.

2.10 Interaction among these factor groups

This chapter will consider the relative importance of linguistic, cultural and interactive differences. While the cognitive factor (and the *Cognitive Prominence Principle*) and the interactive factor (and the *Social Agreement Principle*) have both been studied, it has not been possible to consider the degree to which language choice (and word position) can be isolated as a separate influence. The present study, with its focus on parallel recordings of variation in Spanish, English, and Japanese will hopefully permit such a comparative analysis. For example, one initial hypothesis will be that with the *NEG* in an early sentence position Spanish will permit higher prominence percentages than English or Japanese.

A second hypothesis is that with the greater emphasis on agreement in Japanese culture (Ambady et al. 1996; Yamada 1992; 2002) the prominence percentages will be consistently lowest in Japanese, both because of the default sentence position for *-nai,* and because of this cultural preference.

Given that there is a broad range of prosodic dialectal variation in English (e.g., Thomas and Carter 2006; Arvaniti 2007; Arvaniti and Garding 2007; Ladd et al. 2009), Japanese (e.g., Sugitou et al. 1997), and Spanish (e.g., Sosa 1999; Estebas-Vilaplana 2007) but no studies to date which allude to dialect-specific patterns for choosing "focal" prominence, we will assume that while the specific contour used—or the lack of one—may vary in different dialect groups, any differences in occurrence of focal accent can be ascribed to socio-cultural rather than dialect factors. We will try to answer these questions: To what degree does language itself, and the default *NEG* position influence prominence options? To what degree do (sub)cultural variations in "preference for agreement" influence options? These questions will be addressed in the following section.

3. Research methodology

Section 2.1 discussed the acoustic software used to permit accurate sociophonetic analysis of prosodic prominence; such software is used by ToBI coders as well as sociophoneticians (Syrdal et al. 2001; Shattuck-Hufnagel, Veilleux and Brugos 2005). Section 2.2's review of the literature showed that negatives "should" be prosodically prominent, but subsequent sections reviewed evidence that social situation can counterbalance the *Cognitive Prominence Principle.* It seems clear that, at least in English, the social situation strongly influences whether negatives will be prominent, and we will address the hypotheses that speakers from certain social groups emphasize negatives more than those from other groups, and that different situations may be treated differently in different cultures. As already discussed, in order to address these questions, we will analyze data from "parallel corpora." That is, except for the variables to be considered in the analysis—in this case, language, culture and region—demographics, stance and footing of the speakers are held as constant as possible. While the intention is to present information on friendly conversations, in each language *NEG* from newscasts have been measured as well, to permit a baseline comparison of "informative" stance with the evidence from social interactions.

3.1 Corpus choice

It is always difficult to determine how much data is needed for an adequate sample for any sociophonetic study. One rule of thumb is that the more variables to be compared, the greater the number of tokens needed to fill the cells. Another rule of thumb is that the more common the variable, the smaller the corpus needed to access sufficient tokens: e.g., analysis of a common consonant requires a much smaller corpus for the investigation of sufficient tokens than analysis of, say, a rarely used lexical item. In the present case, we are examining a discourse level phenomenon—"disagreements," which varies radically with social situation and would rarely occur in classic "Interview Style", where the interviewer is trained to appear supportive, and not to voice opinions which might be disagreed with. We also have hypothesized that situational stance, turn footing, and demographic variables will influence the results significantly, so (at least for conversational corpora) we need a very large sample to provide sufficient information for inspection of these variables, while holding other factors steady. We have been quite fortunate to have access to cross-linguistic equivalent/parallel corpora of both newscasts and friendly conversations which provide sufficient data for comparative analysis of this discourse feature.

This chapter will analyze the phonetic realization of prominence in these two parallel corpora for the three language communities. For every social group studied to date we can now show that the *Cognitive Prominence Principle* is limited by the *Social Agreement Principle* and that, at a finer analytical level, subcultural social groups vary their prosodic behavior quite extensively, with social situation and turn-footing both critical to the prosodic choices made by the speakers. Table 5.1 presents the corpora to be analyzed for this study. The demographic groups which can be isolated are men vs. women, speakers from different dialect areas of the same language, and demographically similar speakers who live in different countries and speak different languages. Unfortunately, due to idiosyncrasies of the corpus, age is not one of the demographic factors which can be considered.

Table 5.1 Number of Speakers in Each Corpus

	News		CallFriend		CF
	Men	Women	Men	Women	Total
US English N	6	3	8e[9]; 4nc; 4y; 2w	6e; 6nc; 4y;2w	36
US English S	—	—	6a; 4s	6; 2s	18
Costeño Spanish	—	—	5	4	9
Serrano Spanish	9	7	6	4	10
Tokyo Japanese	3	3	4	0	4
Sapporo Japanese	—	—	0	4	4

The American English corpus was further divided into speakers from the rful- South (a),[7] those from formerly rless Southern regions (s), the NorthEast (e),[8] the West (w), the Inland North (nc), and—following the claims of Tannen (1981, 1984) and Schiffrin (1984)—speakers from a strongly Ashkenazy-Jewish background from Eastern Seaboard cities (y).

3.1.1 Informative corpus

The Linguistics Data Consortium (henceforth LDC: www.ldc.upenn.edu) has collected large samples of newscasts (N) in several languages. While the materials were initially collected for the National Institute of Standards and Technology's (henceforth NIST, formerly known as the Bureau of Standards) benchmark studies for speech recognition, obviously the informative nature of the genre provides a perfect "foil," or comparison, for conversational material. Analysis of the use of *NEG* in newscasts will permit us to see if "informative" tokens with no possible disagreement are primarily prominent as projected, and will allow us to compare the relative importance of the *Cognitive Prominence* and *Social Agreement Principle*s. Newscasts in Spanish (*Hub4*) and English (*English Broadcast News*) available from the LDC (and taped in the 1990s) will be compared with newscasts recorded directly from TV programs broadcast in Japan in 2002.

The demographics of the speakers in the News corpus are listed on the two left-hand columns of Table 5.2.

English: The 1996 Broadcast News Speech Corpus (LDC97S44/66/71) contains a total of 104 hours of broadcasts from radio networks with corresponding time aligned transcripts. We analyzed a cross-section of those read newscasts and all the news readers use the neutral *koiné* often referred to as "NPR (i.e., National Public Radio) English," although the analyzed data were gathered from ABC and NBC, not from NPR. For newsbroadcasts, with only informative stance, 100 *NEG* tokens were deemed sufficient.

Japanese: The Japanese broadcast news corpus contains a total of eight hours of nationally televised evening newscasts from NHK (Tokyo), TBS (Tokyo), and TV-Asahi (Tokyo) in 2002; all the newscasters are trained speakers of the Japanese broadcast *koiné* referred to as *kyootsuu-go* ("common language") or *hyoojun-go* ("standard language"). The first 161 tokens from these newscasts were then transcribed and analyzed by the second author's team.

Spanish: The *Hub4* corpus (LDC98S74) contains speech and aligned transcripts of 30 hours of broadcast newscasts from Televisa (Miami), Univisión (Mexico) and Voice of America (VOA) broadcasts to Latin America read by Mexican and "Miami" speakers of Spanish; the preferred international broadcast standard for Latin American Spanish in the United States is Mexican (Ahrens 2004). Here again, the first 100 tokens were coded.

3.1.2 Conversational corpora

Previous studies (Labov 1972; Yaeger 1974; Yaeger-Dror 2001; Di Paolo and Faber 1990; Eckert and Rickford 2001; Tucker 2007) have consistently demonstrated that the more self-conscious speakers are, the less rule-governed their sociophonology is. If this is true for vowel or consonant phonology, which for most speakers only tangentially varies with "footing" and other situational factors, it is likely to be true for prosody, which is most susceptible to situational variation.

Luckily, several large parallel conversational corpora are available from LDC. To maximize comparability, we have chosen friendly conversations from several cultures, referred to on the LDC website as the "CallFriend" (CF) corpus; conversations in US English, Japanese and Latin American Spanish transcribed at the University of Arizona are available both through LDC and on the Talkbank website (www.talkbank.org/data/CA). The sound quality of all the conversations is quite good, and almost all conversations to date appear to be primarily "unmonitored"; that is, speakers appear unself-conscious about local variation and display minimal evidence of the accommodation to the coparticipant which is known to occur when the conversationalists are strangers to each other or the interview situation requires an external microphone. When there were obvious "power" asymmetries, a file was discarded from the present analysis. These phone calls permit the analysis of how specific variables are used in the same social situation—phone conversations between close friends, initiated by one of the conversational participants.

Speakers were solicited by the LDC to participate in this telephone speech collection effort via the internet and personal contacts, so all speakers were from similarly educated middle-class social backgrounds; this is confirmed by the level of education shown for speakers. There is a total of 60 calls for each call set (English/Southern, English NonSouthern—CF_NENG:LDC96S46; CF_SENG:LDC96S47; Spanish Coastal/Noncoastal—LDC96S57, CF_Sp:LDC96S58; also Hub5—LDC98S70/T27 and LDC98S70; Japanese—LDC96S53); each caller placed a telephone call via a toll-free robot operator maintained by the LDC to a callee of his or her choice. Recruits were given no guidelines concerning what they should talk about, but were told to call close friends. All participants knew that these calls would be recorded. Upon successful completion of the call, the caller was paid $20 (and given the free long-distance telephone call). Documentation for each call includes home region, sex, age, education, callee area code, and the aligned transcript. As discussed earlier, to the best of our ability only phone calls between friends of the same sex, age and regional background were transcribed for analysis, and only transcribed calls were analyzed.

All conversations took place in the 1990s (as did all newscasts but those in Japanese). Almost all phone calls were between intimates and equals, but since the cultural underpinnings may influence the relative importance of the *Social Agreement Principle*, in light of the studies by Tannen (1981, 1984) and Schiffrin (1984) discussed previously, the dialect and region of all callers were carefully noted.

English: All calls between immediate family members were discarded, except in a few (2 Northern, 2 Southern) cases. For the moment, these four cross-generational conversations have not been isolated but are still included in the corpus under analysis. Each data set was run both without the cross-generational calls, and then with them. The only change in the results was that with the addition of the family calls, age became a significant factor, and the other factor groups became more significant but did not change.

Japanese: While power is assumed to be more significant as a variable in Japanese culture than in the US or Latin America, these conversations were chosen to be as free of hierarchy as possible. Within the Japanese language corpus, there was a confound since all the men transcribed were from the Kanto region (Eastern Japan, e.g., Tokyo), and were in their 20s, while all of the women were from Hokkaido and were in their 40s. As a result, it is unclear whether differences between conversations were due to speaker sex, to age grading, or to region.

Spanish: Conversations which met the criteria for this study were transcribed in their entirety and can be found online with the other CallFriend conversations (talkbank.org). This subcorpus required greater dialect "triage" than the others.—LDC coded speakers as "Caribbean" or "NonCaribbean" based on a rough estimate of dialect region. However, dialect region does not actually follow the the borders of countries, and we recoded speakers as "*Costeños*" ("Coastal") or "*Serranos*" ("Mountain") based on their dialect characteristics (Canfield 1963, 1981). Given that the *Costeño* cultural pattern is more socially symmetrical than the *Serrano* (Brown and Gillman 1960), this distinction is particularly important for discourse analysis. While all speakers in these calls reciprocally addressed each other with *tú*, the calls coded as *Serrano* were made between Mexicans, or Colombians from the Bogotá region (Canfield 1963/1981); most of the Venezuelans are coded as *Costeños* for the purposes of this analysis. Only one conversation was analyzed from speakers who were not both from the same region and only one in which speaker-sex differed.

The columns on the right of Table 5.1 show the number of speakers in each cell.

3.1.3 Individual speaker variables

For the Varbrul Analysis, each speaker's unique code categorized him/her by sex (MFG),[9] age (by decade) and dialect/region (as specified before). Except for two men from the deep south, all speakers were middle class; as already noted, the canvassing strategy elicited calls from mostly computer-literate speakers, many with graduate degrees, and most telephone dyads were limited to those with identical demographics.

Except for the cross-generational calls discussed earlier, all dyads were symmetrical. To the analysts, even the exceptions appeared to be quite "solidary" and "reciprocal" (Brown and Gillman 1960).

As Tables 5.1 and 5.2 show, each speaker was also coded for situation, with the newscasters (N) isolated from casual conversationalists (CF). The number of *NEG* tokens analyzed and discussed here is found on Table 5.2, along with the number of tokens from situations which are alluded to in passing.[10] Note that there are fewer tokens for the Japanese CF corpus than for the others, not because the speakers use fewer of *NEG* tokens, but because fewer phone calls have been analyzed; the average number of tokens per speaker is not surprisingly low.

Table 5.2 Number of Tokens for Each Situation

Situation	Spanish	Japanese	English
News	100	161	100
Debate	—	287	530
SWB	—	—	505
CF	450	299	1626
Mean *NEG* tokens / CF speaker	22	37	34

3.2 Coding the dependent variable

Acoustic measurements of fundamental frequency, amplitude, and duration were used to determine the prosodic prominence of *NEG* tokens in each of the three languages sampled. Table 5.3 provides the coding choices for the dependent variable, and Figure 5.1 provides a sample sentence. In the example, taken from the Kennedy-Nixon debates, we see that the first token of *not* is, indeed, prominent. The second *NEG*—for which we see the coding—is nonprominent (N) albeit uncontracted (F[ull]), but the following word (*presume*) is prominent (R). Each token of *NEG* was displayed and the relevant parameters were analyzed and coded on the "VARBRUL" tier. The full transcript was also monitored carefully, since a larger context is needed to permit accurate analysis of what will be referred to in this chapter as the **footing** of each turn, which will be discussed in Section 3.6. The coding tier allowed all tokens to be coded as they were analyzed and permitted quick access to questionable tokens, with the coding, the sound file, and the pitchtrack all bound together in one file.[11] Table 5.3 presents this dependent variable and its coding.[12]

In each case at least two people were involved in the coding: the primary coder and the primary researcher for the corpus. Questions that arose were discussed among the coauthors to insure that coding would be as similar as possible for the three corpora. Pitchworks permits the coding tier to be exported into a file directly analyzable by Goldvarb (Sankoff, Tagliamonte, and Smith 2005).

English: The pitch accent of the *NEG* was determined with coding choices roughly parallel to the ToBI system (cf. Syrdal et al. 2001; Shattuck-Hufnagel et al. 2005) with modifications necessitated by variation found in each language. As shown on Table 5.3, tokens were later recoded into a binary system, with Prominence (+) being the Application of the rule. To compare the results with Hirschberg's (1990, 1993) and O'Shaughnessy's (O'Shaughnessy and Allen 1983), only variations on H* were considered as applications in the final English and Spanish studies, with L and v recoded with N and A as nonapplications (-), as shown on Table 5.3 in the "recode" column.

Japanese: The Japanese research group found that almost all the occurrences of prominent—*nai* -*NEG*—were realized as H*+L. L* and its permutations cannot occur in Japanese, so even if L*, or L*+H had been included as an application, it would not have changed the analysis. [13]

Table 5.3 presents the dependent variable as coded.

Spanish: Navarro-Tomás (1944), Sosa (1999), Face (2001, 2002) all agree that the narrower the focus, the higher the F0 peak on a Spanish word. Beckman et al. (2005), Estebas-Vilaplana (2006) and others have pointed out that, at least for reading intonation in isolated sentences, the preferred noncontrastive focus of Iberian Spanish is L*+H; that is, there is a low F0 prominence on the accented syllable, with a rise late in that syllable or in subsequent syllables. This L*+H contour is much rarer in English and is not documented for other languages studied to date, nor in the American Spanish dialects discussed by Navarro Tomás or those in the present corpus. However, even in Iberian Spanish, both narrow focus and cases where the focal word does not have subsequent unstressed syllables, H*, or at least L+H*, is much more likely to occur. In addition, there is some controversy over whether the pitch peak is on the accented syllable only or whether F0 continues to rise til the end of the word. "The peak is on the stressed syllable when it is last, but after the stressed syllable when it is not final." (Face 2002)

While no previous prosodic studies of the use of *NEG* have been attempted for any Spanish-speaking corpus, since "*no*" is only one syllable long the type of rise on the target syllable should not vary with focus. The default assumption is that H* will be more likely to occur on a *NEG* than L* (although either prominence option would still be relevant for this study).

Table 5.3 Prosodic Variation: The Dependent Variable

ENG/S	RECODE	JAPAN[13]	SIGNIFICANCE	TOBI CORRELATE	COMMENT
N	-	N	Neutral	-	no amp. or F0 prominence
A	-	A	Amplitude	L*	Louder, but no F0 prominence
-	-	D	Duration	L*	Duration increase
H	+	—	High	H*	most common prominence
R	+	—	Rising	H+H*; L+H*; H*; %H	variations on H*
^	+	P	Rise+fall	H*+L; H*-L%	occurs frequently
F	+	-	Falling	H*+L; H*-L%	
L	-	—	Low	L*	Bolinger's "pick": rare
v	-	—	Fall-rise	L*+H	occurs more rarely

Only {NALv} are considered nonapplications in English and Spanish, but only N was considered a nonapplication for Japanese. Non-occurring options are designated "—" in the appropriate cell. All tokens were recoded as + or -.

3.3 Coding for morphology of negation

As the previous discussion shows, it is likely that prominence is morphosyntactically constrained in each of the languages under analysis.

English: Table 5.4e demonstrates that there are various ways to express negation in English, and the most common is referred to by Tottie (1991) as

"*Not*-negation." Because it is (by far) the most common form, only full or contracted *Not*- negation in full declarative sentences are analyzed here. (The reasons for limiting the analysis in this way are discussed in greater detail in Yaeger-Dror et al. 2002.) It is also true that the full form of *not*-negation and affixal negative forms are more frequent in writing and in informative interactions, so by only considering the most reducible form of negation, we are actually minimizing the degree to which situation influences the likelihood of *NEG* prominence. In the present study, then, the only morphological coding included is the distinction between contracted and full *NEG*, while the rarer negation types will not be analyzed.

Table 5.4e Morphology

CODE	TOTTIE'S TERMINOLOGY	EXAMPLES	SAMPLE SENTENCES
F	*not-negation [*NEG*]	is not,	It is not really possible.
C	*not-negation [*NEG*]	isn't, 's not	It isn't really possible.
—	*No*-negation	nowhere, never, nothing,	I never did that!
—	Affixal negation	imperfect, irrespective, nonstop	I am incapable . . .
—	Conjunctive negation	but, however, in contrast,	But I talk a good game.

Tottie (1991) found *not*-negation to be the dominant form of negation in English. In this study, only Full and Contracted *not*-negatives in declarative sentences are coded for English; the other forms of negation are not.

Japanese: The morphology of Japanese *NEG* is more complicated than that for English or Spanish: The present study focuses only on the most common type, *nai* negation, with all the four subtypes of conjugations (following verbals, nominals, adjectives, and adjectival nouns) included, as found in Table 5.4j.

Negation involving *nai* is realized in two morphological structures: *nai* is cliticized to the verb as an auxiliary verb (e.g., *hanasu* "speak" /*hanasa-nai* "do not speak"; *iku* "go" /*ika-nai* "do not go"), or it is realized as an independent adjective preceded by nominals (e.g., *suru koto ga nai* "(I) do not have anything to do."), adjectives (e.g., *oishiku wa nai* "(It) is not delicious.") or adjectival nouns (e.g., *kirei de wa nai* "(It) is not pretty.") It can be assumed that the morphologically independent use of *nai* should be perceptually more salient than when it is cliticized. As in English, the clitic-*NEG* is much more common: 74% of the tokens are "auxiliary-nai" in conversation. Moreover, just as in English, the other forms of negation become more common in preplanned-broadcast statements, the percentage rising from 26% in conversation to 37% in newscasts.

Analysis of reading passages or isolated sentences has demonstrated that *nai*'s position within the sentence influences the probability that it will receive focal prominence; prosodic prominence on *nai* is closely linked to syntactic dislocation (the movement of linguistic elements to the post-predicate position). Takano (2002, 2008) found that postposed elements supplant the unmarked position for *nai*, shifting it forward and creating a prosodic environment theoretically more favorable to pitch prominence on *nai*. However, as in English, the likelihood of occurrence of these more complex structures is low. Language specific constraints interact with communicative requirements of specific social situations. At the moment, although the verbal affix is most common and is similar to NEG in other languages, the small number of phone calls analyzed to date led us to code all *nai* for the analysis.

Table 5.4j Morphology: Japanese

CODE	GRAMMATICAL	FORM	SAMPLE SENTENCES	GLOSS
X	**Auxiliary Verb**	**Verbs + *nai***	*Eigo wa hanasa-nai.* English TOP speak-NEG	(I) do not speak English.
N	**Nominal-**	**Nominals + *nai***	*Suru koto ga nai* do things SUB NEG	(I) do not have anything to do.
A	**Adjective-**	**Adjectives + *nai***	*Oishiku (wa) nai.* delicious TOP NEG	(It) is not delicious.
D	**Adjectival-noun-**	**Adjectival Nouns +*nai***	*Kirei de wa nai.* Pretty COP TOP NEG	(It) is not pretty.
—	**Affixal negation**	**prefix *hi-*, *hu-*, *mu-*, *bu-***	*hi-kooshiki; hu-ben, etc.*	Unofficial; inconvenience, etc.
—	**Conjunct negation**	**Placed before *nai***	*Zenzen okashiku nai.*	(It's) not funny at all.

TOP = topic marker
SUB = subject marker
COP = copula

Spanish: Table 5.4s demonstrates that there are also various ways to express negation in Spanish. By far the most common is "*No*-Negation." Again because it is the most common form, the simplest, and most similar to the NEG form analyzed for English, we will analyze here only *No*-Negation in full declarative sentences, so no coding for morphology is needed for the Spanish corpus.

Table 5.4s Morphology

CODE	TOTTIE TERMINOLOGY	EXAMPLES	SAMPLE
-	***no***-negation [*NEG*] ***n***-negation **affixal** negation	*No es* *nada, nunca,* *imperfecto, incapaz . . .*	*No es posible.* *¡Nunca hizo eso!* *Soy incapaz . . .*
	Conjunctive negation	*Pero, aunque . . .*	*Pero te lo dije.*

The morphology of Spanish is simpler than that for English, so no coding for morphology is required, since only "no-negation" is included in the analysis.

3.4 Coding for sentence position: End vs. Other

As already discussed in Section 2.3, ToBI analysis of readings in all three languages has found that pitch range tends to become narrower toward the end of the intonation phrase (Arvaniti 2007; Jun 2005; Ladd 2008; Pierrehumbert 1980; Sosa 1999); this is irrelevant if *Cutler's Corollary* prevails, but to the degree that prosody can be constrained by sentence position, it should allow total freedom for prominence on Spanish *NEG*, a somewhat constrained freedom on English *NEG*, and should constrain Japanese *NEG* most effectively.

Previous quantitative corpus studies support that claim: Yaeger-Dror (2002a), Banuazizi (2003) and Hedberg and Yaeger-Dror (2008) all found that sentential position influences the likelihood that a *NEG* token will be prominent in English; the study of Japanese has now shown sentential position to be a significant factor as well. In Spanish, of course, *NEG* cannot be sentence final except with one word utterances, which are not under discussion here, so sentence position (End vs. Other) is only coded for Japanese[14] and English.

3.5 Coding for environmental adjacent prominence

One of our initial hypotheses was that if a word adjacent to a *NEG* is prominent, prominence on the *NEG* itself will be less likely.

Unfortunately, while this is theoretically a reasonable hypothesis, reality is far more complicated (Yaeger-Dror 2002a): the analyst must consider not only the likelihood of prominence, but which side of the negative the prominence is on, whether both preceding and succeeding words are prominent and whether the prominent word upgrades or downgrades the force of the disagreement; these factors must then be supplemented by coding for the situation, stance and footing of the turn.

The segment shown on Figure 5.1 is a case in point:

(1) While we do *not* take the credit for it, I would not *presume* to . . . (K/N1: Richard Nixon, 1960.)[15]

Nixon does not say:

(1') I would ***not*** presume to but
(1) I would not pre***sume*** to

Given the fact that this variable was much more complicated than our first coding permitted, the issue will be discussed in a later publication. [16]

3.6 Interactive stance and footing

We showed in Section 2.7 that each corpus was uniformly of a single **stance**, so there was no need to code for stance separately in this study. However, within each of the corpora, turn **footing** was found to vary significantly, and was coded as an independent variable. Table 5.5 shows the coding options relevant to the analysis here. There is a definite cultural preference for one or another footing in the different languages, or, to be more accurate, in the different societies, but some patterns are consistent. In radio news broadcasts all *NEG* are informative, while in the CallFriend conversations approximately a quarter of all tokens are used supportively by each group of speakers, confirming our initial assumption that the CallFriend conversations are fairly comparable as well.

For the conversations sampled, three turn footings appeared to be used in the same way by all the speakers and presented no coding problems: Supportive (S), Informative (I) and Remedial (R). All tokens were coded by one researcher and checked by another. Other coded options were created because of their importance within a given culture. For example, self-protective (P) tokens were initially incorporated into the coding scheme to facilitate analysis of our Japanese corpus. Once the factor was incorporated into the coding scheme, we found that the American political debaters frequently use a self-protective stance, as in sentence (2). Although its use was much more limited in the CallFriend data, where a conversationalist infers that the interlocutor disagrees with him/her there may be a self-protective use of negation as in sentence (3), cited from the Switchboard (SWB) corpus.

(2) Now I *don't* wanna get into a debate with you all.—George Bush, Sr.

(3) I *don't* wanna deny them their rights!—SWB 2709n.[17]

Hedged, self-corrective or self protective tokens were coded, but in the runs reported here, these factors were discarded from the Goldvarb analysis. The analysis of these turn footings will be presented elsewhere, and only Supportive, Remedial, and Informative footings are included in the analysis reported here.

Table 5.5 Turn-Footings Coded in Study

CODE	RECODE	SIGNIFICANCE	SAMPLE SENTENCE	SOURCE
I	**I**	**I**nformative	the surveillance system is not that sinister.	BUR News
S	**S**	**S**upportive	I agree, they don't write anything like they use'to.[18]	SWB 2281
R	**R**	**R**emedial	He simply doesn't know what he's talking about.	K/N
C	-	Self-**C**orrect	I don't know- I don't know the immigration laws.	swb 2709
P	-	Self-**P**rotect	Y'know, I don't wanna deny them their rights!	swb 2709
H	-	**H**edge	If I'm not mistaken . . .	ALL

Specific turn-footings coded in this study; after initial analyses, the final analysis discussed here includes only the first three footings, with the others excluded from the analysis.

Other independent factor groups were significant for one language or another. However, those significant as independent variables for at least two of the languages are those discussed here: Corpus/Situation/Stance (News, CallFriend), Footing (Supportive, Remedial, Informative) Morphology (Full, Cliticized), Sentence Position (End, Other), and speaker characteristics (gender, region).[19]

4. The analysis

Once all the tokens were coded, and those tokens not included in this analysis were discarded, a Goldvarb statistical analysis (Sankoff et al. 2005) determined the degree to which one or another factor group influenced the likelihood of prominence. Table 5.6 displays those variables which the Goldvarb showed to be a significant influence on prosodic variation of ***NEG*** tokens, which are discussed here. The Goldvarb weights are found on Table 5.7.

Table 5.6 Cross-Linguistic Comparison of Different Factor Groups: Aside from "Situation," All Comparisons Are for CF Data

FACTOR GP	SIGNIFICANCE	SPANISH	JAPANESE	N. ENGLISH	S. ENGLISH
Situation[20]	Stance	N>CF	N>CF	N >CF	—
Morphology cf. Table 5.4	Full/clitic	—	Vb>Adj	F>c	F>c
Footing cf. Table 5.5	SIR	ns	S>I>R	S>I>R	S>I>R
SPosition	E(nd) vs. o(ther)	—	o>E	o>E	o>E
Sex	M F	F>M	M ~F*	F>M	F>M
Region[21]	(See Table 5.1)	Cos>Ser	Tok~Ho*	W>nc>y>E	S>A

Table 5.7 Comparing Goldvarb Factor Weights for Applications (= NEG prominence) Cross-Linguistically in the CF Calls That Have Been Analyzed

FACTOR GP	SIGNIFICANCE	SPANISH	JAPANESE	ENGLISH
Situation		-	N>CF .55>.38	
Morphology Cf. Tables 5.4ejs	Factor Wts	-	Vb>Adj .54>.38	-
Position End≠Other	Factor Wts.	-	.41<.64	.62>.48(S) .59>.49 (all)
Footing cf. Table 5.5	SIR Factor Wts	ns	S>I>R .93>.47>.44	.71>.52>.495 (S) .66>.50<.52 (all)
Sex	M/F Factor Wts	F>M .73>.25	M~F*	F>M>GayMen .59~.49>.26
Region[21]	Factor Wts	Cost>Ser .62>.27	Tok~Ho*	W>nc>S>y>E>A .62>.61>.53>.5>.47>.43

N.B.: Symbols and abbreviations as in Table 5.6.

* As in previous tables, there is a three way confound for Japanese CF speakers with age, sex, and region. There is, similarly, a confound for age in the CF conversations.

4.1 Situation

First the newscasts were run separately for each language group; newscast NEG were pitch prominent greater than half the time for both English and

Spanish, although even in English prominence did not peak over 90% as it had for the isolated sentence readers (O'Shaughnessy and Allen 1983) or the news re-readers (Hirschberg 1990) discussed earlier. In English 78% of Newscast tokens were prominent, in Spanish 58%, and in Japanese 39% (Yaeger-Dror et al 2002, 2003, Takano 2008).

The different CallFriend corpora were run separately, and then the Call-Friend and News subcorpora were run together (for the Japanese Corpus). Situation (News vs. CallFriend) is consistently significant across all corpora, but for the English and Spanish corpora we determined that it was inappropriate to run the two situations together.

With regard to footing, the newscasters' *NEG* were uniformly coded as Informative. All other results on the table are for CF calls.

4.2 Morphology

As implied in the discussion of morphology, we expected that full *not* tokens (coded as F on Table 5.4e) are overall significantly more likely to be prominent than contracted *not* (coded as C) in American English conversations; however, within the CF corpus, there were so few Full tokens in the CF declarative sentences that the factor group did not enter the CF-only regressions, and are not found on Table 5.7.

On the other hand, there is more variation within the Japanese CF calls: the Japanese cliticized-*nai* (i.e., auxiliary *nai* [coded as X on Table 5.4j]) are more likely to be prominent (.55) than the remaining morphologically independent "*nai*" (i.e., nominals, adjectives, adjectival nouns + "*nai*" [coded as N, A, D respectively on Table 5.4j]) (.40). Further analysis shows that this distinction is noteworthy in "Informative" footing of *-nai*: the "cliticized" *nai* tends to receive more prominence (36%) than the "morphologically independent" *-nai* (21%). We infer that this systematic pattern is closely linked to the degree of perceptual salience of the negative *-nai* in different morphological positions and the speaker's (perhaps tacit) intent to augment communicative efficiency in telephone conversations in which verbal signals are the only medium to rely on. Note that the same tendency is also observed in more information-laden registers such as news broadcast and political debates data as well (Takano 2008).

Given that—as shown on Table 5.4s—there are no morphological *NEG* variants considered in Spanish, morphology is irrelevant to the discussion of Spanish variation.

4.3 Sentence position

As we see on Table 5.7, in Japanese *NEG* is less likely to be prominent when it occurs within five morae of the end of a sentence (E), than in other (O) positions. This is consistent with expectations based on earlier studies. The opposite is true for French conversations and debates (Yaeger-Dror 2002a,b), English debate and MacLaughlin Group data (Yaeger-Dror 2002a, b; Hedberg and Yaeger 2008), and for these CF English conversations on Table 5.7 where sentence final *NEG* actually favors prominence (.59>.49).

Another factor related to sentence position cannot be ignored. Early in the chapter, we noted that while the three groups of speakers are differentiated by their cultures, language may be a significant factor as well. We know that prominence is more likely to occur early in a sentence, and that there are syntactic techniques available in each of these languages (albeit infrequently used) for "raising" an important element toward the beginning of a sentence. We suggested that to the degree that purely linguistic considerations are significant, the Spanish speakers (with *NEG* early in the sentence) should be much more likely to have a high percentage of prominence than the American speakers, while the Japanese speakers (with *NEG* most consistently at the end of the sentence) will have the lowest percentage. This is clearly not the case. In conversation the Spanish speakers, who cannot "hide" a disagreement at the end of a sentence, or by reduce it with cliticization, are actually far more likely to reduce the negatives than speakers who have more syntactic freedom.

When we look at the actual results for the speakers from these different groups, we find we are lucky to have the comparison-corpus of Newscasts, which show that the *Cognitive Prominence Principle* is not irrelevant to the Latin American speaker: Spanish Newsbroadcasts (58%) English Newsbroadcasts (78%) both out-emphasize Japanese (39%). However, cross-linguistic differences in CallFriend data contradict both initial hypotheses: the Hispanic conversationalists are by far the least likely to emphasize remedial negatives (4%), while the Japanese (29%) and Americans (31%) are more likely to do so, despite our preconceptions about culture or our expectation that sentential position would influence the likelihood of prominence occurring in remedial turns. Clearly, neither a purely linguistic nor a purely cultural hypothesis is viable, and further analysis is called for, preferably with a larger CF sample which would permit all data to be run with "language" as one of the factor groups.

We see that the language with least opportunity to "lower" a cognitively critical negative to a less prominent position (i.e., Spanish) most consistently disallows the negative to be emphasized prosodically in actual interactions, while the language which permits the most syntactic freedom (Japanese) allows most prosodic freedom as well. It is also quite clear that the prosodic variation in all languages analyzed to date supports the *Cognitive Prominence Principle* in informative situations or sentence reading, but supports the *Social Agreement Principle* in interactive situations.

The analysis of prosodic variation appears to be a productive technique for determining distinctions among situations, both within and across cultures. The dissimilarities between cultures (even cultures that we would initially expect to be quite similar) are at least as great as the distinctions between different registers within a single culture. We had initially expected that confrontational registers—like political debates and readings of literary dialogue—would be quite different from polite social occasions—like the conversations-for-class-consumption between two friends. In fact, the polite registers used less pitch prominence than the confrontational registers in both cultures. However, the differences between the American and Spanish versions of News or CallFriend were as salient as the differences between the situations within each culture.

4.4 Footing

Table 5.7 shows that both English and Japanese conversationalists' supportive negatives (S) are significantly more likely to be prominent than those found in informative (I) or remedial (R) turns—with factor weights of .89>.47>.44 for Japanese Supportive>Informative>Remedial tokens, and .66>.50<.52, for English. This difference was not significant for the Spanish speakers, for whom there were so few prominent tokens that the difference between the footing of the different turns was not significant.[20]

Yaeger-Dror et al. (2002, 2003) and Takano (2008) both found that the reverse is the case for political debates—that is, the remedial negatives (R) are significantly more likely to be prominent than the Supportive ***NEG*** both in political debates (Yaeger-Dror et al. 2002, 2003; Takano 2008) and in political "discussion" programs (Hedberg and Yaeger-Dror 2008; Takano 2008). The Goldvarb results for debates are on Table 5.8, with Remedial tokens (R) favoring prominence more than either Informative (I) or Supportive (S) tokens.

Table 5.8 Factor Weights for **Footing** in Political Debates in English and Japanese

FACTOR GP	SIGNIFICANCE	SPANISH	JAPANESE	ENGLISH
cf. Table 5.5	footing	ns	(S) I<R	S<I<R
Debate	Factor Wts	—	- .42<.55	.22<.46<.56 (all)

4.5 Speaker characteristics

4.5.1 Male/Female

To our own amazement, Table 5.7 shows that women are significantly more likely to emphasize a remedial *NEG* than the men in both Spanish and English friendly conversations; the question is still open for Japanese conversations due to the confound with region, age, and sex discussed earlier. Surprisingly, if the hedges, self protective and self corrective tokens are included in the analysis, the significance is even more striking.

4.5.2 Region/ Class/ Ethnicity

Given the input from Tannen and others (Blum-Kulka et al 1989; DeFina, Schiffrin, and Bamberg 2003; Gumperz 1982; Kiesling and Paulston 2005; Liebscher and O'Cain 2009) who maintain that speakers of specific ethnic backgrounds or from specific regions are more (or less) likely to emphasize disagreements, and given the evidence that there are significant differences between the emphasis on *NEG* in different social groups (Goodwin et al. 2002; Jefferson 2002; Yaeger-Dror 2002a, b; Song 1994), one primary purpose in undertaking the present study was to determine relative *NEG* prominence of speakers from different regions.

While region is significant, the results for English are surprising: Californians and other Westerners (W) have the reputation of being laid back, nonconfrontational (Tannen 2005[1984]) and unlikely to disagree, while New Yorkers and Philadelphia Jews have a reputation for being adversarial as "a form of sociability" (Schiffrin 1984; Tannen 1981, 1984), but region and ethnicity are consistently significant in more complicated ways. When Northern and Southern calls are pooled, Table 5.7 shows that speakers from the West (W: .62) are most likely to emphasize remedial negatives, with Inland Northern speakers (nc: 61) coming in a close second. The Southerners from formerly rless areas (S: .51) and NY Jews (y: .50) were actually less likely to emphasize negatives; among the Northerners, other speakers from the Eastern Seaboard appear less likely to emphasize remedial negation (E: .47), while those from Appalachia (a: .43) are least likely to focus on disagreement.

Given the size of the corpus, doubtless, the factor weights would have been even stronger if 2 of the Eastern speakers had not been coded as Gay. Obviously, a larger sample of parallel conversations from these regional groups will allow a clearer picture to be drawn, but the pattern thus far certainly does not support a conjecture (based on the claims of Tannen (1981, 2005/1984) and Schiffrin [1984]) that New Yorkers, and Ashkenazi Jews will emphasize remedial negatives more than other English speakers.

On the other hand, the fact that in the Spanish CF corpus *Costeño* speakers are more likely to emphasize remedial negations than *Serrano* speakers fits the local stereotypes and our expectations based on Brown and Gillman (1960). Our preliminary ongoing comparison of Kanto and Kansai disagreements from an expanded Japanese corpus also supports the local stereotype—that Kansai speakers are actually more likely to emphasize remedial *NEG* than Kanto speakers (Yaeger-Dror et al. 2009). More within language comparisons are underway.

5. Conclusions

The sociophonetic studies which can be carried out today with downloadable software could not have been carried out at home even a few years ago. Although the tools for prosodic analysis are still being refined, the present study shows that they are already adequate for an elaborate analysis of variation in prosodic strategies. We have the necessary software to process not just the concordances and statistical results needed for studies of large text corpora, but even digitized sound for analysis of large speech corpora. The LDC sound archives provide a plethora of corpora for comparative analysis of speakers from different regions and different cultures. The primary focus of this investigation was on the use of negatives as carriers of information and as carriers of remedial disagreement between coparticipants in an interaction. Such a study would not have been feasible at all before the recent advances in technology which have made it possible to store large corpora and to carry out acoustic and statistical analysis of such large corpora. Only these advances have made it possible to supersede the analyses made in the 1980s based on smaller corpora, which often were composed of isolated sentences (O'Shaughnessy and Allen 1983) or newscasts (Hirschberg 1990).

As we saw, speech analysts and cognitive scientists have maintained that negatives carry critical information, and therefore should be pitch prominent, but their data have been based on "informative" registers or read sentences. Our evidence confirms that purely informative negatives used in informative situations (like the read newscasts studied by Hirscherg 1990, 1993) are likely to be prominent, and therefore support the *Cognitive Prominence Principle* while conversational data contradicts this claim; nor can adversarial interactive data (like political debates or Crossfire-genre programs) be construed as supporting this principle. Not surprisingly, adversarial interactions reveal that the *Social Agreement Principle* is likely to be inverted in this type of genre rather than merely neutralized.

Our results do not support the hypothesis that a language's default position for simple *NEG* has an influence on prosodic strategies (much less that it results from such strategies), but it does support a tentative conclusion that speakers from specific ethnic or regional backgrounds differ significantly from each other within each of the societies studied.

6. Where do we go from here?

The present study was initiated because the data from read sentences (so commonly used in phonetic analysis) differ radically from what was patently obvious from analysis of conversational interaction. Even today, many of those who create industrial applications for speech assume that reading style differs from, say, human-computer interaction or conversations between strangers in only minor ways. However, these researchers now need to project what people will say (and how they will say it) in an expanding array of different social situations. It is sociolinguists who have the expertise to collect and analyze data from an expanding pool of interactive settings in order to isolate the relevant variables for future analyses of speech.

6.1 Incorporating the social into sociophonetics

The issue of social situation is of particular interest in sociophonetic analysis of prosodic variation, particularly when, as in this case, the different societies are purported to have radically different ways of viewing the task being accomplished. Preliminary evidence has shown that native speakers of different languages do not have the same rules for emphasis on negation. One conclusion of Yaeger-Dror (2002) is that French speakers are perceived as confrontational by Americans partly because they do not reduce the prominence on negatives in informative turns, but only in remedial turns, while, as we see here, Americans reduce *NEG* in informative turns as well, if the social occasion itself is supportive. On the other hand, the French were much more sparing of prominence in political debate than the Americans. In the present instance, we find that Japanese and Spanish speakers are even more strongly influenced by the social setting than Americans.

Even in informative footing turns in friendly phone calls, the Spanish speakers almost never use prominence on the negative, although newscasters use prominence more than half the time. Japanese speakers are much more carefully attuned to the situational footing than either the US or Latin American speakers and vary prominence with the footing much more radically.

Obviously, many opportunities for misunderstanding arise in intercultural communication and a more nuanced approach to foreign language teaching would doubtless have an effect not only on classroom presentation but on cross-cultural communication in general. It is clear that careful analysis of negation in different cultures will have an impact on language teaching, on how well people from different cultures communicate in the real world, and on how computer systems interpret speech, as well as on linguistic theory.

These studies will be useful not just for our own theoretical research, but for the applied fields of automatic speech recognition and synthesis, as well as for the pedagogy of foreign languages so that learners will sound more like actual conversationalists, and less like classroom drones.

6.2 Socio-theoretical ramifications

Coupland (2001) isolates two types of register variation. One he refers to as "dialect style" and the other as "ways of speaking." He hypothesized that there is a clear distinction between those variables which are linguistic ("dialect style") and those which are influenced by cultural rules for interaction ("ways of speaking"). The use of negation is relevant to both and both must be taken into consideration to permit an adequate analysis of negation strategies, although the present study has considered only the importance of "ways of speaking" to this variation.

Coupland also suggests that both "dialect style" and "ways of speaking" vary relative to three goals: instrumental, identity, and relational. Further study will be needed to substantiate claims that variation in negation strategies occurs relative to each of these three "goals."

Notes

1 This study was begun with NSF# sbs9809884, and the Spanish segment of the analysis was supported by a UA SBSRI Grant. Work on the political panels was facilitated by grants from the Kennedy Library and the White House Historical Foundation. None of the analysis of news broadcasts or CallFriend would have been possible without the assistance of Mark Liberman and Dave Graff of LDC

for their permission to make the files publicly available and to Brian MacWhinney for the subcontract awarded to our group for transcription. Thanks are also due to our conscientious transcribers Alan and Sara Beaudrie, Tatiana Cerene, Sarah Longstaff, and Tomoe Nakamura. Earlier versions of this chapter have been presented at the LSA, CLIC/LISO 2002, NWAV05 (Granadillo and Yaeger-Dror 2002a, 2002b, Di Paolo, Foulkes, and Yaeger-Dror 2005), as well as at invited talks, in the UK and Japan, as well as in the US, and we are most grateful for feedback received from attendees at those talks. We would especially like to acknowledge many interesting discussions with Atissa Banuazizi, Sharon Deckert, Marianna Di Paolo, Kathy Ferrara, Charles and Marjorie Goodwin, Kerry Green, Greg Guy, Nancy Hedberg, John Heritage, Gail Jefferson, Miriam Locher, John Paolillo, Patti Price, Manny Schegloff, Juan Sosa, and Tim Vance.

2 In this chapter, the unmarked reference to Spanish or English will assume that American dialects are under discussion.

3 For example, the following programs are available either as freeware (e.g,, Praat: Boersma and Weenik 2006; Akustyk: Plichta 2006) or for a fee (e.g., Pitchworks: Tehrani 2006; Wavesurfer: Sjölander and Beskow 2006).

4 Syrdal et al. 2001, Shattuck-Hufnagel, Veilleux, and Brugos 2005, Jun 2006, and Fagyal and Yaeger-Dror forthcoming: all include recent discussions of ToBI and its categorization of pitch accents for English.

5 Bilmes (1997) presents evidence that interruptions are also more overt in debates; see also Hayashi (1996).

6 "Remedial" (Goffman 1971) is the cover term preferred here.

7 While a few of the speakers from the deep south were from a nonacademic background, their results have not been tallied for the present analysis.

8 New England, Rhode Island, New Jersey, etc.

9 Two of these "Eastern" speakers were Gay, and their conversation differed from others in the CF set; later these two men were recoded "G."

10 We will also refer to Political debates (PD) discussed in Yaeger-Dror et al. 2002, 2003. Panel discussions (PP) discussed in Yaeger-Dror et al. 2003, and in Hedberg and Yaeger-Dror 2008. The LDC Switchboard corpus (SWB) is discussed in Yaeger-Dror et al. 2003, and CallHome (CH) in Banuazizi 2002.

11 These tiers are all saved in one Pitchworks file (Tehrani 2006), but the same effect is achieved with Praat (Boersma and Weenik 2006), where tiers are saved as separate files.

12 To permit comparison with Bolinger (1978) the coding scheme also permitted an analysis using L* as an application value, but the low number of tokens coded with L* or L*+H obviated the need for such an analysis.

13 Japanese is a pitch accent language. The tonal pattern of a word is predictable based on the location of its lexical accent and the number of moras involved, though there is a great deal of dialectal variation. See Venditti (2005) and Jun (2005) for a detailed discussion of Japanese prosodic patterns. As with the English and Spanish data, tokens of A or D were very rare, providing further evidence

that Bolinger's claim (that cross-linguistically, the primary prominence type for negatives would be equivalent to ToBI L*) is untenable in any corpus analyzed to date. As far as possible, the same criteria were used for Japanese as for the other two languages.

14 In Japanese, "End" signifies less than 5 morae from the end of a sentence, while "Other" signifies more than 5 morae from the end.

15 Note that the first *NEG* token is prominent despite occurring inside a dependent clause, while the second cedes prominence to the adjacent verb.

16. For example, in the English conversational corpus, contrary to expectations, if the preceding word emphasizes the force of the negation and is prominent, then the likelihood of a prominent *NEG* is greatly reduced (with a Goldvarb weighting of .26), whereas if the emphasis follows the *NEG* the Goldvarb weighting is (.63), and with focus on both sides (.61) *NEG* prominence is significantly more likely to occur than when there is no environmental prominence (.56), so only a preceding emphasis disfavors application of the rule, at least in English! This factor group is not included in the present discussion, but will be analyzed in a later publication.

17 If examples are cited without attribution, they are not found in the corpora. Those with attribution include data from CallFriend (CF . . .), from presidential debates (with the debater mentioned), from Switchboard (SWB), or CallHome (CH).

18 Some clearer examples of Supportive turns [but without *NEG*] are cited here from Bravo 2009: The original citation is in Spanish, and the translations appear on pp.772f.

(3) —original, p763:
B: lo que tampoco queremos es ir de maratón porque entonces-
A: no no claro!
B: We don't want to do a marathon either, cause, then-
> A: No, no, of course not.

(12) —original p767:
A: . . . porque yo tengo el cuerpo to' etropea'o, sí yo no voy mal encaminá!
B: tú tienes el cuerpo estropeado?
A: oy que no!
B: tú flipas!
A: so that's what I need! [laser surgery] Because my body is totally trashed!
B: YOUR body trashed?
A: you bet!
> B: you're out of your mind!

That is, a turn can be marked as "supportive" if it is agreeing with a preceding negative, or even if it is disagreeing with a negative self-assessment by the interlocutor, and is therefore supportive rather than remedial in intent.

19 As shown on Table 5.2, to test the assumptions of Tannen (1984) and Schiffrin (1984)—"region" encompasses not just the dialect or cultural region, but ethnicity.

20 Other situations had also been analyzed in previous English and Japanese corpus studies and the results are of interest for comparison: US political "discussion" programs (such as Crossfire, MacLaughlin Group) have even higher ***NEG*** prominence percentages than political debates which have been analyzed (Kennedy/Nixon, Bush/Carter, Bush/Clinton/Perot—see further discussion in Yaeger-Dror et al. 2003)—(78%>55%)—and both are significantly more likely to use prominent ***NEG*** in remedial turns than nonadversarial conversations (Yaeger-Dror et al. 2003, Hedberg and Yaeger-Dror 2008, Takano 2008). Face-to-face interactions are not less likely to use prominent ***NEG*** than telephone interactions in Japanese (33%~29%-Takano 2008), but in most English Face to Face conversations studied the there is less prominence (Yaeger-Dror 1985) (3%<31%), even in face to face group therapy sessions there's less prominence (Yaeger-Dror 1985) (13%<31%), phone conversations between strangers (such as the Switchboard corpus (Yaeger-Dror et al. 2003)—13%<31%) or with immediate family members (as in the Call-Home corpus analyzed by Banuazizi 2003—13%<31%); these are all significantly less likely to use prominent ***NEG*** than the CallFriend calls studied here (Yaeger-Dror et al. 2003; Banuazizi 2003), as shown in the following table.

Overall prominence percentages of ***NEG*** in different corpora of English analyzed to date. Note that the News tokens are all informative, but in conversation the percentages are for remedial tokens.

Corpus	%	Reference
Hirschberg's BUR News	97	Hirschberg 1990, 1993
LDC News	78	Present paper
Political Panel Discussions	78	Hedberg and Yaeger-Dror 2008
Presidential debates	49–65	Yaeger-Dror et al. 2003
Group therapy session	13.3	Yaeger-Dror 1985
SWB	13	Yaeger-Dror et al. 2003
CH	13	Banuazizi 2003
CF	31	Present paper
Face to Face	2.5	Yaeger-Dror 1985, 2002

21 Note again that all **Japanese** men were from the *Kanto* (eastern Japan) region, here marked "Tok" for Tokyo, and all women were from **Ho**kkaido (3) or the *Kansai* (Western Japan) region (1). The 8 **Spanish** women are divided evenly between ***Costeño*** and ***Serrano***, and the men were also almost evenly divided. Note that there were no Southern US English news readers, in our sample. Within the US North, the regions were roughly divided into West (=W), Inland North (=nc), East (=E), and Ashkenazy (=y), while Southern speakers, based on Feagin's work and the *ANAE*, are divided into those from formerly "rless" areas (=S) and those from fully "rful" areas (=A).

References

Agha, Asif and Stanton E. F. Wortham. 2005. Special issue: Discourse across speech events: Intertextuality and interdiscursivity in social life. *Journal of Linguistic Anthropology* 15.

Ahrens, Frank. 2004. Accent on higher TV ratings. *Washington Post*, A1.

Ambady, Nalini, Jan Koo, Fiona Lee, and Robert Rosenthal. 1996. Linguistic and nonlinguistic politeness in two cultures. *Journal of Personality and Social Psychology* 70: 996–1011.

Applefield, David. 1997. *Paris Free Voice*. April–May.

Arvaniti, Amalia. 2007. On the presence of final lowering in British and American English. In C. Gussenhoven and T. Riad (eds), *Tone and tunes, Vol. 2: Experimental studies in word and sentence prosody*. Berlin/New York: Mouton de Gruyter, 317–347.

Amalia Arvaniti and Gina Garding. 2007. Dialectal variation in the rising accents of American English. In J. Cole and J. Hualde (eds), *Laboratory phonology 9*. Berlin/New York: Mouton de Gruyter, 547–576.

Azuma, Junichi. 1992. Nihongo no inritsu taikei (Prosodic systems of Japanese). *Proceedings of International Symposium on Japanese Prosody*: 53–61.

Banuazizi, Atissa. 2003. Information status and pitch prominence: Variation in the prosodic realization of NOT-negation in American English, NWAVE 32: Philadelphia, October.

Beckman, Mary, Manuel Díaz-Campos, Julia McGory, and Terrell Morgan. 2002. Intonation across Spanish in the tones and break indices framework. *Probus* 14: 9–36. http://www.ling.ohio-state.edu/~mbeckman/Sp_ToBI/Sp_ToBI_Jul29.pdf (accessed February 5, 2010).

Beckman, Mary and Janet Pierrehumbert. 1986. Intonational structure in Japanese and English. *Phonology Yearbook* 3: 255–309.

Befu, Harumi. 1980. A Critique of the group model of Japanese society, *Social Analysis* 5/6: 29–43.

Benguerel. Andre-Pierre. 1970. *Some physiological aspects of stress in French*. Ann Arbor, MI: Phonetics Laboratory, University of Michigan.

Bilmes, Jack. 1997. Being interrupted. *Language in Society* 26: 507–531.

Blaauw, Eleonora. 1995. *On the perceptual classification of spontaneous and read speech*. Utrecht: Brill.

Blum-Kulka, Shoshana, Juliane House, and Gabriele Kasper (eds). 1989. *Cross-cultural pragmatics: Requests and apologies*. Norwood, NJ: Ablex.

Boersma, Paul, and David Weenink. 2006. Praat: Doing phonetics by computer (Version 4.4.30). http://www.praat.org/(accessed February 8, 2010).

Bolinger, Dwight. 1978. Intonation across languages. In J. Greenberg (ed.) *Universals of Language II*. Stanford, CA: Stanford University Press, 471–524.

Bravo, Diana. 2009. (Im)politeness in Spanish-speaking socio-cultural contexts. Special issue: *Pragmatics* 18 (4).

Brown, Penelope and Stephen Levinson. 1978. Universals of language usage: Politeness phenomena. In Esther Goody (ed.), *Questions and politeness*. Cambridge: Cambridge University Press, 56–289.

Brown, Roger and Albert Gilman. 1960. The pronouns of power and solidarity. In Thomas A. Sebeok (ed.), *Style in language*. Cambridge MA: MIT Press, 253–276.

Bunnell, H. Timothy and William Idsardi (eds). 1996. Proceedings of the International Conference on Spoken Language Processing, Philadelphia: University of Delaware and Alfred I. duPont Institute.

Canfield, D. Lincoln. 1963. *La pronunciación del español en América*, Bogotá: Instituto Caro y Cuervo.

Canfield, D. Lincoln. 1981. *Spanish pronunciation in the Americas*. Chicago: University of Chicago Press.

Carroll, Raymonde. 1988. *Cultural misunderstandings*. Chicago: University of Chicago Press.

Chu-Carroll, Jennifer and Nancy Green (eds). 1998. Applying machine learning to discourse processing. *Papers from the 1998 AAAI Spring Symposium*, Menlo Park, CA: AAAI Press.

Clayman, Steven. 2002. Disagreements and third parties: dilemmas of neutralism in panel news interviews. *Journal of Pragmatics* 34: 1385–1401.

Clayman, Steven and John Heritage. 2002. The *news interview: Journalists and public figures on air*. Cambridge: Cambridge University Press.

COLING-ACL (ed.). 1998. *Proceedings of the COLING-ACL Workshop on Discourse Relations and Discourse Markers*. Montreal: McGill University Press.

Couper-Kuhlen, Elizabeth. 1992. Contextualizing discourse: The prosody of interactive repair. In Peter Auer and Aldo Di Luzio (eds), *The contextualization of language*. Amsterdam: John Benjamins, 337–364.

Coupland, Nikolas. 2001. Language, situation, and the relational self. In Eckert and Rickford (eds), 185–210.

Coussé, Evie, Steven Gillis, Hanne Kloots, and Marc Swerts. 2004. The influence of the labeller's regional background on phonetic transcriptions: Implications for the evaluation of spoken language resources. *4th International Conference on Language Resources and Evaluation*: Lisbon.

Cutler, Ann, Delphine Dahan, and Wilma van Donselaar. 1997. Prosody in the comprehension of spoken language. *Language and Speech* 40: 141–201.

Dahan, Delphine and Jean-Marc Bernard. 1997. Interspeaker variability in emphatic accent production in French. *Language and Speech* 39 (4): 341–374.

Danieli, Morena, Juan Maria Garrido, Massimo Moneglia, Andrea Panizza, Silvia Quazza, and Marc Swerts. 2004. Evaluation of consensus on the annotation of prosodic breaks in the Romance corpus of spontaneous speech "C-ORAL-ROM." Paper presented at the 4th International Conference on Language Resources and Evaluation: Lisbon.

De Fina, Anna, Deborah Schiffrin, Michael Bamberg (eds). 2003. *Discourse and identity, Studies in Interactional Sociolinguistics* 23. Cambridge, UK: Cambridge University Press.

Di Cristo, Albert. 1998. Intonation in French. In Daniel Hirst and Albert Di Cristo (eds), *Intonation systems: A survey of 20 languages*. Cambridge: Cambridge University Press, 195–218.

Di Paolo, Marianna and Alice Faber. 1990. Phonation Differences and the phonetic content of the tense-lax contrast in Utah English. *Language Variation and Change* 2: 155–204.
DiPaolo, Marianna, Paul Foulkes, and Malcah Yaeger-Dror. 2005. Toward best practices in sociophonetics. NWAV, New York University.
DiPaolo, Marianna and Malcah Yaeger-Dror (eds). To appear. *Sociophonetics: A Student Guide.* New York: Routledge.
Eckert, Penelope and John Rickford (eds). 2001. *Style and sociolinguistic variation.* Cambridge: Cambridge University Press.
Englebretson, Robert (ed.). 2007. *Stancetaking in discourse: Subjectivity, evaluation, interaction.* Philadelphia: John Benjamins.
Estebas-Vilaplana, Eva. 2007. Sp_ToBI, 4 dialects. http://www2.ilch.uminho.pt/eventos/PaPI2007/Extended-Abstract-Sp-ToBI.PDF (accessed February 8, 2010.)
Face, Timothy. 2001. Focus and early peak alignment in Spanish intonation. *Probus* 13: 223–246.
Face, Timothy. 2002. Local intonational marking of Spanish contrastive focus. *Probus* 14: 71–92.
Fagyal, Zsuzsanna. 2004. Action des médias et interactions entre jeunes dans une banlieue ouvrière de Paris. *Cahier de Sociolinguistique* 9: 41–60.
Goffman, Erving. 1971. *Relations in public.* New York: Basic Books.
Goffman, Erving. 1981. *Forms of talk.* Oxford: Blackwell.
Goodwin, Charles and Majorie Goodwin. 1995. Interstitial argument. In Alan Grimshaw (ed.), *Conflict talk.* Cambridge: Cambridge University Press, 85–117.
Goodwin, Marjorie. 2006a. Participation, affect, and trajectory in family directive/response sequences. *Text and Talk* 26: 513–541.
Goodwin, Marjorie. 2006b. *The hidden life of girls: Games of stance, status, and exclusion.* Malden, MA: Blackwell.
Goodwin, Marjorie, Charles Goodwin, and Malcah Yaeger-Dror. 2002. Multi-modality in girls' game disputes. *Journal of Pragmatics* 34 (10–11): 1621–1649.
Grabe, Esther. 2002. Variation adds to prosodic typology. Paper presented at Aix-en-Provence, France, April 11–13. http://www.isca-speech.org/archive/sp2002 (accessed February 5, 2010).
Grabe, Ether, Brechtje Post, and Francis Nolan. 2002. Intonational variation in the British Isles: The IViE Corpus. Paper presented at Aix-en-Provence, France, April 11–13. http://www.isca-speech.org/archive/sp2002 (accessed February 5, 2010).
Grabe, Esther, Brechtje Post, Francis Nolan, and Kimberley Farrar. 2000. Pitch accent realization in four varieties of British English. *Journal of Phonetics* 28: 161–185.
Grabe, Esther, Burton Rosner, Jose Garcia Albea, and Xiaolin Zhou. 2003. Perception of English intonation by English, Spanish, and Chinese listeners. *Language and Speech* 46 (4): 375–401.
Granadillo, Tania and Malcah Yaeger-Dror. 2002a. If *negatives are critical, why aren't they prominent?*Los Angeles: CLIC/LISO.
Granadillo, Tania and Malcah Yaeger-Dror. 2002b. *Pitch prominence occurs on critical information-No!* San Francisco: Linguistic Society of America.

Grosz, Barbara and Candace Sidner. 1986. Attention, intentions, and the structure of discourse. *Computational Linguistics* 12: 175–204.

Gumperz, John. 1982. *Discourse strategies.* Cambridge: Cambridge University Press.

Hattori, Shiro. 1933. Akusen to hoogen (accents and dialects). *Kokugo Kagaku Kooza* Volume 7, No. 45. Tokyo: Meiji Shoin.

Hayashi, Takuo. 1996. Politeness in conflict management: A conversation analysis of dispreferred message from a cognitive perspective. *Journal of Pragmatics* 25 (2): 227–255.

Hedberg, Nancy and Juan M. Sosa. 2003. Pitch contours in negative sentences. Paper presented at the 15th International Congress of Phonetic Sciences, Barcelona.

Hedberg, Nancy and Malcah Yaeger-Dror. 2008. The effect of informational and interactive factors on the prosodic prominence of negation. Paper presented at the Linguistic Society of America, Chicago.

Heritage, John. 2002a. The limits of questioning negative interrogatives and hostile question content. *Journal of Pragmatics.* 34(10/11): 1427–1446.

Heritage, John. 2002b. Oh-prefaced responses to assessments: A method of modifying agreement/disagreement. In Cecilia Ford, Barbara Fox and Sandra A. Thompson (eds), *The language of turn and sequence.* Oxford: Oxford University Press, 196–224.

Hirschberg, Julia. 1993. Pitch accent in context: Predicting prominence from text. *Artificial Intelligence* 63: 305–340.

Hirschberg, Julia. 2000. A corpus-based Approach to the study of speaking style. In Horne (ed.), 335–350.

Hirschberg, Julia and Christine Nakatani. 1996. A prosodic analysis of discourse segments in direction giving monologues. Proceedings of the 34th Annual Meeting of the Association for Computational Linguistics: Santa Cruz, CA.

Hirst, Daniel and Albert Di Cristo (eds). 1998. *Intonation systems: A survey of twenty languages*, Cambridge: Cambridge University Press.

Hoare, Rachel. 2000. Linguistic competence and regional identity in Brittany: Attitudes and perceptions of identity. *Journal of Multilingual and Multicultural Development* 21: 324–346

Holtgraves, Thomas. 1997a. Yes, but. Positive politness in conversational arguments. *Journal of Language and Social Psychology* 16: 222–239.

Horne, Merle. 2000. *Prosody: Theory and experiment.* Dordrecht/Boston/London: Kluwer Academic.

Hutchby, Ian. 1996. *Confrontation talks: Arguments, asymmetries, and power on talk radio.* Mahwah, NJ: Lawrence Erlbaum Associates.

IEEE (ed.). 1997a. IEEE Workshop on Speech Recognition and Understanding. Santa Barbara, CA.

Ishida, Takeshi. 1984. Conflict and its accomodation: Omote-Ura and Uchi-Soto relations. In Ellis S. Krauss, Thomas P. Rohlen, and Patricia G. Steinhoff (eds), *Conflict in Japan.* Honolulu: University of Hawaii Press, 16–38.

Ishihara, T. (2003). A phonological effect on tonal alignment in Tokyo Japanese. Paper presented at the *Proceedings of the 15th International Congress of Phonetic Sciences*: Barcelona, 615–619.

Jacobs, Scott. 2002. Language and interpersonal communication. In Mark L. Knapp and John Daly (eds), *Handbook of interpersonal communication, Vol 3.* Thousand Oaks, CA: Sage, 213–239.

Jefferson, Gail. 2002. Is "no" an acknowledgment token? Comparing American and British uses of (+)/(-) tokens. *Journal of Pragmatics* 34 (10–11): 1345–1383.

Jun, Sun-Ah (ed.). 2005. *Prosodic typology: The phonology of intonation and phrasing.* Oxford: Oxford University Press.

Kakavá, Christina. 2002. Opposition in modern Greek discourse: Cultural and contextual constraints. *Journal of Pragmatics* 34 (10–11): 1537–1568.

Kato, Akiko. 2004. *Japanese speakers' use of not-negation.* Unpublished SLAT dissertation, University of Arizona.

Kaufmann, Anita. 2002. Negation and prosody in British English: A study based on the London-Lund Corpus. *Journal of Pragmatics* 34 (10–11): 1473–1494.

Kiesling, Scott F. and Christina Bratt Paulston (eds). 2005. Intercultural discourse and communication: The essential readings. Malden, MA: Blackwell.

Koori, Shiro. 1989a. Fookasu jitsugen ni okeru onsei to tsuyosa, jizoku jikan, F0 no yakuwari (Intensity, duration the role of F0 in focus). *Onsei Gengo* 3: 29–38.

Koori, Shiro. 1989b. Kyoochoo to intoneeshon (Emphasis and intonation). In M. Sugitou (ed.), *Kooza Nihongo to Nihongo Kyooiku, Vol. II.* Tokyo: Meiji Shoin, 316–342.

Krauss, Ellis S., Thomas P. Rohlen, and Patricia G. Steinhoff (eds). 1984. *Conflict in Japan.* Honolulu: University of Hawaii Press.

Kroskrity, Paul V. (ed.). 2000. *Regimes of language: Ideologies, polities, and identities.* Santa Fe, NM: School of American Research Press.

Kurzon, Dennis. 2001. The politeness of judges: American and English judicial behavior. *Journal of Pragmatics* 33: 61–85.

Labov, William. 1972. *Sociolinguistic patterns.* Philadelphia: University of Pennsylvania Press.

Labov, William and David Fanshel. 1977. *Therapeutic discourse: Psychotherapy as conversation.* New York: Academic Press.

Ladd, D. Robert. 2008. *Intonational phonology.* Cambridge: Cambridge University Press.

Ladd, D. Robert, Astrid Schepman, Laurence White, Louise May Quarmbya, and Rebekah Stackhouse. 2009. Structural and dialectal effects on pitch peak alignment in two varieties of British. *English Journal of Phonetics* 37: 145–161.

Lempert, Michael. 2009. On 'flip-flopping': Branded stance-taking in U.S. electoral politics. *Journal of Sociolinguistics* 13: 223–248.

Levin, Harry, Carole Schaffer, and Catherine Snow. 1982. The prosodic and paralinguistic features of reading and telling stories. *Language and Speech* 25: 43–54.

Liberman, Mark. 1992. Comments, IRCS Workshop on Prosody in Natural Speech.

Licari, Carmen and Stefania Stame. 1990. The Italian morphemes 'no' and 'niente' as conversational markers. *Acta Linguistica Hungarica* 38: 163–173.

Liebscher, Grit and Jennifer Dailey-O'Cain. 2009. Language attitudes in interaction. *Journal of Sociolinguistics* 13: 195–222.

Locher, Miriam A. 2004. *Power and politeness in action: Disagreements in oral communication*. Berlin/New York: Mouton de Gruyter.

Maynard, Douglass. 1989. How children start arguments. *Language in Society* 14: 1–29.

McLemore, Cynthia A. 1991. *The pragmatic interpretation of English intonation: Sorority speech*. PhD dissertation: The University of Texas at Austin.

Mendoza-Denton, Norma. 1999. Turn initial 'no': Collaborative opposition among Chicana adolescents. Paper presented at Pragma 99 Symposium on Disagreement: A Cross-Linguistic, Cross-Cultural Comparison: Tel Aviv.

Mennen, Ineke. 2007. Phonetic and phonological influences in non-native intonation: An overview for language teachers. In Jurgen Trouan and Ulrike Gut (eds), *Non-native prosody: Phonetic descriptions and teaching practice*. Berlin: Mouton de Gruyter, 53–76.

Mills, Sara. 2003. *Gender and politeness*. Cambridge: Cambridge University Press.

Mills, Sara. 2004. Class, gender and politeness. *Multilingua* 23: 171–190.

Morel, Mary-Annick. 1995. Valeur énonciative des variations de hauteur mélodique en français. *French Language Studies* 5: 189–202.

Navarro-Tomás, Tomás. 1944. *Manual de entonación española*. New York: Hispanic Institute.

Nevalainen, Terttu. 1992. Intonation and discourse type. *Text* 12 (3): 397–427.

Ochs, Elinor, Emanuel Schegloff, and Sandra Thompson (eds). 1996. *Interaction and grammar*. Cambridge: Cambridge University Press.

Okamoto, Shigeko. 1994. 'Gendered' speech styles and social identity among young Japanese women. In Mary Bucholtz, Laurel Sutton, Caitlin Hines (eds), *Cultural performances*. Berkeley, CA: Berkeley Women and Language Group, 569–581.

O'Rourke, Erin. 2005. *Intonation and language contact*. Unpublished PhD thesis. Champagne/Urbana: University of Illinois.

O'Shaughnessy, Douglas and Jon Allen. 1983. Linguistic modality effects on fundamental frequency. *Journal of the Accoustical Society of America* 74: 1155–1171.

Pierrehumbert, Janet and Mary Beckman. 1988. *Japanese tone structure*. Cambridge, MA: MIT Press.

Pike, Kenneth and Carol McKinney. 1996. Understanding misunderstandings as cross-cultural emic clash. In Kurt R. Jankowsky (ed.), The *mystery of cultural contacts: Historical reconstruction and text analysis: An emic approach*. Washington, DC: Georgetown University Press, 39–64.

Platt, Polly. 1998. *French or foe*. Paris: Distribooks.

Plichta, Bartłomiej. 2006. Akustyk: A free Praat plug-in for sociolinguists. http://bartus.org/akustyk/ (accessed February 9, 2010).

Sacks, Harvey (ed.). 1992. *Harvey Sacks' lectures on conversation*. Oxford: Blackwell.

Sagisaka, Yoshinori, Nick Campbell, and Noriko Higuchi (eds). 1997. *Computing prosody: Computational models for processing spontaneous speech*. New York: Springer.

Sankoff, David, Sali Tagliamonte, and Eric Smith. 2005. Goldvarb X: A variable rule application for Macintosh and Windows. http://individual.utoronto.ca/tagliamonte/Goldvarb/GV_index.htm (accessed February 6, 2010).

Schegloff, Emanuel, Gail Jefferson, and Harvey Sacks. 1977. The preference for self-correction in the organization of repair in conversation. *Language* 53: 361–382.
Schiffrin, Deborah. 1984. Jewish argument as sociability. *Language in Society* 13: 311–335.
Schilling-Estes, Natalie. 1998. Situated ethnicities: Constructing and reconstructing identity in the sociolinguistic interview. Paper presented at NWAVE 27: Athens, GA, October 1–4.
Scott, Suzanne. 2002. Linguistic feature variation within different types of disagreements: An empirical investigation. *Text* 22 (2): 301–328.
Shattuck-Hufnagel, S., N. Veilleux, and A. Brugos. 2005. The new ToBI homepage, and tutorial in ToBI. http://anita.simmons.edu/~tobi/ (accessed February 9, 2010).
Silverman, Kim, Mary Beckman, John Pitrelli, Mari Ostendorf, Colin Wightman, Patti Jo Price, Janet Pierrehumbert, and Julia Hirschberg. 1992. ToBI: A standard for labeling English prosody. Proceedings of the 1992 International Conference on Spoken Language Processing (ICSLP) II: Banff, CA, October 12–16.
Simon-Vandenbergen, Anne-Marie. 2000. The functions of I think in political discourse. *International Journal of American Linguistics* 10 (1): 41–63.
Sjölander, Kåre and Jonas Beskow. 2006. Wavesurfer download and user's manual. URL: http://www.speech.kth.se/wavesurfer/documentation.html (accessed February 7, 2010).
Song, Kyong-Sook. 1994. The dynamics of gender in Korean argumentative conversational discourse. In Mary Bucholtz, Laurel Sutton, and Caitlin Hines (eds), *Cultural performances*. Berkeley, CA: Berkeley Women and Language Group, 651–667.
Sosa, Juan. 1999. *La entonación del español*, Madrid: Cátedra.
Sugitou, Miyoko. 1982. Oosaka hoogen ni okeru kyoochoo no onkyooteki tokuchoo (Acoustic properties of emphasis in the Osaka dialect). *Shooin Kokubungaku*, 19: 55–63.
Sugitou, Miyoko, Ryouichi Sato, Shinji Sanada, Masanobu Kato, and Shuichi Itabashi (eds). 1997. *Shohougen no Akusento to Intoneeshon* (Accents and intonation of Japanese regional dialects). Tokyo: Sansei-do.
Suleiman, Camelia, Daniel O'Connell, and Sabine Kowal. 2002. 'If you and I, if we, in this later day, lost that sacred fire.' Perspective in political interviews. *Journal of Psycholinguistic Research* 31 (3): 269–287.
Swerts, Marc and Carel van Wijk. 2005. Prosodic, lexico-syntactic and regional influences on word order in Dutch verbal endgroups. *Journal of Phonetics* 33 (2): 243–262.
Syrdal, Ann, Julia Hirschberg, Julie T. McGory, and Mary Beckman. 2001. Automatic ToBI prediction and alignment to speed manual labeling of prosody. *Speech Communication* 33 (1–2): 135–151.
Takano, Shoji. 2002. A variationist study of prosodic focus in naturally occurring interactions: the case of the negative 'nai' in Hokkaido Japanese. *Journal of the Phonetic Society of Japan* 6 (3): 25–47.

Takano, Shoji. 2008. Variation in prosodic focus of the Japanese negative "nai": Issues of language specificity, interactive style and register. In Kimberly Jones and Tsuyishi Ono (eds), *Style shifting in Japanese.* Amsterdam/Philadelphia: John Benjamins, 285–327

Tannen, Deborah. 1981. New York Jewish conversational style. *International Journal of the Sociology of Language* 30: 133–149.

Tannen, Deborah. 2005 [1984]. *Conversational style: Analyzing talk among friends.* New York: Oxford University Press.

Tehrani, Henry. 2006. Documentation for Pitchworks. http://www.sciconrd.com/pitchworks.html (accessed February 9, 2010).

Thomas, Erik and Philip M. Carter. 2006. Prosodic Rhythm and African American English. *English World-Wide* 27 (3): 331–355.

Thomas, Erik and Jeffrey Reaser. 2004. Delimiting perceptual cues used for the ethnic labeling of African American and European American voices. *Journal of Sociolinguistics* 8 (1): 54–87.

Ting-Toomey, Stella, Ge Gao, Paula Trubisky, Zhizhong Yang, Hak Soo Kim, Sung-Ling Lin, and Tsukasa Nishida. 1991. Culture, face maintenance and styles of handling interpersonal conflict: A study in 5 cultures. *International Journal of Conflict Management* 2: 275–296.

Tottie, Gunnel. 1991. *Negation in English speech and writing.* San Diego: Academic.

Tucker, Benjamin V. 2007. *Spoken word recognition of the American English flap.* Unpublished PhD Thesis. Tuscon: University of Arizona.

Tucker, Benjamin V. and Natasha Warner. 2007. Inhibition of processing due to reduction of the American English Flap. Proceedings of ICPhS XVI: Saarbrucken, August 6–10.

Venditti, Jennifer. 2005. The J ToBI model of Japanese intonation. In Sun Ah Jun (ed.), *Prosodic typology: The phonology of intonation and phrasing.* Oxford: Oxford University Press, 172–200.

Watt, Dominik, Anne Fabricius, and Tyler Kendall. To appear. Vowel normalization. In Marianna Di Paolo and Malcah Yaeger-Dror (eds). Best practices in sociophonetics. New York: Routledge.

Watts, Richard J. 2003. *Politeness.* Cambridge: Cambridge University Press.

Wierzbicka, Anna. 1994. Cultural scripts: A new approach to the study of cross-cultural communication. In Martin Pütz (ed.), *Language contact and language conflict.* Amsterdam: John Benjamins, 69–87.

Yaeger, Malcah. 1974. Speaking style: Some phonetic realizations and their significance. *Pennsylvania Working Papers on Linguistic Change and Variation* I: 1–60.

Yaeger, Malcah. 1979. *Context determined variation in Montreal French vowels.* PhD Dissertation, Philadelphia: University of Pennsylvania.

Yaeger-Dror, Malcah. 1985. Intonational prominence on negatives in English. *Language and Speech* 28: 197–230.

Yaeger-Dror, Malcah. 1996. Intonation and register variation. In Jennifer Arnold, Renée Blake, Brad Davidson, Scott Schwenter, and Julie Solomon (eds), *Sociolinguistic variation: Data, theory, and analysis*. Stanford: CSLI, 243–260.

Yaeger-Dror, Malcah. 2001. Primitives for the analysis of register. In Penelope Eckert and John Rickford (eds), *Style and sociolinguistic variation*. Cambridge: Cambridge University Press, 170–185.

Yaeger-Dror, Malcah. 2002a. Register and prosodic variation, a cross language comparison. *Journal of Pragmatics* 34: 1495–1536.

Yaeger-Dror, Malcah (ed.). 2002b. Special issue on Disagreement and negation. *Journal of Pragmatics* 34: 10–11.

Yaeger-Dror, Malcah and Zsuzsanna Fagyal. To appear. Chapter 10. Analyzing prosody. In Di Paolo and Yaeger-Dror (eds).

Yaeger-Dror, Malcah, Lauren Hall-Lew, and Sharon Deckert. 2002. It's not, or isn't it? Using large corpora to determine the influences on contraction strategies. *Language Variation and Change* 14: 79–118.

Yaeger-Dror, Malcah, Lauren Hall-Lew, and Sharon Deckert. 2003. Situational variation in prosodic strategies. In Charles F. Meyers and Pepi Leistyna (eds), *Corpus analysis: Language structure and language use*. Amsterdam: Rodopi.

Yaeger-Dror, Malcah, Shoji Takano, Carol Rinnert, and Ian Willey. 2009. Comparison of Japanese and American Predisagreements. Poster presented at International Pragmatics Association Congress: Melbourne, June.

Yamada, Haru. 1992. *American and Japanese business discourse: A comparison of interactional styles*. Norwood, NJ: Ablex.

Yamada, Haru. 2002. *Different games, different rules: Why Americans and Japanese misunderstand each other*. Oxford: Oxford University Press.

Chapter 6

An Emerging Gender Difference in Japanese Vowel Devoicing

Terumi Imai, Wittenberg University

1. Introduction

The Japanese high vowels /i/ and /u/ (the latter phonetically [ɯ]) tend to be devoiced when they occur between voiceless consonants or after a voiceless consonant and before a pause (Sakuma 1929; Martin 1952; Han 1962; McCawley 1968; Kawakami 1977; Nihon Housou Kyoukai (NHK) 1985; Vance 1987; Maekawa 1983, 1988; Sugito 1988; Kondo 1994, 1995; Nagano-Madsen 1994, 1995; Tsuchida 1997; Yuen 1997; Varden 1999). This phenomenon has been studied extensively in terms of its mechanism and phonetic environments in the field of phonetics (Sakuma 1929; Martin 1952; Han 1962; Sawashima 1971; Sawashima and Niimi 1974; Kawakami 1977; Yoshioka 1981; Yoshioka, Löfqvist, and Hirose 1982; Maekawa 1983; Beckman and Shoji 1984; Nihon Housou Kyoukai (NHK) 1985; Sugito 1988; Jun and Beckman 1993; Kondo 1994, 1995; Nagano-Madsen 1994, 1995; Tsuchida 1997), but this study investigates the social aspects of vowel devoicing in Tokyo Japanese, particularly the effects of gender and age and how these factors influence the rate of vowel devoicing.

I will give an overview of Japanese vowel devoicing and the factors that play a major role in this phenomenon in Section 2. Next, the data collection and analysis techniques are discussed in Section 3. Section 4 summarizes the results of the statistical analyses, and Section 5 concludes the chapter with future research suggestions.

2. Japanese vowel devoicing

2.1 What is vowel devoicing?

Although the most unmarked, or natural, realization of a vowel is a voiced vowel, when a high vowel occurs between voiceless consonants, it tends to be devoiced in Japanese as in [ki̥ta] 'north' and [tsu̥tʃi] 'soil.' There are different approaches to this phenomenon, but most phoneticians agree that it occurs because of the overlap of the glottal gestures: the glottis is open for the preceding voiceless consonant and the following consonant, but in order to produce a voiced vowel, the glottis must be closed. This movement of the glottis—open, closed, open again—requires more effort than keeping it open and therefore causes the devoicing of the vowel. Thus, a devoiced vowel is a vowel produced while the glottis is open. A completely devoiced vowel does not show a periodic wave, has no clear formants in a spectrogram, shows a drop in intensity and no pitch track, and there is no audible voicing, although there is mora preservation.

Here are some examples: Figures 6.1 and 6.2 show two tokens of a same word, /see+katsu#hi/ 'living expenses,' produced by different speakers. Figure 6.1 shows the token with a voiced vowel and Figure 6.2 with a devoiced vowel. The upper window shows the sound wave and the lower window shows the spectrogram. The thick black dotted line in the middle of the spectrogram shows the pitch track, and the thin white line above the pitch track shows the intensity. In Figure 6.1, the periodic wave for /u/ in the third syllable is rather small compared to others, but we can still see the clear formants for the vowel /u/. There is a clear pitch track, which remains stable until it reaches the final syllable. Intensity also rises where the vowel /u/ is produced. Thus, we can say all the four vowels in this word are voiced.

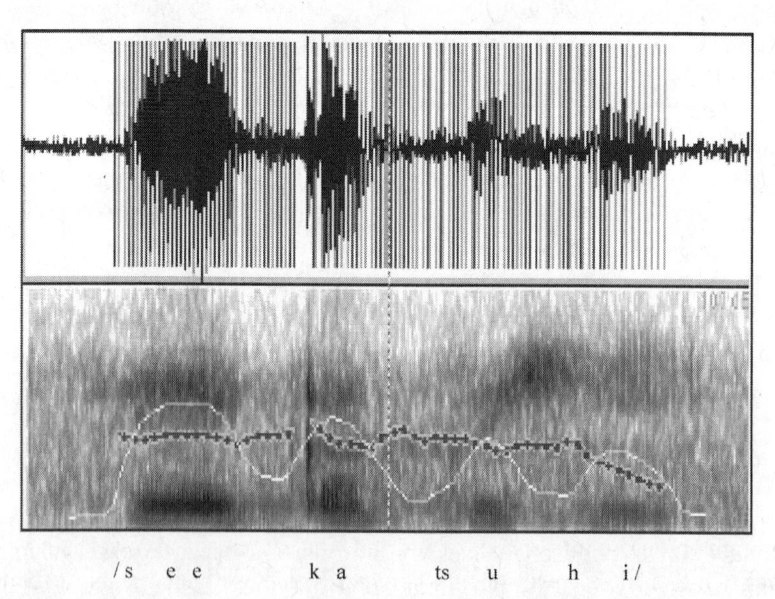

Figure 6.1 /see+katsu#hi/ ('living expenses') with a voiced vowel.

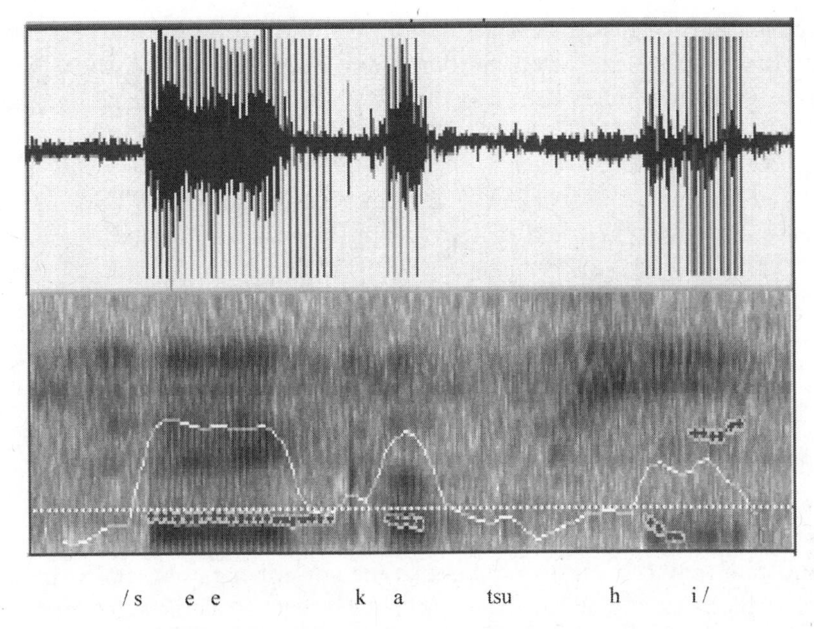

Figure 6.2 /see+katsu#hi/ ('living expenses') with a devoiced vowel.

Figure 6.2 shows a devoiced token of the same word. There are no formants, periodic wave peak, pitch track, nor intensity movement where the vowel /u/ should be. There is a small intensity rise where /ts/ is released, but nothing else. This is the devoiced /u/.

There were cases in which it is hard to determine voicing. In this study, if three of the preceding criteria were met, the vowel was coded as devoiced. For example, if there were no periodic wave, no clear formants, no intensity (and no audible voicing), but there was a pitch track in the vowel's position, I nevertheless regarded the vowel as devoiced.

2.2 Factors that affect vowel devoicing

There are many factors that affect the likelihood of devoicing; linguistic factors include the preceding and following consonant identity, pitch accent of the target vowel, the existence of potentially devoiceable vowels before and/or after the target vowel, and the morpheme boundary type. The preceding and following consonant identity is important because vowel devoicing occurs between voiceless consonants, and previous studies show that there is a difference in their effect on vowel devoicing depending on the type of consonant—that is, if it is a stop, a fricative, or an affricate (Han 1962; Kawakami 1977; Maekawa 1983; Nagano-Madsen 1995; Kondo 1997; Yuen 1997). Previous studies also report that the devoicing of accented vowels is avoided (Sakuma 1929; Han 1962; Sakurai 1985; Maekawa 1988; Kondo 1993; Sugito and Hirose 1988; Nagano-Madsen 1995), that consecutive devoicing is avoided (Sakuma 1929; Martin 1952; Han 1962; Kawakami 1977; Maekawa 1988; Tsuchida 1997), and that devoicing is avoided at some morpheme boundaries (Sakurai 1985; Vance 1987, 1992; Kondo 1997; Tsuchida 1997). I will not report on the linguistic factors here; they are reported along with social factors highlighted here in Imai (2004).

Social factors used in this study include age, sex, and speech style. There have not been many sociolinguistic studies done on Japanese vowel devoicing, and there is only one study that I know of that included sex and speech style. Yuen (1997) found that as degree of formality increases, speech rate decreases, vowel length increases, and, therefore, devoicing decreases. This correlation of voicing (or non-devoicing), speech rates, and vowel length was significant ($p<0.05$). He also found that the vowel length of males is indeed shorter than that of females, that males have faster speech rates than females, that males devoice more than females, and that women devoiced much less in the most formal style than men did.

Age differences in vowel devoicing have been assumed, particularly in association with accent; older generations are said not to devoice accented vowels while younger generations do (NHK 1985; Sakurai 1985; Tsuchida 1997), but no sources are cited in those statements, and there is no systematic and extensive study that focuses on age differences. There has been no study investigating age differences in vowel devoicing among Tokyo dialect speakers.

The results of Yuen's study seem to suggest that Japanese vowel devoicing is a nonstandard feature because it is known that nonstandard features are more likely to occur in more casual styles, and women are reported, in many sociolinguistic studies, to use more standard features than men, and to use more prestigious, or standard forms, in more formal styles than men. Vowel devoicing, however, is considered a standard feature of the Tokyo dialect, itself considered to be a standard dialect, according to the general perception of Japanese speakers and to prescriptive authority, such as dictionaries. We often find comments by Japanese linguists linking the "crispness" and "briskness" of Tokyo (standard) dialect to vowel devoicing and the "softness" and "mildness" of Kansai dialect to a lack of vowel devoicing. In order to understand this apparent contradiction between the perceived standard variety (Tokyo) and the use of one feature of it (devoicing) by atypical speakers of the standard (males) and in atypical situations (informal), it is necessary to look more closely at the social factors that might affect Japanese vowel devoicing, including age, sex, and speech style.

3. Data

3.1 Data collection

The data used in this study came from 21 men and 21 women, all of whom grew up in the Tokyo area. Most of them were also born there and have at least one parent who grew up in Tokyo. There are three age groups: 15 were in the younger age group, 14 were in the middle group, and 13 respondents made up the older group. Originally, I also included three social classes: 14 participants were considered working class, 16 were classified as lower middle class, and 12 respondents made up the upper middle class group. However, this distinction did not show a statistical significance.

Data were collected through sociolinguistic interviews, which were recorded on tape. An interview consisted of three stages. First, I asked the respondent some demographic questions—where they were born and raised, where their parents were born and raised, their occupation, their parents' occupation, where they live now, what they like to do for leisure, and so on. Then they were asked to read a word list and a reading passage. The word list consisted of 90 words, phrases, or short sentences, containing all the possible combinations of the preceding and following voiceless consonants, including a pause, for both high vowels. The reading passage used as many words from the word list as possible without becoming too long (1.5 pages). The entire interview session was recorded, and they ranged from 20 minutes to 2.5 hours in length.

3.2 Data analysis

The recorded data were transferred and digitized using the sound analysis program Praat in order to determine the voicing of the vowels. After the acoustic analysis was done, all the necessary data was input in an Excel spreadsheet, and a statistical analysis was done using Goldvarb (a logistic regression program) to find out significant factors and the relative significance of the values within each factor. Goldvarb is capable of dealing with the very small numbers in some cells that may arise in the study of conversational data. The total number of tokens (vowels) used for the statistical analyses is over 30,000.

4. Results

4.1 Speech style

The results of the statistical analyses show that speech style is a significant factor in Japanese vowel devoicing. Respondents devoiced most in *conversation*, and more in *reading passage* than in *word list*. In other words, the more casual the speech style, the more likely devoicing occurs. This confirms the results obtained in Yuen 1997. Table 6.1 and Table 6.2 show the results of a Goldvarb run for speech style for the vowels /i/ and /u/ respectively.

Table 6.1 Speech Style for /i/—Goldvarb

	Speech Style	Weight	Number (devoiced/total)
1	Conversation	0.816	1585/1785
2	Reading passage	0.486	1097/1732
3	Word list	0.335	1799/3740

Table 6.2 Speech Style for /u/—Goldvarb

	Speech Style	Weight	Number (devoiced/total)
1	Conversation	0.742	1585/1785
2	Reading passage	0.590	1097/1732
3	Word list	0.330	1799/3740

In Table 6.1, only conversational style promotes the devoicing of /i/, and the word list and reading passage styles demote it, even though devoicing is more likely to occur in reading passages than in word lists. In Table 6.2, both the conversational and reading passage styles are promoters for the devoicing of /u/, and only the word list style demotes it. However, the general order is the same: the more casual the style, the more likely devoicing occurs.

4.2 Age and sex

One surprising result of the current study is the interaction between age and sex. When the two categories were cross-tabulated, there was a significant difference between young males and young females, but there was little sex difference between other age groups. Younger males devoice most, younger females least, and the rest fall in between, as shown in Figure 6.3 for /i/ and Figure 6.4 for /u/.

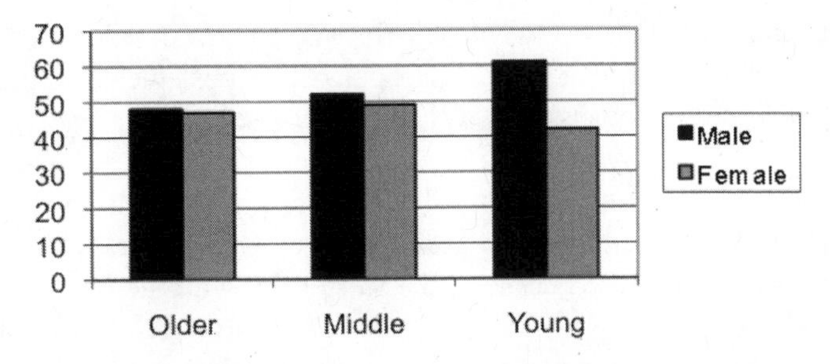

Figure 6.3 Age and sex for /i/.

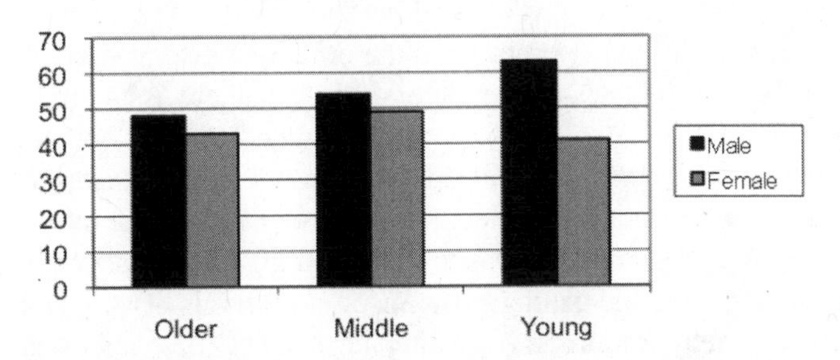

Figure 6.4 Age and sex for /u/.

Both figures show a similar pattern, with the sex differences within the same age group slightly larger for /u/.

5. Discussion

These results suggest that vowel devoicing is a nonstandard feature because, as mentioned earlier, young males tend to be attracted to the covert prestige associated with nonstandard features, and nonstandard features usually occur in more casual speech style. Moreover, younger females tend to be attracted to the overt prestige associated with standard features, and standard features usually occur in more formal speech styles. This may explain why younger males devoice most and younger females devoice least. However, there are studies that show native speakers' perception of vowel devoicing as standard. For example, Maekawa (1988) states that if the final vowel in the polite copula /desu/ in sentence-final position is not devoiced, it sounds "strange." He also states that, in a consecutive devoicing environment, such as /ʃukufuku/, "celebration," where all the vowels are potentially devoiced, only certain patterns are actually used out of the possible combinations of devoiced and voiced vowels, and if the speaker does not use one of the possible patterns, that also sounds strange. Another example is Sakuma's (1929) comment that if someone does not devoice the high vowels in a devoicing environment, they sound like they are from somewhere in the western part of Japan, implying that those people in the western part are nonstandard speakers, "hillbillies," or people who don't know how to speak "properly." Furthermore, the *Japanese Pronunciation and Accent Dictionary* specifies which vowels should be devoiced in standard Japanese. These facts point towards the standard status of vowel devoicing.

How do we account for this? One thing that is clear is that younger speakers are doing something different from the other age groups. No matter what the reason for this pattern is, the data show that there is language change (or at least age-grading) going on among younger speakers. Moreover, there appears to be a new meaning attached to vowel devoicing; it is used to signal a gender difference among younger speakers, not degree of standardness.

I'd like to suggest a possible reason for this language change or age-grading. Japanese has considerable gender differences at all levels of language—use of honorifics, self-reference terms, voice pitch level, and so on—and is particularly well-known for sentence-final particle differences. However, Okamoto (1995) shows that younger female speakers actually use more masculine sentence-final forms than feminine ones. Also, it has been reported that younger females are using more and more "male language." This could suggest that linguistic gender differences are lessening among younger speakers. If this is the case and if younger male and female speech are becoming similar in terms of some linguistic features, such as sentence-final particles and vocabulary, it is possible to hypothesize that younger people may try to express gender differences in another form. This could be manifested in their use of vowel devoicing—less devoicing is feminine, and more devoicing is masculine, with no regard, except perhaps historically, to its standard or nonstandard status. Perhaps because of the association of vowel devoicing with more casual speech style, triggering more devoicing in young males' speech, the association has arisen. Once extensive use of devoicing among young males has established, young females may have felt the need to distinguish themselves from males, resulting in less devoicing. This differentiation does not extend to older age groups because they still maintain the traditional gender differences in other areas.

There have been many recent studies done on Japanese women's language (Shibamoto 1985; Haig 1990; Ide and McGloin 1990; McGloin 1990; Okamoto 1995; Ide 1997; Ide and Yoshida 1999; Okamoto and Shibamoto 2004). Okamoto and Shibamoto (2004) suggest that the relationship of language and gender is complex, not direct and fixed, and that there are many factors to be considered when we talk about women's language: sexual orientation, social and contextual diversity, and the speaker's beliefs about language use. So, young females' increased use of men's language may not mean women's language is disappearing. However, it is still true that there is a new meaning attached to vowel devoicing among younger speakers as a group, as the results of this study show.

If we take the hypothesis suggested here seriously, our next question is, "How much devoicing is standard and how much is nonstandard?" If vowel devoicing is a standard feature and young males are devoicing more and young females devoicing less, we might think the standard amount of devoicing is somewhere in the middle, approximately where the rest of the groups are. If standard speakers feel (subconsciously, of course) that Kansai (western Japan) speakers are not devoicing enough, are the female speakers taking a risk of sounding like Kansai speakers? Probably not. Young females are attracted to standard speech, and those young females sound very standard to the ears of standard speakers. They are within the territory of standard devoicing. One might argue that there are other features that distinguish Tokyo speakers from Kansai speakers, such as pitch accent, although vowel devoicing is still a good parameter (cf. Morris 2003). The questions here is, then, how much devoicing do Kansai speakers have compared to Tokyo speakers? Are the environments in which devoicing occurs different in the two major dialects of Japanese? The answer to these questions has to wait until another production study on Kansai speakers is done.

In conclusion, a detailed acoustic study of Japanese vowel devoicing revealed the emerging gender difference among younger speakers of the Tokyo dialect. If we had not considered this factor, Japanese women's language may have appeared to be on the way to merging with men's language, but that is not the case at the phonetic level, at least in terms of the use of vowel devoicing. A study of Kansai speakers' vowel devoicing rates is needed to determine the standard amount of vowel devoicing in Japanese. Moreover, more systematic study is needed of younger speakers' speech on multiple levels (lexicon, phonetics, morphology, syntax, etc.) to reveal the social correlates of current language change in Tokyo Japanese.

References

Beckman, Mary and Atsuko Shoji. 1984. Spectral and perceptual evidence for CV coarticulation in devoiced /si/ and /syu/ in Japanese. *Phonetica* 41: 61–71.

Haig, John H. 1990. A phonological difference in male-female speech among teenagers in Nagoya. In Ide and McGloin (eds), 5–22.

Han, Mieko Shimizu. 1962. Unvoicing of vowels in Japanese. *Study of Sounds* 10: 81–100.
Ide, Sachiko (ed.). 1997. *Joseigo no sekai.* Tokyo: Meiji Shoin.
Ide, Sachiko and Naomi Hanaoka McGloin (eds). 1990. *Aspects of Japanese women's language.* Tokyo: Kuroshio.
Ide, Sachiko and Megumi Yoshida. 1999. Sociolinguistics: Honorifics and gender differences. In Natsuko Tsujimura (ed.), *The handbook of Japanese linguistics.* Malden, MA: Blackwell, 444–480.
Imai, Terumi. 2004. *Vowel devoicing in Tokyo Japanese: A variationist approach.* Doctoral dissertation, East Lansing: Michigan State University.
Jun, Sun-Ah and Mary E. Beckman. 1993. A gestural-overlap analysis of vowel devoicing in Japanese and Korean. Paper presented at the Annual Meeting of the Linguistic Society of America: Los Angeles.
Kawakami, Shin. 1977. *Nihongo onsei gaisetsu.* Tokyo: Oofuusha.
Kondo, Mariko. 1993. The effect of blocking factors and constraints on consecutive vowel devoicing in Standard Japanese. Poster presented at LabPhon 4: Oxford, August 11–14.
Kondo, Mariko. 1994. Mechanisms of vowel devoicing in Japanese. *Proceedings of the 1994 International Conference on Spoken Language Processing*, Vol. 2, 479–482. Yokohama, September.
Kondo, Mariko. 1995. Temporal adjustment of devoiced morae in Japanese. *Proceedings of the 13th International Congress of Phonetic Sciences*, Vol. 3, 61–64. Stockholm, August 13–19.
Kondo, Mariko. 1997. *Mechanisms of vowel devoicing in Japanese.* Doctoral dissertation, University of Edinburgh.
Maekawa, Kikuo. 1983. Kyotsugo ni okeru Boin no Museika no Kakuritsu ni tsuite. [Probabilities for the occurrence of vowel devoicing in Common Japanese]. *Gengo no Sekai* 1–2: 69–81.
Maekawa, Kikuo. 1988. Boin no museika. [Vowel devoicing]. In Miyoko Sugito (ed.), *Koza Nihongo to Nihongo Kyoiku*, Vol.2, Tokyo: Meiji Shoin, 135–153.
Martin, Samuel. 1952. Morphophonemics of standard colloquial Japanese. Supplement to *Language*: *Journal of the Linguistic Society of America* 28 (8), pt. 2. Language dissertations, no. 47. Baltimore: Linguistic Society of America.
McCawley, James. 1968. *The phonological component of a grammar of Japanese.* The Hague: Mouton.
McGloin, Naomi Hanaoka. 1990. Sex differences and sentence-final particles. In Ide and McGloin (eds), 23–41.
Morris, Midori Yonezawa. 2003. *Perception of devoicing variation and the judgment of speakers' region in Japanese.* Doctoral dissertation, East Lansing: Michigan State University.
Nagano-Madsen, Y. 1994. Vowel devoicing rates in Japanese from a sentence corpus. Lund University, Department of Linguistics Working Papers 42a: 117–127.

Nagano-Madsen, Y. 1995. Effect of accent and segmental contexts on the realization of vowel devoicing in Japanese. *Proceedings of the 13th International Congress of Phonetic Sciences*, Vol. 3, 564–567. Stockholm, August 13–19.

Nihon Housou Kyoukai (NHK; ed.) 1985. *Nihongo hatsuon akusento jiten* [Japanese Pronunciation and Accent Dictionary]. Tokyo: Nihon Hoosoo Shuppan Kyookai.

Okamoto, Shigeko. 1995. "Tasteless" Japanese: Less "Feminine" speech among young Japanese women. In Kira Hall and Mary Bucholtz (eds), *Gender articulated: Language and the socially constructed self.* New York: Routledge, 297–325.

Okamoto, Shigeko and Janet S. Shibamoto Smith (eds). 2004. *Japanese language, gender, and ideology: Cultural models and real people.* New York: Oxford University Press.

Sakuma, Kanae. 1929. *Nihon onseigaku.* [Japanese phonology] Tokyo: Kyoubunsha.

Sakurai, S. 1985. Kyoutsuugo-no Hatsuon-de Chuui Subeki Kotogara [On the pronunciation of Standard Japanese]. In Nihon Hoosoo Kyookai (ed.), *Nihongo Hatsuon Akusento Jiten* [Japanese Pronunciation and Accent Dictionary]. Tokyo: Nihon Hoosoo Shuppan Kyookai, 128–134.

Sawashima, Masayuki. 1971. Devoicing of vowels. *Annual Bulletins* 5, Research Institute of Logopedics and Phoniatrics, University of Tokyo.

Sawashima, Masayuki and S. Niimi. 1974. Laryngeal conditions in articulations of Japanese voiceless consonants. *Annual Bulletin of the Research Institute of Logopedics and Phoniatrics* 8: 13–17.

Shibamoto, Janet S. 1985. *Japanese women's language.* Orlando: Academic Press.

Sugito, Miyoko. 1988. Nihon no 8 Toshi ni okeru Boin no Museika [Vowel Devoicing in Eight Cities in Japan]. *Osaka Shoin Women's College Collected Essays* 25: 1–10.

Sugito, Miyoko and Hajime Hirose. 1988. Production and perception of accented devoiced vowels in Japanese. *Annual Bulletin of the Research Institute of Logopedics and Phoniatrics* 22: 21–39.

Tsuchida, Ayako. 1997. *Phonetics and phonology of Japanese vowel devoicing.* Doctoral dissertation, Ithaca, NY: Cornell University.

Vance, Timothy. 1987. *An introduction to Japanese phonology.* Albany, NY: SUNY Press.

Vance, Timothy. 1992. Lexical phonology and Japanese vowel devoicing. In Diane Brentari, Gary N. Larson, and Lynn A. MacLeod (eds), *The joy of grammar.* Philadelphia: John Benjamins, 337–350.

Varden, Kevin J. 1999. *On high vowel devoicing in Standard Modern Japanese: Implications for current phonological theory.* Doctoral dissertation, Seattle: University of Washington.

Yoshioka, Hirohide. 1981. Laryngeal adjustments in the production of the fricative consonants and devoiced vowels in Japanese. *Phonetica* 38: 236–251.

Yoshioka, Hirohide, Anders Löfqvist, and Hajime Hirose. 1982. Laryngeal adjustments in Japanese voiceless sound production. *Journal of Phonetics* 10: 1–10.

Yuen, Chris L. 1997. *Vowel devoicing and gender in Japanese.* MA thesis, San Diego: University of California.

Part II
Studies of Perception

Chapter 7

Regional Stereotypes and the Perception of Japanese Vowel Devoicing

Midori Yonezawa Morris, Gettysburg College

1. Introduction

Vowel devoicing in the Tokyo dialect is a common topic in Japanese phonology. A general description of such devoicing (e.g., Vance 1987) notes that the high vowels /i/ and /u/ are devoiced between voiceless consonants, as in /k*i*kan/ "time period" and /k*u*kan/ "linear section," and between a voiceless consonant and a pause, as in /hon des*u*/ "It's a book." Studies of different aspects of devoicing in the Tokyo dialect have been extensively reported, but devoicing in non-Tokyo dialects, like the Kinki dialect, spoken in the Kyoto-Osaka area, has not yet been as fully studied; it is widely believed, however, that devoicing does not occur in Kinki. In fact, although previous studies are limited, devoicing in Kinki may occur as frequently as in Tokyo, at least in the environments described previously. This suggests that the general belief about devoicing in Kinki and actual pronunciation may be contradictory.

Some sociolinguistic studies have reported that people can ascertain language varieties based on speech samples but that their judgments can be affected by social information, such as gender, ethnicity, and region (e.g., Niedzielski 1999). In Japanese, accentuation, for example, which is formed by the placement of high pitch on a mora, is phonemic, and different pitch patterns in words with the same segments are clues to different varieties (Warner 1997). Devoicing experiments, in which the participants are asked to make judgments about which variety they hear, may not be as definitive because of the allophonic status of devoicing and the possible gap between general belief about and actual pronunciation in Kinki. In making judgments on a speaker's region, if Tokyo respondents use devoicing to identify Tokyo and nondevoicing to identify non-Tokyo, and if Kinki people relate devoicing to non-Kinki and nondevoicing to Kinki, then they actually hear allophonic differences and use them as clues, but they also use regional stereotypes rather than actual regional use.

I conducted a perception experiment to examine how Tokyo and Kinki people judge a speaker as a local or a non-local person based on devoicing variation and pitch accent pattern. This chapter reports the results of their judgments, focusing on voicing variants. It also reports how social factors such as gender and age affect judgments.

2. Previous studies

2.1 Vowel devoicing in the Tokyo dialect

In previous studies, different aspects of devoicing in the Tokyo dialect have been extensively reported. Those include physiological characteristics (Yoshioka 1981), phonology, and variability (Imai 2004; Han 1962; Sugito 1969). Devoicing is avoided when a devoiceable vowel is in an accented (high-pitched) mora (Vance 1987; and others), in a mora that carries intonation (Vance 1987), in a successive devoicing environment (Kondo 1999; and others), in an unaccented high-pitched mora (Han 1962), and at a morpheme boundary (Tsuchida 1997; and others). Han (1962) suggested some features that affect frequency of devoicing, and Sugito (1969, 1988) also reported variation in devoicing. Imai (2004) reported environments and features that promote devoicing in production based on a large amount of production data. Maekawa (1983) states that vowel devoicing may be required as a norm in the society, and it is prescribed in dictionaries and in the training of announcers and teachers of Japanese. Yuen (1997) and Imai (2004) point out, however, that devoicing also has a non-standard character because vowels are devoiced more frequently by men and in casual and rapid speech.

2.2 Vowel devoicing in the Kinki dialect

Generally it is believed that vowel devoicing does not occur in the Kinki dialect or it is described as "less frequent in Kinki" (Tsujimura 1996). Data from previous studies, however, show that devoicing does occur there and with more than minimal frequency. In a large sound database (Tahara et al. 1998), 33 out of 40 tokens of devoiceable vowels were devoiced. Nakai (1991) reported that sentences ending /u/ in Kinki were regularly devoiced by elementary school children, and Sugito (1969, 1988) shows variation in devoicing in Kinki as well as in Tokyo. Finally, Fujimoto (2004) found that devoicing in Kinki is very individual and that some Kinki speakers devoice vowels as frequently as those in Tokyo do.

The data on devoicing in Kinki in these previous studies, however, are taken from very limited phonological environments or social variants, and the devoiceable vowel is not always compared with a vowel in the same phonological environment; for example, if /u/ is the last sound in a word with HL (high then low pitch) in Tokyo but LH (low then high pitch) in Kinki, /u/ is unaccented in the first but accented in the second. Kinki speakers may avoid devoicing in such cases because of accentuation, just as Tokyo speakers would, and such comparisons would lead to an inaccurate evaluation of overall devoicing rates.

Table 7.1 Variation in Devoicing

	Tokyo	Subjects	Osaka (Kinki)	Subjects
	Devoiced	Nondevoiced	Devoiced	Nondevoiced
Sugito (1969)	65.8%	34.2%	29.4%	70.6%
Sugito (1988)	55.6%	44.2%	32.2%	67.8%
Fujimoto (2004)	74.8%	25.2%	56.0%	44.0%
Yoshioka (1981)	56.5%	43.5%	N/A	N/A
Tahara et al. (1988)	N/A	N/A	82.5%	17.5%

Table 7.1 shows the devoicing rates in several studies. The rates by Tokyo speakers are quite similar in Sugito (1969), Sugito (1988), and Yoshioka (1981). The rate for Osaka (Kinki) speakers is higher in Fujimoto (2004) than in Sugito (1969) and Sugito (1988) and even higher in Tahara et al. (1998), but the vowels in Tahara's data are all in the optimal devoicing environment—a high vowel between two voiceless consonants in an unaccented mora. Re-calculated devoicing rates in just this environment for the other studies are shown in Table 7.2. The devoicing rate in Tahara's data (Kinki, Table 7.1) and the three data sets of the tokens in similarly unaccented morae (Tokyo) in Table 7.2 are quite comparable. It will be necessary to collect a larger amount of more controlled Kinki production data to determine the distribution and variation of devoicing before making such comparisons. Nevertheless, these more recent comparisons make it possible to assume that the devoicing rate in Kinki is not all that different from that in Tokyo, at least in the environment where devoicing is most frequent, and I take this as a tentative assumption.

Table 7.2 Devoicing Variation in Different Positions (Tokyo Subjects)

	Unaccented		Accented	
	Devoiced	Nondevoiced	Devoiced	Nondevoiced
Yoshioka (1981)	76.8%	23.2%	16.1%	83.9%
Fujimoto (2004)	78.5%	21.5%	71.0%	29.0%
Morris	80.6%	19.4%	N/A	N/A

2.3 Perception of dialects and attitudes toward them

Labov (1972) discusses the benefits of sociolinguistic investigation derived from isolating a significant linguistic variant that may serve as an index of social identity, and there are many studies of dialect perception within this general framework. Kerswill (1985) shows that respondents judge those who speak a mixture of dialects along a continuum in Norwegian accurately, but they cannot describe the differences they based their judgments on. Preston (1996) shows that people can identify the regions from which different speech samples came based on the degree of distinctiveness of dialects, but with no focus on specific features. Purnell, Idsardi, and Baugh (1999) show that people can discriminate the ethnicity of the speakers of three different varieties of English with minimal phonetic clues. Strand (1999) shows that people draw boundaries between minimal pairs in accordance with a gender difference in pronunciation while looking at "typical" or "nontypical" faces. Niedzielski (1999) shows that people identify phonetic details based on stereotypes about the regions where speakers are from rather than on accurate acoustic facts.

3. Assumptions

It seems quite reasonable then to collect quantitative data from Tokyo and Kinki people to examine how they use variation in devoicing in making judgments of a speaker's region. In this study, my assumptions are the following:

1. People may be able to identify someone's dialect region based on forms they are not aware of and cannot describe accurately.

2. Such judgments may be affected by social information or stereotype, as well as linguistic information.

Japanese speakers tend to believe that devoicing is a standard norm and that it does not occur in non-Tokyo areas, including perhaps especially Kinki, even though, as suggested before, Kinki speakers may devoice vowels as frequently as Tokyo speakers in the most general environments, that is, in unaccented morae between voiceless consonants.

Therefore both Tokyo and Kinki people tend to use stereotypical criteria. That is, for Tokyo people, a devoicer is a Tokyo person and a nondevoicer is a non-Tokyo person, and for Kinki people, a devoicer is a non-Kinki person and a nondevoicer is a Kinki person. It is important to note, however, that, neither Tokyo nor Kinki people suffer from linguistic insecurity, and both recognize prestige in their own dialects.

4. Methods

In my experiment, I presented a test tape that consisted of a word list to Tokyo and Kinki people and asked them to judge for each word whether the speaker was from the same region as their own. I chose the words so that voicing variation would be the only difference they could use in making judgments. Words as in (1a) and (1b) have only one devoiceable vowel in the most general devoicing environment and have the same accent pattern in Tokyo and Kinki. For comparison, I also used words that contain no devoiceable vowel and are pronounced in different pitch accents in Tokyo and Kinki as in (1c) and words that contain no devoiceable vowel and are pronounced in the same pitch accents as in (1d).

	Word	Gloss	Speaker	Devoicing/Accent
(1a)	ataf*u*ta	'hurriedly'	J	Devoiced
	atafuta	'hurriedly'	K	Nondevoiced
(1b)	nadesh*i*ko	'a pink'	K	Devoiced
	michihide	'by high and low tides'	M	Nondevoiced
(1c)	kawari	'replacement'	H	LHH (Tokyo)
	kawari	'replacement'	G	HHH (Kinki)
(1d)	tabun	'probably'	E	

Tables 7.3 and 7.4 show how the responses were tabulated. The responses I expected were:

1. Tokyo respondents would judge Tokyo pitch accent and devoiced tokens as "from the same region."

2. Kinki respondents would judge Tokyo pitch accent and devoiced tokens as "not from the same region,"

3. Tokyo respondents would judge Kinki pitch accent and nondevoiced tokens as "not from the same region."

4. Kinki respondents judge Kinki pitch accent and nondevoiced tokens as "from the same region."

The opposite response for each token is counted as "unexpected." "Neutral" tokens were always expected to be judged as like the respondent's own.

Table 7.3 Tabulation (Tokyo Respondents) PA = Pitch Accent

Type	Expected	Unexpected
Devoiced	From the same region	Not from the same region
Tokyo PA	From the same region	Not from the same region
Nondevoiced	Not from the same region	From the same region
Kinki PA	Not from the same region	From the same region
Neutral	From the same region	Not from the same region

Table 7.4 Tabulation (Kinki Respondents) PA = Pitch Accent

Type	Expected	Unexpected
Devoiced	Not from the same region	From the same region
Tokyo PA	Not from the same region	From the same region
Nondevoiced	From the same region	Not from the same region
Kinki PA	From the same region	Not from the same region
Neutral	From the same region	Not from the same region

I analyzed the responses, determining the significant phonological and social factors for the judgments, using a multivariate logistic regression program (Goldvarb).

5. Results and discussion

5.1 Token types

Tables 7.5 and 7.6 show the results by token types for both Tokyo and Kinki respondents. Accent patterns are obvious clues, and the expected judgments dominated. Both Tokyo and Kinki people also tended to judge tokens with voicing variation as expected; that is, devoiced tokens were judged as "Tokyo" or "non-Kinki," and nondevoiced tokens as "non-Tokyo" or "Kinki."

These results suggest that the respondents tended to make judgments based on regional stereotypes of devoicing, which may not match actual distribution of devoicing, at least in the most general devoicing environments.

Table 7.5 Results by Token Types (Tokyo) N (%)

Type	Expected	Unexpected	Total
Devoiced	1712 (70.11)	730 (29.89)	2442 (100)
Tokyo PA	377 (67.20)	184 (32.80)	561 (100)
Nondevoiced	1174 (59.90)	786 (40.10)	1960 (100)
Kinki PA	507 (86.22)	81 (13.78)	588 (100)
Neutral	155 (73.81)	55 (26.19)	210 (100)
Total	3925 (68.13)	1836 (31.87)	5761 (100)

Table 7.6 Results by Token Types (Kinki) N (%)

Type	Expected	Unexpected	Total
Devoiced	1765 (52.17)	1618 (47.83)	3383 (100)
Tokyo PA	724 (86.84)	131 (15.32)	855 (100)
Nondevoiced	1505 (54.69)	1247 (45.31)	2752 (100)
Kinki PA	777 (87.60)	110 (12.40)	887 (100)
Neutral	275 (88.42)	36 (11.58)	311 (100)
Total	5046 (61.63)	3142 (38.37)	8188 (100)

Comparison of the Tokyo and Kinki results for different pitch accent patterns reveals further differences. For the Tokyo respondents, it seems that a non-local feature induces the response "non-local" more easily than a local feature induces the response "local." That is, a Tokyo pitch accent is not such a good clue for "local" in Tokyo, while the Kinki accent is as good for Kinki identification of local as the Tokyo accent is for identification of nonlocal. Tables 7.7 and 7.8, derived from Tables 7.5 and 7.6, show these differences more clearly (expected results only).

Table 7.7 Tokyo Results PA = Pitch Accent

Pitch Accent	%
Tokyo PA (i.e., "local")	67.20
Kinki PA (i.e., "nonlocal")	86.22

Table 7.8 Kinki Results PA = Pitch Accent

Pitch Accent	%
Tokyo PA (i.e., "nonlocal")	86.84
Kinki PA (i.e., "local")	87.60

Perhaps these different patterns reflect the different positions and values of local varieties in Tokyo and Kinki. The Kinki dialect functions to bond people due to its long history in the area, while Tokyo people may well have a smaller sense of solidarity due to the short history of its status as a standard variety and perhaps even due to a lesser sense of local identity in an area where many residents have immigrated from other regions of the country. These results show a similar tendency to ones reported in such studies as Preston (1996), in which regional varieties are valued by their speakers along such different dimensions as "correctness" and "pleasantness."

5.2 Voicing variants

The main results of this study, however, have to do with the perception of devoicing. Tables 7.9 and 7.10 summarize the results for voicing variants, with both percentages and weights obtained from Goldvarb. Again, both Tokyo and Kinki respondents tended to judge the speaker's region based on the stereotypical criterion of devoicing, a low-level allophonic feature. In other words, their judgments are promoted by a feature that is only putatively their own—devoicing in Tokyo and nondevoicing in Kinki. This is a weaker tendency in Kinki, as shown by lower percentages and a smaller range of weights. This weaker tendency for expected judgments of voicing variants in Kinki also supports the idea that there are higher devoicing rates in Kinki speech than believed. If Kinki people devoice vowels as frequently as in Tokyo speech, at least in the most optimal environments, they may well not use devoicing variation efficiently as a criterion in making judgments. It is possible that Kinki people assume that devoicing is a non-Kinki feature based on the higher nondevoicing rate in certain low-frequency devoicing environments (e.g., accented morae), but confirmation of that interpretation would require a different study.

Table 7.9 Tokyo Results by Voicing Variants

Voicing	%/Weight
Devoiced	70.11/0.552
Nondevoiced	59.90/0.436

Table 7.10 Kinki Results by Voicing Variants

Voicing	%/Weight
Nondevoiced	54.69/0.521
Devoiced	52.17/0.483

5.3 Gender of the speaker

Tables 7.11, 7.12, and 7.13 show the results of perception of voicing variants by gender of the speaker. The results with Tokyo devoiced-nondevoiced combined data and Kinki devoiced-nondevoiced separated data are not significant. Tokyo results for devoiced and nondevoiced show that women's voices promote the expected responses; that is, female devoicers tended to be judged as Tokyo and female nondevoicers tended to be judged as non-Tokyo. This suggests that Tokyo respondents are more sensitive to the stereotype that women are more likely users of the standard. In contrast, the Kinki results show that men's voices promote expected responses. Respondents may associate a covert prestige idea with men's voices, perhaps assuming that male nondevoicers are tough and/or cool-sounding Kinki persons and that male devoicers are not.

Table 7.11 Results by Gender of the Speaker (Tokyo, Devoiced)

Gender	Weight
Female	0.542
Male	0.444

Table 7.12 Results by Gender of the Speaker (Tokyo, Nondevoiced)

Gender	Weight
Female	0.588
Male	0.436

Table 7.13 Results by Gender of the Speaker (Kinki, Combined)

Gender	Weight
Male	0.521
Female	0.479

5.4 Gender of the Respondent

Tables 7.14, 7.15, 7.16, and 7.17 show the results by gender of the respondent. The results for Tokyo devoiced and Kinki combined data are not significant. In all cases that are significant, women respondents are promoters of the expected response, indicating they may be more sensitive to voicing status in general and perhaps matching assumptions about the standard character of vowel devoicing.

Table 7.14 Results by Gender of the Respondent (Tokyo, Combined)

Gender	Weight
Female	0.524
Male	0.466

Table 7.15 Results by Gender of the Respondent (Tokyo, Nondevoiced)

Gender	Weight
Female	0.556
Male	0.421

Table 7.16 Results by Gender of the Respondent (Kinki, Devoiced)

Gender	Weight
Female	0.543
Male	0.470

Table 7.17 Results by Gender of the Respondent (Kinki, Nondevoiced)

Gender	Weight
Female	0.528
Male	0.459

5.5 Age of the respondent

Finally, Tables 7.18 and 7.19 show the results of combined data by age of the respondent. In the Tokyo results, a mild age-grading pattern is indicated, again matching the assumption that vowel devoicing is a standard form, which the youngest and oldest have less concern with. The Kinki results do not show an age-grading pattern, with only the youngest age group as a demoter. This might indicate linguistic change, but that is not confirmed. It should be noted that, in recent studies, Fujimoto (2004) shows that the devoicing rate in Osaka is higher than those given in Sugito (1969) and Sugito (1988) and that the devoicing rate in accented morae in Tokyo is much higher than Yoshioka's findings (1981). The limited phonological environments and varieties of social factors in these earlier reports must be considered, however, and extensive production data in Kinki must be collected and examined carefully, but Fujimoto's (2004) results may also indicate evidence of linguistic change.

Table 7.18 Results by Age of the Respondent (Tokyo)

Age Group	Weight
23–29, 30–39 (middle)	0.517
18–22, 40–49 (youngest and oldest)	0.469

Table 7.19 Results by Age of the Respondent (Kinki)

Age Group	Weight
23–29, 30–39, 40–49, 50–59 (middle and oldest)	0.506
18–22 (youngest)	0.468

6. Conclusion

Two main points should be made.

1.) Devoicing variation contributes to respondent judgment, but the identification strategy comes principally from stereotypes rather than from knowledge of actual regional patterns of devoicing and nondevoicing.

2.) The Tokyo results by gender of the speaker, gender of the respondent, and age of the respondent all suggest that vowel devoicing is an indicator of standard speech associated with Tokyo and that nondevoicing is a nonstandard form.

Additionally, the Kinki results are inconsistent in many cases because devoicing is not such a good clue for Kinki people in judging a speaker as "non–Kinki." The general belief that Kinki people do not devoice may come from lower devoicing rates in some phonological environments rather than in the most general ones.

In order to have clear interpretation of the results of this experiment and to make legitimate comparisons of production and perception of devoicing between Tokyo and Kinki Japanese, it is essential to obtain a large amount of production data, taking into account both phonological environments and social factors.

References

Fujimoto, Masako. 2004. Boinchô to boin no museika no kankei: Tokyo hôgen washa to Osaka hôgen washa no hikaku [Relationship between length of the vowel and devoicing: Comparisons between Tokyo speakers and Osaka speakers]. *Kokugogaku* 55 (1).

Han, Mieko Shimizu. 1962. Unvoicing of vowels in Japanese. *Onsei no Kenkyû* [Study of sounds] 10: 81–100, Nihon Onsei Gakkai.

Imai, Terumi. 2004. *Vowel devoicing in Tokyo Japanese: A variationist approach.* PhD dissertation, East Lansing: Michigan State University.

Kerswill, Paul E. 1985. Native dialect and dialect mixing in Bergen: A perception experiment. *Cambridge Papers in Phonetics and Experimental Linguistics 4.*

Kondo, Mariko. 1999. Syllable weight and syllable structure in Japanese. Presentation at the 9th Japanese/Korean Linguistics Conference, The Ohio State University.

Labov, William. 1972. *Sociolinguistic patterns.* Philadelphia: University of Pennsylvania Press.

Maekawa, Kikuo. 1983. Kyôtsûgo ni okeru boin no museika no kakuritsu ni tsuite [On probabilities of vowel devoicing in the language for mutual understanding]. *Gengo no Sekai* 1 (2): 69–81.

Nakai, Ykihiko. 1991. Terebi shutsuen-ji no akusento: Kinki chihô no shôgakusei ga Kinki rôkaru no bangumi ni shutsuen suru baai [Accents in appearing on a TV program: The case of elementary school children in Kinki appearing in a program broadcast locally in Kinki]. Script for the presentation at the 52nd Conference of Nihon Hôgen Kenkyûkai [Japanese Dialect Studies Association].

Niedzielski, Nancy. 1999. The effect of social information on the perception of sociolinguistic variables. *Journal of Language and Social Psychology* 18 (1): 62–85.

Preston, Dennis R. 1996. Where the worst English is spoken. In Edgar Schneider (ed.), *Focus on the USA*, Amsterdam: John Benjamins, 297–360.

Purnell, Thomas, William Idsardi, and John Baugh. 1999. Perceptual and phonetic experiments on American English dialect identification. *Journal of Language and Social Psychology* 18 (1): 10–30.

Strand, Elizabeth A. 1999. Uncovering the role of gender stereotypes in speech perception. *Journal of Language and Social Psychology* 18 (1): 86–100.

Sugito, Miyoko. 1969. Tokyo, Osaka ni okeru musei–boin ni tsuite [A study of voiceless vowels in Tokyo and Osaka]. *Onsei no Kenkyu* [Study of Sounds] 14: 249–264.

Sugito, Miyoko. 1988. Nihon no 8 toshi ni okeru boin no museika [Vowel devoicing in 8 cities in Japan]. *Osaka Shôin Women's College Collected Essays* 15: 1–10.

Tahara, Hiroshi, et al. 1998. Jinmonkon Database Vol. 2 (CD–ROM). Kanagawa, Japan: Sôgô Kenkyû Daigakuin Daigaku.

Tsuchida, Ayako. 1997. *Phonetics and phonology of Japanese vowel devoicing.* Doctoral dissertation, Ithaca: Cornell University.

Tsujimura, Natsuko. 1996. *An introduction to Japanese linguistics.* Oxford: Blackwell.

Vance, Timothy. 1987. *An introduction to Japanese phonology.* Albany: SUNY Press.

Warner, Natasha. 1997. Recognition of accent patterns across dialects in Japanese. *Proceedings of the 23rd Annual Meeting of the Berkeley Linguistics Society*, 364–375.

Yoshioka, Hirohide. 1981. Laryngeal adjustments in the production of the fricative consonants and devoiced vowels in Japanese. *Phonetica* 38: 236–251.

Yuen, Chris L. 1997. *Vowel devoicing and gender in Japanese.* MA thesis, University of California, San Diego.

Chapter 8

Phonetic Detail, Linguistic Experience, and the Classification of Regional Language Varieties in the United States

Cynthia G. Clopper, The Ohio State University

1. Introduction

The perception of linguistic and social categories in spoken language has been studied in cognitive psychology and speech science for over 50 years. Researchers in these fields have examined how linguistic information is processed perceptually and cognitively as well as the role of talker-specific and social information in spoken language processing. While the primary goals of speech scientists have not been to understand sociolinguistic variation or the relationship between language and social interaction, the methods that they have developed are a virtually untapped resource for sociophoneticians. Experimental studies of speech perception provide quantitative, empirical insights into the perception and representation of linguistic and sociolinguistic variation without relying on the potentially unreliable impressions of linguistically naïve participants.

Peterson and Barney (1952) were among the first speech scientists to explore the role of inter-talker variability in speech perception. They recorded a large number of talkers (men, women, and children) producing hVd utterances and then played the samples back to a group of listeners and asked them to identify the vowels. Overall vowel identification accuracy was quite good, particularly for those vowels that are located in relatively uncrowded regions of the vowel space (such as /i/ and /u/). However, vowels that were involved in dialect shifts were more likely to be misidentified, particularly in cases of mergers (such as /ɑ/ and /ɔ/). Peterson and Barney (1952) interpreted these findings as the result of the interaction of the linguistic experiences of the talkers and the listeners. They also conducted an acoustic analysis of the hVd utterances, which confirmed a high degree of variability between the talkers in absolute formant frequency values within a given vowel category, but a consistent pattern of relationships between the vowels across talkers. These early findings suggest that speech perception involves processing multiple sources of phonetic detail, including linguistic and talker-specific information.

The invention of the pattern playback synthesis system in the 1950s allowed speech scientists to examine the relationship between fine acoustic details and the perception of phonological categories using synthetic stimulus materials. In what has become a classic set of experiments, Liberman et al. (1957) presented listeners with synthetic CV syllables and asked them to identify the initial consonant. The syllables formed a continuum from /be/ to /de/ to /ge/ and were created by modifying the transition of the second formant between the consonant and the vowel along a continuum from sharply rising (/be/) to sharply falling (/ge/). Despite the relatively small acoustic difference between any two neighboring syllables on the continuum, the listeners identified each individual stimulus item consistently as /b/, /d/, or /g/. That is, the listeners perceived a continuum of synthetic speech samples as though they were categorical, with a sharp shift from /b/ to /d/ responses in the early part of the continuum and a shift from /d/ to /g/ responses in the later part of the continuum.

Liberman et al. (1957) then conducted a paired comparison discrimination task using an ABX paradigm. On each trial, the listeners were presented with three stimulus items and were asked to indicate whether the last token (X) was the same as the first (A) or second (B) item. In all cases, the A and B stimulus items were one-step neighbors on the continuum and the X stimulus was acoustically identical to either A or B. Liberman et al. (1957) found that the listeners responded at chance if they had previously identified the A and B stimulus items as the same consonant and well above chance if they had previously identified the A and B stimuli as different consonants. That is, within-category consonant discrimination was difficult, whereas between-category discrimination was not. Taken together, the results of these phoneme identification and discrimination experiments suggest that phoneme perception is categorical, at least at some levels of processing, and that even small changes in the acoustic signal can result in categorical shifts in perception.

However, when Pisoni (1973) replicated these two experiments with a continuum of vowels from /i/ to /ɪ/, he found a sharp boundary in the identification task, but a much weaker decline in performance for between-category discrimination. Although the primary pattern of results across the two sets of stimulus materials is similar, Pisoni's (1973) findings suggest that the categorical perception of phonemes has limits. In particular, consonants and vowels may be processed differently, particularly with respect to the discrimination of acoustically similar tokens.

By the mid-1970s, speech scientists had also begun to investigate the perception of social sources of variation in the speech signal. For example, Lass et al. (1976) asked naïve listeners to categorize unfamiliar talkers by gender based on isolated vowel productions. They found that the listeners were well above chance in the gender identification task even when the stimulus materials were whispered or degraded by lowpass filtering. This finding suggests that acoustic information about the talker is available in very short speech samples, even in the absence of a laryngeal source or formant structure, and that naïve listeners are able to access that information in an explicit gender categorization task.

Speech scientists have also examined the interaction between linguistic and social information in spoken language processing. Mullennix and Pisoni (1990) found evidence of interference between linguistic and social information in a speeded classification task with multiple talkers. In one condition, listeners were asked to categorize isolated words produced by male and female talkers as beginning with either a /p/ or a /b/. In a second condition, listeners were asked to categorize the same stimulus materials by the gender of the talker (i.e., male or female). In both cases, the listeners were instructed to ignore the unattended dimension and to respond as quickly as possible after each stimulus was presented. When the word-initial phoneme and the gender of the talker were uncorrelated, significant increases in response time were found as the variability in the unattended dimension increased. That is, in the phoneme identification task, the listeners were slower to respond when the stimulus materials were produced by more different talkers. Similarly, in the gender identification task, the listeners were slower to respond when more different words were presented. This result suggests that talker-specific information such as gender is perceived and processed in parallel with linguistic information and can also interfere with rapid phoneme processing.

More recently, Strand (1999) examined the categorical perception of the place of articulation of voiceless fricatives. She developed several continua of stimulus materials that ranged from /s/ to /ʃ/ by manipulating the frequency of the fricative noise. The continua varied in terms of their perceived gender and gender typicality, so that the "voices" were either male or female and either prototypical or non-prototypical of their gender. The overall results replicated the earlier categorical perception results of Liberman et al. (1957) and revealed a sharp shift between /s/ and /ʃ/ responses near the midpoint of the continuum. However, Strand (1999) also found that the gender of the talker had a significant effect on the location of the perceived category boundary. The perceived /s/~/ʃ/ boundary was higher in frequency for the female voices than the male voices. In addition, the perceptual boundaries for the non-prototypical voices were closer together on the continuum than the boundaries for the prototypical voices. Thus, identical acoustic signals were judged differently depending on the acoustic context in which they were presented, suggesting an interaction between contextual information about the talker and the perception of linguistic categories.

Taken together, the results of these studies contribute to our understanding of the nature of naïve listeners' perception of both linguistic and social information in the speech signal. Naïve listeners can explicitly identify both linguistic and social categories from short speech samples. The perception of linguistic categories is significantly affected by both small acoustic changes in the stimulus materials and variation due to surrounding acoustic context.

In addition to examining the effects of talker differences on perception, the methods described previously can also be applied to investigations of the role of the listener's background in speech perception and spoken language processing. By comparing the performance by multiple groups of listeners with different backgrounds or experiences in the same task, we can explore the relationship between linguistic experience and spoken language processing. For example, Tees and Werker (1984) investigated the effects of linguistic experience on the discrimination of Hindi retroflexed and dental stops. Native English listeners with early exposure to Hindi and those with five years of experience with Hindi as adults performed the task well above chance. Native English listeners with only one year of experience with Hindi and those trained on the two phoneme categories in the laboratory exhibited chance performance on the same task. Thus, familiarity with a given phoneme contrast affects the perception of those phonemes in an explicit discrimination task. We would predict that a listener's experience would similarly affect the perception of both linguistic and social categories in the speech of talkers from familiar and unfamiliar dialects.

A number of researchers have recently begun to apply speech science methods to sociophonetic perception research. Carefully designed perception experiments with naïve listeners have provided new insights into what naïve listeners know about sociolinguistic variation, including how linguistic contrasts are perceived cross-dialectally and how social sources of information in the speech signal are perceived. The role of the listener's experience with variation has also been examined by comparing performance in these types of tasks across different listener populations. Sociophonetic studies of the perception of linguistic categories have focused primarily on vowel identification tasks, while the studies of social categories have typically examined the perception of regional dialect variation in the United States.

2. Perception of linguistic categories

Some of the most well-documented sources of regional dialect variation in the United States are ongoing shifts in the vowel systems of northern and southern varieties of American English (see e.g., Labov, Ash, and Boberg 2005; Thomas 2001). As a result, most of the cross-dialect perception research dealing with linguistic categories has focused on vowel perception. Using both natural and synthetic stimulus materials, vowel perception has been examined in vowel identification and word recognition tasks. The word recognition tasks have typically included multiple conditions, in which the words were presented in isolation, in semantically neutral sentence contexts, and/or in semantically predictable sentence contexts. In addition, vowel identification performance by local listeners has been compared to responses to the same set of stimulus materials by non-local listeners. The results of these studies provide insights into the perception of well-documented regional vowel shifts by naïve listeners, the role of linguistic context in producing cross-dialect lexical interference, and the role of familiarity with a given variety in perception.

In one set of studies, Labov and Ash (1998) used two different tasks to obtain converging evidence for the effects of linguistic context and the listener's region of origin on vowel perception. First, they asked naïve listeners in Birmingham, Philadelphia, and Chicago to identify naturally produced Birmingham vowels in kVd utterances in an open-set identification task. They found that the Birmingham listeners were more accurate overall than the other two listener groups, although the same vowels which were difficult for the Philadelphia and Chicago listeners were also difficult for the Birmingham listeners.

Labov and Ash (1998) then conducted a word recognition task, in which they played progressively longer samples of speech in semantically predictable contexts and asked listeners to identify the target word. The speech samples were again produced by Birmingham speakers and the listeners were from Birmingham, Philadelphia, and Chicago. The region of origin of the listeners significantly affected word recognition accuracy for the phrase-length utterances. The Birmingham listeners were again more accurate than the non-local listeners, although overall performance varied greatly depending on the target vowel. Region of origin was not a significant factor in determining performance for the word-length and sentence-length utterances due primarily to floor and ceiling effects, respectively. Thus, Labov and Ash (1998) found evidence of an interaction between linguistic context and region of origin of the listener in the perception of local vowels.

Using a classic categorical perception paradigm, Rakerd and Plichta (2003) asked naïve listeners to identify a series of synthetic vowel stimuli as /ɑ/ or /æ/. The stimulus materials were constructed such that the middle part of the continuum was ambiguous between a fronted /ɑ/ characteristic of the Northern Cities Chain Shift (NCCS) and an unshifted /æ/ typical of many varieties of American English. The vowel stimuli were embedded in monosyllabic words which were presented in isolation and at the end of semantically neutral sentences. Half of the carrier sentences contained Northern Cities shifted vowels and the other half contained unshifted vowels. Rakerd and Plichta (2003) found that two factors interacted to cause a perceptual category boundary shift: region of origin of the listener and preceding linguistic context. Listeners from the upper peninsula of Michigan, where the NCCS is not common, perceived the /ɑ/~/æ/ category boundary at the same point on the continuum regardless of the context of the stimulus item.

However, listeners from the Detroit area, where the NCCS is common among local white speakers, perceived the boundary at a more fronted location along the continuum when the stimulus item was preceded by a carrier phrase containing Northern Cities shifted vowels, but not in isolation or the unshifted context. Like the results of Labov and Ash's (1998) word recognition study, these findings suggest that both the listener's region of origin and the linguistic context of the utterance can affect the perception of local vowel category boundaries.

Niedzielski (1999) also used continua of synthetic vowel stimuli to examine the perception of the NCCS in Detroit. In her task, she asked listeners to match the vowel sound in a target word to one token from a set of synthetic vowel stimulus items. While all of her target items were produced by a single female speaker with Northern Cities shifted vowels, her listeners did not always select the most acoustically-similar synthetic vowels as the best match. In particular, Niedzielski (1999) manipulated the biases of her listeners by telling half of them that the talker was from Detroit. The other half of her listeners were told than the talker was from Canada. Niedzielski (1999) found that the listeners who believed the talker was from Detroit tended to select canonical unshifted vowels as the best match, whereas the listeners who believed the talker was from Canada tended to select the most acoustically-similar vowels as the best match. As in the studies by Strand (1999) and Mullennix and Pisoni (1990), in which linguistic and social information in the speech signal were found to interact in perception, the results of this study suggest that the listener's beliefs about a talker can have a significant impact on the perception of the linguistic information in the speech of that talker.

Taken together, these studies have applied methods developed by speech scientists to explore important research questions in sociophonetics and have extended our understanding of the perception of vowel categories by naïve listeners. In particular, these findings have shown that vowel perception is more complex than a simple mapping between the acoustic signal and a phonological vowel category representation. The listener's experience with specific varieties, the extent to which the relevant variety is made available through linguistic context, and the beliefs that the listener has about the talker can all affect the mapping between the acoustic signal and the cognitive representation of the vowel category. Additional sociophonetic research is needed to determine the limits of naïve listeners' abilities to adapt to unfamiliar dialects, the role of category mismappings on spoken language processing and speech recognition, and the relationship between category boundaries in perception and production.

3. Perception of social categories

Much of the research in variationist sociolinguistics has focused on documenting the acoustic properties of socially-based variation. Labov et al. (2006) have undertaken an enormous project to document, describe, and ultimately define regional phonological variation in the United States. However, far less is known about naïve listeners' perception and representation of this important source of inter-talker variability. Over the past 15 years, a number of studies have used methods developed in cognitive psychology and speech science to explore the explicit categorization and discrimination of regional varieties of American English. These studies have all used samples of naturally-produced speech, typically sentence-length or longer, which contain multiple dialect-specific target words or phonemes. The listener populations have been manipulated to include listeners from different regional backgrounds and with different degrees of geographic mobility to explore the role of these two listener-related factors in perception. The results of these studies provide insights into the cognitive dialect categories naïve listeners construct through their interactions with people from their own and other dialect regions, the kinds of phonological variants that naïve listeners find salient, and the role that these acoustic details play in social category construction.

In one early study, Preston (1993) used a dialect identification task to explore naïve listeners' ability to identify the regional background of unfamiliar talkers. The stimulus materials were short extracts of narratives produced by nine male talkers from nine different cities on a north-south continuum between Michigan and Alabama. He asked adult listeners in Michigan and southern Indiana to listen to each sample and then indicate which city they thought the talker was from. The results revealed that the listeners had difficulty distinguishing between northern and midland talkers, but that they were more accurate in distinguishing northern from southern talkers. In addition, the region of origin of the listeners (Michigan vs. Indiana) had a significant effect on their responses. The Michigan listeners perceived the north-south boundary at a more northern location along the geographic continuum than the Indiana listeners. Thus, region of origin affects the perception of social categories, such as regional dialect, as well as the perception of local vowel systems (e.g., Labov and Ash 1998).

More recently, Clopper and Pisoni (2004, 2006; Clopper, Conrey, and Pisoni 2005) have used forced-choice perceptual categorization tasks to explore the role of listener background in dialect perception. In the first of a series of studies, we asked undergraduate listeners to categorize a set of male talkers by regional dialect based on sentence-length utterances (Clopper and Pisoni 2004). The listeners were shown a map of the United States with six dialect regions drawn and labeled on it and were asked to listen to each short sample of speech and select the region that they thought the talker was from. Overall performance was quite poor in this six-alternative forced-choice categorization task; average accuracy was only 30%. However, performance was statistically above chance, which is 17% in a six-alternative task, confirming that while the task was difficult for the listeners, their responses were not entirely random. Unlike the perception of talker gender, which is robust to degradation (Lass et al. 1976), dialect categorization is quite difficult for naïve listeners, even under ideal listening conditions.

The large number of errors produced by the listeners allowed us to quantitatively investigate their patterns of confusions. A clustering analysis of the listeners' responses revealed a perceptual similarity structure that broadly corresponded to the phonological variation present in the speech signals. The listeners tended to confuse northern varieties with one another, southern varieties with one another, and western varieties with one another, but made fewer errors between these three broader dialect categories. We replicated these results with several different sets of sentence materials, as well as with a group of female talkers (Clopper et al. 2005), and with two groups of mixed male and female talkers from different corpora (Clopper et al. 2005; Clopper and Pisoni 2006). Figure 8.1 shows the overall accuracy on the six-alternative dialect categorization task in the four different experiments.

We also examined the effects of the listener's region of origin and geographic mobility on forced-choice categorization performance. Like Preston (1993), we found that region of origin was an important factor in the perception of the regional dialect of unfamiliar talkers. The listeners in our first experiment (Clopper and Pisoni 2004) correctly categorized more talkers from regions that they had lived in than from regions that they had not lived in. In addition, those listeners who had lived in multiple different dialect regions prior to attending college performed better overall than the listeners

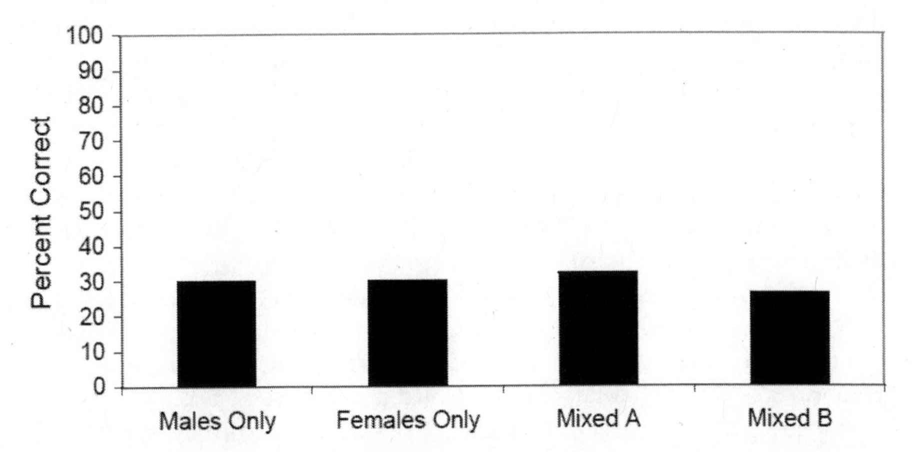

Figure 8.1 Percent correct categorization performance in four six-alternative forced-choice dialect categorization tasks: male talkers only (Clopper and Pisoni 2004), female talkers only (Clopper et al. 2005), and two sets of mixed male and female talkers (Mixed A: Clopper et al. 2005; Mixed B: Clopper and Pisoni 2006).

who had lived only in Indiana, suggesting that geographic mobility is also an important factor in the perception of dialect variation.

Several possible explanations may account for why explicit categorization of unfamiliar talkers by regional dialect is difficult for naïve listeners. First, the acoustic characteristics of the different regional dialects may not be salient enough for naïve listeners to use them to create accurate cognitive categories for regional variation in the United States. However, it may also be that the listeners can clearly differentiate talkers from different regions, but that they have difficulty assigning the correct category labels to those groups either because the cognitive mappings between acoustic properties and regional dialect labels do not match those proposed by sociolinguists (and provided by the experimenter in these tasks) or because naïve listeners have a different set of categories altogether.

The results of an analysis of the response biases of the listeners in one of the forced-choice categorization tasks suggests that naïve listeners may have a different acoustics-to-label mapping than sociolinguists. Clopper and Pisoni (2006) reported an asymmetric response bias for midwestern listeners for talkers from the northeastern United States. In particular, Mid-Atlantic talkers were frequently miscategorized as New Englanders, but the New England talkers were rarely miscategorized as Mid-Atlantic talkers. In addition, performance was much more accurate on the Mid-Atlantic talkers than the New England talkers overall. This finding suggests that when the listeners in our experiment were making their categorization judgments, they may have been relying on different mappings between acoustic characteristics of the speech signal and regional labels than those predicted based on descriptive variationist research (e.g., Labov et al. 2006). We have conducted two additional experiments which allowed us to investigate the role of category labels in the perception of regional dialects of American English.

First, a free classification experiment was developed to investigate naïve listeners' classification behavior in the absence of experimenter-provided dialect regions or labels (Clopper and Pisoni 2007). The listeners were asked to group a set of unfamiliar talkers by regional dialect based on sentence-length utterances. They were permitted to make as many groups as they wanted with as many talkers in each group as they wished. Two sets of talkers from six different regional dialects of American English produced the stimulus materials. One set of talkers included only males and was identical to the talkers who produced the stimulus materials in our original forced-choice categorization task (Clopper and Pisoni 2004). The second set of talkers included both males and females and was identical to the second set of mixed male and female talkers from our earlier categorization task (Clopper and Pisoni 2006). By using the same sets of talkers and stimulus materials, we could directly compare the results of the free classification experiments to the forced-choice categorization experiments.

Given that the pattern of errors produced by the listeners in our earlier forced-choice categorization experiments consistently revealed three broad dialect categories, we predicted that the naïve listeners would exhibit a relatively high tolerance for within-group acoustic variability and make a relatively small number of groups in the free classification task. Instead, however, the listeners made an average of eight to ten groups of talkers, suggesting that they were able to represent fine-grained acoustic differences between the talkers. However, their grouping accuracy was still rather poor overall, which may indicate attention to talker-specific differences instead of dialect-specific variation. Thus, the difficulties naïve listeners exhibit in explicit categorization tasks may reflect poorly specified perceptual dialect categories, and not simply a mismatch between the experimenter-provided labels and the listeners' own cognitive categories.

Multidimensional scaling analyses of the aggregate free classification data revealed two primary dimensions of perceptual dialect similarity: geography (northern vs. southern varieties) and distinctiveness (many vs. few characteristic properties). When both male and female talkers were used, gender was also revealed to be an important dimension of perceptual similarity (Clopper and Pisoni 2007). This finding suggests a strong interaction between dialect and gender in perception, similar to the perceptual interference effects reported for linguistic categories and talker gender (e.g., Mullennix and Pisoni 1990; Strand 1999). Additional research is needed to explore the role of talker gender in perception and the apparent inability of listeners to ignore this important source of talker variability in speech processing.

The results of the free classification experiment were consistent across two different sets of stimulus materials and for listeners with different regions of origin and degrees of geographic mobility. However, as in the previous forced-choice categorization experiments (Preston 1993; Clopper and Pisoni 2004), the region of origin of the listeners had a significant effect on their performance in the free classification task. Listeners tended to perceive greater similarity between their own dialect and neighboring dialects than between more geographically distant dialects. Geographic mobility attenuated this effect and resulted in greater discrimination overall.

In a second experiment, we used a paired comparison similarity ratings task to examine the perceptual similarity of dialects in more detail (Clopper, Levi, and Pisoni 2006). In this experiment, the listeners were presented with pairs of talkers and after listening to one sentence produced by each talker, were asked to rate the similarity of the talkers' dialects on a seven-point similarity scale. Only four dialect regions were represented in the paired comparison similarity ratings task. We reduced the set of talkers in this experiment to make the number of pairwise comparisons manageable and used a subset of the male and female talkers from our earlier forced-choice categorization and free classification tasks (Clopper and Pisoni 2006; Clopper and Pisoni 2007).

While the listeners consistently assigned higher ratings to talkers from the same dialect region than to talkers from different dialect regions, the mean ratings for both same-dialect and different-dialect pairs were near the middle of the range, again suggesting relatively poor performance overall. The mean ratings for the same-dialect and different-dialect pairs are shown in Figure 8.2. In addition, talker gender was found to be an important factor in this experiment; same-gender pairs were consistently rated as more similar than different-gender pairs, despite instructions to ignore talker gender in making the dialect similarity judgments (Clopper et al. 2006). This finding again suggests interference between two different sources of social information in an explicit perceptual task.

Multidimensional scaling analyses of the aggregate similarity data revealed the same two dimensions of perceptual similarity that were obtained in the earlier free classification experiment (Clopper and Pisoni

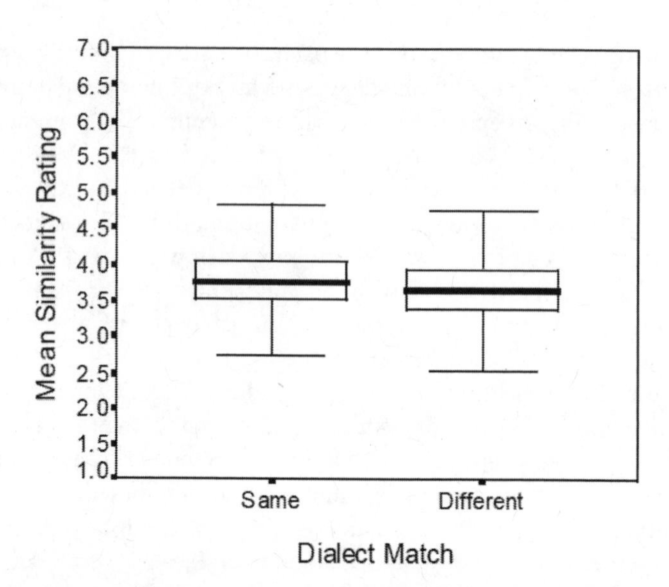

Figure 8.2 Mean similarity ratings for the same-dialect and different-dialect talker pairs in the paired comparison perceptual similarity ratings task (Clopper et al. 2006).

2007): geography and distinctiveness. The results of the similarity ratings task thus provide converging evidence with the free classification results for poor mapping between dialect-specific variation and cognitive dialect categories, but a consistent pattern of perceptual similarity related to geography and phonological distinctiveness.

Taken together, the results of these studies on the perception of dialect variation suggest that American listeners have rather poorly specified dialect categories. The results of the free classification and similarity ratings tasks suggest that these poorly specified categories are not simply the result of a mismatch between experimenter-provided labels and clusters of specific phonological properties, but may instead be the result of inconsistent mappings between phonetic details and dialect labels. That is, the listeners may not have well-established connections between linguistic variability and cognitive dialect representations, which leads to poor performance in the explicit dialect perception tasks.

Despite the relatively low levels of performance overall, the linguistic experience of the listener emerged as an important factor in dialect classification performance across several different tasks. In particular, region of origin affected the perception of local varieties such that local varieties were more confusable than non-local varieties. Geographic mobility, on the other hand, served to create more fine-grained distinctions among different varieties, perhaps reflecting more robust cognitive representations of dialect variation, and attenuating the locality effect. Additional research is needed to determine whether listeners can be trained to perform these types of tasks more accurately, at what levels of performance they reach an asymptote, and the relationship between specific acoustic properties and dialect classification performance.

4. New directions

Sociophonetic research on the perception of dialect variation has revealed several major findings that complement earlier speech science research on the perception of linguistic and social categories. First, the results of the vowel identification tasks (Labov and Ash 1998; Rakerd and Plichta 2003) suggest that linguistic context is an important factor in the perception of shifted vowel systems. When the semantic context is sufficient to predict the target word, recognition performance is good, regardless of the match between the dialects of the talker and the listener (Labov and Ash 1998). However, when the semantic context is ambiguous, word recognition is impaired for non-local listeners (Labov and Ash 1998; Rakerd and Plichta 2003). Second, the dialect classification and discrimination studies provide evidence for poorly-specified perceptual dialect categories. The results of the free classification task (Clopper and Pisoni 2007) and the similarity ratings task (Clopper et al. 2006) in particular suggest that naïve listeners have difficulty mapping acoustic variability to specific dialect representations.

Finally, in both the vowel identification and dialect classification experiments, the linguistic experience of the listeners was an important factor in determining performance. First, region of origin had a significant effect on the listeners' ability to adapt to vowel shifts in the vowel identification tasks (Labov and Ash 1998; Rakerd and Plichta 2003). Listeners also showed greater accuracy overall in categorizing talkers from their own dialect region in the dialect classification task (Clopper and Pisoni 2004), as well as a tendency to perceive their own dialect as more similar to neighboring dialects than to more geographically distant varieties (Clopper 2004; Clopper and Pisoni 2006). Second, geographic mobility had a significant effect on the listeners' classification behavior. Geographically mobile listeners were more accurate in their categorization judgments overall (Clopper and Pisoni 2004) and exhibited greater discrimination between their own dialects and neighboring dialects

(Clopper and Pisoni 2007). Both of these effects are most likely related to the listeners' overall familiarity with the phonological systems of different dialects. While some evidence suggests that dialect familiarity can develop through exposure to national and local media (Stuart-Smith, Timmins, and Pryce 2005), the effects of linguistic experience obtained in the vowel identification and dialect classification studies discussed previously suggest that a listener's personal experience with variation as a result of where he or she has lived also plays a significant role in dialect familiarity.

The representation of phonetic detail in memory and the role of linguistic experience in perception and cognitive processing can both be accounted for by exemplar-based models of spoken language. The two primary properties of exemplar models are that every experience (e.g., utterance) is represented and stored in long term memory and that recognition of a new stimulus results from the comparison of that stimulus to the previously stored exemplars. The new stimulus is identified as being the "same" as the stored exemplar(s) it is most similar to. Representational strength of the exemplars is assumed to decay over time and different representations can be assigned different weights, so that recently encountered stimuli or previous exemplars produced by the same talker are given more weight than others in perception and recognition. Exemplar models have been proposed to account for a range of linguistic phenomena, including vowel perception (Johnson 1997), lexical access (Goldinger 1996), and phonological change (Pierrehumbert 2001, 2002).

Pierrehumbert's (2001, 2002) model of the lexicon includes representations of lexical, phonological, and phonetic information. Representations of individual words are linked to their constituent phonemes which, in turn, are linked to phonetic elements. In order to account for the perception and representation of dialect variation, several additional levels of representation must be added. As shown in Figure 8.3, a model of speech perception that can account for the sociophonetic research described previously would also include representations of talker, dialect, semantic, and non-linguistic social information. In this model, it is assumed that representations at all information levels take the form of exemplars, but this is not a crucial assumption of the model. Abstract, symbolic representations could also be assumed as long as the connections between the various sources of information permitted the same effects of phonetic detail and linguistic experience to emerge.

The core linguistic component of the model includes the phonetic, phonological, lexical, and semantic representations. In general, the connections are assumed to be bidirectional. Bottom-up acoustic-phonetic information can be used to identify phonological categories, which can then be used to identify lexical items. On the other hand, top-down semantic information

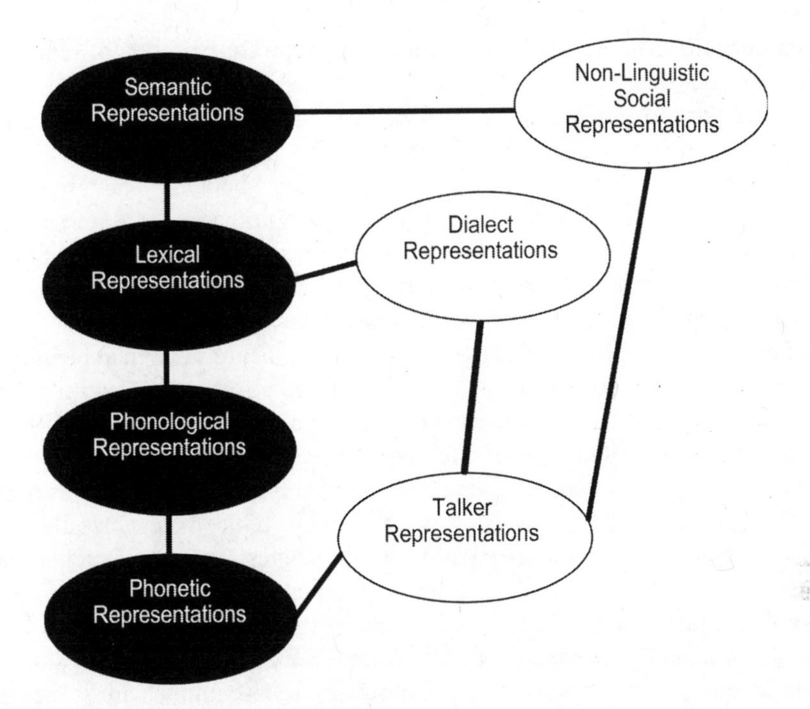

Figure 8.3 Levels of representation in an exemplar-based model of the perception and representation of dialect variation.

can also be used to identify lexical items, which can then specify phonological categories.

The representation of cross-dialect phonological differences requires a match between two utterances at the lexical level, and a mismatch or ambiguous or overlapping representations at the phonological level. For example, in order for a listener to learn that a talker has a *pen~pin* merger, the listener must encounter the phonological form /pɪn/ in a lexical context which unambiguously requires the lexical item *pen*. As Labov and Ash (1998) found, in semantically predictable contexts, listeners are able to adapt to unfamiliar vowel shifts as a result of the interaction between phonological and semantic information. Without any supporting semantic information (as in Rakerd and Plichta's neutral contexts, 2003), the listener assumes a match between his or her dialect and the dialect of the talker and does not adjust the mapping between phonological and lexical representations. In the model in Figure 8.3, the dialect representations are connected to the lexical representations to capture this important role of the lexicon in the construction of representations of phonological variation.

Dialect representations are also connected to talker-specific representations. In order to assign specific phonological phenomena to a given dialect category, the listener must know something about the background of the talker. That is, an individual talker may exhibit the *pen~pin* merger, but until the listener learns that the talker is from the southern United States, a link between the southern dialect category and the *pen~pin* merger cannot be established. Once connections have been made between dialect and phonological representations, however, these connections can then be used in explicit dialect categorization tasks. Thus, a listener's experience with dialect variation is crucial for the formation of robust dialect representations. When a listener encounters an unfamiliar talker with the *pen~pin* merger, the listener can access his or her dialect representations in order to make a guess as to the talker's regional background. However, the results of the dialect classification experiments (Clopper and Pisoni 2004, 2006) suggest that this particular part of the system is not well-specified for most listeners. This is likely the result of failures in the acquisition process. Given that we do not ever learn the regional background of many of the talkers we encounter, it is likely that the connections between phonological and dialect representations are somewhat sparse, making explicit dialect categorization of unfamiliar talkers difficult.

Individual talker representations are also connected to phonetic representations. Most listeners can accurately identify friends and family over the telephone based on very short utterances and listeners can also be trained to identify unfamiliar talkers in the laboratory (Nygaard, Sommers, and Pisoni 1994). The identification of an individual talker is based on idiosyncratic aspects of the talker's voice which are reflected in the phonetic representations of that talker's speech, including voice quality, pitch, and talker-specific instantiations of phonological categories (Pittam 1994). Thus, individual talker representations must be connected to the fine phonetic details of the talker's speech that are available at the level of phonetic representation.

Finally, non-linguistic social representations account for listeners' performance in attitude judgment tasks. Naïve listeners make highly consistent judgments about the intelligence or kindness of unfamiliar talkers, and their judgments correlate with dialect and/or language prestige (Ryan and Giles 1982). The interpretation of these results typically assumes that when listeners are asked to assess the intelligence of an unfamiliar talker based on a short sample of speech, they first activate a dialect representation and then respond based on the connections between that representation and stereotypes about that dialect that are stored as non-linguistic social information. Since these judgments typically reflect social stereotypes, they are also connected to other semantic representations, as well as individual talker representations.

The model shown in Figure 8.3 supplements a relatively traditional model of phonology (the black ovals) with representations of some of the kinds of social information (the white ovals) that have been shown to affect speech perception and spoken language processing. In particular, the model suggests mechanisms for the interference between linguistic and social information in speech perception, the poorly defined dialect representations exhibited by naïve listeners in the dialect classification tasks, and the role of acoustic and semantic context in the perception of local and non-local vowel systems. The bidirectional connections between the nodes account for perceptual learning of linguistic and social categories as well as later recognition of those categories. The model can also be interpreted with respect to second dialect acquisition and speech production more generally, where similar kinds of relationships would be predicted to exist.

The model in Figure 8.3 also suggests several future directions for sociophonetic perception research. First, the nature of the connections between the phonological information and the dialect representations must be more fully described. The specific phonological variants that are salient to naïve listeners have not been identified and the role of mediation by semantic information and the lexicon in constructing dialect representations must be investigated in much greater detail. Second, the role of dialect mismatch between the talker and the listener should be further explored at the level of word recognition and spoken language processing. Most of the existing research on dialect perception is focused on the explicit identification of either phonological or social categories, but cross-dialect interference in speech perception may have deeper implications for sociolinguistic interaction, models of language processing, and listener populations with speech, language, or hearing impairments. Finally, we have only scratched the surface of questions relating to linguistic experience and the ability of naïve listeners to access specific dialect representations in both speech perception and production. In all three of these research areas, speech science can provide baseline methods and results on which to build a research program in sociophonetics.

Acknowledgments

This work was supported by grants from the National Institutes of Health to Indiana University (T32 DC00012 and R01 DC00111) and to Northwestern University (F32 DC007237).

References

Clopper, Cynthia G., Brianna L. Conrey, and David B. Pisoni. 2005. Effects of talker gender on dialect categorization. *Journal of Language and Social Psychology* 24 (2): 182–206.

Clopper, Cynthia G., Susannah V. Levi, and David B. Pisoni. 2006. Perceptual similarity of regional dialects of American English. *Journal of the Acoustical Society of America* 119: 566–574.

Clopper, Cynthia G. and David B. Pisoni. 2004. Homebodies and army brats: Some effects of early linguistic experience and residential history on dialect categorization. *Language Variation and Change* 16: 31–48.

Clopper, Cynthia G. and David B. Pisoni. 2006. Effects of region of origin and geographic mobility on perceptual dialect categorization. *Language Variation and Change* 18: 193–221.

Clopper, Cynthia G. and David B. Pisoni. 2007. Free classification of regional dialects of American English. *Journal of Phonetics* 35: 421–438.

Goldinger, Stephen D. 1996. Words and voices: Episodic traces in spoken word identification and recognition memory. *Journal of Experimental Psychology: Learning, Memory, and Cognition* 22 (5): 1166–1183.

Johnson, Keith. 1997. Speech perception without speaker normalization: An exemplar model. In Keith Johnson and John W. Mullennix (eds), *Talker variability in speech processing.* San Diego: Academic Press, 145–165.

Labov, William and Sharon Ash. 1998. Understanding Birmingham. In Cynthia Bernstein, Thomas Nunnally, and Robin Sabino (eds), *Language variety in the South revisited.* Tuscaloosa: University of Alabama Press, 508–573.

Labov, William, Sharon Ash, and Charles Boberg. 2006. *Atlas of North American English.* New York: Mouton de Gruyter.

Lass, Norman J., Karen R. Hughes, Melanie D. Bowyer, Lucille T. Waters and Victoria T. Bourne. 1976. Speaker sex identification from voiced, whispered, and filtered isolated vowels. *Journal of the Acoustical Society of America* 59 (3): 675–678.

Liberman, Alvin M., Katherine Safford Harris, Howard S. Hoffman, and Belver C. Griffith. 1957. The discrimination of speech sounds within and across phoneme boundaries. *Journal of Experimental Psychology* 54 (5): 358–368.

Mullennix, John W., and David B. Pisoni. 1990. Stimulus variability and processing dependencies in speech perception. *Perception and Psychophysics* 47 (4): 379–390.

Niedzielski, Nancy. 1999. The effect of social information on the perception of sociolinguistic variables. *Journal of Language and Social Psychology* 18 (1): 62–85.

Nygaard, Lynne C., Mitchell S. Sommers, and David B. Pisoni. 1994. Speech perception as a talker-contingent process. *Psychological Science* 5 (1): 42–46.

Peterson, Gordon E. and Harold L. Barney. 1952. Control methods used in a study of the vowels. *Journal of the Acoustical Society of America* 24: 175–184.

Pierrehumbert, Janet B. 2001. Exemplar dynamics: Word frequency, lenition and contrast. In Joan Bybee and Paul Hopper (eds), *Frequency and the emergence of linguistic structure.* Amsterdam: John Benjamins, 137–157.

Pierrehumbert, Janet B. 2002. Word-specific phonetics. In Carlos Gussenhoven and Natasha Warner (eds), *Laboratory Phonology VII*. Berlin: Mouton de Gruyter, 101–140.

Pisoni, David B. 1973. Auditory and phonetic memory codes in the discrimination of consonants and vowels. *Perception and Psychophysics* 13 (2): 253–260.

Pittam, Jeffery. 1994. *Voice in social interaction*. London: Sage.

Preston, Dennis R. 1993. Folk dialectology. In Dennis R. Preston (ed.), *American dialect research*. Philadelphia: John Benjamins, 333–378.

Rakerd, Brad and Bartlomiej Plichta. 2003. More on perceptions of /a/ fronting. Paper presented at New Ways of Analyzing Variation 32: Philadelphia, October 9–12.

Ryan, Ellen Bouchard and Howard Giles (eds). 1982. *Attitudes towards language variation*. London: Edward Arnold.

Strand, Elizabeth A. 1999. Uncovering the role of gender stereotypes in speech perception. *Journal of Language and Social Psychology* 18 (1): 86–100.

Stuart-Smith, Jane, Claire Timmins, and Gwilym Pryce. 2005. Explaining phonological variation and change in an urban vernacular: Does television play a role? Paper presented at New Ways of Analyzing Variation 34: New York, NY, October 20–23.

Tees, Richard C. and Janet F. Werker. 1984. Perceptual flexibility: Maintenance or recovery of the ability to discriminate non-native speech sounds. *Canadian Journal of Psychology* 38 (4): 579–590.

Thomas, Erik R. 2001. *An acoustic analysis of vowel variation in New World English*. Durham, NC: Duke University Press.

Chapter 9

Perceptions of /a/ fronting Across Two Michigan Dialects

Bartłomiej Plichta, University of Minnesota Twin Cities and Brad Rakerd, Michigan State University

1. Ishpeming and Detroit

It would be difficult to find two Michigan cities more different than Ishpeming, in the Upper Peninsula, and Detroit, in Southeastern Lower Michigan (Figure 9.1). Ishpeming is a working-class town, known for iron-mining activities, lumbering, marble quarrying, and winter sports. Its population is mostly of Scandinavian origin. Detroit, on the other hand, is a large metropolitan area and is known for being a center of the American automotive industry. Detroit is a very dynamic, ethnically and linguistically diverse city.

The most recent US Census (2000) data shows population density to be among the highest in Michigan in the Metropolitan Detroit area and among the lowest around Ishpeming. The Detroit suburbs are among the more affluent areas in Michigan. The Ishpeming area, on the other hand, ranks as one of the poorest. Finally, fewer than 70% of the inhabitants of the Detroit area were born in Michigan, as compared to over 90% in Ishpeming.

These demographics make the urban and suburban areas of Southeastern Lower Michigan particularly prone to adopting and spreading new language norms (Labov 2001), while the more conservative, older populations of the Upper Peninsula would not be expected to participate in major sound change phenomena at nearly the same pace. It is, therefore, not surprising that the dialects of English spoken by the upwardly-mobile, white members of the dynamic and diverse speech communities of Metropolitan Detroit have been found to exhibit some of the most advanced stages of the Northern Cities Chain Shift (NCCS), while the dialects of English spoken in the Upper Peninsula rarely shows elements of NCCS (Labov, Ash, and Boberg 2006). Instead, the latter are under some Canadian influence.

Figure 9.2 shows the vowel systems of two young, white female talkers from the Detroit area. For both, NCCS is well advanced, with multiple

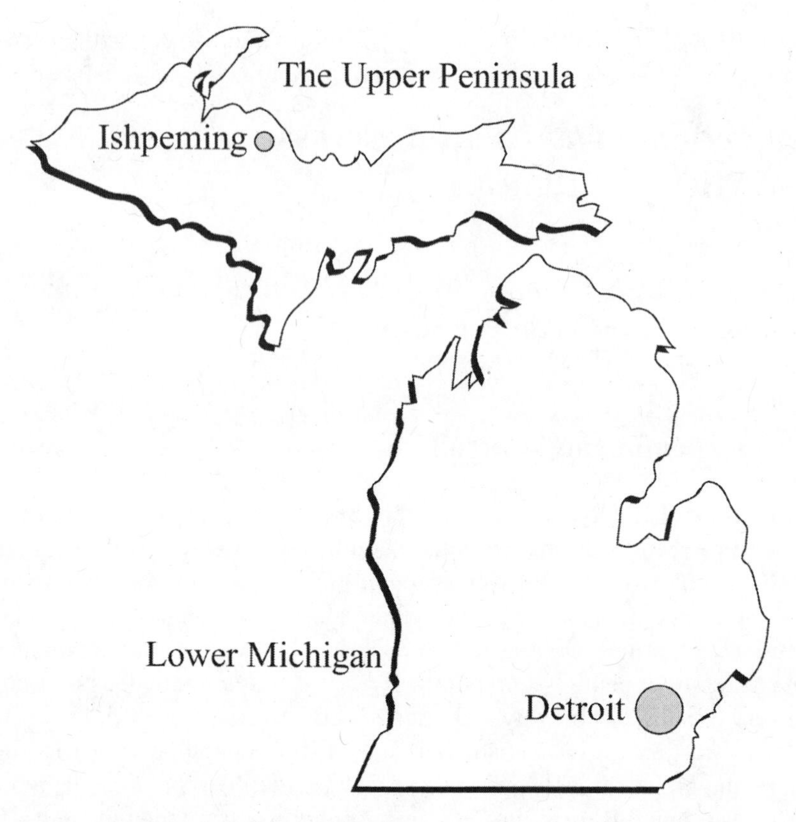

Figure 9.1 Ishpeming and Detroit, Michigan.

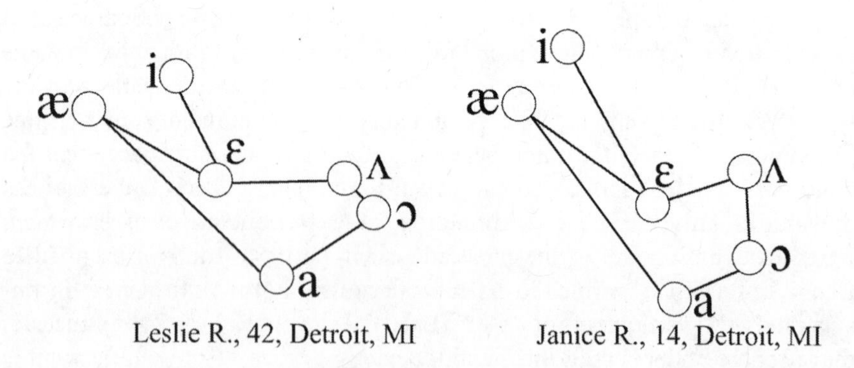

Figure 9.2 Sample vowel systems of Detroit females, from Labov et al. (1997), with permission.

vowel shifts, including /a/ fronting, /æ/ fronting and raising, and /ɛ/ lowering. Shifts of this kind represent a substantial source of acoustical variation in the production of vowels and a potential source of confusion for vowel perceivers. A possibility entertained in the present study is that perceivers who have knowledge of NCCS will minimize their confusion by taking its influences into account when they interpret vowel cues. In other words, their larger perception of a talker's dialect will set a frame for the perceptual identification of vowels that participate in NCCS.

To test this possibility, we compared listeners' perceptions of vowel tokens that might be subject to /a/ fronting, depending on whether those tokens occurred (a) at the end of sentences produced by a talker from the Detroit area whose speech showed clear evidence of NCCS (including /a/ fronting); or (b) at the end of sentences produced by a talker from the Ishpeming area whose speech showed no evidence of NCCS. The details of that test and its results are presented in Section 4. Section 2 first summarizes several findings regarding the phenomenon of talker normalization, which is a vowel perception effect closely related to the sociophonetic effect under study here. Section 3 then describes a field-based method of data collection that we employed to gather the perceptual data that are reported here.

2. Talker normalization in vowel perception

The speech signals that a listener must process are extremely variable. The sources of this variability are of several different kinds. One of the most notable is between-talker variation in vocal tract size, especially overall vocal tract length (VTL). VTL varies across both age (children vs. adults) and gender (women vs. men), and it directly affects the formant frequencies of all vowels produced by a talker (Fant 1970). Effects of VTL variation can be substantial. As an example, the formant frequencies of the vowel /æ/, as in "back," produced by male and female talkers from the same speech community can differ by as much as 300 Hz along $F1$ and $F2$. Differences of this magnitude are large enough to produce overlap between the formant frequencies of neighboring vowel categories (Peterson and Barney 1952). Despite this, perceivers are generally accurate in their categorization of vowels. This strongly suggests that an adjustment for VTL differences is made routinely, as part of the vowel perception process. This adjustment is commonly referred to as talker normalization (Strange 1999).

2.1 Intrinsic normalization

Proponents of intrinsic normalization theory argue that there is sufficient information within the spectral content of the vowel itself to support a listener's normalization computation. Two of the most convincing studies of intrinsic normalization are those by Miller (1989) and Syrdal and Gopal (1986). Miller demonstrated that the monophthongal vowels of American English can be represented as distinct clusters or "target zones" within a three-dimensional perceptual space, where the dimension correspond to: (i) the difference between the center frequencies of formants three and two (*F*3-*F*2); (ii) the difference between formants two and one (*F*2-*F*1), and the difference between formant one and a sensory reference (*F*1-SR). Miller examined a number of speech corpora in this way, and found that essential vowel category contrasts can be accurately represented by means of this model.

Syrdal and Gopal used a Bark transformation to devise a two-dimensional model of vowel recognition based primarily on the perception of critical distance, in Bark (Chistovich 1985). Their evidence for intrinsic normalization came from successful discriminant analysis of vowels. The discriminant plane resulting from the analysis was delimited by parameters derived from the ratios of Bark-transformed *F*1-*F*0, *F*2-*F*1, and *F*3-*F*2.

A limitation of these studies is that they did not expressly include substantial sources of sociolinguistic variability as it relates to vowels. Both studies used the Peterson and Barney corpus, which contains a well-documented but limited database of formant values from a select set of monosyllabic words, all produced in /hVd/ context. Very little is known about the speakers' dialect history, however, and no direct attempt was made to capture dialectal variation within the corpus. Other test corpora were similarly lacking in documented sociolinguistic variability.

To illustrate the potentially important role of sociolinguistic variation, a Bark analysis similar to that of Syrdal and Gopal (1986) was applied here to a corpus of monophthongal vowels elicited from 26 NCCS speakers and, for comparison, to the vowels of the Peterson and Barney corpus. Figure 9.3(a) shows a two-dimensional plot of the Peterson and Barney data delimited by *F*3-*F*2 and *F*1-*F*0 in the discriminant plane. It can be seen that each vowel occupies its own unique spot in the discriminant space (delimited by the ellipses), which suggests that with intrinsic normalization there should be very little vowel confusion. Results for the NCCS vowel set are quite different. There is substantial overlap among /a/, /ɛ/, /ʌ/, and /ɔ/ in this corpus, which suggests that vowel confusion would be more likely to occur in communities where NCCS is in progress (Preston, this volume). These results also suggest that in such communities the success of intrinsic normalization strategies is less likely.

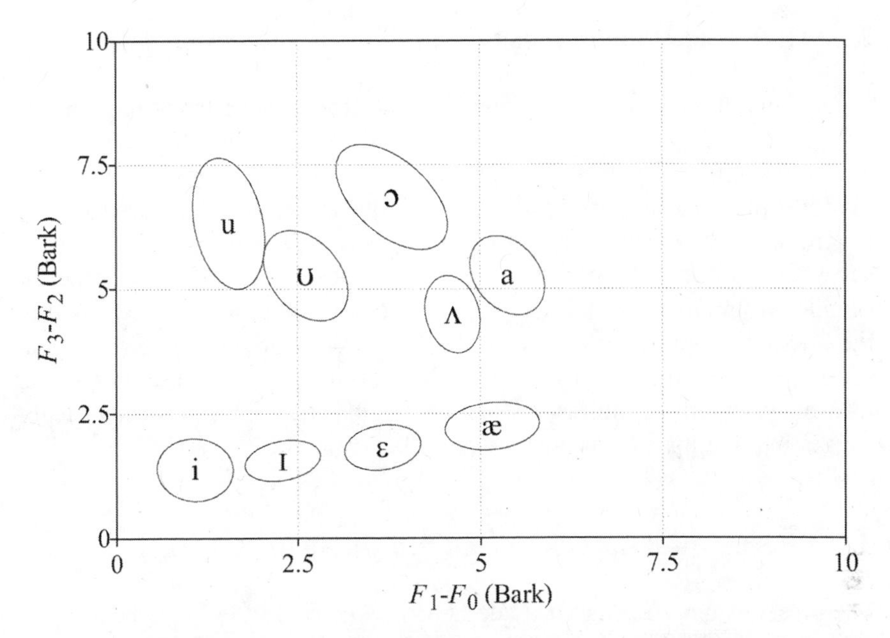

Figure 9.3a A two-dimensional discriminant analysis of Bark-transformed formant values for vowels in the Peterson and Barney (1952) corpus.

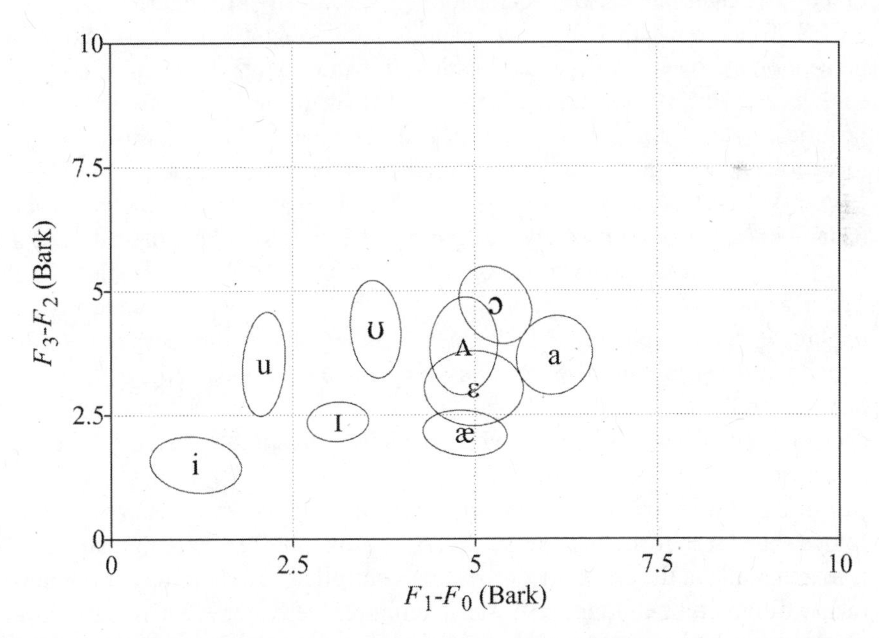

Figure 9.3b A two-dimensional discriminant analysis of Bark-transformed formant values for vowels in a corpus of 26 adult NCCS speakers.

2.2 Extrinsic normalization

Proponents of extrinsic normalization argue that vowel perception requires a frame of reference that is established based on information obtained from sources beyond the vowel itself. Ladefoged and Broadbent (1957) showed that this information can come from an earlier portion of an utterance that is in progress. They synthesized multiple versions of a lead-in sentence ("Please say what this word is.") by modifying its formant structure to simulate speech samples from talkers with differing vocal tract characteristics. Then each of the alternative forms was presented to listeners followed immediately by a set of common target words. The notable finding was that variations in the lead-in systematically influenced perception of target word vowels, strongly suggesting that listeners normalize for talker differences in real time.

3. Perception data collected "in the field"

The present study, like that of Ladefoged and Broadbent, asked whether perception of a vowel occurring at the end of an utterance may be influenced by information conveyed earlier in that utterance. But in this case the information of particular interest was sociophonetic, specifically information regarding NCCS. To learn whether and how this information might influence a listener's perception of vowels, we needed to gather data about a rather large inventory of speech samples. We also needed to test listeners who had diverse sociophonetic histories, and who resided in distant parts of Michigan. A decision was therefore made to conduct data collection for this study in the field, so much as possible.

Variationist sociolinguistic research has been dominated by fieldwork (Chambers 1995). Traditionally, sociolinguists prefer to collect their data at a place of the subject's own choosing, such as the home or place of employment. The argument of observer's paradox (Labov 2001) demands that fieldworkers not create an atmosphere in which the authenticity and naturalness of the language sample is compromised. Studies of speech perception, on the other hand, have generally been conducted in laboratory settings, where the environmental acoustics are well controlled and where the fidelity of stimulus presentation can be assured.

In designing the current sociophonetic speech perception study, a conscious effort was made to observe the main principles of sociolinguistic field research while at the same time providing controlled and rigorous experimental conditions to the extent possible. Therefore, the experiment was run at a quiet place of each participant's own choosing, with the stimulus presentation and response collection achieved by means of a portable (laptop) computer.

Some respondents chose to have the experiment run at their own house, while others chose a public library, quiet study room or a vacant conference room.

3.1 The Protocol

During testing, a respondent was asked to sit quietly and to face the computer, which was placed in a well-lighted location within easy reach and view. Instructions were presented on the computer screen to lead the respondent through all aspects of testing, and to pace the test sessions. The audio capability of modern portable computers is close in quality to that of older speech laboratory workstations. Speech stimuli were presented to respondents binaurally, at a comfortable listening level, via closed, flat-response headphones (Koss R80) that provided both high quality audio reproduction and also attenuation of any background noise. The respondent's decisions about stimuli were reported to the computer by means of button presses directed through the built-in touchpad.

Test results were written to a database in real time. The database was later merged dynamically with demographic information about the respondent into a data file that could be cross-tabulated to obtain information about individual respondents and/or about groups of respondents.

4. The present study

4.1 Talkers and listeners

As noted previously, the present study asked whether listeners would interpret vowel tokens that might by subject to /a/ fronting differently, depending on whether those tokens occurred in sentences spoken by a talker from the Detroit area of Southeastern Lower Michigan where NCCS is active, or by a talker from the Ishpeming area of the Upper Peninsula where NCCS effects are minimal. A second important variable in the study concerned the sociophonetic backgrounds of the listeners themselves. The study respondents were selected to include one subgroup from Lower Michigan who had had extensive listening experience with NCCS, and a second subgroup from the Upper Peninsula who had had much more limited experience.

4.2 Respondents

The respondents were 18 young adults (ages 19—34) of European-American descent. Nine of them (4 men, 5 women) were recruited from the Detroit area of Lower Michigan; nine (5 men, 4 women) were recruited from the Ishpeming area of the Upper Peninsula. To participate in this study, an individual had to have been born and raised in one of these regions and to have never left there for more than a year. It was also required that the person be a native speaker of English.

4.3 An /a/-to-/æ/ Vowel Continuum

Fronting of /a/ primarily affects the frequency of the second formant (Labov, Yeager, and Steiner 1972). We therefore generated a continuum of synthetic vowels that varied from /a/ to /æ/ along the $F2$ dimension. The continuum was based on real vowel formant data obtained from two young, middle-class, adult male talkers. One of these talkers, referred to here as *Talker LM*, was from the Detroit area, the other, *Talker UP*, was from Ishpeming. Talkers LM and UP were selected to be matched, so much as possible in physical size, in voice fundamental frequency, and in the general characteristics of their vowel systems. Figure 9.4 shows a comparison of acoustic properties of their vowels obtained by LPC analysis of 4 pronunciations of 50 vowel tokens in a broad range of consonantal contexts (see Appendix 9.1). It can be seen that the overall range of

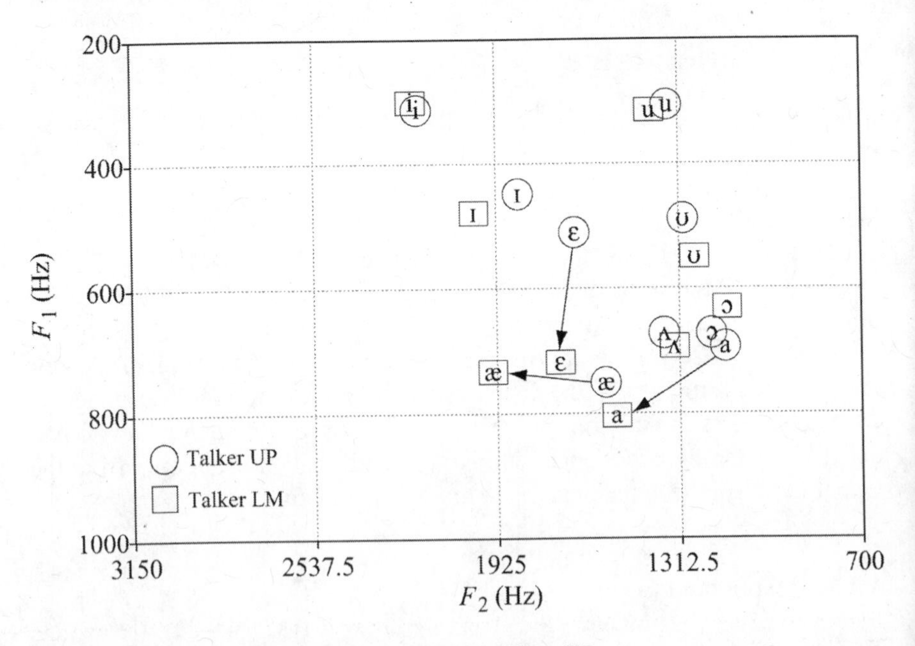

Figure 9.4 Vowel systems of Talker LM and Talker UP.

variation in $F1$ and $F2$ was very similar for the two talkers. It can also be seen that corresponding vowels were generally very similarly placed within the $F1$/$F2$ space, except in instances where an effect of NCCS would be expected.

A parametric speech synthesizer (Sensimetrics 1997) was used to generate the /a/-to-/æ/ synthetic vowel series. Each vowel item was synthesized with a fundamental frequency contour that fell linearly from 120 Hz at onset to 100 Hz at offset. With the exception of $F2$, formant frequencies were fixed at approximately the mid-point of the range between /a/ and /æ/, as produced by both talkers ($F1$ = 750 Hz, $F3$ = 2500 Hz, $F4$ = 3500 Hz).

The frequency of $F2$ was varied from stimulus item to stimulus item. In all seven different vowel stimuli were created, with $F2$ values ranging from 1245 Hz to 1443 Hz in 33 Hz steps. Pilot testing showed that listeners' perceptions regularly transitioned from /a/ to /æ/ within this interval.

4.3 "Hot—hat" and "sock—sack"

The complete vowel series was embedded in each of two CVC syllable frames, with appropriate formant transitions imposed at onset and offset. The first frame was /hVt/, which yielded a word series that varied from "hot" to "hat" along the continuum. The second frame was /sVt/, which varied from "sock" to "sack." Figure 9.5 shows the endpoint stimuli from each of these word series.

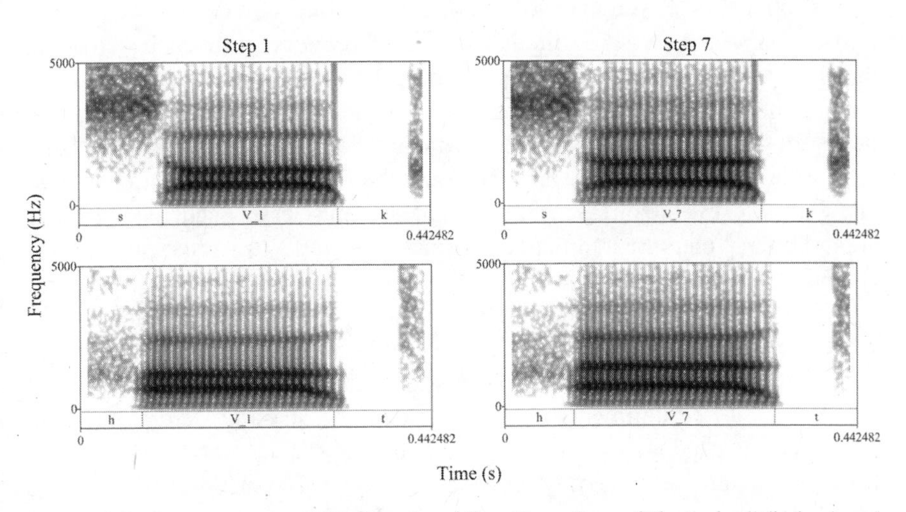

Figure 9.5 Spectrograms of the Step 1 and Step 7 versions of "hot—hat" (below) and "sock—sack" (above).

4.4 Target words in citation-Form: The qualifying test

A condition of participation in the main experiment (referred to below as the sociophonetic test) was that a listener had to be sensitive to the acoustical variations in *F*2 that were represented across the stimulus set. Accordingly, prior to participating in the main experiment, all listeners completed a qualifying test in which they were asked to categorize the vowel heard in each item of the "hot"—"hat" word series, and each item of the "sock"—"sack" word series, with the words presented in citation form.

Over the course of this test each word item was presented a total of four times. The order of these presentations was randomized and different on every test run. After a word was presented, the respondent's task was to decide whether the target vowel sounded more like /a/ (as in "hot" or "sock") or /æ/ (as in "hat" or "sack"). The choice was then reported by pressing the appropriate button on the computer's touchpad. The entire citation-form test was completed at a single sitting, in about 30 minutes time.

4.5 Psychometric functions and cross-over points

Figure 9.6 shows the results of the qualifying test, which was passed by all 18 of respondents. The panel at the top shows /a/ and /æ/ psychometric functions for the UP respondents; the panel at the bottom shows them for the LM respondents. Psychometric functions are plots showing the percentage of trials on which a vowel stimulus was heard as /a/ or /æ/ at each step along the continuum. Note that the seven steps of the vowel continuum are ordered from right to left. This is to agree with "standard" vowel space plots, like those shown in Figures 9.2 and 9.4, which order *F*2 frequency values from right to left to show their consonance with the front-back dimension of vowels. The lowest value of *F*2 for the present stimulus series occurred at step #1 (1245 Hz). *F*2 incremented thereafter (in 33 Hz steps) to its maximum value (1443 Hz) at step 7.

It can be seen that the UP and LM groups responded similarly across the vowel series. Both heard /a/ nearly 100% of the time at steps 1 and 2, and then a progressively declining percentage of the time thereafter. The percentage of /æ/ judgments was complementary, starting at zero, and then incrementing gradually to virtually 100% by steps 6–7. The *cross-over point* between /a/ and /ae/ is marked in each panel with a dashed line. It occurred at step 4.7 for UP listeners, and at 4.8 for LM listeners. These cross-over points provide a best estimate of the positioning of the perceptual category

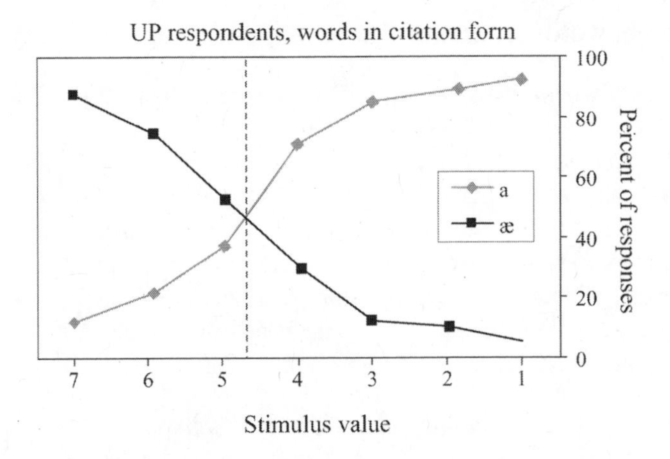

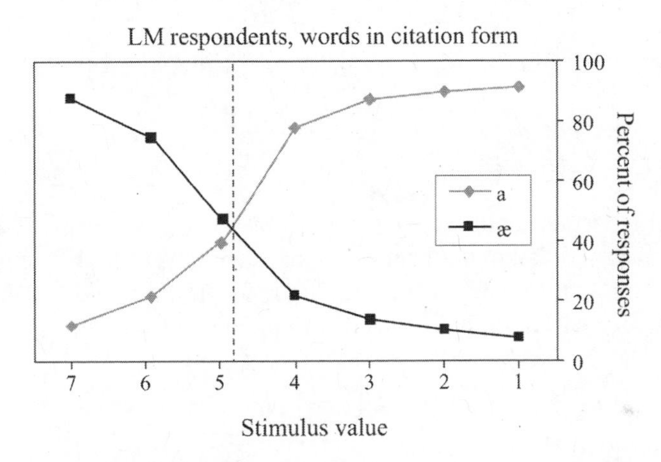

Figure 9.6 Results of the qualifying test. The upper panel shows the probability that a vowel stimulus item was judged as /æ/ (dark line) or /a/ (light line) by respondents from the UP (n=9). The lower panel shows the results for respondents for LM (n=9).

boundary between /a/ and /æ/ for each group. A subject-by-subject analysis showed no significant difference between the cross-over point means for the two respondent groups ($t(16) = 0.24$; $p > 0.05$). This indicates that even though there were a number of specific phonetic differences between the UP and LM vowel systems (especially regarding vowels /æ/, /ɛ/, and /a/, see Figure 9.4), both groups shared a similar general representation of the /a/—/æ/ category boundary.

4.6 Target words in sentence carriers: The sociophonetic test

For the sociophonetic test, the target words were embedded in sentence carriers produced by Talker LM and by Talker UP. Both talkers recorded the same set of four semantically neutral sentences. The recordings were made in a quiet place with a close-talking, flat-response microphone (Sennheiser HMD25–1) and a digital audiotape recorder (Tascam DA-P1). Each sentence contained a broad sampling of vowels, to include specific exemplars of /a/ and /æ/. At the end of each sentence, the talker produced the syllable "uh" in order to complete the sentence prosodically, and as a "filler" to be digitally replaced by the synthetic word stimuli. The recorded sentences were as follows:

1. *Bob was positive that he heard his wife, Shannon, say "uh."*
2. *Cathy's card was blue and said: "pot", while Mary's was black and said: "uh."*
3. *The key to winning the game of boggle is to know lots of short words like "uh."*
4. *It turned out that the most common response to question thirty-two on last week's test was: "uh."*

The finalized stimulus set was created by pairing Talker LM's four carrier sentences and Talker UP's four sentences with every /hVt/ and /sVk/ target word item, in the manner shown in Figure 9.7. The syllable "uh" at the end of the sentence was digitally replaced with the target word items.

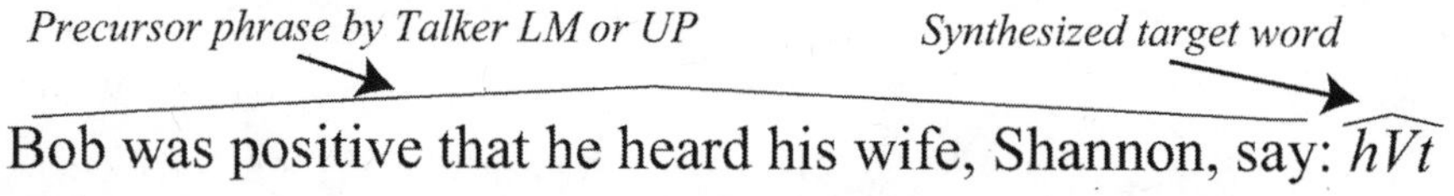

Precursor phrase by Talker LM or UP *Synthesized target word*

Bob was positive that he heard his wife, Shannon, say: $\widehat{hVt}$

Figure 9.7 Sentence-carrier stimulus design. A sentence produced by Talker UP or LM was digitally joined to an /hVt/or /sVk/ target word.

4.7 Testing

On sentence-carrier test trials, a single sentence stimulus (selected at random from the full set available) was presented. The listener's task was to attend carefully to the vowel heard in the last word of the sentence and to report (by means of a touchpad response) whether it sounded more like "hat" or "hot" (or "sack" or "sock"). There were a total of 112 test stimuli for the sentence-carrier test (2 talkers x 4 sentences x 2 syllable frames x 7 vowel steps). Each of these was judged four times over the course of the test, for a total of 448 trials. The randomized stimuli were presented in eight blocks of 56 trials each. The experiment was administered in two 30-minute parts, with a 30-minute break in between.

4.8 Results for the UP Respondents

The UP subgroup of respondents were selected for this study based on their longtime residence in the Upper Peninsula of Michigan, and correspondingly, on their limited experience with speech that was strongly influenced by NCCS. Figure 9.8 shows the UP respondents' results for the sociophonetic test. The psychometric functions plotted in the upper panel of the figure are for vowel items presented in sentences produced by Talker UP. The functions in the bottom panel are for vowels items in sentences produced by Talker LM.

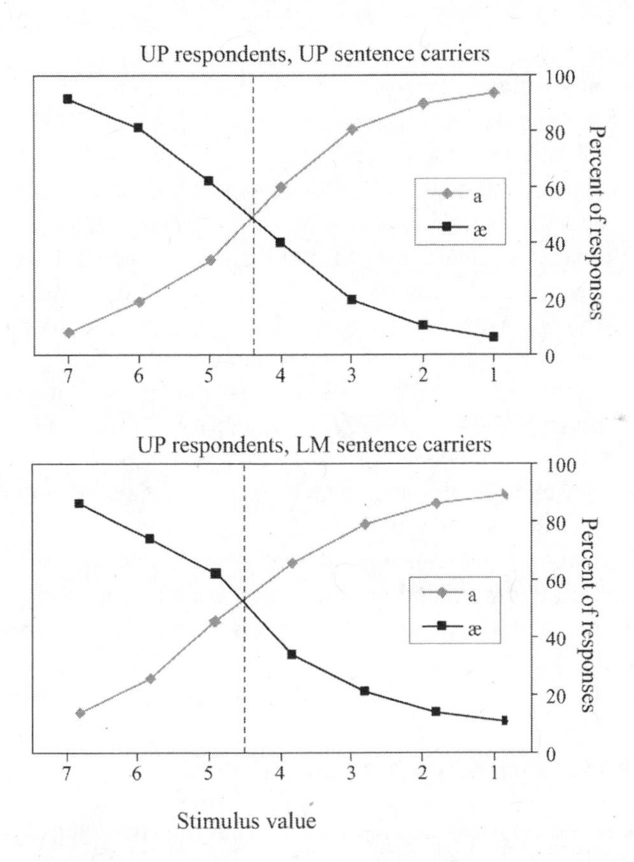

Figure 9.8 Psychometric functions for the UP respondents. The upper panel shows responses for sentence carriers produced by Talker UP; the lower panel shows responses for sentence carriers produced by Talker LM.

The response patterns were very similar for the two talkers, with the /a/-to-/æ/ cross-over point occurring at steps 4.3 for Talker UP, and at step 4.5 for Talker LM. There was no statistical difference between these two values ($t(8) = 0.96$; $p > 0.05$). This strongly suggests that the respondents from the UP did not take NCCS influences into account when interpreting vowel cues.

4.9 Results for the LM respondents

The LM respondents had resided in Southeast Lower Michigan throughout most of their lives and they were highly familiar with speech marked by NCCS. Figure 9.9 shows the LM respondents' results for the sociophonetic test. There is strong evidence that they were sensitive to the dialectal difference between the two talkers. For Talker UP (upper panel) the cross-over from /a/ to /æ/ occurred at step 4.3. For Talker LM (lower panel), the result was significantly different ($t(8) = 4.34$; $p < 0.002$), with the cross-over occurring at step 5.4, more than a full step further *front* (i.e., at a higher value of $F2$) along the continuum than for Talker UP.

Another point to be made about the response profile for the LM respondents is that it was very similar to that of the UP respondents when the talker was from the UP and had a speech pattern that showed little evidence of NCCS. This can be seen by comparing the upper panels of Figures 9.8 and 9.9, both of which show a crossover value of 4.3. But a cross-over difference of 0.9 continuum steps arose when the talker was from Lower Michigan and exhibited NCCS (compare the results for Talker LM shown in the lower panels of the figures; cross-over = 4.5 for UP respondents and 5.4 for LM respondents.) Apparently the LM respondents formed a perceptual representation of NCCS speech—a representation that included /a/ fronting—and when they encountered a talker whose speech pattern was consistent with that representation it modulated their perceptual interpretation of the available vowel cues. The UP respondents, on the other hand, had no such representation (and showed no vowel shift), presumably owing to their much more limited experience with speakers who exhibit NCCS.

5. The role of the speech community

The results of the present study showed: (1) that information about a talker's dialect can play a significant role in vowel identification; and (2) that this effect is constrained by listener-dependent sociolinguistic factors. Specifically, it

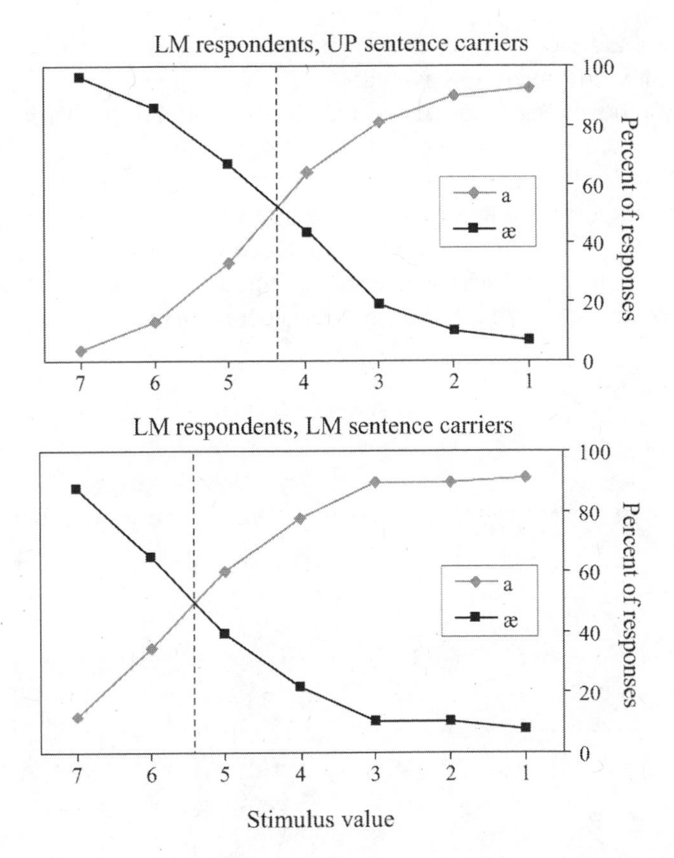

Figure 9.9 Psychometric functions for the LM respondents. The upper panel shows responses for sentence carriers produced by Talker UP; the lower panel shows responses for sentence carriers produced by Talker LM.

was found here that listeners from Detroit, Michigan were sensitive to NCCS-influenced vowels—as revealed in individual talkers' sentence productions—while listeners from Ishpeming, Michigan were not. When trying to account for this pattern of results, one is drawn to the notion of speech community. Speech community is typically defined as a group of speakers united on the basis of their shared language characteristics, as well as regional and social attributes (Wolfram and Schilling-Estes, 1998).

The speech communities of Ishpeming, in the Upper Peninsula, and Detroit, in Lower Michigan, differ from each other substantially in regard to their adoption of NCCS. The dialectally diverse Detroit-area populations have been exposed to a number of NCCS pronunciation features, and the middle and upper-middle-class European Americans (such as the participants of the present study) are likely to have adopted at least some of these features in their own productions. Thus, the range of available phonetic variants of the vowels /a/ and /æ/ in the community is substantial, and far greater than the range found in the more dialectally conservative populations of the Upper Peninsula. Exposure to these variants on an everyday basis appears to be a critical factor in the formulation of NCCS-sensitive perceptual representations for vowels. In essence, the speech community acts as a dialectal filter that is used actively in the speaker-hearer negotiation of vowel identity.

Appendix 9.1

Wordlist used to elicit vowel samples from talker LM and talker UP.

1. jaw
2. job
3. knock
4. lid
5. lot
6. nasty
7. pot
8. set
9. shed
10. heat
11. shot
12. sit
13. soothe
14. nag
15. man
16. caught
17. head
18. cod
19. coat
20. sought
21. test
22. hut
23. wheat
24. but
25. bag
26. move
27. bit
28. book
29. boot
30. rude
31. but
32. sad
33. cap
34. cot
35. dad
36. bead
37. left
38. bet
39. dead
40. did
41. hat
42. sat
43. hit
44. should
45. shut
46. hook
47. hot
48. cat
49. mat
50. cut

References

Chambers, J. K. 1995. *Sociolinguistic theory: Linguistic variation and its social significance*. Oxford: Blackwell.

Chistovich, Ludmilla. 1985. Central auditory processing of peripheral vowel spectra. *Journal of the Acoustical Society of America* 77 (3): 789–805.

Fant, Gunnar. 1970. *Acoustic theory of speech production with calculations based on X-ray studies of Russian articulations* ([2d] ed.). The Hague: Mouton de Gruyter.

Labov, William. 2001. *Principles of linguistic change: social factors.* Oxford: Blackwell.

Labov, William, Sharon Ash, and Charles Boberg. 2006. *The atlas of North American English: Phonetics, phonology, and sound change.* Berlin/New York: Mouton de Gruyter.

Labov, William, Malcah Yeager, and Richard Steiner. 1972. *A Quantitative study of sound change in progress*. Philadelphia: U.S. Regional Survey.

Ladefoged, Peter and Donald E. Broadbent. 1957. Information conveyed by vowels. *Journal of the Acoustical Society of America* 1 (29): 99–104.

Miller, James D. 1989. Auditory-perceptual interpretation of the vowel. *Journal of the Acoustical Society of America* 85 (5): 2114–2134.

Peterson, Gordon and Harold Barney. 1952. Control methods used in a study of vowels. *Journal of the Acoustical Society of America* 24: 175–184.

Sensimetrics. 1997. HLsyn (Version 2.2). Cambridge: Sensimetrics Corporation.

Strange, Winifred. 1999. Perception of vowels: Dynamic constancy. In J. M. Pickett (ed.), *The acoustics of speech communication.* Boston: Allyn and Bacon, 153–165.

Syrdal, Ann K. and H.S. Gopal. 1986. A perceptual model of vowel recognition based auditory representation of American English vowels. *Journal of the Acoustical Society of America* 79 (4): 1086–1100.

U.S. Census Bureau. 2000. United States Census 2000. http://www.census.gov/main/www/cen2000.html (accessed February 10, 2010).

Wolfram, Walt and Natalie Schilling-Estes. 1998. *American English: Dialects and variation*. Malden, MA: Blackwell.

Chapter 10

Belle's Body Just Caught the Fit Gnat: The Perception of Northern Cities Shifted Vowels by Local Speakers

Dennis R. Preston, Oklahoma State University

This chapter addresses four questions concerning the comprehension of single words in areas where a dramatic vowel shift is underway or near completion.

1.) Do locals have an advantage in understanding words that contain advanced tokens of change-in-progress vowels? Labov and Ash (1997) say yes, but Plichta (2004) says not particularly for isolated words. Both show an advantage for locals when the words are placed in carrier phrases (the latter even when the phrases contain no semantic or pragmatic clues to the target word's identity).

2.) Can the notion "local" also reflect demographic details (e.g., sex, age, status, urbanity, ethnicity) in such studies of comprehension? Labov and Ash (1997) suggest an advantage for more locally oriented speakers, and such orientation can obviously be related to demographic identities in many cases.

3.) When vowels are misunderstood, are they misunderstood in the direction of the position of vowels in the pre-shifted system (Labov and Ash 1997) or in the direction of vowel positions in the newer one?

4.) What historical, phonetic, perceptual, and other characteristics of the vowels involved influence their different comprehension rates?

This chapter investigates the degree to which such factors influence the comprehension of single-word tokens in the "Northern Cities (Chain) Shift" (NCS), a vowel rotation in which the vowels /æ/, /ɑ/, /ɔ/, /ɛ/, /ʌ/, and /ɪ/ are no longer in the positions of the traditional vowel quadrangle associated with American English. Figure 10.1 shows that traditional positioning and the arrows indicate the direction of movement of the NCS.

Figure 10.2 shows the F1-F2 positions of nine vowels of American English from two previous studies in which single word comprehension tasks played a part. The dotted line shows the position of these vowels in the Peterson and Barney study (1952), and the solid line links the vowel positions determined by Hillenbrand et al. (1995). Since the vowel samples played in the present

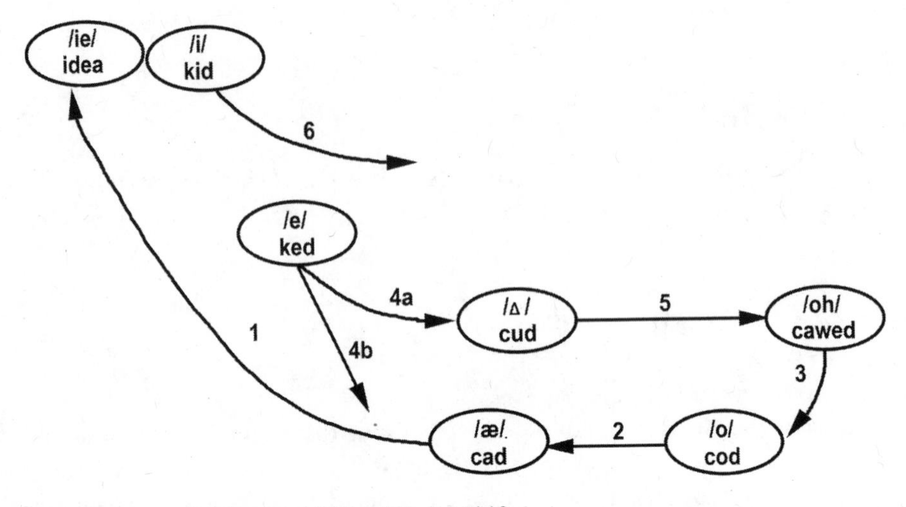

Figure 10.1 The Northern Cities (Chain) Shift.

study were all from female speakers, only female vowel positions are shown from these two earlier studies. The Peterson and Barney values are very much those of the typical vowel quadrangle associated with American English vowels (as in Figure 10.1). The Hillenbrand et al. positions, however, show influence of the NCS: some /ɪ/ lowering and backing; /ɛ/ lowering and backing, /æ/ fronting and raising, /ɑ/ fronting, and /ɔ/ lowering and fronting; only the backing of /ʌ/ is not represented, and that is a late step in the NCS process.

The single word comprehension test results for Peterson and Barney for the six vowels involved in the NCS are shown in Table 10.1. Seventy respondents heard seventy-six speakers (men, women, and children) say each vowel twice, for a total of 10,640 hearings of each vowel. Two of the speakers were not born in the United States, and a few learned English as a second language. Most of the women and children were said to be "from the "Middle Atlantic speech area," but the men "represented a much broader regional sampling of the United States; the majority of them spoke General American." The hearers were said to represent "much the same dialectal distribution as the group of speakers," and thirty-two of the speakers were among the hearers (Peterson and Barney 1952: 177). Table 10.1 shows that comprehension rates were very good—around .90; /ɑ/ was least well understood, at a rate of .87. Some of the scores are not shown here since they involved non-NCS vowels.

Table 10.1 shows that the Hillenbrand et al. results are also very good, in spite of the apparently shifted position of the NCS tokens. The 139 talkers were again men, women, and children, but they were predominantly from

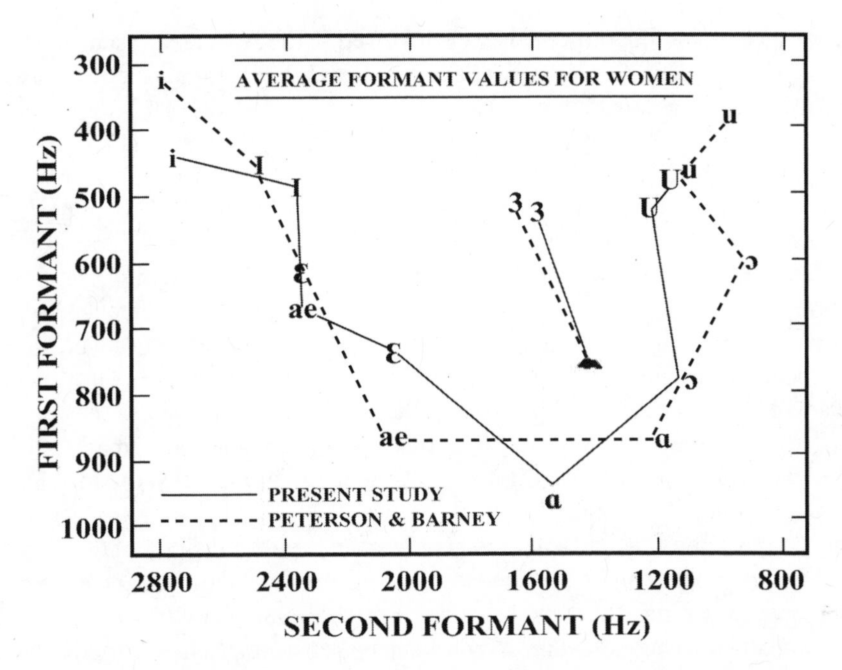

Figure 10.2 Comparison of Peterson and Barney with Hillenbrand, et al. (1995: 3103, women only)

Table 10.1 Percent Correct (for NCS Vowel Tokens Only) in Three Single-Word Comprehension Studies

Vowel	% Correct	
	Peterson & Barney 1952	Hillenbrand et al, 1995
ɪ	92.9	98.8
ɛ	87.7	95.1
æ	96.5	94.1
ɑ	87.0	92.3
ɔ	92.8	82.0
ʌ	92.2	90.8

southeastern and southwestern Michigan, a fact reflected in the NCS shift of their vowels. There were twenty undergraduate student listeners from Western Michigan University. None were recruited from the talker population, but all were at least minimally trained in phonetics and were predominantly from the same region. Each hearer heard each vowel of the twelve tested once from each talker, but only the vowels involved in the NCS are presented here. Except for /ɔ/ (.82), the results are again better than .90 for all vowels (based on about 2,780 hearings of each).

Although the Peterson and Barney results are perhaps not too surprising, from the position of the vowels in the Hillenbrand et al. representation seen in Figure 10.2, one might have expected worse results. It is important to remember, however, that the results are overall—i.e., Hillenbrand et al. do not divide the results for either hearers or talkers by sex. We might assume, therefore, that the perhaps more conservative (i.e., less NCS influenced) pattern of the male speakers helped improve the overall scores. Moreover, since the hearers were undergraduate students from Western Michigan University, many of them would have been under the same NCS influence as the speakers, and that may also have improved the comprehension rate. Finally, since the hearers were all at least minimally phonetically trained, that too may have provided some advantage.

At best, however, Hillenbrand et al. was an accidental study of the ability of locals to understand NCS vowels. First, the men and children speakers did not have such radically shifted systems, and the values shown in Figure 10.2 for women are averages; some may have been considerably less shifted. Additionally, there was no discrimination among hearers; some were undoubtedly younger women from urban southeastern Michigan whose systems would have been even more advanced than that seen in Figure 10.2. Others, however, may have been young men or women from central or northern Michigan or even the Upper Peninsula of Michigan where the shift has had moderate, little, or even no influence. Some would not have been Michiganders at all, and their dialect backgrounds are unknown.

The current study focuses on the ability of locals who have been shown to participate in the NCS to various degrees (Evans et al. 2000) to understand single word items that are radically shifted to positions in the new system, as shown in Figure 10.3.

The following advanced NCS tokens (all spoken by young women from urban southeastern Michigan) were played (twice) for the respondents: *bag, cut, big, can, bond, bed (=bud), hawk, done, sock, tin, hot, caught, pat, Ben (=bun), dawn, bed (=bad).* All likely misunderstandings are real words, e.g., *bag* as *beg* or *big*; *cut* as *caught*, etc. An acoustic analysis of these tokens showed that seven were considerably shifted in the direction of the NCS (*Ben [=bun], bed = [bad], pat, caught, cut, tin,* and *sock*), and they are the ones reported on here. Four vowels not involved in the NCS (*boot, beet, bait,* and *boat*) were also included in the test but showed little or no misunderstanding, with correct comprehension rates of .96, .98, .98, and .99, respectively.

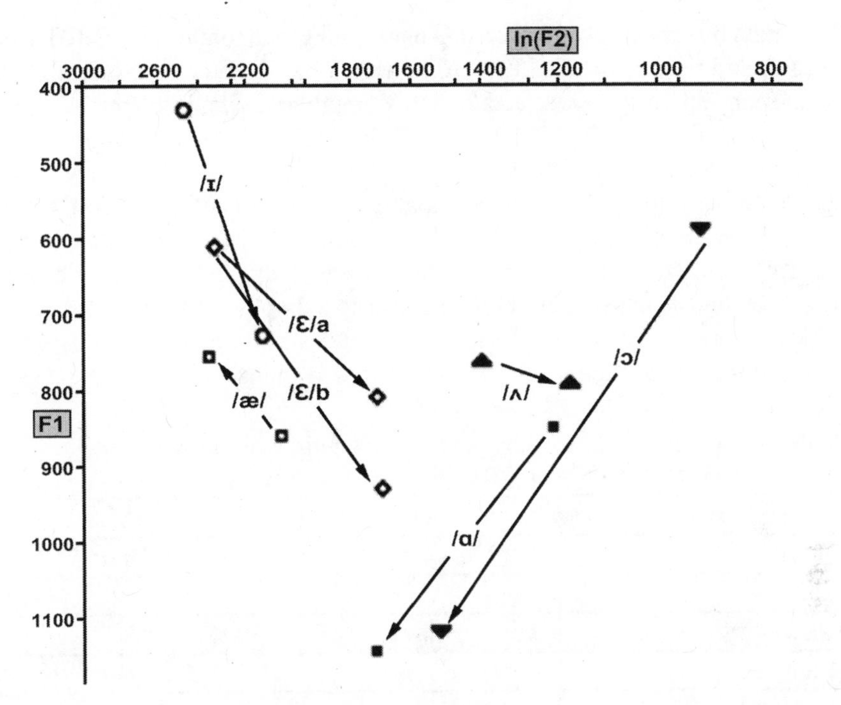

Figure 10.3 A comparison of the Peterson and Barney 1952 means for female speakers (base of arrow) and the tokens played in the current study (tip of arrow) on a Bark scale.

In contrast, the best NCS vowel comprehension rate was .90 for the vowel /ɛ/ (i.e., *bed*, when shifted into the area of /æ/; see 4b in Figure 10.1). The respondents wrote down the word they heard, and items were judged correct if the intended vowel was indicated, not the entire word (e.g., *pet* was judged correct for *bed*).

To avoid age-related hearing loss and to make use of a large pool of respondents, young listeners (ages 15–30 years of age) only are reported on here. The five groups studied were as follows:

1. USM = Southern urban Michiganders, European-American (N=70)
2. ASM = Southern urban Michiganders, European-American immigrants from Appalachia (N=2)
3. RSM = Southern rural Michiganders, European-American (N=17)
4. MM=Mid-Michigan rural Michiganders, European-American (N=39)
5. AASM = Southern urban Michiganders, African-American (N=24)

These five groups were entered as one factor group for the VARBRUL run, and sex and the six vowels of the NCS were also tabulated as factor groups. The dependent variable was accuracy of comprehension of the vowel.

Based on previous work in the area (e.g., Evans et al. 2000), I expected the groups to be ordered as follows as regards comprehension, if comprehension can be linked to the degree of participation in the shift: USM > RSM > MM > AASM > ASM.

Table 10.2 shows the overall results of the study, and these single word tokens obviously cause considerable confusion. Two vowels, /ɔ/ and short /ɛ/ (= [ʌ]), do not even reach the .50 level. Ash 1988 also found less than .50 comprehension by Chicagoans of radically shifted /ɔ/and /ɛ/.

Table 10.2 GOLDVARB Weights and Percentages for Factors Influencing the Comprehension of NCS Vowels

Factor Group	Weight	%
Female	n.s.	0.66
Male	n.s.	0.62
USM	n.s.	0.66
RSM	n.s.	0.66
ASM	n.s.	0.64
MM	n.s.	0.61
AASM	n.s.	0.57
ɛ =[æ]	0.819	0.90
ɑ	0.809	0.90
æ	0.582	0.74
ʌ	0.566	0.73
ɪ	0.406	0.58
ɔ	0.290	0.46
ɛ =[ʌ]	0.093	0.18

There is some rearrangement of the order of groups from the prediction given previously, but the group that has completed or nearly completed the NCS (USM) is the one which comprehends best, and one of the groups that has been shown to participate least in the NCS (AASM) comprehends worst. The rural speakers from southern Michigan (RSM), since they are closer to the areas where the change has already taken place and in greater contact with speakers of it, are equal to the USM group and ahead of the Mid-Michigan (MM) group, which is farther geographically from the centers of change. Although there are only two respondents in the Appalachian immigrant group (ASM), their comprehension rate is slightly behind the RSM group although they all live in urban areas. As earlier work has shown, however (e.g., Evans 2001), the younger members of this group, although not completely culturally integrated into surrounding urban southeastern Michigan, are apparently are very well integrated linguistically. The lower ranking for this group in the aforementioned prediction would have been realized only if older speakers (immigrants themselves from such areas as Kentucky, Tennessee, and West Virginia) had been included. The prejudice against their so-called hillbilly speech was considerable when they came to southeastern Michigan, and the grandchildren of immigrants have given it up entirely and participate in local patterns of use and change.

Table 10.3 Correctness Percentages for All Ages among Three Research Groups

	Young	Middle	Old
MM	.70	.70	.65
AASM	.68	.68	.60
ASM	.76	.66	.64

Note: NB: These scores are higher than those shown in Table 10.2 since they include correct recognition of the non-NCS vowels /i/, /u/, /o/, and /e/.

Table 10.3 provides additional data from middle aged and older speakers and shows again how the youngest ASM speakers are even better comprehenders of these items than the RSM and AASM respondents, both of whom have been in Michigan longer, the AASM respondents even in urban southeastern Michigan longer. But the change is greater from oldest to youngest for this group, and it is more recent, occurring between the middle and younger age groups almost entirely.

Although, as Table 10.2 shows, neither group nor sex was significant, both show trends in the expected direction; women are more advanced speakers of the NCS, and they apparently comprehend somewhat better. These trends, and one for status, can also be seen in the data for the ASM, MM, and AASM data only for which those categories are available.

These results allow me to return to two of the questions asked at first. There does appear to be a clear advantage in comprehension for local groups where local is understood as a regional term; the shift is strongest in the urban

Table 10.4 Overall Correct Responses for Status and Age Groups (MM, ASM, and AASM only)

Age	Young	Middle	Older
	61	55	49

Status	Middle	Working	
	60	54	

areas of southeastern Michigan, and that group (USM) leads in comprehension. Although it is weaker in production in rural southern Michigan (RSM), those speakers appear equal to urban residents in comprehension, but the rural Mid-Michigan (MM) group lags behind. It is possible to conclude from these data that local people more intensely involved in linguistic change are better comprehenders of even single word exemplars of that change. This is similar to the findings of Labov and Ash (1997), who found a local advantage, although it was better expressed when tokens were embedded in carrier phrases. This finding is, however, different from that of Plichta (2004), who found that locals did not continue to interpret advanced resynthesized tokens of an NCS vowel as the same as less advanced ones unless those words were embedded in carrier phrases.

In both these earlier studies, however, the nonlocals were not geographically close to the center of the change; they were from completely different speech areas (e.g., Chicago or Philadelphia hearers listening to Birmingham speakers or Upper Peninsula Michigan speakers listening to increasingly advanced tokens of an NCS vowel).

The second question asked in the present study addressed demographic characteristics of the hearers, and Tables 10.2 and 10.4 suggest that there are such features that prefer comprehension:

Ethnicity—European American
Sex—female
Age—younger
Status—middle

As much previous work has shown, these are the characteristics of speakers most advanced in the shift.

The third question asked if vowels were misunderstood as "pre-shift" or "post-shift" items. For example, imagine a case of /ɛ/ backing (along track "a" in Figure 10.1). It moves into a position occupied by /ʌ/ in the pre-shift system, but since /ʌ/ has backed into a position closer to the pre-shift position of /ɔ/, the moved /ɛ/is now perhaps closer to fronted /ɑ/ in the post-shift system than anything else in the emerging system. Table 10.5 shows, however, that misunderstandings are indeed based on pre-shift positions.

Table 10.5 Correct and Incorrect Vowel Identification

Item	Total	/ɛ/	/ɑ/	/æ/	/ʌ/	/ɪ/	/ɔ/	/ɛ/	other
/ɛ/ = /æ/	142	128	*0*	**8**	0	0	0	x	6
/ɑ/	143	*1*	129	**13**	0	0	0	x	3
/æ/	142	**34**	0	108	0	*0*	0	x	0
/ʌ/	143	0	11	1	104	0	**24**	x	3
/ɪ/	142	**58**	1	*0*	0	83	1	x	0
/ɔ/	142	0	**71**	3	0	0	66	x	2
/ɛ/ = /ʌ/	142	x	2	1	**109**	1		25	4

Gray shading shows correct answers; bold type shows the most frequent mistakes—overwhelmingly "pre-shift" items. Italic type shows possible misunderstandings if the "post-shift" effect had been at work. For example, /ɑ/ is misunderstood most frequently as /æ/, even though /æ/ has shifted. If a post-shift interpretation were at work, then one might expect misunderstandings of /ɑ/ as /ɛ/ (following the "b" line of Figure 10.1), but only one such misunderstanding occurred.

A re-examination of Figure 10.3, the Bark plot of the Peterson and Barney (base of arrow) and experimental (point of arrow) vowels in question, also shows this pre-shift effect to be at work except for the misunderstandings of /ʌ/ as /ɔ/.

What about the individual vowels? The bottom section of Table 10.2 shows the GOLDVARB results for this factor group. What are some phonetic facts about these vowels that might account for this order? Here is a list of assumptions:

1. Recency—the oldest changes in the NCS should be best understood.
2. Phonetic clue—vowels which give some distinctive clue to their identity other than formant positions should be better understood.

3. Phoneme class—vowels not involved in complex, historical phoneme word-class changes should be better understood.
4. Distinctness—vowels at a greater distance from those with which they might be confused should be better understood. This distinctness will be considered in terms of pre-shift positions only due to the findings shown in Table 10.5 and Figure 10.1.
5. Chromaticity—vowels which, as a result of F2 changes, bring about some chromatic change (e.g., +round → -round) may be more poorly understood.
6. Formant perceptual strategy—vowels which, as a result of F2 changes, bring about a change in formant perceptual strategy may be more poorly understood.

Two other features that might have been considered were not. First, the identity of the words and the words that they might have been misunderstood as were not considered since both seem to have more or less equal familiarity as lexical items. Second, no consonant environments (as determined by Stevens and House 1963, for example) had any effect on the realization of these samples so that they might have been reordered in comprehension.

These assumptions are assigned scores in Table 10.7. The higher the score, the less likely the vowel will be understood. The numbers assigned to the order of the shift are taken from previous studies (e.g., Labov 1994: 195). No points were assigned short i and e on the historical dimension, reflecting the relatively uncomplicated history those vowels have had from Old English to Modern English; there has been very little historical category change for words with these vowels. Only short æ had no point assigned to it for phonetic distinctiveness on the basis of its acquiring an inglide; no other vowel gains a specific phonetic character that would distinguish it from surrounding items. Shifted vowels that overlapped or came very close to the preshifted form that they might be confused with (short e, open oh, and short i) were given a point. /ʌ/ was given a point for the confusion that additional roundness might cause (with open oh), and open oh was given one for its loss of roundness (which might contribute to its confusion with short o). Finally, short e was given a point due to the fact that its change from a front to central vowel results in a change in perceptual strategy, i.e., central and back vowels are perceived on the basis of a central weighting between F1 and F2; front vowels are perceived on the basis of a distinct weighting of F1 and a central weighting between F2 and F3 (Strange 1999: 154–155).

These scores reflect the comprehension rates fairly well and suggest that NCS order and other phonetic factors enter into the ability of local speakers to comprehend radically shifted vowels even in single word presentations.

Table 10.6 Ranking of Phonetic Facts Influencing Comprehension of NCS Vowels

Item	NCS	Historical class	Phonetic clue	Distinct	Round	PS	Total
1 short æ	1	1	0	0	0	0	2
2 short o	2	1	1	0	0	0	4
3 wedge ʌ	5	1	1	0	1	0	8
4 short e	4	0	1	1	0	1	7
5 open oh	3	1	1	1	1	0	7
6 short i	6	0	1	1	0	0	8

Note: higher scores = worse comprehension; "PS" indicates a change in perceptual strategy.

Wedge /ʌ/ is, however, a bit of a puzzle. Why is its comprehension rate (GoldVarb .64) nearly as good as the rates for short æ (.70) and o (.67), the earliest moved elements of the shift? It is not only late moved but also scored for lack of phonetic distinctiveness and development of a potentially confusing roundness feature. I can offer only two suggestions. First, open oh moved so much earlier (and lost its roundness characteristic) that any confusion with it is simply ruled out. That, however, would deny the pre-shift effect that seems clearly to be in operation here. Second, perhaps wedge √ has moved so slightly back along the F2 trajectory, as seen in Figure 10.7, that misunderstanding is less likely than for the other more dramatic shifts.

In conclusion, how do these results compare with previous studies of local comprehension of shifted tokens (Labov and Ash 1997, Rakerd and Plichta, 2003)? Labov and Ash say "There is a consistent local advantage in the recognition of advanced forms of the local vernacular" (566). The young, European American, southeastern Michigan group was indeed best here, although Rakerd and Plichta suggest this advantage is related to the use of carrier phrases. That is not the case here.

Labov and Ash also note that "Words heard in isolation are most consistently identified with less advanced forms . . ." (566). That is also true here, in almost every case.

Labov and Ash further note that "The ability to recognize advanced forms . . . is greater among high school students than college students and greater among African-American subjects than white subjects" (567). This study also shows that local subjects who are more advanced in the shift themselves are better at comprehension.

Finally, various historical and phonetic elements play a role in the comprehension of vowels involved in dramatic change, some features of which modify the effect of the order of change of elements in a direction that better matches comprehension rates.

By now the title should be clear: I heard "Belle's body just caught the fit gnat," but the Michigander said "Bill's bawdy jest cut the fat knot." OK; so my pragmatic organizer is shot to hell. (And I didn't really hear anybody say that anyway.)

References

Ash, Sharon. 1988. Contextless vowel identification. A paper presented to the 17th annual meeting of NWAVE (New Ways of Analyzing Variation in English): Montreal, October 29.

Evans, Betsy. 2001. *Dialect contact and the Northern Cities Shift in Ypsilanti, Michigan*. Doctoral dissertation, East Lansing: Michigan State University.

Evans, Betsy, Rika Ito, Jamila Jones, and Dennis R. Preston. 2000. Change on top of change: Social and regional accommodation to the Northern Cities Shift. *Taal en Tongval* (A special issue to honor Dr. Jo Daan on her ninetieth birthday, ed. by Hans Bennis, Hugo Ryckeboer, and Jan Stroop) 52 (1): 61–86.

Hillenbrand, James, Laura A. Getty, Michael J. Clark, and Kimberlee Wheeler. 1995. Acoustic characteristics of American English vowels. *Journal of the Acoustical Society of America* 97 (5): 3099–3111.

Labov, William. 1994. *Principles of linguistic change: Internal factors*. Oxford: Blackwell.

Labov, William. 1996. The organization of dialect diversity in North America. A paper presented to the 4th International Conference on Spoken Language Processing: Philadelphia, October 6. (Available at http://www.ling.upenn.edu/phonoatlas/)

Labov, William and Sharon Ash. 1997. Understanding Birmingham. In Cynthia Bernstein, Thomas Nunnally, and Robin Sabino (eds), *Language variety in the South revisited*. Tuscaloosa/London: The University of Alabama Press, 503–578.

Peterson, Gordon E. and Harold L. Barney. 1952. Control methods used in a study of the vowels. *The Journal of the Acoustical Society of America* 24 (2): 175–184.

Rakerd, Brad and Bartłomiej Plichta. 2003. More on perceptions of /a/ fronting. A paper presented to the 32nd annual meeting of NWAVE (New Ways of Analyzing Variation in English). Philadelphia, October 11.

Stevens, Kenneth N. and Arthur S. House. 1963. Perturbation of vowel articulations by consonantal context: An acoustical study. *Journal of Speech and Hearing Research* 6 (2): 111–128.

Strange, Winifred. 1999. Perception of vowels: Dynamic consistency. In J.M. Pickett (ed.), *The acoustics of speech communication*. Boston: Allyn and Bacon, 153–165.

Chapter 11

Linguistic Security, Ideology, and Vowel Perception

Nancy Niedzielski, Rice University

1. Introduction

Recent technological advances have greatly increased the sociophonetician's ability to capture a vast array of very different types of data. Powerful and easily available programs like Praat have allowed sociophoneticians the ability to capture even the slightest variation in the acoustic signal, revealing, as this volume shows, degrees of variability in production that would be impossible to discover using auditory methods alone. Programs such as Praat offer an additional tool, however: the ability to manipulate the acoustic signal. Researchers can synthesize and resynthesize speech relatively quickly, and the results are of high enough quality to be used in perceptual work. More recent technology, such as eye-tracking and brain-imaging, have allowed the sociophonetician to discover in even more intricate detail how sociophonetic variation is perceived. Thus, work on the both the production *and* the perception of variation have become important components of sociophonetics, and interesting and complex interactions between the two of these components moves forward our understanding of language variation and change.

While research on the perception of sociophonetic variation using these varied methodologies has offered valuable insight into both implicit and explicit knowledge of variation, it has placed questions regarding social cognition firmly at the forefront: what do people *know* about sociophonetic variation? While decades of research on language attitudes and ideologies have shown that knowledge of variation is often not accurate, it is not clear exactly why such inaccurate "knowledge" persists in the face of even substantial counter-evidence.

In the following sections, I examine some of the findings from recent work on the perception of talker variation, not only in sociophonetics, but in psychology as well. I will suggest that different methodologies from these two fields offer insights into what human perceivers know implicitly, and suggest that while the more accurate implicit knowledge is crucial in the process of language change, language attitudes affect the often less accurate explicit knowledge, but that this serves to create and maintain self-identity, particularly in the case of the linguistically secure speaker.

2. Research on implicit knowledge

At its most basic level, implicit knowledge of variation is revealed through processes such as language accommodation. According to Communicative Accommodation Theory (Giles and Coupland 1991), speakers move towards (or, in some cases, away from) their interlocutors during conversation. Early studies revealed that this happened at broad discourse levels such as speech volume, speech rate, and gestures, but research on speech perception in psychology reveals that this occurs at much more fine-grained, perhaps phonetic levels. For instance, research on shadowing (e.g., Goldinger 1998) shows that listeners can determine with surprising accuracy whether a lexical item was produced as a "shadow" of another speaker's production of that item. Figure 11.1 shows that subjects are able to match the item that was produced as a shadow at levels significantly above chance, and they are even more accurate if the item is produced after several repetitions of shadowing, and if the item is a lower-frequency lexical item. Interestingly, the bottom graph shows that the tendency of speakers to accommodate to others diminishes with time; subjects were less accurate if the shadow was delayed. This suggests that speakers are implicitly aware of low-level features of their interlocutors' production, even to the extent that they mimic those features in their own production.

Studies looking more overtly at the perception of language variation reveal to what degree subjects are aware of the patterning of variation in their speech communities. Hay, Warren, and Drager (2006) tested subjects' abilities to distinguish lexical items involved in a merger in progress in New Zealand English (specifically the "beer/bear" merger). Subjects were asked to identify lexical items presented aurally, and following the test, they were asked what age they thought the speaker was. They found that subjects were more accurate in distinguishing potentially merged lexical items if they thought that the speakers were older, suggesting an implicit awareness of the fact that the merger is correlated with age.

Koops, Gentry, and Pantos (2008) also tested implicit knowledge of the correlation between mergers and age, this time in Houston, Texas. Older Anglo speakers who are native to Houston merge high and mid front lax vowels pre-nasally, while these vowels are unmerging in the dialect of younger Anglos. Language attitude tests show that Houstonians correlate the merger with region, particularly urban

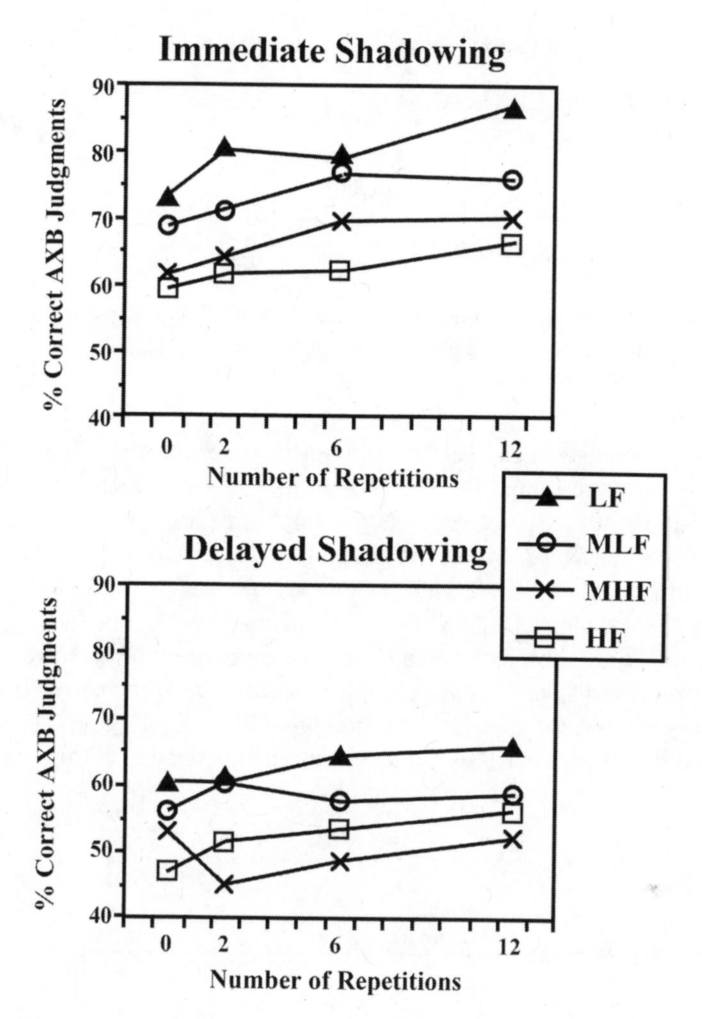

Figure 11.1 Accuracy of subjects' judgments of shadowed lexical items, according to number of repetitions of shadows, and frequency of lexical items. (HF = "high frequency," etc.; Goldinger 1998.)

versus rural, but not age. However, Koops et al. (2006) suggest that Houstonians are in fact implicitly aware that this feature is associated with age. They used eye-tracking technology to determine to what extent subjects fixate on potentially homophonous competitors presented on a computer monitor (as shown in Figure 11.2); in the middle of the screen, is a photograph of one of three women: a "young" woman, a "middle-aged" woman, and an "older" woman.

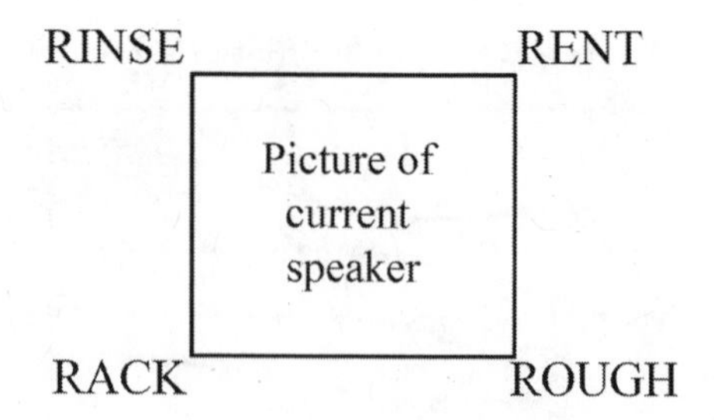

Figure 11.2 Screen subjects view as they hear "rinse" presented aurally. In the center is one of three photographs of women varying in age.

The eye-tracker measures the amount of time that the subjects look at the words printed around the subjects. Figure 11.3 displays the results: the perceived age of the speaker affects the amount of time spent looking at the competitor ("rent"), so that a photograph of an older woman causes the subjects to look at what would more likely be a homophonous lexical item in an older person's dialect. Thus, while Houstonians do not claim explicit knowledge of the correlation between age and the unmerging of these vowels, the eye-tracker reveals that they have implicit knowledge of the correlation.

I suggest that the fact that Houstonians fail to offer age a factor in the unmerging of these vowels as evidence that the knowledge of this correlation

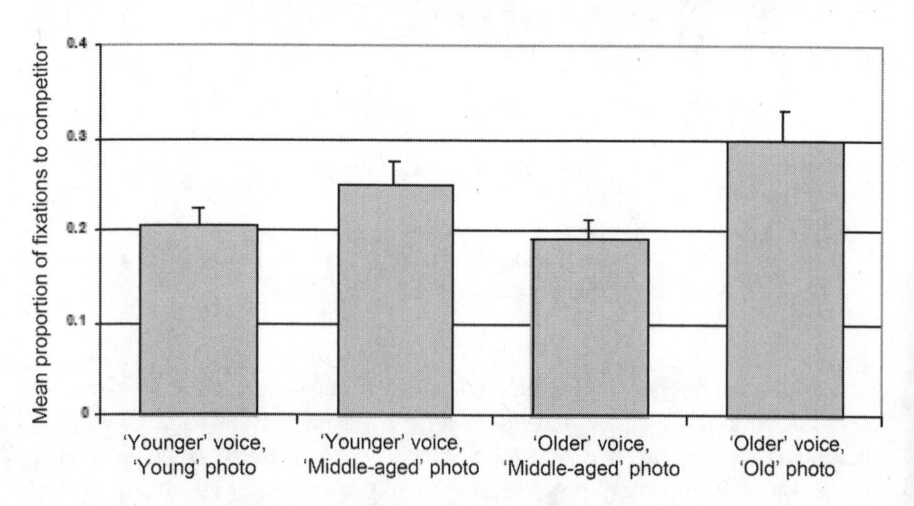

Figure 11.3 Number of fixations on the competing lexical item, by actual and perceived age of speaker (Koops, Pantos and Gentry 2006).

is implicit, rather than explicit. An even more dramatic demonstration of the fact that knowledge about speaker variation can be completely implicit comes from work on what Vitevitch (2003) calls "change deafness." In this set of experiments, he asked subjects to shadow a speaker producing a relatively long list of lexical items, some of which he labeled "hard" and some of which he labeled "easy" (based on, among other things, the amount of phonological distracters an item had). In the middle of the shadowing task, he gave subjects a rest-break, and upon their return from the break, they continued the shadowing task. Some of the subjects, however, were now shadowing a different speaker. In Figure 11.4 are the results of the reaction times after the rest break. What Vitevitch found was that, *regardless of whether the subjects detected the change in speaker,* the reaction times were longer. In other words, even without explicit awareness that the speaker had changed, the subjects reacted as if they had implicit awareness of this fact (particularly with "hard" lexical items), by showing a statistically significant increase in reaction times, comparable to those subjects who did detect the speaker change, rather than those subjects for whom the speaker was not changed.

Finally, brain-imaging studies suggest that exposure to different phonemic contrasts actually causes different neural responses. In Conrey, Potts, and Niedzielski (2005), neural activity of speakers with and without the front lax

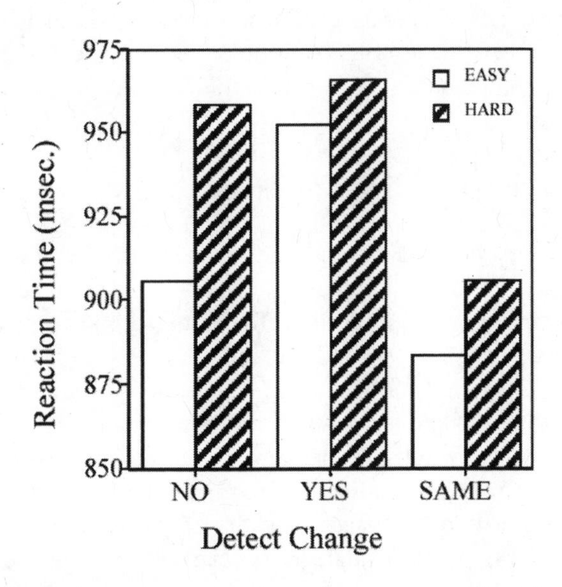

Figure 11.4 Shadowing task reaction times, by awareness of speaker change (Vitevitch 2003).

vowel merger prenasally (as illustrated previously in the Koops et al. study) in Houston, Texas was recorded while subjects heard a sentence like "Sign the check with a pen" or "Sign the check with a *pin." For non-merged speakers, the second sentence is ungrammatical, but it is acceptable for those that do not make the pin/pen distinction. Those subjects with the merger exhibited a reduced late positive event-related potential component, compared to those without the merger, in response to hearing potentially ungrammatical sentences. This suggests that implicit phonological knowledge affects even neural activity (or perhaps vice versa), and suggests that such knowledge has a demonstrated neurological component.

This set of research on implicit knowledge of speaker and language suggests a mechanism by which sociolinguistic indicators—that is, variables below the level of conscious awareness—can spread through a given speech community with the speed and systematicity seen in variable after variable (such as the regular 100 Hz raising of (aw) in Philadephia by decade, shown in Labov [2001]). Shadowing tasks reveal that speakers accommodate towards even low-level variation immediately, and that there is greater accommodation with increased numbers of repetitions. The research on mergers shows that there is implicit knowledge of the correlation between, in these instances, age and variation, even if subjects do not reveal this knowledge explicitly. Thus, contact can produce immediate accommodation, which with lengthened and stronger ties can become more permanent, and, furthermore, people have intricate knowledge of how variation patterns in their community, even if they are not able to consciously express this knowledge.

3. Research on explicit knowledge

Researchers from various different fields have used several different methods in the investigation of language attitudes and language ideology. For instance, the work of perceptual dialectologists (e.g., Preston 1989, Preston 1999, Long and Preston 2002, and the authors therein) on US English provides information about non-linguists' impressions of dialect boundaries, regional definitions of standard English, and the regions in which respondents believe that "correct" English is spoken. Social psychologists (e.g., myriad studies including and since Lambert 1967, Giles 1970, Giles and Powesland 1975) investigate attitudes towards speakers of various dialects, and the perceived standardness of those dialects is revealed through the degrees and types of prestige assigned to their speakers. Language attitude work (e.g., Lippi-Green 1997) has provided ample information about the forms that are considered "incorrect" or nonstandard, and the perceived users of such forms. Such studies attempt to collect what given sets of subjects "know" about how language patterns in their speech communities, and, as most studies reveal, much of the work involves prescriptive ideology.

Sociophonetic work on the perception of vowel tokens in the Detroit area (Niedizelski 1999) shows that subjects react in perceptual tests if they "know" even low-level phonetic features of a speaker's dialect, even if that knowledge is inaccurate. In a number of studies (e.g., Preston 1989, Niedzielski and Preston 1999), Anglo middle-class residents of southeastern Michigan have demonstrated high degrees confidence in the correctness of their own variety of American English, or what Labov 1966 called *linguistic security*. Perhaps the clearest demonstration of this is Figure 11.5. In this figure, results of a ranking task are presented: subjects from southeastern Michigan were asked to label the correctness of the dialects spoken in each state, with the darker shades representing the highest degrees of "correctness." As is apparent from an examination of the figure, Michigan—and only Michigan—receives the highest correctness ranking. This phenomenon of ranking their own speech as the most correct is confirmed by the interviews presented in Niedzielski and Preston (1999). Michigan residents unequivocally offer their variety as an example of correct American English, often referring to theirs as the variety closest to what dictionaries or grammar books prescribe.

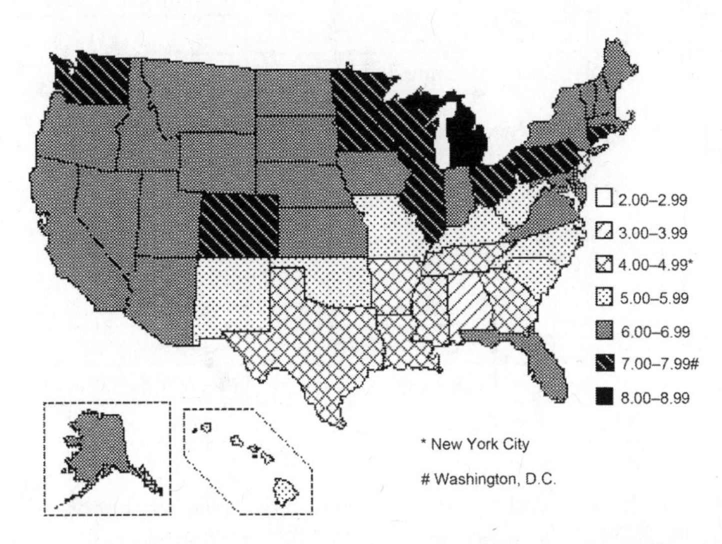

Figure 11.5 Correctness rankings of Michigan residents (Preston 1989).

However, as many sociophonetic studies have shown, the vowel systems of speakers from this area are rapidly diverging from what most Americans—including most Michiganders—consider "standard." As participants in the Northern Cities Shift (NCS), which encompasses speakers from not only Michigan but Ohio, Illinois, Wisconsin, and New York, their vowels have shifted dramatically away from values offered as those found in "standard American English" (SAE), for example those offered in Peterson and Barney (1952).

Speakers in Michigan appear to have no explicit awareness of this, and they reveal this even in perceptual tasks. Tables 11.1 and 11.2 present the results of a perception task given to 42 Michigan residents, in which they were asked to choose from a list of synthesized vowels the vowel that best matched a vowel that they heard in a Michigan speaker. Specifically, after hearing a Michigan speaker produce a sentence containing the words "last" and "pop" (both of which contain a shifted vowel: /æ/ and /a/ respectively), the subjects were asked to listen to a set of six synthesized tokens, and to choose the token that they thought the speaker produced. They were given the option of listening to the sentence as many times as they wished (although few listen more than once), and were then to record their choice.

Table 11.1 Formants of Tokens of "last" Played for Respondents (N=42) and Responses

Token #	F1	F2	Label of Token	# and % of Retspondents Who Chose Each oken
1	900	1530	hyper-standard	4 (10%)
2	775	1700	canonical /æ/	38 (90%)
3	700	1900	actual vowel produced	0

Table 11.2 Formants of Tokens of "pop" Played for Respondents (N-42) and Responses

Token #	F1	F2	Label of Token	# and % of Respondents Who Chose Each Token
1	770	1050	hyper-standard	4 (10%)
2	900	1400	canonical /a/	36 (86%)
3	700	1600	actual vowel produced	2 (5%)

These tables reveal that few of the respondents chose the token that was the actual vowel the speaker produced. In fact, none of the respondents chose the vowel that matched the speaker's /æ/, and only two of the respondents chose the actual token representing the speaker's /a/. Instead, most respondents chose tokens that were produced from formants that matched those found in Peterson and Barney (1952)—vowels that are considered "standard." Even more intriguing, the remainder of the respondents chose tokens that I have labeled "hyper-standard." This label refers to the fact that these tokens are farther from the actual token then even the standard token—farther back and lower in the case of /æ/, and farther back in the case of /a/.

In other words, the respondents did *not* choose the NCS token as the one that best-matched the vowel of a fellow Michigan speaker, but rather chose the one that conformed to their notion of a standard. While it did not conform to what the speaker produced, it is consistent with the notion that Michigan speakers are SAE speakers. This gives us a picture of speakers who believe that they are speaking a standard variety of a language, but who do not in fact find actual features in their own dialect to be standard. I suggest that their notions of standardness come not from the acoustic evidence they are presented with every day as they talk to their cohorts, but from the fact that their sense of linguistic security allows them to filter out evidence incongruent with their beliefs.

In other words, their ideological beliefs of themselves as standard speakers causes them to misidentify vowel tokens in their own speech, if they are being explicitly asked about those tokens. I suggest that this is a direct result of the linguistic security that these speakers display. In short, speakers in regions characterized by high degrees of linguistic security (i.e., speakers who believe that their regional dialect is "standard") have a great deal at stake in their self-stereotype, and this causes them to filter out information (in this case, acoustic evidence) that runs counter to their own beliefs. Giddens (2000) offers a suggestion of precisely why these speakers would do this:

> [T]he plethora of available information is reduced via routinised attitudes which exclude, or reinterpret, potentially disturbing knowledge. From a negative point of view, such closure might be regarded as prejudice, the refusal seriously to entertain views and ideas divergent from those an individual already holds; yet, from another angle, avoidance of dissonance forms part of the protective cocoon which helps maintain ontological security. (187)

Thus, (routinized) language attitudes can inhibit the acquisition of accurate knowledge of language variation, if there is a cost to such acquisition. In the case of Anglo Detroiters, that cost is the surrender of their identity as speakers of Standard American English, a high cost indeed.

4. Discussion

In Figure 11.6 I offer a model of how implicit and explicit knowledge interacts with speaker identity for our linguistically secure speaker, based on an earlier model of speaker identity first proposed in Meyerhoff and Niedzielski (1994). In our earlier model of speaker identity, we proposed that individuals' identities could be cognized as a sphere that had two poles: one corresponding to an ingroup, or "personal" identity, and one corresponding to an outgroup, or "group" identity. We suggested that people "spin" this sphere towards one pole or the other, based on the type of interaction they are engaged in. I add to this model of speaker identity the notion of a filter, which allows varying degrees of acoustic information to be acquired. As the model suggests, more information is allowed near the group identity pole—that is, more acoustic information about a speaker is acquired if the interaction is with an outgroup, or less personal, interlocutor. This allows for the implicit information to be acquired, even in immediate contexts. However, less information is allowed in at the personal end, as in the case of the Detroiters, when they interact with a speaker that they believe to be an ingroup member. Their routinized language beliefs filter out more of the acoustic information, as a mechanism to avoid the "disturbing knowledge" that Giddens speaks of—knowledge that would threaten their own self-identity as a speaker of standard English.

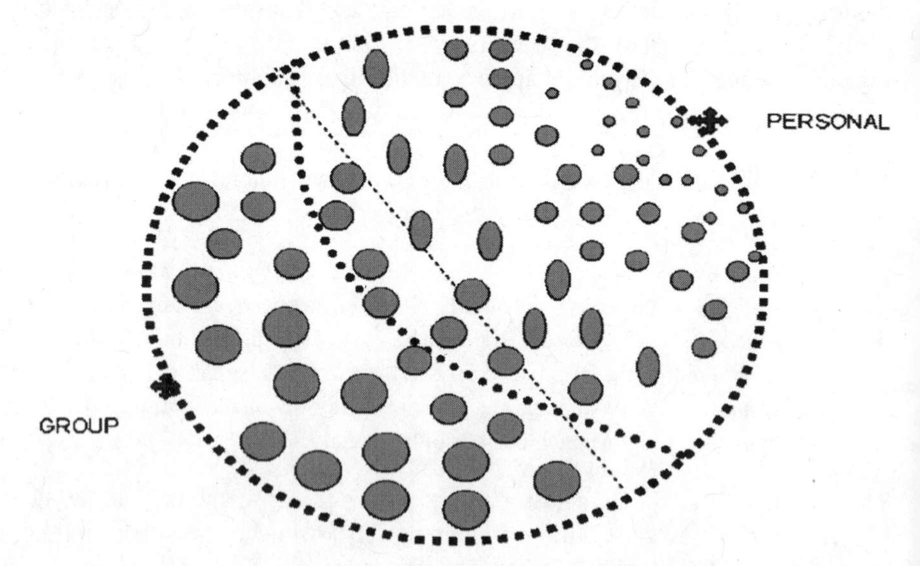

Figure 11.6 A proposed model of speaker identity for a linguistically secure speaker (based on Meyerhoff and Niedzielski 1994).

In this chapter I have claimed that work in both sociophonetics and psychology suggests ways in which implicit knowledge allows language change to progress in a subconscious but systematic way. Furthermore, I suggest that explicit knowledge is often inaccurate due to language attitudes, particularly in the case of the linguistically secure speaker. I offer a filter model for why, even with long-term exposure to acoustic evidence to the contrary, speakers would persist in their beliefs of (often inaccurate) "knowledge" about language variation.

Future sociophonetic work will perhaps reveal clearer interactions between language attitudes and these two types of knowledge, and the role that each plays in the production and perception of language variation.

References

Conrey, Briana, Geoffrey Potts, and Nancy Niedzielski. 2005. Effects of dialect on merger perception: ERP and behavioral correlates. *Brain and Language* 95 (3): 435–449.

Giddens, Anthony. 2000. *Modernity and self-identity: Self and society in the late modern age.* Stanford, CA: Stanford University Press.

Giles, Howard. 1970. Evaluative reactions to accents. *Educational Review* 22 (3): 211–227.

Giles, Howard and Nikolas Coupland. 1991. *Language: Contexts and consequences.* Florence, KY: Wadsworth.

Giles, Howard and Peter F. Powesland. 1975. *Speech style and social evaluation.* London: Academic Press.

Goldinger, Stephen. 1998. Echoes of echoes? An episodic theory of lexical access. *Psychological Review* 105 (2): 251–279.

Hay, Jennifer and Katie Drager. In press. Stuffed toys and speech perception. *Linguistics.*

Hay, Jennifer, Paul Warren, and Katie Drager. 2006. Factors influencing speech perception in the context of a merger-in-progress. *Journal of Phonetics* 34: 458–484.

Koops, Christian, Elizabeth Gentry, and Andrew Pantos. 2008. The effect of perceived speaker age on the perception of PIN and PEN vowels in Houston, Texas. *University of Pennsylvania Working Papers in Linguistics* 14: 2 (Selected papers from NWAV 36). http://repository.upenn.edu/pwpl/vol14/iss2/ (accessed February 10, 2010). .

Labov, William. 1966. *The social stratification of English in New York City.* Washington DC: Center for Applied Linguistics.

Labov, William. 2001. *Principles of linguistic change: Social factors.* Oxford: Blackwell.

Lambert, Wallace E. 1967. A social psychology of bilingualism. *Journal of Social Issues* 23 (2): 91–109.

Lippi-Green, Rosina. 1997. *English with an accent.* London: Routledge.

Long, Daniel and Dennis Preston, eds. 2002. *Handbook of perceptual dialectology, vol. 2.* Amsterdam: John Benjamins.

Meyerhoff, Miriam, and Nancy Niedzielski. 1994. Resistance to creolization: An interpersonal and intergroup account. *Language and Communication* 14 (4): 313–330.

Niedzielski, Nancy. 1999. The effect of social information on the perception of sociolinguistic variables. *Journal of Language and Social Psychology* (Special issue: Attitudes, perception, and linguistic issues, ed. by Lesley Milroy and Dennis R. Preston) 18: 162–185.

Niedzielski, Nancy and Dennis Preston. 1999. *Folk linguistics.* Berlin: Mouton de Gruyter.

Preston, Dennis R. 1989. *Perceptual dialectology.* Dordrecht: Foris.

Vitevitch, M. S. 2003. Change deafness: The inability to detect changes in talkers' voices. *Journal of Experimental Psychology: Human Perception and Performance* 29: 333–342.

Chapter 12

Identification of African American Speech

Erik R. Thomas, North Carolina State University;
Norman J. Lass, West Virginia University;
Jeannine Carpenter, Duke University

1. Introduction

Among the most heavily researched topics in the sociolinguistics of speech perception is the issue of the discriminability of African American and European American voices. This issue involves at least four research questions. First, can listeners distinguish African Americans and European Americans on the basis of voice alone? Second, do demographic differences among speakers and listeners affect discriminability? Third, what features are listeners capable of accessing in order to make ethnic identifications of voices? Finally, what features do listeners access in real-life situations where they have opportunities to identify speakers as African American or European American? The first three questions appear to be more or less resolved. It is the last question that has proved most intractable.

A large number of studies have addressed the first question, that of whether listeners can identify voices as African American or European American (Dickens and Sawyer 1952; Stroud 1956; Hibler 1960; Larsen and Larsen 1966; Bryden 1968a, 1968b; Buck 1968; Tucker and Lambert 1969; Shuy et al. 1969; Shuy 1970; Alvarenga 1971; Koutstaal and Jackson 1971; Abrams 1973; Irwin 1977; Lass et al. 1978; Lass et al. 1979; Lass et al. 1980; Bailey and Maynor 1989; Haley 1990; Hawkins 1992; Walton and Orlikoff 1994; Trent 1995; Baugh 1996; Purnell, Idsardi, and Baugh 1999; and Foreman 2000). The earliest of these studies, Dickens and Sawyer (1952), is over 50 years old, which demonstrates the sustained interest in discriminability of ethnicity. These studies utilized a wide variety of research techniques that are summarized in Thomas and Reaser (2004a). For example, the length of the stimuli varied from utterances consisting of several sentences to, in the case of Walton and Orlikoff (1994), utterances of a single vowel. Nevertheless, the answer to the question of whether listeners can distinguish

African American voices from European American voices is, in general, yes. In fact, accuracy rates in all but a few of these studies fell in the range of 70% to 90%.

A number of studies also have affirmatively answered the second question, that of whether demographic differences among speakers and/or listeners affect identification rates. A few studies have reported that some listeners have difficulty identifying African Americans whose English sounds quite standard (Buck 1968; Tucker and Lambert 1969; Abrams 1973; Baugh 1996). Similarly, African Americans whose speech shows features typical of local European American vernaculars also confound listeners (Wolfram 2001; Mallinson 2002; and Thomas and Reaser 2004a). Some studies (Bailey and Maynor 1989; Haley 1990; Thomas and Reaser 2004a) have reported that younger African Americans can be easier to identify than older African Americans, though it should be noted that the listeners in these experiments were college-aged. Demographic features of listeners also affect discrimination ability. Alvarenga (1971), Haley (1990), Hawkins (1992), and Foreman (2000) all found differences among listener groups in the accuracy of their identifications; in each case, the differences probably had to do with the listeners' familiarity with speakers of both ethnicities. Foreman (2000) reported most explicitly that the best identification was by listeners with extensive contact with both groups.

Investigators have approached the third question, what features listeners can access for identifications, in a piecemeal fashion. Two earlier studies, Roberts (1966) and Bryden (1968a), reported that reading errors cued identifications of a speaker as African American. Subsequent inquiries have focused on phonetic attributes. Vowel quality was found to influence identifications by Lass, Almerino, Jordan, and Walsh (1980), Graff, Labov, and Harris (1986), Purnell et al. (1999), and Thomas and Reaser (2004). The latter three studies found that quality differences of particular vowels—/o/ as in *coat*, /au/ as in *how*, and the /ɛ/ in *hello*—affected identifications. Some counterevidence is provided by Bryden (1968a), though he examined only /u/, as in *too*. Foreman (2000) performed an experiment to demonstrate that intonation could serve as a cue, though Koutstaal and Jackson (1971) had found earlier that intonation could not be the only cue that listeners used. Both Hawkins (1992) and Walton and Orlikoff (1994) report that overall F0 level serves as a cue, with lower F0 associated with African Americans; both of these studies focused on male speakers. Walton and Orlikoff (1994) also reported that two voice quality features, jitter and shimmer, were correlated with ethnic identifications, and Purnell et al. (1999) noted the same for the harmonics-to-noise ratio (itself a cover feature for other voice quality factors). The conclusion emerging from these many studies is simply that listeners are capable of accessing a variety of cues under experimental conditions.

The fact that listeners access a particular cue during an experiment in which their attention may be artificially drawn to that cue does not demonstrate that they utilize that cue under more natural conditions. However, only experiments can tease out the effects of different cues. Hence, a different kind of experiment, one that compares the effects of cues, is called for. Purnell et al. (1999) and Thomas and Reaser (2004b) are perhaps the only studies that have compared the effects of different cues directly. Other studies, including Alvarenga (1971), Lass et al. (1978), Lass et al. (1980), and Thomas and Reaser (2004a), have done so indirectly by using such techniques as playing stimuli backward or using lowpass-filtered stimuli. Purnell et al. (1999) used guises uttered by the same speaker as stimuli, which, while eliminating spurious factors due to individual differences in speakers' voices, could introduce other sources of error if the impersonator cannot control all the cues that are relevant for identification of ethnicity.

These issues related to ethnic identification of voices have real implications for society. A better understanding of how listeners distinguish the ethnicity of voices would make it easier to demonstrate how ethnic profiling can take place, as in the denial of appointments for jobs or residences on the basis of the ethnic identification over the telephone. Purnell et al. (1999) discuss the legal implications of ethnic profiling in some detail. The ability to distinguish ethnicity can also perpetuate stereotypes, as when children identify the voices of cartoon characters and associate them with personality traits exhibited in the cartoon; see Lippi-Green (1997: 79–103). However, in certain cases, ethnic identification of voices could have desirable consequences. For example, patients who have lost the ability to speak and who are African Americans may desire speech synthesis equipment that can produce a voice that matches their personal identity better than the dialect-neutral synthesizers now available. The social importance of the ethnic discrimination of voices necessitates further research into the mechanisms of such distinctions. In order to explore these mechanisms, we devised two experiments, henceforth called Experiments A and B, comparing the effects of different phonetic cues in ethnic discrimination.

For both of these experiments, the stimuli were taken from a corpus of speech obtained from students at North Carolina State University. Thirty-six students, divided approximately evenly between African Americans and European Americans, were recorded in a soundproof booth performing several tasks. They answered a few demographic questions and then recounted a familiar children's tale (in order to elicit spontaneous speech), read a list of sentences, read a dialog, and read a list of words. The sentences were designed so that they either highlighted or avoided specific items, such as a particular vowel. The stimuli for both of the experiments described here came from the recorded sentences.

An earlier experiment (Thomas and Reaser 2004b) was also based on this corpus, but included stimuli from the speakers' spontaneous speech and the dialog. In that experiment, the stimuli were subjected to three treatments: they were left unmodified, they were monotonized, and they were lowpass-filtered at 660 Hz. Monotonization eliminates F0-dependent information, such as jitter and most aspects of intonation. The lowpass filtering was designed to eliminate most of the discernable aspects of vowel quality differences that are correlated with ethnic differences, since those differences depend largely upon F2 and lowpass filtering at 660 Hz nearly always removes F2. A variety of acoustic measurements were obtained on the stimuli. The results showed that vowel quality differences—mostly those having to do with /o/, /u/, or /æ/ (as in *bat*)—were important cues for the ethnicity of all speakers. Of the vowel quality differences that were analyzed, the glide of /o/ showed the highest level of significance. However, the sex of the speaker made a difference for other cues. Phonation emerged as the most important cue for the ethnicity of male speakers, with breathier speech associated with African Americans. However, phonation showed no correlation at all with identifications of ethnicity for female speakers. Conversely, F0-dependent factors proved significant for female speakers but not for male speakers.

2. Experiment A

Experiment A was designed to compare the effects of /o/ and /æ/ against each other and against certain features of voice quality and prosody. Numerous studies have found that European Americans, both inside and outside the South, tend to show more fronted variants of /o/ than African Americans do (Hall 1976; Graff et al. 1986; Thomas 1989a, b, 2001; Thomas and Bailey 1998; Fridland 2003). In fact, the fronting of /o/ represents part of a general fronting of /o/, /u/, and /ʊ/ (as in *good*) that, as a whole, is more advanced among European Americans than among African Americans. A smaller number of studies have reported a tendency for the front vowels /æ/, /ɛ/ (as in *bet*), and /ɪ/ (as in *bit*) to be higher in African American English than in European American English (see Thomas 2001). An advantage of focusing on /o/ and /æ/ is that they represent the back vowel subsystem and the front lax vowel subsystems, respectively, and thus are relatively independent of each other.

2.1 Methods

Of the 36 speakers who were part of the corpus of recordings, 12 were selected for this experiment. They were selected on the basis of ratings they were given by a panel of sociolinguists as to how African American or European American they sounded. The three speakers of each ethnicity/sex combination (i.e., African American females, etc.) who were rated as sounding most typical of their ethnicity were selected. Readings of six sentences were taken for each of the selected speakers. The first two sentences feature /æ/ prominently, the next two feature /o/ prominently, and the last two were intended as control sentences because they do not include /æ/, /o/, /ai/ (as in *sight* or *side*), /au/, or /u/, all of which are known to serve as ethnic markers:

After that, Hattie got sad and came back to the pad.
Pat sat on a hat, a cat, a bat, and a tack. (Apologies to Dr. Seuss.)
Joe hoped he could go shop for a stove.
Hoke showed up when smoke came in his Geo.
She got up early and went in first.
He dropped three books on Ted's front seat.

The stimuli were subjected to three treatments. One was to leave them unmodified. The second was monotonization. The third was conversion of all vowels to schwa. Both the monotonization and the conversion to schwa were conducted using the Kay Analysis Synthesis Laboratory (ASL), which is a linear predictive coding synthesizer. For monotonization, F0 was set at 120 Hz for male speakers and 200 Hz for female speakers. For schwa conversion, formant values were set at F1=500 Hz, F2=1500 Hz, and F3=2500 Hz for male speakers and F1= 600 Hz, F2= 1800 Hz, and F3= 3000 Hz for female speakers. The ASL performed monotonization quite well, but left many of the schwa-converted stimuli with extraneous noise.

All listeners who served as subjects heard all the stimuli: schwa-converted stimuli in the first section of the experimental recording, monotonized stimuli in the second section, and unmodified stimuli in the final section. Within each section, the order of stimuli was randomized and stimuli were presented to subjects in sets of five. A voice announced the beginning of each new section and set. Several stimuli at the beginning of each section served to acclimate listeners to the task and responses to them were excluded from analysis. Three types of listeners served as subjects: European Americans in Raleigh, North Carolina (mostly undergraduate students at North Carolina State University), African Americans in Raleigh, and European Americans at West

Virginia University. Subjects were asked to circle, for each stimulus, either *African American* or *European American* on an answer sheet. Results from subjects with hearing impairments, from those whose first language was not English, and from those of ethnicities other than African American or European American were excluded from the numerical analyses.

2.2 Results and discussion

Levels of accuracy of ethnic identifications by listener group, experimental treatment, and sex of speaker are given in Table 12.1. Three general trends are evident in Table 12.1. First, the West Virginia listeners showed lower accuracy than the two North Carolina groups of listeners. The speakers who produced the stimuli were North Carolinians, and the West Virginians often associated Southern dialect features by some European American speakers with African American identity. However, they probably also had less daily contact with African Americans than North Carolinians do and thus may be less familiar with African American speech. Second, while the monotonized stimuli were identified with only slightly less accuracy than the unmodified stimuli, the schwa-converted stimuli were identified with considerably less accuracy. This finding suggests that vowel quality information is more important than F0-dependent information, but the noise that the synthesizer created on some of the schwa-converted stimuli may have distracted listeners. Third, female speakers were consistently identified with slightly lower accuracy than male speakers.

Table 12.1 Overall Accuracy Levels in Experiment A

Treatment	North Carolina African American listeners (n=11)		North Carolina European American listeners (n=33)		West Virginia European American listeners (n=39)	
	male speakers	female speakers	male speakers	female speakers	male speakers	female speakers
unmodified	97.0%	95.5%	97.5%	94.8%	85.7%	80.7%
monotonized	91.3%	89.0%	94.1%	91.0%	79.0%	77.1%
schwa-converted	78.0%	62.3%	81.9%	64.3%	73.7%	60.2%

Table 12.2 shows the same data broken down into stimuli featuring /æ/ prominently, stimuli featuring /o/ prominently, and control stimuli. It can be observed that, in most cases, the three types of stimuli do not differ much in

the accuracy by which they were identified. In some cases, control stimuli were identified more accurately than corresponding /æ/ or /o/ stimuli. This result seems to contradict the notion that vowel quality is a crucial cue, and suggests that other cues not controlled for, such as timing, amplitude, or certain features of voice quality, may play important roles. The similarity in accuracy levels for /æ/ and /o/ stimuli makes it difficult to determine which of those two vowels is a better cue.

Table 12.2 Accuracy Levels by Sentence Type

Treatment	North Carolina African American listeners (n=11)		North Carolina European American listeners (n=33)		West Virginia European American listeners (n=39)	
	male speakers	female speakers	male speakers	female speakers	male speakers	female speakers
unmodified /æ/	100%	96.6%	98.9%	93.9%	84.1%	76.8%
unmodified /o/	92.0%	96.6%	96.2%	93.9%	85.7%	83.2%
unmodified control	98.9%	93.2%	97.3%	96.6%	87.2%	82.0%
monotonized /æ/	94.3%	94.3%	96.2%	91.7%	81.4%	82.3%
monotonized /o/	86.4%	92.0%	92.0%	90.5%	79.3%	72.3%
monotonized control	93.2%	80.7%	93.9%	90.9%	76.2%	76.8%
schwa- converted /æ/	84.1%	63.6%	84.9%	68.2%	79.3%	63.7%
schwa- converted /o/	70.5%	61.4%	76.0%	65.3%	68.9%	54.9%
schwa- converted control	79.5%	62.0%	84.9%	59.4%	72.9%	61.9%

Several phonetic measurements were obtained on the stimuli using the Praat acoustic analysis software in order to facilitate statistical analysis. The mean F0 for each stimulus was measured because some previous studies have reported that African Americans show a lower overall F0 than European Americans (Hollien and Malcik 1962; Hudson and Holbrook 1981, 1982; Hawkins 1993; Walton and Orlikoff 1994). F0 was determined using the autocorrelation method described in Boersma (1993). The maximum F0 and the standard deviation of F0 were measured for each stimulus in an attempt to gauge intonational differences. Some European Americans, mainly females, show a wide range of F0 values within an utterance, largely because they produce an especially high peak, usually near the beginning of the utterance. Other studies, however, have found that African Americans show a wider pitch range (Tarone,1973; Loman 1975; Hudson and Holbrook

1981, 1982; Jun and Foreman 1996), though this feature of African American English is associated with speech acts that are not represented in the stimuli. In addition, some studies (Loman 1975; Jun and Foreman 1996; Wolfram and Thomas 2002) have reported that African Americans show constant alternations of pitch, or more intonational pitch accents, that European Americans lack, and this feature might affect the standard deviation of F0. The degree of breathiness, which the results of Thomas and Reaser (2004b) showed to be an important cue, was measured using the Cepstral Peak Prominence (CPP) method described in Hillenbrand, Cleveland, and Erickson (1994) and Shrivastav and Sapienza (2003). Vowel quality was gauged in several steps. First, measurements of the first four formants were taken in the center of the vowel for /æ/, 35 ms from the onset of the vowel for the nucleus of /o/, and 35 ms from the offset of the vowel for the glide of /o/. Then, formant values were converted from Hz to Bark using the formula given in Traunmüller (1990). Finally, the frontness of both the nucleus and glide of /o/ was indicated by the value Z_4-Z_2 (i.e., Bark-converted F4 minus Bark-converted F2), while the height of /æ/ was indicated by the value Z_2-Z_1. These Bark-difference metrics serve to normalize vowel quality across speakers and are inspired by Syrdal and Gopal (1986), though the Z_4-Z_2 and Z_2-Z_1 values yield more consistent results than the metrics that Syrdal and Gopal proposed. Analysis of jitter (local variation in F0) and shimmer (local variation in amplitude), which Thomas and Reaser (2004b) found not to be correlated with ethnic identification, was omitted.

Multiple regression was applied to the stimuli, as shown in Table 12.3. Table 12.3 is broken into three parts according to listener group, a, b, and c. A factor was excluded from the analysis when it was neutralized by an experimental treatment; i.e., measures of F0 were excluded from analyses of monotonized stimuli and measures of vowel quality were excluded from analyses of schwa-converted stimuli. Necessarily, measures of vowel quality were also excluded from analyses of the control stimuli. Cells in the table are shaded if the factor represented in that cell reached statistical significance.

Several trends are evident in Table 12.3. One is that fewer cells reached statistical significance for the West Virginia listeners than for either of the North Carolina groups. This result is undoubtedly related to the lower degree of identification accuracy that the West Virginians showed. Another is that vowel quality factors were the ones that most often reached significance. This result may not be surprising, considering that the stimuli were designed to highlight vowel quality. F0 measures showed some erratic patterns, especially for schwa-converted stimuli, but in most cases a higher mean F0 was associated with African Americans and a higher maximum F0 with European *le 12.3* Multiple Regression Results By Listener Group and Sentence Type

y to Coefficient Signs
r mean and max F0, + =Afr. Ams. show higher F0,—=Eur. Ams. show higher F0.
r CPP, + = Eur. Ams. breathier,—=Afr. Ams. breathier.
r /æ/, + =Afr. Ams. show more raising,—=Eur. Ams. show more raising.
r /o/, + =Eur. Ams. show more fronting,—=Afr. Ams. show more fronting.
r std. dev. of F0, + =Afr. Ams. show wider F0 range,—=Eur. Ams. show wider F0 range
p values and coefficient signs for North Carolina African American listeners
=11; coefficient sign shown in parentheses when p≤.10)

Treatment	speaker sex	mean F0	max F0	CPP (a measure of breathiness)	vowel quality nu=nucleus, gl=glide	standard deviation of F0	R^2
mod /æ/	male	.794	.968	.945	.090 (+)	.693	.963
mod /o/	male	.675	.971	.978	nu .816 gl .866	.775	.813
mod control	male	.068 (+)	.060 (-)	.672	—	.898	.945
mod /æ/	female	.713	.039 (-)	.036 (-)	.010 (+)	.299	.986
mod /o/	female	.042 (+)	.061 (-)	.945	nu .006 (+) gl .065 (+)	.040 (-)	.99998
mod control	female	.035 (+)	.058 (-)	.400	—	.085 (+)	.849
ono /æ/	male	—	—	.630	.008 (+)	—	.831
ono /o/	male	—	—	.037 (-)	nu .295 gl .084 (+)	—	.820
ono control	male	—	—	.551	—	—	.219
ono /æ/	female	—	—	.993	.001 (+)	—	.905
ono /o/	female	—	—	.903	nu .0009 (+) gl .051 (+)	—	.988
ono control	female	—	—	.597	—	—	.049
hwa /æ/	male	.472	.757	.462	—	.823	.897
hwa /o/	male	.924	.662	.635	—	.674	.758
hwa control	male	.978	.526	.930	—	.282	.930
hwa /æ/	female	.529	.207	.593	—	.445	.525
hwa /o/	female	.037 (-)	.055 (-)	.230	—	.054 (-)	.825
hwa control	female	.167	.043 (+)	.894	—	.043 (+)	.819

(continued)

Table 12.3 Multiple Regression Results By Listener Group and Sentence Type *(continued)*

b. p values and coefficient signs for North Carolina European American listeners (n=33; coefficie sign shown in parentheses when p≤.10)

Treatment	speaker sex	mean F0	max F0	CPP	vowel quality nu=nucleus, gl=glide	standard deviation of F0	R^2
unmod /æ/	male	.831	.938	.995	.096 (+)	.655	.956
unmod /o/	male	.663	.992	.864	nu .928 gl .875	.684	.791
unmod control	male	.058 (+)	.046 (-)	.860	—	.900	.956
unmod /æ/	female	.884	.057 (-)	.249	.015 (+)	.325	.978
unmod /o/	female	.245	.355	.331	nu .062 (+) gl .179	.464	.999
unmod control	female	.056 (+)	.095 (-)	.058 (-)	—	.123	.798
mono /æ/	male	—	—	.719	.004 (+)	—	.871
mono /o/	male	—	—	.049 (-)	nu .950 gl .138	—	.748
mono control	male	—	—	.238	—	—	.222
mono /æ/	female	—	—	.075 (+)	.00005 (+)	—	.971
mono /o/	female	—	—	.930	nu .0003 (+) gl .093 (+)	—	.992
mono control	female	—	—	.289	—	—	.184
schwa /æ/	male	.045 (+)	.117	.306	—	.474	.960
schwa /o/	male	.519	.252	.678	—	.057 (-)	.923
schwa control	male	.563	.567	.691	—	.429	.725
schwa /æ/	female	.449	.103	.560	—	.856	.774
schwa /o/	female	.130	.617	.298	—	.152	.823
schwa control	female	.923	.488	.295	—	.409	.594

(continued)

le 12.3 Multiple Regression Results By Listener Group and Sentence Type *(continued)*

p values and coefficient signs for West Virginia European American listeners (n=39; coefficient gn shown in parentheses when p≤.10)

Treatment	speaker sex	mean F0	max F0	CPP	vowel quality	standard deviation of F0	R^2
mod /æ/	male	.675	.805	.774	.089 (+)	.670	.961
mod /o/	male	.668	.951	.856	nu .822 gl .789	.713	.721
mod control	male	.100 (+)	.103 (-)	.558	—	.956	.917
mod /æ/	female	.564	.232	.987	.103 (+)	.662	.870
mod /o/	female	.677	.429	.444	nu .144 gl .852	.266	.991
mod control	female	.049 (+)	.095 (-)	.061 (-)	—	.124	.807
ono /æ/	male	—	—	.752	.003 (+)	—	.875
ono /o/	male	—	—	.050 (-)	nu .874 gl .113	—	.757
ono control	male	—	—	.371	—	—	.135
ono /æ/	female	—	—	.109	.00003 (+)	—	.975
ono /o/	female	—	—	.335	nu .007 (+) gl .215	—	.912
ono control	female	—	—	.237	—	—	.223
hwa /æ/	male	.317	.612	.556	—	.989	.865
hwa /o/	male	.364	.371	.522	—	.178	.711
hwa control	male	.115	.105	.150	—	.112	.922
hwa /æ/	female	.354	.332	.463	—	.870	.634
hwa /o/	female	0.54 (-)	.122	.927	—	.534	.916
hwa control	female	.245	.302	.961	—	.371	.428

Americans. Finally, some differences from the results of Thomas and Reaser (2004b) appeared. Unlike the earlier study, the glide of /o/ showed lower levels of significance than the nucleus and CPP (breathiness) reached significance for only a few cells. The differences were probably due to the fact that a smaller set of speakers was used for this study than for the earlier study, and the speakers selected for Experiment A apparently had different voice characteristics than the larger sample.

In general, the results from Experiment A show that vowel quality is a key factor that listeners access to make ethnic identifications, but by no means the only one. F0 seemed to play a role as well. The standard deviation of F0 did not seem to provide the most satisfactory measure of intonational differences, which are too complex to be captured by a one-dimensional metric. The West Virginians clearly had more difficulty with ethnic identification than the North Carolinians. Nevertheless, a question that is left unanswered is whether they are really poorer at ethnic identification as a whole or the nature of the stimuli used in this experiment confounded them. This question and the problem of capturing intonation are addressed in Experiment B.

3. Experiment B

Experiment B was designed to test vowel quality and prosody against each other directly. Experiment A, as well as the earlier experiments in Thomas and Reaser (2004a, b), put more emphasis on vowel quality than on prosody, and a design placing equal emphasis on these two factors was desirable. In addition, the same listener groups as in Experiment A were used in order to gain a more complete understanding of how they differ in accessing cues.

3.1 Methods

Four sentences from the corpus of recordings were chosen for Experiment B. Two feature diagnostic vowels prominently—/o/ and /æ/, respectively—while the other two do not include any vowel known to be diagnostic for African American vs. European American identity:

Joe hoped he could go shop for a stove.
Pat sat on a hat, a cat, a bat, and a tack.
Buckwald's trunk got filled up this month with junk.
We went to the shop to get some milk.

Four examples of each sentence read by African American males, by European American males, by African American females, and by European American females were selected. Unlike in Experiment A, the same speakers were not used for each sentence. Instead, examples of each sentence were selected that showed features of vowel quality and intonation typical of the ethnicity of the speaker, as judged by Thomas. Then, for each sentence, utterances by African American males and European American males were paired with each other, as were utterances by African American females and European American females. The same two speakers were not paired with each other more than once; i.e., if speaker x was paired with speaker y for the first sentence, he or she was not paired with speaker y for any of the other three sentences.

Next, a Praat script was prepared in order to perform synthesis. The script was designed so that the F0 contours and segmental durations could be swapped for each of the paired utterances, syllable by syllable. The result for each pair of speakers was four stimuli: the unmodified sentence uttered by the African American, the unmodified sentence uttered by the European American, the sentence uttered by the African American but with the prosody of the European American substituted, and the sentence uttered by the European American but with the prosody of the African American substituted. On a larger scale, the experiment involved a 2x2x2x2x4 design in that it included male/female x African American/European American x presence/absence of diagnostic vowels x unmodified/prosody-swapped x 4 speakers.

As in Experiment A, the order of the stimuli was randomized and the stimuli were presented in groups of five, with a voice announcing "Set 1," "Set 2," etc. at the beginning of each grouping. However, there was no need to group the stimuli into sections for Experiment B. As before, several stimuli at the beginning of the experimental recording served to acclimate listeners to the task and responses to them were excluded from analysis. Once again, African Americans at North Carolina State University, European Americans at North Carolina State University, and European Americans at West Virginia University served as subjects for the experiment and were asked to circle either *African American* or *European American* for each stimulus. Results from listeners who reported hearing impairments, whose first language was not English, or who were not African American or European American were excluded from analysis.

Accuracy of identification for each of the independent factors is plotted in Figure 12.1. Stimuli with diagnostic vowels were identified more accurately than those without diagnostic vowels, unmodified stimuli were identified more accurately than prosody-swapped stimuli, stimuli uttered by males were identified more accurately than those uttered by females, and stimuli uttered

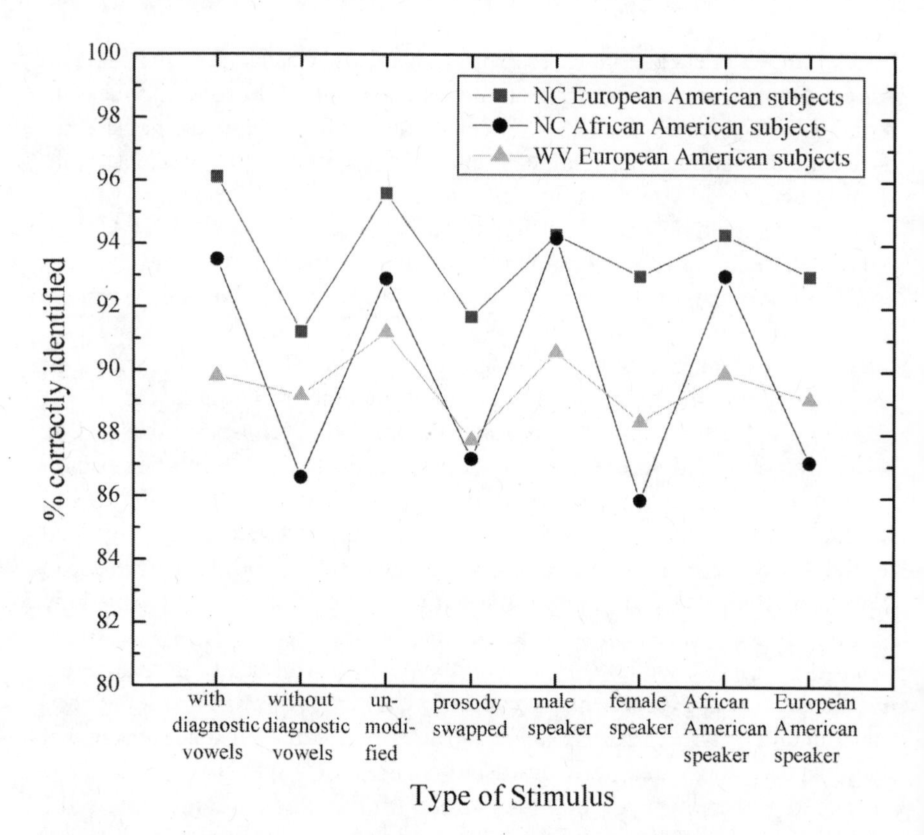

Figure 12.1 Results of Experiment B for each independent variable.

by African Americans were identified more accurately than those uttered by European Americans. Additionally, the strength of each of these trends varies for each listener group, with the African American listeners showing the strongest effects for each independent variable. Accuracy rates overall were quite high, rising to over 96% for stimuli with diagnostic vowels identified by North Carolina European Americans. The fact that identification rates were well over 80% regardless of what kind of stimulus was involved suggests that factors other than vowel quality and prosody were being accessed by listeners. The most likely candidates for other cues are voice quality features, such as phonation.

Interactions of independent variables were important in two cases. Figure 12.2 shows the interaction of presence/absence of diagnostic vowels with natural/swapped prosody. Here, the two North Carolina listener groups behaved

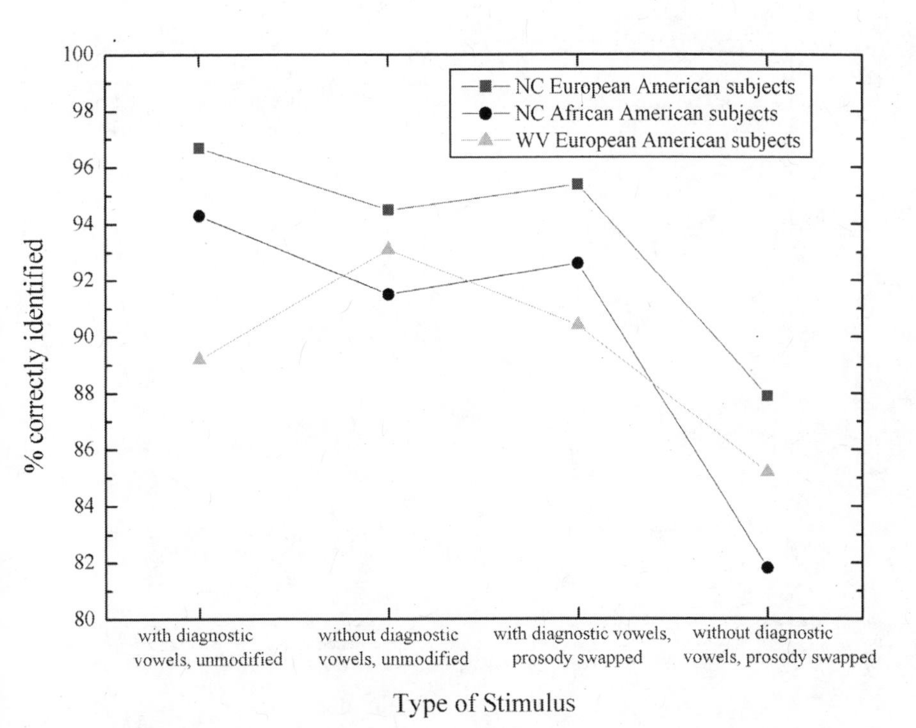

Figure 12.2 Interaction between presence/absence of diagnostic vowels and natural/swapped prosody in Experiment B.

similarly. For the North Carolinians, accuracy rates were quite high for stimuli with both diagnostic vowels and natural prosody. Accuracy dropped only slightly when either the diagnostic vowels were absent or the prosody was swapped, but it dropped steeply when listeners lacked both diagnostic vowels and natural prosody to serve as cues. This result suggests that listeners rely on a suite of cues, and if one is missing, they can rely on another, but the absence of multiple cues is what creates difficulty.

Figure 12.3 shows the interaction of sex of speaker with natural/swapped prosody. In this comparison, the two European American listener groups behave similarly. For the European American listeners, the prosody swapping decreases accuracy rates by about 8% for male speakers but makes virtually no difference for female speakers. For African American listeners, however, prosody swapping decreases accuracy rates for both male and female speakers.

In Experiment B, accuracy of identification, rather than correlation with phonetic measurements taken on the stimuli, was the object of the statistical

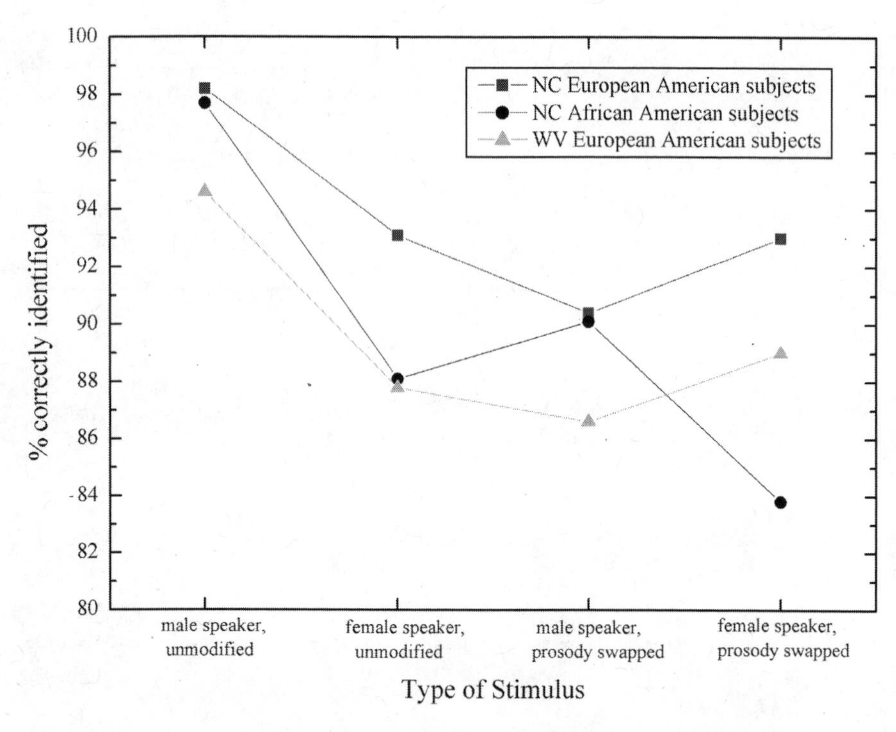

Figure 12.3 Interaction between sex of speaker and natural/swapped prosody in Experiment B.

analysis. Logistic regression was applied to the results plotted in Figure 12.1. The main effects are shown in Table 12.4. All four independent variables proved significant for the African American listeners. For the North Carolina European Americans, presence/absence of diagnostic vowels and natural/swapped prosody showed significant effects, but sex and ethnicity of speaker did not. For the West Virginia listeners, only natural/swapped prosody proved significant, though sex of speaker nearly did.

It is clear that different groups of listeners base their identifications on different sets of cues. For African Americans, the fact that they identify males more accurately than females suggests that they associate features of African American English most strongly with African American *male* identity, or perhaps features of European American English most strongly with European American male identity. The failure of the West Virginians to show any significant effect for presence/absence of diagnostic vowels probably has to do with the fact that the speakers were from North Carolina.

Table 12.4 Logistic Regression Results by Listener Group and Independent Variable

Independent variable	North Carolina African American listeners (n=11)	North Carolina European American listeners (n=24)	West Virginia European American listeners (n=25)
presence/absence of diagnostic vowels	χ^2=18.57 p<.0001	χ^2=33.35 p<.0001	χ^2=0.48 p<.4900
natural/swapped prosody	χ^2=12.58 p<.0004	χ^2=17.63 p<.0001	χ^2=8.81 p<.0030
sex of speaker	χ^2=25.44 p<.0001	χ^2=0.93 p<.3351	χ^2=3.79 p<.0515
ethnicity of speaker	χ^2=13.83 p<.0002	χ^2=2.45 p<.1177	χ^2=0.33 p<.5664

West Virginians are not exposed on a daily basis to North Carolina vowels, and hence they are not sensitive to variants—for example, /o/ with a fronted glide—that are common in North Carolina but not in West Virginia. At the same time, the low proportion of African Americans in West Virginia, particularly in northern West Virginia, where the university is located, may have made the West Virginia subjects less sensitive to vowel variants such as raised /æ/ that typify African American English. At any rate, the fact that the West Virginians were not accessing vowel variation to any significant degree probably explains their poor performance in Experiment A, which put a heavy emphasis on vowel variation.

4. Conclusion

The results of the two experiments described here paint a more complicated picture of ethnic identification than previous work. First, it appears that no single cue serves as the silver bullet for listeners. Instead, listeners rely on several cues, including cues from segmental quality, prosody, and voice quality. In fact, what cue is most important may not be the appropriate question to ask. Listeners exhibit a degree of flexibility. Both experiments, though especially Experiment A, as well as the earlier results from Thomas and Reaser (2004b), suggest that listeners shift the cues they use depending on the sex of the speaker. Furthermore, as Experiment B suggested, they may shift the cues they use depending on what information is available to them in the speech that they hear.

Another finding of these experiments is that different groups of listeners have different repertoires of cues that they are capable of accessing. The clearest example of such a difference is the result from Experiment B that North Carolinians used both vowel quality and prosody as cues, while West Virginians used prosody but not vowel quality. This conclusion should not be surprising, considering that individuals have greatly varying experiences. It provides a mechanism for the findings of Alvarenga (1971), Haley (1990), Hawkins (1992), and Foreman (2000), noted previously, that groups differ in their levels of accuracy for ethnic identification.

The findings described here certainly do not exhaust what can be ascertained about how listeners distinguish African Americans from European Americans. Voice quality remains a potential source of cues that researchers have hardly tapped. The earlier results for phonation are promising, and further experimentation with phonation is planned. More specific information about what aspects of prosody listeners utilize would also be desirable. African American English is by far the most heavily investigated dialect (or group of dialects) of American English, and its identification by listeners is perhaps the most intensively studied perceptual issue in American sociolinguistics. Yet it is still not thoroughly understood. Understanding ethnic identification more completely would aid in understanding how stereotyping occurs and combating its effects.

Acknowledgments

Research for this chapter was supported by NSF grant BCS-0213941. We wish to thank Andrew G. B. Grimes for his help in preparing the Praat script used for Experiment B.

References

Abrams, Albert S. 1973. *Minimal auditory cues for distinguishing Black from White talkers*. Doctoral dissertation, New York: CUNY.

Alvarenga, Joyce E. 1971. *An investigation of the ability of listeners to differentiate race on the basis of tape recorded evidence*. Master's thesis, New York: CUNY.

Bailey, Guy and Natalie Maynor. 1989. The divergence controversy. *American Speech* 64 (1): 12–39.

Bailey, Guy and Erik Thomas. 1998. Some aspects of African-American Vernacular English phonology. In Salikoko S. Mufwene, John R. Rickford, Guy Bailey, and John Baugh (eds), *African-American English: Structure, history and use*. London/New York: Routledge, 85–109.

Boersma, Paul. 1993. Accurate short-term analysis of the fundamental frequency and the harmonics-to-noise ratio of a sampled sound. *Proceedings of the Institute of Phonetic Sciences* 17: 97–110.
Bryden, James D. 1968a. An acoustic and social dialect analysis of perceptual variables in listener identification and rating of Negro speakers. Final report, U.S. Office of Education. ED 022 186.
Bryden, James D. 1968b. The effect of signal bandwidth compression on listener perception. *Journal of the Speech and Hearing Association of Virginia* 9: 6–13.
Buck, Joyce F. 1968. The effects of Negro and White dialectal variations upon attitude of college students. *Speech Monographs* 35 (2): 181–186.
Dickens, Milton and Granville M. Sawyer. 1952. An experimental comparison of vocal quality among mixed groups of Whites and Negroes. *Southern Speech Journal* 17: 178–185.
Foreman, Christina. 2000. Identification of African-American English from prosodic cues. *Texas Linguistic Forum* 43: 57–66.
Fridland, Valerie. 2003. Network strength and the realization of the Southern Vowel Shift among African Americans in Memphis, Tennessee. *American Speech* 78 (1): 3–30.
Graff, David, William Labov, and Wendell A. Harris. 1986. Testing listeners' reactions to phonological markers of ethnic identity: A new method for sociolinguistic research. In David Sankoff (ed.), *Diversity and diachrony: Amsterdam studies in the theory and history of linguistic science, vol. 53*. Amsterdam/Philadelphia: John Benjamins, 45–58.
Haley, Kenneth. 1990. Some complexities in speech identification. *The SECOL Review* 14: 101–113.
Hall, Joan Houston. 1976. *Rural southeast Georgia speech: A phonological analysis.* Doctoral dissertation, Atlanta: Emory University.
Hawkins, Francine Dove. 1993. Speaker ethnic identification: The roles of speech sample, fundamental frequency, speaker and listener variations. Doctoral dissertation, College Park: University of Maryland.
Hibler, Madge Beatrice. 1960. A comparative study of speech patterns of selected Negro and White kindergarten children. Doctoral dissertation, Los Angeles: University of Southern California.
Hillenbrand, James, Ronald A. Cleveland, and Robert L. Erickson. 1994. Acoustic correlates of breathy vocal quality. *Journal of Speech and Hearing Research* 37: 769–778.
Hollien, Harry and Ellen Malcik. 1962. Adolescent voice change in Southern Negro males. *Speech Monographs* 29 (1): 53–58.
Hudson, Amelia I. and Anthony Holbrook. 1981. A study of reading fundamental vocal frequency of young black adults. *Journal of Speech and Hearing Research* 24: 197–201.
Hudson, Amelia I. and Anthony Holbrook. 1982. Fundamental frequency characteristics of young black adults: Spontaneous speaking and oral reading. *Journal of Speech and Hearing Research* 25: 25–28.

Irwin, Ruth Beckey. 1977. Judgments of vocal quality, speech fluency, and confidence of Southern Black and White speakers. *Language and Speech* 20: 261–266.

Jun, Sun-Ah and Christina Foreman. 1996. Boundary tones and focus realization in African-American intonation. Paper presented at the 3rd joint meeting of the Acoustical Society of America and the Acoustical Society of Japan: Honolulu, December 6.

Koutstaal, Cornelis W. and Faith L. Jackson. 1971. Race identification on the basis of biased speech samples. *Ohio Journal of Speech and Hearing* 6: 48–51.

Larsen, Vernon S. and Carolyn H. Larsen. 1966. Reactions to pronunciations. In Raven I. McDavid, Jr. and William M. Austin (eds), *Communication barriers to the culturally deprived.* Cooperative Research Project 2107. Washington, DC: Office of Education, U.S. Department of Health, Education, and Welfare. Papers paginated separately.

Lass, Norman J., Celest A. Almerino, Laurie F. Jordan, and Jayne M. Walsh. 1980. The effect of filtered speech on speaker race and sex identifications. *Journal of Phonetics* 8: 101–112.

Lass, Norman J., Pamela J. Mertz, and Karen L. Kimmel. 1978. The effect of temporal speech alterations on speaker race and sex identifications. *Language and Speech* 21 (3): 279–290.

Lass, Norman J., John E. Tecca, Robert A. Mancuso, and Wanda I. Black. 1979. The effect of phonetic complexity on speaker race and sex identifications. *Journal of Phonetics* 7: 105–118.

Lippi-Green, Rosina. 1997. *English with an accent: Language, ideology, and discrimination in the United States.* London/New York: Routledge.

Loman, Bengt. 1975. Prosodic patterns in a Negro American dialect. In Håkan Ringbom, Alfhild Ingberg, Ralf Norrman, Kurt Nyholm, Rolf Westman, and Kay Wikberg (eds), *Style and text: Studies presented to Nils Erik Enkvist.* Stockholm: Språkförlaget Skriptor AB, 219–242.

Mallinson, Christine. 2002. The regional accommodation of African American English: Evidence from a Bi-ethnic Mountain Enclave Community. MA Thesis, North Carolina State University.

Purnell, Thomas, William Idsardi, and John Baugh. 1999. Perceptual and phonetic experiments in American English dialect identification. *Journal of Language and Social Psychology* 18 (1): 10–30.

Roberts, Margaret M. 1966. *The pronunciation of vowels in Negro speech.* Unpublished PhD dissertation, Columbus: The Ohio State University.

Shrivastav, Rahul and Christine M. Sapienza. 2000. Objective measures of breathy voice quality obtained using an auditory model. *Journal of the Acoustical Society of America* 114 (1): 2217–2224.

Shuy, Roger W. 1970. Subjective judgments in sociolinguistic analysis. In James E. Alatis (ed.), *Report of the Twentieth Annual Round Table Meeting on Linguistics and Language Studies.* Washington, DC: Georgetown University Press, 175–188.

Shuy, Roger W., Joan C. Baratz, and Walter A. Wolfram. 1969. *Sociolinguistic factors in speech identification.* National Institute of Mental Heath Research Project No. MH 15048–01. Washington, DC: Center for Applied Linguistics.

Stroud, Robert Vernon. 1956. A study of the relations between social distance and speech differences of White and Negro high school students of Dayton, Ohio. Unpublished MA thesis, Bowling Green, Ohio: Bowling Green State University.
Syrdal, Ann K. and H. S. Gopal. 1986. A perceptual model of vowel recognition based on the auditory representation of American English vowels. *Journal of the Acoustical Society of America* 79: 1086–1100.
Tarone, Elaine E. 1973. Aspects of intonation in Black English. *American Speech* 48: 29–36.
Thomas, Erik R. 1989a. The implications of /o/ fronting in Wilmington, North Carolina. *American Speech* 64 (4): 327–333.
Thomas, Erik R. 1989b. Vowel changes in Columbus, Ohio. *Journal of English Linguistics* 22 (2): 205–215.
Thomas, Erik R. 2001. *An acoustic analysis of vowel variation in New World English.* Publication of the American Dialect Society 85. Durham NC: Duke University Press.
Thomas, Erik R. and Guy Bailey. 1998. Parallels between vowel subsystems of African American Vernacular English and Caribbean Anglophone creoles. *Journal of Pidgin and Creole Languages* 13: 267–296.
Thomas, Erik R. and Jeffrey Reaser. 2004a. Delimiting perceptual cues used for the ethnic labeling of African American and European American voices. *Journal of Sociolinguistics* 8: 54–86.
Thomas, Erik R. and Jeffrey L. Reaser. 2004b. An experiment on cues used for identification of voices as African American or European American. Paper presented at the 3rd decennial conference on Language Variety in the South (LAVIS), Tuscaloosa, AL: April 15.
Traunmüller, Hartmut. 1990. Analytical expressions for the tonotopic sensory scale. *Journal of the Acoustical Society of America* 88 (1): 97–100.
Trent, Sonja A. 1995. Voice quality: Listener identification of African-American versus Caucasian speakers. *Journal of the Acoustical Society of America* 98 (5): 29–36.
Tucker, G. Richard and Wallace E. Lambert. 1969. White and Negro listeners' reactions to various American-English dialects. *Social Forces* 47: 463–468.
Walton, Julie H. and Robert F. Orlikoff. 1994. Speaker race identification from acoustic cues in the vocal signal. *Journal of Speech and Hearing Research* 37: 738–745.
Wolfram, Walt and Erik R. Thomas. 2002. *The development of African American English: Evidence from an isolated community.* Oxford, UK/Malden, MA: Blackwell.
Wolfram, Walt, Erik R. Thomas, and Elaine W. Green. 2000. The regional context of earlier African-American speech: Evidence for reconstructing the development of AAVE. *Language in Society* 29 (3): 315–345.

Part III
Studies of Perception and Production

Chapter 13

Phonetic Detail in the Perception of Ethnic Varieties of US English

Thomas C. Purnell, University of Wisconsin–Madison

1. Introduction

While this chapter is concerned with the way acoustic cues of ethnically affiliated speech are selected and perceived, it also highlights the complex way social group and language interact phonetically. Results from the analysis of two data sets support the claim that the mapping of acoustic characteristics onto perceptual cues is neither linear nor entirely transparent. The chapter proceeds as follows. In Section 2, perceptual dialectology frames the issue of perceiving ethnically affiliated dialects. The link between an utterance and the reaction to that utterance as emphasized in perceptual dialectology is argued to be somewhat opaque given non-linear or non-transparent layering of phonetic information. Understanding the phonetic non-linearity requires analytical techniques which are also non-linear and uncover latent linguistic factors. The next two sections provide just such analyses of acoustic characteristics and perceptual cues. Section 3 reports a reanalysis of a southeastern Wisconsin dialect strongly influenced by ethnically affiliated immigrant languages, while Section 4 offers a reanalysis of characteristics and cues to African American English, Chicano English and Standard American English. The analysis in both Section 3 and Section 4 allow exploratory *post-hoc* analysis of acoustic characteristics in order to see whether a non-linear acoustic model has the same ability to distinguish dialects as a model driven by perception results. Finally, Section 5 concludes the chapter with a general discussion about the mapping of acoustic characteristics onto perceptual cues.

2. Ethnically affiliated dialects and perceptual dialectology

Perception of ethnically affiliated varieties of American English is influenced by the fluctuating and static properties of the ethnicity-speech connection.

Ethnicity is generally a moving target for researchers because, among other reasons, ethnicity often transcends geo-political boundaries. Examples related to the ethnic groups examined in this study include American English speakers with ties to perceived African or German ancestry found across many geographic locations. Another indication that ethnicity is a potential illusion is that ethnic group membership has fluid temporal and situational characteristics. Baugh (e.g., 1988) found that consonant cluster reduction among African American Vernacular speakers is influenced more by familiarity than ethnicity. Nonetheless, ethnically affiliated speech is afforded some perceptual substance since ethnicity can sometimes be attributed to geographic regions, e.g., German in Lancaster County, Pennsylvania, and southeastern Wisconsin. Additionally, characteristics of ethnic speech patterns attain a degree of perceptual reality as seen in metathesis and cluster reduction in African American English (Rickford 1999 among many others). Finally, the "reality" of ethnically affiliated dialects in the US contributes to social problems dealing with race and ethnicity (e.g., "linguistic profiling," Baugh 2000), and reflects shared knowledge between speakers and listeners.

It makes sense, then, to place the perception of ethnically affiliated dialects within the context of a paradigm accentuating the role that the listener has in the preservation of speech patterns. Perceptual dialectology (Preston 1989, 1997, 2002 et al.) allows for such a focus by defining dialect as listener-centric and social boundary-sensitive. It is listener-centric because it is "an assessment of . . . 'attitudes'" (Preston 2002: 95). This additional notion of dialect as an abstract, perceptual category adds to many traditional notions of dialect.[1] Perceptual dialectology is also sensitive to folk speech boundaries and is in line with the concept of dialect as a social boundary index. At the core of perceptual dialectology is the observation that research on how people react to others' speech or what they say about a speaker because of the speaker's dialect is just as important as what is uttered (Preston 1997, 2000).[2] This orientation to linguistic research is illustrated in Figure 13.1.

Preston's intention in his presentation of Figure 13.1 is to depict not only the speech act (*a*) and reactions to that act (*b* and *c* in the inner triangle), but also linguists' prioritization of research based on what is going on when someone talks (the outer triangle). Preston (and Hoenigswald before him) acknowledges that linguists have been preoccupied with the act of speaking (a') and with determining who and who is not an authentic or legitimate representative of some such speech community based on their speech. Instead, Preston argues that listeners cluster speakers into folk or cognitive categories by what is said (c' and *c*) and how they react (b' and *b*), and that this

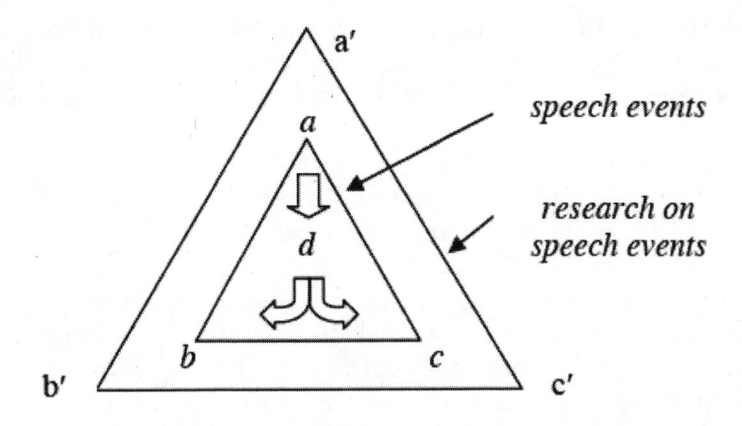

a = what people say a' = states and processes which govern *a*

b = how people react to a b' = attitudes and beliefs governing *b*

c = what people say about a c'= attitudes and beliefs governing *c*

d = the underlying acoustic/cognitive processes giving rise to *b* and *c* from *a*

Figure 13.1 The Hoenigswald-Preston observation (adapted from Preston, 1997).

clustering says something very important about the relation the speech cues have with society.

Yet this depiction also invites the question as to how a reaction occurs in the first place and whether listeners' responses are socially variable at the perceptual level. The relation between what a speaker says and listeners' reactions, beliefs and comments about the speaker (Figure 13.1*d*) should not be seen as a transparent or uninteresting one. Nevertheless, our understanding of the vector between speech acts and speech reactions is often confounded by an interface rendered opaque by properties of the acoustics of a speech act itself. If the acoustic characteristic-perception cue interface, lying between the speech act and response to that action, is rule governed, then we need to ask some customary questions: What are the guiding principles? Are these principles transparent and automatic? Are these principles universal, or do they allow for variation?

It should be acknowledged that there are internal constraints on the interface beyond the acoustic characteristics of speech that arise from processes of folk psychological essentialism and general perceptual categorization. Basic processes involved in categorization and concept acquisition (Wisniewski 2002: 475) are no doubt active in dialect perception.[3] The existence of these perceptual processes gives rise to a folk principle of transparency, which superficially contradicts acoustic opacity. This belief in transparency can be stated as: absent dissonant evidence, a speaker of a variety affiliated with a certain social or geographical group *X* is an authentic or credible *X*-ian. This is considered to be a case of psychological essentialism, i.e., " . . . people's concepts contain the belief that things have essences or underlying natures that make them what they are" (Wisniewski 2002: 501).[4] This is also assumed in the matched guise perception paradigm where listeners display the ability to believe that a speaker is of a certain ethnicity just because they produce an utterance with characteristics peculiar to a specific speech community.[5] For example, in a forced-choice matched guise experiment, a subject might respond that a speaker is African American on the basis of hearing the speaker say [æks] for *ask*. What is important within the context of Figure 13.1 is that the operating procedures behind the belief of transparency often make use of a reduced set of acoustic triggers. That is, matched guise studies show that one need not have an "authentic" speaker, just one who can produce the features well enough to trigger the identification by listeners. Such perceived ethnicity via perceptual cues is emphasized in this chapter by the reanalysis of previously reported ethnically affiliated data.

Regarding the role of phonetic aspects as an additional internal process, we have known for some time that phonetics fosters variation in general by providing multiple pathways to perception. To begin with, phonetic speech events are often highly complex and redundant with respect to both articulation and acoustics affording listeners a "family" of cues to attend to. Lisker (1986) observes this stabilizing effect of a many-to-one relation holding between perceptual cues and the voicing contrast in English coda obstruents (the difference between the words *bid* and *bit*). Voicing, Lisker and others have found, is reflected in pitch, formants, duration of vowel or consonant, amount of glottal pulsing, etc. The upshot of this multi-layering of gesture, acoustic characteristic and perceptual cue ensures correct perception of phonemes (MacNeilage 1970).

We might expect, then, that every acoustic cue has some role to play in the perception of speech, even if it is just a supporting one. Yet, not all acoustic characteristics are perceptual cues. By way of example, Abramson (1986) considered the perception of word initial geminate stops in Pattani Malay to come from four significant acoustic characteristics. However, he discovered later that amplitude differences on the following vowel are the perceptually salient feature for Pattani Malay speakers (Abramson 1991). This finding suggests that part of what is commonly thought to be our "phonetic knowledge" is the learned ability to follow particular perceptual cues.

The issues involved with the non-linear and seemingly non-transparent association between articulation, acoustics and perception can be framed by two sets of research questions having to do with the region between speech act and listeners' reactions. The first set of questions pertains to issues that are external to this chapter but central to the field of historical linguistics, such as why and how this relationship developed. This is the evaluation problem, the embedding problem and the actuation problem of Weinreich et al. (1968). Understanding the phonetic link between utterance and reaction (Figure 13.1) requires answers to the following set of questions:

1. What acoustic cues overlap with other cues? Are there latent factors underlying the set of measurements?
2. What acoustic characteristics are or are not members of the set of significant perceptual cues?
3. Within the set, which of the significant perceptual cues are stronger than others?
4. Is there variation even in the acoustic-perceptual relation, i.e., does the selection of cues, or the weighting of cues, vary by language, dialect, accent, etc.?

The main goal of this chapter is to address these four questions and demonstrate variation in the region between speech act and action. The presentation of the data sets, all previously reported, uses statistical methods, which emphasize potential many-to-many associations between acoustic characteristic and perceptual cue. As such, it contributes answers to questions about variability in the assignment of acoustic characteristics to perceptual cues, highlighting differences between a "perceptual" analysis using acoustic data alone and a "perceptual" analysis linking the two kinds of data.

3. Example 1: Wisconsin English

3.1 Background

Wisconsin English provides an interesting example of how an ethnically affiliated dialect can influence the surrounding dominant varieties.[6] A series of studies compared recordings of Wisconsin residents from four different eras to non-Wisconsin controls.[7] Of interest is the occurrence of apparent post-vocalic obstruent devoicing (e.g., /d/ > [t]) among the Wisconsin English speakers. The Wisconsin English speakers were divided into four groups based on their birth date:

- group 1: 1866 to 1892 (N=5)
- group 2: 1899 to 1918 (N=9)
- group 3: 1920 to 1939 (N=9)
- group 4: 1966 to 1986 (N=5)

The control group consisted of subjects not from Wisconsin who were approximately as old as the third group. The sound files of speakers in groups 1 and 2, and one speaker from group 3 come from the Wisconsin English Language Survey (WELS; Cassidy 1948) and the Dictionary of American Regional English (DARE; Cassidy 1985). Most of the sound files of the youngest test group came from the University of Wisconsin Xray Microbeam database (Westbury 1994). The remainder of the test subject recordings is from speakers living in Watertown, Wisconsin.

The studies reporting this data make two claims, which, in essence, follow the general pattern of linguistic change outlined by Labov (1972: 39). First, German plus other devoicing languages located in one geographic area (Polish, Dutch, some dialects of Yiddish, etc.) fostered interlanguage substrate properties initially. Since then, the distinctive acoustic characteristics were reallocated as a regional feature, distinct from general American English. The saliency of this dialect pattern as reflected in comedy routines at the national level contextualizes this phenomenon within the purview of perceptual dialectology.[8]

Second, the acoustic characteristics of vowel duration and percent glottal pulsing appear to hold a significant trading relation such that an observed weak acoustic characteristic, in vowel duration for example, is noticed to be strengthened by a complementary characteristic, percent glottal pulsing. This observation contrasts with reports in the literature of a more universal characteristic of post-vocalic obstruents as a change in first formant and fundamental frequency (Kingston and Diehl 1994, 1995; Stevens and Blumstein 1981; Stevens 2000). What Purnell et al. (2005b) report instead is that for each of their test groups, the degree of the relation holding between duration and pulsing distinguished one group from another. For example, the data set with the more recent birth dates unexpectedly reveals reduced glottal pulsing for voiced as well as voiceless tokens. This is a dramatically different pattern than that observed for speakers born 30 to 40 years earlier, but somewhat like the oldest group which displayed a preference for glottal pulsing as the dominant acoustic characteristic of post-vocalic voicing. The middle two groups were observed having greater balance between vowel duration and pulsing. This pattern of a younger group adopting the forms of an earlier group reflects the, now old, observation by Labov that "[g]roup A is adopted as a reference group by group B, and the feature is adopted and exaggerated . . ." (1972: 39). In the context of the present study, group A is represented by older Wisconsin English groups (groups 1 and 2), and group B by the youngest group (group 4). In short, this pattern of younger speakers exaggerating a form of an earlier reflex of the voicing distinction should not be unexpected by sociolinguists.

Within the context of the acoustic-perceptual interface identified on the Hoenigswald-Preston observation (Figure 13.1), the trading relation between duration and pulsing found in the Purnell et al. data raises the following overlapping questions:

> Are the significant articulatory or acoustic characteristics also perceptually significant cues? That is, would we expect a change in fundamental frequency to be the strongest perceptual cue as opposed to vowel duration even though it is not a significant measure across test subject groups? Another question is, are there latent factors underlying the articulatory or acoustic characteristics, e.g., a "low frequency" hypothesis, that listeners might be paying attention to rather than to the specific values of the characteristics? Within each speaker group, if latent factors are present, are these underlying factors identifiable as perceptual cues to the voicing distinction? Or, is the acoustic-perception link in Figure 13.1(d) transparent?

The present chapter answers these questions by testing whether or not there is variation across groups with respect to the variables selected or the weight of the variables contributing to the model.[9] One test hypothesis is that there is variation. Given the reported acoustic variation already across the test subject groups, it is hypothesized that the variation reflects a split between the Wisconsin English speakers and the control subjects. Another test hypothesis is that acoustic significance does not necessarily imply perceptual significance nor does perceptual significance imply acoustic significance.

3.2 Methodology

Seven main acoustic measures were collected as potential predictors in this model: vowel duration; the duration of the consonantal gap (for stops) or frication (for fricatives); the duration of glottal pulsing in the gap; the percentage of glottal pulsing in the gap (% glottal pulsing); the ratio of the vowel duration to the gap duration (V:C ratio); the change in F1 from beginning of offset to where it disappears (usually in the consonant); and the corresponding change in F0.[10] We expect that vowel duration, percent glottal pulsing, duration of glottal pulsing and the V:C ratio are larger for voiced tokens than voiceless ones. F0, F1 and consonant duration were then transformed so that the voiced values for all measures were larger than the measures for voiceless tokens. Since the values for these three measures are linear, the transformation was also linear using reference points to reverse the values.[11]

The appropriateness of statistical tests applied to these measures focused on the lack of truly independent variables and the identification of underlying latent factors, both of which are important in understanding the phenomena of post-vocalic obstruent voicing. Regarding variable independence, many acoustic characteristics of obstruent voicing overlap in non-experimentally controlled tokens such that perhaps none of the purportedly independent variables are in fact independent, but rather co-vary with each other. Additionally, a hint that at least one latent factor is operable in post-vocalic obstruent voicing is found in the literature when references are made to a "low frequency property" (Stevens and Blumstein 1981; Kingston and Diehl 1994, 1995). This latent property is often thought to identify a combined percept involving the acoustic characteristics of glottal pulsing, consonant duration, F1 and F0. Thus, one prediction for an analysis looking for underlying factors would be the emergence of a "low frequency property" aligned with the appropriate acoustic characteristics. Tatsuoka (1970: 2) among others notes that overlapping measures, such as the overlap of acoustic measures in the case at hand, distorts a statistical relation across groups implied by univariate analyses.

As a demonstration of how inconsistently the acoustic measures co-vary with each other, correlation matrices are shown in Tables 13.1 and 13.2 for groups 2 and 3. Bilateral correlation comparisons of seven measures are shown for both voiced tokens (the upper right triangle of data) and voiceless tokens (the lower left triangle of data). Inconsistent co-variation is seen when comparing which variables correlate with vowel duration for voiced tokens. For group 3 voiced tokens (Table 13.2), the distribution of values of pulsing duration, percent glottal pulsing and the V:C ratio significantly correlate with the distribution of vowel duration. However, for group 2 (Table 13.1), only V:C ratio significantly correlates with vowel duration for voiced tokens. Additionally, for both voiced and voiceless tokens, the percent of glottal pulsing (i.e., the pulsing duration divided by the consonant gap duration) is correlated with both the pulsing duration and consonant gap duration for both groups of speakers. However, the inferential correlation, i.e., between pulsing duration and consonant gap duration, is significant for voiced tokens, but not voiceless tokens.

ble 13.1 Correlation Matrix for Group 2 (1920–1939)

	Vowel Duration	Pulsing Duration	% Glottal Pulsing	V:C Ratio	Change in F0	Change in F1	Consonant Gap Duration
owel uration		0.181	0.039	0.558***	-0.218	-0.089	-0.082
ulsing uration	-0.035		0.324*	-0.368*	0.260	-0.104	-0.564***
Glottal ulsing	-0.340	0.546**		0.292	0.454**	0.144	0.579***
:C Ratio	0.482*	-0.241	0.297		-0.069	0.190	0.606***
hange F0	-0.224	-0.152	-0.339	0.021		0.434**	0.155
hange F1	-0.389	-0.125	-0.063	-0.085	-0.50		0.209
onsonant ap uration	-0.3459	-0.206	0.531**	0.567**	-0.211	0.292	

Voiceless

Voiced

p = 0.05, ** p = 0.01, *** p = 0.001, **** p = 0.0001

ble 13.2 Correlation Matrix for Group 3 (1920–1939)

	Vowel Duration	Pulsing Duration	% Glottal Pulsing	V:C Ratio	Change in F0	Change in F1	Consonant Gap Duration
owel uration		-0.425*	-0.453*	0.538*	-0.301	0.352	-0.238
ulsing uration	0.237		0.766****	-0.065	0.374*	-0.529**	0.389**
Glottal ulsing	-0.180	0.548**		0.346	0.390*	-0.452*	0.823****
:C Ratio	0.200	-0.121	0.411*		0.006	0.198	0.606***
hange n F0	-0.241	0.299	0.360*	-0.106		-0.241	0.248
hange n F1	0.076	0.136	0.153	-0.009	-0.158		-0.198
onsonant ap uration	-0.439*	-0.267	0.424*	0.652****	0.136	-0.203	

Voiceless

Voiced

p = 0.05, ** p = 0.01, *** p = 0.001, **** p = 0.0001

Because independence of acoustic characteristics of postvocalic obstruent voicing is inconsistent, the statistical analysis examining overlapping measures proceeded in three stages. The heart of the analysis is the use of canonical coefficients, which explain the relation between distinct acoustic variables (predictors) in a many-to-many fashion. This multivariate approach differs sharply from a univariate analysis of several measures.

In terms of which acoustic measures make a significant contribution to the perception of obstruents, predictors were first identified using a discriminant analysis of voicing by speaker group based on a forward stepwise procedure. Typically, a forward stepwise analysis uses only those measures conservatively below the 0.15 significance level. Although Costanza and Afifi (1979) recommend using significance levels where $0.10 < p < 0.20$, they note that the point of raised significance levels is to widen the scope of important variables unless it was known that few variables stopped the procedure early. Such significance levels, as will be seen, yield an uneven number of potentially significant measures across groups. In order to facilitate a between-group comparison and to allow for the inclusion of several low-frequency properties previously claimed to be important to postvocalic voicing, a predetermined number of steps were set to four. In other words, the model used only the first four measures in order to identify the most inclusive subset of variables from which we assume the perceptual cues will come. Adding and taking away insignificant variables in a stepwise fashion involved using variables with univariate significance over the α limit of 0.05 in all groups (maximally 0.12, 0.77, 0.36, 0.35, and 0.06, respectively across groups 1 through 5 in Table 13.3). Again, the reason for considering variables above 0.05 is that the pool of perceptual cues includes the strongest, albeit not entirely strongly significant, acoustic variables. While inclusion of more measures over fewer works against the criterion of parsimony, the multivariate analysis technique has the ability to identify more border-line variables that would not be found using a univariate analyses of several measures, allowing confirmation of whether the strongest acoustic characteristics are in fact the strongest perceptual cues.

The second step in the analysis is a canonical discriminant analysis reducing the top four variables for each group to one dimension. Rather than trying to understand the voicing distinction on a fairly obtuse four-dimensional relation, we can reduce the dimensions to one less than the number of contrasts; a canonical discriminant analysis can only yield an *n-1* category analysis. Assuming that voicing is phonetically distinctive at some level by a binary feature (e.g., [spread glottis] for aspirating languages such as English, and [slack vocal folds] for voicing languages such as Spanish; see Iverson and Salmons 2003), then only one dimension is possible.[12] For each group, the multivariate significance is compared to the individual significance values (using significance levels and r^2 correlation coefficients). This comparison is the test of whether the multivariate analysis is stronger than parallel univariate analyses: the closer the univariate and multivariate squared correlation coefficients are to each other, the less likely the multivariate approach provides insight into the distinction between groups. Canonical coefficients of the linear combination of the measures are then computed. Assuming that the multivariate approach provides a stronger account of the variation in the data (by a higher squared coefficient value), the Mahalanobis distance between the means of the voicing categories is calculated. This distance accounts for the statistical distribution of the data based on the correlation between the acoustic measures used by the model.

Even though the canonical discriminant analysis only finds one factor among the acoustic measures because there are only two voicing categories, we can explore the reduction of dimensions using principal component analysis from the basis of the four most significant measures themselves. This difference in analysis is one of perspective: if the analysis proceeds from the number of categories, then only one factor is possibly considered (canonical discriminant analysis); if the analysis proceeds from the number of measures in the model, then the goal of the analysis is to account for the most variation within the categories (principal component analysis). This third analytical procedure, then, informs our interpretation of which factors might be active within the voiced or voiceless categories. The result of this step allows us to understand the differences between voiced and voiceless tokens at different stages over time and with varying temporal distance to immigrant language influences.

It will be assumed that the within-category weights contribute to the across-category weight. In other words, we could expect that two measures contribute to one factor among voiceless tokens, while two different measures contribute to a factor distinguishing voiced tokens. However, two assumptions simplify the cross-category interpretation: the same four measures are used for both voiced and voiceless models within each group; and, binary grouping of the four measures are assumed to fall consistently into the same two (and only two) principal components for both the voiced and voiceless tokens. The criteria for the binary grouping proceed by an examination of the strongest correlation for all of the voiced and voiceless components for any one measure (four values compared per measure; see Table 13.6). Plots of the two measures along the two component dimensions, multiplied by their individual eigenvector (i.e., weight), provide graphic insight into how well the voiced and voiceless tokens may be distinguished from each other (Figures 13.3 through 13.8).

Since some of the third group's data were presented for an identification evaluation in a forced-choice perceptual experiment (Purnell et al. 2005a), we compare the acoustic and perceptual data where appropriate. Nineteen subjects listened to the data, responding to the final sound in each word they heard. Only three of the listeners did not report a dialect region in Wisconsin or southern Minnesota. The error rates for the group 3 tokens which were considered important were those over 10%: /t/ as [d], 10%; /s/ as [t], 11%; /s/ as [z], 18%; and /z/ as [s], 33%. Thus, a parallel analysis is conducted on the group 3 data that was presented in the perception experiment. The voicing category is transformed based on the error rates over 10%, i.e., if a /z/ target token was perceived as either [t] or [s] more than 10% of the time, then it was coded as voiceless. There are three possible expectations with respect to this data. First, we might expect that the subjects will use a Wisconsin English set of weighted measures, most like group 4 given the proximity in age. Second, we could expect that the listeners use a Wisconsin English set of weighted measures parallel to group 3, given that this is the input to the experiment. Third, we might expect that the listeners use a default, network English set of weighted measures, i.e., more like the controls in group 5.

3.3 Results

Results of the stepwise and canonical discriminant analyses are shown in Tables 13.3 through 13.7. The stepwise analysis results are shown in Table 13.3. Per the stepwise process outlined previously, for each group the four strongest measures are listed in descending order of the degree to which they contribute to the overall strength of the statistical model for that group. For example, percent glottal pulsing, vowel duration, change in F1, and change in F0 are the four measures for group 1 that show relative statistical significance. They are listed in their present order, not because of their univariate significance (compare vowel duration, p=0.0787, with change in F1, p=0.0756), but because of their contribution to the squared canonical correlation value (a resultant 0.485 and 0.523, respectively). Each line of data on Table 13.3 represents the final model output given the addition of the variable on that line along with any variable already added to the model. Of interest is the value for the average squared canonical correlation (ASCC) on the last line for each group because this value depicts the degree of well-separated discriminant space and approximates the amount of variation accounted for by the measures accepted into the model. For the ASCC values, a value of 1 represents the greatest distinction between groups, and thus how separate voiced tokens are from voiceless ones in perceptual space. Overall, voicing is signaled less well by four measures in the group with the most recent birth dates (0.351) and the control group (0.399) as compared to the groups with older birth dates (0.550, 0.479, 0.518, respectively). Table 13.3 reveals how important percent glottal pulsing and vowel duration are to the data and the diminished statistical effect of a changing F1. Percent glottal pulsing is present in all groups, and as the strongest measure in all four Wisconsin English groups. Moreover, it never has a significance value of more than 0.03. Vowel duration is present in all groups with the exception of group 2. Change in F0 appears in three groups (groups 1, 3, and 4) as the third or fourth strongest measure, never reaching significance below 0.10. Change in F1 appears somewhat strong in group 1 ($p<0.10$), but inconsistently weak in group 3 ($p=0.3640$). Table 13.3 also yields an interesting observation that the measures selected from the transformed perception data reflects the selection of group 5 measures instead of the group 3 or group 4 measures.

As mentioned previously, a common method of conducting a forward stepwise discriminant analysis is to set a significance threshold between 0.10 and 0.20. Such a threshold would allow a greater degree of strength to the models for groups 2, 3, and 4. For group 2, in fact, only one measure, percent glottal pulsing would model the data. The three other measures in the model for group 2 add no more than 0.02 to the ASCC value. That is, adding the three measures only accounts for 2% of the variation in the data. For groups 3 and 4, only percent glottal pulsing and vowel duration would make the significance cut-off. The additional two measures account for an additional 1% and 2% of the data variation, respectively.

Once the individual measures were selected for all groups using the forward stepwise discriminant analysis, a canonical discriminant analysis was conducted to verify whether a multivariate analysis is stronger than a univariate one in terms of distinguishing voiced tokens from voiceless ones. Table 13.4 shows the univariate values for the four measures listed by descending r^2 values for each group, while Table 13.5 shows relevant multivariate values for each group. The squared canonical coefficients (SCC) in Table 13.5 represent the amount of variation accounted for by the predictor variables as a group. For the first three test groups, the significant variables in the model (those whose inclusion is within the alpha limit) account for over 50% of the variation (55%, 57% and 52%, respectively). In comparison, the amount of variation accounted for by the significant predictors is below 40% for the fourth test group (35%) and the controls (40%). The model for the perceptual group 3 data accounts for 46% of the variation. Comparing the SCC value for each group in Table 13.5 with the best individual r^2 value in Table 13.4

Table 13.3 Results of Stepwise Discriminant Analysis Using a Forward Method for Four Test Groups of WI English Speakers and One Control Group

Group, Variable	Partial r^2	F	p > F	Average squared canonical correlation
1: 1866–1892 (df=4, 41; N voiced=30, voiceless=16)				
% glottal pulsing	0.446	35.4	0.0001	0.446*
vowel duration	0.070	3.2	0.0787	0.485*
change in F1	0.070	3.3	0.0756	0.523*
change in F0	0.057	2.5	0.1231	0.550*
2: 1899–1918 (df=4, 58; N voiced=38; voiceless=25)				
% glottal pulsing	0.460	51.9	0.0001	0.460*
pulsing duration	0.030	1.8	0.1830	0.476*
C gap duration	0.005	0.3	0.5945	0.478*
V:C ratio	0.002	0.1	0.7658	0.479*
3: 1920–1939 (df=4, 147; N voiced=79, voiceless=73)				
% glottal pulsing	0.347	79.6	0.0001	0.347*
vowel duration	0.248	49.1	0.0001	0.509*
change in F0	0.013	1.9	0.1684	0.515*
change in F1	0.006	0.8	0.3640	0.518*
4: Perception (df=4, 55; N voiced=42, voiceless=18)				
vowel duration	0.209	15.3	0.0002	0.209*
% glottal pulsing	0.152	10.2	0.0023	0.329*
V:C ratio	0.138	8.9	0.0042	0.421*
pulsing duration	0.063	3.7	0.0600	0.457*
5: 1966–1986 (df=4, 61; N voiced=42; voiceless=24)				
% glottal pulsing	0.283	25.3	0.0001	0.283*
vowel duration	0.068	4.6	0.0366	0.331*
change in F0	0.016	1.0	0.3196	0.342*
C gap duration	0.014	0.9	0.3505	0.351*

(continued)

Table 13.3 Results of Stepwise Discriminant Analysis Using a Forward Method for Four Test Groups of WI English Speakers and One Control Group *(continued)*

Group, Variable	Partial r^2	F	p > F	Average squared canonical correlation
6: Controls (df=4, 93; N voiced=52; voiceless=46)				
pulsing duration	0.233	29.1	0.0001	0.233*
V:C ratio	0.144	16.0	0.0001	0.343*
vowel duration	0.035	3.5	0.0664	0.366*
% glottal pulsing	0.052	5.1	0.0261	0.399*

*$p<0.05$

we see that for groups 3 and 5 the multivariate analysis accounts for more than an additional 15% of the variation, whereas for group 1 the multivariate analysis accounts for an additional 10% and, for group 4, an additional 7% of variation. Group 2 has the slightest difference between the two values (2%) largely because one measure, percent glottal pulsing, carries the most statistical weight for that group. The strongest difference occurs in the group 3 perception data where the multivariate model accounts for 25% more variation than the strongest univariate measure. Strength of the multivariate analysis is that the five non-perception study groups in Table 13.5 are significant, while some of the measures' univariate F values—change in F1 for groups 1 and 3, change in F0 for groups 3 and 4, specifically—are above the usual 0.05 significance level. On Table 13.6, the accounted-for difference across groups is mirrored by the total-sample standardized canonical coefficients (TSSCC). This value is suggestive of the discriminatory power between the acoustic predictors with respect to some underlying factor pertaining to the voicing contrast. The TSSCC value indicates that when the tokens are standardized, the percent glottal pulsing receives the highest coefficient for all Wisconsin English groups (1.036, 1.030, 1.170, and 0.864, respectively) and the perception data (2.026), and the second highest coefficient for the control group (0.639). When vowel duration is present (i.e., excluding group 2 and including the group 3 perception data), it has the second strongest TSSCC value except for the control group where it has the strongest value. Figure 13.2 presents the changing difference between vowel duration and the percent glottal pulsing. First, it is worth pointing out the shared pattern across all of

Table 13.4 Univariate Results of Canonical Discriminant Analysis

Group, Variable	F	*p*	r^2
1: 1866–1892 (df = 1, 44)			
% glottal pulsing	35.43	0.0001	0.446
change in F0	6.28	0.0160	0.125
vowel duration	4.28	0.0445	0.087
change in F1	2.91	0.0951	0.062
2: 1899–1918 (df = 1, 86)			
% glottal pulsing	107.89	0.0001	0.557
pulsing duration	42.62	0.0001	0.331
C gap duration	24.82	0.0001	0.224
V:C ratio	5.25	0.0244	0.058
3: 1920–1939 (df = 1, 150)			
% glottal pulsing	79.64	0.0001	0.347
vowel duration	31.22	0.0001	0.172
change in F0	1.22	0.2717	0.008
change in F1	0.02	0.8773	0.000
3: Perception (df = 1, 58)			
vowel duration	15.29	0.0002	0.209
pulsing duration	9.71	0.0029	0.143
% glottal pulsing	7.22	0.0094	0.111
V:C ratio	1.01	0.3197	0.017
4: 1966–1986 (df = 1, 64)			
% glottal pulsing	25.26	0.0001	0.283
vowel duration	7.86	0.0067	0.109
C gap duration	7.60	0.0076	0.106
change in F0	1.49	0.2270	0.023
5: Controls (df = 1, 96)			
pulsing duration	29.08	0.0001	0.233
% glottal pulsing	20.15	0.0001	0.174
vowel duration	16.13	0.0001	0.144
V:C ratio	4.98	0.0280	0.049

Table 13.5 Multivariate Results of Canonical Discriminant Analysis

Group	Squared Distance Between Means	F	Squared Canonical Coefficients	Eigenvalue
1: 1866–1892 (df = 4, 41)	5.15	12.52*	0.550	1.222†
2: 1899–1918 (df = 4, 83)	5.29	27.95*	0.574	1.347†
3: 1920–1939 (df = 4, 147)	4.25	39.46*	0.518	1.074†
3: Perception (df = 4, 55)	3.88	11.59*	0.457	0.846†
4: 1966–1986 (df = 4, 61)	2.27	8.26*	0.351	0.542†
5: Controls (df = 4, 93)	2.62	15.46*	0.399	0.665†

*p<0.0001
†cumulative eigenvalue = 1.000

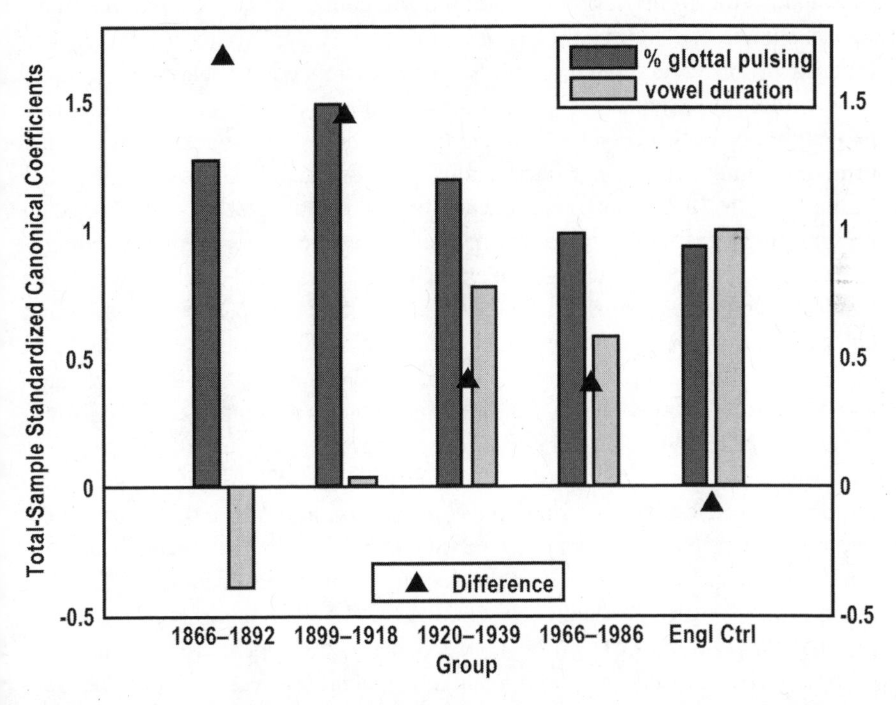

Figure 13.2 Plot of the difference between the important measures with regard to their total-sample standardized canonical coefficient.

the Wisconsin English speaker groups where percent glottal pulsing is greater than vowel duration. For the controls, there is a fairly equal relation between the two measures. Second, note that the differential relation favoring percent glottal pulsing is most extreme in older groups. Third, that all other things being equal, the youngest speakers mirror the group immediately preceding it, i.e., the 1920–1939 group, and not the controls.

To this point, the analysis has focused on the voiced-voiceless comparison. Tables 13.6 and 13.7 compare within-group variation. That is, the principal component analysis explains how latent factors may shape the within-category data, and provides insight into the variability of the weighting of variables such as percent glottal pulsing and vowel duration, which dominate all five groups' data. The cumulative proportion for the second principal component by voicing category on Table 13.7 reveals how much within-category variation is accounted for by the measures used by the model. The voiceless tokens in each group ranged from 63% (group 4) to 85% (group 2). The voiced tokens in each group ranged from 65% (group 3) to 87% (group 2). Group 3 perception data had similar results with the voiced and voiceless tokens (63% and 89%, respectively). All of the eigenvalues on Table 13.7 exceed a value of 1, although the eigenvalues for group 4, group 5, and the perceptual group 3 data in the multivariate canonical discriminant analysis (Table 13.5) do not reach a value of 1. In order to visualize the separation of tokens by voicing, the strongest eigenvectors for the relevant principal component for voiced and voiceless tokens were used as weights of each measure. The addition of the two strongest measures per principal component were plotted against each other and shown in Figure 13.3 through Figure 13.8. Selection of the component eigenvector was established by finding the largest absolute value and then using the same component assignment for voiced and voiceless tokens. Coherence should prevail over these resultant groupings. Consider, for example, the first group. The voiceless first component eigenvector for percent glottal pulsing (0.541) and the voiced first component eigenvector for vowel duration (0.610) suggest that these two measures are grouped together. Such a grouping suggests a latent factor of TEMPORAL CHANGE, while the other pair of measures, change in F0 and change in F1, suggests a competing latent factor of SPECTRAL CHANGE.[13] The grouping of percent glottal pulsing and pulsing duration in group 2 suggests a latent factor of PULSING in contrast to CONSONANT DURATION (consonant gap duration and V:C ratio). The latent factors in group 3 mirror group 1. The first latent factor for group 4 is the TEMPORAL CHANGE factor (percent glottal pulsing, vowel duration). However, the coherence of an interpretation of the grouping of consonant gap duration and change in F0 is less clear (independent from the other two measures). The latent factors in group 5 represent RELATIVE DURATION (percent glottal pulsing, V:C ratio) as the first component

Table 13.6 Measure Values for Multivariate Results of Canonical Discriminant Analysis and Principal Component Analysis

Group, Variables	Total-Sample Standardized Canonical Coefficients	Voiceless Tokens Eigenvector, Principal Component		Voiced Tokens Eigenvector, Principal Component	
		1	2	1	2
1: 1866–1892 (df = 1, 44)					
% glottal pulsing	1.036	0.541†	-0.393	0.513†	0.213
change in F0	0.375	0.428	0.622†	0.594	0.128†
vowel duration	-0.519	-0.490†	0.546	0.610†	-0.124
change in F1	-0.459	0.534	0.401†	-0.114	0.961†
2: 1899–1918 (df = 1, 86)					
% glottal pulsing	1.030	0.617	0.360†	0.316	0.761†
pulsing duration	0.484	0.209	0.763†	-0.432	0.642†
C gap duration	0.174	0.593†	-0.278	0.648†	0.087
V:C ratio	0.105	0.472†	-0.459	0.542†	-0.037
3: 1920–1939 (df = 1, 150)					
% glottal pulsing	1.170	0.631†	0.093	0.675†	0.263
vowel duration	0.800	-0.637†	0.081	-0.593†	0.471
change in F0	-0.147	0.320	-0.698†	0.437	0.296†
change in F1	0.106	0.306	0.706†	0.035	-0.788†
4: Perception (df = 1, 150)					
vowel duration	1.651	0.137	0.798†	-0.518	0.440†
pulsing duration	-0.920	0.581†	-0.183	0.608†	0.129
% glottal pulsing	2.026	0.705†	-0.278	0.593†	0.388
V:C ratio	-1.298	0.385	0.502†	-0.101	0.800†
5: 1966–1986 (df = 1, 64)					
% glottal pulsing	0.864	-0.349	0.795†	0.606	0.219†
vowel duration	0.492	0.487	0.388†	-0.048	-0.716†
C gap duration	0.229	0.426†	0.443	0.721†	0.072
change in F0	-0.223	0.678†	-0.147	-0.333†	0.659
6: Controls (df = 1, 96)					
pulsing duration	0.502	-0.024	0.821†	0.532	0.503†
% glottal pulsing	0.639	0.651†	0.405	0.534†	-0.449
vowel duration	0.678	-0.457	0.386†	-0.459	0.558†
V:C ratio	0.205	0.606†	-0.112	-0.472†	-0.484

† Identifies the eigenvector used for plots of component 1 X component 2

Table 13.7 Multivariate Results of Principal Component Analysis

Group	Voiceless Tokens Principal Component Eigenvalue		Voiced Tokens Principal Component Eigenvalue	
	1	2	1	2
1: 1866–1892	1.865 (0.466)	1.197 (0.765)	1.733 (0.433)	1.017 (0.688)
2: 1899–1918	1.964 (0.491)	1.452 (0.854)	2.146 (0.537)	1.318 (0.866)
3: 1920–1939	1.484 (0.371)	1.144 (0.657)	1.373 (0.343)	1.214 (0.647)
3: Perception	1.641 (0.410)	1.134 (0.694)	2.121 (0.530)	1.453 (0.893)
4: 1966–1986	1.437 (0.359)	1.065 (0.625)	1.565 (0.391)	1.074 (0.660)
5: Controls	1.655 (0.414)	1.359 (0.753)	1.716 (0.429)	1.176 (0.723)

Note: Cumulative proportions appear in parentheses.

and ABSOLUTE DURATION (pulsing duration, vowel duration) as the second component. Thus, we can observe the contrast between temporal and spectral cues to voicing in Wisconsin English, the combination of percent glottal pulsing and vowel duration in Wisconsin English, the dominance of pulsing in group 2, and the opposition—rather than the combination—of percent glottal pulsing and vowel duration in group 5. It is interesting to note that the grouping of the group 3 perceptual data, which parallel group 5 in terms of measures selected by the model, follow the Wisconsin English models which place vowel duration and percent glottal pulsing on opposite dimensions (specifically, like group 2 and not like group 4). The latent factors for the perceptual group 3 data might, then, be interpreted as PULSING and VOWEL DURATION.

Visual relations between variables are depicted in eigenvector plots in Figures 13.3 through 13.8. Since we would like to know how measures relate to each other and how this relation changes over time, we use the eigenvectors as weights for each measure. The plots show the sums of two measures times the actual value for the appropriate measure. The goal of these plots is to depict the variable space so that we can understand the contribution of each variable to the overall discriminant space. In the case at hand, pairs of measures are used for each axis and the best principal component across both voiced and voiceless tokens.

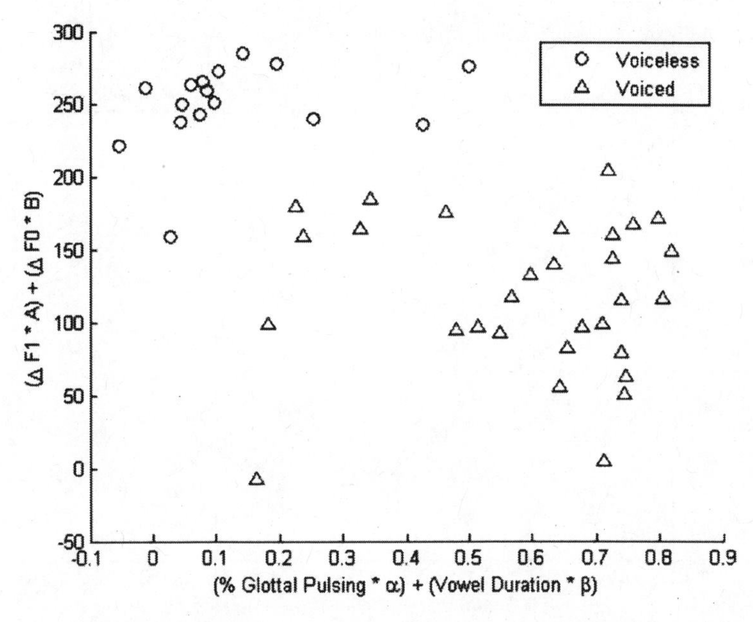

Figure 13.3 Plot of Group 1 eigenvectors from principal component analysis.

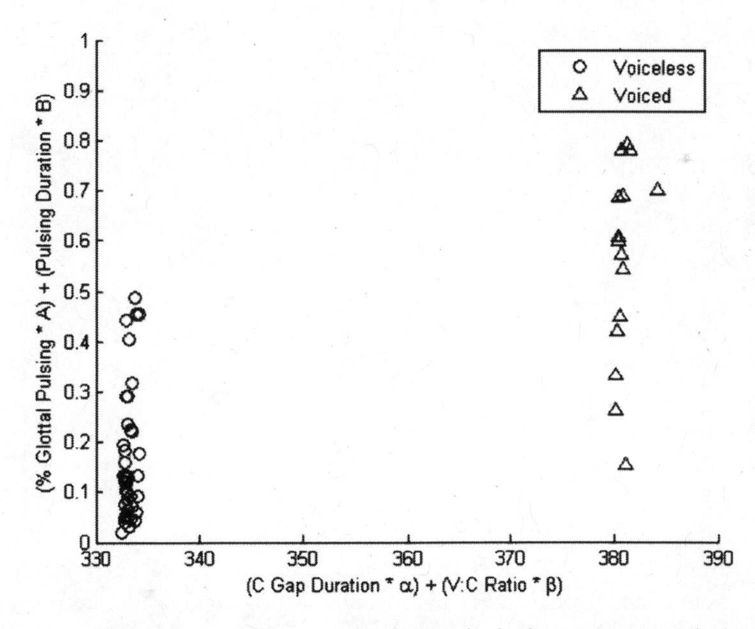

Figure 13.4 Plot of Group 2 eigenvectors from principal component analysis.

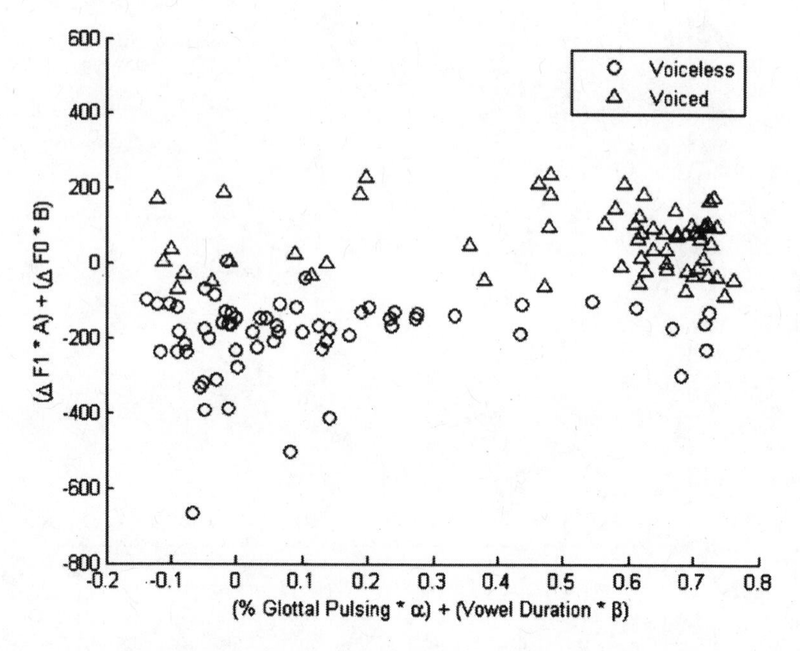

Figure 13.5 Plot of Group 3 eigenvectors from principal component analysis.

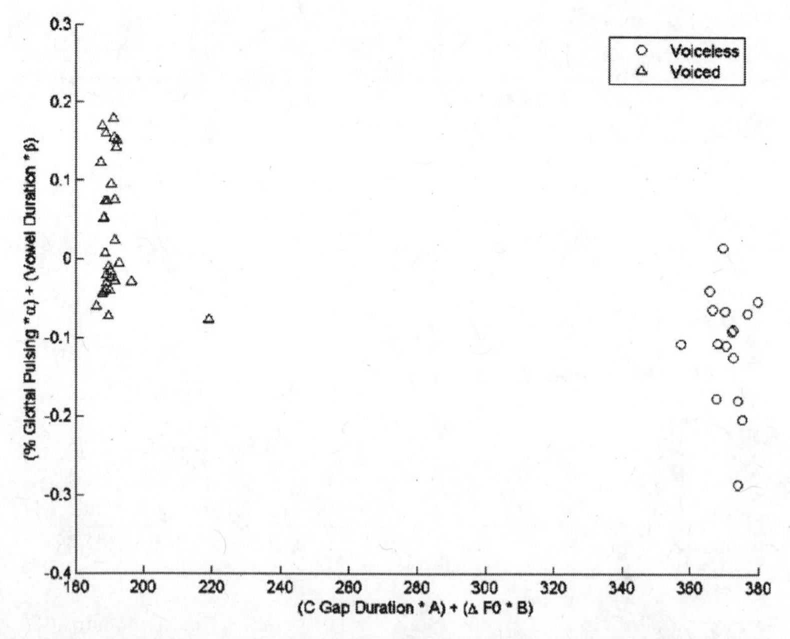

Figure 13.6 Plot of Group 4 eigenvectors from principal component analysis.

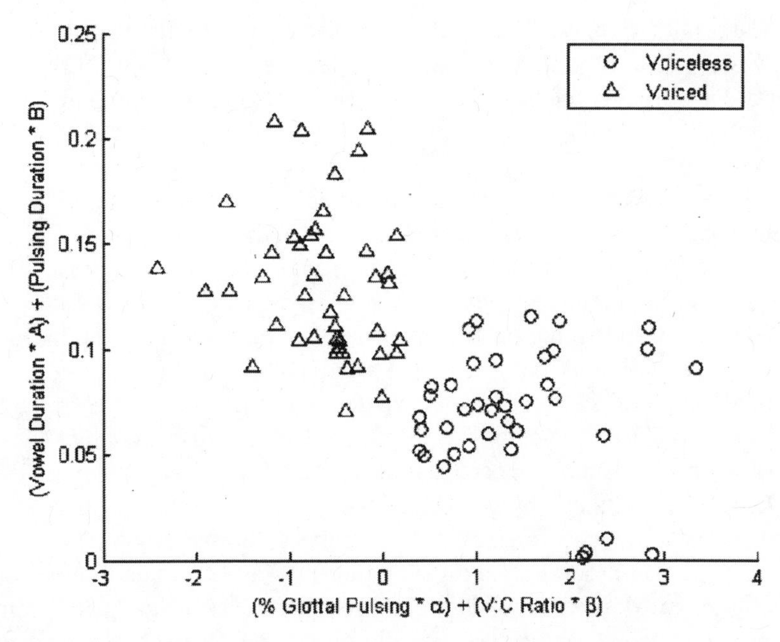

Figure 13.7 Plot of Group 5 eigenvectors from principal component analysis.

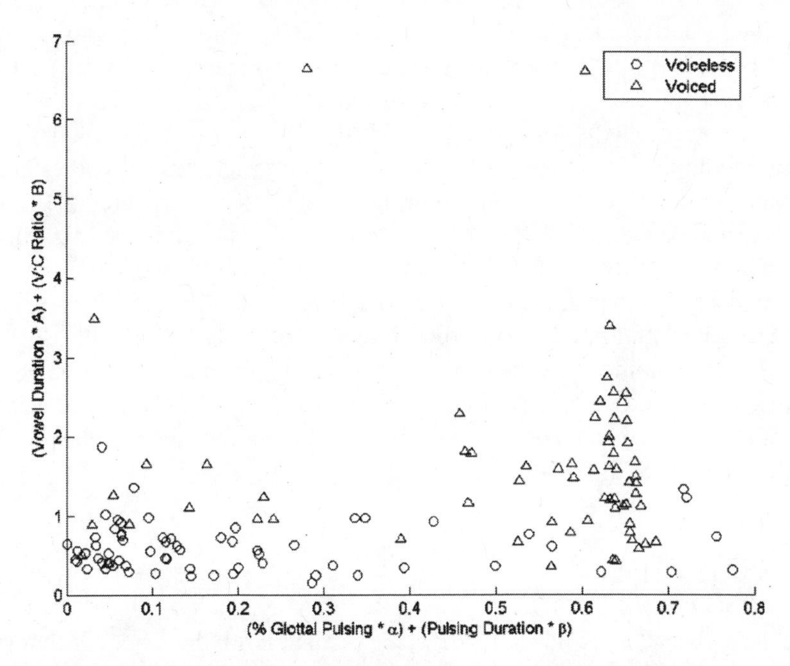

Figure 13.8 Plot of Group 3 Perceptual eigenvectors from principal component analysis.

The results from this type of study can also be used to distinguish an analysis, which is based on trading relations or feature enhancement. If two measures are in a trading relation, then we can see that when one measure is weak for some category member (e.g., the percent glottal pulsing is below 50% of the consonant for voiced tokens), then an opposing measure is strong (e.g., the vowel duration would be longer, compensating for the low pulsing). Thus, we expect that these two values are complementary and either display a significant negative correlation or display no significant correlation. In contrast, if two measures are in an enhancement relation, then we can see that both features are simultaneously strong, or display a significant positive correlation. In the papers by Purnell et al. (2005a, b), the argument is made for a trading relation between vowel duration and percent glottal pulsing for Wisconsin English post-vocalic obstruent voicing. This differs from the claim in work by Kingston and Diehl that measures of post-vocalic obstruent voicing are enhancing. Correlations were calculated by voicing category (voiced, voiceless) and by data group for the four measures identified as strongest for that group. The correlation between vowel duration and glottal pulsing was examined for all groups except group 2 which did not identify vowel duration as a significantly strong measure. The two measures were significantly correlated for some, but not all instances. Group 1 voiceless tokens show a significant negative correlation (-0.5330, p<0.05), but not the voiced tokens (0.3176, p >0.05). Conversely, for the group 3 perception data the voiced tokens show a significant negative correlation (-0.4529, p <0.05) while the voiceless tokens do not (-0.1795, p =0.3340). For group 3 and group 5 the voiceless tokens (-0.3331, p <0.01; -0.3019, p <0.05) and the voiced tokens (-0.2846, p <0.05; -0.4411, p <0.01) show that vowel duration and percent glottal pulsing are negatively significant. Neither group 4 voiceless or voiced tokens are significant for the two measures (0.0160, p =0.9410 and 0.0626, p =0.6938, respectively). Thus, when there is a significant correlation, it is only negative. This tentatively argues in favor of a trading relation model rather than an enhancement one for all cases that use vowel duration and percent glottal pulsing, including group 5 controls. Additionally, Purnell et al. (2005b) claimed that the group 4 data was interesting because the voiced tokens had moved very close to the voiceless tokens (paralleling final devoicing of a native German control). The closeness of voiced and voiceless tokens might account for the lack of significant correlation.

3.4 Conclusions

The larger task at hand is to describe variation in the phonetic component through which a speaker is perceived by a listener as belonging to an ethnically affiliated speech community. The specific case at hand involves a marker of certain European immigrant communities (final devoicing). The first hypothesis we tested was whether there was a statistically significant difference between Wisconsin English speakers (those who may have integrated this low-level ethnically-affiliated cue) and the American English controls (who we assume from experience do not use devoicing in the same way). We found that all groups share the importance of percent glottal pulsing in signaling the voicing distinction, and most Wisconsin English groups share vowel duration as an important measure of voicing. However, while additional measures contribute to the models, the set of important measures is not uniform across all groups. Additionally, the amount of variation the set of measures accounts for and the individual contribution to the model varies by the varying eigenvector weights. The second hypothesis we tested with this data was whether an analysis of the acoustic data and an analysis of the acoustic data in light of perception results are identical. Thus the relation depicted by Figure 13.1(d) is important. The group 3 perception data showed an interesting pattern in which the measures which appear important are those of group 5, yet the weighting—via the identification of latent factors—appears aligned to a Wisconsin English group (group 2). It is unclear from this data how ages of speaker and listener interacts with weighting of acoustic cues as they are used in perception. However, findings of the principal component analysis suggest that Wisconsin English speakers use vowel duration and percent glottal pulsing in a trading relation. These findings conflict with Kingston and Diehl's claim that speakers of American English use enhancement.

Three issues make the study of Wisconsin English devoicing particularly interesting. First, the variables are low-level phonetic attributes and not segmental ones. Second, this study explores variation in consonants in a way that is largely overlooked by sociolinguists.[14] Third, the low-level phonetic cues are tied to the sub-segmental distinctive features in a robust statistical fashion. The canonical discriminant analysis can reveal only one latent factor across the entire data, VOICING, assuming binary features. We now turn to a case where low-level variation will be examined across three ethnically affiliated groups, thereby opening the possibility for more than one latent factor.

4. Example 2: "hello" in three dialects

4.1 Background

The second set of data which shows variation in the mapping of acoustic characteristics to perceptual cues comes from experiments using a tri-dialectal male subject speaking in three dialects (Purnell et al. 1999): African American English (AAE), Chicano English (ChE), and Standard American [Northern] English (SAE). There, it was reported that utterances like "Hello, I'm calling about the apartment you have advertised in the paper" spoken in these three dialects were identified accurately in a matched guise experiment. When the word "hello" from this test phrase was played to listeners by itself, the dialect used in producing that word was identified better than chance. The interpretation made by Purnell et al. (1999) was that the speaker produced some identifiable acoustic characteristic that acted as a trigger for dialect identification.[15] The goal of the present study is to understand this trigger in light of questions raised previously regarding the relation between acoustic characteristics and perceptual cues, and the presence of latent factors.

For comparison purposes it is worth noting that Thomas and his colleagues find differences in acoustics and perception of (Southern) White English and African American English from both source (intonation, creakiness) and filter (vowels) properties.[16, 17] This finding confirms what was reported by Purnell et al. regarding the acoustics of the dialects. We will also see that the similar acoustic characteristics identified by Thomas participate in the cross-dialectal co-variation when using discriminant analyses. What is unclear from previous work is the weighting of acoustic characteristics as perceptual cues, and the relative transparency in Figure 13.1(d) where the focus is primarily across social group. The results from §3 suggest that in the present data we should find latent factors at work and that source and filter characteristics may not be equally weighted.

4.2 Methodology

In the Purnell et al. 1999 study, the solitary "hello" tokens were selected for measurement because they had been used in a perceptual experiment and produced results indicating that speakers must be listening to phonetic information instead of phonological, lexical or grammatical details. In the present study, the same tokens were re-measured. The measurements in the present study were selected to characterize our understanding of the interface in the perceptual dialectology model in Figure 13.1 and of the source and filter cue differences across racially affiliated dialects. So, although this new set of measurements includes a number of the same measures used earlier, it does not use all of them, e.g., harmonic-to-noise ratio, jitter, shimmer and segment durations. The first set of acoustic measures was those that are for the most part filter-oriented, such as vowel steady state characteristics for both vowels. Specifically, these measures included F1, F2 and F3 using both hertz and transformed bark values, and the relational measures of F3-F2 and F3-F1 in bark during the vowel steady state.[18] The acoustic measures which are source oriented and which represent measures for either the voiced portion of the word or the entire word included (a) overall glottal airflow characteristics (glottal period, open quotient, average closure of glottis and period size, peak of glottal closure, maximum airflow declination rate), and (b) pitch characteristics (mean, minimum, maximum, standard deviation, peak, initial, final and difference in pitch). The last set of acoustic measures—reflecting a combination of both source and filter characteristics—includes intensity characteristics such as the mean, minimum, maximum, standard deviation, peak, initial, final, and difference in root mean square. Because pitch, intensity, and spectra capture overlapping information of the source and filter (e.g., vowels have certain inherent pitch and intensity), this data set has a potential to be driven by a latent factor or factors and is suitable for discriminant analysis. Results from a perceptual experiment using the "hello" tokens were reported in Purnell et al. 1999. The model so far for this data (Tables 13.4 and 13.5) has been based on the acoustic measures associated with the dialect that the speaker intended on producing. Instead of using the dialect classification of the tokens based on what the speaker intended to produce, the next model relates the acoustic measures to the dialect the listeners perceived the tokens as. The perceived dialect was assigned by a combined frequency over 66%, e.g., AAE tokens were recategorized as SAE if subjects responded that the AAE token was an SAE token 66% of the time.

4.3 Results

Results of a forward stepwise and canonical discriminant analyses are shown in Tables 13.8 through 13.11. The forward stepwise analysis in Table 13.8 reveals the importance of vowel space measures, primarily the expected backness difference of /ɛ/ and /o/ across the dialects (not between vowels). An ASCC nearing 1 for the acoustic data (specifically, 0.82) indicates a strong acoustic distinction among the dialects by the following predictor measures: vowel backness (/ɛ/ F3-F2 Z, /o/ F2 Z), vowel intensity (RMS standard deviation, initial value), glottal airflow (maximum airflow declination rate), and vowel height (/ɛ/ F1 Z). A less strong overall ASCC value of 0.620 was found for the perception data. The measures of note also include vowel backness (/o/ F2 Hz, /ɛ/ F3-F2 Z), vowel intensity (change in RMS), and vowel height (/ɛ/ F1 Z, /o/ F3-F1 Z). Of note is the identification of one linear backness measure in hertz for the perception data (/o/ F2 Hz) and another non-linear backness measure in bark for the acoustic data (/o/ F2 Z). Unlike hertz, which is an acoustic measure, bark is a transformation of hertz along a psycho-acoustic dimension (Traunmüller 1990).

Use of these seemingly disparate cues by listeners is consistent with stream segregation and perceptual grouping associated with other processes in audition-based cognition (Bregman 1990).[19] Univariate results are shown on Table 13.9 and multivariate results appear on Tables 13.10 and 13.11. Unlike in the analysis on obstruent voicing, we see two latent factors emerge in Table 13.10. Although the univariate r^2 for /ɛ/ backness is fairly high, (0.655, Table 13.9), the multivariate model increases the r^2 value by over 20% (to 0.870, Table 13.10). For the perception data it is clear that the first factor r^2 (0.768, Table 13.10) is much higher than the best univariate r^2 (0.455, Table 13.9).

The principal component analysis used to identify within-group variation indicates that for some measures such as those used in the canonical discriminant analysis, three latent factors emerge for both acoustic and perceptual data. Following the procedure from §3, the strongest value across all

Table 13.8 Results of Stepwise Discriminant Analysis Using a Forward Stepwise Method for AAE, ChE and SAE "hello" Tokens (α= 0.10 to enter model)

Variable	Partial r^2	F	$p > F$	Average squared canonical correlation
Acoustics (df = 12, 46)				
/ɛ/ F3-F2 (Z)	0.655	25.609	0.0001	0.327*
/o/ F2 (Z)	0.584	18.259	0.0001	0.588*
RMS Standard Deviation	0.405	8.507	0.0015	0.681*
RMS Initial Value	0.312	5.450	0.0112	0.722*
Maximum Flow Declination Rate	0.341	4.942	0.0083	0.791*
/ɛ/ F1 (Z)	0.199	2.732	0.0872	0.816*
Perception (df = 10, 46)				
/o/ F2 (Hz)	0.455	11.255	0.0003	0.227*
/ɛ/ F3-F2 (Z)	0.378	7.888	0.0021	0.378*
Change in RMS	0.343	6.523	0.0053	0.506*
/ɛ/ F1 (Z)	0.245	3.889	0.0344	0.570*
/o/ F3-F1 (Z)	0.273	4.328	0.0254	0.620*

Note: Each dialect had ten representative tokens.
*$p<0.001$

Table 13.9 Univariate Results of Canonical Discriminant Analysis

Variable	F	p	r^2
Acoustics (df = 2, 27)			
/ɛ/ F3-F2 (Z)	25.61	0.0001	0.655
/o/ F2 (Z)	16.98	0.0001	0.557
RMS Standard Deviation	11.57	0.0002	0.462
/ɛ/ F1 (Z)	4.11	0.0276	0.234
Maximum Flow Declination Rate	1.51	0.2395	0.101
RMS Initial Value	1.14	0.3361	0.078
Perception (df = 2, 27)			
/o/ F2 (Hz)	11.26	0.0003	0.455
/ɛ/ F1 (Z)	5.12	0.0130	0.275
/ɛ/ F3-F2 (Z)	4.65	0.0184	0.256
Change in RMS	3.31	0.0518	0.197
/o/ F3-F1 (Z)	0.76	0.4760	0.054

Table 13.10 Multivariate Results of Canonical Discriminant Analysis

Group	Squared Distance Between Means	F	Squared Canonical Coefficients	Eigenvalue
Acoustics (df = 6, 22)				
AAE—ChE	31.42	21.34*		
AAE—SAE	31.34	21.28*		
ChE—SAE	17.25	11.72*		
CAN1			0.870	6.683
CAN2			0.762	3.195†
Perception (df=5,23)				
AAE—ChE	15.48	9.50*		
AAE—SAE	5.76	4.21*		
ChE—SAE	15.20	14.56*		
CAN1	0.768		0.768	3.309
CAN2	0.473		0.473	0.896†

*p<0.01
†cumulative eigenvalue = 1.000

Table 13.11 Eigenvectors for Multivariate Results of the First Three Principal Components

	1	2	3
Acoustics			
/ɛ/ F3-F2 (Z)	-0.396	-0.335	0.580†
/o/ F2 (Z)	0.475†	-0.049	0.117
RMS Standard Deviation	0.448	0.565†	0.040
/ɛ/ F1 (Z)	0.357	-0.121	0.703†
Maximum Flow Declination Rate	-0.493†	0.359	0.020
RMS Initial Value	-0.218	0.650†	0.392
Perception			
/o/ F2 (Hz)	-0.383	-0.310	0.662†
/ɛ/ F1 (Z)	-0.562†	0.310	-0.085
/ɛ/ F3-F2 (Z)	0.113	0.894†	0.223
Change in RMS	0.393	0.026	0.694†
/o/ F3-F1 (Z)	0.609†	-0.091	-0.152

† Identifies the eigenvector used for plots.

components identifies the factor to which a specific measure likely falls for the interpretation of the latent factors. An interpretation of Table 13.11 reveals that there are different and similar latent factors to acoustic and perceptual data. The factors appearing active for the acoustic data are by and large divided by overall vowel quality: first MID-BACK VOWEL, then INTENSITY, then MID-FRONT VOWEL. In contrast, the factors appearing active for the perception data are by the two features of vowel quality: first VOWEL HEIGHT, then /ɛ/ BACKNESS, and /o/ BACKNESS. That HEIGHT precedes BACKNESS should be unsurprising in light of the primacy of vowel height across languages (Ladefoged and Maddieson 1996). BACKNESS would then provide a secondary division of vowels within each vowel height.

Three graphic representations of the “hello” data are shown in Figures 13.9 through 13.11. Since the three strongest measures (Table 13.9) for both the acoustic and perception data fall into distinct latent factors (Table 13.11), the raw values for those three measures were plotted against each other. In the plot of acoustic features (Figure 13.9), the space discriminating the three dialects is somewhat unclear. However, in the plot of the perceptual data (Figure 13.10), the data is more distinct across dialect. One reason for the efficacy of two /ɛ/ variables is seen in the need to distinguish the SAE /ɛ/ which display a wider backness variation than the other two dialects (Figure 13.11).

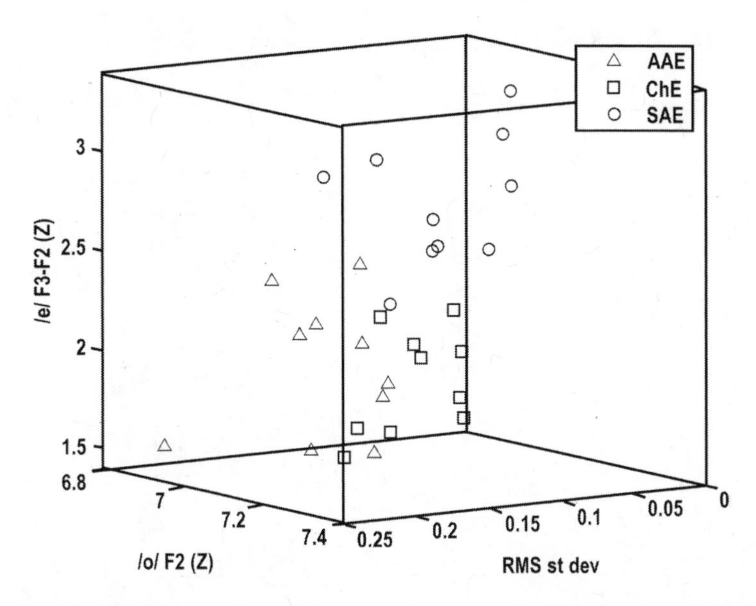

Figure 13.9 Plot of the best variables identified by canonical discriminant analysis with reference to intended and perceived dialects.

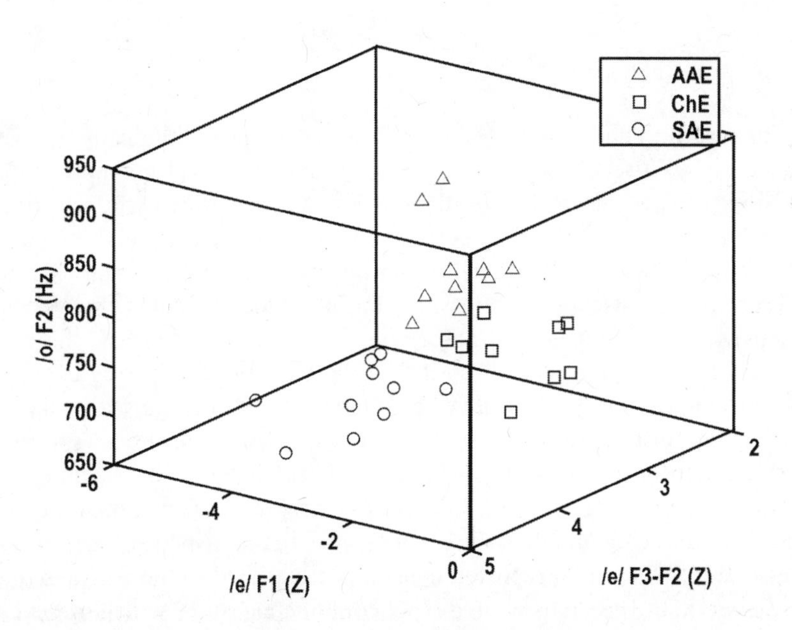

Figure 13.10 Plot of the two best variables identified by canonical discriminant analysis.

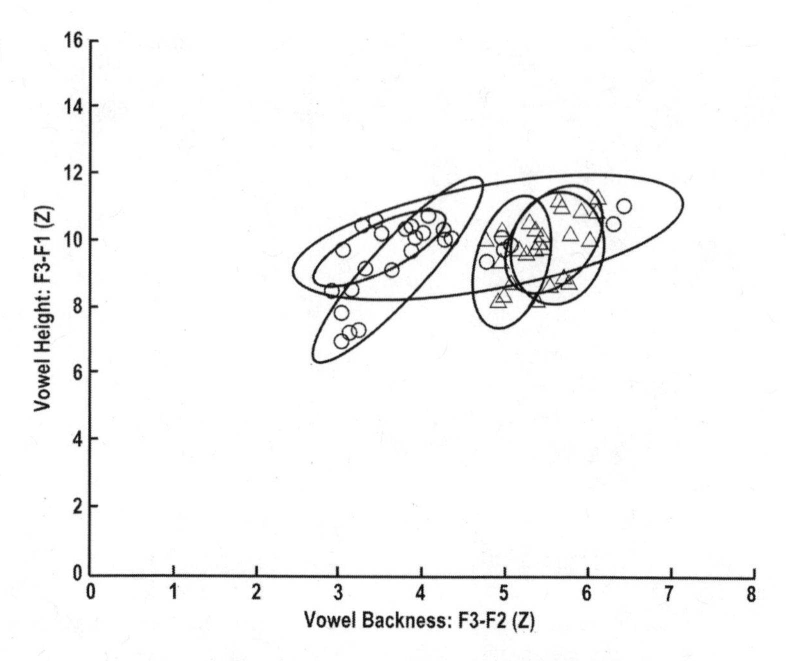

Figure 13.11 Vowel space for vowels in "hello" (inner ellipses for /ɛ/ and /o/ = AAE; wider /ɛ/ ellipsis = SAE).

4.4 Summary

Again, discriminant analyses suggest that variation by ethnically affiliated dialect can occur in the interface between acoustics and perception. Specifically, we saw that the three dialects are well separated in discriminant space, both acoustically and perceptually (ASCC is nearing 1 and the models account for 60% to 80% of the variation). However, there was an observable difference in the selection of measures for latent factors and in the weight of measures across acoustic and perceptual analyses. Nevertheless, the dominant factor (or factors) is the tension in the vowel space distinguishing /ɛ/ from /o/. As such, it is instructive to compare these findings with what was reported earlier (cf. creaky voice and vowel formant differences reported in Thomas and Reaser, 2004, Thomas, this volume, Roeder, this volume). Purnell et al. (1999) reported that F2 in /ɛ/ was important for distinguishing SAE from AAE and ChE, and that the F0 peak also distinguished AAE from SAE tokens. While these two reported measures are related to the findings in the present work, the previous work did not combine measures which might have increased the statistical discrimination of tokens in conjunction with other measures while not being statistically significant on their own. In the present study there do appear to be such measures that are not statistically significant but which reflect underlying source and filter factors.

5. Conclusion

In sum, from these two exploratory experiments involving ethnically affiliated dialect data, we can observe variation in the mapping of acoustic characteristics to perceptual cues. We can respond affirmatively to the overarching question of whether the mapping of acoustic characteristics to perceptual cues allows for variation. For the two data sets previously mentioned we identified three questions regarding the interface between the acoustic characteristics and perceptual cues. The first question was: what acoustic characteristics do or do not serve as perceptual cues? Using a forward stepwise discriminant analysis, the reduced set of predictors in experiment 1 focused largely on vowel duration and percent glottal pulsing, while the set of predictors in experiment 2 focused largely on the vowel space of the two vowels in "hello." The second question asked about the relevant strength of cues. For the Wisconsin English data in experiment 1, while vowel duration and percent glottal pulsing were identified as acoustic variables with strong predictor qualities, the contribution they make to the predictor model varied over subject groups. Also, a change in F1 (claimed by Kingston and Diehl to be a strong factor) was only a mild consideration in the data. For the "hello" data in experiment 2, vowel space was generally stronger than intensity, which in turn was stronger than glottal airflow and pitch. The third question was whether or not there is variation in the acoustic-perception relation, i.e., either in the selection of cues or the weighting of cues. In both analyses the set of perceptually strong measures were not identical to the set of acoustically strong measures. Moreover, both data sets reveal some quirky behavior. For the Wisconsin English data, the perceptual data highlighted the selection of more standard measures, but weighted them like the older Wisconsin English weights. For the "hello" data there was a preference for filter (vowel space) information over source information, although both analyses included at least one intensity measure.

A number of findings contribute directly to the importance of examining the acoustic-perception mapping in light of perceptual dialectology beyond just allowing for variation. The re-analysis of "hello" tokens by intended dialect showed a marked difference to the analysis by perceived dialect. The difference in identified factors calls for more in-depth understanding of how

Figure 13.1a is transformed into Figure 13.1b and 13.1c. Perceptual dialectology presupposes the use of crucial percepts that are further assumed to derive from a set of acoustic characteristics. What we see in this chapter is that these assumptions, while not fatal to the progress made in investigating data at Figure 13.1a, 13.1b, and 13.1c, require a non-axiomatic approach. As such, future research should investigate how experimentally manipulated cues relate to the perceived dialect as well as to the intended dialect.

Notes

1 Compare, for example, the role of dialect as subordinate variety (Chambers and Trudgill 1998: 3), or as a regional or historical derivative (Romaine 2002: 310; Hock 1991: 380–381).
2 Preston's work is based on Hoenigswald (1966). See also the related conception of this claim in Figure 1 in Bradac et al., 2001: 146.
3 An example of an important issue bearing on the perception of ethnically affiliated dialects is how close the input is to the prototype or exemplar, e.g., Attitude Representation Theory (Lord and Lepper 1999), and Structural Alignment Theory (Markman and Gentner 1993).
4 See also Medin 1989; Yamauchi 2005.
5 The matched guise paradigm has been used across languages (Lambert et al. 1960) and dialects (Purnell et al. 1999).
6 The Wisconsin English data presented herein is the product of collaborative work with Jennifer Mercer, Joe Salmons and Dilara Tepeli.
7 See Purnell et al. 2005a,b; Salmons et al. 2006; Tepeli et al. 2008.
8 For example, the pronunciation of "The Bears" used in a Saturday Night Live skit about Chicago sport fans saying *da Bears* with a final [s] is often, ironically enough, used disparagingly by Wisconsinites about the Chicago football team.
9 The weight is approximated by the amount of variation a measure accounts for and the correlation coefficients and eigenvectors assigned by the statistical model.
10 For a more detailed description of the methodology see Purnell et al. 2005a, b.
11 The change in F0 was transformed by

$$\frac{(-1^* \Delta_{F0})}{100},$$

where Δ_{F0} is the original change in F0. The change in F1 was transformed by

$$\frac{(-1^* \Delta_{F1})}{100},$$

where Δ_{F1} is the original change in F1. The duration of the consonant gap or frication was transformed by

$(0.400 - \Delta_{cons})$

where Δ_{cons} is the original duration of the consonant gap or frication.

12 The implication of assuming a binary feature system underlying human language is that children could use such modeling techniques as canonical discriminant analysis to bootstrap redundant acoustic measures onto a specific distinctive feature opposition because the net result can only be a single canonical factor.

13 The use of uppercase letters has two uses in this chapter. The first use is the convention of naming latent factors with all uppercase letters in the statistical literature. The second use of uppercase follows the convention seen in Docherty (1992) to symbolize the general concept of voicing in the speech stream (see also Purnell et al. 2005b, Figure 1).

14 Docherty (1992) and Docherty and Foulkes (1999) are two exceptions already mentioned.

15 A further portion of the data dealt with housing discrimination, and showed that in setting appointments to view apartments, the voice of the speaker on the phone influences whether or not the apartment would or would not be shown to the speaker. This finding of the relation between housing discrimination and voice perception was confirmed by Massey and Lundy (2001) and Squires and Chadwick (2006).

16 See Thomas and Bailey (1998) Thomas (1999), Thomas and Reaser (2001, 2004), and Thomas (this volume).

17 The terms *source* and *filter* (Fant [1960]; Flanagan [1965]; Stevens and House [1961]) provide an important distinction in the articulation of speech sounds where the former term refers to the generation of a complex acoustic wave (*initiation* and *phonation* in terms of Abercrombie [1967]), while the latter refers to the shaping of that wave with a specific tongue-lip-velum configuration (Abercrombie's *articulation*).

18 Bark was calculated per Traunmüller (1990).

19 An upshot of this finding may be that the brain uses multiple many of the multiple measures described in Adank et al. (2004).

References

Abercrombie, David. 1967. *Elements of general phonetics.* Chicago: Aldine Publishing Company.

Abramson, Arthur S.1986. The perception of word-initial consonant length: Pattani Malay. *Journal of the International Phonetic Association* 16: 8–16.

Abramson, Arthur S. 1991. Amplitude as a cue to word-initial consonant length: Pattani Malay. Paper presented at the 12th International Congress of Phonetic Sciences: Aix-en-Provence, Université de Provence.

Adank, Patti, Roel Smits, and Roeland van Hout. 2004. A comparison of vowel normalization procedures for language variation research. *Journal of the Acoustical Society of America* 116 (5): 3099–3107.

Baugh, John. 1988. *Black street speech: Its history, structure and survival.* Austin: University of Texas Press.

Baugh, John. 2000. *Beyond ebonics: Linguistic pride and racial prejudice.* Oxford: Oxford University Press.

Bradac, James J., A.C. Cargile, and J.S. Hallett. 2001. Language attitudes: Retrospect, conspect, and prospect. In W. P. Robinson and Howard Giles (eds), *The new handbook of language and social psychology.* New York: John Wiley, 137–155.

Bregman, Albert S. 1990. *Auditory scene analysis: The perceptual organization of sound.* Cambridge, MA: MIT Press.

Cassidy, Frederic G. 1948. On collecting American dialect. *American Speech* 23 (3/4): 185–193.

Cassidy, Frederic G. (ed.). 1985. *The dictionary of American regional English.* Cambridge, MA: Harvard University Press.

Chambers, Jack K. and Peter Trudgill, Peter. 1998. *Dialectology.* Cambridge: Cambridge University Press.

Costanza, M.C. and A. A. Afifi. 1979. Comparison of stopping rules in forward stepwise discriminant analysis. *Journal of the American Statistical Association* 74: 777–785.

Docherty, Gerard J. 1992. *The timing of voicing in British English obstruents.* Berlin: Foris Publications.

Docherty, Gerard J. and Paul Foulkes. 1999. Derby and Newcastle: Instrumental phonetics and variationist studies. In Paul Foulkes and Gerard J. Docherty (eds), *Urban Voices.* London: Arnold, 47–71.

Fant, Gunnar. 1960. *Acoustic theory of speech production.* The Hague: Mouton.

Flanagan, James L. 1965. *Speech analysis synthesis and perception.* Berlin: Springer-Verlag.

Hock, Hans Henrich. 1991. *Principles of historical linguistics.* Berlin: Mouton de Gruyter.

Hoenigswald, Henry M. 1966. A proposal for the study of folk-linguistics. In William Bright (ed.), *Sociolinguistics: Proceedings of the UCLA Sociolinguistics Conference, 1964.* The Hague: Mouton, 16–26.

Iverson, Gregory K. and Joseph C. Salmons. 2003. Laryngeal enhancement in Early Germanic. *Phonology* 20: 43–74.

Kingston, John and Randy L. Diehl. 1994. Phonetic knowledge. *Language* 70 (3): 419–454.

Kingston, John and Randy L. Diehl. 1995. Intermediate properties in the perception of distinctive feature values. In Bruce Connell and Amalia Arvaniti (eds), *Phonology and phonetic evidence: Papers in laboratory phonology IV.* Cambridge: Cambridge University Press, 7–27.

Labov, William. 1972. *Sociolinguistic patterns.* Philadelphia: University of Pennsylvania Press.

Ladefoged, Peter and Ian Maddieson. 1996. *The sounds of the world's languages.* Oxford: Blackwell.

Lambert, Wallace E., Richard C. Hodgson, Robert C. Gardner, and Stanley Fillenbaum. 1960. Evaluational reactions to spoken languages. *Journal of Abnormal and Social Psychology* 60 (1): 44–51.

Lisker, Leigh. 1986. "Voicing" in English: A catalogue of acoustic features signaling /b/ versus /p/ in trochees. *Language and Speech* 29 (1): 3–11.

Lord, Charles G. and Mark R. Lepper. 1999. Attitude Representation Theory. In Mark P. Zanna (ed.), *Advances in experimental social psychology*. San Diego: Academic Press, 265–343.

MacNeilage, Peter F. 1970. Motor control of serial ordering of speech. *Psychological Review* 77 (3): 182–196.

Markman, Arthur B. and Dedre Gentner. 1993. Structural alignment during similarity comparisons. *Cognitive Psychology* 25 (2): 431–467.

Massey, Douglas S. and Garvey Lundy. 2001. Use of Black English and racial discrimination in urban housing markets: New methods and findings. *Urban Affairs Review* 36 (4): 452–469.

Medin, D. L. 1989. Concepts and conceptual structure. *American Psychologist* 44 (12) 1469–1481.

Preston, Dennis R. 1989. *Perceptual dialectology: Nonlinguists' views of areal linguistics*. Dordrecht: Foris.

Preston, Dennis R. (ed.). 1997. *Handbook of perceptual dialectology, Vol. I.* Amsterdam: John Benjamins.

Preston, Dennis R. 2000. Some plain facts about Americans and their language. *American Speech* 75 (4): 398–401.

Preston, Dennis R. 2002. Perceptual dialectology. In Jan Berns and Jaap van Marle (eds), *Present-day dialectology*. Berlin: Mouton de Gruyter, 57–104.

Purnell, Thomas C., William J. Idsardi, and John Baugh. 1999. Perceptual and phonetic experiments on American English dialect identification. *Journal of Language and Social Psychology* 18 (1): 10–30.

Purnell, Thomas, Joseph Salmons, and Dilara Tepeli. 2005. German substrate effects in Wisconsin English: Evidence for final fortition. *American Speech* 80 (2): 135–164.

Purnell, Thomas, Joseph Salmons, Dilara Tepeli, and Jennifer Mercer. 2005. Structured heterogeneity and change in laryngeal phonetics: Upper Midwestern final obstruents. *Journal of English Linguistics* 33 (4): 307–338.

Rickford, John R. 1999. *African American vernacular English: Features, evolution, educational implications*. Oxford: Blackwell.

Romaine, Suzanne. 2002. Dialect and dialectology. In R. Mesthrie (ed.), *Concise encyclopedia of sociolinguistics*, Oxford: Elsevier Science, 310–08.

Salmons, Joseph, Jennifer Mercer, Dilara Tepeli, and Thomas Purnell. 2006. Deutsche Spuren im amerikanischen Englischen? Auslautverhärtung in Wisconsin. In Nina Berend and Elisabeth Knipf-Komlósi (eds.), *Sprachinselwelten—The World of Language Islands*. Frankfurt: Peter Lang, 205–225.

Squires, Gregory D. and Jan Chadwick. 2006. Linguistic profiling: A continuing tradition of discrimination in the home insurance industry? *Urban Affairs Review* 41 (3): 400–415.

Stevens, Kenneth N. and Arthur S. House. 1961. An acoustical theory of vowel productions and some of its implications. *Journal of Speech and Hearing Research* 4: 303–320.

Stevens, Kenneth N. and Sheila E. Blumstein. 1981. The search for invariant acoustic correlates of phonetic features. In Peter D. Eimas and Joanne L. Miller (eds), *Perspectives on the study of speech*. Hillsdale, NJ: Lawrence Erlbaum Associates, 1–38.

Stevens, Kenneth N. 2000. Diverse acoustic cues at consonantal landmarks. *Phonetica* 57 (2–4): 139–151.

Tatsuoka, Maurice M. 1970. *Discriminant analysis: The study of group differences*. Champaign, IL: Institute for Personality and Ability Testing.

Tepeli, Dilara, Joseph Salmons, and Thomas Purnell. 2008. Was bleibt bestehen? Der deutsche Einfluß auf das Amerikanische. In Josef Raab and Jan Wirrer (eds.), *Die deutsche Präsenz in den USA - The German presence in the U.S.A.* Münster: LIT Verlag, 745–763.

Thomas, Erik R. and Guy Bailey. 1998. Parallels between vowel subsystems of African American vernacular English and Caribbean Anglophone creoles. *Journal of Pidgin and Creole Languages* 13: 267–296.

Thomas, Erik R. 1999. A first look at African-American vernacular English intonation. Toronto: *NWAVE*.

Thomas, Erik R. and Jeffrey Reaser. 2001. A perceptual experiment on the ethnic labeling of Hyde County, North Carolina. *SECOL 62*, Knoxville, TN.

Thomas, Erik R. and Jeffrey Reaser. 2004. Delimiting perceptual cues used for the ethnic labeling of African American and European American voices. *Journal of Sociolinguistics* 8: 54–87.

Traunmüller, Hartmut. 1990. Analytical expressions for the tonotopic sensory scale. *Journal of the Acoustical Society of America* 88 (1): 97–100.

Weinreich, Uriel, William Labov, and Marvin Herzog. 1968. Empirical foundations for a theory of language change. In Winfred P. Lehmann and Yakov Malkiel (eds), *Directions for historical linguistics*. Austin: University of Texas Press, 95–195.

Westbury, John R. 1994. X-Ray microbeam speech production database user's handbook (Version 1.0). Madison: Waisman Research Center, University of Wisconsin.

Wisniewski, Edward J. 2002. Concepts and categorization. In Douglas Medin (ed.), *Steven's handbook of experimental psychology: Memory and cognitive processes*. New York: John Wiley & Sons, 467–531.

Yamauchi, Takashi. 2005. Labeling bias and categorical induction: Generative aspects of category information. *Journal of Experimental Psychology-Learning Memory and Cognition* 31 (3): 538–553.

Chapter 14

Sound Judgments: Perception of Indexical Features in Children's Speech

Paul Foulkes, University of York; Gerard Docherty and Ghada Khattab, Newcastle University; Malcah Yaeger-Dror, University of Arizona

1. Introduction

One of the defining features of human language is that it displays systematic variation at all levels of structure, from syntax to fine-grained features of pronunciation. Certain aspects of this variation result from biological differences across speakers. One example of biologically-constrained variation is the markedly different levels of fundamental frequency typical of men, women, and children, which result to a large extent from gross differences in laryngeal anatomy and physiology. Variation may also derive from learned patterns of behavior, acquired as a consequence of a speaker's regional, social, linguistic, and cultural background. Regional accent is a clear case in point.

When we speak we therefore offer a wealth of information about ourselves through the linguistic and phonetic alternatives we use. Listeners can and do take notice of such alternatives. Several studies have investigated which variable cues listeners can identify, how they are identified, and what interpretations listeners make of them. It has been shown, for example, that cues related to speaker gender, or to individual talkers, can affect linguistic processing such as lexical identification or phoneme categorization (e.g., Johnson 1997, Strand 1999, Hawkins and Smith 2001). Sociolinguistic studies, meanwhile, have established that listeners evaluate variants (positively or negatively), linking them to aspects of personality such as intelligence and friendliness (e.g., Giles and Powesland 1975). Furthermore, listeners can identify, with varying degrees of accuracy, aspects of a talker's social, ethnic and regional background (e.g., van Bezooijen and Gooskens 1999; Purnell, Idsardi, and Baugh 1999; see further Thomas 2002 for an excellent summary of speech perception work which bears on sociolinguistic issues).

In this chapter we describe an experiment in which listeners were asked to identify the sex of children from their speech. The study has two broad aims. First, it seeks to enhance our understanding of the range of cues used by listeners in performing the task of gender identification. Although a number of studies have addressed this issue previously (reviewed subsequently), results have been somewhat inconsistent and at times vague. Secondly, our specific interest is in the role played by fine-grained phonetic variants in listeners' responses. It is well known from sociolinguistic studies that segmental features may vary quantitatively within a community. A particular form may therefore be indexical of a social group. For instance, men might use statistically more of a particular variant than women do in the same type of interactional speech style. However, little work has been carried out to assess whether listeners show any awareness of such statistical associations between phonetic forms and social categories.

We begin with a brief review of previous work on identifying speaker sex, and of sex-correlated variation in speech. In Section 3 we then outline the dialect and sociolinguistic variables of interest for our study. Section 4 explains the experimental method we adopted, and the results are discussed in Section 5. The final section summarizes the findings and identifies opportunities for further work.

2. Listener identification of speaker sex—Previous studies and possible cues

We might expect that judging the sex of a speaker is relatively straightforward, at least for adult talkers engaged in everyday interaction. This perhaps explains why few studies have tested listeners' ability to distinguish the sex of adult male and female talkers. One of the few studies to include a formal identification test of speaker sex (as part of a larger project) reports a 100% success rate (Krauss, Freyberg, and Morsella 2002: 621).

For adults, as noted earlier, a particularly robust cue to speaker sex is provided by the fundamental frequency (f0) of the speaker's voice. Based on analysis largely of western European languages, the average f0 for male speakers is around 120 Hz while that for females is around 220 Hz (e.g., Fant 1956). Klatt and Klatt (1990) estimate that female f0 averages around 1.7 times that of males.

However, f0 is neither an infallible nor an invariant cue to speaker sex. First of all, there is considerable overlap in the f0 ranges used by adult males and females, such that a high pitched male voice may be mistaken for a low pitched female voice, or vice versa. For f0 in normal conversation Fant (1956) identifies the maximal male range as 50–250Hz, while that for women overlaps the male range at 120–480 Hz. Künzel (1987) presents data from 100 Germans which indicate that around 35% of males have an average f0 higher than the female baseline of 120 Hz. Moreover, f0 is subject to variation in response to many factors. Analysis of speech in contexts other than regular conversation shows, for example, that male f0 can be much higher under stress (Boss 1996), when a speaker attempts to counter ambient noise (e.g., Lane and Tranel 1971), and in telephone speech or when reading aloud (Hirson, French, and Howard 1995). It also appears that average male f0 may deviate markedly from the often-cited mean of 120 Hz when we consider different languages and non-standard dialects. French and Harrison (2005), for instance, report a mean of 105 Hz for 22 Caribbean males in Birmingham, UK, while the average for speakers of Urdu has been reported to be as high as 186 Hz (Peter French, personal communication).

Although f0 may be an obvious cue in many instances, it does not always provide unambiguous information about a speaker's sex. What is more, in the case of prepubescents, f0 may not be a helpful cue at all. The gross differences we can observe in f0 across males and females result from the physiological changes which occur in male voices at the onset of puberty (the "breaking" of the voice; Mackenzie Beck 1997). Males have a lower f0 because their vocal folds are larger and more massive, and thus they vibrate more slowly than those of females. With children there are no such major physiological differences (although there is some evidence that small physical differences in vocal tract anatomy emerge well before puberty, e.g., King 1952; Crelin 1973).

Nevertheless, there is abundant evidence that children's speech manifests phonetic differences which listeners can access to identify the sex of the talker. Several studies report response rates well above chance on sex identification tests (reviewed by Perry, Ohde, and Ashmead 2001). However, it is less clear which cue(s) are the most useful for listeners.

Given that f0 is such an important cue for adult talkers, it is understandable that several studies have assessed whether f0 differs for boys and girls, and also whether f0 is used by listeners to judge the sex of child talkers. For example, Günzburger et al. (1987) asked listeners to judge the sex of 17 children, and then recruited a group of blind listeners who rated the three best identified boys and three best identified girls on a number of perceptual scales. The clearest result from the latter part of the study was that the best identified girls were consistently rated as high pitched, while the boys were just as consistently given low pitch ratings. However, the consensus is that average f0 plays at best only a secondary role in listeners' perceptions of sex for child talkers (Weinberg and Bennett 1971; Bennett and Weinberg 1979b; Perry et al. 2001). As expected, f0 has generally been found not to differ systematically or consistently between boys and girls in the way that it does for adults. Presumably it therefore cannot function as a robust cue for speaker sex. Weinberg and Bennett (1971), for instance, report no statistical differences between boys and girls aged 5 and 6, while Lee, Hewlett and Nairn (1995) found significant differences to emerge only from age 12. Perry et al. (2001) identified differences for 16-year-olds (and no differences for 4-, 8- or 12-year-olds), but their focus was on f0 of single vowels extracted from carrier phrases. Some studies in fact report girls to have lower f0 than boys matched for age (e.g., Sachs et al. 1973 for children aged 4 to 14, Günzburger et al. 1987 for Dutch-speaking children aged 7 and 8). By contrast, those studies that have found boys to have lower f0 than girls have usually been based on analysis of short and non-spontaneous materials such as sustained isolated vowels (e.g., Hasek, Singh, and Murry 1980 for ages 7 to 10), or small speaker samples (e.g., Sorenson 1989, reporting significant differences at ages 6, 8, 9 and 10, with three children of each sex per age category). Lieberman (1967) also describes findings from a small study, but his data are nonetheless noteworthy. A ten month old baby boy was recorded with a mean f0 of 390Hz when playing with his mother, but 340 Hz in a similar 20 minute play session with his father. A similar effect was found with a 13-month-old girl (average 390 Hz with the mother and 290 Hz with the father). The implication of these finding is that the children were adjusting their overall f0 level in relation to that of their interlocutor. However, it is clear that f0 does not play the same role in cueing the sex of child talkers as it does for adults.

In dismissing average f0 as an important cue, several studies have suggested that listeners can gain more reliable information from relative vowel formant frequencies and spacing. Perry et al. (2001) found systematic differences in formant values for four-year-olds, with boys giving lower first and second formant values than girls. Children therefore display the same patterns found to a more marked degree for adults. It remains unclear whether these effects are the product of emerging differences invocal tract dimensions, whether boys and girls are imitating the differences that can be observed between adults, or both. Listeners do, however, seem inclined to attribute low F1 and F2 values to boys (Bennett and Weinberg 1979b, Perry et al. 2001).

Few other possible contributors to the identification of talker sex have been identified, and fewer still tested. Sachs et al. (1973: 81) suggest intonation and voice quality as possible cues, commenting also that boys in their study had a "more forceful, definite rhythm," although these parameters are not tested in their study. Günzburger, Bresser, ter Keurs (1987), however, offer some support that intonation patterns might affect listener response in sex identification tasks. Among the perceptual scales used by their blind listener group was "monotonous—melodious." The boys who were most successfully identified were given high "monotonous" ratings, while girls were given high "melodious" ratings. This suggests that a wide intonation range might be taken as an indicator of female speech. Production studies of adult talkers, however, fail to reveal a consistent pattern which would explain why listeners might make this inference. Syrdal's (1996) analysis of the 160 speaker Switchboard corpus, for instance, did find that women had a much wider f0 range than men, whereas Henton's (1989) review of earlier research suggested the opposite general trend. Henton's own study, based on a sample of ten Americans, yielded no significant differences for speaker sex. In comparing these studies it should also be borne in mind that Syrdal's data were collected from telephone calls. Telephone transmission introduces various acoustic and phonetic effects into the speech signal, both via the technical effects of passing the signal through a handset and telephone line, and also because speakers may behave differently when speaking on a telephone (e.g., Moye 1979; Summers et al. 1988; Byrne and Foulkes 2004).

Voice quality covers a wide array of phonetic cues (Laver 1980), only a small number of which have been addressed in production studies where speaker sex has been at issue. Phonatory differences have received the most attention. Breathy phonation has been identified regularly as a characteristic of female speech (e.g., Thorne et al. 1983; Henton and Bladon 1985; Klatt and Klatt 1990; Hillenbrand, Cleveland, and Erickson 1994), although there is often considerable variation within the male and female speaker groups tested. Creak has been attributed both to males (Henton and Bladon 1988 for British English speakers) and females (Syrdal 1996 for American English speakers), which might indicate regionally- or sociolinguistically-governed patterning. Stuart-Smith's (1999) detailed study of Glasgow speech identified both creaky phonation and nasalization as consistent features of male speech, while females were found to use phonation that is more whispery. In spite of such observations on voice quality, however, these do not appear to have been tested in either production or perceptual studies of children's speech.

The Günzburger et al. (1987) study suggested that overall amplitude or intensity of speech may be relevant in understanding listeners' responses to child talkers, with the blind listener group rating boys as "loud" and girls as "soft." Again, however, this seems not to have been the subject of formal testing in perceptual studies. Production studies do offer some support, though.

For example, Markel, Prebor, and Brandt (1972) found that adult males spoke, on average, with a greater intensity than females in interview tasks (the overall male average was 76.1 dB compared with that for females of 69.5 dB).

A final parameter for consideration is articulation rate. Bennett and Weinberg (1979a) considered rate as a possible factor in listeners' judgments, but found no differences in rate when they compared the speech of boys and girls and therefore concluded it would not be likely to affect listeners. A number of studies of adult speech production have also reported no differences in rate (Ryalls et al. 1994, Syrdal 1996, Robb, Maclagan, and Chen 2004). There is, however, some evidence for rate differences in other studies. Byrd (1994) analysed rate for 630 talkers in the TIMIT corpus, using two spoken sentences per subject. She found that men spoke on average 6.2% faster than women (the male mean was 4.69 syllables per second, compared with the female mean of 4.42). Yuan, Liberman, and Cieri (2006) also claim a small but significant effect, again with males speaking faster than females. Their findings are derived from analysis of several large corpora of telephone speech from English and Chinese speakers.

From this brief review of previous studies we can conclude that, while male and female talkers differ on a number of phonetic dimensions, the consistency and systematicity of these features is variable, and the evidence for their value in judgments of speaker sex is sketchy. Moreover, although a number of phonetic features have been addressed in perceptual studies, researchers have not previously assessed the role played by gender-correlated sociolinguistic variables. It is well known that gender patterning in sociolinguistic variable studies is extremely widespread (see the review by Chambers 2003). For example, males (at least in western societies) typically use higher proportions of non-standard variants than females of the same age, social background and community. What remains unclear is whether listeners can recognize the statistical associations between sociolinguistic variants and speaker sex in the way that has been shown for associations with ethnicity, social class, and region.

We move on now to describe the experiment we carried out to test listeners' perceptions of gender-correlated variables. This experiment was originally designed as a pilot study to probe listeners' ability to identify speaker sex from a range of phonetic cues: sociolinguistic variables were our main concern, but we also sought to test the effects of cues such as voice quality and rate, following the predictions made by other researchers which were reviewed previously. We chose to exploit the fact that we had access to a large number of recordings of speech from pre-school children, for whom no gross f0 differences would be expected. With respect to f0, then, we are assuming that children's voices are in principle androgynous, enabling us to test the contribution of other phonetic factors in listeners' perception of sex.

3. Dialect focus: Sex-correlated patterns in Tyneside voiceless stops

Tyneside is a large conurbation in the north-east of England, with the city of Newcastle upon Tyne as its hub. The dialectology and sociolinguistics of the region have been studied as extensively as any in the British Isles (e.g., Heslop 1892, Pellowe et al. 1972, Pellowe and Jones 1978, Local 1982, Jones-Sargent 1983, Jones 1985). The wide interest in Tyneside is undoubtedly a reflection both of the strong and distinctive cultural identity of the region, and also the singular character of its dialect. The Tyneside dialect, commonly referred to as Geordie, is in many respects very different from other non-standard varieties of British English in lexis, syntax, and both segmental and suprasegmental phonology and phonetics (see e.g., Watt and Milroy 1999, Local, Kelly, and Wells 1986, Beal 1993, 2004, and for example sound files www.ncl.ac.uk/necte/ and www.phon.ox.ac.uk/IViE/). The dialect is one that lay listeners find relatively easy to recognize, and its saliency is also testified by copious dialect literature (e.g., Dobson's popular lexicon and grammar *Larn Yersel' Geordie*, and several characters in the Newcastle-based adult comic *Viz*).

Two large empirical projects were executed in Tyneside in the 1990s, the first with adult subjects (Milroy, Milroy, and Docherty 1997) and the second with children and their mothers (Docherty et al. 2002). We draw on the findings and materials of both of these studies here. The adult study is henceforth referred to as the PVC project (an abbreviation of its full title, *Phonological Variation and Change in Contemporary British English*). The child study is abbreviated to ESV (*The Emergence of Structured Variation in the Speech of Tyneside Infants).* The fieldwork design and methods of data collection and analysis have been reported in detail elsewhere (for PVC see Docherty et al. 1997 and for ESV Foulkes et al. 2005), but Table 14.1 provides a summary of the main features of each project.

The work of the first two authors has focused on consonantal variation, with a particular interest in voiceless stops. Auditory and acoustic analysis of voiceless stops reveals rich, complex and often very subtle patterns of variation (see in particular Docherty et al. 1997, Docherty and Foulkes 1999, 2005, Foulkes et al. 2005, Foulkes and Docherty 2006). The plain oral stops [p t k], characteristic of standard English, are also found in Tyneside. However, /p t k/ in Tyneside English may be spirantized, pre-aspirated and/or voiced, while /t/

Table 14.1 Fieldwork Summary for Tyneside Projects

	PVC	ESV
speakers	32 adults	53 children + mothers
age range	15–27, 45–67	1;11—4;1
social class	MC and WC	WC
sex	males and females	males and females
spoken materials	45-minute free conversations in pairs + wordlists	free play sessions including toy-bag and picturebook tasks
location	subjects' homes	subjects' homes
recording media	Sony TCD D-10 Pro II DAT Sennheiser microphone	Sony TCD-D10 Pro II DAT Trantec lapel microphone

can be also realized as a tap or [ɹ]. Most distinctive of all is the range of highly localized variants involving laryngeal constriction. Intersonorant /p t k/ (in *water, winter*) are generally realized with full or partial voicing and a period of creaky phonation either before or after the oral constriction. Wells (1982) transcribes these variants as [p͡ʔ t͡ʔ k͡ʔ] although we prefer [b̰ d̰ g̃] to reflect the fact that such tokens tend to be voiced. These local variants are very salient to the ears of outsiders, and are undoubtedly an example of a stereotype in the sense used by Labov (1994: 78). Glottal stops similar in form to those found in other dialects (i.e., fully voiceless and with a complete occlusion) are relatively rare. Docherty and Foulkes (1999, 2005) discuss subtle variation in production of glottal and glottalized forms in Tyneside English, but for the purposes of the present study we group together as a single category all types of variant which contain a laryngealized element.

Patterns of variant usage are constrained by a wide range of internal and external factors, including style (e.g., formality of speech), lexical identity (especially with respect to [ɹ] for /t/; Wells 1982), social characteristics of the speaker and interlocutor, conversational function (e.g., in turn endings—see also Local et al. 1986) and prosody (e.g., articulation rate and phonological context, Docherty 2007).

We focus here on two patterns which were especially clear in previous analyses. Both relate to correlations between variant usage and gender. First, in word-medial intersonorant contexts two main variants are found in the community: plain [p t k] and the local laryngealized variants. In free conversation the latter dominates for most speaker groups, while the plain variants are largely restricted to females (see Figure 14.1, which shows quantified data drawn from the PVC project). As expected for a stereotype variable, the laryngealized forms decrease in more formal styles, being instead replaced by the standard plain variants. For older females in particular the style shift is absolute; that is, local laryngealized variants are not used at all in formal speech styles. Thus, notwithstanding style, age, and class effects, we can observe that plain variants are statistically much more likely to occur in female speech.

In word-final pre-pausal context a different set of variants is found. Here laryngealized or glottal forms are very rare. Instead, plain [p t k] are the default forms for most speakers (a pattern which, incidentally, differentiates Tyneside from most other British accents, where glottal stops are usually frequent in this context). For young women, though, pre-aspirated [ʰp ʰt ʰk] are emerging as a favored form. Our analysis of word-list data showed that 70% of tokens produced by young women were pre-aspirated (Docherty and Foulkes 1999). Pre-aspiration was considerably less frequent for younger males (35%). The overall rate of pre-aspiration was also much lower for older speakers in

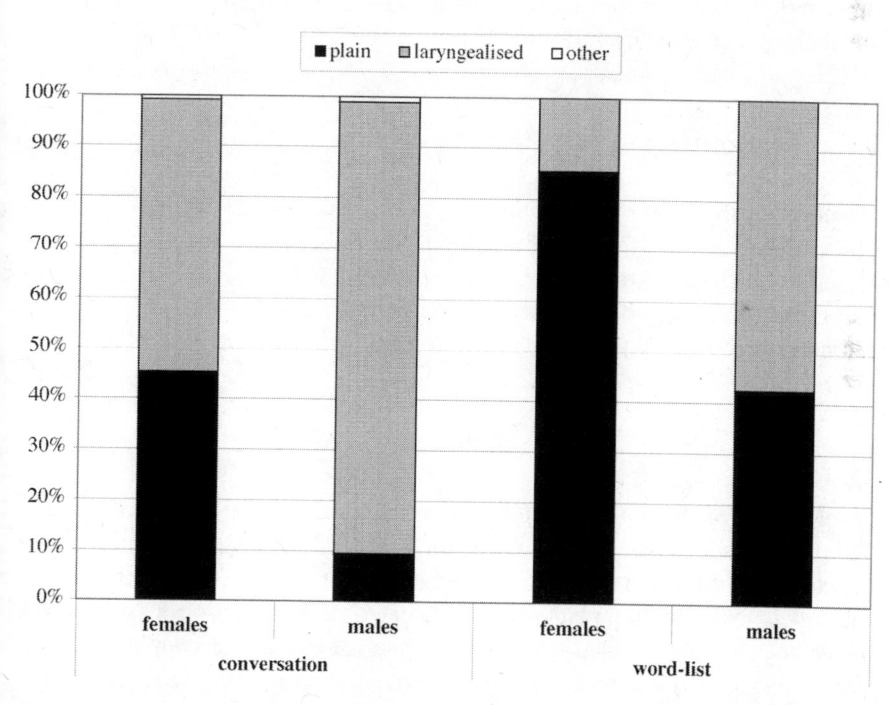

Figure 14.1 Variant usage for word-medial (p,t,k) by sex and speaking style, Tyneside adults (N tokens: conversation = 1,764 for females, 1,628 for males; word-list = 571 for females, 572 for males).

the PVC sample, but the sex pattern was consistent (23% for older women compared with less than 1% for the older men).

Variant usage is of course influenced by a complex range of factors, as noted in passing above, and any generalization about a single factor inevitably represents an oversimplification. However, the patterns reported here for Tyneside are sufficiently clear for us to infer that the variants of voiceless stops are indexical of gender. Plain variants in intersonorant position and pre-aspirated variants in pre-pausal context are far more frequent in the speech of females than males.

The question at issue in the remainder of this study is whether members of the speech community under investigation can recognize such patterns. That is, do native users of the Tyneside dialect infer patterns of indexicality from sociolinguistic variables akin to those which have been identified in studies of speech production? In our specific case example, do Tynesiders recognize that males and females use variants of voiceless stops in statistically different ways? Do they have implicit or explicit knowledge of patterns of variation, such that they can associate a particular variant with aspects of a speaker's social background?

4. Method

As noted earlier, the experiment was designed to probe the role of various phonetic cues in listeners' identification of a talker's sex. Assuming that f0 would not differ markedly for children, we constructed a simple listening test using samples of children's speech as stimuli. The task for listeners was to indicate whether they judged the child to be a boy or a girl.

4.1 Speakers

In our corpus of children's speech we identified six individuals who produced the full range of sociophonetic variants under investigation. That is, examples were found in each child's recording of both plain and laryngealized variants in word-medial context, and both plain and pre-aspirated variants in pre-pausal contexts. Three boys and three girls were chosen to provide a balanced sample. The children were among the older ones in the corpus, with an age range from 3;0 to 4;1, although the age of the child was not used as a criterion for selection. Instead we targeted those children whose speech was relatively well developed and fluent, and whose recordings contained ample material suitable for the experiment.

4.2 Stimuli

From the six children's recordings we extracted a total of 67 tokens for the listening test (Table 14.2). The extraction was performed using the editing tools in the Praat software program. The tokens extracted consisted mostly of single words, with four of the tokens being two word phrases. 27 tokens were single syllable words, 33 contained two syllables, five contained three, and two were four syllable items. Fifty-three of the tokens contained a voiceless stop in medial or final position, with the other 14 being fillers. We were not concerned with including the same number of tokens for each variant or context. The 53 tokens of interest were selected because they were the only ones available in the six recordings which (i) we could extract without problem (e.g., they were spoken in isolation rather than in a continuous sentence, which might lead to clipping of part of the extracted token), and (ii) which were not affected by background noise or overlapping speech from someone else present during the recording. Of the total of 67 tokens, 32 (47.7%) were taken from boys and 35 (52.3%) from girls.

Table 14.2 Stimuli Used in Listening Test

stimuli	**variants**	**n**	**variants**	**n**	**N**	**examples**
medial	plain [p t k]	20	laryngealized [b̰ d̰ g̃]	12	32	*jumper, letters, chicken, the water*
pre-pausal	plain [p t k]	7	pre-aspirated [ʰp ʰt ʰk]	14	21	*up, cat, look, fell out*
fillers					14	*bath, bumble bee, blue*
Total					67	

The extracted tokens were compiled into a new (.wav) sound file for the purposes of the listening test. Each stimulus in the test consisted of three consecutive repetitions of a token. A gap of 1.5 seconds was inserted between each token repetition, and a longer gap of 5 seconds separated adjacent stimuli.

4.3 Listeners

Three listener groups were recruited for the experiment. The listeners were drawn from staff and students at the home universities of the authors. Some students who participated had some training in linguistics. However, none of the students was at an advanced level and none knew either the purpose of the experiment or had awareness of the first two authors' previous work on Tyneside English. The first (experimental) group consisted of 20 natives of the Tyneside region. The other two groups were selected as controls for comparison with the Tynesiders. One consisted of 35 native British English speakers from regions other than Tyneside. They are referred to henceforth as the "non-local UK" listener group. Although we would predict some familiarity with varieties of British English, we assumed this group would have little awareness of the indexicality of sociolinguistic variables specific to Tyneside. The other control group consisted of 114 American students. These participants came from a range of geographical backgrounds but were all resident at the time of the experiment in Tucson, Arizona. We assumed that this group had little or no knowledge of phonological variation in British English. No formal testing was carried out of speech or hearing disorders, but none of the listeners reported any such problems.

4.4 Listening tests

The tests were conducted on campus at the participating universities. The British listeners participated in the tests in computer laboratories. The test sound file was played through standard audio programs, with listeners wearing good quality headphones. The American group heard the sound file via high quality amplification in a classroom setting. Although not wearing headphones, both laryngealization and pre-aspiration could be heard clearly by the administrator (the fourth author, who was positioned furthest away from the amplifier).

Listeners were given an answer sheet consisting of a transcription of the stimulus and two responses, "boy" and "girl" (Figure 14.2). The structure of the test was outlined verbally by the test administrators, who also explained that all the children came from Newcastle upon Tyne, UK. Listeners were instructed to judge whether the speaker of each stimulus was a boy or a girl, and to circle the appropriate answer. They were warned that they would find the test difficult, but further instructed to provide an answer for each stimulus even if they had to guess to do so.

1. cat	BOY	GIRL
2. letters	BOY	GIRL
3. bath	BOY	GIRL

Figure 14.2 Sample of answer sheet.

A training test was provided which consisted of three stimuli presented in the same format as the main test. After the completion of the training test listeners had the opportunity to ask questions about the test (and, in the case of the British groups, the audio programs). In practice the only questions raised concerned modification to the volume of sound playback. The main test was thus administered a few minutes after the training test. Despite reports that they found the task difficult, listeners performed as instructed, offering answers to each stimulus with only two exceptions.

4.5 Analysis

While our main point of interest was in the effect of the sociolinguistic variants on sex identification, we anticipated that the stimuli would also display variation along other parameters which might influence listener response. Following discussions with some of the participants after the test, and in light of predictions derived from previous linguistic research, we coded the stimuli for a number of factors. In addition to the sociolinguistic variant, each stimulus was also measured for f0 and amplitude. Quantification of f0 was performed for the obvious reason that f0 is a key cue to speaker sex for adults, and it was therefore possible that f0 differences might influence response for the child data. f0 was measured in Praat, recording the average f0 value across the whole stimulus. Amplitude was also measured in Praat and recorded as a mean for the stimulus, as a reflection of its overall loudness. Two further factors were coded for auditorily: articulation rate and voice quality. For speech rate the first three authors judged each token to be "normal," "slow," or "fast." For voice quality we recorded judgments of "modal," "breathy," and "creaky." In both cases the majority decision was taken as the final classification. We restricted ourselves to these simple taxonomies because the stimuli seemed to us to differ most clearly through phonation type, and because these labels approximated the kinds of comments listeners reported when discussing how they arrived at their responses. We subsequently made a more objective analysis of rate in terms of syllables per second. We made no attempt to analyze formant values or spacing, since previous studies which have identified formant differences in child speech have done so with fully controlled materials such as prolonged vowels spoken in isolation (Bennett and Weinberg 1979b, Perry et al. 2001).

Statistical analysis involved binary logistic regression in the first instance in order to explore the overall variance in the data. Regression analyses were carried out for each listener group, with separate runs for word-medial responses and pre-pausal responses. The dependent variable was response ("boy" or "girl"), and the independent variables were amplitude, f0, rate, voice quality and variant (plain versus laryngealized for the run on medial responses, plain versus pre-aspirated for pre-pausal responses). Post hoc analysis was performed using chi square tests.

5. Results

Since the listening test yielded a binary outcome we report all results arbitrarily in terms of "girl" responses.

5.1 Overall responses

Although we were not concerned with how accurate listeners were in identifying the sex of the speaker, it is worth reporting that the proportion of correct responses was very similar for the three listener groups (Table 14.3). Moreover, the figures approached chance level at 50%, which was perhaps to be expected. The proportion of "girl" responses, however, was slightly higher than "boy" responses for all three groups (recall also that more of the tokens did in fact come from girls' speech). Neither the correct responses nor the "girl" responses differed significantly across the two British listener groups. However, the American group gave significantly fewer correct responses than the non-local UK group (chi sq = 5.992, df = 1, $p < .025$).

Table 14.3 Overall Distribution of Results

listener group	correct responses (%)	"girl" responses (%)	N
Tynesiders	48.7	52.0	1,340
non-local UK	49.4	53.3	2,343
Americans	46.5	51.4	7,648

5.2 Logistic regression analysis

The results of the exploratory logistic regression analyses are summarized in Table 14.4. Unsurprisingly the results were complex, as is to be expected when we consider the number of factors included in the analysis, and the fact that the stimuli were both small in number and relatively uncontrolled. All factors were returned as significant in one or more of the runs for at least one of the listener groups.

Table 14.4 Factors Returned as Significant in Logistic Regression Analysis

word-medial stimuli					
group	**amplitude**	**f0**	**voice quality**	**rate**	**variant**
Tynesiders	**				
non-local UK	***	**			
Americans	***	***	***	(*)	
pre-pausal stimuli					
group	**amplitude**	**f0**	**voice quality**	**rate**	**variant**
Tynesiders	(*)	**	***	*	
non-local UK	***	***	***	**	
Americans	(*)	***	**	***	***

(*) $p < .1$, * $p < .05$, ** $p < .01$, *** $p < .001$

We refrain from reading too much into the regression results, since further tests would need to be carried out using more controlled data to clarify the patterns observed. What is clear, however, is that the sociolinguistic variants do play a role in listener response, albeit a relatively small one compared with other factors, and much more clearly for pre-pausal responses than for medial ones. In light of the overall complexity in the data we continue with an exploration of responses in relation to each of the main factors.

5.3 Results by amplitude

The regression analyses showed amplitude to be a significant factor in the responses by non-local UK listeners for both medial and pre-pausal stimuli, and by Americans for medial stimuli (Table 14.4). Figure 14.3 enables us to take a closer look at the patterns in the responses. It shows responses in the form of scatter plots, for the three listener groups separately. Results for medial and pre-pausal stimuli are pooled. The vertical axis represents the proportion of 'girl' responses given by listeners, while the horizontal axis indicates the mean amplitude of the stimulus (in dB). Each data point indicates responses to an individual stimulus. Trend lines are also included for each listener group.

Figure 14.3 indicates a consistent and clear pattern for all three groups. While relatively louder tokens are readily perceived as being either "boy" or "girl," relatively quieter tokens (those with lower amplitude values) elicited more "girl" responses. The effect is clearest for the quietest tokens, i.e., those to

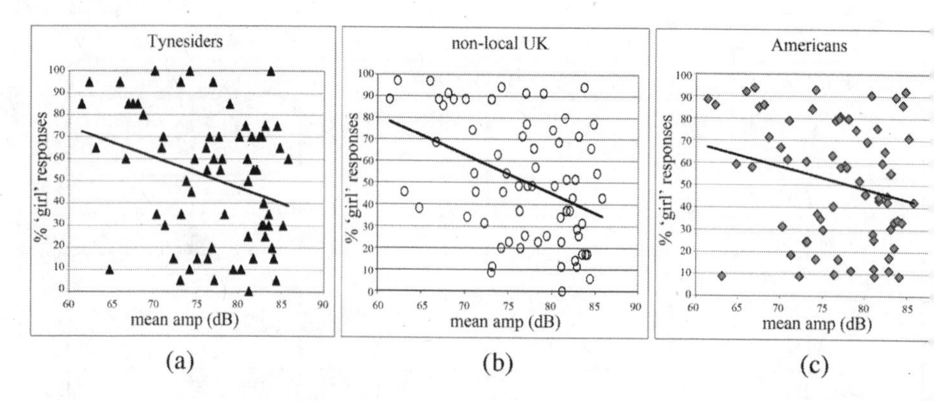

Figure 14.3 Percentage of "girl" responses by amplitude of stimulus; (a) Tynesiders, (b) non-local UK, (c) Americans.

the left hand side of the scatter plots. Results of correlation analyses are summarized in Table 14.5. The negative correlations are significant for all listener groups when all tokens are considered together. When medial tokens are examined alone the correlations are again significant for all three listener groups. For pre-pausal tokens taken alone the correlation is significant only for the non-local UK group, but the negative trend is maintained for the other groups.

Table 14.5 Correlation Analysis Results, Responses by Amplitude

		Tynesiders	non-local UK	Americans
all stimuli (df=65)	*r*	–.300	–.409	–.236
	p	< .01	< .0005	< .05
medial only (df=30)	*r*	–.362	–.434	–.310
	p	< .025	< .01	< .05
pre-pausal only (df=19)	*r*	–.273	–.466	–.137
	p	n.s.	< .025	n.s.

5.4 Results by f0

f0 was returned as a significant factor in five of the six regression analyses (Table 14.4). Closer analysis of the results, however, fails to reveal a clear pattern. Figure 14.4 shows responses in the form of scatter plots, following the same format as Figure 14.3.

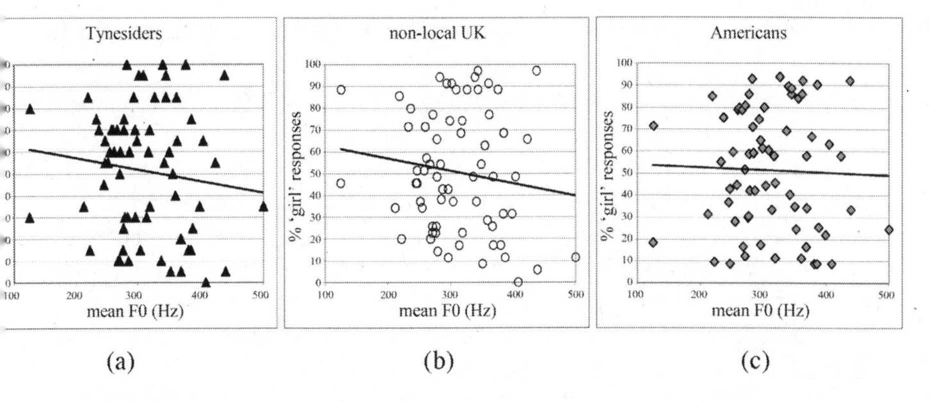

Figure 14.4 Percentage of "girl" responses by f0 of stimulus; (a) Tynesiders, (b) non-local UK, (c) Americans.

For adults high f0 is usually associated with female speakers and low f0 with males. In light of this we might predict that stimuli with high f0 would be more likely to elicit "girl" responses from listeners in our test. This was not the case in our test. The trend lines in fact indicate an effect in the opposite direction, with low f0 stimuli eliciting more "girl" responses from all listener groups. However, none of the correlations were close to significance. The plots in Figure 14.4 present all stimuli together, with no division according to the phonological context of the voiceless stop. Further exploration of the f0 data with reference to phonological context fails to clarify the picture. When stimuli with a word-medial or pre-pausal /p t k/ are analyzed separately the correlations remain nonsignificant.

It is clear that to understand the relationship between f0 and listener response requires further research. We might offer a partial explanation for our findings, however, with reference to the relationship between f0 and amplitude. As Figure 14.3 showed, quiet stimuli elicited more "girl" responses while more "boy" responses were given for louder tokens. As is well known, louder speech typically leads to an increase in f0, as the increased airflow required to raise amplitude will also (unless the speaker makes compensatory adjustments) lead to faster rate of vocal fold vibration. Quiet speech may by contrast involve relatively low f0. What we see in Figure 14.4, then, might in fact be an indirect reflection of the loudness of the stimuli. We therefore tested whether there was any correlation between the f0 and amplitude measures in our data. When all stimuli were considered there was indeed a positive—but non-significant—correlation. That is, louder stimuli had higher f0, and quieter stimuli lower f0, but the effect was not marked. We also considered the fact that listeners might only show a clear pattern of responses for stimuli with extremely high or low f0 values. When we examined the f0 and amplitude measures in more detail we found a much stronger positive correlation when only those stimuli with extremely low f0 values were considered. We arbitrarily tested for f0 and amplitude correlations with the 10, 12, 15, and 20 stimuli which had lowest f0. The correlation coefficient reached significance for the 12, 15, and 20 stimuli with lowest f0. No significant correlations were found in a similar set of comparisons with the highest f0 stimuli. Thus, in summary, stimuli with very low f0 may be eliciting high numbers of "girl" responses because they are also quiet. This remains, however, an issue which demands further exploration in future experiments.

5.5 Results by voice quality

Voice quality was not generally identified as a significant factor in the regression analyses, the only exception being for American listeners with pre-pausal stimuli (Table 14.4). Nevertheless we present the main effects here for completeness, and because a predictable trend did emerge in the responses. Figure 14.5 represents the proportion of "girl" responses for the three groups, with tokens divided according to whether they were coded as modal, creaky, or breathy. The number of stimuli in the creaky and breathy categories is small (6 creaky and 4 breathy from the total of 67), but it is noteworthy that the breathy tokens elicited the highest proportion of "girl" responses from all groups.

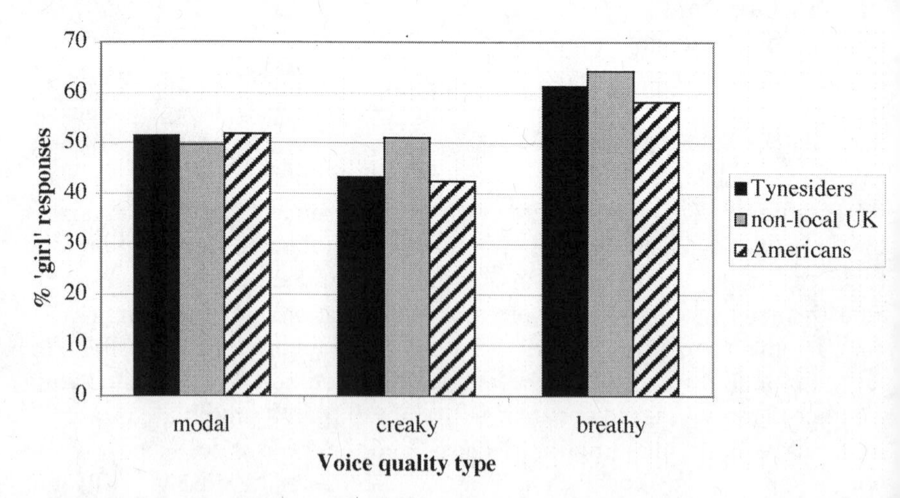

Figure 14.5 Percentage of "girl" responses by voice quality.

5.6 Results by articulation rate

The data are arranged in Figure 14.6 according to our auditory categorization by articulation rate. As was the case with voice quality, the number of stimuli in the non-modal categories is fairly small (n=13 in each case). The emergent trend in this particular analysis was variable across the listener groups. Both British groups gave fewer "girl" responses to fast stimuli than they did slow stimuli. For the Americans the reverse pattern was found.

Following the regression analysis we took an objective measure of articulation rate, in terms of syllables per second for each token (Künzel 1997). The results of this more detailed analysis failed to clarify the picture, however, with no significant correlation emerging between articulation rate and responses.

5.7 Results for word-medial variants

No variant was returned as a significant factor in the regression analysis for stimuli with medial /p t k/. However, when we compare the listener groups we do find evidence for a significant difference in responses.

Figure 14.7 shows the proportion of "girl" responses for medial tokens containing plain and laryngealized variants separately. For both the non-local UK

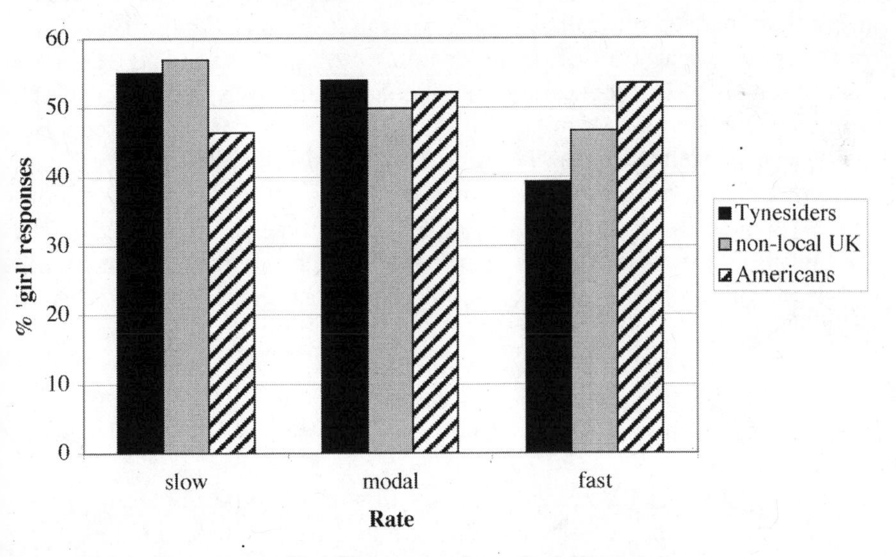

Figure 14.6 Percentage of "girl" responses by articulation rate.

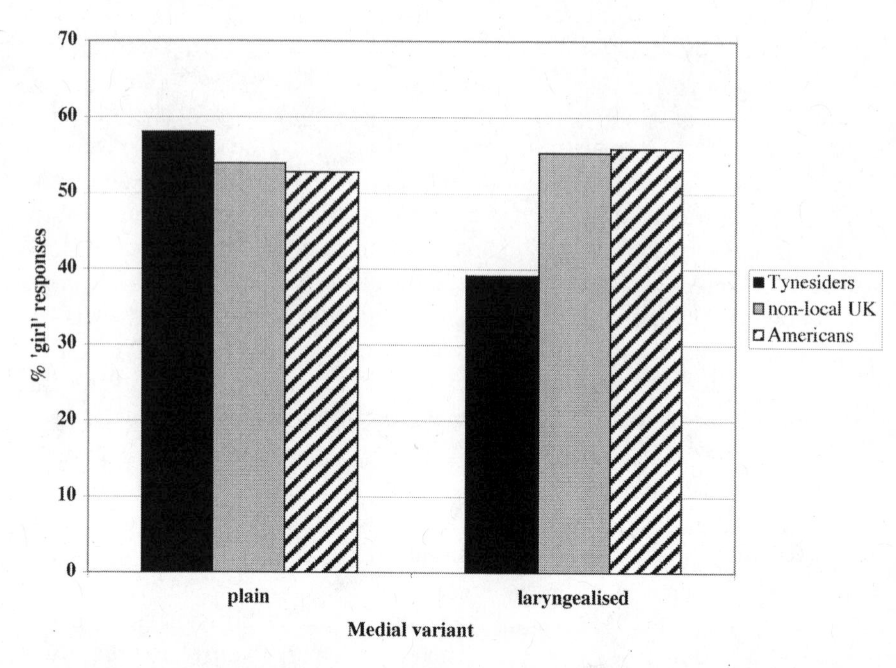

Figure 14.7 Percentage of "girl" responses to word-medial tokens by listener group and variant.

and American listeners the proportion of "girl" responses is approximately equal when they hear stimuli with plain or laryngealized tokens. For the Tynesiders, however, there is a clear difference according to variant. With plain tokens the proportion of "girl" responses (58%) is similar to that from the non-locals and Americans, and with no significant difference according to listener group. But with laryngealized tokens the Tyneside listeners gave significantly fewer "girl" responses (39%) than they did for plain tokens (chi sq = 21.289, df = 1, $p < .001$). The Tynesiders furthermore gave significantly fewer "girl" responses to the laryngealized tokens than either of the control groups (Tynesiders versus non-local UK: chi sq = 15.803, df = 1, $p < .001$; Tynesiders versus Americans: chi sq = 22.608, df = 1, $p < .001$; no difference between the two control groups).

5.8 Results for pre-pausal variants

Finally, Figure 14.8 illustrates responses to stimuli with pre-pausal /p t k/. The variant was shown to be significant for all three listener groups in the regression analyses. The data in Figure 14.8 enable us to explore these patterns more fully.

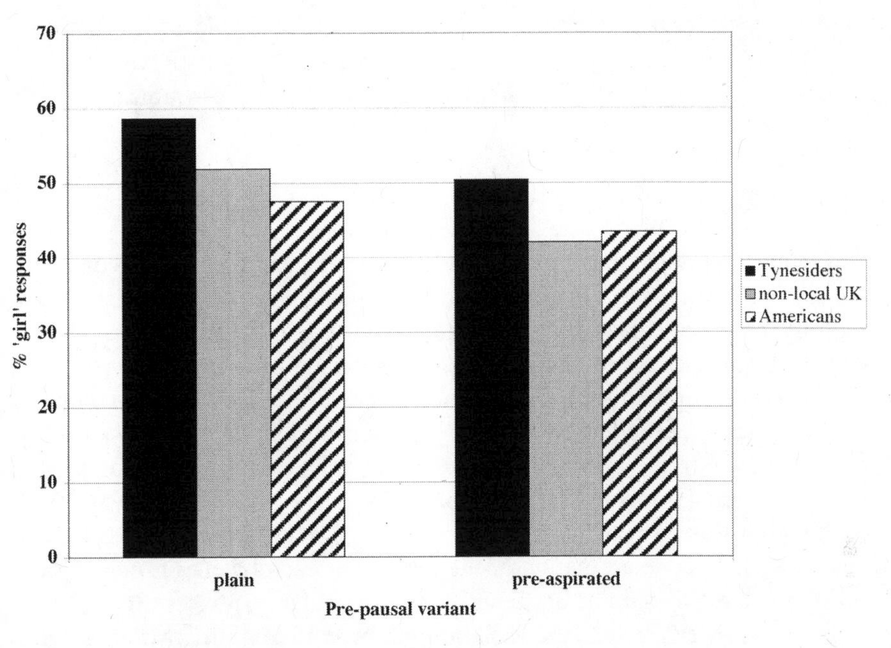

Figure 14.8 Percentage of "girl" responses to pre-pausal tokens by listener group and variant.

First, we can see that all listener groups gave fewer "girl" responses to stimuli with pre-aspirated [ʰp ʰt ʰk] than they did with plain variants. This effect was significant for both the non-local UK group (chi sq = 6.325, df = 1, $p < .025$) and also the Americans (chi sq = 3.86, df = 1, $p < .05$). Note that this finding might appear to go against our predictions based on patterns observed in speech production. However, the Tyneside listeners were the only group which did *not* give a significantly lower number of "girl" responses to pre-aspirated tokens compared with plain tokens. Furthermore, for the pre-aspirated stimuli the local listeners gave significantly more "girl" responses than both the control groups (compared with non-local UK listeners: chi sq = 4.978, df = 1, $p < .05$; compared with Americans: chi sq = 4.621, df = 1, $p < .05$). There was no difference between the two non-local groups.

6. Discussion

As explained in the introduction, this experiment had two main aims: to explore the range of cues used by listeners in judging a speaker's sex or gender, and to assess whether listeners show awareness of statistical associations between a speaker's social background and fine-grained sociolinguistic variants. We turn now to a discussion of the findings with respect to these aims.

6.1 Cues in identifying the sex of a speaker

In Section 2 we noted that previous studies have yielded somewhat inconsistent conclusions with respect to the question of which cues are used by listeners in judging the sex of child talkers. In general, f0 has been dismissed as a relevant cue since children do not display the systematic sex-correlated differences in f0 observable for adults. Several other cues have been mentioned in previous studies, but with little formal study of their value in identification tasks.

In our study the effect of f0 was just as unclear as in previous studies (Weinberg and Bennett 1971, Bennett and Weinberg 1979b, Perry et al. 2001). Although it was returned as a significant factor in the exploratory regression analyses, detailed examination of the results for each listener group showed no significant correlations between f0 and particular responses (Section 5.4). There was a weak negative correlation between f0 and proportion of "girl" responses, such that stimuli with low f0 tended to elicit more "girl" identifications. However, this may be an artefact of the overall correlation between f0 and amplitude: louder tokens tend also to have higher f0, quieter tokens have lower f0. As we saw in Section 5.3, there was a consistent and clear effect in the data when we analyze the results with respect to amplitude. Quieter tokens are readily attributed to girls by all three listener groups. A further issue to consider in assessing the role of f0 is that we used short samples. It may be that considerably longer samples are required in order to gain a meaningful measure of f0 (Nolan 1983, for example, argues that samples should be at least 30 seconds in duration).

The contribution of amplitude has not, to our knowledge, been formally tested before, but it has certainly been identified as a potential cue, for example by Günzburger et al. (1987). Although all three listener groups responded to amplitude differences in a similar way, we refrain from suggesting that this might be a universal cue for judging a talker's sex. The association of quiet speech with female talkers almost certainly reflects a social convention for the listener groups concerned, which may also vary markedly according to the type of talk involved.

Voice quality has also been mentioned as a cue to speaker sex by other researchers (e.g., Sachs et al. 1973). The results of our experiment offer support to this hypothesis, with all listener groups giving more "girl" responses to breathy stimuli (Section 5.5). This pattern coincides with the findings of speech production studies, where breathy phonation has often been identified as a characteristic of female talkers (e.g., Henton and Bladon 1985). As with the results for amplitude we resist the temptation to highlight voice quality as a potentially universal cue to sex, however. First, our analysis focused solely on broadly defined aspects of phonation quality. Voice quality is far more complex than phonation alone (Laver 1980). Other aspects of vocal setting, such as marked differences in supralaryngeal settings, may also affect sex identification or override the perceptual effects of phonatory differences. Secondly, the perceptual association of voice qualities with particular categories of speaker is certainly another socially-constructed convention, and one which may differ markedly across speech communities, languages, and types of speech. Biemans (2000) found no clear gendered pattern for breathiness with Dutch speakers, and concludes that this is not as "salient" a feature in Dutch as it is in English (165). Another example is provided by Wolof, where breathiness appears not to be a marker of gender but of high status "noble" speech, along with low overall f0, slow tempo, low volume and a narrow f0 range (Irvine 1998).

Articulation rate was included as a factor in the analysis despite conflicting results from previous studies of adult speech production and inconclusive outcomes in perceptual tests. Our results with respect to rate proved both interesting and variable. The British listeners rated faster stimuli as more likely to be spoken by boys, whereas slow stimuli were attributed to girls. For the Americans the opposite pattern emerged. The British listeners' responses are predictable in light of studies such as those by Byrd (1994) and Yuan et al. (2006), which found men to speak significantly faster than women. Note that both studies documented the significance of speech rate for American English speakers who were generally of a middle-class background. While British listeners' responses followed expectations based on these studies, American listeners' responses did not. However, regional patterns for speech rate may be more significant than projections based on Byrd or Yuan et al would reveal. Specifically, in this case, sociolinguists in the south-west United States have noted a "John Wayne" effect whereby men appear to use a low narrow f0 range, to speak more slowly, and to talk less than women (Lauren Hall-Lew, personal communication). Analysis of these factors in a corpus of Arizona speech has not yet been completed, but given that the US listener sample was dominated by Arizona natives makes it likely that regional gendered speech patterns are relevant to the results obtained here. Clearly more investigation is required to explore these effects further, but it seems to us once again that any associations between rate and gender are likely to vary across social groups. It is also prudent to conclude from this aspect of the analysis that a single word or short phrase may not be sufficient for listeners to draw any firm conclusions about the sex of the speaker.

A final observation can be made with respect to the overall success rate of listeners in the identification task. Correct responses for all groups were close to chance, at just over 50% (Table 14.3). This is markedly lower than in other similar experiments (for example, Weinberg and Bennett 1971: 74%; Sachs et al. 1973: 81%; Meditch 1975: 79%; Bennett and Weinberg 1979a: 68%; Edwards 1979: 84%; Günzburger et al. 1987: 74%). One likely reason for our lower scores is the relatively short duration of the samples we used. The better scores reported in other studies have mostly been derived when longer stimuli have been used. For example, Weinberg and Bennett (1971) used 30 seconds of spontaneous speech, Meditch (1975) used 2 minutes, Edwards (1979) a 99 word passage, and the 74% score for Günzburger et al. (1987) was achieved with sentence stimuli. However, other studies have still achieved higher identification rates with samples at least as short as ours. The listeners in Bennett and Weinberg (1979b) gave 65% correct responses on isolated vowels and 66% on whispered vowels. The correct responses in Günzburger et al. (1987) dropped to 55% overall with isolated vowels, but for boys this was still significantly above chance at 57%. A further factor in our relatively low score may therefore be our use of uncontrolled, spontaneous materials rather than comparable materials for all speakers such as sustained vowels. The more natural material contains a range of variable phonetic features, and it is possible that cues relevant to gender identification might vary in salience across the stimuli. It is also possible that different cues to gender may conflict with one another in listeners' perceptions, and thus make the judgement task more difficult.

6.2 Listener awareness of sociolinguistic variants

Our second principal interest was whether judgements of speaker sex were influenced by fine-grained phonetic variants.

With respect to word-medial (p, t, k) our results indicate that the presence of a particular variant did make a difference to listener response, but only for the Tyneside group. This finding follows from the prediction we made in respect of gendered patterns in speech production. In Tyneside English plain stops are strongly associated with female speech. Local listeners' responses appear to display tacit awareness of this gendered pattern, with plain tokens eliciting significantly more "girl" identifications than laryngealized tokens did. Neither control group showed any difference in response patterns to the two variants. This was also predicted, since we assume that listeners who are not intimately familiar with the Tyneside dialect will not be aware of any sociolinguistic patterning in respect of variables such as voiceless stops.

The results for pre-pausal (p, t, k) were less clear than those for medial stops. However, they can still be interpreted as supportive of our initial hypothesis. Although all groups gave fewer "girl" responses to pre-aspirated tokens, contrary to our expectations, it is important to remember that the natural stimuli used in the test contain many other potential cues to gender. As suggested earlier, these other cues might override any perceptual contribution from a subtle phonetic feature such as pre-aspiration. More importantly, the Tynesiders gave significantly more "girl" responses to the pre-aspirated tokens than did either the non-local UK group or the American group. The results therefore again suggest that local listeners might indeed derive information about the sex of the speaker from the pre-pausal variants. Specifically, it is possible that they interpreted pre-aspiration as an indicator of female speech more frequently than the other listener groups did.

7. Concluding comments

The findings of our exploratory study support and extend previous research on understanding how listeners make judgments about a speaker's sex. Although the task of identifying a child's sex from a short sample was difficult, listeners' perceptions were affected by a number of factors. Clear and consistent effects were exerted by amplitude and phonation quality, with quieter stimuli and breathy phonation leading to an increased percept that the talker was female. Articulation rate also affected responses, but with variable effects across listener groups. The role of f0 was less clear, and our results therefore conform with those recorded in previous experiments. It further appears, however, that listeners' judgments are also affected by their own sociolinguistic background. With respect to gendered sociolinguistic variants, listeners who were familiar with the dialect of the talkers registered different results from those who were not. We have evidence, then, that listeners do indeed show tacit awareness of statistical associations between categories of speaker and linguistic variants.

Naturally, these findings all deserve more thorough investigation. A profitable line for future research will be to use controlled materials to examine the effects of each cue in isolation, or in specific combinations. Use of synthetic or resynthesized speech will permit manipulation of specific parameters in the stimuli chosen for listening tests. It may also be of value to test the perceptual effects of stimuli which are longer, or of a different structure.

Given the role played by sociolinguistic variants in the identification task, and the socially variable nature of other cues such as voice quality, it is furthermore of interest to ask whether *any* cues might exert a universal effect on listeners. It seems possible, perhaps even likely, that all perceptual cues have a variable effect, determined according to social context. The relative strength of a cue may differ according to the linguistic, social and regional backgrounds of both the speaker and the listener, and the communicative purpose of the spoken material. We are only just beginning to understand the variable nature of acoustic cues on speech perception in general. It appears that the intersection of sociolinguistics and speech perception is fertile territory for further investigation.

Acknowledgments

Versions of this material were presented at NWAV33 (University of Michigan, 2004), the BAAP Colloquium (University of Cambridge, 2004), and seminars at the University of Pennsylvania and North Carolina State University. We are grateful to colleagues at those meetings for their comments. We also record our thanks to Bill Haddican for comments on a draft of this chapter and to David Howard for advice on statistical analysis.

References

Beal, Joan. 1993. The grammar of Tyneside and Northumbrian English. In James Milroy and Lesley Milroy (eds), *Real English: The grammar of English dialects in the British Isles*. London: Longman, 187–213.

Beal, Joan. 2004. Geordie Nation: Language and identity in the North-east of England. *Lore and Language* 17: 33–48.

Bennett, Suzanne and Bernd Weinberg. 1979a. Sexual characteristics of preadolescent childrens' voices. *Journal of the Acoustical Society of America* 65 (1): 179–189.

Bennett, Suzanne and Bernd Weinberg. 1979b. Acoustic correlates of perceived sexual identity in preadolescent children's voices. *Journal of the Acoustical Society of America* 66 (4): 989–1000.

Biemans, Monique. 2000. *Gender variation in voice quality*. PhD dissertation, Utrecht: University of Utrecht.

Boss, Dagmar. 1996. The problem of F0 and real-life speaker identification: A case study. *Forensic Linguistics: The International Journal of Speech, Language and the Law* 3 (1): 155–159.

Byrd, Dani. 1994. Relations of sex and dialect to reduction. *Speech Communication* 15 (1–2): 3954.
Byrne, Catherine and Paul Foulkes. 2004. The mobile phone effect on vowel formants. *The International Journal of Speech, Language and the Law* 11 (1): 83–102.
Chambers, J. K. 2003. *Sociolinguistic theory* (2nd ed.). Oxford: Blackwell.
Crelin, Edmund S. 1973. *Functional anatomy of the newborn*. New Haven, CT: Yale University Press.
Docherty, Gerard J. 2007. Prosodic factors and sociophonetic variation: speech rate and glottal variants in Tyneside English. *Proceedings of the 15th International Congress of Phonetic Sciences*: 1517–1520.
Docherty, Gerard J. and Paul Foulkes. 1999. Newcastle upon Tyne and Derby: Instrumental phonetics and variationist studies. In Foulkes and Docherty (eds), 47–71.
Docherty, Gerard J. and Paul Foulkes. 2005. Glottal variants of /t/ in the Tyneside variety of English. In William J. Hardcastle and Janet Mackenzie Beck (eds), *A figure of speech: A Festschrift for John Laver*. London: Lawrence Erlbaum Associates, 173–199.
Docherty, Gerard J., Paul Foulkes, Barbara Dodd, and Lesley Milroy. 2002. The emergence of structured variation in the speech of Tyneside infants. Final report to the United Kingdom Economic and Social Research Council, grant R000 237417. http://www.regard.ac.uk (accessed February 15, 2010).
Docherty, Gerard J., Paul Foulkes, James Milroy, Lesley Milroy, and David Walshaw. 1997. Descriptive adequacy in phonology: A variationist perspective. *Journal of Linguistics* 33: 275–310.
Edwards, John R. 1979. Social class differences and the identification of sex in children's speech. *Journal of Child Language* 6 (1): 121–127.
Fant, Gunnar. 1956. On the predictability of formant levels and spectrum envelopes from formant frequencies. In Morris Halle, Horace G. Lunt, Hugh McLean, and Cornelis H. van Schooneveld (eds), *For Roman Jakobson: Essays on the occasion of his sixtieth birthday*. The Hague: Mouton, 109–120.
Foulkes, Paul and Gerard J. Docherty (eds). 1999. *Urban voices: Accent studies in the British Isles*. London: Arnold.
Foulkes, Paul and Gerard J. Docherty. 2006. The social life of phonetics and phonology. *Journal of Phonetics* 34: 409–438.
Foulkes, Paul, Gerard J. Docherty, and Dominic J.L. Watt. 2005. Phonological variation in child directed speech. *Language* 81 (1): 177–206.
French, J. Peter and Philip T. Harrison. 2005. Lay-witness voice description and identification: Considerations of shouting, pitch and accent. Paper presented at the Annual Conference of the IAFPA: Marrakesh, Morocco.
Giles, Howard and Peter F. Powesland. 1975. *Speech style and social evaluation*. New York: Academic Press.
Günzburger, Deborah, A. Bresser, and M. ter Keurs. 1987. Voice identification of prepubertal boys and girls by normally sighted and visually handicapped subjects. *Language and Speech*, 30: 47–58.

Hasek, Carol S., Sadanand Singh, and Thomas Murry. 1980. Acoustic attributes of preadolescent voices. *Journal of the Acoustical Society of America*, 68 (5): 1262–1265.

Hawkins, Sarah and Rachel Smith. 2001. Polysp: A polysystemic, phonetically-rich approach to speech understanding. *Rivista di Linguistica*, 13 (1): 99–188.

Henton, Caroline. 1989. Fact and fiction in the description of female and male pitch. *Language and Communication* 9 (4): 299–311.

Henton, Caroline and Anthony Bladon. 1985. Breathiness in normal female speech: Inefficiency versus desirability. *Language and Communication* 5 (3): 221–227.

Henton, Caroline and Anthony Bladon. 1988. Creak as a sociophonetic marker. In Larry Hyman and Charles N. Li (eds), *Language, speech and mind: Studies in honor of Victoria A. Fromkin*. London: Routledge, 3–29.

Heslop, Richard Oliver. 1892. *Northumberland words*. London: Truebner.

Hillenbrand, James, Ronald A. Cleveland, and Robert L. Erickson. 1994. Acoustic correlates of breathy vocal quality. *Journal of Speech and Hearing Research* 37: 769–778.

Hirson, Allen, Peter French, and David Howard. 1995. Speech fundamental frequency over the telephone and face-to-face: Some implications for forensic phonetics. In Jack Windsor Lewis (ed.), *Studies in general and English phonetics*. London: Routledge, 230–2–40.

Irvine, Judith. 1998. Ideologies of honorific language. In Bambi B. Schieffelin, Kathryn A. Woolard, and Paul V. Kroskrity (eds), *Language ideologies: Practice and theory*. Oxford: Oxford University Press, 51–67.

Johnson, Keith. 1997. Speech perception without speaker normalization: An exemplar model. In Keith Johnson and John Mullennix (eds), *Talker variability in speech processing*. San Diego: Academic Press, 145–165.

Jones, Val. 1985. Tyneside syntax: a presentation of some data from the Tyneside Linguistic Survey. In Wolfgang Viereck (ed.), *Focus on England and Wales*. Amsterdam: John Benjamins, 163–177.

Jones-Sargent, Val. 1983. *Tyne Bytes. A computerised sociolinguistic study of Tyneside*, Frankfurt am Main: Peter Lang.

King, Elbert W. 1952. A roentgenographic study of pharyngeal growth. *The Angle Orthodontist* 22 (1): 23–37.

Klatt, Dennis H. and Laura C. Klatt. 1990. Analysis, synthesis, and perception of voice quality variations among female and male talkers. *Journal of the Acoustical Society of America* 87 (2): 820–857.

Krauss, Robert M., Robin Freyberg, and Ezequiel Morsella. 2002. Inferring speakers' physical attributes from their voices. *Journal of Experimental Social Psychology* 38: 618–625.

Künzel, Hermann J. 1987. *Sprechererkennung: Grundzüge Forensischer Sprachverarbeitung*. Heidelberg: Kriminalistik-Verlag.

Künzel, Hermann J. 1997. Some general phonetic and forensic aspects of speaking tempo. *Forensic Linguistics: The International Journal of Speech, Language and the Law* 4: 48–83.

Labov, William. 1994. *Principles of linguistic change: Internal factors.* Oxford: Blackwell.

Lane, Harlan and Bernard Tranel. 1971. The Lombard sign and the role of hearing in speech. *Journal of Speech and Hearing Research*, 14: 677–709.

Laver, John 1980. *The phonetic description of voice quality.* Cambridge: Cambridge University Press.

Lee, Alison, Nigel Hewlett, and Moray Nairn. 1995. Voice and gender in children. In S. Mills (ed.), *Language and gender: Interdisciplinary perspectives.* Harlow: Longman, 194–204.

Lieberman, Philip. 1967. *Intonation, perception and language.* Cambridge, MA: MIT Press.

Local, John K. 1982. Modelling intonational variability in children's speech. In Suzanne Romaine (ed.), *Sociolinguistic variation in speech communities.* London: Arnold, 85–103.

Local, John K., J. Kelly, and William H.G. Wells. 1986. Towards a phonology of conversation: Turntaking in Tyneside. *Journal of Linguistics* 22 (2): 411–437.

Mackenzie Beck, Janet. 1997. Organic variation of the vocal apparatus. In William J. Hardcastle and John Laver (eds), *The handbook of phonetic sciences.* Oxford: Blackwell, 256–297.

Markel, Norman M., Layne D. Prebor, and John F. Brandt. 1972. Biosocial factors in dyadic communication: Sex and speaking intensity. *Journal of Personality and Social Psychology* 23 (1): 11–13.

Meditch, Andrea 1975. The development of sex-specific speech patterns in young children. *Anthropological Linguistics* 17: 421–433.

Milroy, Lesley, James Milroy, and Gerard J. Docherty. 1997. Phonological variation and change in contemporary spoken British English. Final report to the United Kingdom Economic and Social Research Council, grant R000 234892. http://www.regard.ac.uk (accessed February 15, 2010).

Moye, Laurie S. 1979. *Study of the effects on speech analysis of the types of degradation occurring in telephony*, Harlow: Standard Telecommunication Laboratories.

Nolan, Francis. 1983. *The phonetic bases of speaker recognition.* Cambridge: Cambridge University Press.

Pellowe, John and Val Jones. 1978. On intonational variety in Tyneside speech. In Peter Trudgill (ed.), *Sociolinguistic patterns in British English*, 101–121.

Pellowe, John, Graham Nixon, Barbara M.H. Strang, and Vincent McNeany. 1972. A dynamic modelling of linguistic variation: The urban (Tyneside) linguistic survey. *Lingua* 30 (1): 1–30.

Perry, Theodore L., Ralph N. Ohde, and Daniel H. Ashmead. 2001. The acoustic bases for gender identification from children's voices. *Journal of the Acoustical Society of* America 109: 2988–2998.

Purnell, Thomas, William Idsardi, and John Baugh. 1999. Perceptual and phonetic experiments in American English dialect identification. *Journal of Language and Social Psychology* 18 (1): 10–30.

Robb, Michael P., Margaret A. Maclagan, and Yang Chen. 2004. Speaking rates of American and New Zealand varieties of English. *Clinical Linguistics & Phonetics* 18 (1): 1–15.

Ryalls, John, Guylaine De Lorze, Nathalie Lever, Lisa Ouellet, and Céline Larfeuil. 1994. The effects of age and sex on speech intonation and duration for matched statements and questions in French. *Journal of the Acoustical Society of America* 95 (4): 2274–2276.

Sachs, Jacqueline, Philip Lieberman, and Donna Erickson. 1973. Anatomical and cultural determinants of male and female speech. In Roger W. Shuy and Ralph W. Fasold (eds), *Language attitudes: Current trends and prospects*. Washington DC: Georgetown University Press, 74–84.

Sorenson, David N. 1989. A fundamental frequency investigation of children ages 6–10 years old. *Journal of Communication Disorders* 22: 115–123.

Strand, Elizabeth. 1999. Uncovering the role of gender stereotypes in speech perception. *Journal of Language and Social Psychology* 18 (1): 86–99.

Stuart-Smith, Jane. 1999. Glasgow: Accent and voice quality. In Foulkes and Docherty (eds), 203–222.

Syrdal, Ann K. 1996. Acoustic variability in spontaneous conversational speech of American English talkers. In H. Timothy Bunnell and William Idsardi (eds), *Proceedings of ICSLP 96* (4th International Conference on Spoken Language Processing), Vol. 1, 438–441. Newark: University of Delaware.

Thomas, Erik R. 2002. Sociophonetic applications of speech perception experiments. *American Speech* 77: 115–147.

Thorne, Barrie, Cheris Kramarae, and Nancy Henley (eds). 1983. *Language, gender and society*. Rowley, MA: Newbury House.

Van Bezooijen, Renée and Charlotte Gooskens. 1999. Identification of language varieties: The contribution of different linguistic levels. *Journal of Language and Social Psychology* 18 (1): 31–48.

Van Summers, W., David B. Pisoni, Robert H. Bernacki, Robert I. Pedlow, and Michael A. Stokes. 1988. Effects of noise on speech production: Acoustic and perceptual analyses. *Journal of the Acoustical Society of America* 84: 917–928.

Watt, Dominic J.L. and Lesley Milroy. 1999. Patterns of variation and change in three Tyneside vowels: Is this dialect levelling? In Foulkes and Docherty (eds), 25–46.

Weinberg, Bernd and Suzanne Bennett. 1971. Speaker sex recognition of 5- and 6-year-old children's voices. *Journal of the Acoustical Society of America* 50: 1210–1213.

Wells, John C. 1982. *Accents of English* (3 vols.). Cambridge: Cambridge University Press.

Yuan, Jiahong, Mark Liberman, and Christopher Cieri. 2006. Towards an integrated understanding of speaking rate in conversation. Paper presented at the ICSLP conference: Pittsburgh PA, September 17–21.

Chapter 15

Avant-garde Dutch: A Perceptual, Acoustic, and Evaluational Study

Renée van Bezooijen, Radboud University and
Vincent J. van Heuven, Leiden University

1. Introduction

In the present study we will target a vowel shift in present-day Dutch. It is the most conspicuous feature of a new variety of Dutch "discovered" and described by Stroop (1998), who christened it Polder Dutch. Here we will refer to the new variety by the more interpretable name of Avant-garde Dutch (for details on the background of the variety we refer to Van Heuven, Van Bezooijen, and Edelman 2005). The clearest phenomenon in avant-garde Dutch is a change affecting the closing low-mid diphthong /ɛi/, which is said to undergo a process of lowering. According to Stroop, the lowering would be especially noticeable in the speech of relatively young, highly educated and politically progressive women.

We aim to present an integrated study of various properties of the ongoing change. We will do this by presenting three separate studies. The first study uses a perceptual approach to test the claim that avant-garde women are more prone to adopt the new variety than male speakers. The second study tries to determine the acoustic basis of the difference in realization of /ɛi/ by female and male speakers. The third evaluational study aims to determine the gender-related attractiveness and other subjective features of Avant-garde Dutch. Below, the aims of the three studies will be presented in more detail.

1.1 The phonetics of Avant-garde Dutch

Avant-garde Dutch differs from the standard language only in its phonetics, so it is an accent rather than a dialect. Stroop presents the change as a chain shift, whereby the low-mid diphthongs /ɛi, œy, ɔu/ are lowered. As a result, the onset of the low-mid diphthongs assumes a position very close to open /a:/,

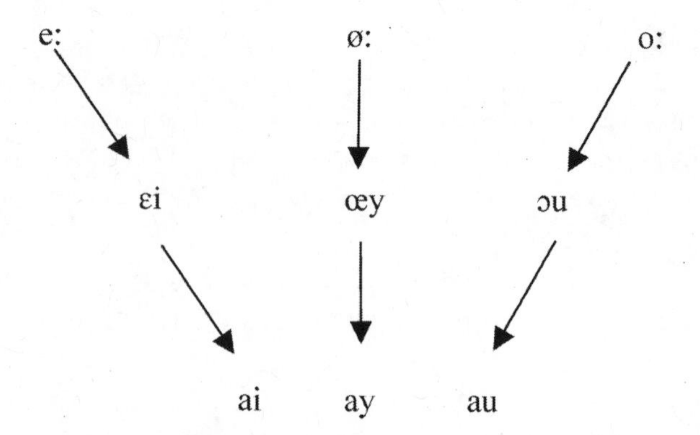

Figure 15.1 Shift of long vowels and diphthongs in Avant-garde Dutch (after Stroop 1999: Figure 4).

so that the three diphthongs are no longer clearly differentiated in their onsets. However, the end points of the diphthongs—which may possibly be lowered as well—still differentiate adequately between the front unrounded /ɛi/, the front rounded /œy/, and the back rounded /ɔu/. As a consequence of the lowering of the low-mid diphthongs the tense high-mid vowels /e:, ø:, o:/, which have slight diphthongization in the standard language, are also somewhat lowered and more noticeably diphthongized. The entire chain is illustrated in Figure 15.1, which shows how the onsets of both the high-mid vowels and of the low-mid diphthongs have shifted to more open positions.

It remains unclear from the descriptions provided whether the degree of diphthongization is affected by the sound change. If it is only the onset of the diphthongs that is more open, and the end point remains stable, then the strength of diphthongization (the size of the diphthong trajectory) should have increased. However, if the onset and the endpoint have been lowered together, then the strength of diphthongization should have remained the same.

1.2 The socio-linguistics of Avant-garde Dutch

Stroop (1998) claims that Avant-garde Dutch is typically used by (relatively) young, highly educated, progressive Dutch women, who wish to make a statement through speech that they are unconventional and emancipated. He notices the variety among women with high-prestige social positions such as authors, actors, film producers, artists, left-wing politicians, high-ranking academics, and pop-singers. The typical, first-generation speaker of Avant-garde Dutch has a higher-middle-class background, an environment traditionally dominated by Standard Dutch, and is between 25 and 40 years of age. As the variety is spreading, Stroop hears it more and more often among students and salesgirls of a younger age as well. According to Stroop it is difficult to find men with an Avant-garde Dutch accent matching the typical, highly educated Avant-garde Dutch women, especially above age 30. However, among very young teenagers he thinks that the number of boys speaking Avant-garde Dutch is increasing rapidly. Stroop regards Avant-garde Dutch as a sociolect rather than a regiolect, as it seems to be socially conditioned rather than geographically; its speakers come from all regions of the Netherlands.

1.3 Aims of the study

The first aim of this study is to clarify the phonetics of the sound change in so far as it relates to the pronunciation of the diphthong /ɛi/. This sound has been advanced by Stroop (1998: 25) as the major exponent of the new variety. In doing this, we will concentrate on possible male-female differences. We will test the hypothesis that highly educated, progressive female speakers deviate more from Standard Dutch when realizing /ɛi/ than men with comparable social characteristics, both perceptually and acoustically. The acoustic analysis necessarily involves the issue of cross-gender speaker normalization. To supplement the analysis of the gender-related production of avant-garde /ɛi/ we designed an evaluation study to verify Stroop's ideas. The study focussed on linguistically naive people's perception of Avant-garde Dutch as compared to Standard Dutch and two other accents of present-day Dutch. We expected young female listeners to be more positive towards Avant-garde Dutch than older female listeners and both young and old male listeners, and we expected this effect to be independent of regional origin.

2. Study 1: Perception of Avant-garde /ɛi/

2.1 Speakers and speech materials

To test the idea that women lead the sound change, we should compare groups of male and female speakers that are equivalent in all socio-linguistically relevant aspects, such as socio-economic status and age. Preferably, the speakers should not be aware of the fact that their speech is being recorded for linguistic analysis, and their speech should be spontaneously produced rather than read out from paper. To aggravate matters, the type of speaker we were targeting is not easily accessible. These are typically well-known public figures, celebrities who will not be easily persuaded to participate in a scientific study. As a feasible alternative we decided to record a televised series of weekly talk shows featuring precisely the type of speakers that we were looking for. The particular talk show, Het Blauwe Licht (The Blue Light), was produced by the "highbrow" VPRO television network in the Netherlands. In each show two guests discussed recent television programs, press photos and newspaper articles.

From the winter season of 1998–1999 onwards, the first 16 male and 16 female Dutch-speaking guests who appeared in the television talk show were recorded. The mean ages of the men and women were the same (47 years of age). Per speaker some 6 minutes of speech were recorded. For each speaker 10 tokens of the target diphthong /ɛi/ were selected from the recordings, along with 5 tokens of /i/ and 5 tokens of /a/. Tokens to be selected into the database preferably occurred before obstruents in stressed syllables of content words. Multiple tokens of the same word by the same speaker were avoided (for details see Edelman 2002).

2.2 Procedure

Both authors independently judged the vowel height of the onsets of the 320 /ɛi/ tokens along a scale from 0 (maximally close onset) to 10 (maximally open onset). Tokens were made audible with a minimal acoustic context of 500 ms both preceding and following the target diphthong token. The scores for perceived onset height were averaged per speaker, for each rater separately, so that 32 pairs of onset height scores were obtained. The scoring was done with substantial between-rater consistency, as is evidenced by the correlation coefficient that was found between the 32 pairs of scores, $r = 0.80$ ($p < 0.001$).[1]

2.3 Results

Figure 15.2 presents the perceptual ratings collapsed over both raters (after Z-normalization per rater) for the 16 male and 16 female speakers, ordered pair-wise from left to right in ascending order of conservatism, i.e., in descending order of perceived openness of the /ɛi/ onset. It is quite clear from Figure 15.2 that the female speakers lead the male counterparts in the lowering of the /ɛi/ onsets; in the ordering, every female member of the pair has a more open onset than the male counterpart, $t(15) = 6.61$ ($p < 0.001$, one-tail).

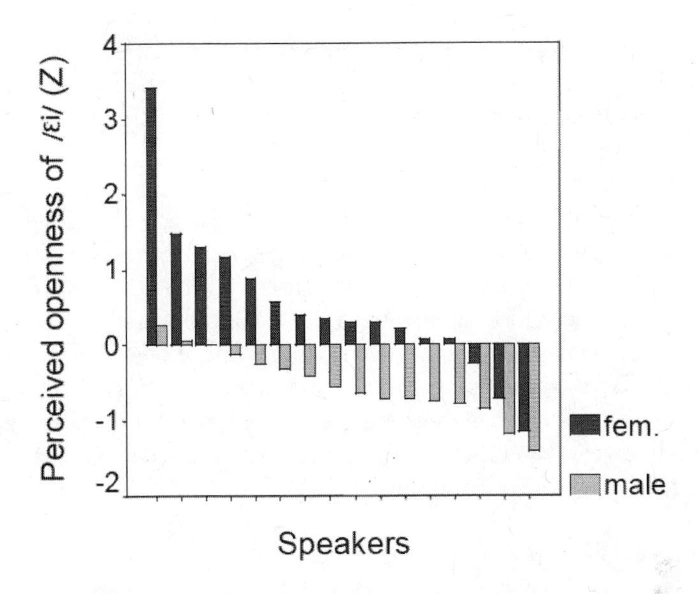

Figure 15.2 Perceived openness of /ɛi/ onset (mean judgments obtained from two raters, after Z-normalization per rater) for 16 male and 16 female speakers. Individuals are ordered within sexes from left to right in ascending order of conservatism as determined by their openness score.

If it is true that the /ɛi/ onset lowering in incipient only in the female part of the Dutch avant-garde, it makes sense that there should be a greater range of /ɛi/ openness values among the female speakers than among the corresponding group of male speakers. This prediction is clearly borne out by the data in Figure 15.2. The female scores range between +3.5 Z and –1 Z, whereas the male scores are roughly between 0 and –1 Z.

3. Study 2. Acoustics of Avant-garde /ɛi/

3.1 Acoustic measurement of vowel quality

Vowel quality, and change of vowel quality in diphthongs, can be quantified by measuring the center frequencies of the lower resonances in the acoustic signal. Specifically the center frequency of the lowest resonance of the vocal tract, called first formant frequency or F1, corresponds to the articulatory and/or perceptual dimension of vowel height. For an average male voice, the F1 values range between 200 Hertz (Hz) for a high (close) vowel /i/ to some

800 Hz for a low (open) vowel /a/. The second formant frequency (or F2) reflects the place of maximal constriction during the production of the vowel, i.e., the front vs. back dimension, such that the F2 values range from roughly 2200 Hz for front /i/ down to some 600 Hz for back /u/.

The relationship between the formant frequencies and the corresponding perceived vowel quality is not linear. For instance, a change in F1 from 200 to 300 Hz brings about a much larger change in perceived vowel quality (height) than a numerically equal change from 700 to 800 Hz. Over the past decades an empirical formula has been developed that adequately maps the differences in Hertz-values onto the perceptual vowel quality domain, using the so-called Bark transformation (for a summary of positions, see Hayward 2000). Using this transformation, the perceptual distance between any two vowel qualities can be computed from acoustic measurements. We used the Bark formula as given by Traunmüller (1990):

$$\text{Bark} = [(26.81 \times F) / (1960 + F)] - 0.53$$

where F represents the measured formant frequency in Hertz. Given that the first and last portions of any vowel, monophthongs and diphthongs alike, are strongly influenced by (the articulation place of) the neighboring consonants, it is customary to sample the formant values for the starting point of the diphthong at one-quarter of the time-course of the diphthong, and to measure the formants for the endpoint of the diphthong at 75% of its duration. The degree of diphthongization is then expressed as the distance in Barks between the onset and the offset vowel quality. In terms of the traditional vowel diagrams used by impressionistic linguists and phoneticians, this procedure is the equivalent of measuring the length of the arrow that represents the diphthong.

3.2 Acoustic processing

The audio recordings were digitally sampled (16 kHz, 16 bits) and stored on computer disk. Using the Praat speech processing software (Boersma and Weenink 1996) the beginnings and end points of the target vowels were located in oscillographic and/or spectrographic displays. Formant tracks for the lowest two formants (F1, F2) were then computed at 25, 50, and 75% of the duration of the target vowel (for details see Van Heuven et al. 2005).

Figure 15.3 illustrates the measurements. It shows the wide-band spectrogram of a target diphthong /ɛi/ with the formant tracks drawn through the lowest two formants as white lines. The duration of this diphthong token was

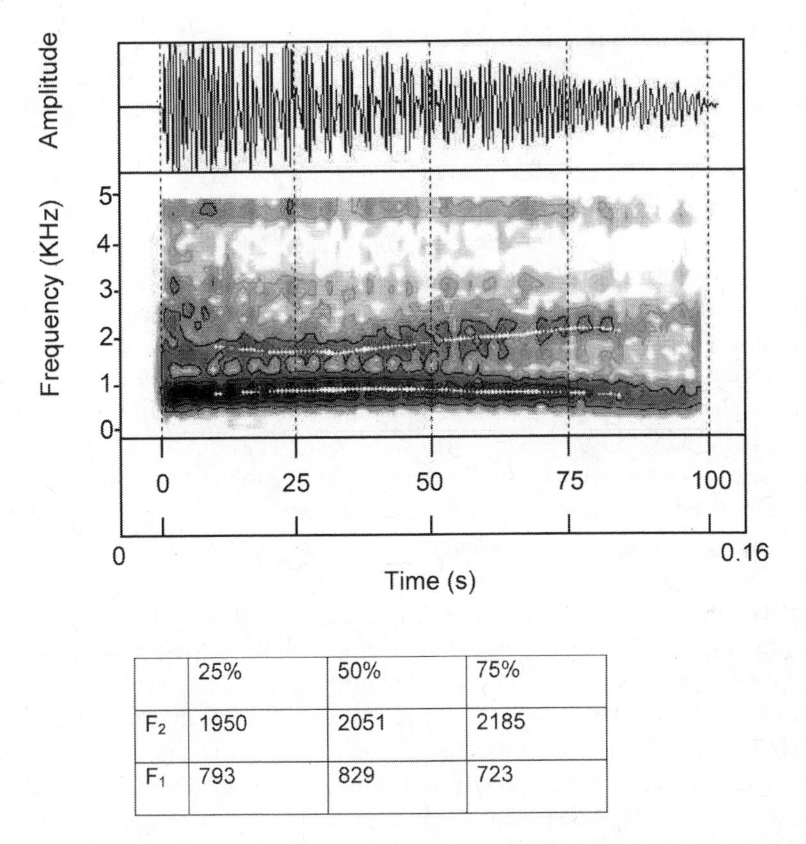

	25%	50%	75%
F_2	1950	2051	2185
F_1	793	829	723

Figure 15.3 Oscillogram, wide-band spectrogram and superimposed formant tracks for F1 and F2 of an utterance containing /ɛi/, as spoken by a female speaker. Formant values (in Hertz) extracted at 25, 50, and 75% of the duration of the diphthong are listed below the figure.

measured to be ca. 150 ms. Segmentation lines have been drawn at the onset and offset of the target diphthong (0 and 100% duration, respectively), as well as at one, two and three quarters of the diphthong durations (25, 50, and 75% duration, respectively). The center frequencies of F1 and F2 extracted at the three temporal measurement points are listed below the figure. The figure shows that the /ɛi/ token is a true diphthong. F1 starts at a rather high frequency (over 800 Hz) and drops to lower values as time progresses. This reflects the closing gesture made during the articulation of the diphthong. At the same time the F2 steadily rises, thereby widening the gap between the first and second formant, a sign of the tongue shifting to a more fronted articulation.

3.3 Vowel normalization

Formant values measured for perceptually identical vowels may differ between individuals. The larger the differences are between two speakers in shape and size of the cavities in their vocal tracts, the larger the differences in formant values of perceptually identical vowel tokens will be. Given that the vocal tracts of women are some 15% smaller than those of men, comparison of formant values is hazardous across speakers of the opposed sex. Numerous attempts have been made, therefore, to factor out the speaker-individual component from the raw formant values such that phonetically identical vowels spoken by different individuals would come out with the same values. None of these vowel normalization procedures have proven fully satisfactory (Labov 2001: 157–164).

Broadly, two approaches to the normalization problem have been taken in the literature (see also Nearey 1989). The first approach, called intrinsic normalization, tries to solve the problem by considering only information that is contained in the single vowel token under consideration, typically by computing ratios between pairs of formant values such as F1/F0, F2/F1.[2] The alternative, extrinsic normalization, looks at tokens of all the vowels in the phoneme inventory of a speaker and expresses the position of one vowel token relative to the other tokens within the individual speaker's vowel space.

For the purpose of the present study we adopted a hybrid solution, which combines virtues of both intrinsic and extrinsic normalization. The intrinsic part of our normalization is just a transformation of the measured formant values from Hertz into Bark. The extrinsic part of the procedure is a new implementation of what has been called "end-point normalization" in the literature. A vowel token is scaled according to its relative position between the extreme (lowest and highest) values for F1 and F2 found for the individual speaker. Since the study is limited to the sound change in /ɛi/—a front, unrounded vowel—we only require reference vowels that allow us to determine the individual implementation of the front region of the speaker's vowel space. All that is required, therefore, is a reliable estimation of the speaker's /i/ (maximally high front vowel) and /a/ (maximally open front vowel). We made the explicit assumption that the point vowels /i/ and /a:/ do not participate in the sound change in progress that affects the Dutch mid vowels (as is also implied by Stroop's vowel diagram, which does not indicate any involvement of the point vowels /i, a:, u/ (1998: 28; see also our Figure 15.1).

In some cases, the vowel tokens of a speaker were dispersed in a perfectly regular fashion, with the five tokens of /i/ compactly clustered in the left-hand corner of the acoustic vowel space, the five tokens of /a/ in the open-central area, and the tokens of the target diphthong /ɛi/ in between. In other cases there was overlap between the phoneme categories (see Van Heuven et al. 2005 for a detailed presentation of unproblematic and problematic types of speakers). In view of the susceptibility of the reference point vowels to reduction (centralization) we selected the single most extreme (i.e., front-most) token within the speaker's /i/ cluster as the high-front endpoint of the dimension, and the most extreme (i.e., most open) /a/ token as the other endpoint. Consequently, the speaker's /i/ token with the highest F2 value and the /a/ token with the highest F1 value were adopted as the extremes of the speaker-individual vowel height dimension.

This procedure allowed us to express vowel height speaker-individually as a relative measure. The spectral distance between the extreme /i/ token and the extreme /a/ token was set at 100%, such that /i/ has 100% vowel height and /a/ 0%. When some /ɛi/ onset finds itself exactly midway between the extreme /i/ and /a/ tokens, its relative height will come out as 50% (for details of the computations, see Van Heuven et al. 2005).

We then defined a relative spectral change measure for the speaker-individual degree of diphthongization in the /ɛi/ tokens. First we computed the Euclidian distance in the Bark-transformed F1 by F2 plane between onset (at the 25% temporal point) and offset (at the 75% point) and then took this distance as a percentage of the total distance between extreme /i/ and /a/ of the speaker. A relative glide measure of 25% would then indicate that the /ɛi/ glide extends along one quarter of the entire front edge of the speaker's vowel diagram. The smaller the percentage, the shorter the length of the arrow representing the diphthongal glide in the traditional impressionistic vowel diagram.

3.4 Results

The speaker-normalized measures of (relative) vowel height of the /ɛi/ onset and of the magnitude of the diphthongization are shown in Figures 15.4 and 15.5, respectively. In these figures the values have been plotted separately for the male and female speakers, in ascending order of conservatism.

It is obvious from Figure 15.4 that the female speakers, on the whole, have lower /ɛi/ onsets than the males. There are one man and one woman with an extremely open /ɛi/ onset of 20% vowel height. It seems that the change from [ɛi] to [ai] has been completed for these two speakers. At the conservative end of the scale, there is one woman with a higher (i.e., more conservative) /ɛi/ onset than the most conservative of the male speakers. For the 2 × 14 remaining speakers the women consistently lead in the change from [ɛi] to [ai]. The effect of sex is significant by a paired *t*-test, $t(15) = 5.46$ ($p < 0.001$, one-tail).

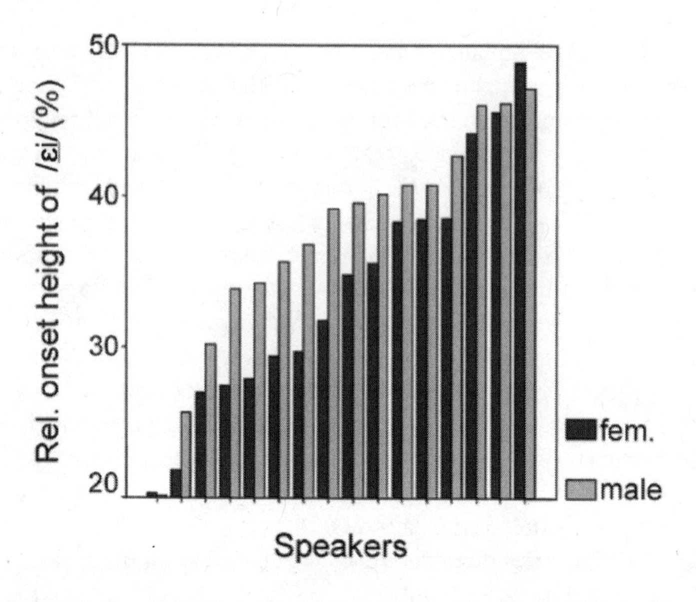

Figure 15.4 Relative vowel height of /ɛi/ onset for 16 male and 16 female speakers. Individuals are ordered within sexes from left to right in ascending order of conservatism (as determined by the relative height of their /ɛi/ onsets).

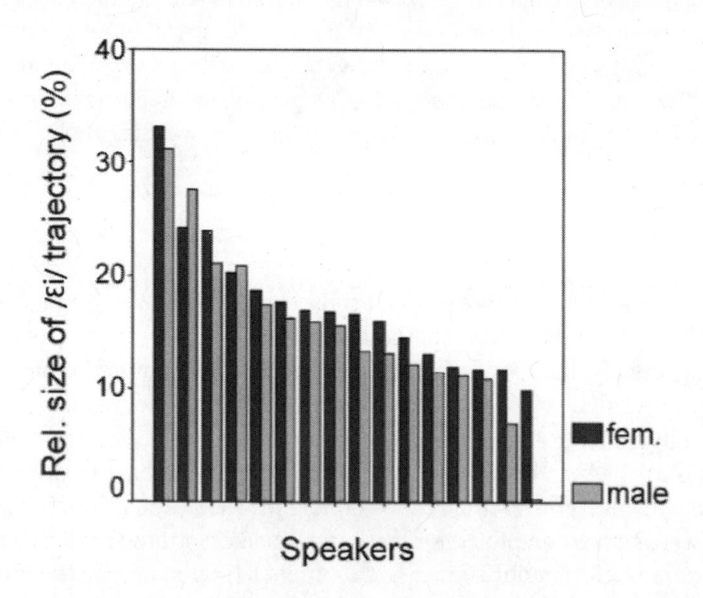

Figure 15.5 Relative magnitude of diphthongization of /ɛi/ for 16 male and 16 female speakers. Individuals are ordered within sexes from left to right in ascending order of conservatism (as determined by the magnitude of diphthongization).

Figure 15.5 reveals the same state of affairs with respect to the (normalized) magnitude of the spectral change in the diphthongs. The women generally have a larger difference between onset and offset of the diphthongs than the men, $t(15) = 2.93$ ($p = 0.005$, one-tail).

Figures 15.4 and 15.5 together indicate that the phonetics of the sound change in progress are best characterized as a combined lowering and spectral enhancement of the low-mid diphthong: the onset changes from low-mid to fully low but the offset remains more or less stationary, such that a larger spectral distance has to be covered between onset to offset. The correlation between onset lowering and strength of diphthongization is significant for the female speakers, $r = 0.48$ ($p = 0.030$, one-tail) but not for the males, $r = 0.17$ (ins.). This finding strengthens the claim that the sound change in progress is predominantly found with female speakers.

3.5 Relationship between perception and acoustic measures

Both raters obtained moderate, but highly significant, correlations between their perceptual openness scores for the /ɛi/ onsets and the normalized height index computed from the acoustic formant measurements, with $r = -0.69$ (N = 32, $p < 0.001$) for RB and $r = -0.62$ for VH (N = 32, $p < 0.001$). The correlation coefficients are negative since 0% vowel height corresponds to the maximum openness score on the perceptual scale from 0 to 10. The correlation coefficients improve substantially, however, if only the ratings and acoustic indices obtained for the 16 female speakers are taken into account, with $r = -0.80$ (N = 16, $p < 0.001$) for VH and $r = -0.79$ (N = 32, $p < 0.001$) for RB.

These correlations illustrate that the relationship between perception and acoustics is quite strong for the female speakers but poorer for the males. Although the male speakers are concentrated towards the non-low extreme of the acoustic onset height dimension, there are a few men who have acoustically low /ɛi/ onsets, but who are not perceived as having particularly open onsets. Closer inspection of the acoustic data revealed that these men did not feature the stronger diphthongal glide that would be expected to accompany the low /ɛi/ onsets. In fact, the male speaker with the perceptually most open /ɛi/ onset had virtually no diphthongal glide at all. The women with extremely low /ɛi/ onsets, however, did have the corresponding stronger glides. It would appear, therefore, that our perception of onset height in the diphthong /ɛi/ is co-determined by the size of the closing gesture.

In view of the preceding findings it is difficult to claim that our relative acoustic measure (even after normalization) corresponds in a straightforward fashion with perceived vowel openness. It would appear that the acoustic measure either underestimates the perceived openness of vowels in female voices, or—more likely—that it overestimates the perceived openness of vowel produced by men. It is important, in this context, to note that our perception of vowel onset in closing diphthongs seems to have been influenced by the magnitude of the diphthongal glide. More specifically, it seems to be the case that a rather open /ɛi/ onset is perceived as relatively close when the diphthongal glide is (almost) absent. It is unclear at this stage how this effect—if it were found to be reproducible with other phonetically trained listeners—should be explained.

4. Study 3: Evaluation of Avant-garde /ɛi/

4.1 Method

4.1.1 Speakers

Listeners heard the speech of twelve women. Three of the speakers spoke Avant-garde Dutch, three spoke Dutch with a typically Amsterdam accent, three spoke different variants of Randstad Dutch (the Randstad, or City Belt, is the heavily urbanized western part of the Netherlands), and three spoke Standard Dutch. Avant-garde Dutch is the focus of this study, the three other varieties served as reference points. Randstad and Amsterdam Dutch were chosen as reference conditions because some people consider Avant-garde Dutch as "just another Randstad accent." We were curious to see whether Avant-garde Dutch would be evaluated different from regional accents from the Randstad. Standard Dutch was included as the traditional norm for spoken Dutch.

The speakers of Avant-garde Dutch had been selected by Stroop as good representatives of Avant-garde Dutch, mainly on the basis of their realization of /ɛi/. The three speakers with an Amsterdam accent were all born and raised in Amsterdam; they manifested some typical Amsterdam features such as palatalization of /n/, /s/ and /t/, and rounding of /a:/. The three speakers with a Randstad accent originated from smaller towns in the Randstad. Their accents were not identical but all had clear Randstad elements, such as devoicing of /v/ and /z/ and diphtongization of /e:/ and /o:/. The three representatives of Standard Dutch had been judged by a panel of five phoneticians to speak (almost) perfect Standard Dutch. They had none of the Avant-garde Dutch, Amsterdam or Randstad features characteristic of the other three groups of speakers.

According to Stroop (1998), typical speakers of Avant-garde Dutch are of the female sex, between 25 and 40 years of age, and highly educated. The speakers of Avant-garde Dutch in the present experiment fit this profile well. This also holds for the speakers of the other accents. Thus the listeners were confronted with speech samples from a socially homogeneous group of speakers.

4.1.2 Speech material

Utterances referring to the origin, profession, personality, and opinions of the speakers were excluded from the listening materials, so that the contents of the stimuli could not influence the judgments. The selected utterances were digitally excised from their original context (radio and television programs, sociolinguistic interviews) and placed in a random order, separated by pauses of 400 ms. This procedure resulted in semantically neutral speech samples, composed of unrelated utterances with a total duration of about 25 s per speaker. The speech samples were placed in two random orders, A and B.

4.1.3 Listeners

A total of 160 listeners took part in the experiment. They fell into eight groups of 20 listeners each. Each group was defined by three variables: gender ("male" and "female"), age ("young" and "old"), and regional origin ("west" and "east"). The younger listeners were mostly in their early twenties and the older ones in their late forties. The subjects from the west had spent the greater part of their lives in the western provinces of Noord-Holland, Zuid-

Figure 15.6a Origin of female listeners.

Figure 15.6b Origin of male listeners.

Holland, or Utrecht, the subjects from the east in the provinces of Overijssel, Gelderland, Noord-Brabant, and Limburg, i.e., the south-eastern part of the Netherlands, bordering on Germany and Belgium. The origin of the listeners is indicated in Figures 15.6a and 15.6b. The listeners' educational level was high, in accordance with that of the speakers.

4.1.4 Task and procedure

The listeners expressed their reactions to the speech samples by ticking six 7-point scales, with opposite terms on either side. The scales had been selected on the basis of their supposed relevance for ongoing change in the standard language. They included: *broad—standard, diverging—normal, old fashioned—modern, ugly—beautiful, sloppy—polished, not my cup of tea—my cup of tea.* Within each listener group half of the subjects heard the speech samples in order A and the others in order B. The stimuli were preceded by practice samples, composed in the same manner of semantically neutral utterances.

4.2 Results

The reliability of the scales, assessed by means of Cronbach's alpha, was high, for the eight separate groups as well as for groups combined. Only one coefficient remained below .80, namely *modern* as judged by the young male listeners from the east, but most coefficients exceeded .90. This means that the listeners within and across the various listener groups made clear and similar distinctions among the speech samples along the six judgment dimensions: they agreed to a high degree on the characteristics of the stimuli. Apparently, the six scales were indeed relevant to differences among the accents judged.

The principal purpose of this study was to compare the reactions towards different language varieties of four particular social groups, namely young women, old women, young men, and old men. We therefore ran a series of ANOVAs in which these four groups constituted the four levels of one factor Group. Group thus refers to specific combinations of age and gender of listener. Two more factors were included, i.e., Variety of speaker, also with four levels (Avant-garde Dutch, Standard Dutch, Randstad Dutch, Amsterdam Dutch), and Region of listener, with two levels (west and east). For each analysis there was one dependent variable, which consisted of the ratings on one particular scale, averaged over the 20 listeners in each of the original eight groups as described in section 4.1.3.

The main results of these analyses, which were run separately for each of the six judgment scales, are given in Table 15.1. Listed are the main effect of the factor Variety, the second-order interactions of Variety with Group and of Variety with Region, and the third-order interaction between Variety, Group, and Region. Not listed are the main effects of Group and Region, nor the interaction between these two factors. They point to general tendencies in the judgment behavior of the listeners, independently of particular accents, and are therefore irrelevant to the aim of this research.

Table 15.1 Analyses of Variance on All Listeners: F-ratios and Significances

	Main effects and Interactions			
Scale	V	V×G	V×R	V×G×R
Standard	229.56*	3.18**	0.63	0.21
Normal	149.91*	3.75**	0.70	0.91
Modern	35.75*	1.17*	0.84	0.62
Beautiful	144.47*	4.22**	0.20	0.36
Polished	213.18*	7.14**	0.18	1.02
My cup of tea	124.68*	4.72**	0.89	0.56

*$p < 0.05$; **$p < 0.01$. V = Variety of speaker, G = Group of listener, R = Region of listener.

Table 15.1 shows that all six scales yield a significant effect of Variety, so for all six aspects judged the listeners perceived systematic differences among the accents. In five cases there is a significant Variety×Group interaction: with respect to *standard, normal, beautiful, polished* and *my cup of tea* there are systematic differences between the reactions of (some of) the groups of listeners towards (some of) the varieties judged. There is only one scale that does not show an interaction between Variety and Group, namely *modern*. This means that in this case the four groups of listeners hold similar views on the varieties presented to them. Also, none of the interactions involving Region is significant, which indicates that the regional origin of the listeners never plays a role in the judgments. So the judgments by the listeners from the western part of the Netherlands are similar in all respects to those by listeners from the eastern part.

To gain further insight into the differential behavior of the four listener groups towards the four varieties, we ran a second series of ANOVAs, separately for the younger female, the younger male, the older female, and the older male listeners, the only remaining factors being Variety and Region. As expected, for all four groups the factor Variety again had a significant effect on the ratings for each of the six scales, whereas the factor Region never had any effect.

We were especially interested, of course, in the nature of the effect of Variety, i.e., whether and in what way the groupings of the four accents by the younger female listeners deviated from those made by the other three groups. To this end, post-hoc tests (Tukey's HSD) were run as part of the analyses, the results of which are shown in Table 15.2. In this table subsets appear on separate lines. Accents that were not judged to be significantly different from each other (joined by a plus sign) are within the same subset. An accent that was perceived by listeners as significantly different from all other accents forms an independent (one-member) subset.

Table 15.2 Results of Post-Hoc Analyses ($p < 0.05$), with Accents Ordered from Highest to Lowest Rating

	Male young	Male old	Female young	Female old	All listeners
Standard	S Av+R A	S Av+R A	S+Av R A	S Av+R A	S Av R A
Normal	S+Av Av+R A	S Av+R A	S+Av R A	S Av+R A	S Av R A
Modern	Av+R+S S+A	Av+S+R A	Av+S+R S+R+A	Av+S S+R A	Av S+R A
Beautiful	S Av+R A	S R+Av+A	S+Av R A	S R+Av A	S Av+R A
Polished	S Av+R A	S R+Av Av+A	S Av R A	S R Av A	S Av+R A
My cup of tea	S Av+R A	S R+Av A	Av+S R A	S R+Av A	S Av R A

Note: Groups including Avant-garde Dutch are underlined. S = Standard Dutch, Av = Avant-garde Dutch, R = Randstad Dutch, A = Amsterdam Dutch.

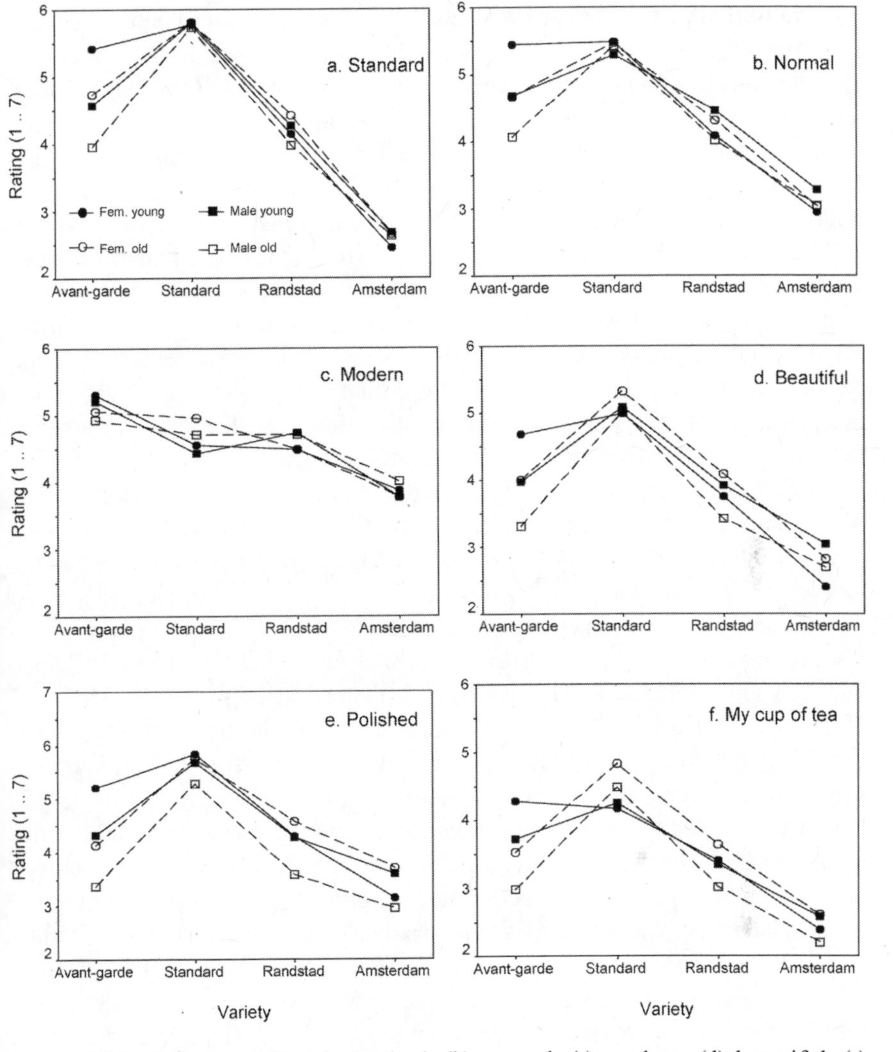

Figure 15.7 Judgments for (a) standard, (b) normal, (c) modern, (d) beautiful, (e) polished and (f) my cup of tea.

To facilitate the interpretation of the post-hoc analyses, the corresponding judgment data are shown graphically in Figures 15.7a through 15.7f. In these figures the factor Region is not presented, since it had no effect on the ratings. Represented are the four sex-by-age listener groups along the horizontal axis and the scale ratings for the four varieties, averaged over 40 listeners per group, along the vertical axis.

We will start with the scale *modern*, which differs in a number of ways from the other scales. First, the distinctions among the accents are much less clear for *modern* than for the other scales. This appears from Figure 15.7c, where the *modern* ratings for the four accents can be seen to be concentrated within a relatively narrow range (between 3.8 and 5.3). It can also be deduced from the post-hoc results in Table 15.2, where, at least for the separate groups, most accents are clustered together and hardly any constitute a subset by themselves. Second, *modern* is the only scale where Avant-garde Dutch has been systematically given the highest rating. In the separate groups it shares the first position with Standard Dutch and often Randstad Dutch. However, for all listeners together it differs significantly from these two accents. Important for the purpose of this study is the finding that in the case of *modern*, which is the least evaluative and most descriptive of the six scales, the judgments of the younger females are similar to those of the other listeners.

All other scales show diverging judgments by the younger women for Avant-garde Dutch. The post-hoc results in Table 15.2 show similar patterns of groupings in this respect for three scales, namely *standard*, *beautiful*, and *my cup of tea*. Whereas the young males, the old males, and the old females group Avant-garde Dutch together with Randstad Dutch, the younger females group it with Standard Dutch. The difference is clearly visible in Figures 15.7a-d-f. For the young women there is a wide gap between the judgments for Randstad Dutch and Avant-garde Dutch, and only a small gap or no gap at all between the judgments for Avant-garde Dutch and Standard Dutch. For the other three groups of listeners, however, the situation is reversed: hardly any or no gap between the judgments for Randstad Dutch and Avant-garde Dutch, and a wide gap between Avant-garde Dutch and Standard Dutch (except perhaps for the young males in the judgment of *my cup of tea*, which we will come back to later). So, young females perceive the Avant-garde Dutch accent to be equally *standard*, *beautiful*, and *their cup of tea* as Standard Dutch, whereas the three other groups assign Avant-garde Dutch a significantly lower second rank, together with regional accents from the Randstad. Here, the evaluations of the younger females are clearly more positive.

In judging *polished*, it appears from the post-hoc results in Table 15.2 and the data in Figure 15.7e that the young females agree with the other listeners that Standard Dutch is the single most *polished* accent of the four. In fact, *polished* is the only scale which shows that the young females indeed distinguish Avant-garde Dutch from Standard Dutch. For all four groups, the high *polished* ratings for Standard Dutch are consistently separated by a fairly wide gap from the other accents further down the scale. However, whereas the young males and the old males consider Avant-garde Dutch to be equally *polished* as Randstad Dutch and whereas the older females consider Avant-garde Dutch to be even less *polished* than Randstad Dutch, the younger females place Avant-garde Dutch above the Randstad accents. Again the young women are found to hold a more positive attitude towards Avant-garde Dutch than the other listeners.

Finally, the scale *normal* shows again a (slightly) different pattern. According to the post-hoc results in Table 15.2, neither the young males nor the young females differentiate between the degree of normalcy of Avant-garde Dutch and Standard Dutch, whilst the other two groups judge Avant-garde Dutch to be significantly less *normal* than Standard Dutch. The data in Figure 15.7b are not convincing in this respect, as the gap between the judgments for Avant-garde Dutch and Standard Dutch is hardly any smaller for the young males than for the older females. However, statistically speaking the young males side here with the young females. Both young groups of listeners express a greater degree of habituation to Avant-garde Dutch than the older listeners. In the case of *normal* there is a sex-independent generation gap.

4. General discussion

The results that were obtained from the acoustic analysis of 320 targets diphthongs (10 tokens of /ɛi/ for each of 16 male and 16 female speakers) allow us to answer the phonetic issues raised in the introduction. The phonetic characterization of /ɛi/ in the emerging Avant-garde variety of Standard Dutch is that it has a lowered onset. The offset, or end-point of the diphthong, tends to keep its original vowel height, so that the quality change between the onset and offset of the diphthong has increased accordingly. The analysis bears out that the onset of the new /ɛi/ variety [ai] has the phonetic quality of a low front vowel, close to or even identical to the Dutch tense monophthong /a:/ that was used as a reference vowel in the present study. The phonetic quality was therefore judged correctly by Stroop (1998).

Sociolinguistically, the data bear out that the avant-garde variant of /ɛi/ is more strongly present in the female speaker group than in the male counterparts. This was shown acoustically and even more clearly in the perceptual judgments by two expert listeners of degree of onset lowering. Although extremely progressive and conservative speakers are found among both sexes, the women lead the change quite noticeably, especially in the middle portion of the range. This conclusion supports Stroop's (1998) observation that the avant-garde variety of standard Dutch was initiated by women in precisely the socio-economic group that we targeted in this study.

Methodologically, although cross-speaker and especially cross-gender comparison of acoustic measures of vowel quality are hazardous in principle, the procedure that we applied in our study, i.e., recording reference vowels and performing partial extrinsic speaker normalization on Bark-transformed formant measurements, affords useful comparison across vowels produced by male and female speakers. As far as we have been able to ascertain, we are the first to have adopted this specific normalization procedure, which is a mixture of extrinsic and intrinsic normalization. It bears a resemblance to Gerstman's (1968) end-point normalization, but differs from it in two details: (i) our procedure specifically looks for the front-most /i/ and the open-most /a/ in the front vowel continuum only, while the Gerstman procedure indiscriminately adopts the lowest and highest F1 and F2 values in an entire vowel set as the end-points, and (ii) our procedure is applied after Bark-transformation, which is a form of intrinsic normalization.

It should be reiterated that our acoustic procedure should only be used with caution when making comparisons between steady-state vowels and dynamic vowels such as the diphthongs in our study. We suspect that onset of a closing diphthong is heard with a more open vowel quality as the diphthongal gesture is larger. This effect, if indeed it can be shown to exist in a full-scale psychophysical experiment with static and dynamic vowel sounds, should be modeled in future vowel normalization procedures. Only then can acoustic measurements be used as a fully adequate substitute for (expert) human perception of vowel quality and quality change in diphthongs.

The evaluation study, in which samples of Avant-garde Dutch mainly characterized by the typical realization of /ɛi/ were judged by groups of listeners, confirmed the hypothesis that young women are more positive towards Avant-garde Dutch than other listeners. Generally speaking, young women place Avant-garde Dutch on an equal footing with Standard Dutch, giving these two varieties the highest ratings, whereas other listeners place it together with Randstad Dutch in second position. Only with respect to *polished* do the young females place Standard Dutch above Avant-garde Dutch. So our experiment lends strong support to the real-life observations by Stroop (1998). It indeed appears to be the young Dutch women who favour Avant-garde Dutch. In fact, there is no evidence in our results that men or older women even distinguish Avant-garde Dutch from regional accents from the Randstad, since it is judged significantly different from these on none of the scales. There is little evidence that Avant-garde Dutch would be spreading among young males.

Also in accordance with Stroop's (1998) views is the finding that people's regional origin is irrelevant. The same attitudes towards Avant-garde Dutch are indeed held by people from the west of the Netherlands and those from the east. In this respect, too, Stroop (1998) seems to have been right about the social meaning of Avant-garde Dutch in present day Dutch society. Our evaluation data show that the new variety is powered by young, assertive and highly educated women both in the west and the east of the country. They consistently hold more positive attitudes towards this variety, making it plausible that they speak it more consistently as well.

Notes

1 As a precaution the second author judged the onset height of the 320 tokens a second time a few days later. His within-rater consistency was found to be considerable, with $r = 0.82$ (N = 32, $p < 0.001$).
2 When formant values are rescaled to Bark, the numerical difference (F1–F2; F2–F1, etc.) is preferred over the ratio.

References

Boersma, Paul and David Weenink. 1996. Praat: A system for doing phonetics by computer, version 3.4. Report of the Institute of Phonetic Sciences Amsterdam, 132.

Edelman, Loulou. 2002. De trendsetters van het Poldernederlands. De uitspraak van (ei) door vrouwen en mannen [The trendsetters of Polder Dutch. The pronunciation of (ei) by men and women]. MA thesis, The Netherlands: Linguistics program, Nijmegen University.

Gerstman, Louis J. 1968. Classification of self-normalized vowels. *IEEE Transactions Audio Electro-acoustics* AU-16: 78–80.

Hayward, Katrina. 2000. *Experimental phonetics*. Harlow: Pearson Education.

Labov, William. 1991. *Principles of linguistic change. Social factors*. Oxford: Blackwell.

Nearey, Terrance M. 1989. Static, dynamic, and relational properties in vowel perception. *Journal of the Acoustical Society of America* 85 (5): 2088–2113.

Stroop, Jan. 1998. *Poldernederlands. Waardoor het ABN verdwijnt* [Polder Dutch. What makes Standard Dutch disappear?]. Amsterdam: Bert Bakker.

Stroop, Jan. 1999. Young women's farewell to Standard Dutch. Paper presented at the New Methods in Dialectology Conference, X: St. John's, Newfoundland, Canada, August 1–6. http://hum.uva.nl/poldernederlands/english/stjohnspaper_engels.htm (accessed February 10, 2010).

Traunmüller, Hartmut. 1990. Analytical expressions for the tonotopic sensory scale. *Journal of the Acoustical Society of America* 88 (1): 97–100.

Van Heuven, Vincent J., Renée Van Bezooijen, and Loulou Edelman. 2005. Pronunciation of /ɛi/ in avant-garde Dutch: A cross-sex acoustic study. In Markku Filppula, Juhani Klemola, Marjatta Palander, and Esa Penttilä, (eds), *Dialects across borders*. Amsterdam: John Benjamins, 185–210.

Chapter 16

Aspects of the Acoustic Analysis of Imitation

Betsy E. Evans, University of Washington

1. Introduction

This chapter explores the analysis of imitation, an area of sociolinguistic research that has received little attention, largely due to an assumption that speakers can "perform" only gross stereotypical characteristics of other varieties. However, results from the study of imitation in other subfields of linguistics, especially forensic linguistics, indicate that sociolinguists should consider imitation more seriously. An exploration of existing acoustic research on imitation will be presented in order to establish the current state of this kind of research and target future directions this field could take.

Firstly, it is useful to clarify here what is meant by imitation. For the purposes of this chapter, imitation refers to the conscious use of a variety that is not the speaker's usual vernacular. Some might call such speech activities "performance," "style," "imitation," or even "metaphoric shift." This difficulty in defining what imitation is probably contributes to imitation not being taken seriously as a topic of research. In addition, definitions of imitation often suit the purpose of the research. However, more importantly, imitation has received little attention from sociolinguists due to the prominence in sociolinguistics of the "vernacular principle" (Labov 1972: 112). Much time and effort have been devoted to developing methods of data collection/interviewing that avoid the observer's paradox so that we can study the "vernacular" (see Milroy and Gordon 2003). Clearly, imitation is a case in which the speaker is paying a great deal of attention to his/her speech, thus leading researchers to set imitation aside.

In addition, for many years, linguists have assumed that it is not possible for a speaker to modify his/her speech in a systematic way. Labov (1972: 215) has stated that he doubts if a speaker can master more than one dialect:

> Although one can achieve a certain amount of insight working with bilingual informants, it is doubtful if as much can be said for "bidialectal" informants, if indeed such speakers exist. We have not encountered any nonstandard

> speakers who gained good control of a standard language, and still retained control of the nonstandard vernacular. Dialect differences depend upon low-level rules which appear as minor adjustments and extensions of contextual conditions, etc. It appears that such conditions inevitably interact, and although the speaker may indeed appear to be speaking the vernacular, close examination of his speech shows that his grammar has been heavily influenced by the standard. He may succeed in convincing his listeners that he is speaking the vernacular, but this impression seems to depend upon a number of unsystematic and heavily marked signals.

Very little research has been conducted that explores bidialectalism (see Hazen 2001), and it seems that for many the conclusion about imitation is still the same: "Ash . . . did a test survey of individuals who were asked to disguise their voices over the telephone. The subjects modified tempo, voice quality, and intonation, but none modified the segmental features specific to their geographical dialect" (Labov 1994: 111). In a study of European American imitation of African American Vernacular English and African American imitation of European American speech, Preston (1993) found that "both performances, with the exception of white uses of pronunciation and voice characteristics, may be said to make limited use of low-level linguistic features" (1993: 337).

Nevertheless, there is documentation to the contrary. In Schilling-Estes' (1998) study of Okracoke "brogue" (the traditional speech of Okracoke Island, North Carolina) found regular patterning in the "performance" and "normal" speech of an informant named Rex. She examined the first and second formants of the diphthong /ay/ in his "performance" and "regular" speech. In both styles she found regular patterning with regard to phonological environments in relation to both the height and backness of /ay/. Her findings "suggest that the patterns of linguistic variation observed in self-conscious speech are not necessarily different from, or less regular than, those observed in non-self-conscious speech" (1998: 64).

In summary, the prioritization of vernacular speech and assumption that dialect differences depend upon inaccessible low-level rules have led to a lack of research on imitation, especially that of an acoustic nature, in sociolinguistics. What is the truth of this matter? This unanswered question about whether imitations are the employment of only a few stereotypical linguistic features, or, if at a phonological level, simply inaccurate (at least at the level of acoustic realization and/or detailed contextual specification) reflects a gap in sociolinguistic research. In addition, all of these factors contribute to preventing a combined body of comparable research to emerge within the field.

Related fields, however, have not ignored the utility of the study of imitation. The relevance of imitation to applied linguistics has led to a variety of studies of its role in second language acquisition, some suggesting that imitation is a plausible learning and modeling behavior (e.g., Markham 1997), and many focusing on the inability of adult learners to achieve native-like proficiency. Research on imitation in speech and hearing science is also well-known (e.g., Zetterholm 2002). In addition, the study of imitation in forensic linguistics, such as speaker identification, speaker profiling, voice line-ups has been carried out for some time (see Hollien 2002). The study of imitative behavior in child language acquisition (e.g., Richards 1986) and speech pathology is also well known (e.g., Dillon et al. 2004; Snow 2001). Many of these studies of imitation show us the effects of external speech alteration such as that done by Molina de Figueiredo and de Souza Britto (1996), who showed that acoustic alterations from disguising the voice by speaking with a pencil in the mouth can create significant differences in the quality of the vowels. In addition, many of the imitation studies use auditory methods (e.g., Reich 1981; Markham 1997, 1999; Masthoff 1996; Schlichting and Sullivan 1997).

Arguably, though, a very important (but certainly not the only) justification for the study of imitation is the exploration of the flexibility and limitations of the human language faculty, but the discussion here is limited to a few of the small collection of acoustic studies of imitation in which internally disguised or imitated speech was examined. For example, Endres, Bambach, and Flösser (1971) explored the ability to both disguise and imitate. With regard to disguise, respondents were invited to read a text with a disguise of their choice three times. The mean formant frequencies of their /a:/, /i:/, and /n/ in these recordings were compared to those of their normal speech. Results indicated that "there is possibility of considerably changing the formant structure of vowels and vowel-like sounds as well as the mean pitch frequency by deliberate disguise of the voice" (1847). In addition, Endres et al. explored the ability of professional imitators to imitate other speakers by examining existing tape recordings of imitations and the imitators' normal speech. In this case, by comparing the mean formant frequencies of /a/, /e/ and /i:/ they found that "the imitator can change the formant positions of his voice within certain limits" but do not reach an exact match in frequency position. Another study that involved professional imitators was carried out by Zetterholm (2002). She studied two professional and one semi-professional impersonator and their ability to imitate famous people (all of whom had different dialects from the impersonators). Auditory and acoustic methods were used. Results showed "large" differences in the imitators' own voices and imitations[1], and perceptual tests confirmed the success of the imitators' efforts. Zetterholm also concluded that, while the imitations were generally accurate, there were some features of the target voices (e.g., voice quality) that were more difficult for the imitators to reproduce.

Rogers (1998) examined the possibility for non-native speakers to speak with a less strong foreign accent than they usually do. This was prompted by his forensic work with a threatening message recorded on an answering machine. The recording appeared to be made by a Cantonese speaker of English. Rogers compared the recording to the speech of the suspect. He concluded through auditory and acoustic analyses that the suspect's and recorded voice were unlikely to belong to the same individual as the suspect showed consistent differences in accent while speaking English from the voice on the tape (e.g., differences in the spectral sections of [s]). He further concluded that non-native speakers can imitate a stronger accent than they normally have but not a weaker one. Lindsey and Hirson (1999) showed that speakers with "disordered" /r/ could produce "standard" /r/ by measuring F3 of respondents' /r/ in their normal speech and when imitating recordings of speakers with "standard" /r/. Three of five subjects judged to have nonstandard /r/ were able to produce standard /r/ while imitating a taped stimulus with standard /r/. This is especially interesting in light of Rogers' (1998) conclusions about the inability of non-native speakers to approximate a more "native" accent and again highlights the need for research on a person's ability to modify a speech idiosyncrasy.

The issue of F0 as a unique feature is widely debated (e.g., Braun 1995; Gfroerer and Wagner 1995; Boss 1996). Künzel (2000), for example, studied the effects of and preferences for a different type of voice disguise with regard to F0. Respondents were invited to read material presented by the investigator using raised or lowered pitch or in a denasalized (while pinching the nose) manner. Five recordings were made with six-week intervals. Mean fundamental frequency was then determined for undisguised and disguised speech. Künzel's results indicate that speakers changed F0 consistently according to the F0 in their "normal" speech. That is, speakers with higher-than-average F0 tend to increase their F0 levels and speakers with lower-than-average F0 tend to disguise their voice by lowering F0. Künzel concluded that, in terms of identification of speakers, "a speaker's natural level of fundamental frequency can be predicted with a reasonable error margin from his/her disguised values" (173).

It seems that a common procedure for studies of imitation involves respondents who have been instructed how to disguise their voice or professional imitators. What could be learned by exploring the ability of non-professionals to imitate a dialect different from their own?

2. An exemplary study

My own work on imitation has explored the ability of a member of the general public (e.g., not a professional impersonator) to imitate another dialect. This case study[2] involves a 29-year-old psychologist called Noah born in Morgantown, West Virginia, an area near the border of the North and South Midlands dialect areas of the US (Kurath 1949: Figure 3). He lived there until the age of 23, but his parents were natives of Detroit, a decidedly northern speech area. Because the respondent had adequate input of both "South Midlands" (or, more exactly, "native Morgantown") and "non-South Midlands" speech, there is good reason to believe that he could have control over both varieties. It is not unpredictable that his "usual" vernacular speech reflects a conservative northern system, as will be shown subsequently, given the social status of South Midlands speech in the community of Morgantown, the home of West Virginia University. The question addressed in this study is how accurate his command of those elements of South Midlands speech that do not appear in his "usual" speech is. The respondent read a word list and a reading passage with items deliberately selected to reflect differences in "Northern" and "Southern" US speech. After some discussion, he was asked to re-read the word list and reading passage in the "West Virginia" style of the people from his home town. This word list/reading passage format allowed Noah to use his mental representation of that dialect but prevented him from assuming a persona such as "good ole boy sheriff" or using a catch phrase like "y'all come back now." It has been observed by Preston (1993, 1996) that a respondent's performance was improved by the use of a catch phrase or persona: "'non-performed' performances reflect a rather more systematic knowledge of the variety" (1996: 63).

Noah's performances were compared first to a "conservative" Northern vowel system, presumably not unlike his parents' and not unlike one he would have learned as a "university-oriented" child in Morgantown, in spite of surrounding Midland speech. Of course, his Detroit parents might have shown some incipient tendency towards the "Northern Cities Shift" (e.g., Labov 1994: 177 et passim) and that possibility is taken into consideration here. Figure 16.1 shows a conservative vowel system for Untied States English, with no influence of either the Northern Cities or Southern Vowel Shift (e.g., Labov 1994: 211 et passim).

Noah's vowels are then compared to the configuration of the so-called "Southern Vowel Shift" (Figure 16.2). If his vowels in both his normal and imitation systems correspond to the conservative system, we may conclude that there is little low-level skill in imitation (the claim of most earlier

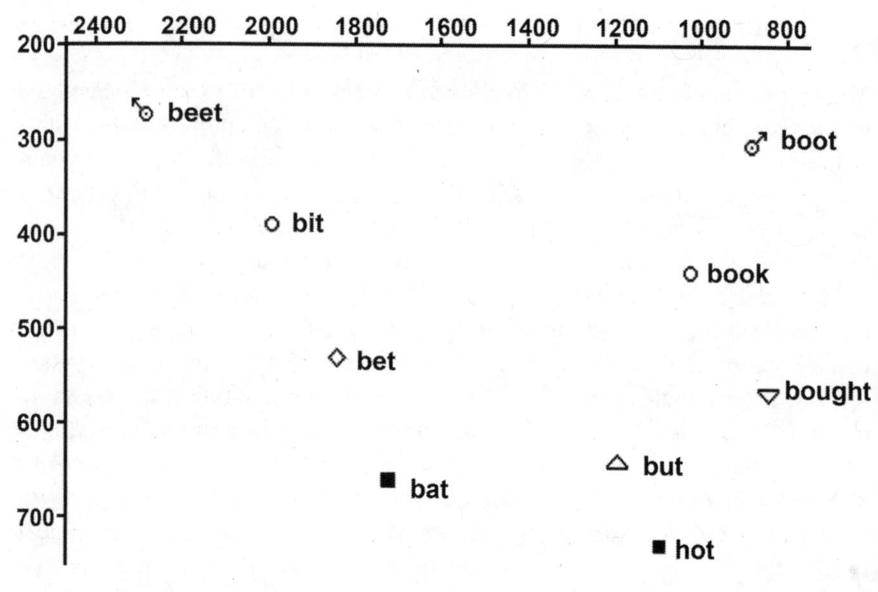

Figure 16.1 Conservative American English vowels, based on F1 and F2 scores from Peterson and Barney (1952).

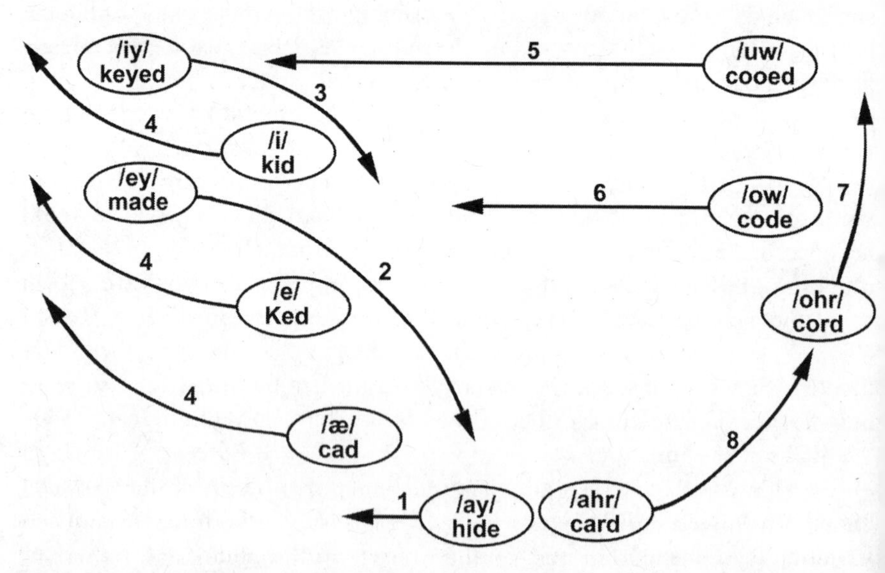

Figure 16.2 The Southern Shift (Labov, Ash, and Boberg 1997).

sociolinguistic research). If, however, the normal performance conforms to the conservative system and the imitation system conforms (or at least in part conforms) to the Southern Vowel Shift system, then we may conclude that imitative or performance ability is rather more precise than expected.

2.1 Results

A comparison of Noah's normal and imitation speech reveals the systematic differences between them. Figure 16.3 displays the mean scores for Noah's "normal" and WV imitation vowel system where an "X" marks the position of the mean score of Noah's vowels in his normal system, and an arrow points to its position in the imitation system. In general, if we compare the mean scores of the vowels of Noah's usual speech to a conservative "Midwestern" system, such as that represented in Figure 16.1 (or Kurath and McDavid, 1961), we find a great deal of correspondence. For example, [iy] "peel" is higher and more front than [ey] "paid"; [æ] "apple" is in a low front position, and [ow] "hope" is mid and back. The only significant deviation is the fronted position of [uw] "food," which is higher but more front than [ow][3].

The imitation system, on the other hand, bears a great resemblance to the Southern Shift (Figure 16.2), which consists of the backing and lowering of the tense front vowels [iy] and [ey], the fronting and raising of the lax front vowels [ɪ] and [e], the raising and backing of low vowels, the fronting of the back vowels [ow] and [uw], and the reduction of the diphthongs [ay], [aw], and [oy]. We might expect the respondent's imitation of West Virginia speech, to reflect some characteristics of the Southern Vowel Shift as Morgantown, West Virginia borders on the region identified as belonging to the Southern Shift (Labov, Ash, and Boberg 2006). As can be seen in Figure 16.3, Noah's imitation speech demonstrates just such elements. Figure 16.3 not only demonstrates the similarities of his imitation system to the Southern Shift but also the very wide range of differences between his normal and imitation systems.

Noah's normal system mean scores are indicated by boxes. Arrows point to the imitation mean score.

In order to gauge the perceptual success of Noah's imitation, a "matched guise" (Lambert et al. 1960) tape was created with Noah's "normal" and "West Virginian" speech and five other male speakers; three from West Virginia (Charleston—in the southern part of the state, Parkersburg—west of Morgantown but also near the north south division of the state, and

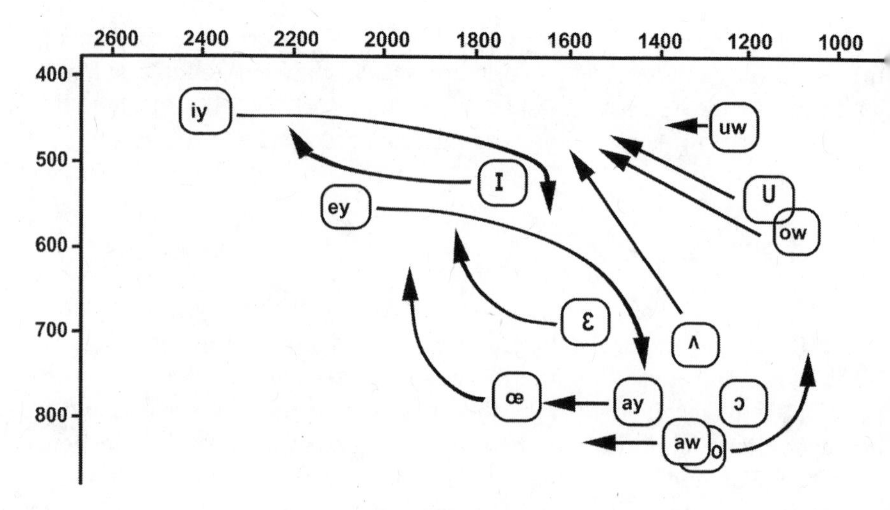

Figure 16.3 Noah's normal and imitation systems.

Keyser—in the northern and eastern part of the state); one from an Inland North dialect (as were Noah's parents), and another South Midlands speaker not from West Virginia. Respondents (n=69) were recruited at the University of West Virginia in Morgantown, WV and asked to listen to the tape and indicate whether they believed each speaker was from West Virginia or not using a five-point scale.

1. "you are *sure* that the speaker grew up in West Virginia"
2. "you *think* the speaker grew up in West Virginia"
3. "you *don't know* if the speaker grew up in West Virginia"
4. "you *think* that the speaker *did not* grow up in West Virginia"
5. "you are *sure* that the speaker *did not* grow up in West Virginia"

Figure 16.4 shows the mean scores for all speakers. The mean score for the Charleston speaker (1.67) indicates that respondents felt sure that he grew up in West Virginia and suggests that "southern" speech is a salient characteristic for such an indentification. The mean score for Noah's imitation (1.93) in conjunction with t-test results showed the difference between the mean scores for the imitation and Charleston speaker to be not significant (.08). Thus it seems that the respondents perceived the imitation to be as likely to be from West Virginia as the Charleston speaker. Mean scores for the other speakers on the tape show that respondents weren't sure or perceived those

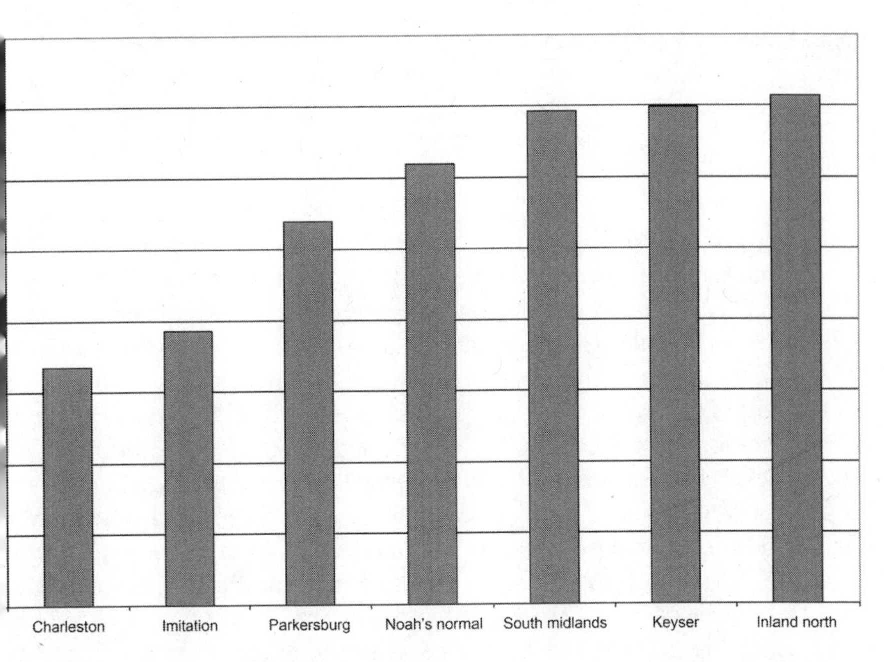

Figure 16.4 Mean scores for all speakers.

speakers to be from elsewhere, even for the Keyser speaker, who is from West Virginia.

3. Conclusions

In terms of objections to the general study of imitation described previously, it is clear that we need to reconsider previous notions about the character of imitation speech and the utility in studying it. It has been shown before that some individuals are capable of quite accurately producing a variety of speech that is acoustically different from their everyday repertoire; that is, the consistency and accuracy present in the performances questions the notion of "vernacular" speech. This kind of data requires reconsideration of what comprises a person's "vernacular" and therefore the primacy of the "attention to speech" paradigm.[4] We must also expand our expectations of the ability of the human linguistic repertoire. LePage and Tabouret-Keller (1985: 182) pointed out that speakers can proactively assert a style if they have the motivation and ability, and "style" has become an important area of study in sociolinguistics (e.g., Eckert and Rickford 2001; Coupland 2003). Deeper examination of the social contexts and motivations for both language acquisition and performance/style-shifting could provide insight on "attention to speech" models of style, variation and change, and perception.

Some questions that need exploring are:

Why can some individuals imitate other dialects with great accuracy and others not? In several instances, the ability to accurately imitate another dialect or certain speech features varies from person to person. More research could better establish what governs the individual variation in the levels of accuracy of imitation, a feature that is, arguably, a part of nearly everyone's repertoire. Masthoff (1996: 164) noted that of the respondents he studied, only three of the twenty respondents' disguises masked the respondent's normal voice and that "several speakers who exhibited a strong regional accent in their modal voices never did attempt to obscure this important speaker-specific feature." In light of the accuracy of Zetterholm's (2002) respondents and that of Noah, the question of whether this is due to perceptual salience or simply inability to control regional accent must be asked.

What is the truth about what we can and cannot do—why are there conflicting results on this? (Consider, for example, Roger's [1998] Cantonese speaker of English and Lindsey and Hirson's [1999] non-standard /r/ speakers.) Other issues such as the role of F0 as a unique feature, as mentioned before, could become more clear if more acoustic studies of imitation and its effects on F0 were carried out.

How many/which features of a dialect must be included for a listener to be convinced of authenticity or inauthenticity? (E.g., Noah may have included too many features for the region he imitated but listeners were satisfied.)

What impact does imitation have on language variation and change? Eckert raises the question of language acquisition and change through adoption of features "off the shelf": "We need to ask ourselves what kinds of changes require the kind of repeated exposure that regular social interaction gives, and what kinds can be taken right off the shelf"(2003: 395). Could imitation be the same as "off the shelf" adoption?

The acoustic study of imitation can provide details on the ability and function of the human language faculty and insight into language perception. More research needs to be carried out in this area, so that a body of comparable research can emerge providing a solid base of information from which we can draw answers to the previously asked questions.

Notes

1 For auditory research on how individual speakers vary in their ability to produce and perceive imitation, see Markham 1997, 1999.
2 For more details on the methods and results of this study, see Evans 2002.
3 This could reflect an overall trend among younger speakers of Midwest American English (Ash 1996).
4 Eckert (2003) calls this issue one of sociolinguistics' "elephants in the room."

References

Ash, Sharon. 1996. Freedom of Movement: /uw/-fronting in the Midwest. In Jennifer Arnold, Renée Blake, Brad Davidson, Scott Schwenter, and Julie Solomon (eds), *Sociolinguistic variation: Data theory and analysis. Selected papers from NWAV 23 at Stanford*, Stanford, CA: CSLI Publications, 3–25.

Blomberg, Mats, Daniel Elenius, and Elisabeth Zetterholm. 2004. Speaker verification scores and acoustic analysis of a professional impersonator. *Proceedings of Fonetik 2004*, 84–87. Stockholm, Sweden.

Boss, Dagmar. 1996. The problem of F0 and real-life speaker identification. *Forensic Linguistics* 1 (1): 155–159.

Braun, Angelika. 1995. Fundamental frequency: how speaker-specific is it? *BIPHOL Studies in Forensic Phonetics* 64: 9–23.

Coupland, Nicolas. 2003. Sociolinguistic authenticities. *Journal of Sociolinguistics* 7 (3): 417–431.

Dillon, Caitlin M., Miranda Cleary, David B. Pisoni, and Allyson K. Carter. 2004. Imitation of nonwords by hearing-impaired children with cochlear implants: Segmental analyses. *Clinical Linguistics and Phonetics* 18 (1): 39–55.

Eckert, Penelope and John Rickford. 2001. *Style and sociolinguistic variation*. Cambridge: Cambridge University Press.

Eckert, Penelope. 2003. Elephants in the room. *Journal of Sociolinguistics* 7 (3): 392–431.

Endres, Werner K., W. Bambach, and G. Flösser. 1971. Voice spectrograms as a function of age, voice disguise and voice imitation. *The Journal of The Acoustical Society of America* 49 (6): 1842–1848.

Evans, Betsy E. 2002. An acoustic and perceptual analysis of imitation. In Daniel Long and Dennis R. Preston (eds), *Handbook of perceptual dialectology, Vol. II*. Amsterdam: John Benjamins, 95–112.

Gfroerer, Stefan and Isolde Wagner. 1995. Fundamental frequency in forensic speech samples. In A. Braum and J.-P. Koster (eds), *Studies in Forensic Phonetics*. Trier: Wissenschaftlicher Verlag Trier, 41–48.

Hazen, Kirk. 2001. An introductory investigation into bidialectalism. *University of Pennsylvania Working Papers in Linguistics* 7 (3): 85–99.

Hollien, Harry. 2002. *Forensic voice identification*. San Diego: Academic Press.

Künzel, Hermann J. 2000. Effects of voice disguise on speaking fundamental frequency. *Forensic Linguistics* 7 (2): 149–179.

Kurath, Hans. 1949. *A word geography of the eastern United States*. Ann Arbor: University of Michigan Press.

Kurath, Hans and Raven I. McDavid, Jr. 1961. *The pronunciation of English in the Atlantic states*. Ann Arbor: University of Michigan Press.

Labov, William. 1972. *Sociolinguistic patterns*. Philadelphia: University of Pennsylvania Press.

Labov, William. 1994. *Principles of linguistic change: Internal factors*. Oxford: Blackwell.

Labov, William, Sharon Ash, and Charles Boberg. 1997. A national map of the regional dialects of American English. Retrieved from University of Pennsylvania website: http://www.ling.upenn.edu/phono_atlas/NatonalMap/NationalMap.html.

Labov, William, Sharon Ash, and Charles Boberg. 2006. *The atlas of North American English*. Berlin: Mouton de Gruyter.

Lambert, Wallace E., Richard C. Hodgson, Robert C. Gardner, and Stanley Fillenbaum. 1960. Evaluational reactions to spoken languages. *Journal of Abnormal and Social Psychology* 60 (1): 44–51.

LePage, Robert B. and Andrée Tabouret-Keller. 1985. *Acts of identity: Creole based approaches to language and ethnicity*. Cambridge/New York: Cambridge University Press.

Lindsey, Geoff and Allen Hirson. 1999. Variable robustness of nonstandard /r/ in English: Evidence from accent disguise. *Forensic Linguistics* 6 (2): 278–288.

Markham, Douglas. 1997. *Phonetic imitation, accent, and the learner*. Lund: Lund University Press.

Markham, Douglas. 1999. Listeners and disguised voices: The imitation and perception of dialectal accent. *Forensic Linguistics* 6 (2): 289–299.

Masthoff, Herbert R. 1996. A report on a voice disguise experiment. *Forensic Linguistics* 3 (1): 160–167.

Milroy, Lesley and Matthew Gordon. 2003. *Sociolinguistics: Method and Interpretation*. Oxford: Blackwell.

Molina de Figueiredo, Ricardo and Helena de Souza Britto. 1996. A report on the acoustic effects of one type of disguise. *Forensic Linguistics* 3 (1): 168–175.

Peterson, Gordon E. and Harold Barney. 1952. Control methods used in a study of the vowels. *Journal of the Acoustical Society of America* 24 (2): 175–184.

Payne, Arvila. 1980. Factors controlling the acquisition of the Philadelphia dialect by out-of-state children. In William Labov (ed.), *Locating language in time and space*. New York: Academic Press, 143–178.

Preston, Dennis R. 1993. Talkin Black and talkin White. In Joan H. Hall, Nick Doane, and Dick Ringler (eds), *English Old and New: Studies in language and linguistics in honor of Frederic G. Cassidy*. New York: Garland, 327–355.

Preston, Dennis R. 1996. Whaddayaknow? The modes of folk linguistic awareness. *Language Awareness* 5 (1): 40–77.

Reich, Alan R. 1981. Detecting the presence of vocal disguise in the male voice. *Journal of the Acoustical Society of America* 69 (5): 1458–1461.

Richards, Brian. 1986. The role of imitation. *Cahiers de l'Institut de Linguistique de Louvain* 12 (3–4): 157–174.

Rogers, Henry. 1998. Foreign accent in voice discrimination. *Forensic Linguistics* 5 (2): 203–208.

Schilling-Estes, Natalie. 1998. Investigating "self-conscious" speech: The performance register in Ocracoke English. *Language in Society* 27 (1): 53–83.

Schlichting, Frank and Kirk P.H. Sullivan. 1997. The imitated voice—a problem for voice line-ups? *Forensic Linguistics* 4 (1): 148–165.

Shinan, Lu and Antonio Almeida. 1986. The effects of voice disguise upon formant transitions. *Proceedings of ICASSP '86*. Piscataway, NJ: IEEE Press. 885–888.

Snow, David. 2001. Imitation of intonation contours by children with normal and disordered language development. *Clinical Linguistics and Phonetics* 15 (7): 567–584.

Zetterholm, Elisabeth. 2002. A case study of successful voice imitation. *Logopedics Phoniatrics Vocology* 27 (2): 80–83.

Chapter 17

The Cycle of Production, Ideology, and Perception in the Speech of Memphis, Tennessee

Valerie Fridland, University of Nevada–Reno

1. Introduction

As contemporary research has found, community variation is much more complex than a simple correlation between linguistic forms and the traditional sociological categories routinely explored in early studies. While such methodology has lent insight into the general theory of what motivates sound change by showing, in many cases, similar trends across disparate data samples, researchers such as Coates (1998), Eckert (1989, 2000), Eckert and McConnell-Ginet (1998), Milroy (1980) and Wolfram (1991, 1993) have suggested such a broad and sweeping approach to each community can lose valuable information on how speech choices are functioning and often obscure relationships among socially constructed categories and linguistic variation. Moving research in new directions, studies such as Eckert's in Detroit (1988), Milroy's in Belfast (1980) and Nichols' in Coastal South Carolina (1983) suggested that patterns of variation result from a sensitive balance between socioculturally established roles and speech. Their research found that the selection of sociolinguistic variables is dependent on the density and overlap of community ties and on the varying use of language as linguistic capital among speakers in these communities. Eckert's exploration of communities of practice (2000) also showed that social meaning is simultaneously constructed and represented by the linguistically and socially symbolic choices made by individuals acting as participants in a larger world of meaning. The spread of linguistic change relies crucially on the ideological vantage point of speakers, the conflicting and complementary ideologies surrounding them, and how these are integrated within the social networks in which speakers participate. Still, while recognizing the role of ideology, most of this research relies exclusively on the description of local production patterns, making essentially educated guesses about the meaning behind patterned variation. Without some method of seeing into speaker's heads as they hear and produce linguistic variants, we have no way of knowing whether, for example, use of backed /ʌ/ variants really signals "urbanness" (and what this constitutes for speakers) just because it is found in higher percentages among urban-oriented youths in Detroit. Recognizing that linguistically and socially meaningful speech is formed within locally defined and constructed communities, other recent research has highlighted the importance of pushing beyond descriptive accounts of local speech to a fuller understanding of the perceptions and attitudes behind speakers' linguistic realizations (e.g., Milroy and Preston 1999). Gaining insight into fundamental questions involving the origin, diffusion, and meaning of sound changes requires integrating examination of what speakers do productively, what they hear perceptually and what they believe attitudinally.

In line with this goal of moving toward an integrated analysis, this chapter presents the findings of a multi-project study on vowel variation which, through acoustic analysis, perceptual tests, and a folk dialectology study, sought to provide a unified account of the production, perception, and attitudes surrounding local vowel shifts for Southern speakers from Memphis, Tennessee. Although American dialects generally share the same vowel system, they differ predominately in terms of the phonetic range in which vowel tokens are realized within these prescribed categories. Much work in the variationist paradigm has focused on describing and instrumentally measuring the productive changes affecting the vowels in a variety of American dialects. A recent wealth of such work has lead to a very clear picture of regional differences and similarities, including some fairly dramatic shifts in the relative position of vowels in all three major dialect regions, the North, South, and West. (Eckert 1988, 2000, Feagin 1986; Fridland 2000, 2001, 2003; Fridland and Bartlett 2006; Gordon 2001; Labov 1991, 1994, 2000; Labov, Ash, and Boberg 2005; Thomas 1997, 2001).

Based on these regional shifts, several separate, but interlinked, research projects were designed to get a comprehensive picture of what was going on in the Memphis speech community. The first study was designed to investigate how the relative acoustic positions of vowels are shifting productively in Southern American dialects of English. This part of the project set out to examine the degree of phonetic change in the Memphis community and ethnic group participation in any shifts. Following this descriptive account of local speech, sociophonetic perception tests were designed to better understand how salient these shifts were for local speakers and what social information they carried. This perception portion of the study explored whether the differences emerging in Southern speech symbolize local regional or ethnic identity and which of the changes serve as salient social cues within the region. Following the perception study, a folk dialectology project directly elicited respondents' beliefs about local and national speech. This attitudinal portion of the study examined how Southern speakers' linguistic self-image played a role in assigning particular values to various aspects of the shift and to regional dialects more globally. Based on the results that emerged from these projects, a final follow-up perception study was designed to investigate how these shifts have become meaningful intra-regional prestige markers.

Overall, this project attempts to provide information not typically available through production studies, perception studies, or attitudinal studies alone. By incorporating all three aspects simultaneously within the same community, this research was designed so that, hopefully, each study could inform the others, making the picture of local variation and the motivations behind it emerge much more clearly. At this point, most of this research has been completed, and, while there is much more that needs to be done, each part of this larger project has contributed greater insight into the linguistic choices made by Memphians. The remainder of this chapter will briefly summarize the major findings from this work and discuss the next steps projects such as this one need to take. (More detailed methodology and results discussion can be found in Fridland 2000, 2001, 2003a, b; Fridland and Bartlett 2006; and Fridland, Bartlett, and Kreuz 2004, 2005.)

2. Project description

Before perceptual or attitudinal studies could be performed, it was necessary to determine what Memphians were currently doing in their speech. As the vowel shifts mentioned previously are some of the most important changes affecting US regional dialects, the production study was designed to determine the degree to which Memphis natives were affected by the series of vowel shifts characterized as the Southern Vowel Shift (SVS). Figure 17.1 contrasts the traditional American vowel system with the Southern system affected by SVS shifts. The most characteristic SVS shifts are generally the acoustic reversal of the front tense and lax vowel pairs (iy~ɪ and ey~ɛ). In addition, many Southerners show evidence of fronting in the high back vowels (uw, ʊ) and, less commonly, a similar shift in the /ow/ class. The changes affecting the front vowel sub-system appear to be the most distinguishing shifts in terms of regional differentiation while back vowel fronting has been widely attested in almost every regional U.S. dialect (Ash 1996; Fridland 2000, 2001; Hagiwara 1997; Labov 1994, 2000; Luthin 1987; Thomas 1989). With the lack of information on the participation of African-American groups in vowel changes in the South, measuring the participation of African-Americans in the shift was a priority of this project.

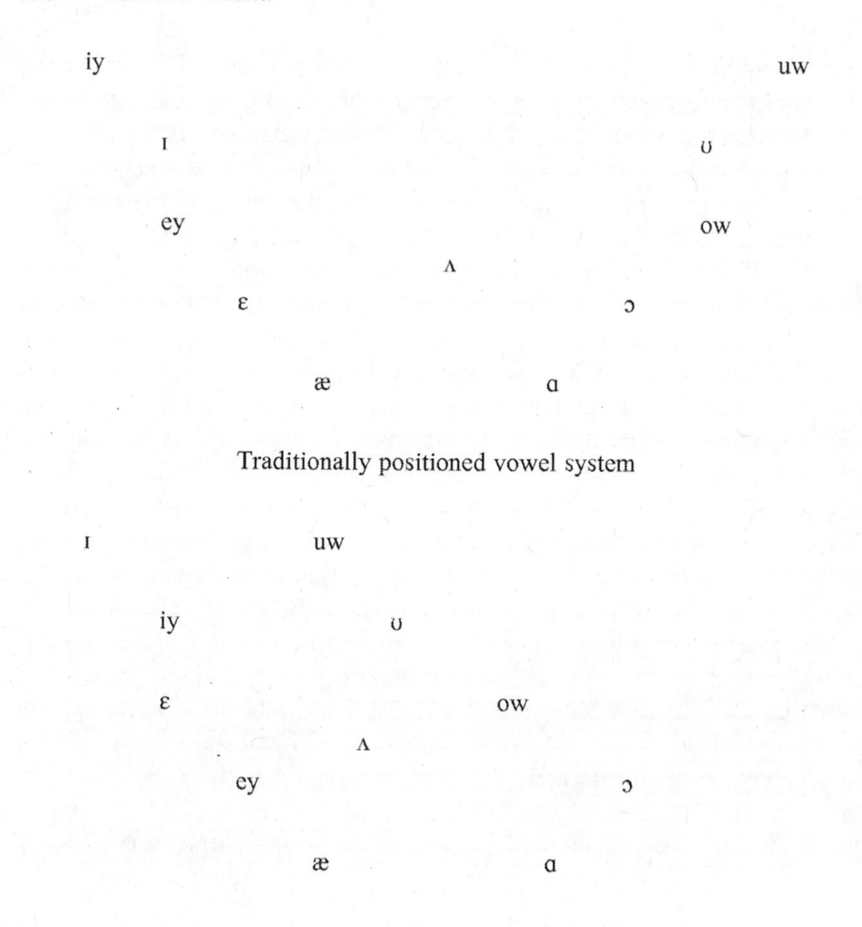

Figure 17.1 Traditional (above) vs. a Southern shifted system (below).

This examination of the Memphis vowel system was approached through the collection and analysis of both spontaneous and elicited (reading passage/ word list) data from 100 native African-American and European-American Memphians in two broad age categories, under 30 and over 40. Thirty-five of those speaker samples have been analyzed. Acoustic analysis was performed on selected vowel tokens from the reading passage and word list using the Kay Elemetrics Computer Speech Lab (CSL) 4300B at a sampling rate of 10 kHz and a low pass filtering rate of 4 kHz. The analysis of each speaker's system was based on a corpus of about 100 tokens. For each vowel, first, second, and third formant readings were selected by examining LPC peaks, spectrograms, energy, and pitch of the signal. Vowels were then plotted on F1/F2 grids and relative vowel positions were examined within each speaker's system.

The production study clearly indicated that all Memphians in the sample were affected by at least some aspects of the SVS. Figure 17.2 illustrates the shape of the vowel system generally found in the Memphis speaker sample. As in this figure, all of the participants showed near or complete reversal of the /ey/ and /ɛ/ classes, but little shift in the /iy/ and /ɪ/ classes. Only older male systems showed even marginal evidence of /iy/ or /ɪ/ shift, while all speakers were strongly affected by /ey/ shift and most speakers, particularly middle aged and older groups, had some shift in the /ɛ/ class (Fridland 2000, 2001). The high back vowel classes, /uw/ and /ʊ/, showed extensive fronting, while the mid-back class, /ow/, was much less often shifted, with significantly more shift in the younger speakers systems (F (32) = 4.69, p < .05) (Fridland and Bartlett 2006). The fronted prelateral /uw/ token, *tool*, an inhibitive environment for shift, shows the extent to which White Memphians have been affected by fronting. Beyond these shifts, /ay/ glide weakening, a characteristic Southern feature, was found widely in White Memphians' speech, both in the typical pre-voiced and free context and also, less frequently, in the pre-voiceless context (Fridland 2003b). In addition, nuclear distinctions still maintained the division between the low back vowel classes, and the /ɔ/ class showed no tendency toward diphthongization (Fridland 2004).

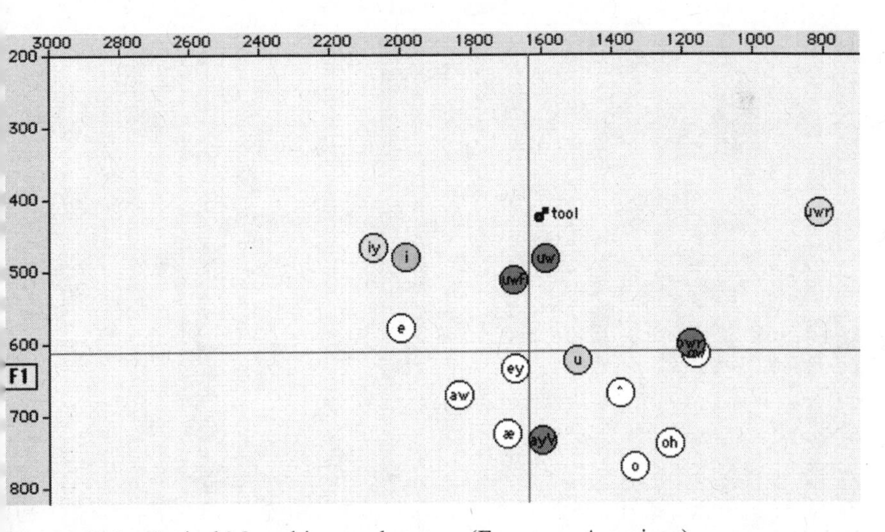

Figure 17.2 Typical Memphis vowel system (European-American).

The production study also found a great degree of similarity in terms of vowel shift participation between European-American and African-American speakers in Memphis (Fridland 2003a). As depicted in Figure 17.3, African-Americans also showed reversed /ey/ and /ɛ/ classes and fronted /uw/ and /ʊ/ classes with no /iy/ and /ɪ/ shift and with no strong shifting of the /ow/ class yet visible. In addition, the two groups showed very similar distributions of shifted tokens within vowel categories, with the same environmental conditioning for /ay/ monophthongization (including pre-voiceless contexts) and back vowel fronting. However, pre-lateral back vowel tokens remain backed for African-American speakers, suggesting fronting is not as advanced in their systems compared to European-Americans. In addition, results suggest that the /ɑ/ and /ɔ/ classes potentially locate a subtle Southern ethnic divide, with European-Americans showing less of a tendency towards diphthongization but more nuclear separation among low-back vowel tokens while African-Americans have greater nuclear overlap but adopt upglides in /ɔ/ to mark the vowel classes' distinction (Fridland 2004).

Once local production norms were established, a perception study was designed to determine how local speakers interpreted these shifts socially. In this study, Memphians were asked to comparably rate a range of vowel frequencies (within each vowel class) as more or less Southern sounding (Fridland, Bartlett, and Kreuz 2004). This study was performed through the administration of a matched guise test using synthesized vowel tokens

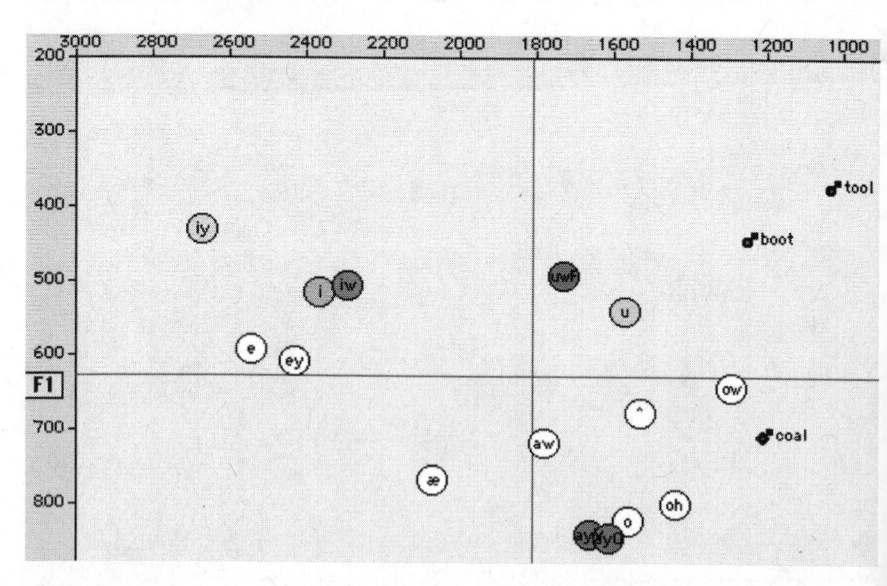

Figure 17.3 Typical African-American vowel system.

manipulated roughly by multiples of 25–50 Hz on vowel height frequencies (F1) and vowel front/back advancement frequencies (F2), respectively. Participants were played two of these slightly altered versions of the same monosyllabic word presented in a two word-set, with each member of the pair having been altered along the first formant (vowel height) or second formant (front/back advancement) dimension. So, for example, the word 'coat,' containing the /ow/ vowel, was played twice for listeners with each pronunciation differing only by how far front the tongue was positioned in the mouth during the vowel's production, a measure which correlates to a specific component frequency in the sound wave that produced that vowel. Thus, by altering the second formant component of the sound wave by adding 100 hertz, it replicates a fronter tongue position during production. All other aspects of the vowel quality were held constant. After hearing the token pair, the participants were asked to determine which pronunciation of the word was the most "Southern" sounding and, in a subsequent test, how educated and pleasant each token sounded.

Even though most subjects reported difficulty hearing differences between each member of the token pair, their responses showed that they were, in many cases, able to accurately select the token most shifted toward Southern norms in each pair. Table 17.1 shows the overall mean accuracy scores in descending order for the Memphis Sample while Table 17.2 lists the shifts in each vowel class by the degree to which they are used productively by Memphians and notes whether the shift is exclusive to the South. A higher mean score indicates a higher accuracy rate for selecting the most shifted vowel as the most southern-sounding. Interestingly, their "Southernness" accuracy was highly dependent on which vowel class was involved, with those vowel classes most actively engaged in productive shift locally being more salient as Southern markers. Vowel duration and gliding also appeared to make such selections easier, as the short vowels showed the lowest overall accuracy rates. Shifts like back vowel fronting that were also found in dialects outside the South appeared to be less socially salient as regional markers than those uniquely used in the South. Relative to their accuracy for the /iy/ and /ey/ classes, participants showed less accuracy picking out the more Southern sounding variant when comparing back vowel variants. However, listeners were better at distinguishing more and less Southern versions of shifted /ow/ variants, a shift that is less common outside the South and one found only in young speakers' systems.

Following the "Southernness" test, participants heard a subset of the synthesized tokens presented one at a time (repeated twice) and were asked to rate how educated and pleasant each token sounded on a 3-point scale (Fridland, Bartlett, and Kreuz 2005). Results from this task suggested that the more the token had been shifted toward Southern Shift norms, the lower

Table 17.1 "Southernness" Test Mean Accuracy Scores: Mean Score Rating the More Southern Word Accurately by Individual Vowel Class and by Vowel Subgroup

Vowel Class	Mean*
/ey/	.84
/iy/	.67
/ow/	.62
/uw/	.54
/ʊ/	.51
/ɛ/	.49
/ɪ/	.39

Note: *A higher mean score indicates a higher accuracy rate for selecting the most shifted vowel as the most southern-sounding.

Table 17.2 Degree of Memphians' Involvement in Shifts Found in Southern Speech

Front vowels:			
Class	Degree	Social aspects	Shift exclusive to South?
iy	Marginal	Older males only	Yes
ɪ	Marginal	Older males only	Yes
ey	extensive	All groups	Yes
ɛ	some	More in Middle/older groups	Yes
Back vowels:			
Class	Degree	Social aspects	Shift exclusive to South?
uw	extensive	all groups	No
ʊ	extensive	all groups	No
ow	some	younger group only	Somewhat

the token was ranked on education and pleasantness (Table 17.3). Whether shifts were shared across regions or exclusive to the South also had an affect, as front vowels shifted toward Southern norms were rated much lower in both education and pleasantness than back vowels shifted front, as found in Southern speech and elsewhere. Taken together, the production study and the perception study cumulatively suggest that shifts in which Memphians were most active productively and which were most unique to the South were also those most acoustically salient to listeners as "Southern" sounding variants. In addition, these locally defining shifts were also those speech samples judged least educated and least pleasant. So, based on these results, it appears that Memphians judge their own speech variety rather harshly.

Table 17.3 Education and Pleasantness Mean Ratings by Shift-Type

	Education	Pleasantness
More Southern front vowels	1.67	1.72
Less Southern front vowels	1.86	1.77
More Southern back vowels	2.11	1.89
Less Southern back vowels	2.14	1.99

Such findings are puzzling as to why Memphians would continue to use variants that local listeners rank as less pleasant and less educated than non-Southern variants. The production studies performed in Memphis clearly showed that several of the Southern Shift variants which were rated least educated and least pleasant were widely found across age, gender, and ethnic groups in Memphis. So, speakers must find some benefit to maintaining their use of these variants, even if they consider them uneducated and unpleasant compared to non-shifted variants. Without greater access to Memphians' language attitudes, it is difficult to determine what was driving participants' responses.

Hoping to gain insight into these results, a study was performed to examine Memphians' attitudes toward their own speech and that spoken elsewhere in the US to supplement this project. Replicating studies in folk dialectology (e.g., Preston 1989, 1993), participants were simply asked to rate all 50 states, New York City, and the District of Columbia on scales of 1 to 10 for correctness and pleasantness and on a scale of 1 to 4 for degree of difference from their own speech. This perceptual dialectology project, in comparison to the earlier production and perception studies, got at the overt stereotypes and attitudes speakers held toward their own speech and that around them, allowing interesting contrast to their actual speech behavior and their more unconscious speech perceptions.

Table 17.4a lists mean scores assigned by Memphians about where correct and pleasant speech is spoken regionally. The higher the mean score, the more correct and pleasant the speech found in the area. Not surprisingly, results suggest that the North/South continuum remains very salient to Memphians, particularly in terms of its correlation with "correct" speech. While

Memphians considered each region to be significantly different from the others on correctness scales (Table 17.4b), the Southern region was considered comparatively most incorrect even by Southerners themselves (Table 17.5). The Northern region, particularly the Upper North, was rated most correct. In contrast, no regions were considered significantly different in terms of pleasantness. In addition, all regions except the South showed lower pleasantness than correctness scores, pointing to a trade-off between correct and pleasant speech. From such results, it would seem that Memphians find their own speech rather pleasant, even if not correct, pointing to an underlying motivation for the variety's perseverance. However, Memphians' behavior on this study stands in contrast to their behavior in the previously-cited "Southernness" perception study, where pleasantness and education ratings decreased as degree of shift toward Southern norms increased. Such results suggest that the more Southern one sounds the less educated and pleasant they seem. Why this disconnect in language attitudes and speech perception behavior?

Table 17.4a Memphis Mean Scores for Each Map Region

Region	**Correctness (0–9)**	**Pleasantness (0–9)**
Southern	4.22 (1.04)	4.94 (1.32)
Upper North	5.88 (1.24)	4.93 (1.35)
All North	5.73 (1.12)	4.94 (1.03)
Midwest	5.32 (1.07)	4.93 (1.03)
West	5.60 (1.13)	5.03 (1.03)

Table 17.4b T-tests Comparing Memphians' Correctness Means by Region

Correctness	
South—All North*	t (165) = 14.69, p < .01
South—West*	t (165) = 13.25, p < .01
South—Midwest*	t (165) = 12.24, p < .01
South—Upper North*	t (165) = 14.47, p < .01
All North*—West	t (166) = 2.33, p < .05
All North*—Midwest	t (166) = 8.04, p < .01
All North—Upper North*	t (166) = 5.88, p < .01
West*—Midwest	t (166) = 4.86, p < .01
West—Upper North*	t (166) = 3.95, p < .01
Midwest—Upper North*	t (166) = 7.40, p < .01

* Indicates the region considered significantly more correct in each pair.

Table 17.5 T-Tests Comparing Memphians' Southern Correctness Scores to Other Regions

	t	df	Sig. (2-tailed)
South—Greater North	-14.680	165	.000
South—West	-13.246	165	.000
South—Mid West	-12.242	166	.000
South—Upper North	-14.400	165	.000

The key to this apparently contradictory behavior may lie in the difference in tasks calling on supra-regional vs. intra-regional identity. The folk dialectology study specifically asked participants to compare speech spoken across the US, drawing attention to the long-standing differences between regional dialects, particularly those of the Southern US. In addition, it also asked participants to make intra-regional comparisons, a task which Memphians showed little hesitancy in doing, as is evidenced in their relative downgrading of Mississippi and Arkansas, the largely rural states sitting on Memphis' borders (Table 17.6). While they viewed these states as significantly less pleasant and educated than their own speech (correctness: MS, $t(167) = 10.95$, $p < .001$, and AK, $t(167) = 10.41$, $p < .001$; pleasantness:MS, $t(166) = 9.21$, $p < .001$, and AR $t(166) = 9.96$, $p < .001$), they did not find the speech spoken in these two states significantly different from their own on the degree of difference task. Apparently, Memphians had clear opinions about Memphis' intra-regional status even while recognizing a shared dialect.

Table 17.6 Memphians' Comparative Ratings of Tennessee, Mississippi, and Arkansas

	Correctness	**Pleasantness**	**Difference**
Southern US	4.22 (1.04)	4.94 (1.32)	1.40 (.58)
TN	4.26 (2.06)	5.62 (2.46)	.54 (1.06)
MS	2.70 (2.12)	4.15 (2.70)	.86 (1.07)
AR	2.81 (1.98)	3.90 (2.38)	.99 (1.09)

In contrast to this folk dialectology task, the "Southernness" accuracy study made no reference to other regions nor did it make any regional claims about where the tokens listeners heard were from, so, presumably, listeners were not forced to recognize the less Southern sounding tokens as explicitly non-Southern. Thus, in rating these tokens on competence and solidarity scales, listeners may not have used "Northern" versus "Southern" dialect criteria at all, but were perhaps instead using only intra-Southern criteria comparing more rural vs. less rural or more educated vs. less educated sounding tokens. So, when rating tokens with greater degrees of Southern shift, the differences Memphians believe to exist between themselves and inhabitants of other states like Mississippi and Arkansas may be coming into play.

To gain more insight into this contradictory behavior, a final perception study was designed to examine whether intra-regional norms associated with urban vs. rural speech played into Memphians' ratings of synthesized vowel tokens (Fridland and Bartlett 2007). For this study, Memphians were given the same synthesized vowel token perception test used in the previous perception study. This time, instead of rating "Southernness," listeners were instructed to rate the relative ruralness of Southern shifted and non-shifted tokens, and, in a separate test, how educated and pleasant the tokens sounded. Participants were considered accurate when they selected the token shifted most toward Southern norms in each token-set as the most rural member of the pair, allowing comparison of ruralness accuracy to Southernness accuracy from the earlier perception study.

Before beginning the test, participants were asked to fill out a brief demographic questionnaire and each participant was asked to define the concept "rural." In order to ensure we knew what participants were responding to conceptually, the analysis was based on participants' ideas of rurality rather than a set definition which may or may not have matched with that held by participants. On review, the definitions predominately broke down into two different categories, those who equated "rurality" with non-urban, agricultural life and those who had no non-urban association with the term at all. Instead, in this second category, the participants clearly did not have any traditional understanding of what this term meant whatsoever, and their answers were often arbitrary. Since some participants had a very different concept of rurality, the data from those whose definitions involved a contrast with urban life/metropolitan lifestyles and those whose definitions did not fit any traditional understanding of rurality were split and run as two separate groups, the traditional definers and the non-traditional definers. The results from the two groups were then compared and the results were also compared to those from the earlier perception studies.

Table 17.7 shows descending mean score results for the traditional and non-traditional definers as well as for the original "Southernness" accuracy perception test. The comparative runs for traditional vs. non-traditional definers within the ruralness test clearly showed that this definitional distinction affected participants' perception and evaluation of vowel variants.

In addition, comparing the results of the traditional defining group on the ruralness test to the participant results from the original Southernness accuracy test shows that these two groups are highly similar in terms of picking out the most Southern shifted token as the most rural or southern sounding tokens, respectively. While both these groups showed accuracy rates significantly different than chance for a number of vowel classes (indicated by asterisks), the non-traditional definers were not significantly different than chance for any vowel class, suggesting that they were quite random in their ratings, as would be expected based on their lack of any clear understanding of the term "rurality."

Table 17.7 Descending Means Comparison for Ruralness and Southernness Studies

R/U Non-Traditional Definition		R/U Traditional Definition		Southernness Accuracy	
ɛ	.55	ey*	.76	ey*	.82
uw	.55	iy*	.68	iy*	.67
ʊ	**.54**	ow*	.63	ow*	.63
ɪ	**.54**	ʊ	.52	uw*	.54
ey	.53	uw	.51	ʊ	.52
iy	.49	ɛ	.48	ɛ	.49
ow	.49	ɪ*	.37	ɪ*	.41

Within the ruralness group, how subjects defined rurality also appeared to affect the ratings of tokens on competence and solidarity measures. Based on their mean ratings on education, participants in the traditional definition group generally found tokens in each class to sound less educated than those who did not define rurality traditionally. Similarly, non-traditional definers felt the tokens sounded more pleasant than traditional definers. In fact, breaking the vowels down by regional shift-type, non-traditional definers gave higher education and pleasantness scores to all vowel classes regardless of whether the token involved shifts towards Southern or non-Southern norms (see mean scores in Table 17.8). Such results suggest that participants' beliefs about the ruralness of speech does affect how they evaluate the relative education and pleasantness associated with such speech. Merely going into the test with the concept of rurality defining the task pulls down raters' assessment of speakers' level of education and pleasantness.

Table 17.8 Traditional/Non-Traditional Definers Education and Pleasantness Mean Scores

	Education		Pleasantness	
	Traditional Definitions	Non-Traditional Definitions	Traditional Definitions	Non-Traditional Definitions
Very Southern Shifted Tokens	1.57 (.304)	1.62 (.391)	1.55 (.370)	1.65 (.413)
Southern Shifted Tokens	2.31 (.437)	2.34 (.403)	1.92 (.466)	2.10 (.469)
Mildly-shifted Tokens	1.94 (.378)	2.03 (.376)	1.94 (.424)	1.99 (.439)
Non-Southern Tokens	2.07 (.255)	2.16 (.258)	1.90 (.303)	1.99 (.322)
Very Non-Southern Tokens	2.26 (.499)	2.41 (.458)	2.00 (.554)	2.19 (.491)

Although their ratings were not highly distinct, some differences also emerged when comparing education and pleasantness ratings for the traditional defining group in the ruralness test to those from the Southernness accuracy test (Table 17.9). With a few exceptions, rural raters tended to be slightly less harsh overall in assigning education and pleasantness ratings compared to Southernness raters. While this difference is generally quite minimal, the trend becomes more apparent when comparing the two groups' ratings of the Southern-shifted tokens on Education and Pleasantness. As can be seen in Table 17.9, rural study participants gave higher ratings in both categories to the Southern-shifted tokens in the /ey/, /uw/ and /ow/ classes compared to the Southernness study participants. The exception to this trend is the /ɛ/ class, the only class that showed an accuracy score below chance (Table 17.7), suggesting listeners were not able to discriminate between Southern and Non-Southern pronunciations. Although in general these differences were slight, it may suggest that, while similar, there is not perfect overlap between participants' concepts of Southernness and rurality. Indeed, several participants indicated that rurality could apply to areas outside the South by, for instance, mentioning other rural areas in the US. So, while rurality is not considered a prestigious trait based on this study's results, it is not exclusively found within the Southern region. Clearly, however, the greater the degree of Southern shift pattern a vowel exhibits, the more rural and Southern it sounds to participants and the less educated and pleasant it becomes. Thus, when comparing different degrees of shift between vowels, participants do appear to base decisions on intra-regional criteria of rurality, among other things, better explaining the seemingly contradictory pattern of results found in the earlier studies.

Table 17.9 Ruralness Test Traditional Definition Means and Southernness Accuracy Test Means for Education and Pleasantness

	Education		Pleasantness	
	Southernness	Rurality	Southernness	Rurality
/ey/ Tokens	1.61 (.316)	1.70 (.314)	1.73 (.432)	1.76 (.426)
/ɛ/ Tokens	1.89 (.405)	1.88 (.437)	1.72 (.451)	1.64 (.397)
/uw/ Tokens	2.34 (.414)	2.34 (.411)	2.01 (.472)	2.04 (.466)
/ow/ Tokens	2.02 (.296)	2.17 (.312)	1.92 (.382)	2.00 (.417)

3. Conclusion

This overview merely highlights some of the major findings so far in this research project in terms of how each aspect of the project helped inform and clarify the work preceding it. Next steps include administering these same studies in research sites outside the South which are affected by different vowel shift patterns. Further research also includes the development of more finely-tuned vowel categorization and discrimination tests to determine how regional dialect experience shapes listeners' perceptual vowel space and category goodness tests. While this research integrating productive, perceptual, and attitudinal approaches is merely a first step on a long road, it will hopefully suggest avenues of possible research to other investigators seeking to provide a more comprehensive and empirically-based explanation of the language variation and change found in our communities. Such a research synthesis should prove to have both theoretical and applied benefits, contributing to basic theories about the nature of sound change and the ability of adult language learners to adjust aspects of their phonological system to issues of cross-dialectal comprehension and computer speech and voice recognition technology development.

Acknowledgment

I gratefully acknowledge the support of the National Science Foundation Linguistics Program BCS-#0132145 and BCS#0001725.

References

Coates, Jennifer (ed.). 1998. *Language and gender: A reader.* Oxford: Blackwell.

Eckert, Penelope. 1988. Adolescent social structure and the spread of linguistic change. *Language Variation and Change* 1: 245–208.

Eckert, Penelope. 2000. *Linguistic variation as social practice.* Oxford: Blackwell.

Eckert, Penelope and Sally McConnell-Ginet. 1998. Communities of practice: Where language, gender, and power all live. In Coates (ed.), 485–494.

Feagin, Crawford. 1986. More evidence for vowel change in the South. In David Sankoff (ed.), *Diversity and diachrony.* Amsterdam/Philadelphia: John Benjamins, 83–95.

Fridland, Valerie. 2000. The Southern vowel shift in Memphis, TN. *Language Variation and Change* 11: 267–285.

Fridland, Valerie. 2001. Social factors in the Southern Shift: Gender, age and class. *Journal of Sociolinguistics* 5 (2): 233–253.

Fridland, Valerie. 2003a. Network strength and the realization of the Southern Vowel Shift among African-Americans in Memphis, TN. *American Speech* 78 (1): 3–30.

Fridland, Valerie. 2003b. Tide, tied and tight: The expansion of /ai/ monopthongization in African-American and European-American speech in Memphis, TN. *Journal of Sociolinguistics* 7: 279–298.

Fridland, Valerie. 2004. The spread of the cot/caught merger in the speech of Memphians: An ethnolinguistic marker? Paper presented at LAVIS III (Language and Variation in the South II) Conference: Tuscaloosa, AL.

Fridland, Valerie and Kathryn Bartlett. 2006. The social and linguistic conditioning of back vowel fronting across ethnic groups in Memphis, TN. *English Language and Linguistics* 10 (1): 1–22.

Fridland, Valerie and Kathryn Bartlett. 2007. Southern or rural? The social perception of regional vowel distinctions. *Southern Journal of Linguistics* 31 (1): 38–62.

Fridland, Valerie, Kathryn Bartlett, and Roger Kreuz. 2004. Do you hear what I hear? Experimental measurement of the perceptual salience of acoustically manipulated vowel variants by Southern speakers in Memphis, TN. *Language Variation and Change* 16: 1–16.

Fridland, Valerie, Kathryn Bartlett, and Roger Kreuz. 2005. Making sense of variation: Pleasantness and education ratings of regional vowel variants. *American Speech* 80 (4): 366–387.

Gordon, Matthew. 2001. *Small-town values and big-city vowels: A study of the Northern Cities Shift in Michigan*. Publication of the American Dialect Society 84. Durham, NC: Duke University Press.

Hagiwara, Robert. 1997. Dialect variation and formant frequency. The American English vowels revisited. *The Journal of the Acoustical Society of America* 102.1: 655–658.

Labov, William. 1991. The three dialects of English. In Penelope Eckert (ed.), *New ways of analyzing variation*. New York: Academic Press, 1–44.

Labov, William. 1994. *Principles of linguistic change: Internal factors*. Oxford: Blackwell.

Labov, William. 2000. *Principles of linguistic change: Social factors*. Oxford: Blackwell.

Labov, William, Sharon Ash, and Charles Boberg. 2005. *The atlas of North American English*. Berlin: Mouton de Gruyter.

Luthin, H. 1987. The story of California ow: The coming-of-age of English in California. In Keith M. Denning, Sharon Inkelas, Faye C. McNair-Knox, and John R. Rickford (eds), *Variation in language: NWAV-XV at Stanford*. Stanford CA: Department of Linguistics, Stanford University.

Milroy, Lesley. 1980. *Language and social networks*. Baltimore: University Park Press.

Milroy, Lesley and Dennis R. Preston (eds). 1999. Special Issue: Attitudes, perception, and linguistic features. *Journal of Language and Social Psychology* 18 (1).

Nichols, Patricia. 1983. Linguistic options and choices for Black women in the rural South. In Barrie Thorne, Cheris Kramerae, and Nancy Henley (eds), *Language, gender and society*. Rowley, MA: Newbury House.

Preston, Dennis R. 1989. *Perceptual dialectology*. Dordrecht: Foris.

Preston, Dennis R. 1993. *Folk dialectology*. In Preston (ed.), 333–378.

Preston, Dennis R. (ed.). 1993. *American dialect research*. Amsterdam: John Benjamins.

Thomas, Erik. 1997. *A compendium of vowel plots*. A publication of the North Carolina Language and Life Project. Raleigh: Department of English, North Carolina State University.

Thomas, Erik. 2001. *An acoustic analysis of vowel variation in New World English*. Publication of the American Dialect Society 85. Durham, NC: Duke University Press.

Wolfram, Walt. 1991. *Dialects and American English*. Englewood Cliffs, NJ: Prentice Hall.

Wolfram, Walt. 1993. Identifying and interpreting variables. In Preston (ed.), 193–222.

Author Index

Subject Index